THE RATING GUIDE TO
LIFE
IN
AMERICA'S
SMALL
CITIES

America's 219 Micropolitan Areas

Map Designed by Valerie Ferenti-Cognetto

THE RATING GUIDE TO

LIFE IN

CLIMATE · DIVERSIONS · ECONOMICS
EDUCATION · ENVIRONMENT
HEALTH CARE · HOUSING · PUBLIC SAFETY
SOPHISTICATION · TRANSPORTATION

AMERICA'S SMALL CITIES

WITH
REPORT CARDS
ON THE
219 MICROPOLITAN
ALTERNATIVES TO
METROPOLITAN
HASSLES

G. SCOTT THOMAS

PROMETHEUS BOOKS
BUFFALO, NEW YORK

94 93 92 91 90   5 4 3 2 1

Library of Congress Cataloging-in-Publication Data

Thomas, G. Scott.
    The rating guide to life in America's small cities / G. Scott
Thomas.
        p.   cm.
    ISBN 0-87975-599-7
    ISBN 0-87975-600-4 pbk. (acid-free paper)
    1. Cities and towns—United States—Ratings. 2. Cities and towns—
United States—Statistics. 3. Urban-rural migration—United States.
I. Title.
HA214.T46   1990
307.76'0973—dc20   89-77457
                                                                  CIP

Contents

Contents

Introduction:

Micropolitan America

Big is better. That is the American credo. We aspire to drive big cars, own big houses, and hold big jobs. We believe size and quality are linked inextricably. Athletes are judged by their salaries, television programs by their quantities of viewers, corporations by their bottom lines. The bigger each is, the more impressed we are.

The same is true of cities. Metropolitan giants like New York City, Los Angeles, and Chicago dazzle the nation with their wealth, glamour, and power. Other large cities dominate their regions and states in a similar manner. More than three-quarters of all Americans—77 percent—now live in metropolitan areas.

It would seem only logical that an urban setting would provide the best possible quality of life. Why else would millions upon millions of people have crowded into our cities? Big *is* better, isn't it?

Not necessarily. Consider these examples of metropolitan unrest:

● The U.S. Department of Housing and Urban Development conducted a national survey in 1978 on perceptions of community life. More than 7,000 Americans, most of them in metro areas, were asked where children

8   could best be raised. Nearly half chose small towns; only 12 percent said big cities. The response was nearly identical to a question about where the friendliest people could be found: 49 percent said small towns, 21 percent picked suburbs, and only 13 percent opted for big cities.

• A 1985 Gallup survey inquired if people would move away from their communities if only they could. Fully 41 percent of those in cities with more than 1 million residents said they wanted out. Only 30 percent living in smaller cities (50,000-500,000 people) and 27 percent in rural areas expressed similar dissatisfaction.

• The *Los Angeles Times* polled more than 2,000 residents of the Los Angeles metro area in February 1989. Asked if the region's quality of life had deteriorated over the previous 15 years, 60 percent said yes; only 17 percent insisted it had improved. About half of the respondents said they had given thought in the previous year to leaving the area.

The traditional outlet for urban stress has been the dream of moving to a tranquil suburb, where the big worries are crabgrass and the wait at the first tee, not crime and the one-and-a-half mile backup on the expressway. But many of these fortresses of serenity have been successfully stormed by the troops of encroaching urbanization. "My suburb has become a city, without any of the amenities," columnist Judy Mann complained in the *Washington Post*. "We have traffic jams that rival New York's. Half-hour commutes have become 45-minute and hourlong commutes."

As older suburbs are becoming just like large cities with their congested streets and climbing crime rates, newer suburbs are quickly becoming too expensive for many urban refugees. The *Washington Post* in 1987 relayed the story of Corby O'Connor, who had moved with her husband and two sons from upstate New York to a Connecticut suburb of New York City. O'Connor was horrified by the $275,000 price tag on her new home, which had less room than the house she had left. "We're tripping over each other," she said. "To live here, you have to live in cramped quarters and all your money goes into real estate. We have no cash. We don't go on vacation. We don't go out very often. Every single day, we're in the red." O'Connor's family is not alone. The *average* price of a home in Orange County, southeast of Los Angeles, was $200,395 in 1989, according to a survey by the American Chamber of Commerce Researchers Association.

The Newest Frontier

The process of elimination provides the answer for Americans seeking quality lives without excessive stress and expense. Big cities are out, as are the suburbs. What's left?

City dwellers have historically scorned small towns for being isolated, placid, and decidedly unmetropolitan. But such contempt loses its strength in light of the obvious deterioration of urban life. Most home buyers now want to move as far from big cities as possible. *Professional Builder,* the national journal for contractors, asked more than 1,000 Americans in 1988 where they would prefer to purchase a new house. Their replies showed a definite anti-metropolitan bias:

	%
Central city	3.5
Close-in suburbs	30.4
Outlying suburbs	33.8
Rural	30.0
Other	2.3

Add the figures for the suburban fringe and rural America, and you have almost two-thirds of the respondents. *New York Times* correspondent John Herbers wrote in his perceptive 1986 book, *The New Heartland,* that these regions distant from big-city influence constitute "the newest American frontier."

Herbers saw middle-class residents of large cities and their suburbs yearning for space and independence, and looking for those qualities beyond metropolitan boundaries. He scoffed at those who dismissed this trend as a passing fad. "Rather, it is an alternative to both the big cities and their massive suburbs, one that a sizeable number of people have chosen," he wrote. "And nothing on the horizon strongly indicates an end to this trend."

Information about these new growth regions is not always easily obtained. The Census Bureau floods libraries and research firms with reports on the 333 officially designated metropolitan areas. The rest of America necessarily takes a back seat. Data for small cities and rural counties are compiled less frequently than are statistics for metros.

This book seeks to provide essential facts to those city residents and suburbanites who are wondering whether to move to a smaller, quieter, safer, less costly community. The following pages focus on 219 "micropolitan" areas, consisting of small cities and their surrounding territories. If you are interested in the technical criteria for inclusion in this book, read the following six rules. If not, be content with the knowledge that all micros offer an alternative to metropolitan life. Now the rules:

1. The central city must have at least 15,000 residents.

2. The county must have at least 40,000 residents, including the population of the central city. Almost all micropolitan areas consist of a single county.

10   3. If a qualifying city has at least 40 percent of its population in each of two counties, the micro area includes both counties.

4. Four states have independent cities that are not located in counties. Any independent city with 15,000 or more residents can qualify for micropolitan status. If the city is larger than 15 square miles, its boundaries become those of the micro. If the city is smaller, it is joined with the adjacent county to form the area.

5. No micropolitan area, with one exception listed below, can have been part of an officially designated metropolitan area, as of June 15, 1989. (The government confuses the situation in the six New England states, where it has two sets of metro areas. One is drawn according to township lines; the other uses counties. This rule employs the latter system.)

6. The federal government lists Decatur, Alabama, as a metro; this book considers it to be a micro. All official metropolitan areas have met a series of criteria established by the Office of Management and Budget, except Decatur. It failed to pass the statistical tests. Congress then stepped in and ordered OMB to list it as a metro in 1988. Several private research firms have decided that Decatur is really a small city and have refused to include it in their metropolitan-area reports.

More than 15 million people live in micropolitan America, nearly 6.5 percent of the nation's population. Small cities account for at least 10 percent of the residents of 20 states. Idaho has the highest proportion of people living in micros: slightly more than 35 percent. Other states with strong small-city representation are New Mexico (32.2 percent), Maine (23.1), New Hampshire (21.8), and Montana (21.0). Ohio has both the largest number of micros, with 15 areas, and the highest total of residents in those communities, approximately 1.1 million. Four states—Hawaii, Massachusetts, New Jersey, and South Dakota—join the District of Columbia in not having any micropolitan areas.

Small Cities Today

Some big cities are better than others. The same is true of micropolitan areas.

This book is designed to help you find the best small city for your needs, using a statistical system to grade the quality of life in each. But before determining the differences between micropolitan communities, it is useful to learn what they have in common:

Youth. Small cities have a greater proportion of young people than does the nation as a whole. Nearly 59 percent of all micros (129 of 219) have median ages that are lower than the average for the whole country. Many are either college towns or the sites of military bases.

Friendliness. Americans believe small-city residents are more outgoing than their big-city counterparts, as indicated by the results of that 1978 HUD survey. They certainly seem to be correct. "Missoula can feel mighty small. People smile and say hello on the street," says writer Elizabeth Gold of the micropolitan area she calls home. She adds jokingly: "Make an enemy and he will show up, without fail, at every party you attend."

Lack of stress. The pace of life is a step slower in small cities than in their hectic metropolitan neighbors. James Rouse, a noted urban planner and developer, contends that large cities are so huge that they prevent people from feeling in control of their lives. "I believe this out-of-scaleness promotes loneliness, irresponsibility, superficial values," he says. "People grow best in small communities where the institutions, which are the dominant forces in their lives, are within the scale of their comprehension and within reach of their sense of responsibility and capacity to manage."

Less education. The residents of micropolitan areas generally have received less schooling than have the people who live in metros. The typical American attends 12.5 years of classes. Fully 65 percent of all micros (143 of 219) have averages that are below that figure. The notable exceptions to this trend are university towns.

Less racial diversity. Most small cities do not offer the mix of racial and ethnic groups that one finds in big cities. Only 28 percent of the nation's micropolitan areas (61 of 219) have a larger share of black residents than does the nation as a whole. Just 11 percent (25 of 219) have a higher proportion of Hispanics than the average for the country.

Lower incomes. Paychecks are definitely lighter in small cities than in big cities. Per capita incomes are lower than the national average in 95 percent of all micros (208 of 219). Keep in mind that it also costs less to live in a small community, so the disparity is not as great as it seems.

Closeness to nature. It can be a frustrating, time-consuming trip to escape from a metro area to your favorite campground or lake. Small cities are often very close to such attractions. "Wages are lower here, but you have to weigh what's important," Vermont speech therapist Steve Libbey told *USA Today.* "Do I want to live near the Metropolitan Museum of Art, or do I want to live somewhere where I can take my kids to see butterflies?"

Closeness to metro areas. Many city dwellers think of the typical small city as being an isolated backwater. The reality is much different: most micropolitan areas are close enough to a big city for day trips or even commuting. Slightly more than 55 percent of the nation's micros (121 of 219) are within 50 miles of the center of a metropolitan area.

After studying this list of qualities—some good, some not so good— you might have decided that the balance tips in favor of micropolitan life.

12 But how do you find the small city that is right for you?

This book grades all 219 micropolitan areas according to their performances in 50 statistical measures, known as categories. All of the numbers used in these categories are the most recent figures publicly available from the federal government and other sources, as of June 15, 1989. They will not be quickly outdated by the 1990 census, since most of its detailed statistics for small cities will be published in 1993 at the earliest.

Each category assigns points to all micros on a scale of 20. The best figures—for example, the very lowest crime rates—earn all 20 points for their communities. The worst statistics—in this case, the very highest crime rates—warrant none. The distance between the upper and lower ends of the scale is evenly divided into 19 intervals, with cities being awarded from one to 19 points depending on where they place.

Five categories that measure different aspects of the same broad field are grouped together. There are ten of these sections, in which each community's five category scores are totaled. Let's say there are three cities you find especially interesting. The section totals allow you to make quick comparisons. Which town offers the best health care? Which of the three has the finest educational system? Just check the numbers.

The obvious last step is to add the ten section totals for each micropolitan area, resulting in a score for the community's overall quality of life. Such final totals can be found at the back of this book, along with "report cards" for the 219 small cities, listing their strengths and weaknesses.

Author Sherwood Anderson, who was unsparingly critical of small-town America in his early works, came to a change of heart just before his death. "The big world outside now is so filled with confusion," he wrote in 1940, "it seemed to me that our only hope, in the present muddle, was to try thinking small."

The statistics and scores in this book are intended to inspire exactly that. Study the ten sections; check out the report cards. You might find that "thinking small" will lead you to a happy home in micropolitan America.

	Components	Population
Alabama		
Athens	Limestone County	51,800
Auburn–Opelika	Lee County	80,800
Decatur	Morgan County	98,800
Enterprise	Coffee County	40,200
Selma	Dallas County	52,700
Talladega	Talladega County	76,500
Alaska		
Fairbanks	Fairbanks North Star Borough	67,600
Arizona		
Bullhead City–Lake Havasu City	Mohave County	76,600
Casa Grande–Apache Junction	Pinal County	98,800
Flagstaff	Coconino County	86,100
Prescott	Yavapai County	84,800
Sierra Vista	Cochise County	91,800
Yuma	Yuma County	86,800
Arkansas		
Blytheville	Mississippi County	58,000
El Dorado	Union County	49,000
Hot Springs	Garland County	75,300
Jonesboro	Craighead County	63,400
Rogers	Benton County	89,000
Russellville	Pope County	43,400
California		
El Centro–Calexico–Brawley	Imperial County	107,000
Eureka	Humboldt County	114,200
Hanford	Kings County	85,900
Madera	Madera County	77,900
San Luis Obispo–Atascadero	San Luis Obispo County	196,700
Colorado		
Grand Junction	Mesa County	89,000
Connecticut		
Torrington	Litchfield County	162,200
Delaware		
Dover	Kent County	105,200

Note: Population figures are estimates from the U.S. Census Bureau for June 30, 1986.

	Components	Population
Florida		
Key West	Monroe County	72,500
Vero Beach	Indian River County	81,000
Georgia		
Brunswick	Glynn County	59,800
Carrollton	Carroll County	64,900
Dalton	Whitfield County	69,300
Gainesville	Hall County	87,100
Hinesville	Liberty County	42,300
La Grange	Troup County	54,200
Rome	Floyd County	78,700
Valdosta	Lowndes County	73,700
Idaho		
Coeur d'Alene	Kootenai County	67,500
Idaho Falls	Bonneville County	70,600
Nampa–Caldwell	Canyon County	90,200
Pocatello	Bannock County	68,100
Twin Falls	Twin Falls County	55,800
Illinois		
Carbondale	Jackson County	60,500
Danville	Vermilion County	91,300
De Kalb	De Kalb County	74,100
Freeport	Stephenson County	49,400
Galesburg	Knox County	56,300
Mattoon–Charleston	Coles County	52,000
Ottawa	La Salle County	108,200
Quincy	Adams County	68,100
Sterling	Whiteside County	62,800
Indiana		
Columbus	Bartholomew County	64,500
Marion	Grant County	77,100
Michigan City–La Porte	La Porte County	106,100
New Castle	Henry County	50,100
Richmond	Wayne County	72,200
Vincennes	Knox County	41,400
Iowa		
Ames	Story County	72,500
Burlington	Des Moines County	44,600
Clinton	Clinton County	53,600
Fort Dodge	Webster County	42,700
Marshalltown	Marshall County	40,500
Mason City	Cerro Gordo County	48,800
Muscatine	Muscatine County	41,300

	Components	**Population**
Kansas		
Hutchinson	Reno County	65,300
Manhattan	Riley County	65,100
Salina	Saline County	50,000
Kentucky		
Bowling Green	Warren County	82,400
Frankfort	Franklin County	44,000
Madisonville	Hopkins County	46,600
Paducah	McCracken County	60,300
Radcliff–Elizabethtown	Hardin County	93,800
Richmond	Madison County	54,900
Louisiana		
Bogalusa	Washington Parish	47,700
Crowley	Acadia Parish	59,600
Hammond	Tangipahoa Parish	92,100
Minden	Webster Parish	46,100
Morgan City	Saint Mary Parish	64,300
New Iberia	Iberia Parish	69,000
Opelousas	Saint Landry Parish	88,400
Ruston	Lincoln Parish	42,600
Maine		
Augusta–Waterville	Kennebec County	112,000
Biddeford	York County	158,800
Maryland		
Salisbury	Wicomico County	69,300
Michigan		
Adrian	Lenawee County	88,800
Marquette	Marquette County	71,300
Mount Pleasant	Isabella County	54,200
Owosso	Shiawassee County	69,000
Traverse City	Grand Traverse County	59,200
Minnesota		
Faribault	Rice County	47,500
Mankato	Blue Earth County	53,200
Winona	Winona County	46,300

	Components	**Population**
Mississippi		
Columbus	Lowndes County	60,200
Greenville	Washington County	70,700
Greenwood	Leflore County	41,300
Hattiesburg	Forrest County	68,300
Laurel	Jones County	63,000
Meridian	Lauderdale County	76,900
Tupelo	Lee County	62,100
Vicksburg	Warren County	51,400
Missouri		
Cape Girardeau	Cape Girardeau County	61,300
Jefferson City	Cole County	63,400
Sikeston	Scott County	40,200
Montana		
Bozeman	Gallatin County	47,800
Helena	Lewis and Clark County	46,400
Missoula	Missoula County	77,700
Nebraska		
Grand Island	Hall County	48,900
Nevada		
Carson City	Carson City (independent city)	36,900
New Hampshire		
Concord	Merrimack County	109,700
Keene	Cheshire County	66,900
Laconia	Belknap County	47,100
New Mexico		
Alamogordo	Otero County	50,200
Carlsbad	Eddy County	52,400
Clovis	Curry County	43,400
Farmington	San Juan County	92,000
Gallup	McKinley County	65,800
Hobbs	Lea County	64,900
Rio Rancho	Sandoval County	51,100
Roswell	Chaves County	56,700

	Components	Population
New York		
Auburn	Cayuga County	79,900
Batavia	Genesee County	58,800
Cortland	Cortland County	47,400
Gloversville	Fulton County	54,600
Ithaca	Tompkins County	87,600
Jamestown	Chautauqua County	143,100
Kingston	Ulster County	164,200
Olean	Cattaraugus County	85,300
Plattsburgh	Clinton County	81,200
Watertown	Jefferson County	90,600
North Carolina		
Eden	Rockingham County	85,500
Goldsboro	Wayne County	97,900
Greenville	Pitt County	98,000
Havelock–New Bern	Craven County	81,100
Kinston	Lenoir County	60,100
Lumberton	Robeson County	106,000
Roanoke Rapids	Halifax County	55,800
Rocky Mount	Edgecombe and Nash counties	130,200
Sanford	Lee County	41,400
Shelby	Cleveland County	86,500
Statesville	Iredell County	88,600
Wilson	Wilson County	64,500
North Dakota		
Minot	Ward County	61,300
Ohio		
Ashland	Ashland County	46,300
Ashtabula	Ashtabula County	101,200
Athens	Athens County	57,600
Chillicothe	Ross County	67,300
East Liverpool	Columbiana County	110,100
Findlay	Hancock County	65,900
Fremont	Sandusky County	62,200
Marion	Marion County	65,300
New Philadelphia	Tuscarawas County	85,500
Portsmouth	Scioto County	82,300
Sandusky	Erie County	77,100
Sidney	Shelby County	44,000
Tiffin	Seneca County	61,600
Wooster	Wayne County	101,200
Zanesville	Muskingum County	84,100

	Components	Population
Oklahoma		
Ardmore	Carter County	47,500
Bartlesville	Washington County	44,900
Chickasha	Grady County	44,500
Duncan	Stephens County	44,600
McAlester	Pittsburg County	43,900
Muskogee	Muskogee County	70,300
Okmulgee	Okmulgee County	40,000
Ponca City	Kay County	52,200
Stillwater	Payne County	64,900
Oregon		
Albany	Linn County	89,000
Bend	Deschutes County	68,700
Corvallis	Benton County	64,600
Grants Pass	Josephine County	68,200
Klamath Falls	Klamath County	57,500
Roseburg	Douglas County	93,200
Pennsylvania		
Butler	Butler County	151,100
Chambersburg	Franklin County	118,700
New Castle	Lawrence County	101,900
Pottsville	Schuylkill County	156,400
Rhode Island		
Newport	Newport County	84,800
South Carolina		
Greenwood	Greenwood County	58,000
Hilton Head Island	Beaufort County	85,600
Myrtle Beach	Horry County	130,600
Orangeburg	Orangeburg County	87,300
Sumter	Sumter County	95,000
Tennessee		
Cleveland	Bradley County	72,300
Columbia	Maury County	53,900
Cookeville	Putnam County	51,100
Morristown	Hamblen County	52,900
Tullahoma	Coffee County	41,300

	Components	**Population**
Texas		
Alice	Jim Wells County	40,300
Bay City	Matagorda County	41,000
Del Rio	Val Verde County	40,000
Greenville	Hunt County	67,100
Huntsville	Walker County	54,100
Lufkin	Angelina County	69,400
Nacogdoches	Nacogdoches County	50,600
Palestine	Anderson County	47,500
Paris	Lamar County	45,000
Utah		
Logan	Cache County	65,500
Vermont		
Rutland	Rutland County	60,000
Virginia		
Blacksburg	Montgomery County	66,100
Fredericksburg	Spotsylvania County and Fredericksburg (independent city)	58,900
Harrisonburg	Rockingham County and Harrisonburg (independent city)	81,400
Martinsville	Henry County and Martinsville (independent city)	74,900
Staunton–Waynesboro	Augusta County and Staunton and Waynesboro (independent cities)	91,500
Winchester	Frederick County and Winchester (independent city)	58,100
Washington		
Aberdeen	Grays Harbor County	62,700
Longview	Cowlitz County	78,700
Port Angeles	Clallam County	53,700
Pullman	Whitman County	40,700
Walla Walla	Walla Walla County	48,000
Wenatchee	Chelan County	49,900

	Components	Population
West Virginia		
Beckley	Raleigh County	84,200
Clarksburg	Harrison County	75,200
Fairmont	Marion County	64,100
Morgantown	Monongalia County	77,700
Wisconsin		
Fond du Lac	Fond du Lac County	90,400
Manitowoc	Manitowoc County	82,200
Marshfield–Wisconsin Rapids	Wood County	77,500
Stevens Point	Portage County	58,700
Wyoming		
Rock Springs	Sweetwater County	47,000

State	Total Population	Micropolitan Population	% Micropolitan
Alabama	4,053,000	400,800	9.9
Alaska	534,000	67,600	12.7
Arizona	3,242,000	524,900	16.2
Arkansas	2,372,000	378,100	15.9
California	26,981,000	581,700	2.2
Colorado	3,267,000	89,000	2.7
Connecticut	3,189,000	162,200	5.1
Delaware	633,000	105,200	16.6
District of Columbia	626,000	0	0.0
Florida	11,675,000	153,500	1.3
Georgia	6,104,000	530,000	8.7
Hawaii	1,062,000	0	0.0
Idaho	1,003,000	352,200	35.1
Illinois	11,548,000	622,700	5.4
Indiana	5,504,000	411,400	7.5
Iowa	2,851,000	344,000	12.1
Kansas	2,461,000	180,400	7.3
Kentucky	3,727,000	382,000	10.2
Louisiana	4,501,000	509,800	11.3
Maine	1,174,000	270,800	23.1
Maryland	4,463,000	69,300	1.6
Massachusetts	5,832,000	0	0.0
Michigan	9,155,000	342,500	3.7
Minnesota	4,216,000	147,000	3.5
Mississippi	2,625,000	493,900	18.8
Missouri	5,066,000	164,900	3.3

Note: Population figures are estimates from the U.S. Census Bureau for June 30, 1986.

State	Total Population	Micropolitan Population	% Micropolitan
Montana	819,000	171,900	21.0
Nebraska	1,598,000	48,900	3.1
Nevada	964,000	36,900	3.8
New Hampshire	1,027,000	223,700	21.8
New Jersey	7,620,000	0	0.0
New Mexico	1,479,000	476,500	32.2
New York	17,772,000	892,700	5.0
North Carolina	6,331,000	995,600	15.7
North Dakota	680,000	61,300	9.0
Ohio	10,752,000	1,111,700	10.3
Oklahoma	3,305,000	452,800	13.7
Oregon	2,698,000	441,200	16.4
Pennsylvania	11,889,000	528,100	4.4
Rhode Island	975,000	84,800	8.7
South Carolina	3,378,000	456,500	13.5
South Dakota	707,000	0	0.0
Tennessee	4,803,000	271,500	5.7
Texas	16,682,000	455,000	2.7
Utah	1,665,000	65,500	3.9
Vermont	541,000	60,000	11.1
Virginia	5,787,000	430,900	7.4
Washington	4,463,000	333,700	7.5
West Virginia	1,919,000	301,200	15.7
Wisconsin	4,785,000	308,800	6.5
Wyoming	507,000	47,000	9.3
U.S. Total	**241,010,000**	**15,540,100**	**6.4**

Glossary of Important Terms

Category. A single statistical measure that is used to assess one aspect of a community's quality of life. There are five categories in each of this book's ten sections.

Central city. The major community in a region; the city or cities that give the area its name. Augusta and Waterville are the central cities of the Augusta–Waterville, Maine, micropolitan area. Aberdeen is the central city of the Aberdeen, Washington, micropolitan area. Also called *core city.*

East. A region that includes Connecticut, Delaware, District of Columbia, Maine, Maryland, Massachusetts, New Hampshire, New Jersey, New York, Pennsylvania, Rhode Island, Vermont, and West Virginia.

Median. The middle number in a group when all figures are arranged according to size. Three communities have 32, 29, and 11 doctors respectively. The median for this group is 29, while the average is 24.

Metro center. The dominant city in an officially designated metropolitan area; there is only one per area. Albany is the metro center of the Albany–Schenectady–Troy, New York, metro area. Tulsa is the metro center of the Tulsa, Oklahoma, metro area.

Metropolitan area. A large city and its suburbs, or a combination of neighboring large cities and their suburbs, that are defined by the federal government as "socially and economically interrelated." There are 333 of these areas. Also called *metro area* or *metro.*

24 **Micropolitan area.** A small city and its surrounding territory, or a combination of neighboring small cities and their surrounding territory. A more precise definition is provided in the introduction of this book. There are 219 of these areas. Also called *micro area* or *micro.*

Midwest. A region that includes Illinois, Indiana, Iowa, Kansas, Michigan, Minnesota, Missouri, Nebraska, North Dakota, Ohio, South Dakota, and Wisconsin.

Per capita. Any figure expressed as a rate per each person living in an area. A region has 2,000 residents who spend a total of $1 million a year in restaurants. That is $500 per capita.

Rates. It is often unfair to compare absolute totals from two communities of different sizes, so the totals are projected to a common rate to put both cities on an equal footing. Community A has 20,000 residents and 400 police officers; community B has 10,000 residents and 30 officers. Rates are commonly, although not always, expressed as a number per 100,000 residents. Community A would have 2,000 officers per 100,000; community B would have 300 per 100,000.

Section. A broad component of a community's quality of life, such as housing or health care. This book identifies ten sections.

South. A region that includes Alabama, Arkansas, Florida, Georgia, Kentucky, Louisiana, Mississippi, North Carolina, Oklahoma, South Carolina, Tennessee, Texas, and Virginia.

Spacing. The interval that carries the same point value in a category. The per capita income category awards 20 points to any community with a figure of $13,250 or more, while no points are given to a town registering $5,649 or less. The spacing is every $400. That means one point is awarded for anything in the range of $5,650-$6,049, two points for $6,050-$6,449, up to 19 points for $12,850-$13,249.

West. A region that includes Alaska, Arizona, California, Colorado, Hawaii, Idaho, Montana, Nevada, New Mexico, Oregon, Utah, Washington, and Wyoming.

1

Climate/ Environment

T he weather is always doing something," Mark Twain once noted slyly. "[It is] always getting up new designs and trying them on people to see how they will go."

People are capable of similar capriciousness. They have tested their environment with a vast array of toxic compounds over the course of this century. The impact of this tinkering with the balance of nature sometimes has been frightening.

There are other parallels between the climate and the environment. Both can affect our health. "There is a clear connection between certain weather conditions and some human diseases," says Alfred Wehner, president of the American Institute of Medical Climatology. The linkage between pollution and selected illnesses has also been established.

Both are of great public interest. Witness the existence of a 24-hour-a-day cable-television channel that does nothing but talk about the weather. Or consider the steady growth in the membership rolls of environmental organizations throughout the 1980s.

Both, in the final analysis, can be reduced to a discussion of people and

26 nature. Climate is what nature forces people to endure, or allows them to enjoy. The state of the environment depends largely on people's needs and intentions. Will they exploit nature, or will they seek to coexist with it?

This section provides an overall picture of what it is like outdoors in each micropolitan area, measuring the balance between people and nature. Four categories rank the cities according to the desirability of their climates. The fifth assesses the potential for environmental danger in each area.

The United States is a nation of meteorological extremes. Its southwestern deserts are often intolerably hot; California's Death Valley once reached 134 degrees. The country's northern reaches are capable of unbearable cold; Alaska has dropped as low as minus 80, Montana minus 70. The Pacific Northwest is awash with endless rainstorms in the winter, while the Great Lakes region is buried under mountainous snowdrifts. And the South does not escape. Its summertime humidity intensifies the impact of its high temperatures.

"I used to tell my friends that the United States was like the little child in a fairy tale," recalled Polish-born mathematician Stanislaw Ulam, who helped develop America's hydrogen bomb. "At [its] birth all the good fairies came bearing gifts, and only one failed to come. It was the one bringing the climate."

Another of America's gifts, a vast continent of natural wonders and resources, is being squandered. The Great Lakes and most of our major rivers have been polluted. Acid rain falls on eastern forests. Our cities are draped in shrouds of smog. The accumulation of carbon dioxide in the atmosphere threatens to produce severe global warming, the "greenhouse effect." Robert Dickinson, a senior scientist at the National Center for Atmospheric Research, warns that the situation is more dangerous than many are willing to admit. "We don't have 100 years [to slow the 'greenhouse effect']," he insists. "We have 10 or 20 at most."

Pollution is a problem almost everywhere in the country, but there is no doubt it is worst in large cities. A 1988 report from the Environmental Protection Agency showed that all of the nation's 24 biggest metropolitan areas were violating federal standards for emission of either carbon monoxide or ozone, or both. New York City averages 86 days of excessive carbon monoxide annually, the worst figure on the list. Los Angeles has the most severe ozone problem, with 143 days over the limit each year.

Ranking micropolitan America. The ideal small city would be one that avoids climatic extremes as much as possible, while also offering the clean environment that is unavailable in large cities. Each area is subjected to tests in five categories to determine how close it comes to perfection:

1. Temperature Extremes: Does the small city have a mild climate, or is it prone to excessively hot and/or cold days?

2. Temperature Variability: Is there a gradual fluctuation in temperatures over the year, or is the swing between seasons an abrupt one?

3. Summer Comfort: Is it warm, without being stiflingly hot, in mid-summer?

4. Snowfall: Does the area receive a reasonable amount of snow each winter, or is it buried under a massive white blanket for months?

5. Potential Environmental Dangers: Has the small city avoided serious pollution, or does it have some sites in need of cleanup?

Temperature Extremes

Joe McGinniss picked the perfect title a decade ago when he wrote his bestseller about life in Alaska. He called it *Going to Extremes.*

The most obvious extreme in Alaska is its climate. The same is true of the southwestern desert. One can be frighteningly cold; the other is often blisteringly hot. Both are memorable. Neither is found pleasant by most people.

This category measures each area's tendency to be cursed with extreme temperatures. It adds the number of days where the thermometer reaches or surpasses 90 degrees in a typical year with the number of days at or below 32 degrees.

Eureka, California, with its pleasant maritime climate, has never had a temperature higher than 86° in its recorded history. It averages only five days annually with a reading below the freezing point.

Bozeman, Montana, is at the opposite end of the scale. Perched 5,950 feet above sea level, Bozeman averages 241 freezing days a year, including seven in June, two in July, and three in August!

Cities on or near the Pacific coast generally do the best in this category. The interior West does worst.

Source. These statistics, published in 1985, are averages of conditions from 1951 through 1980. Derived from: *Climates of the States* (Detroit: Gale Research Co., 1985).

Scoring. Twenty points for 29 days or less; no points for 220 days or more. The spacing is every 10 days.

Temperature Extremes: Highs and Lows

Lowest	Days of 90° or More Or 32° or Less
1. Eureka, Calif.	5
2. San Luis Obispo–Atascadero, Calif.	15
3. Port Angeles, Wash.	41
4. Key West, Fla.	44
5. Aberdeen, Wash.	48
6. Brunswick, Ga.	58
7. Vero Beach, Fla.	59
8. Longview, Wash.	62
9. Albany, Oreg.	70
9. Corvallis, Oreg.	70

Highest	
219. Bozeman, Mont.	241
218. Rio Rancho, N.Mex.	226
217. Fairbanks, Alaska	221
216. Gallup, N.Mex.	218
215. Flagstaff, Ariz.	214
214. Rock Springs, Wyo.	213
213. Idaho Falls, Idaho	212
211. Bend, Oreg.	209
211. Minot, N.Dak.	209
210. Farmington, N.Mex.	207

(Figure following each area name indicates the number of days of 90° or more or 32° or less; figure in parentheses represents rating points.)

Alabama

Athens	112	(11)
Auburn–Opelika	122	(10)
Decatur	112	(11)
Enterprise	118	(11)
Selma	128	(10)
Talladega	131	(9)

Alaska

Fairbanks	221	(0)

Arizona

Bullhead City–Lake Havasu City	192	(3)
Casa Grande–Apache Junction	203	(2)
Flagstaff	214	(1)
Prescott	182	(4)
Sierra Vista	133	(9)
Yuma	172	(5)

Arkansas

Blytheville	140	(8)
El Dorado	140	(8)
Hot Springs	134	(9)
Jonesboro	135	(9)
Rogers	149	(8)
Russellville	149	(8)

California

El Centro–Calexico–Brawley	174	(5)
Eureka	5	(20)
Hanford	124	(10)
Madera	142	(8)
San Luis Obispo– Atascadero	15	(20)

Colorado

Grand Junction	200	(2)

Connecticut

Torrington	144	(8)

Delaware

Dover	121	(10)

Florida

Key West	44	(18)
Vero Beach	59	(17)

Georgia

Brunswick	58	(17)
Carrollton	120	(10)
Dalton	124	(10)
Gainesville	103	(12)
Hinesville	112	(11)
La Grange	123	(10)
Rome	131	(9)
Valdosta	128	(10)

Idaho

Coeur d'Alene	166	(6)
Idaho Falls	212	(1)
Nampa-Caldwell	192	(3)
Pocatello	202	(2)
Twin Falls	206	(2)

Illinois

Carbondale	152	(7)
Danville	154	(7)
De Kalb	164	(6)
Freeport	157	(7)
Galesburg	156	(7)
Mattoon–Charleston	149	(8)
Ottawa	155	(7)
Quincy	149	(8)
Sterling	168	(6)

Indiana

Columbus	153	(7)
Marion	160	(6)
Michigan City–La Porte	156	(7)
New Castle	160	(6)
Richmond	147	(8)
Vincennes	157	(7)

Iowa

Ames	181	(4)
Burlington	162	(6)
Clinton	160	(6)
Fort Dodge	176	(5)
Marshalltown	171	(5)
Mason City	177	(5)
Muscatine	155	(7)

Kansas

Hutchinson	184	(4)
Manhattan	180	(4)
Salina	188	(4)

Kentucky

Bowling Green	142	(8)
Frankfort	150	(7)
Madisonville	139	(9)
Paducah	144	(8)
Radcliff–Elizabethtown	143	(8)
Richmond	120	(10)

Louisiana

Bogalusa	135	(9)
Crowley	112	(11)
Hammond	126	(10)
Minden	144	(8)
Morgan City	102	(12)
New Iberia	101	(12)
Opelousas	108	(12)
Ruston	130	(9)

Maine

Augusta–Waterville	155	(7)
Biddeford	164	(6)

Maryland

Salisbury	108	(12)

Michigan

Adrian	164	(6)
Marquette	200	(2)
Mount Pleasant	167	(6)
Owosso	161	(6)
Traverse City	174	(5)

Minnesota

Faribault	179	(5)
Mankato	181	(4)
Winona	170	(5)

Mississippi

Columbus	150	(7)
Greenville	133	(9)
Greenwood	128	(10)
Hattiesburg	139	(9)
Laurel	134	(9)
Meridian	132	(9)
Tupelo	146	(8)
Vicksburg	106	(12)

Missouri

Cape Girardeau	160	(6)
Jefferson City	178	(5)
Sikeston	143	(8)

Montana

Bozeman	241	(0)
Helena	201	(2)
Missoula	206	(2)

Nebraska

Grand Island	189	(4)

Nevada

Carson City	206	(2)

New Hampshire

Concord	187	(4)
Keene	179	(5)
Laconia	187	(4)

New Mexico

Alamogordo	187	(4)
Carlsbad	185	(4)
Clovis	183	(4)
Farmington	207	(2)
Gallup	218	(1)
Hobbs	170	(5)
Rio Rancho	226	(0)
Roswell	176	(5)

New York

Auburn	144	(8)
Batavia	150	(7)
Cortland	163	(6)
Gloversville	158	(7)
Ithaca	158	(7)
Jamestown	158	(7)
Kingston	161	(6)
Olean	174	(5)
Plattsburgh	164	(6)
Watertown	153	(7)

North Carolina

Eden	116	(11)
Goldsboro	126	(10)
Greenville	129	(10)
Havelock–New Bern	92	(13)
Kinston	126	(10)
Lumberton	122	(10)
Roanoke Rapids	137	(9)
Rocky Mount	129	(10)
Sanford	113	(11)
Shelby	132	(9)
Statesville	137	(9)
Wilson	127	(10)

North Dakota

Minot	209	(2)

Ohio

Ashland	146	(8)
Ashtabula	134	(9)
Athens	160	(6)
Chillicothe	142	(8)
East Liverpool	142	(8)
Findlay	144	(8)
Fremont	150	(7)
Marion	156	(7)
New Philadelphia	139	(9)
Portsmouth	125	(10)
Sandusky	132	(9)
Sidney	153	(7)
Tiffin	142	(8)
Wooster	144	(8)
Zanesville	144	(8)

Oklahoma

Ardmore	148	(8)
Bartlesville	177	(5)
Chickasha	177	(5)
Duncan	161	(6)
McAlester	148	(8)
Muskogee	145	(8)
Okmulgee	163	(6)
Ponca City	175	(5)
Stillwater	171	(5)

Oregon

Albany	70	(15)
Bend	209	(2)
Corvallis	70	(15)
Grants Pass	121	(10)
Klamath Falls	182	(4)
Roseburg	72	(15)

Pennsylvania

Butler	157	(7)
Chambersburg	143	(8)
New Castle	152	(7)
Pottsville	146	(8)

Rhode Island

Newport	143	(8)

South Carolina

Greenwood	136	(9)
Hilton Head Island	84	(14)
Myrtle Beach	80	(14)
Orangeburg	124	(10)
Sumter	124	(10)

Tennessee

Cleveland	123	(10)
Columbia	135	(9)
Cookeville	120	(10)
Morristown	140	(8)
Tullahoma	117	(11)

Texas

Alice	144	(8)
Bay City	117	(11)
Del Rio	143	(8)
Greenville	148	(8)
Huntsville	133	(9)
Lufkin	143	(8)
Nacogdoches	149	(8)
Palestine	123	(10)
Paris	144	(8)

Utah

Logan	168	(6)

Vermont

Rutland	159	(7)

Virginia

Blacksburg	140	(8)
Fredericksburg	161	(6)
Harrisonburg	145	(8)
Martinsville	151	(7)
Staunton–Waynesboro	140	(8)
Winchester	131	(9)

Washington

Aberdeen	48	(18)
Longview	62	(16)
Port Angeles	41	(18)
Pullman	146	(8)
Walla Walla	100	(12)
Wenatchee	151	(7)

West Virginia

Beckley	115	(11)
Clarksburg	155	(7)
Fairmont	130	(9)
Morgantown	130	(9)

Wisconsin

Fond du Lac	166	(6)
Manitowoc	152	(7)
Marshfield–Wisconsin Rapids	183	(4)
Stevens Point	175	(5)

Wyoming

Rock Springs	213	(1)

Temperature Variability

A compelling argument can be made in support of areas that boast four sharply distinct seasons: a sunny summer, a brisk autumn, a white winter and a promising spring. But it is also true that many cities carry this concept too far.

This category ranks each area according to the volatility of its climate. The average low temperature for January, the coldest month in most of the country, is subtracted from the average high for July, typically the warmest month.

Eureka, California, has the smallest swing between hot and cold. Its July mean maximum is 60.3 degrees; its January mean minimum is a mere 19 degrees lower: 41.3. The Coast Range, which reaches its first ridge just ten miles east of the city, traps the moderating influence of the Pacific Ocean's breezes in the Eureka area.

The mountains that virtually surround Fairbanks, Alaska, have the opposite effect. They bar maritime air masses from the city. The result is an erratic climate, with an average high of 71.8 degrees in July and a numbing average low of minus 21.6 degrees in January. The swing is 93.4 degrees between these extremes.

Cities in the Pacific coastal region have the best (smallest) temperature ranges. The worst scores are largely in Midwestern cities away from the Great Lakes.

Source. These statistics, published in 1985, are averages of conditions from 1951 through 1980. Derived from *Climates of the States* (Detroit: Gale Research Co., 1985).

Scoring. Twenty points for 27.9 degrees or less; no points for 85 degrees or more. The spacing is every three degrees.

Lowest	Difference in Degrees Between July Mean Maximum and January Mean Minimum
1. Eureka, Calif.	19.0
2. Key West, Fla.	23.3
3. Aberdeen, Wash.	34.6
4. Port Angeles, Wash.	35.5
5. San Luis Obispo– Atascadero, Calif.	35.7
6. Vero Beach, Fla.	38.1
7. Longview, Wash.	44.4
8. Brunswick, Ga.	47.7
9. Albany, Oreg.	47.8
9. Corvallis, Oreg.	47.8

Highest

219. Fairbanks, Alaska	93.4
218. Minot, N.Dak.	88.0
217. Mankato, Minn.	84.1
216. Faribault, Minn.	82.6
215. Mason City, Iowa	80.3
214. Ames, Iowa	79.8
213. Winona, Minn.	79.5
211. Fort Dodge, Iowa	78.9
211. Marshfield– Wisconsin Rapids, Wis.	78.9
210. Grand Junction, Colo.	78.8

(Figure following each area name indicates difference in degrees between July mean maximum and January mean minimum; figure in parentheses represents rating points.)

Alabama

Athens	58.4	(9)
Auburn–Opelika	57.0	(10)
Decatur	58.4	(9)
Enterprise	53.3	(11)
Selma	55.0	(10)
Talladega	58.4	(9)

Alaska

Fairbanks	93.4	(0)

Arizona

Bullhead City–Lake Havasu City	70.7	(5)
Casa Grande–Apache Junction	70.6	(5)
Flagstaff	67.2	(6)
Prescott	66.6	(7)
Sierra Vista	58.6	(9)
Yuma	63.6	(8)

Arkansas

Blytheville	64.0	(7)
El Dorado	60.2	(9)
Hot Springs	62.1	(8)
Jonesboro	63.5	(8)
Rogers	67.1	(6)
Russellville	64.9	(7)

California

El Centro–Calexico–Brawley	65.0	(7)
Eureka	19.0	(20)
Hanford	60.8	(9)
Madera	62.9	(8)
San Luis Obispo–Atascadero	35.7	(17)

Colorado

Grand Junction	78.8	(3)

Connecticut

Torrington	64.9	(7)

Delaware

Dover	61.9	(8)

Florida

Key West	23.3	(20)
Vero Beach	38.1	(16)

Georgia

Brunswick	47.7	(13)
Carrollton	58.5	(9)
Dalton	60.1	(9)
Gainesville	56.3	(10)
Hinesville	52.6	(11)
La Grange	57.3	(10)
Rome	58.9	(9)
Valdosta	52.8	(11)

Idaho

Coeur d'Alene	64.2	(7)
Idaho Falls	74.5	(4)
Nampa–Caldwell	70.9	(5)
Pocatello	73.5	(4)
Twin Falls	72.3	(5)

Illinois

Carbondale	67.6	(6)
Danville	70.1	(5)
De Kalb	74.3	(4)
Freeport	74.0	(4)
Galesburg	73.2	(4)
Mattoon–Charleston	69.1	(6)
Ottawa	72.0	(5)
Quincy	71.9	(5)
Sterling	75.3	(4)

Indiana

Columbus	68.3	(6)
Marion	69.6	(6)
Michigan City–La Porte	69.6	(6)
New Castle	69.9	(6)
Richmond	67.4	(6)
Vincennes	69.2	(6)

Iowa

Ames	79.8	(2)
Burlington	75.1	(4)
Clinton	74.2	(4)
Fort Dodge	78.9	(3)
Marshalltown	78.2	(3)
Mason City	80.3	(2)
Muscatine	74.0	(4)

Kansas

Hutchinson	75.1	(4)
Manhattan	75.2	(4)
Salina	75.9	(4)

Kentucky

Bowling Green	64.6	(7)
Frankfort	66.6	(7)
Madisonville	64.8	(7)
Paducah	65.7	(7)
Radcliff–Elizabethtown	65.0	(7)
Richmond	62.0	(8)

Louisiana

Bogalusa	54.5	(11)
Crowley	50.6	(12)
Hammond	52.7	(11)
Minden	59.3	(9)
Morgan City	48.5	(13)
New Iberia	49.4	(12)
Opelousas	50.4	(12)
Ruston	58.9	(9)

Maine

Augusta–Waterville	68.4	(6)
Biddeford	67.0	(6)

Maryland

Salisbury	59.3	(9)

Michigan

Adrian	68.9	(6)
Marquette	71.2	(5)
Mount Pleasant	70.1	(5)
Owosso	68.3	(6)
Traverse City	67.6	(6)

Minnesota

Faribault	82.6	(1)
Mankato	84.1	(1)
Winona	79.5	(2)

Mississippi

Columbus	61.1	(8)
Greenville	59.7	(9)
Greenwood	57.5	(10)
Hattiesburg	55.5	(10)
Laurel	56.7	(10)
Meridian	58.3	(9)
Tupelo	61.3	(8)
Vicksburg	54.4	(11)

Missouri

Cape Girardeau	67.9	(6)
Jefferson City	72.9	(5)
Sikeston	66.1	(7)

Montana

Bozeman	67.9	(6)
Helena	75.5	(4)
Missoula	71.1	(5)

Nebraska

Grand Island	78.7	(3)

Nevada

Carson City	68.6	(6)

New Hampshire

Concord	73.6	(4)
Keene	72.6	(5)
Laconia	73.6	(4)

New Mexico

Alamogordo	67.3	(6)
Carlsbad	66.4	(7)
Clovis	68.5	(6)
Farmington	74.9	(4)
Gallup	74.8	(4)
Hobbs	65.3	(7)
Rio Rancho	75.3	(4)
Roswell	66.3	(7)

New York

Auburn	66.6	(7)
Batavia	66.2	(7)
Cortland	67.0	(6)
Gloversville	69.4	(6)
Ithaca	66.5	(7)
Jamestown	65.3	(7)
Kingston	69.3	(6)
Olean	66.9	(7)
Plattsburgh	72.8	(5)
Watertown	71.0	(5)

North Carolina

Eden	60.0	(9)
Goldsboro	59.7	(9)
Greenville	59.7	(9)
Havelock–New Bern	54.7	(11)
Kinston	58.8	(9)
Lumberton	58.2	(9)
Roanoke Rapids	62.0	(8)
Rocky Mount	59.7	(9)
Sanford	59.1	(9)
Shelby	61.3	(8)
Statesville	61.9	(8)
Wilson	59.1	(9)

North Dakota

Minot	88.0	(0)

Ohio

Ashland	66.0	(7)
Ashtabula	62.9	(8)
Athens	67.4	(6)
Chillicothe	66.1	(7)
East Liverpool	65.0	(7)
Findlay	66.4	(7)
Fremont	66.5	(7)
Marion	67.4	(6)
New Philadelphia	64.6	(7)
Portsmouth	63.0	(8)
Sandusky	64.0	(7)
Sidney	68.8	(6)
Tiffin	66.0	(7)
Wooster	65.0	(7)
Zanesville	65.1	(7)

Oklahoma

Ardmore	65.0	(7)
Bartlesville	72.2	(5)
Chickasha	69.9	(6)
Duncan	67.9	(6)
McAlester	66.5	(7)
Muskogee	66.8	(7)
Okmulgee	68.8	(6)
Ponca City	71.7	(5)
Stillwater	70.4	(5)

Oregon

Albany	47.8	(13)
Bend	61.1	(8)
Corvallis	47.8	(13)
Grants Pass	57.6	(10)
Klamath Falls	63.8	(8)
Roseburg	50.3	(12)

Pennsylvania

Butler	67.3	(6)
Chambersburg	64.7	(7)
New Castle	66.3	(7)
Pottsville	65.3	(7)

Rhode Island

Newport	62.0	(8)

South Carolina

Greenwood	59.8	(9)
Hilton Head Island	51.6	(12)
Myrtle Beach	52.6	(11)
Orangeburg	57.4	(10)
Sumter	57.1	(10)

Tennessee

Cleveland	60.1	(9)
Columbia	62.4	(8)
Cookeville	61.4	(8)
Morristown	62.7	(8)
Tullahoma	59.8	(9)

Texas

Alice	49.8	(12)
Bay City	50.4	(12)
Del Rio	59.4	(9)
Greenville	64.2	(7)
Huntsville	56.8	(10)
Lufkin	59.7	(9)
Nacogdoches	60.4	(9)
Palestine	58.2	(9)
Paris	63.8	(8)

Utah

Logan	70.9	(5)

Vermont

Rutland	70.4	(5)

Virginia

Blacksburg	62.0	(8)
Fredericksburg	66.2	(7)
Harrisonburg	65.0	(7)
Martinsville	64.0	(7)
Staunton–Waynesboro	63.6	(8)
Winchester	63.1	(8)

Washington

Aberdeen	34.6	(17)
Longview	44.4	(14)
Port Angeles	35.5	(17)
Pullman	59.6	(9)
Walla Walla	60.4	(9)
Wenatchee	66.7	(7)

West Virginia

Beckley	58.0	(9)
Clarksburg	65.2	(7)
Fairmont	62.4	(8)
Morgantown	62.2	(8)

Wisconsin

Fond du Lac	74.7	(4)
Manitowoc	69.1	(6)
Marshfield–Wisconsin Rapids	78.9	(3)
Stevens Point	78.0	(3)

Wyoming

Rock Springs	75.3	(4)

Summer Comfort

A long, hot summer is the rule for much of America. The Southern interior typically is blanketed by a steamy mixture of sizzling temperatures and sky-high humidity. Residents of the southwestern desert boast of their "dry heat," but the emphasis belongs on the second word. The desert sun can be as merciless as the muggy air blasting forth from the Gulf of Mexico.

Fortunately, there is an escape. This category measures each area's summer comfort level by taking the difference between its average high temperature for July and the arbitrary level of 80 degrees, chosen as a pleasantly warm reading.

The breezes from nearby Lake Ontario keep Watertown, New York, comfortable all summer long. Its mean maximum for July is 79.9 degrees. The temperature usually climbs past 90 degrees only twice in the month. Watertown has never had a day hotter than 97 degrees.

Bullhead City–Lake Havasu City, Arizona, cannot say the same. Its average July day reaches a high of 109.1 degrees. The thermometer tops 90 degrees every single day in a typical July.

Cities in the Northeast and near the Great Lakes offer the most comfortable summers. Desert cities dominate the list of those with the worst scores.

Source. These statistics, published in 1985, are averages of conditions from 1951 through 1980. Derived from *Climates of the States* (Detroit: Gale Research Co., 1985).

Scoring. Twenty points for areas whose mean maximum temperature for July deviates 0.5 degrees or less from 80 degrees; no points for 19.6 degrees or more. The spacing is every one degree.

Lowest Deviation	Deviation of July Mean Maximum from 80°
1. Watertown, N.Y.	0.1*
2. Traverse City, Mich.	0.2
3. Ithaca, N.Y.	0.3
4. Beckley, W.Va.	0.4*
4. Manitowoc, Wis.	0.4*
6. Cortland, N.Y.	0.5
6. Plattsburgh, N.Y.	0.5
8. Augusta–Waterville, Maine	0.6*
8. Newport, R.I.	0.6
10. Albany, Oreg.	0.7
10. Corvallis, Oreg.	0.7
10. Jamestown, N.Y.	0.7
10. Marshfield–Wisconsin Rapids, Wis.	0.7
10. Olean, N.Y.	0.7*

Highest Deviation

219. Bullhead City– Lake Havasu City, Ariz.	29.1
218. Yuma, Ariz.	26.8
217. El Centro–Calexico– Brawley, Calif.	26.6
216. Casa Grande– Apache Junction, Ariz.	26.4
215. Eureka, Calif.	19.7*
214. Madera, Calif.	19.1
212. Del Rio, Tex.	17.7
212. Hanford, Calif.	17.7
211. Ardmore, Okla.	16.1
210. Duncan, Okla.	16.0

* These areas have July mean maximums below 80 degrees. All others have means above 80.

(Figure following each area name indicates deviation of July mean maximum from 80 degrees; figure in parentheses represents rating points.)

Alabama

Athens	9.4 (11)
Auburn-Opelika	10.6 (9)
Decatur	9.4 (11)
Enterprise	11.4 (9)
Selma	12.8 (7)
Talladega	10.6 (9)

Alaska

Fairbanks	8.2*(12)

Arizona

Bullhead City–Lake Havasu City	29.1 (0)
Casa Grande–Apache Junction	26.4 (0)
Flagstaff	1.9 (18)
Prescott	8.7 (11)
Sierra Vista	13.4 (7)
Yuma	26.8 (0)

Arkansas

Blytheville	12.7 (7)
El Dorado	12.6 (7)
Hot Springs	13.4 (7)
Jonesboro	12.1 (8)
Rogers	10.1 (10)
Russellville	13.2 (7)

California

El Centro–Calexico–Brawley	26.6 (0)
Eureka	19.7* (0)
Hanford	17.7 (2)
Madera	19.1 (1)
San Luis Obispo–Atascadero	2.6*(17)

Colorado

Grand Junction	14.0 (6)

Connecticut

Torrington	3.2 (17)

Delaware

Dover	7.5 (13)

Florida

Key West	8.9 (11)
Vero Beach	9.7 (10)

Georgia

Brunswick	9.5 (11)
Carrollton	9.1 (11)
Dalton	9.2 (11)
Gainesville	7.1 (13)
Hinesville	11.8 (8)
La Grange	10.4 (10)
Rome	9.7 (10)
Valdosta	11.8 (8)

Idaho

Coeur d'Alene	6.0 (14)
Idaho Falls	3.7 (16)
Nampa–Caldwell	13.0 (7)
Pocatello	8.6 (11)
Twin Falls	11.3 (9)

---

* July mean maximum below 80°.

Illinois		
Carbondale	9.7	(10)
Danville	6.9	(13)
De Kalb	4.9	(15)
Freeport	3.2	(17)
Galesburg	5.3	(15)
Mattoon–Charleston	6.5	(14)
Ottawa	6.6	(13)
Quincy	7.0	(13)
Sterling	5.6	(14)

Indiana		
Columbus	6.4	(14)
Marion	4.7	(15)
Michigan City–La Porte	4.5	(16)
New Castle	5.5	(15)
Richmond	4.3	(16)
Vincennes	8.5	(12)

Iowa		
Ames	6.4	(14)
Burlington	6.9	(13)
Clinton	5.1	(15)
Fort Dodge	5.2	(15)
Marshalltown	5.2	(15)
Mason City	3.6	(16)
Muscatine	6.1	(14)

Kansas		
Hutchinson	13.9	(6)
Manhattan	11.7	(8)
Salina	12.7	(7)

Kentucky		
Bowling Green	9.2	(11)
Frankfort	7.5	(13)
Madisonville	9.4	(11)
Paducah	10.6	(9)
Radcliff–Elizabethtown	8.7	(11)
Richmond	7.3	(13)

Louisiana		
Bogalusa	12.6	(7)
Crowley	12.1	(8)
Hammond	12.4	(8)
Minden	13.2	(7)
Morgan City	11.6	(8)
New Iberia	11.2	(9)
Opelousas	11.7	(8)
Ruston	12.7	(7)

Maine		
Augusta–Waterville	0.6*	(19)
Biddeford	1.1*	(19)

Maryland		
Salisbury	6.9	(13)

Michigan		
Adrian	3.8	(16)
Marquette	4.7*	(15)
Mount Pleasant	3.2	(17)
Owosso	2.4	(18)
Traverse City	0.2	(20)

Minnesota		
Faribault	4.0	(16)
Mankato	4.5	(16)
Winona	1.4	(19)

Mississippi		
Columbus	12.7	(7)
Greenville	12.7	(7)
Greenwood	12.2	(8)
Hattiesburg	12.4	(8)
Laurel	12.2	(8)
Meridian	12.5	(8)
Tupelo	12.5	(8)
Vicksburg	11.4	(9)

Missouri

Cape Girardeau	11.2	(9)
Jefferson City	10.9	(9)
Sikeston	10.5	(10)

Montana

Bozeman	4.3*	(16)
Helena	3.6	(16)
Missoula	4.8	(15)

Nebraska

Grand Island	9.5	(11)

Nevada

Carson City	9.1	(11)

New Hampshire

Concord	2.6	(17)
Keene	3.5	(17)
Laconia	2.6	(17)

New Mexico

Alamogordo	15.2	(5)
Carlsbad	15.6	(4)
Clovis	11.1	(9)
Farmington	12.7	(7)
Gallup	8.5	(12)
Hobbs	13.3	(7)
Rio Rancho	14.0	(6)
Roswell	13.7	(6)

New York

Auburn	1.6	(18)
Batavia	1.3	(19)
Cortland	0.5	(20)
Gloversville	0.9	(19)
Ithaca	0.3	(20)
Jamestown	0.7	(19)
Kingston	4.1	(16)
Olean	0.7*	(19)
Plattsburgh	0.5	(20)
Watertown	0.1*	(20)

North Carolina

Eden	7.9	(12)
Goldsboro	10.2	(10)
Greenville	9.9	(10)
Havelock–New Bern	8.3	(12)
Kinston	9.5	(11)
Lumberton	9.4	(11)
Roanoke Rapids	9.2	(11)
Rocky Mount	9.9	(10)
Sanford	8.2	(12)
Shelby	8.8	(11)
Statesville	8.4	(12)
Wilson	9.6	(10)

North Dakota

Minot	3.6	(16)

Ohio

Ashland	2.8	(17)
Ashtabula	1.3	(19)
Athens	5.7	(14)
Chillicothe	5.7	(14)
East Liverpool	5.6	(14)
Findlay	3.3	(17)
Fremont	3.4	(17)
Marion	3.3	(17)
New Philadelphia	2.5	(18)
Portsmouth	6.4	(14)
Sandusky	2.7	(17)
Sidney	4.5	(16)
Tiffin	4.3	(16)
Wooster	1.8	(18)
Zanesville	3.7	(16)

Oklahoma

Ardmore	16.1	(4)
Bartlesville	14.7	(5)
Chickasha	15.3	(5)
Duncan	16.0	(4)
McAlester	14.0	(6)
Muskogee	14.1	(6)
Okmulgee	14.1	(6)
Ponca City	13.8	(6)
Stillwater	13.9	(6)

Oregon		
Albany	0.7	(19)
Bend	2.1	(18)
Corvallis	0.7	(19)
Grants Pass	10.4	(10)
Klamath Falls	4.7	(15)
Roseburg	4.2	(16)

Pennsylvania		
Butler	2.8	(17)
Chambersburg	5.1	(15)
New Castle	4.5	(16)
Pottsville	4.3	(16)

Rhode Island		
Newport	0.6	(19)

South Carolina		
Greenwood	10.5	(10)
Hilton Head Island	9.9	(10)
Myrtle Beach	9.2	(11)
Orangeburg	10.7	(9)
Sumter	11.1	(9)

Tennessee		
Cleveland	9.3	(11)
Columbia	9.8	(10)
Cookeville	3.7	(16)
Morristown	8.6	(11)
Tullahoma	8.3	(12)

Texas		
Alice	15.4	(5)
Bay City	12.8	(7)
Del Rio	17.7	(2)
Greenville	14.5	(6)
Huntsville	15.1	(5)
Lufkin	14.5	(6)
Nacogdoches	14.4	(6)
Palestine	13.5	(7)
Paris	15.0	(5)

Utah		
Logan	7.2	(13)

Vermont		
Rutland	1.5	(19)

Virginia		
Blacksburg	2.6	(17)
Fredericksburg	9.8	(10)
Harrisonburg	6.3	(14)
Martinsville	7.9	(12)
Staunton–Waynesboro	5.1	(15)
Winchester	6.5	(14)

Washington		
Aberdeen	11.0*	(9)
Longview	2.8*	(17)
Port Angeles	11.3*	(9)
Pullman	1.8	(18)
Walla Walla	8.8	(11)
Wenatchee	7.9	(12)

West Virginia		
Beckley	0.4*	(20)
Clarksburg	5.1	(15)
Fairmont	3.7	(16)
Morgantown	3.6	(16)

Wisconsin		
Fond du Lac	1.9	(18)
Manitowoc	0.4*	(20)
Marshfield–Wisconsin Rapids	0.7	(19)
Stevens Point	1.5	(19)

Wyoming		
Rock Springs	6.5	(14)

Snowfall

A light snowfall often does wonders for the spirit. It affords an opportunity to dust off the skis and sleds in the garage and try the local slopes. It blankets the drab winter landscape beautifully. And nothing is better to put the family in a holiday mood.

But too much snow is a nuisance. It renders roads impassable, forces you to dust off the shovels and snow blowers as well as the skis, and eventually causes the onset of the dreaded "cabin fever."

This category ranks each area according to its average annual snowfall. A few inches won't hurt a city's score appreciably, but a propensity for blizzards will yield a position near the bottom of the list.

Eight micropolitan areas receive no snowfall at all in a typical year. They are in Arizona, California, and Florida.

Bozeman, Montana, makes up for all of them. It is hit with more than a foot of snow in each month from October through April. This mountain city even got 15 inches of snow in June 1954.

Warm-weather cities obviously offer your best chance of escaping the snow. Cities in upstate New York and Michigan are the most likely to put you under five-foot drifts by February.

Source. These statistics, published in 1985, are averages of conditions from 1951 through 1980 from *Climates of the States* (Detroit: Gale Research Co., 1985).

Scoring. Twenty points for 0.0 inches; no points for 95.1 inches or more. The spacing is every five inches.

Snowfall: Highs and Lows

Lowest	Average Inches of Snow
1. Bullhead City–Lake Havasu City, Ariz.	0.0
1. Casa Grande-Apache Junction, Ariz.	0.0
1. El Centro–Calexico–Brawley, Calif.	0.0
1. Hanford, Calif.	0.0
1. Key West, Fla.	0.0
1. San Luis Obispo–Atascadero, Calif.	0.0
1. Vero Beach, Fla.	0.0
1. Yuma, Ariz.	0.0
9. Alice, Tex.	0.1
9. Brunswick, Ga.	0.1
9. Madera, Calif.	0.1
9. Morgan City, La.	0.1

Highest

219. Bozeman, Mont.	224.8
218. Olean, N.Y.	165.5
217. Jamestown, N.Y.	142.4
216. Marquette, Mich.	116.8
215. Auburn, N.Y.	109.8
214. Watertown, N.Y.	101.3
213. Flagstaff, Ariz.	96.6
212. Traverse City, Mich.	96.3
211. Batavia, N.Y.	93.4
210. Cortland, N.Y.	90.9

(Figure following each area name indicates average inches of snow; figure in parentheses represents rating points.)

Alabama

Athens	2.8	(19)
Auburn-Opelika	0.7	(19)
Decatur	2.8	(19)
Enterprise	0.4	(19)
Selma	0.3	(19)
Talladega	1.0	(19)

Alaska

Fairbanks	66.5	(6)

Arizona

Bullhead City–Lake Havasu City	0.0	(20)
Casa Grande–Apache Junction	0.0	(20)
Flagstaff	96.6	(0)
Prescott	24.1	(15)
Sierra Vista	2.1	(19)
Yuma	0.0	(20)

Arkansas

Blytheville	8.3	(18)
El Dorado	2.6	(19)
Hot Springs	4.9	(19)
Jonesboro	9.0	(18)
Rogers	12.1	(17)
Russellville	5.1	(18)

California

El Centro–Calexico–Brawley	0.0	(20)
Eureka	0.2	(19)
Hanford	0.0	(20)
Madera	0.1	(19)
San Luis Obispo–Atascadero	0.0	(20)

Colorado

Grand Junction	26.1	(14)

Connecticut

Torrington	38.3	(12)

Delaware

Dover	17.5	(16)

Florida

Key West	0.0	(20)
Vero Beach	0.0	(20)

Georgia

Brunswick	0.1	(19)
Carrollton	0.4	(19)
Dalton	2.9	(19)
Gainesville	3.3	(19)
Hinesville	0.3	(19)
La Grange	0.5	(19)
Rome	2.0	(19)
Valdosta	0.4	(19)

Idaho

Coeur d'Alene	61.4	(7)
Idaho Falls	36.4	(12)
Nampa–Caldwell	13.7	(17)
Pocatello	41.8	(11)
Twin Falls	26.5	(14)

Illinois

Carbondale	13.8	(17)
Danville	21.9	(15)
De Kalb	35.5	(12)
Freeport	34.5	(13)
Galesburg	27.5	(14)
Mattoon–Charleston	18.7	(16)
Ottawa	28.0	(14)
Quincy	23.5	(15)
Sterling	34.5	(13)

Indiana

Columbus	17.9	(16)
Marion	28.1	(14)
Michigan City–La Porte	73.0	(5)
New Castle	22.2	(15)
Richmond	23.5	(15)
Vincennes	14.8	(17)

Iowa

Ames	31.9	(13)
Burlington	27.5	(14)
Clinton	32.9	(13)
Fort Dodge	39.5	(12)
Marshalltown	31.3	(13)
Mason City	41.9	(11)
Muscatine	32.3	(13)

Kansas

Hutchinson	16.7	(16)
Manhattan	20.5	(15)
Salina	20.2	(15)

Kentucky

Bowling Green	12.4	(17)
Frankfort	14.0	(17)
Madisonville	11.0	(17)
Paducah	9.9	(18)
Radcliff–Elizabethtown	14.2	(17)
Richmond	18.6	(16)

Louisiana

Bogalusa	0.4	(19)
Crowley	0.4	(19)
Hammond	0.2	(19)
Minden	1.1	(19)
Morgan City	0.1	(19)
New Iberia	0.2	(19)
Opelousas	0.4	(19)
Ruston	1.3	(19)

Maine

Augusta–Waterville	79.5	(4)
Biddeford	72.5	(5)

Maryland

Salisbury	12.3	(17)

Michigan

Adrian	32.4	(13)
Marquette	116.8	(0)
Mount Pleasant	36.8	(12)
Owosso	40.9	(11)
Traverse City	96.3	(0)

Minnesota

Faribault	43.0	(11)
Mankato	38.8	(12)
Winona	47.3	(10)

Mississippi

Columbus	2.2	(19)
Greenville	1.6	(19)
Greenwood	1.8	(19)
Hattiesburg	0.7	(19)
Laurel	0.8	(19)
Meridian	1.2	(19)
Tupelo	2.4	(19)
Vicksburg	1.4	(19)

Missouri

Cape Girardeau	12.3	(17)
Jefferson City	17.6	(16)
Sikeston	8.6	(18)

Montana

Bozeman	224.8	(0)
Helena	48.1	(10)
Missoula	49.1	(10)

Nebraska

Grand Island	30.5	(13)

Nevada

Carson City	26.2	(14)

New Hampshire

Concord	64.4	(7)
Keene	69.2	(6)
Laconia	64.4	(7)

New Mexico

Alamogordo	4.6	(19)
Carlsbad	5.5	(18)
Clovis	12.9	(17)
Farmington	14.2	(17)
Gallup	20.9	(15)
Hobbs	6.5	(18)
Rio Rancho	8.6	(18)
Roswell	11.5	(17)

New York

Auburn	109.8	(0)
Batavia	93.4	(1)
Cortland	90.9	(1)
Gloversville	82.1	(3)
Ithaca	71.9	(5)
Jamestown	142.4	(0)
Kingston	42.6	(11)
Olean	165.5	(0)
Plattsburgh	78.2	(4)
Watertown	101.3	(0)

North Carolina

Eden	12.2	(17)
Goldsboro	5.1	(18)
Greenville	6.4	(18)
Havelock–New Bern	3.2	(19)
Kinston	4.3	(19)
Lumberton	3.0	(19)
Roanoke Rapids	12.7	(17)
Rocky Mount	6.4	(18)
Sanford	7.5	(18)
Shelby	7.3	(18)
Statesville	9.3	(18)
Wilson	5.9	(18)

North Dakota

Minot	39.1	(12)

Ohio

Ashland	40.3	(11)
Ashtabula	72.9	(5)
Athens	24.2	(15)
Chillicothe	21.9	(15)
East Liverpool	24.6	(15)
Findlay	24.3	(15)
Fremont	30.3	(13)
Marion	32.6	(13)
New Philadelphia	28.6	(14)
Portsmouth	18.3	(16)
Sandusky	29.9	(14)
Sidney	24.6	(15)
Tiffin	29.3	(14)
Wooster	36.0	(12)
Zanesville	25.3	(14)

Oklahoma

Ardmore	5.0	(19)
Bartlesville	10.2	(17)
Chickasha	6.1	(18)
Duncan	6.3	(18)
McAlester	6.3	(18)
Muskogee	8.1	(18)
Okmulgee	8.2	(18)
Ponca City	8.1	(18)
Stillwater	8.4	(18)

Oregon

Albany	6.5	(18)
Bend	40.2	(11)
Corvallis	6.5	(18)
Grants Pass	5.4	(18)
Klamath Falls	37.6	(12)
Roseburg	6.2	(18)

Pennsylvania

Butler	41.4	(11)
Chambersburg	32.8	(13)
New Castle	39.3	(12)
Pottsville	32.8	(13)

Rhode Island

Newport	32.5	(13)

South Carolina

Greenwood	2.3	(19)
Hilton Head Island	0.3	(19)
Myrtle Beach	0.9	(19)
Orangeburg	1.6	(19)
Sumter	2.1	(19)

Tennessee

Cleveland	4.1	(19)
Columbia	7.3	(18)
Cookeville	16.5	(16)
Morristown	12.6	(17)
Tullahoma	9.6	(18)

Texas

Alice	0.1	(19)
Bay City	0.2	(19)
Del Rio	0.6	(19)
Greenville	3.5	(19)
Huntsville	0.9	(19)
Lufkin	0.9	(19)
Nacogdoches	1.5	(19)
Palestine	0.5	(19)
Paris	3.8	(19)

Utah

Logan	68.2	(6)

Vermont

Rutland	65.6	(6)

Virginia

Blacksburg	22.0	(15)
Fredericksburg	17.7	(16)
Harrisonburg	25.1	(14)
Martinsville	14.5	(17)
Staunton–Waynesboro	25.9	(14)
Winchester	27.6	(14)

Washington

Aberdeen	9.6	(18)
Longview	6.7	(18)
Port Angeles	6.3	(18)
Pullman	38.6	(12)
Walla Walla	19.9	(16)
Wenatchee	30.7	(13)

West Virginia

Beckley	59.6	(8)
Clarksburg	31.3	(13)
Fairmont	42.0	(11)
Morgantown	32.1	(13)

Wisconsin

Fond du Lac	36.9	(12)
Manitowoc	42.5	(11)
Marshfield–Wisconsin Rapids	49.0	(10)
Stevens Point	42.0	(11)

Wyoming

Rock Springs	49.2	(10)

Potential Environmental Dangers

Water shortages, dead fish in rivers, lakes completely without fish, medical waste washing up on beaches, predictions of global warming: there is considerable evidence that man is still endangering the environment. Pollution is generally much worse in large cities, but not all micropolitan areas have escaped the problem.

This category ranks each area according to its rate of potentially dangerous waste sites. Included are locations listed for investigation or cleanup by the Environmental Protection Agency, the Defense Department, and the states. Each area's total number of such sites is projected to a rate per 1,000 square miles.

Sixty-five micropolitan areas do not have any such danger zones. But Grand Island, Nebraska, has 108, or a rate of 201.1 per 1,000 square miles. Drinking-water wells in the vicinity of the Cornhusker Army Ammunition Plant have been found to be contaminated with high concentrations of the explosive compound RDX. Cleanup is under way.

Areas with no hazardous-waste sites are in all regions of the country. The bulk of the small cities with the worst problems are in the East and the South.

Source. These statistics, published in 1988, are for 1986. Derived from: U.S. Geological Survey, *National Water Summary, 1986* (Washington: U.S. Government Printing Office, 1988).

Scoring. Twenty points for 0.0 hazardous-waste sites per 1,000 square miles; no points for 19.1 or more. The spacing is every one site per 1,000 square miles.

Lowest

(The areas listed below tied with 0.0 specified waste sites per 1,000 square miles.)

1. Alice, Tex.
1. Ashland, Ohio
1. Auburn, N.Y.
1. Auburn–Opelika, Ala.
1. Bend, Oreg.
1. Blytheville, Ark.
1. Bullhead City–Lake Havasu City, Ariz.
1. Cape Girardeau, Mo.
1. Carson City, Nev.
1. Cookeville, Tenn.
1. Crowley, La.
1. Dalton, Ga.
1. De Kalb, Ill.
1. Del Rio, Tex.
1. Eden, N.C.
1. Enterprise, Ala.
1. Findlay, Ohio
1. Fond du Lac, Wis.
1. Fort Dodge, Iowa
1. Freeport, Ill.
1. Gainesville, Ga.

1. Grants Pass, Oreg.
1. Greenville, Miss.
1. Greenville, N.C.
1. Greenville, Tex.
1. Greenwood, Miss.
1. Greenwood, S.C.
1. Hinesville, Ga.
1. Hot Springs, Ark.
1. Huntsville, Tex.
1. Jefferson City, Mo.
1. Key West, Fla.
1. Klamath Falls, Oreg.
1. La Grange, Ga.
1. Lumberton, N.C.
1. Madera, Calif.
1. Marion, Ohio
1. Mason City, Iowa
1. McAlester, Okla.
1. Minot, N. Dak.
1. Morgan City, La.
1. Morristown, Tenn.
1. Mount Pleasant, Mich.
1. Owosso, Mich.

1. Palestine, Tex.
1. Paris, Tex.
1. Plattsburgh, N.Y.
1. Port Angeles, Wash.
1. Prescott, Ariz.
1. Richmond, Ind.
1. Richmond, Ky.
1. Rio Rancho, N.Mex.
1. Roanoke Rapids, N.C.
1. Rogers, Ark.
1. Rome, Ga.
1. Roseburg, Oreg.
1. Roswell, N.Mex.
1. Russellville, Ark.
1. Ruston, La.
1. Stevens Point, Wis.
1. Tiffin, Ohio
1. Tullahoma, Tenn.
1. Tupelo, Miss.
1. Vincennes, Ind.
1. Wilson, N.C.

Highest	**Specified Waste Sites Per 1,000 Square Miles**
219. Grand Island, Neb.	201.1
218. Talladega, Ala.	104.9
217. Newport, R.I.	56.1
216. Fairmont, W.Va.	28.8
215. Morgantown, W.Va.	27.5
214. Hutchinson, Kans.	17.5
213. Goldsboro, N.C.	16.2
212. Myrtle Beach, S.C.	14.0
211. Concord, N.H.	13.9
210. Minden, La.	13.3

(Figure following each area name indicates specified waste sites per 1,000 square miles; figure in parentheses represents rating points.)

Alabama

Athens	1.8	(18)
Auburn–Opelika	0.0	(20)
Decatur	7.0	(13)
Enterprise	0.0	(20)
Selma	2.1	(17)
Talladega	104.9	(0)

Alaska

Fairbanks	2.8	(17)

Arizona

Bullhead City–Lake Havasu City	0.0	(20)
Casa Grande–Apache Junction	0.2	(19)
Flagstaff	0.1	(19)
Prescott	0.0	(20)
Sierra Vista	0.2	(19)
Yuma	0.2	(19)

Arkansas

Blytheville	0.0	(20)
El Dorado	7.6	(12)
Hot Springs	0.0	(20)
Jonesboro	1.4	(18)
Rogers	0.0	(20)
Russellville	0.0	(20)

California

El Centro–Calexico–Brawley	0.5	(19)
Eureka	0.6	(19)
Hanford	1.4	(18)
Madera	0.0	(20)
San Luis Obispo–Atascadero	0.6	(19)

Colorado

Grand Junction	0.6	(19)

Connecticut

Torrington	11.9	(8)

Delaware

Dover	6.7	(13)

Florida

Key West	0.0	(20)
Vero Beach	4.0	(16)

Georgia

Brunswick	4.9	(15)
Carrollton	4.0	(16)
Dalton	0.0	(20)
Gainesville	0.0	(20)
Hinesville	0.0	(20)
La Grange	0.0	(20)
Rome	0.0	(20)
Valdosta	3.9	(16)

Idaho

Coeur d'Alene	1.6	(18)
Idaho Falls	1.6	(18)
Nampa–Caldwell	10.3	(9)
Pocatello	4.5	(15)
Twin Falls	0.5	(19)

Illinois

Carbondale	1.7	(18)
Danville	2.2	(17)
De Kalb	0.0	(20)
Freeport	0.0	(20)
Galesburg	2.8	(17)
Mattoon–Charleston	2.0	(18)
Ottawa	2.6	(17)
Quincy	4.7	(15)
Sterling	1.5	(18)

Indiana

Columbus	4.9	(15)
Marion	4.8	(15)
Michigan City–La Porte	3.3	(16)
New Castle	2.5	(17)
Richmond	0.0	(20)
Vincennes	0.0	(20)

Iowa

Ames	1.7	(18)
Burlington	9.7	(10)
Clinton	2.9	(17)
Fort Dodge	0.0	(20)
Marshalltown	3.5	(16)
Mason City	0.0	(20)
Muscatine	4.5	(15)

Kansas

Hutchinson	17.5	(2)
Manhattan	3.4	(16)
Salina	2.8	(17)

Kentucky

Bowling Green	3.6	(16)
Frankfort	4.7	(15)
Madisonville	3.6	(16)
Paducah	12.0	(8)
Radcliff–Elizabethtown	4.8	(15)
Richmond	0.0	(20)

Louisiana

Bogalusa	1.5	(18)
Crowley	0.0	(20)
Hammond	2.6	(17)
Minden	13.3	(6)
Morgan City	0.0	(20)
New Iberia	1.7	(18)
Opelousas	1.1	(18)
Ruston	0.0	(20)

Maine

Augusta–Waterville	5.7	(14)
Biddeford	4.0	(16)

Maryland

Salisbury	10.6	(9)

Michigan

Adrian	1.3	(18)
Marquette	0.5	(19)
Mount Pleasant	0.0	(20)
Owosso	0.0	(20)
Traverse City	2.1	(17)

Minnesota

Faribault	2.0	(18)
Mankato	2.7	(17)
Winona	4.8	(15)

Mississippi

Columbus	3.9	(16)
Greenville	0.0	(20)
Greenwood	0.0	(20)
Hattiesburg	2.1	(17)
Laurel	1.4	(18)
Meridian	1.4	(18)
Tupelo	0.0	(20)
Vicksburg	1.7	(18)

Missouri

Cape Girardeau	0.0	(20)
Jefferson City	0.0	(20)
Sikeston	2.4	(17)

Montana

Bozeman	0.4	(19)
Helena	0.3	(19)
Missoula	0.4	(19)

Nebraska

Grand Island	201.1	(0)

Nevada

Carson City	0.0	(20)

New Hampshire

Concord	13.9	(6)
Keene	8.4	(11)
Laconia	9.9	(10)

New Mexico

Alamogordo	0.3	(19)
Carlsbad	0.5	(19)
Clovis	0.7	(19)
Farmington	0.2	(19)
Gallup	0.4	(19)
Hobbs	0.9	(19)
Rio Rancho	0.0	(20)
Roswell	0.0	(20)

New York

Auburn	0.0	(20)
Batavia	4.0	(16)
Cortland	2.0	(18)
Gloversville	8.0	(12)
Ithaca	4.2	(15)
Jamestown	0.9	(19)
Kingston	9.7	(10)
Olean	3.8	(16)
Plattsburgh	0.0	(20)
Watertown	0.8	(19)

North Carolina

Eden	0.0	(20)
Goldsboro	16.2	(3)
Greenville	0.0	(20)
Havelock–New Bern	2.9	(17)
Kinston	2.5	(17)
Lumberton	0.0	(20)
Roanoke Rapids	0.0	(20)
Rocky Mount	1.0	(19)
Sanford	3.9	(16)
Shelby	2.1	(17)
Statesville	1.7	(18)
Wilson	0.0	(20)

North Dakota

Minot	0.0	(20)

Ohio

Ashland	0.0	(20)
Ashtabula	11.4	(8)
Athens	2.0	(18)
Chillicothe	2.9	(17)
East Liverpool	3.7	(16)
Findlay	0.0	(20)
Fremont	2.4	(17)
Marion	0.0	(20)
New Philadelphia	1.8	(18)
Portsmouth	1.6	(18)
Sandusky	3.8	(16)
Sidney	4.9	(15)
Tiffin	0.0	(20)
Wooster	1.8	(18)
Zanesville	1.5	(18)

Oklahoma

Ardmore	2.4	(17)
Bartlesville	4.7	(15)
Chickasha	0.9	(19)
Duncan	2.3	(17)
McAlester	0.0	(20)
Muskogee	2.5	(17)
Okmulgee	1.4	(18)
Ponca City	1.1	(18)
Stillwater	2.9	(17)

Oregon

Albany	1.3	(18)
Bend	0.0	(20)
Corvallis	1.5	(18)
Grants Pass	0.0	(20)
Klamath Falls	0.0	(20)
Roseburg	0.0	(20)

Pennsylvania

Butler	8.9	(11)
Chambersburg	11.6	(8)
New Castle	2.8	(17)
Pottsville	6.4	(13)

Rhode Island			Virginia		
Newport	56.1	(0)	Blacksburg	12.8	(7)
			Fredericksburg	7.3	(12)
South Carolina			Harrisonburg	1.1	(18)
Greenwood	0.0	(20)	Martinsville	7.6	(12)
Hilton Head Island	8.6	(11)	Staunton–Waynesboro	3.0	(17)
Myrtle Beach	14.0	(6)	Winchester	9.4	(10)
Orangeburg	1.8	(18)			
Sumter	7.5	(12)	**Washington**		
			Aberdeen	1.0	(19)
Tennessee			Longview	4.4	(15)
Cleveland	3.1	(16)	Port Angeles	0.0	(20)
Columbia	3.2	(16)	Pullman	0.5	(19)
Cookeville	0.0	(20)	Walla Walla	2.4	(17)
Morristown	0.0	(20)	Wenatchee	1.7	(18)
Tullahoma	0.0	(20)			
			West Virginia		
Texas			Beckley	4.9	(15)
Alice	0.0	(20)	Clarksburg	9.6	(10)
Bay City	2.7	(17)	Fairmont	28.8	(0)
Del Rio	0.0	(20)	Morgantown	27.5	(0)
Greenville	0.0	(20)			
Huntsville	0.0	(20)	**Wisconsin**		
Lufkin	1.2	(18)	Fond du Lac	0.0	(20)
Nacogdoches	1.1	(18)	Manitowoc	3.4	(16)
Palestine	0.0	(20)	Marshfield–Wisconsin		
Paris	0.0	(20)	Rapids	1.2	(18)
			Stevens Point	0.0	(20)
Utah					
Logan	1.7	(18)	**Wyoming**		
			Rock Springs	1.6	(18)
Vermont					
Rutland	5.4	(14)			

The Results

Morris Zachuto was enthusiastic when a *New York Times* reporter asked him how he liked his new hometown. "The sky is so clear here," Zachuto replied quickly. "The sun shines a lot. And people are really nice. That's the best part."

Zachuto and his wife had decided a few months earlier to chuck big-city life and move to San Luis Obispo, California. They found the unpolluted skies a pleasant switch from the smoggy Los Angeles to which they were accustomed. Refugees from the chilly North speak just as happily of warm winters and pleasant summers.

The San Luis Obispo–Atascadero area takes first place in the climate/environment section, earning 93 out of a possible 100 points. Situated in a valley about 20 miles from the Pacific Ocean, the region is both warmed by the famed California sun and cooled by sea breezes.

Temperatures reach an average high of 77.4 degrees in July, a far cry from the intense heat that bakes California's interior each summer. The typical mid-winter day has a high in the mid-60s, with an overnight low in the 40s. Snow is rarely seen.

Pollution is not a major concern in the San Luis Obispo–Atascadero area. Two waste sites require cleanup, a rate of just 0.6 sites per 1,000 square miles. And then there are the clear skies that so impressed Morris Zachuto.

The Pacific coast dominates the list of the ten small cities with the best climate/environment scores. San Luis Obispo–Atascadero is joined by three areas each from Washington and Oregon, as well as one from California. All are either on the ocean or close to it. The remaining two slots in the top ten belong to sunny Florida beach towns.

Grand Island, Nebraska, sees its share of clouds and is certainly distant from the ocean. The combination of an exacting climate and serious environmental problems has landed Grand Island in last place in this section, with 31 points. Summers are hot on the plains, with an average high in July just short of 90 degrees. Winters bring more than 30 inches of snow, along with overnight lows in the teens. More than half of all days in Grand Island either top the 90-degree mark or fall below freezing.

The ground-water pollution in the Grand Island area is unmatched in micropolitan America. The army has identified 108 sites needing investigation or cleanup as a result of contamination from an ammunition plant.

Most of the other communities with low climate/environment scores are located in the interior West or the hilly country of the East.

Highest	Rating Points
1. San Luis Obispo–Atascadero, Calif.	93
2. Key West, Fla.	89
3. Albany, Oreg.	83
3. Corvallis, Oreg.	83
5. Port Angeles, Wash.	82
6. Aberdeen, Wash.	81
6. Roseburg, Oreg.	81
8. Longview, Wash.	80
9. Vero Beach, Fla.	79
10. Eureka, Calif.	78
11. Brunswick, Ga.	75
12. Gainesville, Ga.	74
13. Havelock–New Bern, N.C.	72
13. Morgan City, La.	72
15. Cookeville, Tenn.	70
15. Crowley, La.	70
15. Enterprise, Ala.	70
15. New Iberia, La.	70
15. Tullahoma, Tenn.	70
20. Dalton, Ga.	69
20. Eden, N.C.	69
20. Hinesville, Ga.	69
20. La Grange, Ga.	69
20. Lumberton, N.C.	69
20. Opelousas, La.	69
20. Vicksburg, Miss.	69

Lowest

219. Grand Island, Nebr.	31
218. Hutchinson, Kans.	32
217. Fairbanks, Alaska	35
216. Concord, N.H.	38
213. Bozeman, Mont.	41
213. Marquette, Mich.	41
213. Nampa-Caldwell, Idaho	41
212. Laconia, N.H.	42
211. Pocatello, Idaho	43
207. Fairmont, W.Va.	44
207. Flagstaff, Ariz.	44
207. Grand Junction, Colo.	44
207. Keene, N.H.	44

	San Luis Obispo–Atascadero, Calif.	Grand Island, Nebr.
Total Points in Section	93	31
Rank in Section	1	219
Results (and Rating Points)		
Temperature Extremes Days of 90° or more or 32° or less	15 (20)	189 (4)
Temperature Variability Difference in degrees between July mean maximum and January mean minimum	35.7 (17)	78.7 (3)
Summer Comfort Deviation of July mean maximum from 80 degrees	–2.6 (17)	9.5 (11)
Snowfall Average inches of snow	0.0 (20)	30.5 (13)
Potential Environmental Dangers Specified waste sites per 1,000 square miles	0.6 (19)	201.1 (0)

(Figure following each area name indicates the composite score from the five categories in this section.)

Alabama
Athens	68
Auburn–Opelika	68
Decatur	63
Enterprise	70
Selma	63
Talladega	46

Alaska
Fairbanks	35

Arizona
Bullhead City–Lake Havasu City	48
Casa Grande–Apache Junction	46
Flagstaff	44
Prescott	57
Sierra Vista	63
Yuma	52

Arkansas
Blytheville	60
El Dorado	55
Hot Springs	63
Jonesboro	61
Rogers	61
Russellville	60

California
El Centro–Calexico–Brawley	51
Eureka	78
Hanford	59
Madera	56
San Luis Obispo–Atascadero	93

Colorado
Grand Junction	44

Connecticut
Torrington	52

Delaware
Dover	60

Florida
Key West	89
Vero Beach	79

Georgia
Brunswick	75
Carrollton	65
Dalton	69
Gainesville	74
Hinesville	69
La Grange	69
Rome	67
Valdosta	64

Idaho
Coeur d'Alene	52
Idaho Falls	51
Nampa–Caldwell	41
Pocatello	43
Twin Falls	49

Illinois
Carbondale	58
Danville	57
De Kalb	57
Freeport	61
Galesburg	57
Mattoon–Charleston	62
Ottawa	56
Quincy	56
Sterling	55

Indiana
Columbus	58
Marion	56
Michigan City–La Porte	50
New Castle	59
Richmond	65
Vincennes	62

Iowa
Ames	51
Burlington	47
Clinton	55
Fort Dodge	55
Marshalltown	52
Mason City	54
Muscatine	53

Kansas
Hutchinson	32
Manhattan	47
Salina	47

Kentucky
Bowling Green	59
Frankfort	59
Madisonville	60
Paducah	50
Radcliff–Elizabethtown	58
Richmond	67

Louisiana
Bogalusa	64
Crowley	70
Hammond	65
Minden	49
Morgan City	72
New Iberia	70
Opelousas	69
Ruston	64

Maine

Augusta–	
Waterville	50
Biddeford	52

Maryland

Salisbury	60

Michigan

Adrian	59
Marquette	41
Mount Pleasant	60
Owosso	61
Traverse City	48

Minnesota

Faribault	51
Mankato	50
Winona	51

Mississippi

Columbus	57
Greenville	64
Greenwood	67
Hattiesburg	63
Laurel	64
Meridian	63
Tupelo	63
Vicksburg	69

Missouri

Cape Girardeau	58
Jefferson City	55
Sikeston	60

Montana

Bozeman	41
Helena	51
Missoula	51

Nebraska

Grand Island	31

Nevada

Carson City	53

New Hampshire

Concord	38
Keene	44
Laconia	42

New Mexico

Alamogordo	53
Carlsbad	52
Clovis	55
Farmington	49
Gallup	51
Hobbs	56
Rio Rancho	48
Roswell	55

New York

Auburn	53
Batavia	50
Cortland	51
Gloversville	47
Ithaca	54
Jamestown	52
Kingston	49
Olean	47
Plattsburgh	55
Watertown	51

North Carolina

Eden	69
Goldsboro	50
Greenville	67
Havelock–New Bern	72
Kinston	66
Lumberton	69
Roanoke Rapids	65
Rocky Mount	66
Sanford	66
Shelby	63
Statesville	65
Wilson	67

North Dakota

Minot	50

Ohio

Ashland	63
Ashtabula	49
Athens	59
Chillicothe	61
East Liverpool	60
Findlay	67
Fremont	61
Marion	63
New Philadelphia	66
Portsmouth	66
Sandusky	63
Sidney	59
Tiffin	65
Wooster	63
Zanesville	63

Oklahoma

Ardmore	55
Bartlesville	47
Chickasha	53
Duncan	51
McAlester	59
Muskogee	56
Okmulgee	54
Ponca City	52
Stillwater	51

Oregon

Albany	83
Bend	59
Corvallis	83
Grants Pass	68
Klamath Falls	59
Roseburg	81

Pennsylvania
Butler	52
Chambersburg	51
New Castle	59
Pottsville	57

Rhode Island
Newport	48

South Carolina
Greenwood	67
Hilton Head Island	66
Myrtle Beach	61
Orangeburg	66
Sumter	60

Tennessee
Cleveland	65
Columbia	61
Cookeville	70
Morristown	64
Tullahoma	70

Texas
Alice	64
Bay City	66
Del Rio	58
Greenville	60
Huntsville	63
Lufkin	60
Nacogdoches	60
Palestine	65
Paris	60

Utah
Logan	48

Vermont
Rutland	51

Virginia
Blacksburg	55
Fredericksburg	51
Harrisonburg	61
Martinsville	55
Staunton–Waynesboro	62
Winchester	55

Washington
Aberdeen	81
Longview	80
Port Angeles	82
Pullman	66
Walla Walla	65
Wenatchee	57

West Virginia
Beckley	63
Clarksburg	52
Fairmont	44
Morgantown	46

Wisconsin
Fond du Lac	60
Manitowoc	60
Marshfield–Wisconsin Rapids	54
Stevens Point	58

Wyoming
Rock Springs	47

2

Diversions

Having fun is becoming hard work. That's the complaint from millions of Americans who say they are spending more time than ever on their jobs. Making room in their busy schedules for recreation is difficult.

A *Wall Street Journal*–NBC survey in 1986 found that twice as many Americans reported a decline in their leisure time as they got older, compared to those whose free time was on the increase. People in professional and management positions said they were working an average of 45 hours a week; the typical manufacturing employee was putting in 43. Vacation time is also at a premium. Americans average two weeks a year. Their counterparts in every industrialized nation but Japan receive more.

"We think of leisure as a postponed activity," says Richard Bolles, author of a handbook for job hunters, *What Color Is Your Parachute?* "[But] the big joke in our culture is the heart attack that comes a week before that big cruise you've waited for all your life."

It is important that recreational opportunities be readily available to people who lack the time to go hunting for them. This section rates each micropolitan area according to the wealth of options available to those in need of diversions.

But what do people really like to do when they're not stuck behind

64 a desk or in front of a machine? A comprehensive Gallup survey found that sedentary pursuits are common on weeknights. One-third of all Americans say their favorite way of spending an evening is in front of the television set, 14 percent each mention reading or resting, and 13 percent give the broad answer that they like to spend time with their families.

Energy levels are higher on weekends. Fully 43 percent of all Americans say they like to go swimming when they can; that amounts to 75 million people. Other physical activities are nearly as popular: 60 million go bicycling, 56 million enjoy fishing, 49 million run or jog, and 44 million like to strap on their backpacks and hit the country's hiking trails. Millions more go camping, using everything from simple canvas tents to recreational vehicles that often offer more amenities than small homes do. "No one really *needs* an RV," concedes an industry executive. But that doesn't stop hundreds of thousands from buying them annually.

Purchases of any kind are sought by millions of Americans with both time and money to spare. Shopping malls from coast to coast are jammed on Friday and Saturday nights. "Some people say that impulse buying elevates their mood and boosts their energy," says marketing expert Dennis Rook of the University of Southern California. "For them, giving in to the urge is a highly satisfying experience."

Weary shoppers might cap their expeditions with a bite to eat. The National Restaurant Association says dining out has been steadily gaining in popularity for decades. It estimates that 25 percent of the typical family's food dollar was spent on eating away from home in 1955. That figure had risen to 40 percent by 1985.

There is no doubt that large cities offer their residents a better selection of movie theaters, health clubs, stores, and restaurants than small cities can. But many micropolitan areas are tourism centers with no shortage of bright lights. Others provide entertainment for large regions, explaining their unexpectedly broad ranges of activities. Small cities are certainly vastly superior to massive urban areas in allowing the necessary breathing room for outdoor diversions. "We buy access to lower crime rates, the spectacular scenery, and recreational opportunities," says University of Montana economics professor Thomas Power in defense of small-town life.

Ranking micropolitan America. The perfect micropolitan area would offer a strong mixture of urban forms of entertainment with space for open-air activities. There must be equal chances to see a movie, land a fish, go shopping, and dawdle in a park. Each small city is checked in five categories:

1. Amusement Place Availability: Does the area have an enticing selection of theaters, bowling alleys, golf courses, arcades, and the like?

2. Shopping Availability: When you head downtown or to the mall,

will you find a large array of stores, or will the pickings be slim?
    3. Food and Drink: Are local restaurants and taverns popular, or are they avoided by most residents?
    4. Population Density: Is there enough room for your favorite outdoor activity, or is the micropolitan area relatively crowded?
    5. Local Recreation Funding: Is the local government willing to spend money on parks and recreation programs?

Amusement Place Availability

When people in the East decide to play, many head for the bright lights of a South Carolina coastal community, Myrtle Beach.

Myrtle Beach was mapped out in the 1920s, but didn't truly hit its peak as a tourist attraction until the 1974 Arab oil embargo. "A lot of people in the Northeast found us much closer than Florida, and they have been coming back since," remembers Ashby Ward, executive vice president of the Myrtle Beach Chamber of Commerce. His town now draws an estimated 350,000 visitors a week in the summer.

This category ranks each area by its rate of what the government calls "amusement/recreation establishments": things like movie theaters, bowling alleys, golf courses, race tracks, amusement parks, skating rinks, and arcades. Myrtle Beach has 127 of these places, or a rate of 116.1 per 100,000 residents. The national average is 29.1 per 100,000, including metro areas.

Rio Rancho, New Mexico, which depends heavily on nearby Albuquerque for entertainment, had only three amusement places in the government's last survey, or a rate of 8.5 per 100,000.

Several well-known tourist areas lead this list. Southern cities hold most of the slots at the bottom.

Source. These statistics, published in 1984, are for 1982. Derived from U.S. Bureau of the Census, *Census of Service Industries* (Washington: U.S. Government Printing Office, 1984).

Scoring. Twenty points for 86.0 sites or more per 100,000; no points for 9.9 or less. The spacing is every four per 100,000.

Amusement Place Availability: Highs and Lows

Highest	Amusement/Recreation Establishments Per 100,000 Residents
1. Myrtle Beach, S.C.	116.1
2. Key West, Fla.	98.4
3. Carson City, Nev.	72.3
4. Laconia, N.H.	68.2
5. Aberdeen, Wash.	66.9
6. Hot Springs, Ark.	58.8
7. Mason City, Iowa	49.6
8. Twin Falls, Idaho	49.5
9. Ashland, Ohio	47.3
10. Bozeman, Mont.	44.2

Lowest	
219. Rio Rancho, N.Mex.	8.5
218. Hanford, Calif.	9.0
217. Hinesville, Ga.	9.8
216. Crowley, La.	10.2
215. Bay City, Tex.	10.8
214. Auburn–Opelika, Ala.	11.3
213. Opelousas, La.	11.4
212. Greenville, Tex.	11.8
211. Talladega, Ala.	12.0
210. Ruston, La.	12.1

(Figure following each area name indicates the number of amusement/ recreation establishments per 100,000 residents; figure in parentheses represents rating points.)

Alabama

Athens	15.3	(2)
Auburn–Opelika	11.3	(1)
Decatur	16.5	(2)
Enterprise	24.8	(4)
Selma	17.8	(2)
Talladega	12.0	(1)

Alaska

Fairbanks	15.3	(2)

Arizona

Bullhead City–Lake Havasu City	28.9	(5)
Casa Grande– Apache Junction	14.6	(2)
Flagstaff	28.5	(5)
Prescott	26.4	(5)
Sierra Vista	21.1	(3)
Yuma	17.7	(2)

Arkansas

Blytheville	15.2	(2)
El Dorado	20.5	(3)
Hot Springs	58.8	(13)
Jonesboro	30.4	(6)
Rogers	23.7	(4)
Russellville	17.3	(2)

California

El Centro–Calexico– Brawley	20.5	(3)
Eureka	23.7	(4)
Hanford	9.0	(0)
Madera	18.9	(3)
San Luis Obispo– Atascadero	31.2	(6)

Colorado

Grand Junction	30.9	(6)

Connecticut

Torrington	40.2	(8)

Delaware

Dover	36.3	(7)

Florida

Key West	98.4	(20)
Vero Beach	26.4	(5)

Georgia

Brunswick	30.3	(6)
Carrollton	20.3	(3)
Dalton	16.7	(2)
Gainesville	17.9	(2)
Hinesville	9.8	(0)
La Grange	23.7	(4)
Rome	21.4	(3)
Valdosta	23.2	(4)

Idaho

Coeur d'Alene	27.3	(5)
Idaho Falls	28.2	(5)
Nampa–Caldwell	24.5	(4)
Pocatello	32.5	(6)
Twin Falls	49.5	(10)

Illinois

Carbondale	20.9	(3)
Danville	20.4	(3)
De Kalb	21.4	(3)
Freeport	22.2	(4)
Galesburg	28.4	(5)
Mattoon–Charleston	28.7	(5)
Ottawa	31.0	(6)
Quincy	30.7	(6)
Sterling	15.4	(2)

Indiana

Columbus	23.2	(4)
Marion	21.7	(3)
Michigan City–La Porte	18.4	(3)
New Castle	19.3	(3)
Richmond	26.7	(5)
Vincennes	25.9	(4)

Iowa

Ames	30.2	(6)
Burlington	32.8	(6)
Clinton	31.6	(6)
Fort Dodge	33.2	(6)
Marshalltown	28.6	(5)
Mason City	49.6	(10)
Muscatine	24.0	(4)

Kansas

Hutchinson	26.0	(5)
Manhattan	26.9	(5)
Salina	28.3	(5)

Kentucky

Bowling Green	21.2	(3)
Frankfort	37.6	(7)
Madisonville	12.8	(1)
Paducah	27.7	(5)
Radcliff–Elizabethtown	18.4	(3)
Richmond	23.6	(4)

Louisiana

Bogalusa	19.9	(3)
Crowley	10.2	(1)
Hammond	20.0	(3)
Minden	13.5	(1)
Morgan City	37.5	(7)
New Iberia	27.7	(5)
Opelousas	11.4	(1)
Ruston	12.1	(1)

Maine

Augusta–Waterville	26.2	(5)
Biddeford	35.8	(7)

Maryland

Salisbury	26.0	(5)

Michigan

Adrian	30.4	(6)
Marquette	17.8	(2)
Mount Pleasant	37.4	(7)
Owosso	31.6	(6)
Traverse City	39.1	(8)

Minnesota

Faribault	23.2	(4)
Mankato	30.4	(6)
Winona	23.8	(4)

Mississippi

Columbus	30.0	(6)
Greenville	26.0	(5)
Greenwood	23.9	(4)
Hattiesburg	23.6	(4)
Laurel	21.7	(3)
Meridian	25.8	(4)
Tupelo	34.4	(7)
Vicksburg	19.2	(3)

Missouri

Cape Girardeau	31.8	(6)
Jefferson City	20.3	(3)
Sikeston	20.1	(3)

Montana

Bozeman	44.2	(9)
Helena	38.4	(8)
Missoula	41.2	(8)

Nebraska

Grand Island	38.5	(8)

Nevada

Carson City	72.3	(16)

New Hampshire

Concord	37.7	(7)
Keene	23.6	(4)
Laconia	68.2	(15)

New Mexico

Alamogordo	16.8	(2)
Carlsbad	33.7	(6)
Clovis	18.0	(3)
Farmington	19.5	(3)
Gallup	16.3	(2)
Hobbs	31.8	(6)
Rio Rancho	8.5	(0)
Roswell	27.5	(5)

New York

Auburn	23.8	(4)
Batavia	38.8	(8)
Cortland	33.0	(6)
Gloversville	27.3	(5)
Ithaca	31.9	(6)
Jamestown	34.2	(7)
Kingston	35.9	(7)
Olean	35.0	(7)
Plattsburgh	27.3	(5)
Watertown	35.7	(7)

North Carolina

Eden	17.8	(2)
Goldsboro	16.4	(2)
Greenville	29.1	(5)
Havelock–New Bern	17.6	(2)
Kinston	38.3	(8)
Lumberton	14.5	(2)
Roanoke Rapids	18.0	(3)
Rocky Mount	16.0	(2)
Sanford	31.8	(6)
Shelby	28.7	(5)
Statesville	20.2	(3)
Wilson	29.8	(5)

North Dakota

Minot	23.3	(4)

Ohio

Ashland	47.3	(10)
Ashtabula	36.9	(7)
Athens	15.6	(2)
Chillicothe	31.9	(6)
East Liverpool	32.6	(6)
Findlay	27.6	(5)
Fremont	33.7	(6)
Marion	22.3	(4)
New Philadelphia	23.4	(4)
Portsmouth	17.8	(2)
Sandusky	34.4	(7)
Sidney	25.2	(4)
Tiffin	27.7	(5)
Wooster	23.2	(4)
Zanesville	28.4	(5)

Oklahoma

Ardmore	30.4	(6)
Bartlesville	21.2	(3)
Chickasha	25.3	(4)
Duncan	21.5	(3)
McAlester	19.5	(3)
Muskogee	16.2	(2)
Okmulgee	22.3	(4)
Ponca City	32.4	(6)
Stillwater	32.1	(6)

Oregon

Albany	25.4	(4)
Bend	39.2	(8)
Corvallis	32.2	(6)
Grants Pass	35.0	(7)
Klamath Falls	28.6	(5)
Roseburg	24.9	(4)

Pennsylvania

Butler	27.4	(5)
Chambersburg	26.9	(5)
New Castle	32.9	(6)
Pottsville	24.6	(4)

Rhode Island

Newport	30.3	(6)

South Carolina

Greenwood	20.3	(3)
Hilton Head Island	36.2	(7)
Myrtle Beach	116.1	(20)
Orangeburg	17.9	(2)
Sumter	15.5	(2)

Tennessee

Cleveland	21.9	(3)
Columbia	21.4	(3)
Cookeville	32.5	(6)
Morristown	17.8	(2)
Tullahoma	12.6	(1)

Texas

Alice	13.1	(1)
Bay City	10.8	(1)
Del Rio	21.1	(3)
Greenville	11.8	(1)
Huntsville	23.8	(4)
Lufkin	29.6	(5)
Nacogdoches	20.5	(3)
Palestine	26.1	(5)
Paris	25.6	(4)

Utah

Logan	30.7	(6)

Vermont

Rutland	39.7	(8)

Virginia

Blacksburg	26.4	(5)
Fredericksburg	31.1	(6)
Harrisonburg	25.5	(4)
Martinsville	24.2	(4)
Staunton–Waynesboro	28.6	(5)
Winchester	32.7	(6)

Washington

Aberdeen	66.9	(15)
Longview	22.6	(4)
Port Angeles	35.0	(7)
Pullman	27.4	(5)
Walla Walla	18.5	(3)
Wenatchee	38.8	(8)

West Virginia

Beckley	20.7	(3)
Clarksburg	21.8	(3)
Fairmont	26.0	(5)
Morgantown	25.8	(4)

Wisconsin

Fond du Lac	32.4	(6)
Manitowoc	32.3	(6)
Marshfield– Wisconsin Rapids	28.0	(5)
Stevens Point	29.9	(5)

Wyoming

Rock Springs	23.7	(4)

Shopping Availability

Large cities have always been defined by their retail centers. Say "Fifth Avenue" to a person anywhere in America, and he or she is apt to respond quickly: "New York." Likewise, Michigan Avenue means Chicago and Peachtree Street is Atlanta.

Small cities do not have the same high profile, but their Main Streets are every bit as important to their regions as Peachtree is to northwest Georgia. And don't forget the ubiquitous shopping malls. "The mall has become the courthouse square of the '80s," an Indiana editor told the *Wall Street Journal* in 1986.

This category measures each area's retail services by projecting its total number of stores into a rate. The average for the entire country is 598.0 retail outlets per 100,000 residents.

Myrtle Beach, South Carolina, serving a steady torrent of tourists, has 8 department stores, 62 women's clothing stores, 31 shoe stores, 22 florists, and 146 grocery stores. Its grand total is 1,499 retail establishments, or a rate of 1,147.8 per 100,000.

Rio Rancho, New Mexico, is on the other end. Its total number of outlets, 151, is only slightly higher than Myrtle Beach's roster of food stores. "Many people here still work in Albuquerque, so they often do their banking and shopping there," says an official with the Rio Rancho Chamber of Commerce.

Source. These statistics, published in 1988, are for 1986. Derived from U.S. Bureau of the Census, *County Business Patterns* (Washington: U.S. Government Printing Office, 1988).

Scoring. Twenty points for 1,000 stores or more per 100,000; no points for 429.9 and less. The spacing is every 30 per 100,000.

Highest	Retail Establishments Per 100,000 Residents
1. Myrtle Beach, S.C.	1,147.8
2. Bozeman, Mont.	1,083.7
3. Key West, Fla.	1,064.8
4. Brunswick, Ga.	1,003.3
5. Laconia, N.H.	987.3
6. Wenatchee, Wash.	973.9
7. Rutland, Vt.	971.7
8. Traverse City, Mich.	964.5
9. Hattiesburg, Miss.	910.7
10. Grand Island, Nebr.	881.4

Lowest

219. Rio Rancho, N.Mex.	295.5
218. Athens, Ala.	432.4
217. Logan, Utah	435.1
216. Wooster, Ohio	461.5
215. Huntsville, Tex.	465.8
214. Hinesville, Ga.	468.1
213. Owosso, Mich.	469.6
212. Madera, Calif.	473.7
211. Hanford, Calif.	477.3
210. Ashland, Ohio	481.6

(Figure following each area name indicates the number of retail establishments per 100,000 residents; figure in parentheses represents rating points.)

Alabama

Athens	432.4	(1)
Auburn–Opelika	529.7	(4)
Decatur	602.2	(6)
Enterprise	676.6	(9)
Selma	567.4	(5)
Talladega	509.8	(3)

Alaska

Fairbanks	599.1	(6)

Arizona

Bullhead City– Lake Havasu City	707.6	(10)
Casa Grande– Apache Junction	491.9	(3)
Flagstaff	734.0	(11)
Prescott	809.0	(13)
Sierra Vista	585.0	(6)
Yuma	743.1	(11)

Arkansas

Blytheville	569.0	(5)
El Dorado	726.5	(10)
Hot Springs	750.3	(11)
Jonesboro	749.2	(11)
Rogers	553.9	(5)
Russellville	668.2	(8)

California

El Centro–Calexico– Brawley	515.0	(3)
Eureka	784.6	(12)
Hanford	477.3	(2)
Madera	473.7	(2)
San Luis Obispo– Atascadero	722.9	(10)

Colorado

Grand Junction	668.5	(8)

Connecticut

Torrington	699.1	(9)

Delaware

Dover	693.9	(9)

Florida

Key West	1,064.8	(20)
Vero Beach	724.7	(10)

Georgia

Brunswick	1,003.3	(20)
Carrollton	590.1	(6)
Dalton	731.6	(11)
Gainesville	628.0	(7)
Hinesville	468.1	(2)
La Grange	691.9	(9)
Rome	663.3	(8)
Valdosta	875.2	(15)

Idaho

Coeur d'Alene	595.6	(6)
Idaho Falls	640.2	(8)
Nampa–Caldwell	528.8	(4)
Pocatello	607.9	(6)
Twin Falls	686.4	(9)

Illinois

Carbondale	657.9	(8)
Danville	548.7	(4)
De Kalb	585.7	(6)
Freeport	550.6	(5)
Galesburg	666.1	(8)
Mattoon–Charleston	619.2	(7)
Ottawa	751.4	(11)
Quincy	635.8	(7)
Sterling	584.4	(6)

Indiana

Columbus	607.8	(6)
Marion	634.2	(7)
Michigan City– La Porte	568.3	(5)
New Castle	562.9	(5)
Richmond	610.8	(7)
Vincennes	801.9	(13)

Iowa

Ames	693.8	(9)
Burlington	775.8	(12)
Clinton	714.6	(10)
Fort Dodge	777.5	(12)
Marshalltown	684.0	(9)
Mason City	866.8	(15)
Muscatine	651.3	(8)

Kansas

Hutchinson	696.8	(9)
Manhattan	533.0	(4)
Salina	798.0	(13)

Kentucky

Bowling Green	683.3	(9)
Frankfort	593.2	(6)
Madisonville	538.6	(4)
Paducah	830.8	(14)
Radcliff–Elizabethtown	486.1	(2)
Richmond	588.3	(6)

Louisiana

Bogalusa	532.5	(4)
Crowley	513.4	(3)
Hammond	602.6	(6)
Minden	551.0	(5)
Morgan City	569.2	(5)
New Iberia	597.1	(6)
Opelousas	549.8	(4)
Ruston	568.1	(5)

Maine

Augusta–Waterville	650.9	(8)
Biddeford	716.6	(10)

Maryland

Salisbury	686.9	(9)

Michigan

Adrian	580.0	(6)
Marquette	607.3	(6)
Mount Pleasant	549.8	(4)
Owosso	469.6	(2)
Traverse City	964.5	(18)

Minnesota

Faribault	621.1	(7)
Mankato	772.6	(12)
Winona	630.7	(7)

Mississippi

Columbus	671.1	(9)
Greenville	608.2	(6)
Greenwood	753.0	(11)
Hattiesburg	910.7	(17)
Laurel	617.5	(7)
Meridian	702.2	(10)
Tupelo	829.3	(14)
Vicksburg	663.4	(8)

Missouri

Cape Girardeau	845.0	(14)
Jefferson City	654.6	(8)
Sikeston	641.8	(8)

Montana

Bozeman	1,083.7	(20)
Helena	842.7	(14)
Missoula	805.7	(13)

Nebraska

Grand Island	881.4	(16)

Nevada
Carson City	766.9	(12)

New Hampshire
Concord	625.3	(7)
Keene	657.7	(8)
Laconia	987.3	(19)

New Mexico
Alamogordo	571.7	(5)
Carlsbad	650.8	(8)
Clovis	762.7	(12)
Farmington	551.1	(5)
Gallup	518.2	(3)
Hobbs	633.3	(7)
Rio Rancho	295.5	(0)
Roswell	647.3	(8)

New York
Auburn	513.1	(3)
Batavia	590.1	(6)
Cortland	654.0	(8)
Gloversville	518.3	(3)
Ithaca	654.1	(8)
Jamestown	663.9	(8)
Kingston	636.4	(7)
Olean	657.7	(8)
Plattsburgh	571.4	(5)
Watertown	724.1	(10)

North Carolina
Eden	568.4	(5)
Goldsboro	654.7	(8)
Greenville	695.9	(9)
Havelock–New Bern	604.2	(6)
Kinston	740.4	(11)
Lumberton	534.0	(4)
Roanoke Rapids	677.4	(9)
Rocky Mount	693.5	(9)
Sanford	833.3	(14)
Shelby	544.5	(4)
Statesville	647.9	(8)
Wilson	775.2	(12)

North Dakota
Minot	743.9	(11)

Ohio
Ashland	481.6	(2)
Ashtabula	557.3	(5)
Athens	517.4	(3)
Chillicothe	545.3	(4)
East Liverpool	562.2	(5)
Findlay	666.2	(8)
Fremont	551.4	(5)
Marion	569.7	(5)
New Philadelphia	640.9	(8)
Portsmouth	571.1	(5)
Sandusky	683.5	(9)
Sidney	490.9	(3)
Tiffin	581.2	(6)
Wooster	461.5	(2)
Zanesville	643.3	(8)

Oklahoma
Ardmore	743.2	(11)
Bartlesville	781.7	(12)
Chickasha	510.1	(3)
Duncan	627.8	(7)
McAlester	567.2	(5)
Muskogee	581.8	(6)
Okmulgee	482.5	(2)
Ponca City	680.1	(9)
Stillwater	634.8	(7)

Oregon
Albany	578.7	(5)
Bend	850.1	(15)
Corvallis	617.6	(7)
Grants Pass	615.8	(7)
Klamath Falls	716.5	(10)
Roseburg	662.0	(8)

Pennsylvania

Butler	544.7	(4)
Chambersburg	528.2	(4)
New Castle	569.2	(5)
Pottsville	559.5	(5)

Rhode Island

Newport	811.3	(13)

South Carolina

Greenwood	675.9	(9)
Hilton Head Island	772.2	(12)
Myrtle Beach	1,147.8	(20)
Orangeburg	579.6	(5)
Sumter	522.1	(4)

Tennessee

Cleveland	547.7	(4)
Columbia	705.0	(10)
Cookeville	696.7	(9)
Morristown	678.6	(9)
Tullahoma	704.6	(10)

Texas

Alice	600.5	(6)
Bay City	646.3	(8)
Del Rio	585.0	(6)
Greenville	578.2	(5)
Huntsville	465.8	(2)
Lufkin	623.9	(7)
Nacogdoches	662.1	(8)
Palestine	549.5	(4)
Paris	644.4	(8)

Utah

Logan	435.1	(1)

Vermont

Rutland	971.7	(19)

Virginia

Blacksburg	559.8	(5)
Fredericksburg	850.6	(15)
Harrisonburg	646.2	(8)
Martinsville	552.7	(5)
Staunton–Waynesboro	606.6	(6)
Winchester	852.0	(15)

Washington

Aberdeen	764.0	(12)
Longview	603.6	(6)
Port Angeles	765.4	(12)
Pullman	488.9	(2)
Walla Walla	583.3	(6)
Wenatchee	973.9	(19)

West Virginia

Beckley	514.3	(3)
Clarksburg	631.6	(7)
Fairmont	558.5	(5)
Morgantown	545.7	(4)

Wisconsin

Fond du Lac	629.4	(7)
Manitowoc	588.8	(6)
Marshfield–Wisconsin Rapids	741.9	(11)
Stevens Point	615.0	(7)

Wyoming

Rock Springs	576.6	(5)

Food and Drink

Cities, whether large or small, are proof of man's essentially social nature. The existence of restaurants and bars provides further evidence.

This category measures the popularity of eating and drinking establishments in each area. It divides the total amount of money spent in a year at all restaurants and taverns by the number of residents. Tourist areas obviously have an advantage in such a system, since it counts the dollars spent by outsiders without including them in the population base.

Myrtle Beach, South Carolina, benefits from its influx of tourists to land first place in this category. Myrtle Beach's 423 eating and drinking places take in $1,065 per capita annually. That's nearly two and a half times the average for the entire country: $438.

Bogalusa, Louisiana, presents a sharp contrast to Myrtle Beach. It is not a major tourist area, is not located on any important highways, and has only 41 eating and drinking places. Their per capita "take" is $128.

Statistics show Westerners spend more money eating out than do residents of any other region. It is therefore not surprising that Western cities take half of the slots in the top ten. Southern cities generally spend the least on food and drink.

Source. These statistics, published in 1988, are for 1982. U.S. Bureau of the Census, *County and City Data Book* (Washington: U.S. Government Printing Office, 1988).

Scoring. Twenty points for $720 or more; no points for $149 or less. The spacing is every $30.

Food and Drink: Highs and Lows

**Annual Per Capita Spending
At Local Restaurants and Taverns**

Highest	$
1. Myrtle Beach, S.C.	1,065
2. Key West, Fla.	920
3. Fairbanks, Alaska	886
4. Flagstaff, Ariz.	796
5. Traverse City, Mich.	695
6. Morgan City, La.	694
7. Helena, Mont.	659
8. Bozeman, Mont.	631
9. Fredericksburg, Va.	624
9. San Luis Obispo– Atascadero, Calif.	624

Lowest	
219. Bogalusa, La.	128
218. Minden, La.	156
217. Rio Rancho, N.Mex.	159
216. Opelousas, La.	162
215. Blytheville, Ark.	187
214. Talladega, Ala.	191
213. Pullman, Wash.	202
212. Enterprise, Ala.	204
211. Gloversville, N.Y.	207
210. Pottsville, Pa.	209

(Figure following each area name indicates the annual per capita spending in dollars at local restaurants and taverns; figure in parentheses represents rating points.)

Alabama

Athens	215	(3)
Auburn–Opelika	354	(7)
Decatur	277	(5)
Enterprise	204	(2)
Selma	213	(3)
Talladega	191	(2)

Alaska

Fairbanks	886	(20)

Arizona

Bullhead City– Lake Havasu City	428	(10)
Casa Grande– Apache Junction	247	(4)
Flagstaff	796	(20)
Prescott	403	(9)
Sierra Vista	280	(5)
Yuma	471	(11)

Arkansas

Blytheville	187	(2)
El Dorado	256	(4)
Hot Springs	546	(14)
Jonesboro	449	(10)
Rogers	232	(3)
Russellville	337	(7)

California

El Centro–Calexico–Brawley	303	(6)
Eureka	446	(10)
Hanford	337	(7)
Madera	309	(6)
San Luis Obispo– Atascadero	624	(16)

Colorado

Grand Junction	485	(12)

Connecticut

Torrington	311	(6)

Delaware

Dover	413	(9)

Florida

Key West	920	(20)
Vero Beach	501	(12)

Georgia

Brunswick	618	(16)
Carrollton	270	(5)
Dalton	372	(8)
Gainesville	433	(10)
Hinesville	282	(5)
La Grange	290	(5)
Rome	333	(7)
Valdosta	470	(11)

Idaho

Coeur d'Alene	383	(8)
Idaho Falls	435	(10)
Nampa–Caldwell	293	(5)
Pocatello	417	(9)
Twin Falls	417	(9)

Illinois

Carbondale	481	(12)
Danville	362	(8)
De Kalb	418	(9)
Freeport	334	(7)
Galesburg	443	(10)
Mattoon–Charleston	486	(12)
Ottawa	424	(10)
Quincy	414	(9)
Sterling	319	(6)

Indiana

Columbus	438	(10)
Marion	404	(9)
Michigan City–La Porte	372	(8)
New Castle	291	(5)
Richmond	418	(9)
Vincennes	387	(8)

Iowa

Ames	469	(11)
Burlington	427	(10)
Clinton	414	(9)
Fort Dodge	494	(12)
Marshalltown	399	(9)
Mason City	489	(12)
Muscatine	369	(8)

Kansas

Hutchinson	478	(11)
Manhattan	441	(10)
Salina	487	(12)

Kentucky

Bowling Green	484	(12)
Frankfort	408	(9)
Madisonville	265	(4)
Paducah	499	(12)
Radcliff–Elizabethtown	290	(5)
Richmond	466	(11)

Louisiana

Bogalusa	128	(0)
Crowley	242	(4)
Hammond	333	(7)
Minden	156	(1)
Morgan City	694	(19)
New Iberia	538	(13)
Opelousas	162	(1)
Ruston	382	(8)

Maine

Augusta–Waterville	359	(7)
Biddeford	449	(10)

Maryland

Salisbury	506	(12)

Michigan

Adrian	346	(7)
Marquette	362	(8)
Mount Pleasant	377	(8)
Owosso	231	(3)
Traverse City	695	(19)

Minnesota

Faribault	425	(10)
Mankato	501	(12)
Winona	433	(10)

Mississippi

Columbus	283	(5)
Greenville	211	(3)
Greenwood	313	(6)
Hattiesburg	514	(13)
Laurel	270	(5)
Meridian	374	(8)
Tupelo	301	(6)
Vicksburg	366	(8)

Missouri

Cape Girardeau	447	(10)
Jefferson City	402	(9)
Sikeston	346	(7)

Montana

Bozeman	631	(17)
Helena	659	(17)
Missoula	568	(14)

Nebraska

Grand Island	577	(15)

Nevada

Carson City	558	(14)

New Hampshire

Concord	395	(9)
Keene	326	(6)
Laconia	546	(14)

New Mexico

Alamogordo	394	(9)
Carlsbad	316	(6)
Clovis	367	(8)
Farmington	406	(9)
Gallup	473	(11)
Hobbs	438	(10)
Rio Rancho	159	(1)
Roswell	468	(11)

New York

Auburn	247	(4)
Batavia	362	(8)
Cortland	444	(10)
Gloversville	207	(2)
Ithaca	441	(10)
Jamestown	379	(8)
Kingston	380	(8)
Olean	335	(7)
Plattsburgh	373	(8)
Watertown	354	(7)

North Carolina

Eden	271	(5)
Goldsboro	270	(5)
Greenville	432	(10)
Havelock–New Bern	320	(6)
Kinston	294	(5)
Lumberton	212	(3)
Roanoke Rapids	274	(5)
Rocky Mount	377	(8)
Sanford	353	(7)
Shelby	295	(5)
Statesville	328	(6)
Wilson	361	(8)

North Dakota

Minot	466	(11)

Ohio

Ashland	338	(7)
Ashtabula	301	(6)
Athens	339	(7)
Chillicothe	351	(7)
East Liverpool	248	(4)
Findlay	508	(12)
Fremont	321	(6)
Marion	358	(7)
New Philadelphia	350	(7)
Portsmouth	338	(7)
Sandusky	555	(14)
Sidney	322	(6)
Tiffin	281	(5)
Wooster	280	(5)
Zanesville	396	(9)

Oklahoma

Ardmore	398	(9)
Bartlesville	474	(11)
Chickasha	266	(4)
Duncan	337	(7)
McAlester	270	(5)
Muskogee	376	(8)
Okmulgee	211	(3)
Ponca City	395	(9)
Stillwater	439	(10)

Oregon

Albany	364	(8)
Bend	470	(11)
Corvallis	462	(11)
Grants Pass	390	(9)
Klamath Falls	415	(9)
Roseburg	360	(8)

Pennsylvania

Butler	344	(7)
Chambersburg	306	(6)
New Castle	250	(4)
Pottsville	209	(2)

Rhode Island		
Newport	424	(10)

South Carolina		
Greenwood	281	(5)
Hilton Head Island	573	(15)
Myrtle Beach	1,065	(20)
Orangeburg	233	(3)
Sumter	216	(3)

Tennessee		
Cleveland	329	(6)
Columbia	289	(5)
Cookeville	359	(7)
Morristown	315	(6)
Tullahoma	365	(8)

Texas		
Alice	327	(6)
Bay City	380	(8)
Del Rio	351	(7)
Greenville	335	(7)
Huntsville	560	(14)
Lufkin	340	(7)
Nacogdoches	295	(5)
Palestine	237	(3)
Paris	355	(7)

Utah		
Logan	223	(3)

Vermont		
Rutland	459	(11)

Virginia		
Blacksburg	374	(8)
Fredericksburg	624	(16)
Harrisonburg	297	(5)
Martinsville	251	(4)
Staunton–Waynesboro	310	(6)
Winchester	432	(10)

Washington		
Aberdeen	486	(12)
Longview	521	(13)
Port Angeles	462	(11)
Pullman	202	(2)
Walla Walla	377	(8)
Wenatchee	540	(14)

West Virginia		
Beckley	312	(6)
Clarksburg	301	(6)
Fairmont	243	(4)
Morgantown	272	(5)

Wisconsin		
Fond du Lac	417	(9)
Manitowoc	333	(7)
Marshfield–Wisconsin Rapids	409	(9)
Stevens Point	496	(12)

Wyoming		
Rock Springs	486	(12)

Population Density

Perhaps the best reason to escape a metropolitan area for a micropolitan community is to get yourself some room. This is particularly true if you enjoy camping, fishing, hiking, or other outdoor activities.

The 1980 census found that there is little room to enjoy nature in big cities, where the average population density was 3,000.5 persons per square mile. Even when you add the more spacious suburbs, the density of all of the nation's metro areas remains a crowded 299.3 per square mile.

This category estimates each area's outdoor recreation potential by considering its population density. The Rock Springs, Wyoming, area offers the best choice of wide open spaces, with only 4.5 people living in each of its 10,352 square miles.

Newport, Rhode Island, was once a thriving seaport. Robber barons, yachtsmen, and society figures flocked there each summer to live in their massive "cottages." Newport has 1.8 times as many residents as Rock Springs, Wyoming, but only one percent of the space.

The deserts and plains of the West obviously offer the best opportunities for outdoor solitude. Southern and Eastern micropolitan areas are generally the most crowded.

Source. These statistics, published in 1988, are for 1986. Derived from U.S. Bureau of the Census, *Current Population Reports: 1986 Population* (Washington: U.S. Government Printing Office, 1988).

Scoring. Twenty points for 15.9 persons or less per square mile; no points for 301.0 or more. The spacing is every 15 per mile.

Population Density: Highs and Lows

Lowest	Persons Per Square Mile
1. Rock Springs, Wyo.	4.5
2. Flagstaff, Ariz.	4.6
3. Bullhead City– Lake Havasu City, Ariz.	5.8
4. Alamogordo, N.Mex.	7.6
5. Fairbanks, Alaska	9.1
6. Roswell, N.Mex.	9.3
7. Klamath Falls, Oreg.	9.7
8. Prescott, Ariz.	10.4
9. Gallup, N.Mex.	12.1
10. Carlsbad, N.Mex.	12.5

Highest	
219. Newport, R.I.	792.5
218. Morristown, Tenn.	339.1
217. Sandusky, Ohio	292.0
216. New Castle, Pa.	280.7
215. Carson City, Nev.	252.7
214. Paducah, Ky.	240.2
213. Dalton, Ga.	238.1
212. Gainesville, Ga.	229.8
211. Cleveland, Tenn.	221.1
210. Morgantown, W.Va.	214.0

(Figure following each area name indicates the number of people per square mile; figure in parentheses represents rating points.)

Alabama
Athens	92.7 (14)
Auburn–Opelika	132.7 (12)
Decatur	171.8 (9)
Enterprise	59.1 (17)
Selma	54.1 (17)
Talladega	101.6 (14)

Alaska
Fairbanks	9.1 (20)

Arizona
Bullhead City–Lake Havasu City	5.8 (20)
Casa Grande–Apache Junction	18.5 (19)
Flagstaff	4.6 (20)
Prescott	10.4 (20)
Sierra Vista	14.8 (20)
Yuma	15.6 (20)

Arkansas
Blytheville	64.7 (16)
El Dorado	46.5 (17)
Hot Springs	114.6 (13)
Jonesboro	88.9 (15)
Rogers	105.5 (14)
Russellville	52.9 (17)

California
El Centro–Calexico–Brawley	25.6 (19)
Eureka	31.9 (18)
Hanford	61.7 (16)
Madera	36.3 (18)
San Luis Obispo–Atascadero	59.5 (17)

Colorado
Grand Junction	26.9 (19)

Connecticut
Torrington	175.9 (9)

Delaware
Dover	176.8 (9)

Florida
Key West	70.1 (16)
Vero Beach	163.0 (10)

Georgia
Brunswick	145.1 (11)
Carrollton	129.3 (12)
Dalton	238.1 (5)
Gainesville	229.8 (5)
Hinesville	81.8 (15)
La Grange	130.6 (12)
Rome	151.6 (10)
Valdosta	145.4 (11)

Idaho
Coeur d'Alene	54.4 (17)
Idaho Falls	38.4 (18)
Nampa–Caldwell	154.5 (10)
Pocatello	61.2 (16)
Twin Falls	28.7 (19)

Illinois
Carbondale	102.5 (14)
Danville	101.4 (14)
De Kalb	116.9 (13)
Freeport	87.6 (15)
Galesburg	78.2 (15)
Mattoon–Charleston	102.2 (14)
Ottawa	95.0 (14)
Quincy	79.9 (15)
Sterling	92.1 (14)

Indiana

Columbus	157.7	(10)
Marion	185.8	(8)
Michigan City–La Porte	176.8	(9)
New Castle	126.8	(12)
Richmond	178.7	(9)
Vincennes	79.6	(15)

Iowa

Ames	126.3	(12)
Burlington	107.7	(13)
Clinton	77.1	(15)
Fort Dodge	59.5	(17)
Marshalltown	70.7	(16)
Mason City	85.8	(15)
Muscatine	93.4	(14)

Kansas

Hutchinson	51.9	(17)
Manhattan	109.8	(13)
Salina	69.3	(16)

Kentucky

Bowling Green	150.6	(11)
Frankfort	207.5	(7)
Madisonville	84.4	(15)
Paducah	240.2	(5)
Radcliff–Elizabethtown	149.1	(11)
Richmond	123.9	(12)

Louisiana

Bogalusa	70.6	(16)
Crowley	90.7	(15)
Hammond	117.6	(13)
Minden	76.6	(15)
Morgan City	104.9	(14)
New Iberia	117.1	(13)
Opelousas	94.4	(14)
Ruston	90.3	(15)

Maine

Augusta–Waterville	127.9	(12)
Biddeford	157.5	(10)

Maryland

Salisbury	182.8	(8)

Michigan

Adrian	117.9	(13)
Marquette	39.1	(18)
Mount Pleasant	94.1	(14)
Owosso	127.5	(12)
Traverse City	127.0	(12)

Minnesota

Faribault	94.8	(14)
Mankato	71.0	(16)
Winona	73.5	(16)

Mississippi

Columbus	116.4	(13)
Greenville	96.5	(14)
Greenwood	68.3	(16)
Hattiesburg	145.6	(11)
Laurel	90.6	(15)
Meridian	109.1	(13)
Tupelo	137.7	(11)
Vicksburg	86.1	(15)

Missouri

Cape Girardeau	106.2	(13)
Jefferson City	161.7	(10)
Sikeston	95.0	(14)

Montana

Bozeman	19.0	(19)
Helena	13.4	(20)
Missoula	30.1	(19)

Nebraska

Grand Island	91.1	(14)

Nevada

Carson City	252.7	(4)

New Hampshire

Concord	117.2	(13)
Keene	94.1	(14)
Laconia	116.6	(13)

New Mexico

Alamogordo	7.6	(20)
Carlsbad	12.5	(20)
Clovis	30.8	(19)
Farmington	16.7	(19)
Gallup	12.1	(20)
Hobbs	14.8	(20)
Rio Rancho	13.8	(20)
Roswell	9.3	(20)

New York

Auburn	115.0	(13)
Batavia	118.8	(13)
Cortland	94.8	(14)
Gloversville	109.9	(13)
Ithaca	183.6	(8)
Jamestown	134.5	(12)
Kingston	145.2	(11)
Olean	65.3	(16)
Plattsburgh	77.9	(15)
Watertown	71.2	(16)

North Carolina

Eden	150.3	(11)
Goldsboro	176.7	(9)
Greenville	149.4	(11)
Havelock–New Bern	115.5	(13)
Kinston	149.5	(11)
Lumberton	111.7	(13)
Roanoke Rapids	77.1	(15)
Rocky Mount	124.5	(12)
Sanford	159.8	(10)
Shelby	184.8	(8)
Statesville	154.4	(10)
Wilson	172.5	(9)

North Dakota

Minot	30.0	(19)

Ohio

Ashland	109.2	(13)
Ashtabula	144.0	(11)
Athens	113.4	(13)
Chillicothe	97.3	(14)
East Liverpool	206.2	(7)
Findlay	123.9	(12)
Fremont	152.1	(10)
Marion	162.0	(10)
New Philadelphia	150.3	(11)
Portsmouth	134.0	(12)
Sandusky	292.0	(1)
Sidney	107.6	(13)
Tiffin	111.4	(13)
Wooster	181.7	(8)
Zanesville	128.6	(12)

Oklahoma

Ardmore	57.4	(17)
Bartlesville	106.1	(13)
Chickasha	40.2	(18)
Duncan	50.4	(17)
McAlester	35.1	(18)
Muskogee	86.3	(15)
Okmulgee	57.3	(17)
Ponca City	56.7	(17)
Stillwater	93.9	(14)

Oregon

Albany	38.8	(18)
Bend	22.7	(19)
Corvallis	95.1	(14)
Grants Pass	41.6	(18)
Klamath Falls	9.7	(20)
Roseburg	18.5	(19)

Pennsylvania

Butler	191.5	(8)
Chambersburg	153.4	(10)
New Castle	280.7	(2)
Pottsville	200.3	(7)

Rhode Island

Newport	792.5	(0)

South Carolina

Greenwood	128.6	(12)
Hilton Head Island	147.8	(11)
Myrtle Beach	114.3	(13)
Orangeburg	78.5	(15)
Sumter	142.9	(11)

Tennessee

Cleveland	221.1	(6)
Columbia	87.5	(15)
Cookeville	128.1	(12)
Morristown	339.1	(0)
Tullahoma	96.3	(14)

Texas

Alice	46.5	(17)
Bay City	36.4	(18)
Del Rio	12.7	(20)
Greenville	79.9	(15)
Huntsville	68.8	(16)
Lufkin	86.0	(15)
Nacogdoches	53.9	(17)
Palestine	44.1	(18)
Paris	49.0	(17)

Utah

Logan	55.9	(17)

Vermont

Rutland	64.4	(16)

Virginia

Blacksburg	169.5	(9)
Fredericksburg	143.7	(11)
Harrisonburg	93.5	(14)
Martinsville	190.6	(8)
Staunton–Waynesboro	91.0	(14)
Winchester	137.0	(11)

Washington

Aberdeen	32.7	(18)
Longview	69.1	(16)
Port Angeles	30.6	(19)
Pullman	18.9	(19)
Walla Walla	38.1	(18)
Wenatchee	17.1	(19)

West Virginia

Beckley	138.5	(11)
Clarksburg	180.3	(9)
Fairmont	205.4	(7)
Morgantown	214.0	(6)

Wisconsin

Fond du Lac	124.7	(12)
Manitowoc	138.4	(11)
Marshfield– Wisconsin Rapids	96.8	(14)
Stevens Point	72.5	(16)

Wyoming

Rock Springs	4.5	(20)

Local Recreation Funding

It is one thing for an area to be blessed with promising recreational raw material: vast forests, open plains, rivers and lakes suitable for swimming and boating. It is quite another for local government to make the necessary commitment to develop and maintain these resources.

This category ranks each area according to its annual per capita expenditures on parks and recreation facilities. Included is all money spent by county and city governments on playgrounds, picnic areas, beaches, pools, golf courses, piers, and marinas.

Rock Springs, Wyoming, allocated $11.2 million to recreation in the latest budget studied by the federal government. That works out to $269 for every man, woman, and child in the Rock Springs area. The average for the entire country is just $27 per capita.

Bogalusa, Louisiana, places a very light emphasis on government support for recreation. Its total tab was $37,000, which is approximately one dollar for each local resident.

Western cities, led by Rock Springs and Fairbanks, Alaska, show a greater interest than towns of other regions in funding their parks. The smallest financial commitment is expressed by Southern cities.

Source. These statistics, published in 1984, are for 1982. U.S. Bureau of the Census, *Census of Governments: Compendium of Government Finances* (Washington: U.S. Government Printing Office, 1984).

Scoring. Twenty points for $100 or more per capita; no points for $4 or less. The spacing is every $5 per capita.

**Annual Per Capita
Recreation-Related Spending
By Local Governments**

Highest	$
1. Rock Springs, Wyo.	269
2. Fairbanks, Alaska	218
3. New Philadelphia, Ohio	78
4. Hutchinson, Kans.	45
5. Carson City, Nev.	44
6. Vero Beach, Fla.	41
6. Yuma, Ariz.	41
8. Morgan City, La.	40
8. Walla Walla, Wash.	40
10. Fort Dodge, Iowa	39

Lowest	
219. Bogalusa, La.	1
214. Hinesville, Ga.	2
214. Owosso, Mich.	2
214. Portsmouth, Ohio	2
214. Rio Rancho, N.Mex.	2
214. Rome, Ga.	2
206. Ardmore, Okla.	3
206. Augusta–Waterville, Maine	3
206. Butler, Pa.	3
206. Del Rio, Tex.	3
206. El Dorado, Ark.	3
206. Minden, La.	3
206. Palestine, Tex.	3
206. Pottsville, Pa.	3

(Figure following each area name indicates per capita recreation-related spending by local government in dollars; figure in parentheses represents rating points.)

Alabama

Athens	5	(1)
Auburn–Opelika	10	(2)
Decatur	31	(6)
Enterprise	24	(4)
Selma	8	(1)
Talladega	13	(2)

Alaska

Fairbanks	218	(20)

Arizona

Bullhead City– Lake Havasu City	23	(4)
Casa Grande– Apache Junction	16	(3)
Flagstaff	24	(4)
Prescott	12	(2)
Sierra Vista	19	(3)
Yuma	41	(8)

Arkansas

Blytheville	12	(2)
El Dorado	3	(0)
Hot Springs	4	(0)
Jonesboro	4	(0)
Rogers	6	(1)
Russellville	8	(1)

California

El Centro–Calexico– Brawley	19	(3)
Eureka	21	(4)
Hanford	22	(4)
Madera	13	(2)
San Luis Obispo– Atascadero	33	(6)

Colorado

Grand Junction	36	(7)

Connecticut

Torrington	11	(2)

Delaware

Dover	4	(0)

Florida

Key West	14	(2)
Vero Beach	41	(8)

Georgia

Brunswick	32	(6)
Carrollton	14	(2)
Dalton	17	(3)
Gainesville	20	(4)
Hinesville	2	(0)
La Grange	12	(2)
Rome	2	(0)
Valdosta	10	(2)

Idaho

Coeur d'Alene	11	(2)
Idaho Falls	19	(3)
Nampa–Caldwell	9	(1)
Pocatello	16	(3)
Twin Falls	10	(2)

Illinois

Carbondale	10	(2)
Danville	27	(5)
De Kalb	6	(1)
Freeport	24	(4)
Galesburg	14	(2)
Mattoon–Charleston	5	(1)
Ottawa	8	(1)
Quincy	25	(5)
Sterling	21	(4)

Indiana

Columbus	16	(3)
Marion	15	(3)
Michigan City–La Porte	14	(2)
New Castle	10	(2)
Richmond	15	(3)
Vincennes	5	(1)

Iowa

Ames	23	(4)
Burlington	20	(4)
Clinton	20	(4)
Fort Dodge	39	(7)
Marshalltown	20	(4)
Mason City	27	(5)
Muscatine	24	(4)

Kansas

Hutchinson	45	(9)
Manhattan	14	(2)
Salina	17	(3)

Kentucky

Bowling Green	17	(3)
Frankfort	13	(2)
Madisonville	4	(0)
Paducah	11	(2)
Radcliff–Elizabethtown	8	(1)
Richmond	8	(1)

Louisiana

Bogalusa	1	(0)
Crowley	7	(1)
Hammond	9	(1)
Minden	3	(0)
Morgan City	40	(8)
New Iberia	20	(4)
Opelousas	10	(2)
Ruston	5	(1)

Maine

Augusta–Waterville	3	(0)
Biddeford	7	(1)

Maryland

Salisbury	32	(6)

Michigan

Adrian	13	(2)
Marquette	18	(3)
Mount Pleasant	8	(1)
Owosso	2	(0)
Traverse City	8	(1)

Minnesota

Faribault	15	(3)
Mankato	24	(4)
Winona	26	(5)

Mississippi

Columbus	4	(0)
Greenville	14	(2)
Greenwood	11	(2)
Hattiesburg	10	(2)
Laurel	11	(2)
Meridian	10	(2)
Tupelo	9	(1)
Vicksburg	15	(3)

Missouri

Cape Girardeau	17	(3)
Jefferson City	17	(3)
Sikeston	4	(0)

Montana

Bozeman	13	(2)
Helena	18	(3)
Missoula	35	(7)

Nebraska

Grand Island	30	(6)

Nevada

Carson City	44	(8)

New Hampshire

Concord	11	(2)
Keene	12	(2)
Laconia	8	(1)

New Mexico

Alamogordo	11	(2)
Carlsbad	27	(5)
Clovis	11	(2)
Farmington	26	(5)
Gallup	15	(3)
Hobbs	29	(5)
Rio Rancho	2	(0)
Roswell	15	(3)

New York

Auburn	20	(4)
Batavia	14	(2)
Cortland	12	(2)
Gloversville	11	(2)
Ithaca	21	(4)
Jamestown	16	(3)
Kingston	13	(2)
Olean	11	(2)
Plattsburgh	13	(2)
Watertown	10	(2)

North Carolina

Eden	14	(2)
Goldsboro	7	(1)
Greenville	13	(2)
Havelock–New Bern	12	(2)
Kinston	15	(3)
Lumberton	10	(2)
Roanoke Rapids	11	(2)
Rocky Mount	14	(2)
Sanford	21	(4)
Shelby	9	(1)
Statesville	17	(3)
Wilson	14	(2)

North Dakota

Minot	25	(5)

Ohio

Ashland	17	(3)
Ashtabula	7	(1)
Athens	4	(0)
Chillicothe	4	(0)
East Liverpool	5	(1)
Findlay	23	(4)
Fremont	11	(2)
Marion	11	(2)
New Philadelphia	78	(15)
Portsmouth	2	(0)
Sandusky	14	(2)
Sidney	8	(1)
Tiffin	13	(2)
Wooster	9	(1)
Zanesville	5	(1)

Oklahoma

Ardmore	3	(0)
Bartlesville	28	(5)
Chickasha	4	(0)
Duncan	10	(2)
McAlester	6	(1)
Muskogee	22	(4)
Okmulgee	5	(1)
Ponca City	38	(7)
Stillwater	18	(3)

Oregon

Albany	13	(2)
Bend	30	(6)
Corvallis	30	(6)
Grants Pass	27	(5)
Klamath Falls	14	(2)
Roseburg	18	(3)

Pennsylvania

Butler	3	(0)
Chambersburg	5	(1)
New Castle	7	(1)
Pottsville	3	(0)

Rhode Island
Newport	11	(2)

South Carolina
Greenwood	8	(1)
Hilton Head Island	11	(2)
Myrtle Beach	11	(2)
Orangeburg	7	(1)
Sumter	11	(2)

Tennessee
Cleveland	9	(1)
Columbia	12	(2)
Cookeville	7	(1)
Morristown	11	(2)
Tullahoma	15	(3)

Texas
Alice	16	(3)
Bay City	5	(1)
Del Rio	3	(0)
Greenville	7	(1)
Huntsville	15	(3)
Lufkin	13	(2)
Nacogdoches	9	(1)
Palestine	3	(0)
Paris	5	(1)

Utah
Logan	25	(5)

Vermont
Rutland	11	(2)

Virginia
Blacksburg	10	(2)
Fredericksburg	20	(4)
Harrisonburg	11	(2)
Martinsville	6	(1)
Staunton–Waynesboro	13	(2)
Winchester	25	(5)

Washington
Aberdeen	25	(5)
Longview	38	(7)
Port Angeles	31	(6)
Pullman	16	(3)
Walla Walla	40	(8)
Wenatchee	31	(6)

West Virginia
Beckley	4	(0)
Clarksburg	11	(2)
Fairmont	6	(1)
Morgantown	17	(3)

Wisconsin
Fond du Lac	13	(2)
Manitowoc	26	(5)
Marshfield–Wisconsin Rapids	25	(5)
Stevens Point	35	(7)

Wyoming
Rock Springs	269	(20)

The Results

People begin strolling toward Mallory Square in Key West, Florida, about 30 minutes before sunset. They gather in small groups, gazing toward the Gulf of Mexico. Street entertainers and vendors go about their business as the crowd grows. An outsider would find no meaning in any of this activity. Until dark—when the people on the docks break into applause as the flaming red sun sinks below the watery horizon. Then they head back to town.

"Key West is intensely unlike any other place in the Union," boasts a brochure. The nightly sunset ceremony is just one example of its uniquely fun-loving character. More than one million tourists come here annually to dive for sunken treasure, take a turn at deep-sea fishing, lie on the long sandy beaches, and eat at the sidewalk cafés. With Key lime pie for dessert, of course.

The Key West area earns first place in the diversions section, with 78 of a possible 100 points. The completion of the Overseas Highway in 1938, connecting this small coral island with the Florida mainland, opened the way for tourists to flock down the Keys. Key West responded by blossoming with amusement places, shops, restaurants, and bars to serve them. There remains plenty of space under the swaying palms for outdoor activities, particularly those that require water.

Close behind Key West is another Southern ocean town. Myrtle Beach, South Carolina, finishes second in this section. But Western cities hold all of the remaining slots in the top ten, with the exception of the lake resort of Laconia, New Hampshire.

Entertainment is not so readily available in two Pennsylvania cities, New Castle and Pottsville. They tie for last place, each receiving a total of only 18 points. New Castle is a depressed steel town in western Pennsylvania; Pottsville is a struggling coal town in the eastern part of the state. Both suffer from a shortage of stores, restaurants, amusement places, and government funding for parks. "About half of my friends went off to college and never came back," Pottsville development official Edward Dunleavy told a reporter in 1986. "There just wasn't enough here to keep their interest and make a good living."

The irony in New Castle's case is that it exports fun. The city is the home of the Zambelli Internationale Fireworks Manufacturing Company, the biggest supplier of public-display fireworks in the country. More than 1,400 communities from coast to coast thrill to Zambelli shows every Fourth of July.

A majority of the other small cities with low diversions scores are in the South.

Diversions Scores: Highs and Lows

Highest	Rating Points
1. Key West, Fla.	78
2. Myrtle Beach, S.C.	75
3. Fairbanks, Alaska	68
4. Bozeman, Mont.	67
5. Wenatchee, Wash.	66
6. Aberdeen, Wash.	62
6. Helena, Mont.	62
6. Laconia, N.H.	62
9. Missoula, Mont.	61
9. Rock Springs, Wyo.	61
11. Flagstaff, Ariz.	60
12. Bend, Oreg.	59
12. Brunswick, Ga.	59
12. Grand Island, Nebr.	59
15. Traverse City, Mich.	58
16. Mason City, Iowa	57
17. Rutland, Vt.	56
18. Port Angeles, Wash.	55
18. San Luis Obispo–Atascadero, Calif.	55
20. Carson City, Nev.	54
20. Fort Dodge, Iowa	54

Lowest	
218. New Castle, Pa.	18
218. Pottsville, Pa.	18
217. Morristown, Tenn.	19
215. Cleveland, Tenn.	20
215. Wooster, Ohio	20
213. Athens, Ala.	21
213. Rio Rancho, N.Mex.	21
204. Fairmont, W.Va.	22
204. Hinesville, Ga.	22
204. Martinsville, Va.	22
204. Minden, La.	22
204. Morgantown, W.Va.	22
204. Opelousas, La.	22
204. Radcliff–Elizabethtown, Ky.	22
204. Sumter, S.C.	22
204. Talladega, Ala.	22

	Key West, Fla.	New Castle, Pa.	Pottsville, Pa.
Total Points in Section	78	18	18
Rank in Section	1	218*	218*
Results (and Rating Points)			
Amusement Place Availability Amusement/ recreation establishments per 100,000 residents	98.4 (20)	32.9 (6)	24.6 (4)
Shopping Availability Retail establishments per 100,000 residents	1,064.8 (20)	569.2 (5)	559.5 (5)
Food and Drink Annual per capita spending at local restaurants and taverns	$920　(20)	$250　(4)	$209　(2)
Population Density Persons per square mile	70.1 (16)	280.7 (2)	200.3 (7)
Local Recreation Funding Annual per capita recreation-related spending by local governments	$14　(2)	$7　(1)	$3　(0)

*There was a tie for last place.

(Figure following each area name indicates the composite score from the five categories in this section.)

Alabama		Colorado		Indiana	
Athens	21	Grand Junction	52	Columbus	33
Auburn–Opelika	26			Marion	30
Decatur	28	**Connecticut**		Michigan City–	
Enterprise	36	Torrington	34	La Porte	27
Selma	28			New Castle	27
Talladega	22	**Delaware**		Richmond	33
		Dover	34	Vincennes	41
Alaska					
Fairbanks	68	**Florida**		**Iowa**	
		Key West	78	Ames	42
Arizona		Vero Beach	45	Burlington	45
Bullhead City–				Clinton	44
Lake Havasu		**Georgia**		Fort Dodge	54
City	49	Brunswick	59	Marshalltown	43
Casa Grande–		Carrollton	28	Mason City	57
Apache		Dalton	29	Muscatine	38
Junction	31	Gainesville	28		
Flagstaff	60	Hinesville	22	**Kansas**	
Prescott	49	La Grange	32	Hutchinson	51
Sierra Vista	37	Rome	28	Manhattan	34
Yuma	52	Valdosta	43	Salina	49
Arkansas		**Idaho**		**Kentucky**	
Blytheville	27	Coeur d'Alene	38	Bowling Green	38
El Dorado	34	Idaho Falls	44	Frankfort	31
Hot Springs	51	Nampa–Caldwell	24	Madisonville	24
Jonesboro	42	Pocatello	40	Paducah	38
Rogers	27	Twin Falls	49	Radcliff–	
Russellville	35			Elizabethtown	22
		Illinois		Richmond	34
California		Carbondale	39		
El Centro–		Danville	34	**Louisiana**	
Calexico–		De Kalb	32	Bogalusa	23
Brawley	34	Freeport	35	Crowley	24
Eureka	48	Galesburg	40	Hammond	30
Hanford	29	Mattoon–Charleston	39	Minden	22
Madera	31	Ottawa	42	Morgan City	53
San Luis Obispo–		Quincy	42	New Iberia	41
Atascadero	55	Sterling	32	Opelousas	22
				Ruston	30

Maine

Augusta–Waterville	32
Biddeford	38

Maryland

Salisbury	40

Michigan

Adrian	34
Marquette	37
Mount Pleasant	34
Owosso	23
Traverse City	58

Minnesota

Faribault	38
Mankato	50
Winona	42

Mississippi

Columbus	33
Greenville	30
Greenwood	39
Hattiesburg	47
Laurel	32
Meridian	37
Tupelo	39
Vicksburg	37

Missouri

Cape Girardeau	46
Jefferson City	33
Sikeston	32

Montana

Bozeman	67
Helena	62
Missoula	61

Nebraska

Grand Island	59

Nevada

Carson City	54

New Hampshire

Concord	38
Keene	34
Laconia	62

New Mexico

Alamogordo	38
Carlsbad	45
Clovis	44
Farmington	41
Gallup	39
Hobbs	48
Rio Rancho	21
Roswell	47

New York

Auburn	28
Batavia	37
Cortland	40
Gloversville	25
Ithaca	36
Jamestown	38
Kingston	35
Olean	40
Plattsburgh	35
Watertown	42

North Carolina

Eden	25
Goldsboro	25
Greenville	37
Havelock–New Bern	29
Kinston	38
Lumberton	24
Roanoke Rapids	34
Rocky Mount	33
Sanford	41
Shelby	23
Statesville	30
Wilson	36

North Dakota

Minot	50

Ohio

Ashland	35
Ashtabula	30
Athens	25
Chillicothe	31
East Liverpool	23
Findlay	41
Fremont	29
Marion	28
New Philadelphia	45
Portsmouth	26
Sandusky	33
Sidney	27
Tiffin	31
Wooster	20
Zanesville	35

Oklahoma

Ardmore	43
Bartlesville	44
Chickasha	29
Duncan	36
McAlester	32
Muskogee	35
Okmulgee	27
Ponca City	48
Stillwater	40

Oregon

Albany	37
Bend	59
Corvallis	44
Grants Pass	46
Klamath Falls	46
Roseburg	42

Pennsylvania

Butler	24
Chambersburg	26
New Castle	18
Pottsville	18

Rhode Island

Newport	31

South Carolina

Greenwood	30
Hilton Head Island	47
Myrtle Beach	75
Orangeburg	26
Sumter	22

Tennessee

Cleveland	20
Columbia	35
Cookeville	35
Morristown	19
Tullahoma	36

Texas

Alice	33
Bay City	36
Del Rio	36
Greenville	29
Huntsville	39
Lufkin	36
Nacogdoches	34
Palestine	30
Paris	37

Utah

Logan	32

Vermont

Rutland	56

Virginia

Blacksburg	29
Fredericksburg	52
Harrisonburg	33
Martinsville	22
Staunton–Waynesboro	33
Winchester	47

Washington

Aberdeen	62
Longview	46
Port Angeles	55
Pullman	31
Walla Walla	43
Wenatchee	66

West Virginia

Beckley	23
Clarksburg	27
Fairmont	22
Morgantown	22

Wisconsin

Fond du Lac	36
Manitowoc	35
Marshfield–Wisconsin Rapids	44
Stevens Point	47

Wyoming

Rock Springs	61

3

Economics

Political candidates might derive their greatest pleasure from delivering stirring orations on foreign policy or the approaching challenge of the twenty-first century. But they know their audiences are primarily concerned with something more tangible: making a living. Ronald Reagan shrewdly asked in 1980, "Are you better off than you were four years ago?" Jimmy Carter insisted the major issue was nuclear arms control. Reagan easily won the presidency.

Economic anxiety remains common today. A 1987 Gallup poll found that 31 percent of its respondents worried most or all of the time that their income wouldn't be sufficient to meet their bills. Such concern knows few bounds. Fully 26 percent of those with annual salaries between $25,000 and $40,000 admitted to such worries; the same was true of 21 percent of all college graduates.

It is essential that an area offer its residents a fighting chance to overcome their financial apprehensions. This section ranks each small city on its performance in providing the key components of economic stability, including competitive salaries, a growing stock of jobs, and solid employers.

There are opposing schools of thought on the question of whether it is now harder or easier to make ends meet than it was in the past. Each side is armed with its own battery of statistics and emphatic opinions.

102   "The standard of living hasn't been going anywhere for a decade," declared a former Labor Department under secretary, Malcolm Lovell, in 1987. His point had been dramatized a year earlier when the Joint Economic Committee of Congress issued a report on the relative earning power of Americans. Adjusting all of its figures to take inflation into account, the study said a typical 30-year-old man earned the 1986 equivalent of $25,253 back in 1973; the average had dropped to $18,763 by 1983. The buying power of an American household was reported to have been 8 percent higher in 1973 than in 1985.

"The young middle class has experienced a dramatic decline in its ability to pursue the conventional American dream: a home, financial security, and education for their children," concluded Richard Michel, an economist with the Urban Institute.

Not everyone agrees. In September 1987, *Fortune* posed this question on its cover, "Do We Live As Well As We Used To?" The answer inside was resoundingly positive. Reporter Sylvia Nasar presented her own statistical proof. She said the average hourly wage in 1956, expressed in 1986 dollars, was $6.80; it had climbed to $8.80 by 1986. The buying power of a 1987 household was twice that of its counterpart in 1952.

"Is starting out harder?" Nasar asked her readers about life late in the twentieth century. "Starting out was *always* hard," Nasar said. She added that the real problem was not a lack of money, but excessive growth of expectations. Americans wanted more than they could reasonably afford.

One answer is to get more money. Metropolitan areas currently offer higher salaries than those available in small towns. A 1986 Census Bureau study pegged the average metro income about 35 percent higher than the pay in the rest of the country. But prices are also steeper in the big city. It costs $7.63 to have a man's suit dry-cleaned in Seattle, compared to $5.67 in micropolitan Wenatchee, Washington, according with a 1989 survey by the American Chamber of Commerce Researchers Association. A pair of men's jeans, tagged at $20.46 in metropolitan Raleigh, North Carolina, sells for just $17.99 in the nearby small city of Rocky Mount. A six-pack of beer shows the difference in Delaware: $2.86 in big Wilmington, $2.50 in little Dover.

Small cities show signs of becoming more competitive in the future. Many are developing a strong mixture of modern industries, rather than gambling everything on luring one big plant to town. "Society teaches us to try to solve problems with one big solution: the 100-percent solution," Missouri community-development specialist Jack McCall told the *Kansas City Times*. "We're looking for 50 2-percent solutions."

Ranking micropolitan America. The ideal small city would offer its residents secure, well-paying jobs, coupled with the prospect of a more prosperous future. Each area is tested in five categories:

1. Per Capita Income: Does the average person make a good wage, or is he or she struggling to get by?

2. Income Growth: Has history shown that workers can expect sizeable raises, or is the pay level virtually stagnant?

3. Manufacturing Productivity: How healthy is the industrial sector of the local economy?

4. Retail Sales: How about the commercial sector? Are stores doing strong business, or are people holding on to the little money they have?

5. Population Growth: Is an expanding job base attracting people to town, or are people being forced to leave to find work elsewhere?

Per Capita Income

Good times came to the Torrington, Connecticut, area during the 1980s. Torrington was swept along by the tide of economic resurgence that washed over New England. It also benefited from the heightened interest of wealthy New Yorkers in rural real estate. "See that house and pool down there?" a local agent shouted to a *New York Times* reporter as they flew over the area in 1985. "That's a stockbroker who escaped the Hamptons."

Torrington leads the nation's micropolitan areas in per capita money income, which the Census Bureau defines as all regularly received income, not including "lump sum" payments like capital gains or inheritances. The per capita figure for Torrington, determined by dividing the area's total money income by its number of residents (including children) is $13,381. The average for the entire country is $10,797.

Gallup, New Mexico, is as troubled as Torrington is prosperous. Severe poverty on local Indian reservations depresses the area's per capita income to $4,743.

Cities with high income levels are fairly evenly distributed among the regions, but the South has most of the communities with substandard figures.

Source. These statistics, published in 1988, are for 1985. U.S. Bureau of the Census, *Current Population Reports: 1986 Population* (Washington: U.S. Government Printing Office, 1988).

Scoring. Twenty points for $13,250 or more per capita; no points for $5,649 or less. The spacing is every $400 per capita.

Per Capita Income

Highest	$
1. Torrington, Conn.	13,381
2. Fairbanks, Alaska	13,079
3. Bartlesville, Okla.	13,035
4. Key West, Fla.	12,319
5. Vero Beach, Fla.	12,155
6. Newport, R.I.	11,921
7. Concord, N.H.	11,313
8. Rock Springs, Wyo.	11,241
9. Columbus, Ind.	11,209
10. Carson City, Nev.	10,937

Lowest

219. Gallup, N.Mex.	4,743
218. Greenwood, Miss.	5,838
217. Del Rio, Tex.	6,224
216. Greenville, Miss.	6,342
215. Opelousas, La.	6,432
214. Lumberton, N.C.	6,582
213. Bogalusa, La.	6,610
212. Selma, Ala.	6,628
211. Roanoke Rapids, N.C.	6,854
210. Blytheville, Ark.	6,885

(Figure following each area name indicates per capita income in dollars; figure in parentheses represents rating points.)

Alabama

Athens	8,724	(8)
Auburn–Opelika	8,546	(8)
Decatur	9,637	(10)
Enterprise	8,804	(8)
Selma	6,628	(3)
Talladega	7,292	(5)

Alaska

| Fairbanks | 13,079 | (19) |

Arizona

Bullhead City– Lake Havasu City	9,041	(9)
Casa Grande– Apache Junction	7,411	(5)
Flagstaff	8,032	(6)
Prescott	8,944	(9)
Sierra Vista	8,464	(8)
Yuma	8,267	(7)

Arkansas

Blytheville	6,885	(4)
El Dorado	8,787	(8)
Hot Springs	9,429	(10)
Jonesboro	8,700	(8)
Rogers	9,803	(11)
Russellville	8,567	(8)

California

El Centro–Calexico– Brawley	7,170	(4)
Eureka	8,803	(8)
Hanford	7,884	(6)
Madera	8,118	(7)
San Luis Obispo– Atascadero	10,305	(12)

Colorado

| Grand Junction | 9,348 | (10) |

Connecticut

| Torrington | 13,381 | (20) |

Delaware

| Dover | 9,284 | (10) |

Florida

| Key West | 12,319 | (17) |
| Vero Beach | 12,155 | (17) |

Georgia

Brunswick	10,565	(13)
Carrollton	8,449	(7)
Dalton	9,957	(11)
Gainesville	10,196	(12)
Hinesville	7,368	(5)
La Grange	8,651	(8)
Rome	9,476	(10)
Valdosta	8,588	(8)

Idaho

Coeur d'Alene	8,544	(8)
Idaho Falls	9,295	(10)
Nampa–Caldwell	7,900	(6)
Pocatello	8,815	(8)
Twin Falls	8,746	(8)

Illinois

Carbondale	8,351	(7)
Danville	9,358	(10)
De Kalb	9,806	(11)
Freeport	10,392	(12)
Galesburg	9,922	(11)
Mattoon–Charleston	9,167	(9)
Ottawa	10,325	(12)
Quincy	8,949	(9)
Sterling	9,633	(10)

Indiana

Columbus	11,209	(14)
Marion	9,723	(11)
Michigan City– La Porte	9,634	(10)
New Castle	9,128	(9)
Richmond	9,176	(9)
Vincennes	8,321	(7)

Iowa

Ames	10,336	(12)
Burlington	10,377	(12)
Clinton	9,739	(11)
Fort Dodge	9,631	(10)
Marshalltown	10,658	(13)
Mason City	10,288	(12)
Muscatine	10,695	(13)

Kansas

Hutchinson	9,978	(11)
Manhattan	8,386	(7)
Salina	10,377	(12)

Kentucky

Bowling Green	9,002	(9)
Frankfort	10,529	(13)
Madisonville	8,951	(9)
Paducah	9,889	(11)
Radcliff–Elizabethtown	8,191	(7)
Richmond	7,600	(5)

Louisiana

Bogalusa	6,610	(3)
Crowley	7,426	(5)
Hammond	6,963	(4)
Minden	8,021	(6)
Morgan City	8,768	(8)
New Iberia	8,608	(8)
Opelousas	6,432	(2)
Ruston	7,461	(5)

Maine

Augusta–Waterville	9,175	(9)
Biddeford	9,889	(11)

Maryland

Salisbury	10,139	(12)

Michigan

Adrian	9,919	(11)
Marquette	8,143	(7)
Mount Pleasant	7,783	(6)
Owosso	9,869	(11)
Traverse City	9,536	(10)

Minnesota

Faribault	9,515	(10)
Mankato	9,343	(10)
Winona	9,042	(9)

Mississippi

Columbus	7,852	(6)
Greenville	6,342	(2)
Greenwood	5,838	(1)
Hattiesburg	7,765	(6)
Laurel	7,873	(6)
Meridian	8,640	(8)
Tupelo	8,531	(8)
Vicksburg	8,760	(8)

Missouri

Cape Girardeau	9,627	(10)
Jefferson City	10,486	(13)
Sikeston	7,711	(6)

Montana

Bozeman	8,532	(8)
Helena	9,918	(11)
Missoula	9,594	(10)

Nebraska

Grand Island	10,202	(12)

Nevada		
Carson City	10,937	(14)

New Hampshire		
Concord	11,313	(15)
Keene	10,493	(13)
Laconia	10,413	(12)

New Mexico		
Alamogordo	7,967	(6)
Carlsbad	8,458	(8)
Clovis	8,350	(7)
Farmington	7,718	(6)
Gallup	4,743	(0)
Hobbs	9,676	(11)
Rio Rancho	8,658	(8)
Roswell	8,207	(7)

New York		
Auburn	8,931	(9)
Batavia	9,837	(11)
Cortland	8,294	(7)
Gloversville	9,038	(9)
Ithaca	9,751	(11)
Jamestown	9,108	(9)
Kingston	10,532	(13)
Olean	8,084	(7)
Plattsburgh	8,526	(8)
Watertown	8,469	(8)

North Carolina		
Eden	9,046	(9)
Goldsboro	8,095	(7)
Greenville	8,417	(7)
Havelock–New Bern	8,567	(8)
Kinston	7,817	(6)
Lumberton	6,582	(3)
Roanoke Rapids	6,854	(4)
Rocky Mount	8,676	(8)
Sanford	9,606	(10)
Shelby	8,885	(9)
Statesville	9,429	(10)
Wilson	8,634	(8)

North Dakota		
Minot	9,103	(9)

Ohio		
Ashland	9,118	(9)
Ashtabula	8,699	(8)
Athens	7,178	(4)
Chillicothe	8,969	(9)
East Liverpool	8,262	(7)
Findlay	10,903	(14)
Fremont	10,010	(11)
Marion	9,148	(9)
New Philadelphia	8,672	(8)
Portsmouth	7,612	(5)
Sandusky	10,759	(13)
Sidney	9,482	(10)
Tiffin	8,845	(8)
Wooster	9,487	(10)
Zanesville	8,668	(8)

Oklahoma		
Ardmore	9,198	(9)
Bartlesville	13,035	(19)
Chickasha	8,841	(8)
Duncan	9,228	(9)
McAlester	7,829	(6)
Muskogee	8,156	(7)
Okmulgee	7,406	(5)
Ponca City	10,436	(12)
Stillwater	8,916	(9)

Oregon		
Albany	8,586	(8)
Bend	9,255	(10)
Corvallis	10,074	(12)
Grants Pass	7,978	(6)
Klamath Falls	8,295	(7)
Roseburg	8,732	(8)

Pennsylvania

Butler	9,313	(10)
Chambersburg	9,529	(10)
New Castle	8,760	(8)
Pottsville	8,339	(7)

Rhode Island

Newport	11,921	(16)

South Carolina

Greenwood	8,960	(9)
Hilton Head Island	10,771	(13)
Myrtle Beach	8,759	(8)
Orangeburg	6,904	(4)
Sumter	7,158	(4)

Tennessee

Cleveland	9,061	(9)
Columbia	9,053	(9)
Cookeville	8,296	(7)
Morristown	8,385	(7)
Tullahoma	9,171	(9)

Texas

Alice	7,327	(5)
Bay City	10,523	(13)
Del Rio	6,224	(2)
Greenville	9,068	(9)
Huntsville	7,999	(6)
Lufkin	8,677	(8)
Nacogdoches	8,294	(7)
Palestine	8,157	(7)
Paris	8,204	(7)

Utah

Logan	7,387	(5)

Vermont

Rutland	9,537	(10)

Virginia

Blacksburg	9,078	(9)
Fredericksburg	10,479	(13)
Harrisonburg	9,247	(9)
Martinsville	9,619	(10)
Staunton–Waynesboro	9,923	(11)
Winchester	10,675	(13)

Washington

Aberdeen	9,320	(10)
Longview	9,878	(11)
Port Angeles	9,928	(11)
Pullman	8,988	(9)
Walla Walla	9,537	(10)
Wenatchee	9,665	(11)

West Virginia

Beckley	8,311	(7)
Clarksburg	8,436	(7)
Fairmont	8,244	(7)
Morgantown	9,105	(9)

Wisconsin

Fond du Lac	9,557	(10)
Manitowoc	9,468	(10)
Marshfield– Wisconsin Rapids	10,045	(11)
Stevens Point	9,006	(9)

Wyoming

Rock Springs	11,241	(14)

Income Growth

Any community with visions of future greatness must base those dreams on economic expansion. That is particularly true of small cities. Should they be unable to offer the reasonable expectation of a stable, comfortable life, micropolitan areas will lose their brightest residents to the blandishment of their metropolitan neighbors.

This category measures each area's economic growth over a six-year period: specifically, the increase in the per capita money income from 1979 to 1985. The national per capita income grew from $7,295 to $10,797 in those years, a gain of 47.9 percent.

Rio Rancho, New Mexico, which in the past 15 years has spurted to life on the desert near Albuquerque, has seen its average income rocket skyward along with its population total. Rio Rancho's per capita figure was $5,108 in 1979, but up to $8,658 in 1985, an improvement of 69.5 percent.

Fewer than 150 miles west of Rio Rancho is a city with a nearly stagnant income level, Gallup, New Mexico. The Gallup area includes a poverty-stricken Navajo reservation, which the *Los Angeles Times* called "the most expansive ghetto" in the country.

Eastern cities show the most promising income growth rates. The West has most of the cities with slow income expansion.

Source. These statistics, published in 1988, are for 1979 through 1985. U.S. Bureau of the Census, *Current Population Reports: 1986 Population* (Washington: U.S. Government Printing Office, 1988).

Scoring. Twenty points for 68.0 percent or more; no points for 20.4 percent or less. The spacing is every 2.5 percent.

	Per Capita Income Increase From 1979 to 1985
Highest	**%**
1. Rio Rancho, N.Mex.	69.5
2. Newport, R.I.	67.0
3. Torrington, Conn.	63.6
4. Concord, N.H.	63.5
5. Rogers, Ark.	60.7
6. Blacksburg, Va.	60.4
7. Keene, N.H.	59.6
7. Plattsburgh, N.Y.	59.6
9. Biddeford, Maine	59.2
10. Key West, Fla.	58.9
10. Kingston, N.Y.	58.9
10. Laconia, N.H.	58.9
Lowest	
219. Gallup, N.Mex.	13.0
218. Klamath Falls, Oreg.	20.9
217. Bend, Oreg.	21.2
216. Albany, Oreg.	22.7
215. Roseburg, Oreg.	23.5
214. El Centro–Calexico– Brawley, Calif.	24.2
212. Aberdeen, Wash.	25.2
212. Sterling, Ill.	25.2
211. Grants Pass, Oreg.	26.4
210. East Liverpool, Ohio	26.5

(Figure following each area name indicates percentage of growth in per capita income from 1979 to 1985; figure in parentheses represents rating points.)

Alabama

Athens	56.4	(15)
Auburn–Opelika	51.6	(13)
Decatur	52.4	(13)
Enterprise	54.5	(14)
Selma	42.4	(9)
Talladega	46.4	(11)

Alaska

Fairbanks	33.1	(6)

Arizona

Bullhead City–		
Lake Havasu City	35.5	(7)
Casa Grande–		
Apache Junction	39.5	(8)
Flagstaff	42.6	(9)
Prescott	38.7	(8)
Sierra Vista	47.5	(11)
Yuma	43.0	(10)

Arkansas

Blytheville	43.7	(10)
El Dorado	49.5	(12)
Hot Springs	48.3	(12)
Jonesboro	49.0	(12)
Rogers	60.7	(17)
Russellville	53.7	(14)

California

El Centro–Calexico–		
Brawley	24.2	(2)
Eureka	27.8	(3)
Hanford	34.9	(6)
Madera	27.6	(3)
San Luis Obispo–		
Atascadero	46.2	(11)

Colorado

Grand Junction	30.4	(4)

Connecticut

Torrington	63.6	(18)

Delaware

Dover	51.6	(13)

Florida

Key West	58.9	(16)
Vero Beach	52.4	(13)

Georgia

Brunswick	54.5	(14)
Carrollton	54.7	(14)
Dalton	51.3	(13)
Gainesville	57.6	(15)
Hinesville	50.1	(12)
La Grange	51.6	(13)
Rome	52.4	(13)
Valdosta	53.1	(14)

Idaho

Coeur d'Alene	34.6	(6)
Idaho Falls	41.5	(9)
Nampa–Caldwell	37.1	(7)
Pocatello	31.7	(5)
Twin Falls	36.5	(7)

Illinois

Carbondale	38.2	(8)
Danville	34.6	(6)
De Kalb	35.9	(7)
Freeport	40.1	(8)
Galesburg	35.2	(6)
Mattoon–Charleston	37.1	(7)
Ottawa	35.6	(7)
Quincy	34.2	(6)
Sterling	25.2	(2)

Indiana

Columbus	41.0	(9)
Marion	45.1	(10)
Michigan City–La Porte	32.4	(5)
New Castle	42.6	(9)
Richmond	40.9	(9)
Vincennes	34.9	(6)

Iowa

Ames	47.8	(11)
Burlington	38.4	(8)
Clinton	35.7	(7)
Fort Dodge	34.4	(6)
Marshalltown	41.3	(9)
Mason City	39.6	(8)
Muscatine	45.7	(11)

Kansas

Hutchinson	40.3	(8)
Manhattan	46.3	(11)
Salina	39.9	(8)

Kentucky

Bowling Green	48.5	(12)
Frankfort	44.1	(10)
Madisonville	36.4	(7)
Paducah	42.7	(9)
Radcliff–Elizabethtown	50.3	(12)
Richmond	48.6	(12)

Louisiana

Bogalusa	29.8	(4)
Crowley	32.5	(5)
Hammond	32.5	(5)
Minden	39.5	(8)
Morgan City	29.2	(4)
New Iberia	33.0	(6)
Opelousas	35.6	(7)
Ruston	39.3	(8)

Maine

Augusta–Waterville	53.8	(14)
Biddeford	59.2	(16)

Maryland

Salisbury	52.1	(13)

Michigan

Adrian	42.6	(9)
Marquette	31.6	(5)
Mount Pleasant	39.2	(8)
Owosso	42.0	(9)
Traverse City	37.6	(7)

Minnesota

Faribault	52.6	(13)
Mankato	41.4	(9)
Winona	46.8	(11)

Mississippi

Columbus	48.2	(12)
Greenville	35.8	(7)
Greenwood	33.3	(6)
Hattiesburg	44.7	(10)
Laurel	43.6	(10)
Meridian	48.9	(12)
Tupelo	47.9	(11)
Vicksburg	39.8	(8)

Missouri

Cape Girardeau	46.7	(11)
Jefferson City	46.1	(11)
Sikeston	38.6	(8)

Montana

Bozeman	32.1	(5)
Helena	36.5	(7)
Missoula	32.2	(5)

Nebraska

Grand Island	42.5	(9)

Nevada

Carson City	34.2	(6)

New Hampshire

Concord	63.5	(18)
Keene	59.6	(16)
Laconia	58.9	(16)

New Mexico

Alamogordo	48.1	(12)
Carlsbad	39.6	(8)
Clovis	40.1	(8)
Farmington	32.8	(5)
Gallup	13.0	(0)
Hobbs	39.8	(8)
Rio Rancho	69.5	(20)
Roswell	40.8	(9)

New York

Auburn	50.5	(13)
Batavia	47.3	(11)
Cortland	47.4	(11)
Gloversville	51.3	(13)
Ithaca	55.7	(15)
Jamestown	47.4	(11)
Kingston	58.9	(16)
Olean	44.0	(10)
Plattsburgh	59.6	(16)
Watertown	51.2	(13)

North Carolina

Eden	49.6	(12)
Goldsboro	52.2	(13)
Greenville	50.9	(13)
Havelock–New Bern	51.6	(13)
Kinston	44.2	(10)
Lumberton	46.2	(11)
Roanoke Rapids	51.9	(13)
Rocky Mount	53.8	(14)
Sanford	52.0	(13)
Shelby	50.5	(13)
Statesville	53.9	(14)
Wilson	50.1	(12)

North Dakota

Minot	42.5	(9)

Ohio

Ashland	39.9	(8)
Ashtabula	33.4	(6)
Athens	41.0	(9)
Chillicothe	43.5	(10)
East Liverpool	26.5	(3)
Findlay	47.1	(11)
Fremont	43.7	(10)
Marion	37.1	(7)
New Philadelphia	34.7	(6)
Portsmouth	39.9	(8)
Sandusky	43.0	(10)
Sidney	45.2	(10)
Tiffin	38.7	(8)
Wooster	40.2	(8)
Zanesville	41.3	(9)

Oklahoma

Ardmore	42.1	(9)
Bartlesville	46.1	(11)
Chickasha	41.1	(9)
Duncan	34.9	(6)
McAlester	46.3	(11)
Muskogee	38.9	(9)
Okmulgee	40.0	(8)
Ponca City	42.3	(9)
Stillwater	47.1	(11)

Oregon

Albany	22.7	(1)
Bend	21.2	(1)
Corvallis	28.9	(4)
Grants Pass	26.4	(3)
Klamath Falls	20.9	(1)
Roseburg	23.5	(2)

Pennsylvania

Butler	37.3	(7)
Chambersburg	42.8	(9)
New Castle	33.4	(6)
Pottsville	41.7	(9)

Rhode Island

Newport	67.0	(19)

South Carolina

Greenwood	46.4	(11)
Hilton Head Island	56.9	(15)
Myrtle Beach	50.9	(13)
Orangeburg	48.5	(12)
Sumter	49.9	(12)

Tennessee

Cleveland	52.1	(13)
Columbia	46.3	(11)
Cookeville	49.3	(12)
Morristown	49.5	(12)
Tullahoma	49.0	(12)

Texas

Alice	30.8	(5)
Bay City	47.3	(11)
Del Rio	37.0	(7)
Greenville	47.9	(11)
Huntsville	41.7	(9)
Lufkin	39.3	(8)
Nacogdoches	41.7	(9)
Palestine	38.5	(8)
Paris	47.1	(11)

Utah

Logan	36.8	(7)

Vermont

Rutland	56.6	(15)

Virginia

Blacksburg	60.4	(16)
Fredericksburg	53.9	(14)
Harrisonburg	51.7	(13)
Martinsville	54.1	(14)
Staunton–Waynesboro	47.4	(11)
Winchester	56.4	(15)

Washington

Aberdeen	25.2	(2)
Longview	29.8	(4)
Port Angeles	29.5	(4)
Pullman	44.3	(10)
Walla Walla	38.1	(8)
Wenatchee	28.3	(4)

West Virginia

Beckley	33.5	(6)
Clarksburg	36.2	(7)
Fairmont	32.1	(5)
Morgantown	41.0	(9)

Wisconsin

Fond du Lac	40.5	(9)
Manitowoc	38.5	(8)
Marshfield–Wisconsin Rapids	46.6	(11)
Stevens Point	44.1	(10)

Wyoming

Rock Springs	26.6	(3)

Manufacturing Productivity

The press is in love with the concept of a service-based economy. Some pundits have gone so far as to predict that manufacturing will lose its importance in the future.

Don't believe it. "Manufacturing is the traditional route for the relatively low-educated or low-skilled into the middle class," says Steven Malin, an economist for the Conference Board. As such, it promotes local economic stability.

This category estimates the health of each area's manufacturing base. It begins with a statistic known as "value added by manufacture," which is the price of a finished item minus all of the costs (labor, materials, electricity, etc.) to produce it. This figure is then divided by the number of workers in local plants.

Farmington, New Mexico, leads the way with an average of $297,750 value added annually per worker. Carrollton, Georgia, has the lowest total, $13,638. The national average, including all metro areas, is $66,458 value added per worker.

Does this category accurately reflect manufacturing strength? Consider this: Farmington's workers are paid well above the national average. Those in Carrollton receive less money than Georgia's already low state average.

Western cities fare best in this measure, Southern cities the worst.

Source. These statistics, published in 1988, are for 1982. Derived from U.S. Bureau of the Census, *County and City Data Book* (Washington: U.S. Government Printing Office, 1988).

Scoring. Twenty points for $120,000 or more per worker; no points for $24,999 or less. The spacing is every $5,000 per worker.

	Value Added Per Production Worker
Highest	**$**
1. Farmington, N.Mex.	297,750
2. Rock Springs, Wyo.	238,000
3. El Dorado, Ark.	189,692
4. Plattsburgh, N.Y.	162,500
5. Fairbanks, Alaska	157,600
6. Okmulgee, Okla.	157,250
7. Huntsville, Tex.	152,273
8. Gallup, N.Mex.	147,333
9. Pocatello, Idaho	135,000
10. Muscatine, Iowa	131,368
Lowest	
219. Carrollton, Ga.	13,638
218. Casa Grande– Apache Junction, Ariz.	14,722
217. Coeur d'Alene, Idaho	24,316
216. Enterprise, Ala.	24,577
215. Lumberton, N.C.	26,046
214. Myrtle Beach, S.C.	26,203
213. Hilton Head Island, S.C.	28,769
212. Rio Rancho, N.Mex.	29,250
211. Portsmouth, Ohio	29,375
210. Hammond, La.	30,529

(Figure following each area name indicates value added in dollars per production worker; figure in parentheses represents rating points.)

Alabama

Athens	66,771	(9)
Auburn–Opelika	46,957	(5)
Decatur	70,716	(10)
Enterprise	24,577	(0)
Selma	39,658	(3)
Talladega	36,108	(3)

Alaska

Fairbanks	157,600	(20)

Arizona

Bullhead City– Lake Havasu City	33,533	(2)
Casa Grande– Apache Junction	14,722	(0)
Flagstaff	77,867	(11)
Prescott	50,833	(6)
Sierra Vista	48,222	(5)
Yuma	35,500	(3)

Arkansas

Blytheville	57,085	(7)
El Dorado	189,692	(20)
Hot Springs	34,897	(2)
Jonesboro	61,511	(8)
Rogers	51,909	(6)
Russellville	43,083	(4)

California

El Centro–Calexico– Brawley	48,400	(5)
Eureka	48,348	(5)
Hanford	64,591	(8)
Madera	55,704	(7)
San Luis Obispo– Atascadero	73,960	(10)

Colorado

Grand Junction	32,905	(2)

Connecticut

Torrington	61,042	(8)

Delaware

Dover	97,462	(15)

Florida

Key West	43,167	(4)
Vero Beach	37,600	(3)

Georgia

Brunswick	52,308	(6)
Carrollton	13,638	(0)
Dalton	47,136	(5)
Gainesville	41,608	(4)
Hinesville	39,500	(3)
La Grange	43,290	(4)
Rome	46,345	(5)
Valdosta	45,773	(5)

Idaho

Coeur d'Alene	24,316	(0)
Idaho Falls	117,231	(19)
Nampa–Caldwell	53,514	(6)
Pocatello	135,000	(20)
Twin Falls	55,545	(7)

Illinois

Carbondale	49,091	(5)
Danville	64,389	(8)
De Kalb	49,277	(5)
Freeport	65,074	(9)
Galesburg	68,690	(9)
Mattoon–Charleston	64,750	(8)
Ottawa	62,889	(8)
Quincy	85,467	(13)
Sterling	53,717	(6)

Indiana

Columbus	63,775	(8)
Marion	55,099	(7)
Michigan City–		
La Porte	69,093	(9)
New Castle	56,273	(7)
Richmond	42,057	(4)
Vincennes	49,077	(5)

Iowa

Ames	103,368	(16)
Burlington	102,159	(16)
Clinton	74,465	(10)
Fort Dodge	107,250	(17)
Marshalltown	97,394	(15)
Mason City	46,350	(5)
Muscatine	131,368	(20)

Kansas

Hutchinson	55,756	(7)
Manhattan	66,000	(9)
Salina	55,914	(7)

Kentucky

Bowling Green	76,317	(11)
Frankfort	44,037	(4)
Madisonville	51,550	(6)
Paducah	76,500	(11)
Radcliff–		
Elizabethtown	63,000	(8)
Richmond	71,125	(10)

Louisiana

Bogalusa	52,632	(6)
Crowley	31,615	(2)
Hammond	30,529	(2)
Minden	49,636	(5)
Morgan City	54,308	(6)
New Iberia	47,385	(5)
Opelousas	77,750	(11)
Ruston	37,154	(3)

Maine

Augusta–Waterville	61,109	(8)
Biddeford	38,380	(3)

Maryland

Salisbury	53,792	(6)

Michigan

Adrian	59,903	(7)
Marquette	60,750	(8)
Mount Pleasant	66,571	(9)
Owosso	41,520	(4)
Traverse City	40,400	(4)

Minnesota

Faribault	63,182	(8)
Mankato	76,227	(11)
Winona	47,333	(5)

Mississippi

Columbus	48,302	(5)
Greenville	41,692	(4)
Greenwood	37,444	(3)
Hattiesburg	36,933	(3)
Laurel	49,105	(5)
Meridian	49,216	(5)
Tupelo	35,119	(3)
Vicksburg	74,121	(10)

Missouri

Cape Girardeau	83,143	(12)
Jefferson City	77,200	(11)
Sikeston	35,684	(3)

Montana

Bozeman	61,571	(8)
Helena	36,833	(3)
Missoula	37,793	(3)

Nebraska

Grand Island	59,581	(7)

Nevada

Carson City	57,077	(7)

New Hampshire

Concord	39,864	(3)
Keene	52,226	(6)
Laconia	36,333	(3)

New Mexico

Alamogordo	34,200	(2)
Carlsbad	62,959	(8)
Clovis	57,200	(7)
Farmington	297,750	(20)
Gallup	147,333	(20)
Hobbs	62,750	(8)
Rio Rancho	29,250	(1)
Roswell	58,250	(7)

New York

Auburn	73,824	(10)
Batavia	54,156	(6)
Cortland	48,250	(5)
Gloversville	47,804	(5)
Ithaca	50,000	(6)
Jamestown	59,304	(7)
Kingston	46,340	(5)
Olean	62,268	(8)
Plattsburgh	162,500	(20)
Watertown	68,675	(9)

North Carolina

Eden	77,142	(11)
Goldsboro	32,918	(2)
Greenville	79,980	(11)
Havelock–New Bern	45,680	(5)
Kinston	45,662	(5)
Lumberton	26,046	(1)
Roanoke Rapids	36,500	(3)
Rocky Mount	46,321	(5)
Sanford	49,458	(5)
Shelby	33,165	(2)
Statesville	39,826	(3)
Wilson	50,545	(6)

North Dakota

Minot	60,250	(8)

Ohio

Ashland	61,810	(8)
Ashtabula	65,833	(9)
Athens	41,286	(4)
Chillicothe	75,568	(11)
East Liverpool	44,983	(4)
Findlay	89,333	(13)
Fremont	69,544	(9)
Marion	82,273	(12)
New Philadelphia	59,516	(7)
Portsmouth	29,375	(1)
Sandusky	68,303	(9)
Sidney	50,840	(6)
Tiffin	55,129	(7)
Wooster	72,614	(10)
Zanesville	43,054	(4)

Oklahoma

Ardmore	67,231	(9)
Bartlesville	68,000	(9)
Chickasha	62,368	(8)
Duncan	67,231	(9)
McAlester	38,750	(3)
Muskogee	68,525	(9)
Okmulgee	157,250	(20)
Ponca City	82,625	(12)
Stillwater	50,667	(6)

Oregon

Albany	57,817	(7)
Bend	38,696	(3)
Corvallis	59,967	(7)
Grants Pass	44,826	(4)
Klamath Falls	41,750	(4)
Roseburg	35,597	(3)

Pennsylvania

Butler	54,338	(6)
Chambersburg	41,430	(4)
New Castle	53,527	(6)
Pottsville	35,710	(3)

Rhode Island

Newport	77,600	(11)

South Carolina

Greenwood	34,115	(2)
Hilton Head Island	28,769	(1)
Myrtle Beach	26,203	(1)
Orangeburg	38,881	(3)
Sumter	40,800	(4)

Tennessee

Cleveland	45,563	(5)
Columbia	62,026	(8)
Cookeville	41,533	(4)
Morristown	37,422	(3)
Tullahoma	45,436	(5)

Texas

Alice	33,000	(2)
Bay City	79,691	(11)
Del Rio	41,600	(4)
Greenville	55,268	(7)
Huntsville	152,273	(20)
Lufkin	62,951	(8)
Nacogdoches	46,037	(5)
Palestine	32,846	(2)
Paris	90,297	(14)

Utah

Logan	50,485	(6)

Vermont

Rutland	45,711	(5)

Virginia

Blacksburg	37,846	(3)
Fredericksburg	78,672	(11)
Harrisonburg	87,112	(13)
Martinsville	31,408	(2)
Staunton– Waynesboro	64,500	(8)
Winchester	43,778	(4)

Washington

Aberdeen	56,137	(7)
Longview	60,013	(8)
Port Angeles	48,773	(5)
Pullman	40,000	(4)
Walla Walla	49,200	(5)
Wenatchee	86,529	(13)

West Virginia

Beckley	61,667	(8)
Clarksburg	40,875	(4)
Fairmont	50,950	(6)
Morgantown	46,056	(5)

Wisconsin

Fond du Lac	70,254	(10)
Manitowoc	53,049	(6)
Marshfield– Wisconsin Rapids	67,549	(9)
Stevens Point	75,645	(11)

Wyoming

Rock Springs	238,000	(20)

Retail Sales

One way to quickly gauge the economic health of an unfamiliar community is to glance at its shopping areas. One city might have a busy Main Street or a sparkling new mall on the highway out of town; the second might be characterized by vacant storefronts or decaying 1950s-style shopping centers. The difference is obvious.

This category ranks each area according to its annual volume of retail trade. The total amount of money taken in by all stores is divided by the number of local residents. The average for the entire country is $4,595 of retail spending by every man, woman, and child.

Stores in Fairbanks, Alaska, do the briskest business: $7,907 per capita annually. The high figure is due in part to inflation. Alaska has the most expensive cost of living of the 50 states. But it also shows a great willingness to buy. Stores in Fairbanks did $465 million worth of business in the year studied.

Residents of Rio Rancho, New Mexico, generally go to nearby Albuquerque to shop. They spent only $50.8 million at their own stores, $1,399 per person.

Strong retail centers are evenly distributed around the country. Most of their weak counterparts are in the West and South.

Source. These statistics, published in 1988, are for 1982. U.S. Bureau of the Census, *County and City Data Book* (Washington: U.S. Government Printing Office, 1988).

Scoring. Twenty points for $6,500 or more per person; no points for $2,699 or less. The spacing is every $200 per person.

	Annual Retail Sales Per Capita
Highest	**$**
1. Fairbanks, Alaska	7,907
2. Fredericksburg, Va.	7,258
3. Myrtle Beach, S.C.	7,007
4. Traverse City, Mich.	6,824
5. Laconia, N.H.	6,732
6. Salisbury, Md.	6,404
7. Grand Junction, Colo.	6,271
8. Carson City, Nev.	6,269
9. Paducah, Ky.	6,194
10. Salina, Kans.	6,144
Lowest	
219. Rio Rancho, N.Mex.	1,399
218. Pullman, Wash.	2,246
217. Hinesville, Ga.	2,379
216. Athens, Ala.	2,837
215. Sidney, Ohio	2,841
214. Casa Grande–Apache Junction, Ariz.	2,889
213. Bogalusa, La.	3,027
212. Talladega, Ala.	3,099
211. Sierra Vista, Ariz.	3,152
210. Owosso, Mich.	3,160

(Figure following each area name indicates annual retail sales in dollars per capita; figure in parentheses represents rating points.)

Alabama

Athens	2,837	(1)
Auburn–Opelika	3,802	(6)
Decatur	4,135	(8)
Enterprise	3,786	(6)
Selma	3,180	(3)
Talladega	3,099	(2)

Alaska

Fairbanks	7,907	(20)

Arizona

Bullhead City– Lake Havasu City	5,083	(12)
Casa Grande– Apache Junction	2,889	(1)
Flagstaff	5,529	(15)
Prescott	4,076	(7)
Sierra Vista	3,152	(3)
Yuma	4,483	(9)

Arkansas

Blytheville	3,235	(3)
El Dorado	4,365	(9)
Hot Springs	5,157	(13)
Jonesboro	4,996	(12)
Rogers	3,744	(6)
Russellville	4,791	(11)

California

El Centro–Calexico– Brawley	4,330	(9)
Eureka	4,781	(11)
Hanford	3,374	(4)
Madera	3,288	(3)
San Luis Obispo– Atascadero	4,522	(10)

Colorado

Grand Junction	6,271	(18)

Connecticut

Torrington	4,131	(8)

Delaware

Dover	5,504	(15)

Florida

Key West	5,728	(16)
Vero Beach	5,398	(14)

Georgia

Brunswick	5,353	(14)
Carrollton	3,557	(5)
Dalton	5,008	(12)
Gainesville	4,476	(9)
Hinesville	2,379	(0)
La Grange	4,363	(9)
Rome	3,784	(6)
Valdosta	5,153	(13)

Idaho

Coeur d'Alene	4,192	(8)
Idaho Falls	5,810	(16)
Nampa–Caldwell	4,263	(8)
Pocatello	4,635	(10)
Twin Falls	5,174	(13)

Illinois

Carbondale	5,458	(14)
Danville	4,030	(7)
De Kalb	3,692	(5)
Freeport	3,880	(6)
Galesburg	4,790	(11)
Mattoon–Charleston	4,390	(9)
Ottawa	4,854	(11)
Quincy	4,773	(11)
Sterling	3,942	(7)

Indiana

Columbus	4,529	(10)
Marion	4,044	(7)
Michigan City–La Porte	4,085	(7)
New Castle	3,467	(4)
Richmond	5,247	(13)
Vincennes	4,412	(9)

Iowa

Ames	4,481	(9)
Burlington	4,941	(12)
Clinton	4,825	(11)
Fort Dodge	5,267	(13)
Marshalltown	4,416	(9)
Mason City	6,016	(17)
Muscatine	4,371	(9)

Kansas

Hutchinson	4,772	(11)
Manhattan	3,683	(5)
Salina	6,144	(18)

Kentucky

Bowling Green	5,099	(12)
Frankfort	4,129	(8)
Madisonville	4,521	(10)
Paducah	6,194	(18)
Radcliff–Elizabethtown	3,672	(5)
Richmond	4,219	(8)

Louisiana

Bogalusa	3,027	(2)
Crowley	3,491	(4)
Hammond	4,923	(12)
Minden	4,315	(9)
Morgan City	5,123	(13)
New Iberia	5,177	(13)
Opelousas	3,900	(7)
Ruston	3,897	(6)

Maine

Augusta–Waterville	4,967	(12)
Biddeford	4,054	(7)

Maryland

Salisbury	6,404	(19)

Michigan

Adrian	3,687	(5)
Marquette	3,489	(4)
Mount Pleasant	3,647	(5)
Owosso	3,160	(3)
Traverse City	6,824	(20)

Minnesota

Faribault	3,805	(6)
Mankato	5,601	(15)
Winona	4,244	(8)

Mississippi

Columbus	4,335	(9)
Greenville	3,888	(6)
Greenwood	3,718	(6)
Hattiesburg	5,810	(16)
Laurel	4,195	(8)
Meridian	4,926	(12)
Tupelo	5,850	(16)
Vicksburg	4,243	(8)

Missouri

Cape Girardeau	5,453	(14)
Jefferson City	5,793	(16)
Sikeston	4,114	(8)

Montana

Bozeman	6,019	(17)
Helena	5,585	(15)
Missoula	5,730	(16)

Nebraska

Grand Island	6,030	(17)

Nevada

Carson City	6,269	(18)

New Hampshire

Concord	5,158	(13)
Keene	4,434	(9)
Laconia	6,732	(20)

New Mexico

Alamogordo	3,987	(7)
Carlsbad	4,957	(12)
Clovis	4,643	(10)
Farmington	4,860	(11)
Gallup	4,686	(10)
Hobbs	5,512	(15)
Rio Rancho	1,399	(0)
Roswell	5,401	(14)

New York

Auburn	3,508	(5)
Batavia	3,510	(5)
Cortland	3,820	(6)
Gloversville	3,431	(4)
Ithaca	4,059	(7)
Jamestown	3,815	(6)
Kingston	4,281	(8)
Olean	3,393	(4)
Plattsburgh	4,201	(8)
Watertown	4,326	(9)

North Carolina

Eden	3,465	(4)
Goldsboro	3,915	(7)
Greenville	4,615	(10)
Havelock–New Bern	4,331	(9)
Kinston	4,243	(8)
Lumberton	3,322	(4)
Roanoke Rapids	3,947	(7)
Rocky Mount	4,153	(8)
Sanford	4,974	(12)
Shelby	3,394	(4)
Statesville	3,731	(6)
Wilson	4,556	(10)

North Dakota

Minot	5,903	(17)

Ohio

Ashland	3,425	(4)
Ashtabula	3,790	(6)
Athens	3,319	(4)
Chillicothe	3,596	(5)
East Liverpool	3,591	(5)
Findlay	4,742	(11)
Fremont	3,754	(6)
Marion	4,081	(7)
New Philadelphia	4,114	(8)
Portsmouth	3,943	(7)
Sandusky	4,932	(12)
Sidney	2,841	(1)
Tiffin	3,343	(4)
Wooster	3,589	(5)
Zanesville	4,067	(7)

Oklahoma

Ardmore	5,085	(12)
Bartlesville	5,141	(13)
Chickasha	3,863	(6)
Duncan	4,863	(11)
McAlester	3,724	(6)
Muskogee	4,615	(10)
Okmulgee	3,549	(5)
Ponca City	5,104	(13)
Stillwater	4,268	(8)

Oregon

Albany	4,006	(7)
Bend	4,947	(12)
Corvallis	3,668	(5)
Grants Pass	4,771	(11)
Klamath Falls	4,424	(9)
Roseburg	3,803	(6)

Pennsylvania

Butler	3,847	(6)
Chambersburg	3,865	(6)
New Castle	3,724	(6)
Pottsville	3,451	(4)

Rhode Island

Newport	4,463	(9)

South Carolina

Greenwood	4,189	(8)
Hilton Head Island	4,666	(10)
Myrtle Beach	7,007	(20)
Orangeburg	3,273	(3)
Sumter	3,486	(4)

Tennessee

Cleveland	4,263	(8)
Columbia	3,767	(6)
Cookeville	4,218	(8)
Morristown	4,812	(11)
Tullahoma	4,535	(10)

Texas

Alice	4,978	(12)
Bay City	4,569	(10)
Del Rio	4,481	(9)
Greenville	4,252	(8)
Huntsville	4,348	(9)
Lufkin	5,046	(12)
Nacogdoches	4,502	(10)
Palestine	4,210	(8)
Paris	4,738	(11)

Utah

Logan	3,451	(4)

Vermont

Rutland	5,403	(14)

Virginia

Blacksburg	4,026	(7)
Fredericksburg	7,258	(20)
Harrisonburg	3,513	(5)
Martinsville	3,613	(5)
Staunton–Waynesboro	4,262	(8)
Winchester	5,162	(13)

Washington

Aberdeen	4,409	(9)
Longview	4,833	(11)
Port Angeles	4,440	(9)
Pullman	2,246	(0)
Walla Walla	3,956	(7)
Wenatchee	5,556	(15)

West Virginia

Beckley	4,802	(11)
Clarksburg	3,981	(7)
Fairmont	4,729	(11)
Morgantown	3,862	(6)

Wisconsin

Fond du Lac	4,255	(8)
Manitowoc	3,443	(4)
Marshfield– Wisconsin Rapids	5,481	(14)
Stevens Point	4,295	(8)

Wyoming

Rock Springs	5,334	(14)

Population Growth

Rio Rancho, New Mexico, wasn't incorporated as a city until 1981, but it is quickly making up for lost time. There was a steady stream of Northern immigrants to the area even before incorporation. "Now it's mostly young people relocating here from Albuquerque," said Mayor Grover Nash in 1987. Demographers are predicting that Rio Rancho might be New Mexico's second-largest city within 20 years.

Steady population growth is usually a strong indication that an area offers an attractive economic future; population erosion is a warning signal that the local job pool is drying up. This category ranks each area by its population growth from 1980 to 1986, a period when the number of Americans grew 6.4 percent.

Rio Rancho easily leads the rest of micropolitan America with its 48.6 percent gain. The Rio Rancho area had 34,400 residents in 1980. The figure was 51,100 just six years later.

Galesburg, Illinois, watched its numbers fall from 61,607 to 56,300 over the same period: a loss of 8.6 percent. The Midwest has been hit hard by the farm crisis and a loss of manufacturing jobs. All 15 micros in Indiana and Illinois saw their populations decline.

Cities with strong population gains are concentrated in the West and the South.

Source. These statistics, published in 1988, are for 1980 through 1986. U.S. Bureau of the Census, *Current Population Reports: 1986 Population* (Washington: U.S. Government Printing Office, 1988).

Scoring. Twenty points for 38 percent or more; no points for any population loss. The spacing is every 2 percent.

	Population Growth From 1980 to 1986
Highest	%
1. Rio Rancho, N.Mex.	48.6
2. Bullhead City–Lake Havasu City, Ariz.	37.1
3. Vero Beach, Fla.	35.2
4. Hilton Head Island, S.C.	31.0
5. Huntsville, Tex.	29.4
6. Myrtle Beach, S.C.	28.8
7. San Luis Obispo–Atascadero, Calif.	26.5
8. Fairbanks, Alaska	25.3
9. Prescott, Ariz.	24.4
10. Palestine, Tex.	23.7
Lowest	
219. Galesburg, Ill.	–8.6
218. Fort Dodge, Iowa	–7.1
217. Bartlesville, Okla.	–6.7
216. Clinton, Iowa	–6.2
215. New Castle, Ind.	–6.0
214. Aberdeen, Wash.	–5.5
213. Corvallis, Oreg.	–5.3
212. Richmond, Ind.	–5.1
210. New Castle, Pa.	–4.9
210. Quincy, Ill.	–4.9

(Figure following each area name indicates percentage of population increase from 1980 to 1986; figure in parentheses represents rating points.)

Alabama

Athens	12.5	(7)
Auburn–Opelika	6.0	(4)
Decatur	9.5	(5)
Enterprise	4.4	(3)
Selma	–2.4	(0)
Talladega	3.6	(2)

Alaska

Fairbanks	25.3	(13)

Arizona

Bullhead City– Lake Havasu City	37.1	(19)
Casa Grande– Apache Junction	8.6	(5)
Flagstaff	14.8	(8)
Prescott	24.4	(13)
Sierra Vista	7.1	(4)
Yuma	13.9	(7)

Arkansas

Blytheville	–2.5	(0)
El Dorado	1.0	(1)
Hot Springs	6.7	(4)
Jonesboro	0.2	(1)
Rogers	13.9	(7)
Russellville	11.5	(6)

California

El Centro-Calexico– Brawley	16.2	(9)
Eureka	5.2	(3)
Hanford	16.5	(9)
Madera	23.4	(12)
San Luis Obispo– Atascadero	26.5	(14)

Colorado

Grand Junction	9.2	(5)

Connecticut

Torrington	3.5	(2)

Delaware

Dover	7.1	(4)

Florida

Key West	14.7	(8)
Vero Beach	35.2	(18)

Georgia

Brunswick	8.8	(5)
Carrollton	15.2	(8)
Dalton	5.3	(3)
Gainesville	15.2	(8)
Hinesville	12.5	(7)
La Grange	8.4	(5)
Rome	–1.4	(0)
Valdosta	8.4	(5)

Idaho

Coeur d'Alene	13.0	(7)
Idaho Falls	7.0	(4)
Nampa–Caldwell	7.6	(4)
Pocatello	4.1	(3)
Twin Falls	5.4	(3)

Illinois

Carbondale	–1.8	(0)
Danville	–4.1	(0)
De Kalb	–0.7	(0)
Freeport	–0.3	(0)
Galesburg	–8.6	(0)
Mattoon–Charleston	–0.5	(0)
Ottawa	–3.5	(0)
Quincy	–4.9	(0)
Sterling	–4.8	(0)

Indiana

Columbus	–0.9	(0)
Marion	–4.8	(0)
Michigan City–La Porte	–2.4	(0)
New Castle	–6.0	(0)
Richmond	–5.1	(0)
Vincennes	–1.1	(0)

Iowa

Ames	0.2	(1)
Burlington	–3.6	(0)
Clinton	–6.2	(0)
Fort Dodge	–7.1	(0)
Marshalltown	–2.8	(0)
Mason City	0.8	(1)
Muscatine	2.1	(2)

Kansas

Hutchinson	0.5	(1)
Manhattan	2.6	(2)
Salina	2.2	(2)

Kentucky

Bowling Green	14.8	(8)
Frankfort	5.2	(3)
Madisonville	0.9	(1)
Paducah	–1.6	(0)
Radcliff–Elizabethtown	5.5	(3)
Richmond	2.9	(2)

Louisiana

Bogalusa	7.8	(4)
Crowley	5.6	(3)
Hammond	14.2	(8)
Minden	5.5	(3)
Morgan City	0.1	(1)
New Iberia	8.2	(5)
Opelousas	5.1	(3)
Ruston	7.1	(4)

Maine

Augusta–Waterville	1.9	(1)
Biddeford	13.6	(7)

Maryland

Salisbury	7.3	(4)

Michigan

Adrian	–1.3	(0)
Marquette	–3.7	(0)
Mount Pleasant	0.1	(1)
Owosso	–3.1	(0)
Traverse City	7.8	(4)

Minnesota

Faribault	3.0	(2)
Mankato	1.8	(1)
Winona	0.2	(1)

Mississippi

Columbus	5.0	(3)
Greenville	–2.3	(0)
Greenwood	–0.7	(0)
Hattiesburg	3.4	(2)
Laurel	1.8	(1)
Meridian	–0.6	(0)
Tupelo	8.8	(5)
Vicksburg	–0.4	(0)

Missouri

Cape Girardeau	4.3	(3)
Jefferson City	11.9	(6)
Sikeston	1.4	(1)

Montana

Bozeman	11.5	(6)
Helena	7.8	(4)
Missoula	2.2	(2)

Nebraska

Grand Island	2.5	(2)

Nevada

Carson City	15.2	(8)

New Hampshire

Concord	11.6	(6)
Keene	7.8	(4)
Laconia	9.7	(5)

New Mexico

Alamogordo	12.5	(7)
Carlsbad	9.6	(5)
Clovis	3.2	(2)
Farmington	12.9	(7)
Gallup	16.3	(9)
Hobbs	15.9	(8)
Rio Rancho	48.6	(20)
Roswell	10.9	(6)

New York

Auburn	0.1	(1)
Batavia	–1.0	(0)
Cortland	–2.9	(0)
Gloversville	–1.0	(0)
Ithaca	0.6	(1)
Jamestown	–2.6	(0)
Kingston	3.8	(2)
Olean	–0.4	(0)
Plattsburgh	0.6	(1)
Watertown	2.8	(2)

North Carolina

Eden	2.5	(2)
Goldsboro	0.9	(1)
Greenville	8.7	(5)
Havelock–New Bern	14.2	(8)
Kinston	0.4	(1)
Lumberton	4.4	(3)
Roanoke Rapids	1.3	(1)
Rocky Mount	5.7	(3)
Sanford	12.7	(7)
Shelby	3.7	(2)
Statesville	7.4	(4)
Wilson	2.1	(2)

North Dakota

Minot	4.9	(3)

Ohio

Ashland	0.3	(1)
Ashtabula	–2.9	(0)
Athens	2.2	(2)
Chillicothe	3.5	(2)
East Liverpool	–3.0	(0)
Findlay	2.0	(2)
Fremont	–1.6	(0)
Marion	–3.9	(0)
New Philadelphia	1.0	(1)
Portsmouth	–2.7	(0)
Sandusky	–3.2	(0)
Sidney	2.1	(2)
Tiffin	–0.6	(0)
Wooster	3.9	(2)
Zanesville	0.9	(1)

Oklahoma

Ardmore	9.0	(5)
Bartlesville	–6.7	(0)
Chickasha	12.8	(7)
Duncan	2.6	(2)
McAlester	8.2	(5)
Muskogee	4.8	(3)
Okmulgee	2.1	(2)
Ponca City	4.6	(3)
Stillwater	3.9	(2)

Oregon

Albany	–0.5	(0)
Bend	10.5	(6)
Corvallis	–5.3	(0)
Grants Pass	15.8	(8)
Klamath Falls	–2.7	(0)
Roseburg	–0.6	(0)

Pennsylvania

Butler	2.1	(2)
Chambersburg	4.4	(3)
New Castle	–4.9	(0)
Pottsville	–2.7	(0)

Rhode Island		
Newport	4.2	(3)

South Carolina		
Greenwood	3.9	(2)
Hilton Head Island	31.0	(16)
Myrtle Beach	28.8	(15)
Orangeburg	6.2	(4)
Sumter	7.6	(4)

Tennessee		
Cleveland	7.0	(4)
Columbia	5.5	(3)
Cookeville	7.2	(4)
Morristown	7.4	(4)
Tullahoma	7.8	(4)

Texas		
Alice	10.5	(6)
Bay City	8.3	(5)
Del Rio	11.3	(6)
Greenville	21.4	(11)
Huntsville	29.4	(15)
Lufkin	8.1	(5)
Nacogdoches	8.0	(5)
Palestine	23.7	(12)
Paris	6.8	(4)

Utah		
Logan	14.6	(8)

Vermont		
Rutland	2.8	(2)

Virginia		
Blacksburg	4.5	(3)
Fredericksburg	18.4	(10)
Harrisonburg	6.1	(4)
Martinsville	−1.2	(0)
Staunton–Waynesboro	0.6	(1)
Winchester	6.9	(4)

Washington		
Aberdeen	−5.5	(0)
Longview	−1.1	(0)
Port Angeles	4.0	(3)
Pullman	1.4	(1)
Walla Walla	1.2	(1)
Wenatchee	10.8	(6)

West Virginia		
Beckley	−3.0	(0)
Clarksburg	−3.2	(0)
Fairmont	−2.6	(0)
Morgantown	3.6	(2)

Wisconsin		
Fond du Lac	1.6	(1)
Manitowoc	−0.8	(0)
Marshfield–Wisconsin Rapids	6.5	(4)
Stevens Point	2.2	(2)

Wyoming		
Rock Springs	12.7	(7)

The Results

Fairbanks, which traces its existence to the 1902 rush of gold prospectors to the region, has long called itself the Golden Heart of Alaska. But liquid gold is its current lifeblood. Oil from Prudhoe Bay flows through the Fairbanks area along the Trans-Alaska Pipeline, which has been in business since 1977.

Author Joe McGinniss visited Fairbanks as the Arctic-to-Pacific pipeline was being constructed. "A lot of people getting rich quick," he wrote of the boom town. "The population had gone from 12,000 to 60,000 in three years. Two-bedroom apartments were renting for $700 a month."

Things have quieted down a bit since those hectic days in the mid-seventies, although many residents look back on them with fondness. "We had a wonderful time spending all that money," joked Jan Faiks, co-chairwoman of the Alaska Senate Finance Committee. Even the drop in the world price of oil didn't faze Faiks when she talked with a *Washington Post* reporter in 1986. "The Alaskan economy has been cyclical since 1890," she said. "The Alaskan spirit is, 'Okay, this is one of those little downturns for a couple years.' "

Fairbanks is not totally dependent on oil. It is fortunate in having other stable employers, notably the military and the University of Alaska. The result is a city that places first in the economics section with 78 points. Fairbanks offers high salaries, partly attributable to the steep cost of sub-Arctic life. It also has a rapidly expanding population and healthy retail and manufacturing bases.

The next four slots in this section's top five belong to Southern cities, led by Fredericksburg, Virginia. But it is the East that registers the strongest overall performance in the economics rankings, having 7 of the 20 cities with the best scores.

Greenwood, Mississippi, bills itself as the Cotton Capital of the World. A local brochure assures visitors, "In spite of dramatic industrialization in this land of plentiful water and limitless growing room, the Delta is still cotton country and Greenwood is its market place." Another paragraph describes the area's antebellum homes and gracious ways, concluding, "And in control, King Cotton."

Greenwood's economy unfortunately also invites comparisons with the Old South. Well-paying jobs are not easily found, and the area is actually losing population as emigrants search elsewhere for better lives. Greenwood consequently takes last place in the economics section, with 16 of a possible 100 points.

The South has the largest share of small towns with low economics scores, placing five cities in the bottom ten. Three of the remaining five are in the West, two in the Midwest.

Economics Scores: Highs and Lows

Highest	Rating Points
1. Fairbanks, Alaska	78
2. Fredericksburg, Va.	68
3. Vero Beach, Fla.	65
4. Key West, Fla.	61
5. Huntsville, Tex.	59
6. Idaho Falls, Idaho	58
6. Newport, R.I.	58
6. Rock Springs, Wyo.	58
9. Dover, Del.	57
9. Jefferson City, Mo.	57
9. Myrtle Beach, S.C.	57
9. San Luis Obispo–Atascadero, Calif.	57
13. Laconia, N.H.	56
13. Torrington, Conn.	56
15. Concord, N.H.	55
15. Hilton Head Island, S.C.	55
15. Muscatine, Iowa	55
18. Salisbury, Md.	54
19. Carson City, Nev.	53
19. Plattsburgh, N.Y.	53

Lowest

219. Greenwood, Miss.	16
218. Selma, Ala.	18
212. Bogalusa, La.	19
212. Casa Grande–Apache Junction, Ariz.	19
212. Crowley, La.	19
212. East Liverpool, Ohio	19
212. Greenville, Miss.	19
212. Roseburg, Oreg.	19
210. Klamath Falls, Oreg.	21
210. Portsmouth, Ohio	21

	Fairbanks, Alaska	Greenwood, Miss.
Total Points in Section	78	16
Rank in Section	1	219
Results (and Rating Points)		
Per Capita Income Per capita income	$13,079 (19)	$5,838 (1)
Income Growth Percentage of growth in per capita income from 1979 to 1985	33.1 (6)	33.3 (6)
Manufacturing Productivity Value added per production worker	$157,600 (20)	$37,444 (3)
Retail Sales Annual retail sales per capita	$7,907 (20)	$3,718 (6)
Population Growth Percentage of population increase from 1980 to 1986	25.3 (13)	–0.7 (0)

(Figure following each area name indicates the composite score from the five categories in this section.)

Alabama		Colorado		Indiana	
Athens	40	Grand Junction	39	Columbus	41
Auburn–Opelika	36			Marion	35
Decatur	46	**Connecticut**		Michigan City–	
Enterprise	31	Torrington	56	La Porte	31
Selma	18			New Castle	29
Talladega	23	**Delaware**		Richmond	35
		Dover	57	Vincennes	27
Alaska					
Fairbanks	78	**Florida**		**Iowa**	
		Key West	61	Ames	49
Arizona		Vero Beach	65	Burlington	48
Bullhead City–				Clinton	39
Lake Havasu		**Georgia**		Fort Dodge	46
City	49	Brunswick	52	Marshalltown	46
Casa Grande–		Carrollton	34	Mason City	43
Apache		Dalton	44	Muscatine	55
Junction	19	Gainesville	48		
Flagstaff	49	Hinesville	27	**Kansas**	
Prescott	43	La Grange	39	Hutchinson	38
Sierra Vista	31	Rome	34	Manhattan	34
Yuma	36	Valdosta	45	Salina	47
Arkansas		**Idaho**		**Kentucky**	
Blytheville	24	Coeur d'Alene	29	Bowling Green	52
El Dorado	50	Idaho Falls	58	Frankfort	38
Hot Springs	41	Nampa–Caldwell	31	Madisonville	33
Jonesboro	41	Pocatello	46	Paducah	49
Rogers	47	Twin Falls	38	Radcliff–	
Russellville	43			Elizabethtown	35
		Illinois		Richmond	37
California		Carbondale	34		
El Centro–		Danville	31	**Louisiana**	
Calexico–		De Kalb	28	Bogalusa	19
Brawley	29	Freeport	35	Crowley	19
Eureka	30	Galesburg	37	Hammond	31
Hanford	33	Mattoon–Charleston	33	Minden	31
Madera	32	Ottawa	38	Morgan City	32
San Luis Obispo–		Quincy	39	New Iberia	37
Atascadero	57	Sterling	25	Opelousas	30
				Ruston	26

Maine

Augusta–Waterville	44
Biddeford	44

Maryland

Salisbury	54

Michigan

Adrian	32
Marquette	24
Mount Pleasant	29
Owosso	27
Traverse City	45

Minnesota

Faribault	39
Mankato	46
Winona	34

Mississippi

Columbus	35
Greenville	19
Greenwood	16
Hattiesburg	37
Laurel	30
Meridian	37
Tupelo	43
Vicksburg	34

Missouri

Cape Girardeau	50
Jefferson City	57
Sikeston	26

Montana

Bozeman	44
Helena	40
Missoula	36

Nebraska

Grand Island	47

Nevada

Carson City	53

New Hampshire

Concord	55
Keene	48
Laconia	56

New Mexico

Alamogordo	34
Carlsbad	41
Clovis	34
Farmington	49
Gallup	39
Hobbs	50
Rio Rancho	49
Roswell	43

New York

Auburn	38
Batavia	33
Cortland	29
Gloversville	31
Ithaca	40
Jamestown	33
Kingston	44
Olean	29
Plattsburgh	53
Watertown	41

North Carolina

Eden	38
Goldsboro	30
Greenville	46
Havelock–New Bern	43
Kinston	30
Lumberton	22
Roanoke Rapids	28
Rocky Mount	38
Sanford	47
Shelby	30
Statesville	37
Wilson	38

North Dakota

Minot	46

Ohio

Ashland	30
Ashtabula	29
Athens	23
Chillicothe	37
East Liverpool	19
Findlay	51
Fremont	36
Marion	35
New Philadelphia	30
Portsmouth	21
Sandusky	44
Sidney	29
Tiffin	27
Wooster	35
Zanesville	29

Oklahoma

Ardmore	44
Bartlesville	52
Chickasha	38
Duncan	37
McAlester	31
Muskogee	37
Okmulgee	40
Ponca City	49
Stillwater	36

Oregon

Albany	23
Bend	32
Corvallis	28
Grants Pass	32
Klamath Falls	21
Roseburg	19

Pennsylvania

Butler	31
Chambersburg	32
New Castle	26
Pottsville	23

Rhode Island

Newport	58

South Carolina

Greenwood	32
Hilton Head Island	55
Myrtle Beach	57
Orangeburg	26
Sumter	28

Tennessee

Cleveland	39
Columbia	37
Cookeville	35
Morristown	37
Tullahoma	40

Texas

Alice	30
Bay City	50
Del Rio	28
Greenville	46
Huntsville	59
Lufkin	41
Nacogdoches	36
Palestine	37
Paris	47

Utah

Logan	30

Vermont

Rutland	46

Virginia

Blacksburg	38
Fredericksburg	68
Harrisonburg	44
Martinsville	31
Staunton– Waynesboro	39
Winchester	49

Washington

Aberdeen	28
Longview	34
Port Angeles	32
Pullman	24
Walla Walla	31
Wenatchee	49

West Virginia

Beckley	32
Clarksburg	25
Fairmont	29
Morgantown	31

Wisconsin

Fond du Lac	38
Manitowoc	28
Marshfield– Wisconsin Rapids	49
Stevens Point	40

Wyoming

Rock Springs	58

4

Education

Johnny can't read.

The New York Telephone Company requires applicants for entry-level jobs, such as operators and clerks, to pass a basic test on vocabulary and problem-solving. More than 22,000 people took the quiz in the first six months of 1987. Only 16 percent passed.

Johnny can't write.

Congress funded a 1984 project that asked approximately 2,000 high-school students to write letters seeking an imaginary summer job at a swimming pool. Less than 20 percent of these letters were judged to be adequate.

Johnny can't do math, either.

American eighth-graders correctly answered an average of only 46 percent of the questions on an international math test in 1982. Not only was the U.S. score well behind Japan's first-place mark of 64 percent, it was also less than the average score of 52 percent for the 11 competing nations.

These discouraging trends in American education prompted the federal government to issue its famous 1983 report, *A Nation At Risk,* which contended that the country had committed "unthinking, unilateral educational disarmament." Education Secretary William Bennett conceded in 1988 that there was still plenty of cause for worry. "We're seeing progress. We're

140 doing better," he said. "But we're not where we should be. We are still at risk."

Bennett's predecessor at the Education Department, Terrel Bell, once promised, "The future is going to belong to the intelligent." But given the mediocre records of most school systems, how can parents be certain their children are being adequately prepared for the challenges they will face as adults? This section rates each micropolitan area according to its commitment to education, both in terms of popular support and money.

Many Americans remain convinced, despite the abundant evidence to the contrary, that their schools are fine as they are. A 1987 Gallup survey asked its respondents to characterize the U.S. educational system: 48 percent called it strong, 47 percent said it was not. Those with college degrees were the most likely to be critical, while those who dropped out of high school were the most prone to give high marks to American schools.

The situation is particularly severe in large cities. Gene Maeroff, a senior fellow at the Carnegie Foundation for the Advancement of Teaching, spent 18 months visiting urban high schools from coast to coast. He found them to be "large, impersonal places in which students lack a sense of belonging and see no connection between what they are asked to do in the classroom and the world that awaits them outside the school." Maeroff concluded that low student achievement has become accepted as the norm in such schools.

Small cities, with their stronger traditions of school attendance and more stable tax bases, have generally been able to avoid the depressing deterioration of education found in metropolitan centers. Students also have more substantial contact with their teachers in small towns. A 1984 Census Bureau report expressed the number of elementary- and secondary-school teachers as a rate per 10,000 residents. Counties with populations of more than 500,000 average 108 instructors per 10,000 people. The rate becomes more favorable as communities get smaller. Areas with populations of 50,000 to 100,000 typically have 129 teachers per 10,000, while counties of 25,000 to 50,000 do even better: 135 per 10,000 residents.

Ranking micropolitan America. The ideal micropolitan area would place a strong emphasis on education, encouraging its students to graduate from high school and go on to college, perhaps to the local university. Each small city is evaluated in five categories:

1. High School Experience: Are most of the community's adults themselves high-school graduates who understand the value of a diploma, or did a good share place a low priority on their education?

2. High School Dropouts: Do the local schools do a good job of keeping students in class, or is there a high dropout rate?

3. College Influence: Is there a university in town that adds its facilities

and inspiration to the local support for education?

4. Local Education Funding: Is the local government willing to put money behind its words of encouragement?

5. Teacher Compensation: Do the local schools pay enough to attract the best teachers?

High School Experience

It stands to reason that if most of a city's adults are high-school graduates, their area's school system will be better than that of a community whose adults received less education. Someone with a diploma is more likely to support local schools and to insist that his or her children hit the books.

This category ranks each area according to the percentage of people 25 or older who graduated from high school. The national average is 66.5 percent.

Fairbanks, Alaska, has the largest pool of potential supporters for its educational system. Fully 86.6 percent of its adults went all the way through high school. Furthermore, 45 percent of those who are 25 or older have been enrolled in college at some point. That's considerably better than the national average of 32 percent.

The *Wall Street Journal* commented in 1987 that Louisiana "is certainly a leading contender for honors as the state doing least to prepare its young people." Crowley's problems are a case in point. Only 40.1 percent of its adults ever earned high school diplomas.

Most of the cities with high percentages of adults who graduated from high school are in the West. The South has a monopoly on towns with low graduation rates.

Source. These statistics, published in 1988, are for 1980. U.S. Bureau of the Census, *County and City Data Book* (Washington: U.S. Government Printing Office, 1988).

Scoring. Twenty points for 83.0 percent or more; no points for 44.9 percent or less. The spacing is every 2 percent.

Highest	**Percent of Those 25 or Older With Four or More Years of High School**
1. Fairbanks, Alaska	86.6
2. Corvallis, Oreg.	86.1
3. Pullman, Wash.	85.8
4. Ames, Iowa	85.6
5. Manhattan, Kans.	85.5
6. Bozeman, Mont.	84.4
6. Logan, Utah	84.4
8. Helena, Mont.	82.3
9. Missoula, Mont.	81.3
10. Ithaca, N.Y.	80.8

Lowest	
219. Crowley, La.	40.1
218. Opelousas, La.	41.1
217. La Grange, Ga.	41.8
216. Roanoke Rapids, N.C.	42.6
215. Alice, Tex.	43.1
214. Lumberton, N.C.	44.4
213. Eden, N.C.	44.6
211. Dalton, Ga.	44.7
211. Greenwood, Miss.	44.7
210. Martinsville, Va.	45.7

(Figure following each area name indicates percent of those 25 or older with four or more years of high school; figure in parentheses represents rating points.)

Alabama

Athens	50.7	(3)
Auburn–Opelika	62.1	(9)
Decatur	59.9	(8)
Enterprise	56.6	(6)
Selma	53.5	(5)
Talladega	49.1	(3)

Alaska

Fairbanks	86.6	(20)

Arizona

Bullhead City–Lake Havasu City	69.1	(13)
Casa Grande–Apache Junction	55.0	(6)
Flagstaff	74.4	(15)
Prescott	73.9	(15)
Sierra Vista	68.8	(12)
Yuma	61.6	(9)

Arkansas

Blytheville	46.9	(1)
El Dorado	58.0	(7)
Hot Springs	59.9	(8)
Jonesboro	54.0	(5)
Rogers	61.8	(9)
Russellville	57.5	(7)

California

El Centro–Calexico–Brawley	50.9	(3)
Eureka	76.4	(16)
Hanford	58.7	(7)
Madera	60.1	(8)
San Luis Obispo–Atascadero	76.8	(16)

Colorado

Grand Junction	74.5	(15)

Connecticut

Torrington	70.6	(13)

Delaware

Dover	65.4	(11)

Florida

Key West	72.3	(14)
Vero Beach	66.6	(11)

Georgia

Brunswick	61.9	(9)
Carrollton	46.9	(1)
Dalton	44.7	(0)
Gainesville	48.1	(2)
Hinesville	69.4	(13)
La Grange	41.8	(0)
Rome	48.8	(2)
Valdosta	57.1	(7)

Idaho

Coeur d'Alene	75.6	(16)
Idaho Falls	80.6	(18)
Nampa–Caldwell	65.2	(11)
Pocatello	79.2	(18)
Twin Falls	68.2	(12)

Illinois

Carbondale	69.7	(13)
Danville	62.3	(9)
De Kalb	75.2	(16)
Freeport	67.5	(12)
Galesburg	68.4	(12)
Mattoon–Charleston	66.2	(11)
Ottawa	62.1	(9)
Quincy	64.2	(10)
Sterling	62.3	(9)

Indiana

Columbus	68.5	(12)
Marion	62.7	(9)
Michigan City–La Porte	63.7	(10)
New Castle	60.8	(8)
Richmond	63.8	(10)
Vincennes	62.5	(9)

Iowa

Ames	85.6	(20)
Burlington	70.7	(13)
Clinton	70.6	(13)
Fort Dodge	71.4	(14)
Marshalltown	74.7	(15)
Mason City	72.5	(14)
Muscatine	66.4	(11)

Kansas

Hutchinson	71.4	(14)
Manhattan	85.5	(20)
Salina	76.4	(16)

Kentucky

Bowling Green	61.3	(9)
Frankfort	64.0	(10)
Madisonville	49.7	(3)
Paducah	62.9	(9)
Radcliff–Elizabethtown	66.5	(11)
Richmond	54.9	(5)

Louisiana

Bogalusa	49.3	(3)
Crowley	40.1	(0)
Hammond	50.9	(3)
Minden	50.9	(3)
Morgan City	50.0	(3)
New Iberia	49.6	(3)
Opelousas	41.1	(0)
Ruston	64.7	(10)

Maine

Augusta–Waterville	68.2	(12)
Biddeford	67.9	(12)

Maryland

Salisbury	56.3	(6)

Michigan

Adrian	67.8	(12)
Marquette	75.6	(16)
Mount Pleasant	70.8	(13)
Owosso	67.6	(12)
Traverse City	77.2	(17)

Minnesota

Faribault	68.2	(12)
Mankato	75.0	(16)
Winona	66.1	(11)

Mississippi

Columbus	57.9	(7)
Greenville	50.0	(3)
Greenwood	44.7	(0)
Hattiesburg	63.4	(10)
Laurel	55.3	(6)
Meridian	60.7	(8)
Tupelo	58.7	(7)
Vicksburg	59.5	(8)

Missouri

Cape Girardeau	63.8	(10)
Jefferson City	70.1	(13)
Sikeston	51.4	(4)

Montana

Bozeman	84.4	(20)
Helena	82.3	(19)
Missoula	81.3	(19)

Nebraska

Grand Island	74.8	(15)

Nevada

Carson City	78.5	(17)

New Hampshire

Concord	74.0	(15)
Keene	71.9	(14)
Laconia	70.2	(13)

New Mexico

Alamogordo	77.1	(17)
Carlsbad	62.8	(9)
Clovis	70.3	(13)
Farmington	65.1	(11)
Gallup	51.2	(4)
Hobbs	60.0	(8)
Rio Rancho	67.0	(12)
Roswell	63.5	(10)

New York

Auburn	62.3	(9)
Batavia	69.2	(13)
Cortland	66.2	(11)
Gloversville	59.5	(8)
Ithaca	80.8	(18)
Jamestown	65.8	(11)
Kingston	66.8	(11)
Olean	64.8	(10)
Plattsburgh	63.7	(10)
Watertown	64.0	(10)

North Carolina

Eden	44.6	(0)
Goldsboro	56.8	(6)
Greenville	56.8	(6)
Havelock–New Bern	60.9	(8)
Kinston	52.2	(4)
Lumberton	44.4	(0)
Roanoke Rapids	42.6	(0)
Rocky Mount	48.2	(2)
Sanford	56.9	(6)
Shelby	47.4	(2)
Statesville	50.1	(3)
Wilson	48.0	(2)

North Dakota

Minot	74.8	(15)

Ohio

Ashland	69.3	(13)
Ashtabula	65.6	(11)
Athens	67.9	(12)
Chillicothe	57.3	(7)
East Liverpool	63.1	(10)
Findlay	75.8	(16)
Fremont	67.2	(12)
Marion	65.4	(11)
New Philadelphia	62.3	(9)
Portsmouth	54.2	(5)
Sandusky	68.0	(12)
Sidney	63.8	(10)
Tiffin	66.4	(11)
Wooster	65.8	(11)
Zanesville	62.6	(9)

Oklahoma

Ardmore	60.1	(8)
Bartlesville	75.1	(16)
Chickasha	58.1	(7)
Duncan	61.2	(9)
McAlester	54.9	(5)
Muskogee	59.1	(8)
Okmulgee	54.8	(5)
Ponca City	68.0	(12)
Stillwater	74.6	(15)

Oregon

Albany	69.5	(13)
Bend	78.3	(17)
Corvallis	86.1	(20)
Grants Pass	68.1	(12)
Klamath Falls	74.3	(15)
Roseburg	67.9	(12)

Pennsylvania

Butler	69.1	(13)
Chambersburg	58.6	(7)
New Castle	63.2	(10)
Pottsville	56.3	(6)

Rhode Island

Newport	72.0	(14)

South Carolina

Greenwood	49.2	(3)
Hilton Head Island	72.0	(14)
Myrtle Beach	58.5	(7)
Orangeburg	49.3	(3)
Sumter	54.4	(5)

Tennessee

Cleveland	53.0	(5)
Columbia	52.3	(4)
Cookeville	50.0	(3)
Morristown	51.0	(4)
Tullahoma	56.1	(6)

Texas

Alice	43.1	(0)
Bay City	53.6	(5)
Del Rio	51.1	(4)
Greenville	56.6	(6)
Huntsville	60.8	(8)
Lufkin	53.6	(5)
Nacogdoches	57.9	(7)
Palestine	51.4	(4)
Paris	53.1	(5)

Utah

Logan	84.4	(20)

Vermont

Rutland	70.0	(13)

Virginia

Blacksburg	62.0	(9)
Fredericksburg	58.6	(7)
Harrisonburg	55.7	(6)
Martinsville	45.7	(1)
Staunton–Waynesboro	54.3	(5)
Winchester	54.0	(5)

Washington

Aberdeen	67.3	(12)
Longview	71.1	(14)
Port Angeles	73.3	(15)
Pullman	85.8	(20)
Walla Walla	75.2	(16)
Wenatchee	69.1	(13)

West Virginia

Beckley	53.6	(5)
Clarksburg	60.7	(8)
Fairmont	61.8	(9)
Morgantown	66.2	(11)

Wisconsin

Fond du Lac	68.1	(12)
Manitowoc	66.9	(11)
Marshfield– Wisconsin Rapids	67.9	(12)
Stevens Point	68.7	(12)

Wyoming

Rock Springs	76.3	(16)

High School Dropouts

"A mind is a terrible thing to waste."

So goes the tag line to a series of well-known television commercials. But it is also a thought nagging officials in small cities across the country. Their hopes of enticing high-tech industries require an educated work force. Many communities have consequently launched programs to cut their school dropout rates.

This category estimates the dropout problem in each area by calculating the percentage of those between the ages of 16 and 19 who are neither students nor high-school graduates. Those who joined the military are excluded from this figure.

Pullman, Washington, has little to worry about. Only 1.3 percent of its 16- to 19-year-olds fit the definition of a dropout given above; this is substantially better than the national average of 13.4 percent. The long shadow of Washington State University reaches Pullman's high schools, encouraging students to continue their studies.

Carpet-making, not education, is the main industry in Dalton, Georgia. The mills are more attractive than classes to many teen-agers, contributing to a dropout rate of 33.9 percent.

University towns have the lowest high-school dropout figures. The worst problems are in Southern and desert cities.

Source. These statistics, published in 1983, are for 1980. U.S. Bureau of the Census, *Census of Population* (Washington: U.S. Government Printing Office, 1983).

Scoring. Twenty points for 3.9 percent or less; no points for 26.8 percent or more. The spacing is every 1.2 percent.

Lowest	Percent of 16- to 19-Year-Olds Not in School and Not High School Graduates
1. Pullman, Wash.	1.3
2. Ames, Iowa	2.2
3. De Kalb, Ill.	3.3
4. Ithaca, N.Y.	3.5
5. Mankato, Minn.	3.7
6. Athens, Ohio	4.0
6. Mount Pleasant, Mich.	4.0
8. Bozeman, Mont.	4.3
8. Faribault, Minn.	4.3
10. Stillwater, Okla.	4.4

Highest

219. Dalton, Ga.	33.9
218. Gallup, N.Mex.	29.6
217. Yuma, Ariz.	27.8
216. Casa Grande–Apache Junction, Ariz.	26.9
215. Vero Beach, Fla.	26.0
212. Gainesville, Ga.	25.8
212. Hobbs, N.Mex.	25.8
212. Morgan City, La.	25.8
211. Eden, N.C.	25.7
210. Del Rio, Tex.	25.5

(Figure following each area name indicates the percentage of 16- to 19-year-olds not in school and not high-school graduates; figure in parentheses represents rating points.)

Alabama

Athens	18.7	(7)
Auburn–Opelika	7.3	(17)
Decatur	20.1	(6)
Enterprise	12.4	(12)
Selma	16.4	(9)
Talladega	19.7	(6)

Alaska

Fairbanks	13.2	(12)

Arizona

Bullhead City– Lake Havasu City	21.3	(5)
Casa Grande– Apache Junction	26.9	(0)
Flagstaff	12.5	(12)
Prescott	11.6	(13)
Sierra Vista	14.4	(11)
Yuma	27.8	(0)

Arkansas

Blytheville	24.2	(3)
El Dorado	19.0	(7)
Hot Springs	18.2	(8)
Jonesboro	14.9	(10)
Rogers	19.0	(7)
Russellville	17.5	(8)

California

El Centro–Calexico– Brawley	16.2	(9)
Eureka	9.9	(15)
Hanford	19.5	(7)
Madera	19.7	(6)
San Luis Obispo– Atascadero	9.8	(15)

Colorado

Grand Junction	18.7	(7)

Connecticut

Torrington	11.0	(14)

Delaware

Dover	15.5	(10)

Florida

Key West	22.1	(4)
Vero Beach	26.0	(1)

Georgia

Brunswick	22.2	(4)
Carrollton	17.3	(8)
Dalton	33.9	(0)
Gainesville	25.8	(1)
Hinesville	23.3	(3)
La Grange	23.2	(3)
Rome	18.1	(8)
Valdosta	15.3	(10)

Idaho

Coeur d'Alene	11.6	(13)
Idaho Falls	17.4	(8)
Nampa-Caldwell	19.6	(6)
Pocatello	11.8	(13)
Twin Falls	18.7	(7)

Illinois

Carbondale	5.6	(18)
Danville	13.3	(12)
De Kalb	3.3	(20)
Freeport	12.5	(12)
Galesburg	13.4	(12)
Mattoon–Charleston	6.8	(17)
Ottawa	10.9	(14)
Quincy	9.6	(15)
Sterling	12.9	(12)

Indiana

Columbus	15.9	(10)
Marion	13.2	(12)
Michigan City–La Porte	15.9	(10)
New Castle	15.2	(10)
Richmond	15.5	(10)
Vincennes	11.9	(13)

Iowa

Ames	2.2	(20)
Burlington	13.7	(11)
Clinton	9.3	(15)
Fort Dodge	8.6	(16)
Marshalltown	10.5	(14)
Mason City	6.3	(18)
Muscatine	16.7	(9)

Kansas

Hutchinson	14.2	(11)
Manhattan	5.4	(18)
Salina	12.2	(13)

Kentucky

Bowling Green	11.6	(13)
Frankfort	21.9	(5)
Madisonville	21.1	(5)
Paducah	12.8	(12)
Radcliff–Elizabethtown	16.7	(9)
Richmond	12.2	(13)

Louisiana

Bogalusa	13.5	(12)
Crowley	19.8	(6)
Hammond	20.5	(6)
Minden	17.9	(8)
Morgan City	25.8	(1)
New Iberia	21.1	(5)
Opelousas	15.2	(10)
Ruston	5.9	(18)

Maine

Augusta–Waterville	8.1	(16)
Biddeford	12.2	(13)

Maryland

Salisbury	13.6	(11)

Michigan

Adrian	10.6	(14)
Marquette	7.1	(17)
Mount Pleasant	4.0	(19)
Owosso	10.3	(14)
Traverse City	9.5	(15)

Minnesota

Faribault	4.3	(19)
Mankato	3.7	(20)
Winona	5.8	(18)

Mississippi

Columbus	18.4	(7)
Greenville	20.0	(6)
Greenwood	15.4	(10)
Hattiesburg	12.7	(12)
Laurel	18.5	(7)
Meridian	16.5	(9)
Tupelo	19.9	(6)
Vicksburg	16.1	(9)

Missouri

Cape Girardeau	6.5	(17)
Jefferson City	12.1	(13)
Sikeston	19.1	(7)

Montana

Bozeman	4.3	(19)
Helena	8.2	(16)
Missoula	9.9	(15)

Nebraska

Grand Island	9.3	(15)

Nevada

Carson City	19.7	(6)

New Hampshire

Concord	10.7	(14)
Keene	10.6	(14)
Laconia	17.8	(8)

New Mexico

Alamogordo	10.8	(14)
Carlsbad	19.7	(6)
Clovis	17.5	(8)
Farmington	24.0	(3)
Gallup	29.6	(0)
Hobbs	25.8	(1)
Rio Rancho	14.2	(11)
Roswell	18.8	(7)

New York

Auburn	12.5	(12)
Batavia	7.4	(17)
Cortland	8.5	(16)
Gloversville	12.6	(12)
Ithaca	3.5	(20)
Jamestown	9.3	(15)
Kingston	10.8	(14)
Olean	11.5	(13)
Plattsburgh	9.7	(15)
Watertown	12.4	(12)

North Carolina

Eden	25.7	(1)
Goldsboro	11.9	(13)
Greenville	8.9	(15)
Havelock–New Bern	18.8	(7)
Kinston	17.0	(9)
Lumberton	20.9	(5)
Roanoke Rapids	17.8	(8)
Rocky Mount	18.7	(7)
Sanford	14.1	(11)
Shelby	19.4	(7)
Statesville	19.2	(7)
Wilson	16.4	(9)

North Dakota

Minot	7.7	(16)

Ohio

Ashland	7.5	(17)
Ashtabula	11.7	(13)
Athens	4.0	(19)
Chillicothe	11.9	(13)
East Liverpool	10.2	(14)
Findlay	8.2	(16)
Fremont	8.1	(16)
Marion	13.6	(11)
New Philadelphia	11.8	(13)
Portsmouth	12.8	(12)
Sandusky	9.6	(15)
Sidney	12.5	(12)
Tiffin	7.7	(16)
Wooster	15.9	(10)
Zanesville	9.2	(15)

Oklahoma

Ardmore	17.4	(8)
Bartlesville	9.5	(15)
Chickasha	18.4	(7)
Duncan	13.4	(12)
McAlester	13.9	(11)
Muskogee	17.8	(8)
Okmulgee	9.9	(15)
Ponca City	14.0	(11)
Stillwater	4.4	(19)

Oregon

Albany	15.1	(10)
Bend	16.7	(9)
Corvallis	5.4	(18)
Grants Pass	16.0	(9)
Klamath Falls	18.2	(8)
Roseburg	16.5	(9)

Pennsylvania

Butler	6.8	(17)
Chambersburg	11.0	(14)
New Castle	9.3	(15)
Pottsville	11.2	(13)

Rhode Island

Newport	9.0	(15)

South Carolina

Greenwood	12.7	(12)
Hilton Head Island	12.7	(12)
Myrtle Beach	13.7	(11)
Orangeburg	8.9	(15)
Sumter	13.3	(12)

Tennessee

Cleveland	19.3	(7)
Columbia	22.3	(4)
Cookeville	14.4	(11)
Morristown	20.7	(6)
Tullahoma	13.5	(12)

Texas

Alice	19.3	(7)
Bay City	19.7	(6)
Del Rio	25.5	(2)
Greenville	15.7	(10)
Huntsville	11.8	(13)
Lufkin	25.0	(2)
Nacogdoches	10.0	(14)
Palestine	13.7	(11)
Paris	19.6	(6)

Utah

Logan	5.1	(19)

Vermont

Rutland	10.1	(14)

Virginia

Blacksburg	6.8	(17)
Fredericksburg	15.2	(10)
Harrisonburg	14.7	(11)
Martinsville	21.8	(5)
Staunton–Waynesboro	14.4	(11)
Winchester	20.2	(6)

Washington

Aberdeen	15.7	(10)
Longview	13.4	(12)
Port Angeles	12.7	(12)
Pullman	1.3	(20)
Walla Walla	10.9	(14)
Wenatchee	14.7	(11)

West Virginia

Beckley	17.7	(8)
Clarksburg	14.8	(10)
Fairmont	11.5	(13)
Morgantown	7.3	(17)

Wisconsin

Fond du Lac	7.4	(17)
Manitowoc	9.8	(15)
Marshfield– Wisconsin Rapids	5.5	(18)
Stevens Point	7.3	(17)

Wyoming

Rock Springs	24.3	(3)

College Influence

A small city benefits in many ways from having a college within its limits. A university enlivens the local cultural and social life with concerts, lectures, and sporting events. It also provides economic stability. Industries may depart in search of cheap labor and lower taxes, but who ever heard of a college changing its address?

Of course, the chief benefit of a university is educational. The local campus provides facilities, such as large libraries, that would otherwise be unavailable. High-school graduates who wish to pursue college degrees while staying at home have that option.

This category measures the impact of local colleges by taking the percentage of the population between the ages of 18 and 24 who are in school. The national average is 31.8 percent.

Pullman, Washington, has 15,289 college students, almost all of them at Washington State University. Slightly more than 88 percent of its 18- to 24-year-olds are still taking classes.

Hinesville, Georgia, is a military city, not a college town. More than half of its work force is in uniform, based at Fort Stewart or Wright Army Air Field. Only 7.1 percent of the 18- to 24-year-olds in Hinesville are in college.

Source. These statistics, published in 1983, are for 1980. U.S. Bureau of the Census, *Census of Population* (Washington: U.S. Government Printing Office, 1983).

Scoring. Twenty points for 76.5 percent or more; no points for 9.9 percent or less. The spacing is every 3.5 percent.

Highest	Percent of 18- to 24-Year-Olds In College
1. Pullman, Wash.	88.2
2. Blacksburg, Va.	80.6
3. Ames, Iowa	78.0
4. Carbondale, Ill.	77.4
5. Ithaca, N.Y.	77.2
5. Stillwater, Okla.	77.2
7. Corvallis, Oreg.	77.0
7. Mount Pleasant, Mich.	77.0
9. Ruston, La.	76.8
10. Athens, Ohio	75.7

Lowest

219. Hinesville, Ga.	7.1
218. Radcliff–Elizabethtown, Ky.	8.6
217. Rock Springs, Wyo.	10.1
216. Gallup, N.Mex.	12.6
214. Farmington, N.Mex.	13.0
214. Grand Island, Nebr.	13.0
213. Hilton Head Island, S.C.	13.2
212. Morgan City, La.	13.4
211. Carlsbad, N.Mex.	13.7
210. Havelock–New Bern, N.C.	13.8

(Figure following each area name indicates percentage of 18- to 24-year-olds in school; figure in parentheses represents rating points.)

Alabama

Athens	20.4	(3)
Auburn-Opelika	72.1	(18)
Decatur	19.8	(3)
Enterprise	34.2	(7)
Selma	26.5	(5)
Talladega	25.6	(5)

Alaska

Fairbanks	23.5	(4)

Arizona

Bullhead City– Lake Havasu City	16.1	(2)
Casa Grande– Apache Junction	19.3	(3)
Flagstaff	54.3	(13)
Prescott	33.4	(7)
Sierra Vista	25.2	(5)
Yuma	17.5	(3)

Arkansas

Blytheville	17.5	(3)
El Dorado	19.1	(3)
Hot Springs	21.0	(4)
Jonesboro	45.1	(11)
Rogers	20.7	(4)
Russellville	40.7	(9)

California

El Centro–Calexico– Brawley	28.2	(6)
Eureka	46.3	(11)
Hanford	18.6	(3)
Madera	15.8	(2)
San Luis Obispo– Atascadero	57.8	(14)

Colorado

Grand Junction	21.9	(4)

Connecticut

Torrington	24.6	(5)

Delaware

Dover	27.7	(6)

Florida

Key West	15.2	(2)
Vero Beach	17.8	(3)

Georgia

Brunswick	18.0	(3)
Carrollton	39.1	(9)
Dalton	15.4	(2)
Gainesville	23.2	(4)
Hinesville	7.1	(0)
La Grange	23.4	(4)
Rome	29.8	(6)
Valdosta	35.1	(8)

Idaho

Coeur d'Alene	25.0	(5)
Idaho Falls	14.1	(2)
Nampa-Caldwell	27.1	(5)
Pocatello	39.1	(9)
Twin Falls	23.7	(4)

Illinois

Carbondale	77.4	(20)
Danville	20.4	(3)
De Kalb	74.9	(19)
Freeport	20.6	(4)
Galesburg	28.5	(6)
Mattoon–Charleston	66.7	(17)
Ottawa	22.1	(4)
Quincy	28.5	(6)
Sterling	19.2	(3)

Indiana

Columbus	16.8	(2)
Marion	32.9	(7)
Michigan City–La Porte	17.4	(3)
New Castle	15.1	(2)
Richmond	26.5	(5)
Vincennes	44.4	(10)

Iowa

Ames	78.0	(20)
Burlington	23.8	(4)
Clinton	20.7	(4)
Fort Dodge	32.6	(7)
Marshalltown	22.7	(4)
Mason City	29.7	(6)
Muscatine	18.5	(3)

Kansas

Hutchinson	26.2	(5)
Manhattan	51.4	(12)
Salina	29.5	(6)

Kentucky

Bowling Green	55.6	(14)
Frankfort	31.0	(7)
Madisonville	14.5	(2)
Paducah	22.9	(4)
Radcliff–Elizabethtown	8.6	(0)
Richmond	68.4	(17)

Louisiana

Bogalusa	23.4	(4)
Crowley	17.6	(3)
Hammond	36.4	(8)
Minden	20.4	(3)
Morgan City	13.4	(1)
New Iberia	17.2	(3)
Opelousas	20.9	(4)
Ruston	76.8	(20)

Maine

Augusta–Waterville	31.7	(7)
Biddeford	23.8	(4)

Maryland

Salisbury	34.8	(8)

Michigan

Adrian	27.4	(5)
Marquette	42.5	(10)
Mount Pleasant	77.0	(20)
Owosso	19.8	(3)
Traverse City	28.2	(6)

Minnesota

Faribault	58.9	(14)
Mankato	64.1	(16)
Winona	59.4	(15)

Mississippi

Columbus	29.7	(6)
Greenville	20.8	(4)
Greenwood	43.1	(10)
Hattiesburg	53.1	(13)
Laurel	25.7	(5)
Meridian	22.1	(4)
Tupelo	20.1	(3)
Vicksburg	25.6	(5)

Missouri

Cape Girardeau	56.1	(14)
Jefferson City	28.7	(6)
Sikeston	19.7	(3)

Montana

Bozeman	69.4	(17)
Helena	33.2	(7)
Missoula	51.2	(12)

Nebraska

Grand Island	13.0	(1)

Nevada

Carson City	20.8	(4)

New Hampshire

Concord	30.8	(6)
Keene	42.8	(10)
Laconia	15.6	(2)

New Mexico

Alamogordo	16.1	(2)
Carlsbad	13.7	(2)
Clovis	15.2	(2)
Farmington	13.0	(1)
Gallup	12.6	(1)
Hobbs	16.6	(2)
Rio Rancho	22.3	(4)
Roswell	27.6	(6)

New York

Auburn	28.2	(6)
Batavia	25.0	(5)
Cortland	58.2	(14)
Gloversville	21.1	(4)
Ithaca	77.2	(20)
Jamestown	36.9	(8)
Kingston	37.2	(8)
Olean	34.9	(8)
Plattsburgh	41.5	(10)
Watertown	21.2	(4)

North Carolina

Eden	18.3	(3)
Goldsboro	22.8	(4)
Greenville	59.6	(15)
Havelock–New Bern	13.8	(2)
Kinston	30.8	(6)
Lumberton	24.4	(5)
Roanoke Rapids	23.3	(4)
Rocky Mount	22.4	(4)
Sanford	25.3	(5)
Shelby	25.0	(5)
Statesville	20.6	(4)
Wilson	31.8	(7)

North Dakota

Minot	26.6	(5)

Ohio

Ashland	33.0	(7)
Ashtabula	18.2	(3)
Athens	75.7	(19)
Chillicothe	17.9	(3)
East Liverpool	19.0	(3)
Findlay	27.7	(6)
Fremont	19.5	(3)
Marion	20.7	(4)
New Philadelphia	18.2	(3)
Portsmouth	20.1	(3)
Sandusky	24.4	(5)
Sidney	15.8	(2)
Tiffin	25.7	(5)
Wooster	28.9	(6)
Zanesville	25.4	(5)

Oklahoma

Ardmore	17.5	(3)
Bartlesville	22.4	(4)
Chickasha	16.9	(2)
Duncan	15.0	(2)
McAlester	18.7	(3)
Muskogee	23.3	(4)
Okmulgee	39.6	(9)
Ponca City	27.1	(5)
Stillwater	77.2	(20)

Oregon

Albany	22.3	(4)
Bend	21.2	(4)
Corvallis	77.0	(20)
Grants Pass	20.8	(4)
Klamath Falls	28.6	(6)
Roseburg	19.1	(3)

Pennsylvania

Butler	33.7	(7)
Chambersburg	19.2	(3)
New Castle	27.8	(6)
Pottsville	18.8	(3)

Rhode Island

Newport	29.1	(6)

South Carolina

Greenwood	31.2	(7)
Hilton Head Island	13.2	(1)
Myrtle Beach	21.2	(4)
Orangeburg	46.3	(11)
Sumter	27.2	(5)

Tennessee

Cleveland	33.4	(7)
Columbia	22.5	(4)
Cookeville	59.1	(15)
Morristown	22.5	(4)
Tullahoma	24.6	(5)

Texas

Alice	18.8	(3)
Bay City	17.0	(3)
Del Rio	15.5	(2)
Greenville	50.6	(12)
Huntsville	65.8	(16)
Lufkin	17.8	(3)
Nacogdoches	66.7	(17)
Palestine	15.4	(2)
Paris	26.6	(5)

Utah

Logan	59.0	(15)

Vermont

Rutland	31.4	(7)

Virginia

Blacksburg	80.6	(20)
Fredericksburg	30.9	(6)
Harrisonburg	50.0	(12)
Martinsville	23.7	(4)
Staunton–Waynesboro	27.0	(5)
Winchester	22.0	(4)

Washington

Aberdeen	20.9	(4)
Longview	20.2	(3)
Port Angeles	22.0	(4)
Pullman	88.2	(20)
Walla Walla	51.2	(12)
Wenatchee	21.5	(4)

West Virginia

Beckley	18.1	(3)
Clarksburg	25.8	(5)
Fairmont	34.5	(8)
Morgantown	70.0	(18)

Wisconsin

Fond du Lac	30.6	(6)
Manitowoc	20.5	(4)
Marshfield– Wisconsin Rapids	22.4	(4)
Stevens Point	56.4	(14)

Wyoming

Rock Springs	10.1	(1)

Local Education Funding

Nearly everything costs more in Alaska than in the continental United States. Schools are no exception.

A 1986 study by the National Education Association estimated that the state and local governments in Alaska spend 2¼ times the national average per pupil. No other state comes close.

Before you dismiss this statistic as another example of Arctic inflation, consider this: Alaska has the highest high-school graduation rate in America. There obviously is a connection between financial commitment and student performance.

It is unsurprising that Fairbanks, Alaska, leads the nation's small cities in monetary support for education. This category divides each area's local allocation for public schools by its number of residents. Fairbanks spends $1,130 per capita.

Radcliff–Elizabethtown, Kentucky, the home of Fort Knox, cannot be accused of raiding its famous vaults for education funding. Radcliff–Elizabethtown doles out $224 per person to its schools, well below the national average of $451.

Western and Eastern cities are the most generous when it comes to education funding from local governments. The South is the most penurious.

Source. These statistics, published in 1988, are for the 1981–1982 budget year. U.S. Bureau of the Census, *County and City Data Book* (Washington: U.S. Government Printing Office, 1988).

Scoring. Twenty points for $640 or more per capita; no points for $259 or less. The spacing is every $20 per capita.

**Annual Per Capita
Education-Related Spending
By Local Governments**

Highest	$
1. Fairbanks, Alaska	1,130
2. Rock Springs, Wyo.	952
3. Olean, N.Y.	678
4. Watertown, N.Y.	671
5. El Centro–Calexico–Brawley, Calif.	668
6. Gallup, N.Mex.	645
7. Kingston, N.Y.	636
8. Huntsville, Tex.	632
9. Albany, Oreg.	625
10. Cortland, N.Y.	623

Lowest	
219. Radcliff–Elizabethtown, Ky.	224
218. Hinesville, Ga.	234
217. Manhattan, Kans.	239
216. Richmond, Ky.	243
215. Bowling Green, Ky.	255
214. Cookeville, Tenn.	257
213. Columbia, Tenn.	258
212. Cape Girardeau, Mo.	268
211. Blacksburg, Va.	274
210. Frankfort, Ky.	280

(Figure following each area name indicates annual per capita education-related spending by local governments; figure in parentheses represents rating points.)

Alabama

Athens	376	(6)
Auburn–Opelika	284	(2)
Decatur	362	(6)
Enterprise	358	(5)
Selma	337	(4)
Talladega	352	(5)

Alaska

Fairbanks	1,130	(20)

Arizona

Bullhead City– Lake Havasu City	478	(11)
Casa Grande– Apache Junction	556	(15)
Flagstaff	563	(16)
Prescott	395	(7)
Sierra Vista	461	(11)
Yuma	477	(11)

Arkansas

Blytheville	417	(8)
El Dorado	371	(6)
Hot Springs	285	(2)
Jonesboro	317	(3)
Rogers	311	(3)
Russellville	392	(7)

California

El Centro–Calexico– Brawley	668	(20)
Eureka	488	(12)
Hanford	553	(15)
Madera	604	(18)
San Luis Obispo– Atascadero	369	(6)

Colorado

Grand Junction	468	(11)

Connecticut

Torrington	481	(12)

Delaware

Dover	420	(9)

Florida

Key West	338	(4)
Vero Beach	423	(9)

Georgia

Brunswick	408	(8)
Carrollton	368	(6)
Dalton	410	(8)
Gainesville	360	(6)
Hinesville	234	(0)
La Grange	434	(9)
Rome	403	(8)
Valdosta	349	(5)

Idaho

Coeur d'Alene	324	(4)
Idaho Falls	400	(8)
Nampa–Caldwell	349	(5)
Pocatello	348	(5)
Twin Falls	326	(4)

Illinois

Carbondale	336	(4)
Danville	432	(9)
De Kalb	430	(9)
Freeport	393	(7)
Galesburg	357	(5)
Mattoon–Charleston	345	(5)
Ottawa	436	(9)
Quincy	313	(3)
Sterling	491	(12)

Indiana

Columbus	518	(13)
Marion	501	(13)
Michigan City–La Porte	411	(8)
New Castle	448	(10)
Richmond	448	(10)
Vincennes	310	(3)

Iowa

Ames	367	(6)
Burlington	478	(11)
Clinton	495	(12)
Fort Dodge	435	(9)
Marshalltown	492	(12)
Mason City	441	(10)
Muscatine	461	(11)

Kansas

Hutchinson	443	(10)
Manhattan	239	(0)
Salina	460	(11)

Kentucky

Bowling Green	255	(0)
Frankfort	280	(2)
Madisonville	341	(5)
Paducah	323	(4)
Radcliff–Elizabethtown	224	(0)
Richmond	243	(0)

Louisiana

Bogalusa	490	(12)
Crowley	388	(7)
Hammond	407	(8)
Minden	467	(11)
Morgan City	529	(14)
New Iberia	516	(13)
Opelousas	521	(14)
Ruston	311	(3)

Maine

Augusta–Waterville	341	(5)
Biddeford	364	(6)

Maryland

Salisbury	460	(11)

Michigan

Adrian	511	(13)
Marquette	480	(12)
Mount Pleasant	307	(3)
Owosso	498	(12)
Traverse City	475	(11)

Minnesota

Faribault	480	(12)
Mankato	555	(15)
Winona	399	(7)

Mississippi

Columbus	309	(3)
Greenville	351	(5)
Greenwood	406	(8)
Hattiesburg	300	(3)
Laurel	300	(3)
Meridian	291	(2)
Tupelo	379	(6)
Vicksburg	355	(5)

Missouri

Cape Girardeau	268	(1)
Jefferson City	283	(2)
Sikeston	399	(7)

Montana

Bozeman	418	(8)
Helena	577	(16)
Missoula	482	(12)

Nebraska

Grand Island	471	(11)

Nevada

Carson City	453	(10)

New Hampshire

Concord	375	(6)
Keene	460	(11)
Laconia	435	(9)

New Mexico

Alamogordo	488	(12)
Carlsbad	501	(13)
Clovis	555	(15)
Farmington	601	(18)
Gallup	645	(20)
Hobbs	619	(18)
Rio Rancho	433	(9)
Roswell	534	(14)

New York

Auburn	547	(15)
Batavia	608	(18)
Cortland	623	(19)
Gloversville	572	(16)
Ithaca	532	(14)
Jamestown	586	(17)
Kingston	636	(19)
Olean	678	(20)
Plattsburgh	614	(18)
Watertown	671	(20)

North Carolina

Eden	391	(7)
Goldsboro	384	(7)
Greenville	381	(7)
Havelock–New Bern	370	(6)
Kinston	432	(9)
Lumberton	513	(13)
Roanoke Rapids	521	(14)
Rocky Mount	427	(9)
Sanford	468	(11)
Shelby	427	(9)
Statesville	394	(7)
Wilson	430	(9)

North Dakota

Minot	481	(12)

Ohio

Ashland	404	(8)
Ashtabula	458	**(10)**
Athens	397	(7)
Chillicothe	418	(8)
East Liverpool	380	(7)
Findlay	408	(8)
Fremont	426	(9)
Marion	444	(10)
New Philadelphia	400	(8)
Portsmouth	420	(9)
Sandusky	535	(14)
Sidney	428	(9)
Tiffin	367	(6)
Wooster	426	(9)
Zanesville	457	(10)

Oklahoma

Ardmore	460	(11)
Bartlesville	417	(8)
Chickasha	442	(10)
Duncan	406	(8)
McAlester	416	(8)
Muskogee	470	(11)
Okmulgee	381	(7)
Ponca City	398	(7)
Stillwater	317	(3)

Oregon

Albany	625	(19)
Bend	492	(12)
Corvallis	484	(12)
Grants Pass	522	(14)
Klamath Falls	496	(12)
Roseburg	608	(18)

Pennsylvania

Butler	394	(7)
Chambersburg	388	(7)
New Castle	389	(7)
Pottsville	375	(6)

Rhode Island

Newport	485	(12)

South Carolina

Greenwood	405	(8)
Hilton Head Island	283	(2)
Myrtle Beach	370	(6)
Orangeburg	430	(9)
Sumter	442	(10)

Tennessee

Cleveland	290	(2)
Columbia	258	(0)
Cookeville	257	(0)
Morristown	328	(4)
Tullahoma	326	(4)

Texas

Alice	487	(12)
Bay City	581	(17)
Del Rio	468	(11)
Greenville	437	(9)
Huntsville	632	(19)
Lufkin	481	(12)
Nacogdoches	304	(3)
Palestine	521	(14)
Paris	351	(5)

Utah

Logan	492	(12)

Vermont

Rutland	459	(10)

Virginia

Blacksburg	274	(1)
Fredericksburg	494	(12)
Harrisonburg	354	(5)
Martinsville	396	(7)
Staunton–Waynesboro	370	(6)
Winchester	397	(7)

Washington

Aberdeen	522	(14)
Longview	531	(14)
Port Angeles	447	(10)
Pullman	409	(8)
Walla Walla	409	(8)
Wenetchee	497	(12)

West Virginia

Beckley	421	(9)
Clarksburg	426	(9)
Fairmont	391	(7)
Morgantown	333	(4)

Wisconsin

Fond du Lac	429	(9)
Manitowoc	345	(5)
Marshfield– Wisconsin Rapids	479	(11)
Stevens Point	410	(8)

Wyoming

Rock Springs	952	(20)

Teacher Compensation

Competition to hire the best teachers has become intense. Miami, Florida, and Rochester, New York, are leading the way with innovative packages that have substantially increased their teachers' paychecks. Other large cities are digging deep for the extra dollars needed to entice the most promising candidates to their classrooms.

Micropolitan areas are already feeling the pressure from this contest. A Census Bureau report says teachers in counties with fewer than 100,000 residents are paid 24 percent less on average than their metropolitan counterparts.

This category ranks each area according to the average monthly pay given to its public-school teachers. The figure for the entire country is $1,789.

Fairbanks, Alaska, pays its 825 teachers an average of $3,015 a month, nearly $300 more than any other small city. That squares with a National Education Association study that estimated Alaskan teachers receive 35 percent higher salaries than their best-paid colleagues in the continental U.S.

Hinesville, Georgia, gives its teachers just $959 a month. All ten of the lowest-paying areas are in the South. The West generally hands out the largest teacher paychecks.

Source. These statistics, published in 1984, are for 1982. U.S. Bureau of the Census, *Census of Governments: Compendium of Public Employment* (Washington: U.S. Government Printing Office, 1984).

Scoring. Twenty points for $2,430 or more per month; no points for $1,099 or less. The spacing is every $70.

Teacher Compensation: Highs and Lows

	Average Monthly Pay
Highest	**$**
1. Fairbanks, Alaska	3,015
2. Minot, N.Dak.	2,724
3. San Luis Obispo–Atascadero, Calif.	2,322
4. Rock Springs, Wyo.	2,079
5. Eureka, Calif.	2,069
6. Mount Pleasant, Mich.	2,062
7. Aberdeen, Wash.	2,025
8. Kingston, N.Y.	2,021
9. Carson City, Nev.	2,019
10. Newport, R.I.	2,017
Lowest	
219. Hinesville, Ga.	959
218. Vicksburg, Miss.	1,052
217. Meridian, Miss.	1,100
216. Hattiesburg, Miss.	1,108
215. Tupelo, Miss.	1,114
214. Rogers, Ark.	1,120
213. Blytheville, Ark.	1,129
212. Columbus, Miss.	1,138
211. Greenville, Miss.	1,143
210. Jonesboro, Ark.	1,155

(Figure following each area name indicates average monthly pay for teachers in dollars; figure in parentheses represents rating points.)

Alabama

Athens	1,429	(5)
Auburn–Opelika	1,300	(3)
Decatur	1,433	(5)
Enterprise	1,461	(6)
Selma	1,451	(6)
Talladega	1,380	(5)

Alaska

Fairbanks	3,015	(20)

Arizona

Bullhead City– Lake Havasu City	1,540	(7)
Casa Grande– Apache Junction	1,687	(9)
Flagstaff	1,536	(7)
Prescott	1,769	(10)
Sierra Vista	1,649	(8)
Yuma	1,797	(10)

Arkansas

Blytheville	1,129	(1)
El Dorado	1,197	(2)
Hot Springs	1,258	(3)
Jonesboro	1,155	(1)
Rogers	1,120	(1)
Russellville	1,432	(5)

California

El Centro–Calexico– Brawley	1,978	(13)
Eureka	2,069	(14)
Hanford	1,924	(12)
Madera	1,982	(13)
San Luis Obispo– Atascadero	2,322	(18)

Colorado

Grand Junction	1,573	(7)

Connecticut

Torrington	1,797	(10)

Delaware

Dover	1,449	(5)

Florida

Key West	1,645	(8)
Vero Beach	1,418	(5)

Georgia

Brunswick	1,249	(3)
Carrollton	1,212	(2)
Dalton	1,300	(3)
Gainesville	1,417	(5)
Hinesville	959	(0)
La Grange	1,254	(3)
Rome	1,389	(5)
Valdosta	1,159	(1)

Idaho

Coeur d'Alene	1,543	(7)
Idaho Falls	1,392	(5)
Nampa–Caldwell	1,365	(4)
Pocatello	1,469	(6)
Twin Falls	1,438	(5)

Illinois

Carbondale	1,601	(8)
Danville	1,508	(6)
De Kalb	1,518	(6)
Freeport	1,539	(7)
Galesburg	1,636	(8)
Mattoon–Charleston	1,447	(5)
Ottawa	1,864	(11)
Quincy	1,685	(9)
Sterling	1,829	(11)

Indiana

Columbus	1,604	(8)
Marion	1,760	(10)
Michigan City–La Porte	1,658	(8)
New Castle	1,393	(5)
Richmond	1,625	(8)
Vincennes	1,544	(7)

Iowa

Ames	1,638	(8)
Burlington	1,857	(11)
Clinton	1,780	(10)
Fort Dodge	1,580	(7)
Marshalltown	1,762	(10)
Mason City	1,659	(8)
Muscatine	1,427	(5)

Kansas

Hutchinson	1,530	(7)
Manhattan	1,645	(8)
Salina	1,435	(5)

Kentucky

Bowling Green	1,594	(8)
Frankfort	1,478	(6)
Madisonville	1,517	(6)
Paducah	1,431	(5)
Radcliff–Elizabethtown	1,582	(7)
Richmond	1,516	(6)

Louisiana

Bogalusa	1,534	(7)
Crowley	1,403	(5)
Hammond	1,235	(2)
Minden	1,430	(5)
Morgan City	1,635	(8)
New Iberia	1,285	(3)
Opelousas	1,419	(5)
Ruston	1,876	(12)

Maine

Augusta–Waterville	1,256	(3)
Biddeford	1,267	(3)

Maryland

Salisbury	1,742	(10)

Michigan

Adrian	1,970	(13)
Marquette	1,951	(13)
Mount Pleasant	2,062	(14)
Owosso	1,953	(13)
Traverse City	1,922	(12)

Minnesota

Faribault	1,828	(11)
Mankato	1,989	(13)
Winona	1,906	(12)

Mississippi

Columbus	1,138	(1)
Greenville	1,143	(1)
Greenwood	1,249	(3)
Hattiesburg	1,108	(1)
Laurel	1,191	(2)
Meridian	1,100	(1)
Tupelo	1,114	(1)
Vicksburg	1,052	(0)

Missouri

Cape Girardeau	1,319	(4)
Jefferson City	1,447	(5)
Sikeston	1,358	(4)

Montana

Bozeman	1,708	(9)
Helena	1,953	(13)
Missoula	1,618	(8)

Nebraska

Grand Island	1,525	(7)

Nevada

Carson City	2,019	(14)

New Hampshire

Concord	1,367	(4)
Keene	1,247	(3)
Laconia	1,263	(3)

New Mexico

Alamogordo	1,599	(8)
Carlsbad	1,644	(8)
Clovis	1,610	(8)
Farmington	1,591	(8)
Gallup	1,526	(7)
Hobbs	1,829	(11)
Rio Rancho	1,351	(4)
Roswell	1,605	(8)

New York

Auburn	1,799	(10)
Batavia	1,920	(12)
Cortland	1,693	(9)
Gloversville	1,855	(11)
Ithaca	1,800	(11)
Jamestown	1,835	(11)
Kingston	2,021	(14)
Olean	1,704	(9)
Plattsburgh	1,766	(10)
Watertown	1,881	(12)

North Carolina

Eden	1,438	(5)
Goldsboro	1,479	(6)
Greenville	1,363	(4)
Havelock–New Bern	1,460	(6)
Kinston	1,473	(6)
Lumberton	1,477	(6)
Roanoke Rapids	1,406	(5)
Rocky Mount	1,451	(6)
Sanford	1,451	(6)
Shelby	1,476	(6)
Statesville	1,490	(6)
Wilson	1,404	(5)

North Dakota

Minot	2,724	(20)

Ohio

Ashland	1,632	(8)
Ashtabula	1,774	(10)
Athens	1,520	(7)
Chillicothe	1,552	(7)
East Liverpool	1,546	(7)
Findlay	1,610	(8)
Fremont	1,661	(9)
Marion	1,528	(7)
New Philadelphia	1,613	(8)
Portsmouth	1,608	(8)
Sandusky	1,718	(9)
Sidney	1,646	(8)
Tiffin	1,532	(7)
Wooster	1,607	(8)
Zanesville	1,558	(7)

Oklahoma

Ardmore	1,483	(6)
Bartlesville	1,668	(9)
Chickasha	1,404	(5)
Duncan	1,511	(6)
McAlester	1,450	(6)
Muskogee	1,621	(8)
Okmulgee	1,426	(5)
Ponca City	1,423	(5)
Stillwater	1,414	(5)

Oregon

Albany	1,587	(7)
Bend	1,635	(8)
Corvallis	1,927	(12)
Grants Pass	1,897	(12)
Klamath Falls	1,592	(8)
Roseburg	1,659	(8)

Pennsylvania

Butler	1,772	(10)
Chambersburg	1,601	(8)
New Castle	1,673	(9)
Pottsville	1,544	(7)

Rhode Island

Newport	2,017	(14)

South Carolina

Greenwood	1,337	(4)
Hilton Head Island	1,487	(6)
Myrtle Beach	1,255	(3)
Orangeburg	1,216	(2)
Sumter	1,206	(2)

Tennessee

Cleveland	1,364	(4)
Columbia	1,707	(9)
Cookeville	1,302	(3)
Morristown	1,349	(4)
Tullahoma	1,415	(5)

Texas

Alice	1,403	(5)
Bay City	1,563	(7)
Del Rio	1,357	(4)
Greenville	1,256	(3)
Huntsville	1,647	(8)
Lufkin	1,446	(5)
Nacogdoches	1,260	(3)
Palestine	1,499	(6)
Paris	1,454	(6)

Utah

Logan	1,600	(8)

Vermont

Rutland	1,223	(2)

Virginia

Blacksburg	1,362	(4)
Fredericksburg	1,445	(5)
Harrisonburg	1,444	(5)
Martinsville	1,366	(4)
Staunton–Waynesboro	1,276	(3)
Winchester	1,398	(5)

Washington

Aberdeen	2,025	(14)
Longview	1,989	(13)
Port Angeles	1,973	(13)
Pullman	1,920	(12)
Walla Walla	1,962	(13)
Wenatchee	1,970	(13)

West Virginia

Beckley	1,456	(6)
Clarksburg	1,858	(11)
Fairmont	1,559	(7)
Morgantown	1,590	(8)

Wisconsin

Fond du Lac	1,765	(10)
Manitowoc	1,665	(9)
Marshfield– Wisconsin Rapids	1,861	(11)
Stevens Point	1,646	(8)

Wyoming

Rock Springs	2,079	(14)

The Results

Ithaca, New York, gives new meaning to the term "higher education." Cornell University and Ithaca College are perched on steep hills above Cayuga Lake and downtown Ithaca. The elevation of the two institutions is symbolic of their importance to the community. "The major industry is education and research," says a local information booklet.

Cornell, which is partially supported by the state, is the only Ivy League institution based in a micropolitan area. Nearly 18,000 students attend classes on one of the country's most beautiful campuses, a wooded expanse with gorges and waterfalls. The main library has 2.5 million books.

Ithaca College, which bills itself as the largest independent residential college in New York, adds another 5,700 students. There is also Tompkins-Cortland Community College, with an enrollment of 3,500.

This impressive array of institutions of higher learning is the primary reason Ithaca has landed first place in the education section, with 83 points out of a possible 100. Not only are the universities' resources available for community use, but their dedication filters into the elementary and secondary schools. Ithaca has a very low high-school dropout rate and provides education funding well above the national average.

The West dominates this section's list of the ten best communities, holding six of the positions. Corvallis, Oregon, is second nationally in education. The Midwest holds three slots. Ithaca is the only Eastern micropolitan area to make the top ten.

Dalton, Georgia, the self-proclaimed Carpet Capital of the World, has more than 200 carpet mills. Their labor needs have historically taken precedence over education. Many poor teenagers find a steady paycheck considerably more alluring than a high-school diploma. The dropout rate is consequently the highest in micropolitan America.

"You're dealing with a unique situation," Jeffeory White, a Dalton physician, told the *Los Angeles Times*. "The carpet industry . . . is a big, non-unionized industry that results in a stratification of society into either very rich or very poor."

Dalton pays its teachers much less than the national average. The area also lacks the positive influence of any sizeable local college. The result is a score of just 13 points, placing Dalton last in the education section. But it is not alone. All eleven of the cities with the lowest totals are from the South.

Highest	Rating Points
1. Ithaca, N.Y.	83
2. Corvallis, Oreg.	82
3. Mankato, Minn.	80
3. Pullman, Wash.	80
5. Fairbanks, Alaska	76
6. Ames, Iowa	74
6. Logan, Utah	74
8. Bozeman, Mont.	73
9. Helena, Mont.	71
10. De Kalb, Ill.	70
11. Cortland, N.Y.	69
11. Mount Pleasant, Mich.	69
11. San Luis Obispo–Atascadero, Calif.	69
14. Eureka, Calif.	68
14. Faribault, Minn.	68
14. Marquette, Mich.	68
14. Minot, N.Dak.	68
18. Kingston, N.Y.	66
18. Missoula, Mont.	66
20. Batavia, N.Y.	65

Lowest	
219. Dalton, Ga.	13
216. Blytheville, Ark.	16
216. Eden, N.C.	16
216. Hinesville, Ga.	16
215. Gainesville, Ga.	18
213. Greenville, Miss.	19
213. La Grange, Ga.	19
209. Columbia, Tenn.	21
209. Crowley, La.	21
209. Madisonville, Ky.	21
209. Martinsville, Va.	21

	Ithaca, N.Y.	Dalton, Ga.
Total Points in Section	83	13
Rank in Section	1	219

Results (and Rating Points)

High School Experience
Percentage of those 25 or older with four or more years of high school

	Ithaca, N.Y.	Dalton, Ga.
	80.8 (18)	44.7 (0)

High School Dropouts
Percentage of 16- to 19-year-olds not in school and not high-school graduates

	Ithaca, N.Y.	Dalton, Ga.
	3.5 (20)	33.9 (0)

College Influence
Percentage of 18- to 24-year-olds in school

	Ithaca, N.Y.	Dalton, Ga.
	77.2 (20)	15.4 (2)

Local Education Funding
Annual per capita education-related spending by local governments

	Ithaca, N.Y.	Dalton, Ga.
	$532 (14)	$410 (8)

Teacher Compensation
Average monthly pay for teachers

	Ithaca, N.Y.	Dalton, Ga.
	$1,800 (11)	$1,300 (3)

(Figure following each area name indicates composite score from the five categories in this section.)

Alabama
Athens	24
Auburn–Opelika	49
Decatur	28
Enterprise	36
Selma	29
Talladega	24

Alaska
Fairbanks	76

Arizona
Bullhead City– Lake Havasu City	38
Casa Grande– Apache Junction	33
Flagstaff	63
Prescott	52
Sierra Vista	47
Yuma	33

Arkansas
Blytheville	16
El Dorado	25
Hot Springs	25
Jonesboro	30
Rogers	24
Russellville	36

California
El Centro– Calexico– Brawley	51
Eureka	68
Hanford	44
Madera	47
San Luis Obispo– Atascadero	69

Colorado
Grand Junction	44

Connecticut
Torrington	54

Delaware
Dover	41

Florida
Key West	32
Vero Beach	29

Georgia
Brunswick	27
Carrollton	26
Dalton	13
Gainesville	18
Hinesville	16
La Grange	19
Rome	29
Valdosta	31

Idaho
Coeur d'Alene	45
Idaho Falls	41
Nampa–Caldwell	31
Pocatello	51
Twin Falls	32

Illinois
Carbondale	63
Danville	39
De Kalb	70
Freeport	42
Galesburg	43
Mattoon–Charleston	55
Ottawa	47
Quincy	43
Sterling	47

Indiana
Columbus	45
Marion	51
Michigan City– La Porte	39
New Castle	35
Richmond	43
Vincennes	42

Iowa
Ames	74
Burlington	50
Clinton	54
Fort Dodge	53
Marshalltown	55
Mason City	56
Muscatine	39

Kansas
Hutchinson	47
Manhattan	58
Salina	51

Kentucky
Bowling Green	44
Frankfort	30
Madisonville	21
Paducah	34
Radcliff– Elizabethtown	27
Richmond	41

Louisiana
Bogalusa	38
Crowley	21
Hammond	27
Minden	30
Morgan City	27
New Iberia	27
Opelousas	33
Ruston	63

Maine

Augusta–Waterville	43
Biddeford	38

Maryland

Salisbury	46

Michigan

Adrian	57
Marquette	68
Mount Pleasant	69
Owosso	54
Traverse City	61

Minnesota

Faribault	68
Mankato	80
Winona	63

Mississippi

Columbus	24
Greenville	19
Greenwood	31
Hattiesburg	39
Laurel	23
Meridian	24
Tupelo	23
Vicksburg	27

Missouri

Cape Girardeau	46
Jefferson City	39
Sikeston	25

Montana

Bozeman	73
Helena	71
Missoula	66

Nebraska

Grand Island	49

Nevada

Carson City	51

New Hampshire

Concord	45
Keene	52
Laconia	35

New Mexico

Alamogordo	53
Carlsbad	38
Clovis	46
Farmington	41
Gallup	32
Hobbs	40
Rio Rancho	40
Roswell	45

New York

Auburn	52
Batavia	65
Cortland	69
Gloversville	51
Ithaca	83
Jamestown	62
Kingston	66
Olean	60
Plattsburgh	63
Watertown	58

North Carolina

Eden	16
Goldsboro	36
Greenville	47
Havelock–New Bern	29
Kinston	34
Lumberton	29
Roanoke Rapids	31
Rocky Mount	28
Sanford	39
Shelby	29
Statesville	27
Wilson	32

North Dakota

Minot	68

Ohio

Ashland	53
Ashtabula	47
Athens	64
Chillicothe	38
East Liverpool	41
Findlay	54
Fremont	49
Marion	43
New Philadelphia	41
Portsmouth	37
Sandusky	55
Sidney	41
Tiffin	45
Wooster	44
Zanesville	46

Oklahoma

Ardmore	36
Bartlesville	52
Chickasha	31
Duncan	37
McAlester	33
Muskogee	39
Okmulgee	41
Ponca City	40
Stillwater	62

Oregon

Albany	53
Bend	50
Corvallis	82
Grants Pass	51
Klamath Falls	49
Roseburg	50

Pennsylvania
Butler	54
Chambersburg	39
New Castle	47
Pottsville	35

Rhode Island
Newport	61

South Carolina
Greenwood	34
Hilton Head Island	35
Myrtle Beach	31
Orangeburg	40
Sumter	34

Tennessee
Cleveland	25
Columbia	21
Cookeville	32
Morristown	22
Tullahoma	32

Texas
Alice	27
Bay City	38
Del Rio	23
Greenville	40
Huntsville	64
Lufkin	27
Nacogdoches	44
Palestine	37
Paris	27

Utah
Logan	74

Vermont
Rutland	46

Virginia
Blacksburg	51
Fredericksburg	40
Harrisonburg	39
Martinsville	21
Staunton– Waynesboro	30
Winchester	27

Washington
Aberdeen	54
Longview	56
Port Angeles	54
Pullman	80
Walla Walla	63
Wenatchee	53

West Virginia
Beckley	31
Clarksburg	43
Fairmont	44
Morgantown	58

Wisconsin
Fond du Lac	54
Manitowoc	44
Marshfield– Wisconsin Rapids	56
Stevens Point	59

Wyoming
Rock Springs	54

5

Sophistication

Many residents of metropolitan areas shudder at the very thought of moving to a smaller town. They fear they would somehow be cut off from modern life. The otherwise admirable *Places Rated Almanac* condescendingly imagined the tribulations of a transplanted urbanite in a small city:

> You trot down to the public library in your new town, only to find a well-worn selection of fiction, mostly published in the fifties, and a few back issues of *Family Circle* and *Field & Stream*. You search for a theatre or musical event and find your only choice is a concert stop by touring country-and-western performer Clyde McFritter and His Heavy Haulers.

As with most generalizations, this scenario is way off base. There are several small university towns with massive libraries and regular schedules of cultural events that are the envy of many metro areas. Other micropolitan communities provide mental stimulation without colleges. Key West, Florida, is still the home of the literary colony that once included Ernest Hemingway and Tennessee Williams. The Jamestown, New York, area boasts the Chautauqua Institution, which offers daily lectures by national figures and concerts

178 by noted musicians all summer long. *Time* called Chautauqua an "extraordinary cultural encampment, now part arts festival and part religious and philosophical retreat."

Nor are residents in smaller cities out of touch with current events. Cable television brings sessions of Congress on C-Span and the latest headlines on the Cable News Network. The local newsstand carries the national newsmagazines and *USA Today*. And don't forget that most micropolitan areas are relatively near large cities, whose television stations and newspapers are also available to them.

"I have friends in New York who think there's nothing out there till you get to Hollywood," says Charles Kuralt, CBS's famous "On the Road" correspondent. "And boy, is that wrong. That's the big change: this explosion of information."

This section evaluates the intellectual climate of each area, taking into account such things as residents' educational and travel experience, their willingness to get involved in government, and the ease with which they can benefit from the information explosion.

Kuralt's New York friends are certainly college graduates. Very likely they prefer their city because it affords the easy opportunity to meet other educated people with a wide range of backgrounds. They might be interested to know Pullman, Washington, and Ames, Iowa, are among the small cities with higher percentages of college graduates than Manhattan. Or that the proportion of people who come from other parts of the country is larger in Bullhead City–Lake Havasu City, Arizona, than in New York City.

Citizen involvement is also higher in small towns, where it is still possible to get in to see the mayor or a member of the city council. Charles Kuralt again provides evidence of the willingness of small-city residents to do their part. "Let something go wrong, and you can be sure somebody will form a committee, somebody will hire a hall," he says. "The next thing you know, people are at work on the problem."

These citizens are often stirred into action by an item seen in the local newspaper or heard on one of the town's radio or television stations. Small-town journalism doesn't meet the standards set by the *New York Times* or CBS, but it is capable of a product that would be considered excellent in any metro area. Newspapers in nine micropolitan areas proudly display the Pulitzer Prize, the highest award available in their business.

Ranking micropolitan America. The perfect small city would have citizens who are highly educated, well informed on important issues, and willing to get involved when necessary. Each area is tested in five categories:

1. College Education: Does the small city have a large number of residents who received their college diplomas, or are those with advanced

education rare?   **179**

2. Population Influx: Have many local residents had the broadening experience of living in other parts of the country, or are most people natives of the city?

3. Voter Turnout: Do citizens take the trouble to participate in government at the simplest level, or can't they even be troubled to vote?

4. Newspaper Strength: How heavily read is the local paper?

5. Broadcast Outlets: Does the area have a good mixture of radio and television stations, or are there few sources of local news and programming?

College Education

The noted philosopher and educator William James maintained that a college education "ought to have lit up in us a lasting relish for the better kind of man, a loss of appetite for mediocrities." It remains an American article of faith that a university will not only prepare its students for attractive jobs, but will also bestow sophistication upon them.

This category evaluates each area's intellectual climate by calculating the percentage of people 25 or older who have attended college for at least four years. The national average is 16.2 percent.

University towns have a great advantage in this measure. Their faculties are highly educated, while many alumni may also choose to remain in the area after graduation. Pullman, Washington, owes thanks to Washington State University for the 36.8 percent of its residents who went to college for four or more years.

Pottsville, Pennsylvania, was once a coal town. It now concentrates on manufacturing textiles. Pottsville's blue-collar past is reflected in its low rate of those who attended college for four years, just 6.1 percent. Southern and Midwestern industrial cities also have thin ranks of university graduates.

Source. These statistics, published in 1988, are for 1980. U.S. Bureau of the Census, *County and City Data Book* (Washington: U.S. Government Printing Office, 1988).

Scoring. Twenty points for 36.0 percent or more; no points for 7.4 percent or less. The spacing is every 1.5 percent.

College Education: Highs and Lows

	Those 25 or Older With 4+ Years of College
Highest	%
1. Pullman, Wash.	36.8
2. Corvallis, Oreg.	36.6
3. Ithaca, N.Y.	36.3
4. Ames, Iowa	33.9
5. Manhattan, Kans.	31.6
6. Bozeman, Mont.	30.5
7. Stillwater, Okla.	27.4
8. Logan, Utah	27.1
9. Blacksburg, Va.	26.8
10. Carbondale, Ill.	26.4
Lowest	
219. Pottsville, Pa.	6.1
218. Portsmouth, Ohio	7.1
216. Crowley, La.	7.4
216. New Castle, Ind.	7.4
215. Madisonville, Ky.	7.5
214. Sikeston, Mo.	7.7
211. New Philadelphia, Ohio	7.8
211. Roanoke Rapids, N.C.	7.8
211. Talladega, Ala.	7.8
210. Eden, N.C.	8.0

(Figure following each area name indicates the percentage of those 25 or older with four or more years of college; figure in parentheses represents rating points.)

Alabama

Athens	8.7	(1)
Auburn–Opelika	21.6	(10)
Decatur	11.8	(3)
Enterprise	12.2	(4)
Selma	11.3	(3)
Talladega	7.8	(1)

Alaska

Fairbanks	22.0	(10)

Arizona

Bullhead City– Lake Havasu City	8.8	(1)
Casa Grande– Apache Junction	9.3	(2)
Flagstaff	23.2	(11)
Prescott	16.2	(6)
Sierra Vista	13.8	(5)
Yuma	10.9	(3)

Arkansas

Blytheville	8.6	(1)
El Dorado	10.7	(3)
Hot Springs	11.3	(3)
Jonesboro	13.3	(4)
Rogers	11.8	(3)
Russellville	11.8	(3)

California

El Centro–Calexico– Brawley	9.6	(2)
Eureka	18.0	(8)
Hanford	10.2	(2)
Madera	10.7	(3)
San Luis Obispo– Atascadero	19.0	(8)

Colorado

Grand Junction	16.3	(6)

Connecticut

Torrington	18.6	(8)

Delaware

Dover	12.6	(4)

Florida

Key West	15.9	(6)
Vero Beach	15.5	(6)

Georgia

Brunswick	14.9	(5)
Carrollton	11.2	(3)
Dalton	9.7	(2)
Gainesville	12.2	(4)
Hinesville	12.3	(4)
La Grange	10.9	(3)
Rome	11.8	(3)
Valdosta	13.2	(4)

Idaho

Coeur d'Alene	13.8	(5)
Idaho Falls	21.1	(10)
Nampa–Caldwell	12.0	(4)
Pocatello	18.4	(8)
Twin Falls	13.4	(4)

Illinois

Carbondale	26.4	(13)
Danville	9.7	(2)
De Kalb	22.2	(10)
Freeport	11.2	(3)
Galesburg	11.1	(3)
Mattoon–Charleston	16.4	(6)
Ottawa	8.9	(1)
Quincy	10.6	(3)
Sterling	8.7	(1)

Indiana

Columbus	14.8	(5)
Marion	9.7	(2)
Michigan City–La Porte	10.6	(3)
New Castle	7.4	(0)
Richmond	10.1	(2)
Vincennes	9.9	(2)

Iowa

Ames	33.9	(18)
Burlington	11.5	(3)
Clinton	10.8	(3)
Fort Dodge	12.6	(4)
Marshalltown	14.2	(5)
Mason City	13.8	(5)
Muscatine	11.8	(3)

Kansas

Hutchinson	13.2	(4)
Manhattan	31.6	(17)
Salina	15.6	(6)

Kentucky

Bowling Green	16.6	(7)
Frankfort	18.0	(8)
Madisonville	7.5	(1)
Paducah	11.5	(3)
Radcliff–Elizabethtown	10.9	(3)
Richmond	17.8	(7)

Louisiana

Bogalusa	8.6	(1)
Crowley	7.4	(0)
Hammond	11.9	(3)
Minden	8.9	(1)
Morgan City	9.2	(2)
New Iberia	9.7	(2)
Opelousas	8.3	(1)
Ruston	23.7	(11)

Maine

Augusta–Waterville	15.0	(6)
Biddeford	14.4	(5)

Maryland

Salisbury	14.2	(5)

Michigan

Adrian	11.9	(3)
Marquette	17.5	(7)
Mount Pleasant	20.6	(9)
Owosso	9.2	(2)
Traverse City	19.1	(8)

Minnesota

Faribault	16.1	(6)
Mankato	18.3	(8)
Winona	16.4	(6)

Mississippi

Columbus	15.1	(6)
Greenville	12.5	(4)
Greenwood	13.2	(4)
Hattiesburg	17.7	(7)
Laurel	10.1	(2)
Meridian	10.9	(3)
Tupelo	12.5	(4)
Vicksburg	15.7	(6)

Missouri

Cape Girardeau	17.1	(7)
Jefferson City	19.3	(8)
Sikeston	7.7	(1)

Montana

Bozeman	30.5	(16)
Helena	23.9	(11)
Missoula	24.0	(12)

Nebraska

Grand Island	12.9	(4)

Nevada

Carson City	15.8	(6)

New Hampshire

Concord	19.8	(9)
Keene	18.0	(8)
Laconia	16.2	(6)

New Mexico

Alamogordo	14.7	(5)
Carlsbad	11.0	(3)
Clovis	11.5	(3)
Farmington	11.4	(3)
Gallup	10.7	(3)
Hobbs	10.0	(2)
Rio Rancho	14.9	(5)
Roswell	13.5	(5)

New York

Auburn	10.9	(3)
Batavia	11.8	(3)
Cortland	15.1	(6)
Gloversville	9.3	(2)
Ithaca	36.3	(20)
Jamestown	11.8	(3)
Kingston	16.0	(6)
Olean	10.7	(3)
Plattsburgh	14.1	(5)
Watertown	10.3	(2)

North Carolina

Eden	8.0	(1)
Goldsboro	10.8	(3)
Greenville	17.7	(7)
Havelock–New Bern	11.7	(3)
Kinston	10.3	(2)
Lumberton	8.7	(1)
Roanoke Rapids	7.8	(1)
Rocky Mount	9.5	(2)
Sanford	11.5	(3)
Shelby	9.2	(2)
Statesville	9.2	(2)
Wilson	11.3	(3)

North Dakota

Minot	16.2	(6)

Ohio

Ashland	12.4	(4)
Ashtabula	8.1	(1)
Athens	20.3	(9)
Chillicothe	8.7	(1)
East Liverpool	8.5	(1)
Findlay	14.7	(5)
Fremont	9.2	(2)
Marion	9.9	(2)
New Philadelphia	7.8	(1)
Portsmouth	7.1	(0)
Sandusky	11.4	(3)
Sidney	8.5	(1)
Tiffin	9.2	(2)
Wooster	12.6	(4)
Zanesville	8.5	(1)

Oklahoma

Ardmore	11.2	(3)
Bartlesville	24.2	(12)
Chickasha	11.8	(3)
Duncan	11.7	(3)
McAlester	9.3	(2)
Muskogee	12.0	(4)
Okmulgee	8.8	(1)
Ponca City	15.7	(6)
Stillwater	27.4	(14)

Oregon

Albany	10.6	(3)
Bend	16.6	(7)
Corvallis	36.6	(20)
Grants Pass	10.9	(3)
Klamath Falls	12.4	(4)
Roseburg	10.5	(3)

Pennsylvania

Butler	11.7	(3)
Chambersburg	10.3	(2)
New Castle	10.0	(2)
Pottsville	6.1	(0)

Rhode Island

Newport	23.5 (11)

South Carolina

Greenwood	13.8 (5)
Hilton Head Island	21.9 (10)
Myrtle Beach	12.5 (4)
Orangeburg	12.7 (4)
Sumter	11.5 (3)

Tennessee

Cleveland	10.5 (3)
Columbia	8.8 (1)
Cookeville	14.1 (5)
Morristown	9.2 (2)
Tullahoma	13.3 (4)

Texas

Alice	8.8 (1)
Bay City	10.9 (3)
Del Rio	12.2 (4)
Greenville	13.7 (5)
Huntsville	17.7 (7)
Lufkin	11.1 (3)
Nacogdoches	18.3 (8)
Palestine	8.4 (1)
Paris	10.0 (2)

Utah

Logan	27.1 (14)

Vermont

Rutland	16.5 (7)

Virginia

Blacksburg	26.8 (13)
Fredericksburg	15.8 (6)
Harrisonburg	14.7 (5)
Martinsville	8.3 (1)
Staunton–Waynesboro	12.5 (4)
Winchester	11.4 (3)

Washington

Aberdeen	9.8 (2)
Longview	11.0 (3)
Port Angeles	13.8 (5)
Pullman	36.8 (20)
Walla Walla	18.2 (8)
Wenatchee	14.5 (5)

West Virginia

Beckley	9.1 (2)
Clarksburg	10.9 (3)
Fairmont	11.1 (3)
Morgantown	23.9 (11)

Wisconsin

Fond du Lac	11.3 (3)
Manitowoc	9.9 (2)
Marshfield–Wisconsin Rapids	11.4 (3)
Stevens Point	17.5 (7)

Wyoming

Rock Springs	14.0 (5)

Population Influx

Intellectual sparks fly most easily when people of different backgrounds and viewpoints get together. A community of like-minded individuals, in contrast, is often less than stimulating.

This category measures each area's exposure to outside influences, computing the percentage of residents who were born in their current home state. The assumption is the lower the figure, the more varied the mix of people.

Even the most famous landmark of Bullhead City–Lake Havasu City, Arizona, the restored London Bridge, is from out of state. Only 16.3 percent of the area's residents were born in Arizona, well below the national average of 68.2 percent who still live in their state of birth. The rest of the population of Bullhead City–Lake Havasu City breaks this way: approximately 30 percent are from the Midwest, about 30 percent are from another Western state, 13 percent are from the South, and 11 percent from the Northeast.

Such heterogeneity is foreign to Pottsville, Pennsylvania, where 94.3 percent of the residents are natives of the state. Most of the small minority born outside of Pennsylvania hail from somewhere in the Northeast.

It is logical that most of the cities with small percentages of in-state natives are in the West. Southern and Eastern towns have the greatest share of stay-at-homes.

Source. These statistics, published in 1983, are for 1980. U.S. Bureau of the Census, *Census of Population* (Washington: U.S. Government Printing Office, 1983).

Scoring. Twenty points for 18.0 percent or less; no points for 95.1 percent or more. The spacing is every four percent.

	Born in State
Lowest Native Percentage	%
1. Bullhead City–Lake Havasu City, Ariz.	16.3
2. Carson City, Nev.	20.3
3. Fairbanks, Alaska	24.7
4. Grants Pass, Oreg.	28.3
5. Prescott, Ariz.	30.5
6. Vero Beach, Fla.	31.4
7. Key West, Fla.	31.8
8. Coeur d'Alene, Idaho	32.5
9. Hobbs, N.Mex.	33.1
10 Sierra Vista, Ariz.	33.9
Highest Native Percentage	
219. Pottsville, Pa.	94.3
218. Opelousas, La.	93.1
217. Crowley, La.	92.6
216. Gloversville, N.Y.	91.4
215. Alice, Tex.	91.2
214. Manitowoc, Wis.	90.7
213. Watertown, N.Y.	90.2
212. Butler, Pa.	90.1
211. New Iberia, La.	89.9
210. Greenwood, Miss.	89.6

(Figure following each area name indicates percentage of residents born in state; figure in parentheses represents rating points.)

Alabama

Athens	82.6	(4)
Auburn–Opelika	67.3	(7)
Decatur	79.5	(4)
Enterprise	76.5	(5)
Selma	87.5	(2)
Talladega	88.6	(2)

Alaska

Fairbanks	24.7	(18)

Arizona

Bullhead City–Lake Havasu City	16.3	(20)
Casa Grande–Apache Junction	47.7	(12)
Flagstaff	53.0	(11)
Prescott	30.5	(17)
Sierra Vista	33.9	(16)
Yuma	35.6	(15)

Arkansas

Blytheville	62.9	(9)
El Dorado	74.3	(6)
Hot Springs	61.0	(9)
Jonesboro	72.9	(6)
Rogers	42.7	(14)
Russellville	68.9	(7)

California

El Centro–Calexico–Brawley	65.5	(8)
Eureka	64.2	(8)
Hanford	60.4	(9)
Madera	64.3	(8)
San Luis Obispo–Atascadero	59.3	(9)

Colorado

Grand Junction	48.8	(12)

Connecticut

Torrington	70.1	(7)

Delaware

Dover	49.1	(12)

Florida

Key West	31.8	(16)
Vero Beach	31.4	(16)

Georgia

Brunswick	70.6	(7)
Carrollton	79.8	(4)
Dalton	74.0	(6)
Gainesville	82.5	(4)
Hinesville	39.0	(14)
La Grange	73.3	(6)
Rome	78.0	(5)
Valdosta	70.3	(7)

Idaho

Coeur d'Alene	32.5	(16)
Idaho Falls	58.6	(10)
Nampa–Caldwell	45.9	(13)
Pocatello	60.8	(9)
Twin Falls	51.4	(11)

Illinois

Carbondale	75.2	(5)
Danville	78.0	(5)
De Kalb	76.1	(5)
Freeport	77.0	(5)
Galesburg	80.5	(4)
Mattoon–Charleston	80.7	(4)
Ottawa	86.2	(3)
Quincy	78.3	(5)
Sterling	79.2	(4)

Indiana

Columbus	75.8	(5)
Marion	74.5	(6)
Michigan City–La Porte	69.4	(7)
New Castle	74.5	(6)
Richmond	69.7	(7)
Vincennes	82.9	(4)

Iowa

Ames	71.0	(6)
Burlington	74.6	(6)
Clinton	77.7	(5)
Fort Dodge	85.0	(3)
Marshalltown	81.3	(4)
Mason City	79.1	(4)
Muscatine	76.6	(5)

Kansas

Hutchinson	74.7	(6)
Manhattan	46.1	(13)
Salina	72.6	(6)

Kentucky

Bowling Green	76.2	(5)
Frankfort	83.6	(3)
Madisonville	81.1	(4)
Paducah	71.4	(6)
Radcliff–Elizabethtown	51.6	(11)
Richmond	76.8	(5)

Louisiana

Bogalusa	77.0	(5)
Crowley	92.6	(1)
Hammond	82.0	(4)
Minden	76.2	(5)
Morgan City	85.0	(3)
New Iberia	89.9	(2)
Opelousas	93.1	(1)
Ruston	76.3	(5)

Maine

Augusta–Waterville	80.0	(4)
Biddeford	62.7	(9)

Maryland

Salisbury	68.1	(7)

Michigan

Adrian	74.3	(6)
Marquette	75.3	(5)
Mount Pleasant	85.4	(3)
Owosso	86.5	(3)
Traverse City	81.4	(4)

Minnesota

Faribault	78.7	(5)
Mankato	80.3	(4)
Winona	72.2	(6)

Mississippi

Columbus	63.8	(8)
Greenville	84.9	(3)
Greenwood	89.6	(2)
Hattiesburg	77.6	(5)
Laurel	84.8	(3)
Meridian	76.5	(5)
Tupelo	81.1	(4)
Vicksburg	76.4	(5)

Missouri

Cape Girardeau	77.4	(5)
Jefferson City	79.6	(4)
Sikeston	75.5	(5)

Montana

Bozeman	52.9	(11)
Helena	61.9	(9)
Missoula	51.0	(11)

Nebraska

Grand Island	77.9	(5)

Nevada

Carson City	20.3	(19)

New Hampshire

Concord	60.4	(9)
Keene	50.9	(12)
Laconia	59.6	(9)

New Mexico

Alamogordo	36.1	(15)
Carlsbad	51.4	(11)
Clovis	42.0	(14)
Farmington	54.4	(11)
Gallup	74.2	(6)
Hobbs	33.1	(16)
Rio Rancho	60.5	(9)
Roswell	47.7	(12)

New York

Auburn	88.4	(2)
Batavia	89.3	(2)
Cortland	86.3	(3)
Gloversville	91.4	(1)
Ithaca	68.7	(7)
Jamestown	78.0	(5)
Kingston	82.7	(4)
Olean	82.6	(4)
Plattsburgh	77.6	(5)
Watertown	90.2	(2)

North Carolina

Eden	81.8	(4)
Goldsboro	76.1	(5)
Greenville	82.7	(4)
Havelock–New Bern	63.8	(8)
Kinston	88.6	(2)
Lumberton	89.1	(2)
Roanoke Rapids	86.3	(3)
Rocky Mount	88.3	(2)
Sanford	79.1	(4)
Shelby	83.1	(3)
Statesville	83.5	(3)
Wilson	88.3	(2)

North Dakota

Minot	66.1	(8)

Ohio

Ashland	83.7	(3)
Ashtabula	74.9	(6)
Athens	77.5	(5)
Chillicothe	85.0	(3)
East Liverpool	77.6	(5)
Findlay	82.1	(4)
Fremont	83.9	(3)
Marion	80.8	(4)
New Philadelphia	88.4	(2)
Portsmouth	76.6	(5)
Sandusky	77.1	(5)
Sidney	83.7	(3)
Tiffin	86.0	(3)
Wooster	79.2	(4)
Zanesville	87.7	(2)

Oklahoma

Ardmore	72.3	(6)
Bartlesville	56.0	(10)
Chickasha	72.5	(6)
Duncan	69.7	(7)
McAlester	74.1	(6)
Muskogee	70.3	(7)
Okmulgee	71.2	(6)
Ponca City	64.2	(8)
Stillwater	63.7	(8)

Oregon

Albany	48.4	(12)
Bend	43.2	(13)
Corvallis	42.5	(14)
Grants Pass	28.3	(17)
Klamath Falls	42.6	(14)
Roseburg	44.4	(13)

Pennsylvania

Butler	90.1	(2)
Chambersburg	82.4	(4)
New Castle	88.5	(2)
Pottsville	94.3	(1)

Rhode Island

Newport	45.2	(13)

South Carolina

Greenwood	81.9	(4)
Hilton Head Island	41.0	(14)
Myrtle Beach	66.0	(8)
Orangeburg	84.7	(3)
Sumter	70.5	(7)

Tennessee

Cleveland	71.6	(6)
Columbia	85.6	(3)
Cookeville	76.9	(5)
Morristown	79.4	(4)
Tullahoma	73.9	(6)

Texas

Alice	91.2	(1)
Bay City	78.2	(5)
Del Rio	71.7	(6)
Greenville	78.4	(5)
Huntsville	78.8	(5)
Lufkin	84.9	(3)
Nacogdoches	81.2	(4)
Palestine	84.3	(3)
Paris	80.9	(4)

Utah

Logan	68.2	(7)

Vermont

Rutland	68.0	(7)

Virginia

Blacksburg	63.5	(8)
Fredericksburg	65.0	(8)
Harrisonburg	74.3	(6)
Martinsville	80.9	(4)
Staunton–Waynesboro	79.3	(4)
Winchester	67.0	(7)

Washington

Aberdeen	63.4	(8)
Longview	52.1	(11)
Port Angeles	54.1	(11)
Pullman	55.3	(10)
Walla Walla	46.9	(13)
Wenatchee	55.0	(10)

West Virginia

Beckley	80.9	(4)
Clarksburg	85.0	(3)
Fairmont	84.9	(3)
Morgantown	68.6	(7)

Wisconsin

Fond du Lac	88.1	(2)
Manitowoc	90.7	(2)
Marshfield–Wisconsin Rapids	84.8	(3)
Stevens Point	83.1	(3)

Wyoming

Rock Springs	37.4	(15)

Voter Turnout

Americans don't seem to be quite as interested in self-government as they once were. "The central conclusion has to be that American democracy is in trouble," says Curtis Gans, the director of the Committee for the Study of the American Electorate. "We are increasingly becoming a government of, by, and for the few."

Gans and other experts are worried by the nation's declining rate of voter turnout. This category measures each area's level of citizen participation by dividing its total number of voters in the 1984 presidential election by its total number of residents. (The decision was made to use 1984 figures because that was the year of the highest turnout in the past decade.)

Bartlesville, Oklahoma, has been called "an anomalous community" by the *New York Times* because of its large share of affluent, skilled, and educated citizens. Residents held pep rallies and nightly vigils when the locally based Phillips Petroleum Company faced a takeover threat. They showed similar spirit with a turnout index of 54.9, compared with the national average of 38.4.

Midwestern and Western cities generally have the best turnout. The South has the worst record, with Hinesville, Georgia, trailing the pack with an index of just 14.3.

Source. These statistics, published in 1985, are for 1984. Derived from: Richard Scammon and Alice McGillivray, *America Votes* (Washington: Elections Research Center, 1985).

Scoring. Twenty points for 53.0 or more; no points for 14.9 or less. The spacing is every two index points.

Highest	Turnout Index
1. Bartlesville, Okla.	54.9
2. Ames, Iowa	53.0
3. Corvallis, Oreg.	52.7
4. Bozeman, Mont.	50.5
5. Fairbanks, Alaska	49.6
6. Mankato, Minn.	49.5
7. Marshalltown, Iowa	49.0
7. Torrington, Conn.	49.0
9. Helena, Mont.	48.8
10. Galesburg, Ill.	48.2

Lowest

219. Hinesville, Ga.	14.3
218. El Centro–Calexico–Brawley, Calif.	20.8
217. Radcliff–Elizabethtown, Ky.	22.1
216. Gallup, N.Mex.	22.3
215. Valdosta, Ga.	22.5
214. Myrtle Beach, S.C.	22.6
213. Yuma, Ariz.	23.6
212. Sumter, S.C.	23.8
211. Huntsville, Tex.	24.2
210. Hanford, Calif.	24.3

(Figure following each area name indicates turnout index; figure in parentheses represents rating points.)

Alabama

Athens	27.0	(7)
Auburn–Opelika	32.4	(9)
Decatur	36.0	(11)
Enterprise	37.6	(12)
Selma	39.3	(13)
Talladega	30.1	(8)

Alaska

Fairbanks	49.6	(18)

Arizona

Bullhead City– Lake Havasu City	32.7	(9)
Casa Grande– Apache Junction	29.0	(8)
Flagstaff	34.5	(10)
Prescott	41.3	(14)
Sierra Vista	28.7	(7)
Yuma	23.6	(5)

Arkansas

Blytheville	30.6	(8)
El Dorado	38.3	(12)
Hot Springs	45.1	(16)
Jonesboro	35.2	(11)
Rogers	36.0	(11)
Russellville	36.5	(11)

California

El Centro–Calexico– Brawley	20.8	(3)
Eureka	47.2	(17)
Hanford	24.3	(5)
Madera	29.8	(8)
San Luis Obispo– Atascadero	39.1	(13)

Colorado

Grand Junction	38.3	(12)

Connecticut

Torrington	49.0	(18)

Delaware

Dover	31.8	(9)

Florida

Key West	33.2	(10)
Vero Beach	40.0	(13)

Georgia

Brunswick	30.6	(8)
Carrollton	26.2	(6)
Dalton	24.9	(5)
Gainesville	25.8	(6)
Hinesville	14.3	(0)
La Grange	27.0	(7)
Rome	30.9	(8)
Valdosta	22.5	(4)

Idaho

Coeur d'Alene	39.5	(13)
Idaho Falls	41.8	(14)
Nampa–Caldwell	36.1	(11)
Pocatello	41.8	(14)
Twin Falls	39.0	(13)

Illinois

Carbondale	42.8	(14)
Danville	43.4	(15)
De Kalb	42.5	(14)
Freeport	42.8	(14)
Galesburg	48.2	(17)
Mattoon–Charleston	41.0	(14)
Ottawa	44.5	(15)
Quincy	45.0	(16)
Sterling	44.7	(15)

Indiana

Columbus	41.8 (14)
Marion	39.8 (13)
Michigan City–La Porte	37.3 (12)
New Castle	38.0 (12)
Richmond	40.5 (13)
Vincennes	42.2 (14)

Iowa

Ames	53.0 (20)
Burlington	46.7 (16)
Clinton	47.4 (17)
Fort Dodge	46.4 (16)
Marshalltown	49.0 (18)
Mason City	47.0 (17)
Muscatine	36.7 (11)

Kansas

Hutchinson	40.1 (13)
Manhattan	26.8 (6)
Salina	43.9 (15)

Kentucky

Bowling Green	29.3 (8)
Frankfort	43.2 (15)
Madisonville	34.7 (10)
Paducah	42.7 (14)
Radcliff–Elizabethtown	22.1 (4)
Richmond	32.7 (9)

Louisiana

Bogalusa	39.8 (13)
Crowley	41.3 (14)
Hammond	35.4 (11)
Minden	40.5 (13)
Morgan City	38.8 (12)
New Iberia	41.3 (14)
Opelousas	42.1 (14)
Ruston	34.5 (10)

Maine

Augusta–Waterville	47.5 (17)
Biddeford	45.4 (16)

Maryland

Salisbury	35.1 (11)

Michigan

Adrian	37.8 (12)
Marquette	39.8 (13)
Mount Pleasant	34.7 (10)
Owosso	41.2 (14)
Traverse City	43.0 (15)

Minnesota

Faribault	45.3 (16)
Mankato	49.5 (18)
Winona	47.0 (17)

Mississippi

Columbus	30.2 (8)
Greenville	33.1 (10)
Greenwood	36.8 (11)
Hattiesburg	33.1 (10)
Laurel	39.6 (13)
Meridian	35.5 (11)
Tupelo	31.8 (9)
Vicksburg	41.3 (14)

Missouri

Cape Girardeau	40.4 (13)
Jefferson City	42.7 (14)
Sikeston	35.6 (11)

Montana

Bozeman	50.5 (18)
Helena	48.8 (17)
Missoula	47.5 (17)

Nebraska

Grand Island	36.7 (11)

Nevada

Carson City	36.7 (11)

New Hampshire

Concord	37.9 (12)
Keene	37.3 (12)
Laconia	40.5 (13)

New Mexico

Alamogordo	28.1 (7)
Carlsbad	37.0 (12)
Clovis	28.6 (7)
Farmington	30.3 (8)
Gallup	22.3 (4)
Hobbs	29.8 (8)
Rio Rancho	31.8 (9)
Roswell	36.7 (11)

New York

Auburn	42.3 (14)
Batavia	42.9 (14)
Cortland	42.7 (14)
Gloversville	41.4 (14)
Ithaca	43.1 (15)
Jamestown	43.8 (15)
Kingston	45.1 (16)
Olean	40.4 (13)
Plattsburgh	37.5 (12)
Watertown	38.1 (12)

North Carolina

Eden	33.4 (10)
Goldsboro	28.6 (7)
Greenville	33.2 (10)
Havelock–New Bern	24.8 (5)
Kinston	36.5 (11)
Lumberton	26.7 (6)
Roanoke Rapids	32.5 (9)
Rocky Mount	35.4 (11)
Sanford	29.4 (8)
Shelby	31.8 (9)
Statesville	38.0 (12)
Wilson	32.0 (9)

North Dakota

Minot	38.5 (12)

Ohio

Ashland	41.6 (14)
Ashtabula	40.9 (13)
Athens	38.1 (12)
Chillicothe	38.0 (12)
East Liverpool	41.0 (14)
Findlay	42.9 (14)
Fremont	41.8 (14)
Marion	40.5 (13)
New Philadelphia	38.3 (12)
Portsmouth	40.4 (13)
Sandusky	43.0 (15)
Sidney	40.9 (13)
Tiffin	40.0 (13)
Wooster	35.7 (11)
Zanesville	38.2 (12)

Oklahoma

Ardmore	37.5 (12)
Bartlesville	54.9 (20)
Chickasha	35.9 (11)
Duncan	43.3 (15)
McAlester	38.2 (12)
Muskogee	38.7 (12)
Okmulgee	40.5 (13)
Ponca City	43.9 (15)
Stillwater	44.1 (15)

Oregon

Albany	44.6 (15)
Bend	45.2 (16)
Corvallis	52.7 (19)
Grants Pass	41.1 (14)
Klamath Falls	44.1 (15)
Roseburg	42.9 (14)

Pennsylvania

Butler	37.5 (12)
Chambersburg	32.7 (9)
New Castle	42.6 (14)
Pottsville	40.5 (13)

Rhode Island

Newport	40.3 (13)

South Carolina

Greenwood	29.8 (8)
Hilton Head Island	24.7 (5)
Myrtle Beach	22.6 (4)
Orangeburg	33.9 (10)
Sumter	23.8 (5)

Tennessee

Cleveland	31.1 (9)
Columbia	29.7 (8)
Cookeville	32.4 (9)
Morristown	30.5 (8)
Tullahoma	32.6 (9)

Texas

Alice	34.0 (10)
Bay City	33.4 (10)
Del Rio	24.5 (5)
Greenville	31.8 (9)
Huntsville	24.2 (5)
Lufkin	34.3 (10)
Nacogdoches	37.2 (12)
Palestine	28.3 (7)
Paris	32.9 (9)

Utah

Logan	40.4 (13)

Vermont

Rutland	41.7 (14)

Virginia

Blacksburg	29.9 (8)
Fredericksburg	31.0 (9)
Harrisonburg	31.3 (9)
Martinsville	36.3 (11)
Staunton–Waynesboro	36.7 (11)
Winchester	33.4 (10)

Washington

Aberdeen	40.9 (13)
Longview	39.3 (13)
Port Angeles	44.2 (15)
Pullman	41.4 (14)
Walla Walla	40.4 (13)
Wenatchee	42.1 (14)

West Virginia

Beckley	34.6 (10)
Clarksburg	45.8 (16)
Fairmont	42.2 (14)
Morgantown	36.4 (11)

Wisconsin

Fond du Lac	44.6 (15)
Manitowoc	45.5 (16)
Marshfield– Wisconsin Rapids	42.4 (14)
Stevens Point	48.0 (17)

Wyoming

Rock Springs	29.2 (8)

Newspaper Strength

Thomas Jefferson believed newspapers were so essential to an enlightened society that he boldly wrote, "Were it left to me to decide whether we should have a government without newspapers, or newspapers without a government, I should not hesitate a moment to prefer the latter."

The daily paper is still the major source of current information in small cities, covering everything from the doings at City Hall to preparations for the big high-school football clash on Friday night. This category measures the penetration of local papers, dividing their total daily circulation by the number of local residents.

The *Free Lance-Star* of Fredericksburg, Virginia, and the *News* of Hutchinson, Kansas, have the greatest local impact, each with an index of 62.8. The Fredericksburg paper sells 36,962 copies a day, its Hutchinson counterpart 41,035. Both have a substantially better penetration rate than the average index for the nation, including metro areas, of 26.1.

Three micropolitan areas are without daily papers: Hinesville, Georgia; Rio Rancho, New Mexico; and Tullahoma, Tennessee.

Midwestern cities have the best record of newspaper readership. The lowest penetration scores are mainly in the South and the West.

Source. These statistics, published in 1988, are for 1988. Derived from: *Editor and Publisher International Year Book* (New York: Editor & Publisher Co., 1988).

Scoring. Twenty points for 62.0 or more; no points for 4.9 or less. The spacing is every three index points.

Newspaper Strength: Highs and Lows

Highest	Newspaper Index
1. Fredericksburg, Va.	62.8
1. Hutchinson, Kans.	62.8
3. Tupelo, Miss.	58.5
4. Salina, Kans.	58.4
5. Wenatchee, Wash.	54.5
6. Paducah, Ky.	53.3
7. Grand Island, Nebr.	51.0
8. Mankato, Minn.	48.5
9. Carbondale, Ill.	46.4
9. Fort Dodge, Iowa	46.4

Lowest	
217. Hinesville, Ga.	0.0
217. Rio Rancho, N.Mex.	0.0
217. Tullahoma, Tenn.	0.0
216. Eden, N.C.	7.1
215. Casa Grande–Apache Junction, Ariz.	7.6
214. Crowley, La.	8.5
213. Sierra Vista, Ariz.	8.6
211. Bullhead City–Lake Havasu City, Ariz.	8.7
211. Morgan City, La.	8.7
210. Biddeford, Maine	9.3

(Figure following each area name indicates the newspaper index; figure in parentheses represents rating points.)

Alabama

Athens	15.3	(4)
Auburn–Opelika	16.3	(4)
Decatur	26.4	(8)
Enterprise	16.0	(4)
Selma	19.1	(5)
Talladega	20.9	(6)

Alaska

Fairbanks	24.4	(7)

Arizona

Bullhead City–Lake Havasu City	8.7	(2)
Casa Grande–Apache Junction	7.6	(1)
Flagstaff	13.8	(3)
Prescott	16.0	(4)
Sierra Vista	8.6	(2)
Yuma	18.9	(5)

Arkansas

Blytheville	17.4	(5)
El Dorado	22.8	(6)
Hot Springs	24.0	(7)
Jonesboro	38.4	(12)
Rogers	15.1	(4)
Russellville	25.8	(7)

California

El Centro–Calexico–Brawley	15.2	(4)
Eureka	18.0	(5)
Hanford	16.7	(4)
Madera	11.1	(3)
San Luis Obispo–Atascadero	14.6	(4)

Colorado

Grand Junction	32.4	(10)

Connecticut

Torrington	10.0	(2)

Delaware

Dover	21.9	(6)

Florida

Key West	9.7	(2)
Vero Beach	30.0	(9)

Georgia

Brunswick	24.8	(7)
Carrollton	15.7	(4)
Dalton	17.3	(5)
Gainesville	24.7	(7)
Hinesville	0.0	(0)
La Grange	27.8	(8)
Rome	27.4	(8)
Valdosta	24.7	(7)

Idaho

Coeur d'Alene	19.8	(5)
Idaho Falls	35.5	(11)
Nampa–Caldwell	19.2	(5)
Pocatello	27.9	(8)
Twin Falls	36.2	(11)

Illinois

Carbondale	46.4	(14)
Danville	27.7	(8)
De Kalb	15.2	(4)
Freeport	34.6	(10)
Galesburg	34.6	(10)
Mattoon–Charleston	36.7	(11)
Ottawa	30.2	(9)
Quincy	40.5	(12)
Sterling	22.7	(6)

Indiana

Columbus	31.9	(9)
Marion	27.2	(8)
Michigan City–La Porte	28.1	(8)
New Castle	26.7	(8)
Richmond	28.4	(8)
Vincennes	35.2	(11)

Iowa

Ames	13.6	(3)
Burlington	41.0	(13)
Clinton	37.4	(11)
Fort Dodge	46.4	(14)
Marshalltown	33.0	(10)
Mason City	41.6	(13)
Muscatine	26.2	(8)

Kansas

Hutchinson	62.8	(20)
Manhattan	19.8	(5)
Salina	58.4	(18)

Kentucky

Bowling Green	25.6	(7)
Frankfort	23.5	(7)
Madisonville	24.1	(7)
Paducah	53.3	(17)
Radcliff–Elizabethtown	15.7	(4)
Richmond	15.3	(4)

Louisiana

Bogalusa	15.8	(4)
Crowley	8.5	(2)
Hammond	14.3	(4)
Minden	10.2	(2)
Morgan City	8.7	(2)
New Iberia	21.5	(6)
Opelousas	16.9	(4)
Ruston	15.8	(4)

Maine

Augusta–Waterville	41.1	(13)
Biddeford	9.3	(2)

Maryland

Salisbury	36.4	(11)

Michigan

Adrian	18.9	(5)
Marquette	25.4	(7)
Mount Pleasant	20.1	(6)
Owosso	20.3	(6)
Traverse City	45.4	(14)

Minnesota

Faribault	17.9	(5)
Mankato	48.5	(15)
Winona	31.7	(9)

Mississippi

Columbus	23.8	(7)
Greenville	20.6	(6)
Greenwood	21.1	(6)
Hattiesburg	36.2	(11)
Laurel	15.6	(4)
Meridian	29.9	(9)
Tupelo	58.5	(18)
Vicksburg	30.8	(9)

Missouri

Cape Girardeau	27.5	(8)
Jefferson City	34.4	(10)
Sikeston	21.8	(6)

Montana

Bozeman	23.9	(7)
Helena	28.0	(8)
Missoula	36.1	(11)

Nebraska

Grand Island	51.0	(16)

Nevada

Carson City	28.6	(8)

New Hampshire

Concord	20.0	(6)
Keene	24.0	(7)
Laconia	23.6	(7)

New Mexico

Alamogordo	17.9	(5)
Carlsbad	15.9	(4)
Clovis	23.3	(7)
Farmington	17.3	(5)
Gallup	22.1	(6)
Hobbs	15.6	(4)
Rio Rancho	0.0	(0)
Roswell	24.7	(7)

New York

Auburn	21.2	(6)
Batavia	26.8	(8)
Cortland	26.2	(8)
Gloversville	25.6	(7)
Ithaca	23.0	(7)
Jamestown	30.9	(9)
Kingston	13.9	(3)
Olean	29.5	(9)
Plattsburgh	29.1	(9)
Watertown	45.8	(14)

North Carolina

Eden	7.1	(1)
Goldsboro	22.8	(6)
Greenville	17.9	(5)
Havelock–New Bern	19.1	(5)
Kinston	23.0	(7)
Lumberton	14.1	(4)
Roanoke Rapids	20.9	(6)
Rocky Mount	10.2	(2)
Sanford	31.7	(9)
Shelby	20.8	(6)
Statesville	19.3	(5)
Wilson	27.1	(8)

North Dakota

Minot	43.2	(13)

Ohio

Ashland	26.0	(8)
Ashtabula	18.9	(5)
Athens	23.9	(7)
Chillicothe	23.3	(7)
East Liverpool	11.7	(3)
Findlay	38.9	(12)
Fremont	22.0	(6)
Marion	27.6	(8)
New Philadelphia	32.3	(10)
Portsmouth	21.4	(6)
Sandusky	34.4	(10)
Sidney	28.9	(8)
Tiffin	17.5	(5)
Wooster	24.8	(7)
Zanesville	27.4	(8)

Oklahoma

Ardmore	27.6	(8)
Bartlesville	27.6	(8)
Chickasha	12.3	(3)
Duncan	22.8	(6)
McAlester	28.3	(8)
Muskogee	26.5	(8)
Okmulgee	12.3	(3)
Ponca City	24.9	(7)
Stillwater	15.4	(4)

Oregon

Albany	23.9	(7)
Bend	29.8	(9)
Corvallis	19.8	(5)
Grants Pass	26.2	(8)
Klamath Falls	32.2	(10)
Roseburg	21.5	(6)

Pennsylvania

Butler	20.4	(6)
Chambersburg	16.2	(4)
New Castle	19.8	(5)
Pottsville	18.7	(5)

Rhode Island
Newport	18.8	(5)

South Carolina
Greenwood	27.6	(8)
Hilton Head Island	21.4	(6)
Myrtle Beach	23.3	(7)
Orangeburg	18.6	(5)
Sumter	22.4	(6)

Tennessee
Cleveland	22.4	(6)
Columbia	22.4	(6)
Cookeville	16.9	(4)
Morristown	38.3	(12)
Tullahoma	0.0	(0)

Texas
Alice	17.9	(5)
Bay City	14.0	(4)
Del Rio	14.9	(4)
Greenville	17.8	(5)
Huntsville	10.1	(2)
Lufkin	21.3	(6)
Nacogdoches	16.5	(4)
Palestine	22.4	(6)
Paris	28.2	(8)

Utah
Logan	21.5	(6)

Vermont
Rutland	41.0	(13)

Virginia
Blacksburg	15.4	(4)
Fredericksburg	62.8	(20)
Harrisonburg	37.8	(11)
Martinsville	24.5	(7)
Staunton–Waynesboro	32.7	(10)
Winchester	36.9	(11)

Washington
Aberdeen	27.8	(8)
Longview	30.9	(9)
Port Angeles	24.4	(7)
Pullman	22.9	(6)
Walla Walla	31.8	(9)
Wenatchee	54.5	(17)

West Virginia
Beckley	38.3	(12)
Clarksburg	31.3	(9)
Fairmont	22.4	(6)
Morgantown	25.8	(7)

Wisconsin
Fond du Lac	21.7	(6)
Manitowoc	20.2	(6)
Marshfield–Wisconsin Rapids	37.2	(11)
Stevens Point	23.8	(7)

Wyoming
Rock Springs	14.6	(4)

Broadcast Outlets

Minot, North Dakota, will never be mistaken for one of the nation's major broadcasting markets. But it does have a larger choice of local news and entertainment programs than any other micropolitan area.

Minot has four television stations, including affiliates of the three major networks and the Public Broadcasting Service. It also has nine radio stations, one of them a member of National Public Radio.

This category measures the strength of the electronic media in each area. It assigns three points for each TV station and one for each radio outlet. Television operations receive more points because they have higher profiles and generally devote more resources to covering local news than radio does.

Minot earns a broadcast index of 21. The national average is an index of 5.9 points per 100,000 residents. That means if Minot had merely met the norm, it would have had approximately 4 points, the equivalent of just one TV station and a single radio outlet.

Four areas, three in the East, are at the bottom of the list, with no television presence and one radio station. Western cities are the most likely to have large complements of broadcast outlets.

Source. These statistics, published in 1988, are for 1988. Derived from *Broadcasting/Cablecasting Yearbook* (Washington: Broadcasting Publications, Inc., 1988).

Scoring. Twenty points for an index of 20 or more; no points for an index of 0. The spacing is every one index point.

Highest	Broadcast Index
1. Minot, N.Dak.	21
2. Meridian, Miss.	19
2. Roswell, N.Mex.	19
4. Fairbanks, Alaska	18
4. Missoula, Mont.	18
6. Grand Junction, Colo.	17
6. Quincy, Ill.	17
8. Bowling Green, Ky.	16
8. Idaho Falls, Idaho	16
8. Salisbury, Md.	16

Lowest

216. Gloversville, N.Y.	1
216. Newport, R.I.	1
216. Rio Rancho, N.Mex.	1
216. Torrington, Conn.	1
186. 30 tied	2

(Figures following each area name indicate the number of local television (T) and radio (R) stations; figure in parentheses represents rating points.)

Alabama

Athens	3R	(3)
Auburn–Opelika	1T, 5R	(8)
Decatur	6R	(6)
Enterprise	3R	(3)
Selma	1T, 5R	(8)
Talladega	3R	(3)

Alaska

Fairbanks	3T, 9R	(18)

Arizona

Bullhead City–Lake Havasu City	5R	(5)
Casa Grande–Apache Junction	3R	(3)
Flagstaff	1T, 6R	(9)
Prescott	1T, 4R	(7)
Sierra Vista	3R	(3)
Yuma	2T, 6R	(12)

Arkansas

Blytheville	2R	(2)
El Dorado	1T, 5R	(8)
Hot Springs	1T, 7R	(10)
Jonesboro	2T, 6R	(12)
Rogers	1T, 3R	(6)
Russellville	2R	(2)

California

El Centro–Calexico–Brawley	1T, 7R	(10)
Eureka	3T, 6R	(15)
Hanford	1T, 3R	(6)
Madera	2R	(2)
San Luis Obispo–Atascadero	1T, 11R	(14)

Colorado

Grand Junction	2T, 11R	(17)

Connecticut

Torrington	1R	(1)

Delaware

Dover	3R	(3)

Florida

Key West	7R	(7)
Vero Beach	5R	(5)

Georgia

Brunswick	5R	(5)
Carrollton	4R	(4)
Dalton	3R	(3)
Gainesville	7R	(7)
Hinesville	2R	(2)
La Grange	4R	(4)
Rome	1T, 6R	(9)
Valdosta	1T, 8R	(11)

Idaho

Coeur d'Alene	2R	(2)
Idaho Falls	3T, 7R	(16)
Nampa–Caldwell	1T, 9R	(12)
Pocatello	1T, 6R	(9)
Twin Falls	1T, 6R	(9)

Illinois

Carbondale	1T, 3R	(6)
Danville	4R	(4)
De Kalb	3R	(3)
Freeport	3R	(3)
Galesburg	5R	(5)
Mattoon–Charleston	1T, 6R	(9)
Ottawa	2R	(2)
Quincy	4T, 5R	(17)
Sterling	2R	(2)

Indiana

Columbus	3R	(3)
Marion	1T, 3R	(6)
Michigan City– La Porte	5R	(5)
New Castle	2R	(2)
Richmond	1T, 5R	(8)
Vincennes	1T, 4R	(7)

Iowa

Ames	1T, 6R	(9)
Burlington	1T, 4R	(7)
Clinton	4R	(4)
Fort Dodge	1T, 6R	(9)
Marshalltown	3R	(3)
Mason City	2T, 7R	(13)
Muscatine	2R	(2)

Kansas

Hutchinson	1T, 5R	(8)
Manhattan	5R	(5)
Salina	1T, 6R	(9)

Kentucky

Bowling Green	3T, 7R	(16)
Frankfort	4R	(4)
Madisonville	2T, 4R	(10)
Paducah	2T, 5R	(11)
Radcliff– Elizabethtown	1T, 2R	(5)
Richmond	4R	(4)

Louisiana

Bogalusa	2R	(2)
Crowley	3R	(3)
Hammond	4R	(4)
Minden	2R	(2)
Morgan City	2R	(2)
New Iberia	3R	(3)
Opelousas	2R	(2)
Ruston	3R	(3)

Maine

Augusta–Waterville	1T, 8R	(11)
Biddeford	1T, 3R	(6)

Maryland

Salisbury	3T, 7R	(16)

Michigan

Adrian	4R	(4)
Marquette	2T, 4R	(10)
Mount Pleasant	1T, 5R	(8)
Owosso	2R	(2)
Traverse City	2T, 6R	(12)

Minnesota

Faribault	2R	(2)
Mankato	1T, 6R	(9)
Winona	5R	(5)

Mississippi

Columbus	1T, 6R	(9)
Greenville	2T, 5R	(11)
Greenwood	1T, 5R	(8)
Hattiesburg	2T, 9R	(15)
Laurel	4R	(4)
Meridian	4T, 7R	(19)
Tupelo	1T, 4R	(7)
Vicksburg	3R	(3)

Missouri

Cape Girardeau	2T, 6R	(12)
Jefferson City	2T, 5R	(11)
Sikeston	3R	(3)

Montana

Bozeman	1T, 5R	(8)
Helena	1T, 7R	(10)
Missoula	3T, 9R	(18)

Nebraska

Grand Island	2T, 5R	(11)

Nevada

Carson City	2R	(2)

New Hampshire

Concord	1T, 5R	(8)
Keene	1T, 4R	(7)
Laconia	3R	(3)

New Mexico

Alamogordo	5R	(5)
Carlsbad	1T, 4R	(7)
Clovis	1T, 6R	(9)
Farmington	1T, 6R	(9)
Gallup	4R	(4)
Hobbs	5R	(5)
Rio Rancho	1R	(1)
Roswell	4T, 7R	(19)

New York

Auburn	4R	(4)
Batavia	2R	(2)
Cortland	3R	(3)
Gloversville	1R	(1)
Ithaca	7R	(7)
Jamestown	5R	(5)
Kingston	1T, 4R	(7)
Olean	4R	(4)
Plattsburgh	2T, 5R	(11)
Watertown	3T, 6R	(15)

North Carolina

Eden	3R	(3)
Goldsboro	5R	(5)
Greenville	3T, 5R	(14)
Havelock–New Bern	1T, 8R	(11)
Kinston	6R	(6)
Lumberton	4R	(4)
Roanoke Rapids	1T, 3R	(6)
Rocky Mount	5R	(5)
Sanford	4R	(4)
Shelby	3R	(3)
Statesville	4R	(4)
Wilson	4R	(4)

North Dakota

Minot	4T, 9R	(20)

Ohio

Ashland	3R	(3)
Ashtabula	2R	(2)
Athens	1T, 4R	(7)
Chillicothe	1T, 5R	(8)
East Liverpool	2R	(2)
Findlay	3R	(3)
Fremont	2R	(2)
Marion	3R	(3)
New Philadelphia	3R	(3)
Portsmouth	1T, 4R	(7)
Sandusky	1T, 2R	(5)
Sidney	2R	(2)
Tiffin	3R	(3)
Wooster	3R	(3)
Zanesville	1T, 3R	(6)

Oklahoma

Ardmore	1T, 3R	(6)
Bartlesville	1T, 2R	(5)
Chickasha	2R	(2)
Duncan	2R	(2)
McAlester	3R	(3)
Muskogee	4R	(4)
Okmulgee	2R	(2)
Ponca City	3R	(3)
Stillwater	4R	(4)

Oregon

Albany	4R	(4)
Bend	2T, 7R	(13)
Corvallis	1T, 6R	(9)
Grants Pass	3R	(3)
Klamath Falls	1T, 7R	(10)
Roseburg	1T, 4R	(7)

Pennsylvania

Butler	3R	(3)
Chambersburg	3R	(3)
New Castle	2R	(2)
Pottsville	3R	(3)

Rhode Island

Newport	1R	(1)

South Carolina

Greenwood	1T, 4R	(7)
Hilton Head Island	3R	(3)
Myrtle Beach	1T, 4R	(7)
Orangeburg	6R	(6)
Sumter	1T, 5R	(8)

Tennessee

Cleveland	1T, 4R	(7)
Columbia	3R	(3)
Cookeville	1T, 5R	(8)
Morristown	3R	(3)
Tullahoma	2R	(2)

Texas

Alice	3R	(3)
Bay City	2R	(2)
Del Rio	4R	(4)
Greenville	2R	(2)
Huntsville	4R	(4)
Lufkin	1T, 4R	(7)
Nacogdoches	5R	(5)
Palestine	4R	(4)
Paris	4R	(4)

Utah

Logan	5R	(5)

Vermont

Rutland	1T, 5R	(8)

Virginia

Blacksburg	3R	(3)
Fredericksburg	1T, 5R	(8)
Harrisonburg	2T, 7R	(13)
Martinsville	3R	(3)
Staunton– Waynesboro	6R	(6)
Winchester	4R	(4)

Washington

Aberdeen	4R	(4)
Longview	3R	(3)
Port Angeles	2R	(2)
Pullman	1T, 4R	(7)
Walla Walla	7R	(7)
Wenatchee	1T, 6R	(9)

West Virginia

Beckley	1T, 6R	(9)
Clarksburg	2T, 6R	(12)
Fairmont	3R	(3)
Morgantown	1T, 6R	(9)

Wisconsin

Fond du Lac	2R	(2)
Manitowoc	4R	(4)
Marshfield– Wisconsin Rapids	1T, 4R	(7)
Stevens Point	3R	(3)

Wyoming

Rock Springs	1T, 4R	(7)

The Results

A philosopher in search of civic enlightenment would probably expect little from a visit to Fairbanks, Alaska. Its history certainly offers scant encouragement. Fairbanks began as a gold-rush camp. Its rough-and-tumble past also includes the frenzied boom engendered by the oil pipeline. The city didn't even get sewers until the 1940s. ·

Then there is the harsh climate. It seems hardly likely that Fairbanks could attract a good mixture of people from the other 49 states to live near the Arctic Circle. And who would expect local residents to become involved in civic events if it meant leaving a warm house on a winter day with 19 hours of darkness and a temperature of 20 degrees below zero?

Our philosopher would be prepared for a rough frontier town with few educated people and little interest in self-government. Instead, he would find Fairbanks sitting in first place in the sophistication section, with 71 of a possible 100 points.

Fairbanks overcame the awesome barriers to its development with a strong faith in the power of education. No micropolitan area spends more on its schools; none has a higher rate of high-school graduates. The local campus of the University of Alaska ensures a sizeable group of residents with college degrees.

Interest in local events is strong. Few areas have higher voter-turnout rates. Author Neal Peirce gives much of the credit to the media. He once called the Fairbanks newspaper "one of the brightest, best-edited small-city newspapers in America." Its readers hail from all corners of the country. More than three-quarters of the city's residents were born outside of Alaska.

Fairbanks has plenty of company from fellow Western cities in the section's list of the most sophisticated communities. The region landed eight of the top eleven slots. The Midwest took two, the East one.

All 13 cities with the lowest scores are Southern. Lumberton, North Carolina, a racially troubled community with severe poverty, is at the bottom with only 17 points.

Lumberton has few college graduates. The city has a history of reacting sharply to perceived evils. Its county was the first in North Carolina to prohibit the sale of alcoholic beverages in 1886. The local district attorney has won more death-penalty cases than any other American prosecutor.

Lumberton's media have been of little note, with one exception. Two Native American men seized 18 hostages at the offices of the local newspaper in 1988. They said they were protesting the way their people were treated in town.

Highest	**Rating Points**
1. Fairbanks, Alaska	71
2. Missoula, Mont.	69
3. Corvallis, Oreg.	67
4. Idaho Falls, Idaho	61
5. Bozeman, Mont.	60
6. Minot, N.Dak.	59
7. Bend, Oreg.	58
8. Grand Junction, Colo.	57
8. Pullman, Wash.	57
10. Ames, Iowa	56
10. Ithaca, N.Y.	56
12. Bartlesville, Okla.	55
12. Helena, Mont.	55
12. Wenatchee, Wash.	55
15. Mankato, Minn.	54
15. Roswell, N.Mex.	54
15. Salina, Kans.	54
18. Eureka, Calif.	53
18. Klamath Falls, Oreg.	53
18. Quincy, Ill.	53
18. Traverse City, Mich.	53

Lowest

219. Lumberton, N.C.	17
217. Athens, Ala.	19
217. Eden, N.C.	19
213. Alice, Tex.	20
213. Crowley, La.	20
213. Hinesville, Ga.	20
213. Talladega, Ala.	20
207. Carrollton, Ga.	21
207. Columbia, Tenn.	21
207. Dalton, Ga.	21
207. Morgan City, La.	21
207. Palestine, Tex.	21
207. Tullahoma, Tenn.	21

	Fairbanks, Alaska	Lumberton, N.C.
Total Points in Section	71	17
Rank in Section	1	219
Results (and Rating Points)		
College Education Percentage of those 25 or older with four or more years of college	22.0 (10)	8.7 (1)
Population Influx Percentage of residents born in state	24.7 (18)	89.1 (2)
Voter Turnout Turnout index	49.6 (18)	26.7 (6)
Newspaper Strength Newspaper index	24.4 (7)	14.1 (4)
Broadcast Outlets Number of local television and radio stations	3T, 9R (18)	4R (4)

(Figure following each area name indicates composite score from the five categories in this section.)

Alabama

Athens	19
Auburn–Opelika	38
Decatur	32
Enterprise	28
Selma	31
Talladega	20

Alaska

Fairbanks	71

Arizona

Bullhead City–
    Lake Havasu
    City
	37

Casa Grande–
    Apache
    Junction
	26

Flagstaff	44
Prescott	48
Sierra Vista	33
Yuma	40

Arkansas

Blytheville	25
El Dorado	35
Hot Springs	45
Jonesboro	45
Rogers	38
Russellville	30

California

El Centro–
    Calexico–
    Brawley
	27

Eureka	53
Hanford	26
Madera	24
San Luis Obispo– Atascadero	48

Colorado

Grand Junction	57

Connecticut

Torrington	36

Delaware

Dover	34

Florida

Key West	41
Vero Beach	49

Georgia

Brunswick	32
Carrollton	21
Dalton	21
Gainesville	28
Hinesville	20
La Grange	28
Rome	33
Valdosta	33

Idaho

Coeur d'Alene	41
Idaho Falls	61
Nampa–Caldwell	45
Pocatello	48
Twin Falls	48

Illinois

Carbondale	52
Danville	34
De Kalb	36
Freeport	35
Galesburg	39
Mattoon–Charleston	44
Ottawa	30
Quincy	53
Sterling	28

Indiana

Columbus	36
Marion	35
Michigan City– La Porte	35
New Castle	28
Richmond	38
Vincennes	38

Iowa

Ames	56
Burlington	45
Clinton	40
Fort Dodge	46
Marshalltown	40
Mason City	52
Muscatine	29

Kansas

Hutchinson	51
Manhattan	46
Salina	54

Kentucky

Bowling Green	43
Frankfort	37
Madisonville	32
Paducah	51
Radcliff– Elizabethtown	27
Richmond	29

Louisiana

Bogalusa	25
Crowley	20
Hammond	26
Minden	23
Morgan City	21
New Iberia	27
Opelousas	22
Ruston	33

Maine

Augusta–Waterville	51
Biddeford	38

Maryland

Salisbury	50

Michigan

Adrian	30
Marquette	42
Mount Pleasant	36
Owosso	27
Traverse City	53

Minnesota

Faribault	34
Mankato	54
Winona	43

Mississippi

Columbus	38
Greenville	34
Greenwood	31
Hattiesburg	48
Laurel	26
Meridian	47
Tupelo	42
Vicksburg	37

Missouri

Cape Girardeau	45
Jefferson City	47
Sikeston	26

Montana

Bozeman	60
Helena	55
Missoula	69

Nebraska

Grand Island	47

Nevada

Carson City	46

New Hampshire

Concord	44
Keene	46
Laconia	38

New Mexico

Alamogordo	37
Carlsbad	37
Clovis	40
Farmington	36
Gallup	23
Hobbs	35
Rio Rancho	24
Roswell	54

New York

Auburn	29
Batavia	29
Cortland	34
Gloversville	25
Ithaca	56
Jamestown	37
Kingston	36
Olean	33
Plattsburgh	42
Watertown	45

North Carolina

Eden	19
Goldsboro	26
Greenville	40
Havelock–New Bern	32
Kinston	28
Lumberton	17
Roanoke Rapids	25
Rocky Mount	22
Sanford	28
Shelby	23
Statesville	26
Wilson	26

North Dakota

Minot	59

Ohio

Ashland	32
Ashtabula	27
Athens	40
Chillicothe	31
East Liverpool	25
Findlay	38
Fremont	27
Marion	30
New Philadelphia	28
Portsmouth	31
Sandusky	38
Sidney	27
Tiffin	26
Wooster	29
Zanesville	29

Oklahoma

Ardmore	35
Bartlesville	55
Chickasha	25
Duncan	33
McAlester	31
Muskogee	35
Okmulgee	25
Ponca City	39
Stillwater	45

Oregon

Albany	41
Bend	58
Corvallis	67
Grants Pass	45
Klamath Falls	53
Roseburg	43

Pennsylvania
Butler	26
Chambersburg	22
New Castle	25
Pottsville	22

Rhode Island
| Newport | 43 |

South Carolina
Greenwood	32
Hilton Head Island	38
Myrtle Beach	30
Orangeburg	28
Sumter	29

Tennessee
Cleveland	31
Columbia	21
Cookeville	31
Morristown	29
Tullahoma	21

Texas
Alice	20
Bay City	24
Del Rio	23
Greenville	26
Huntsville	23
Lufkin	29
Nacogdoches	33
Palestine	21
Paris	27

Utah
| Logan | 45 |

Vermont
| Rutland | 49 |

Virginia
Blacksburg	36
Fredericksburg	51
Harrisonburg	44
Martinsville	26
Staunton–Waynesboro	35
Winchester	35

Washington
Aberdeen	35
Longview	39
Port Angeles	40
Pullman	57
Walla Walla	50
Wenatchee	55

West Virginia
Beckley	37
Clarksburg	43
Fairmont	29
Morgantown	45

Wisconsin
Fond du Lac	28
Manitowoc	30
Marshfield–Wisconsin Rapids	38
Stevens Point	37

Wyoming
| Rock Springs | 39 |

6

Health Care

Wealth and health—the two vie for the attention of the American mind. People worry about both. A 1987 Gallup poll asked respondents to identify the biggest problem facing them and their families. Economic problems were the easy winner, named by 56 percent. Health woes finished second, mentioned by 6 percent. Concerns of all other types trailed the big two.

Money and health care sometimes create a joint worry. It is becoming increasingly expensive to visit a doctor's office or stay in a hospital. The U.S. Health Care Financing Administration predicted in a 1987 report that the situation can only get worse. Americans spent an average of $1,837 on personal health care in 1986. The study suggests that the figure will grow to $5,551 per person by the year 2000.

Another strain will gradually be placed on the nation's medical system as the new century approaches. An aging population and an expected substantial increase in the number of AIDS patients will expand doctors' caseloads. Hospitals will face a greater demand for available space.

It is essential, in light of these predictions, that an area offer its residents a health-care system that will be able to stand the test of time. This section assesses each small city according to its supply of doctors and hospital beds, its financial commitment to health care, and its current death rate.

216   Advances in the health field constitute one of the most important stories of the twentieth century. An American baby born in 1900 had a life expectancy of 49.2 years. An infant delivered in 1980 could look forward to 73.7 years on the average. If that baby was a white girl, the figure rose above 78.

But the system that allowed such improvement is showing signs of wear. The rows of classified advertisements for nurses in metropolitan newspapers are silent testimony to one of the biggest problems: qualified help is getting harder to find. Many health-care centers also need upgrading. "Hospitals will need enough capital to replace outmoded equipment and invest in nursing homes and home-health-care programs," warned Robert Reed, the chief financial officer of Voluntary Hospitals of America, Inc., back in 1987.

Which brings us again to money. Attracting nurses and buying new equipment require additional revenues. The Health Care Financing Administration reported that 11 percent of America's gross national product went for the nation's health-care bill in 1986. It is projecting an increase to 15 percent by 2000.

Micropolitan areas seeking to maintain quality health services in the face of these trends must be more aggressive. A good example is provided by Saint Joseph's Hospital in Marshfield, Wisconsin. It has a full-time recruiter on the road seeking applicants for staff vacancies.

The trend is also toward group ownership of small-town facilities. Westworld Community Healthcare, a fast-growing California firm, made its name in the mid-1980s by quickly acquiring hospitals in 12 states. All were in micropolitan or rural areas.

Westworld's strategy was to convince local officials that it could efficiently operate a facility that had become a burden on the city or county government. The administrator of one of Westworld's hospitals, Charles Duscha, predicted that this system would allow small towns to retain strong health care: "Communities that once settled for a doctor who was just a warm body don't have to anymore."

Ranking micropolitan America. The ideal micropolitan community would have plenty of doctors, a surplus of hospital space, and a strong government commitment to health care. Each small city is graded in five categories:

1. Doctor Availability: Is there a favorable ratio of doctors to residents, or is it hard to find a convenient family physician?

2. Specialist Availability: Does the area have a strong roster of doctors and surgeons who can handle specialized complaints?

3. Hospital Availability: Is there a large supply of hospital beds locally, or is a room difficult to obtain?

4. Local Health Funding: Does the local government show a willingness **217** to provide the necessary funds for hospitals and other health programs?

5. Death Rate: Does the local health-care system handle a low number of terminal patients, or is there a high death rate, indicating a greater strain on medical resources?

Doctor Availability

New doctors struggle to pay enormous bills for medical-school tuition and the latest equipment. It is understandably appealing to them to establish their practices in metropolitan areas that offer the prospects of more patients and higher fees. The number of doctors in large cities and their suburbs consequently grew by 85 percent between 1970 and 1986; the increase in small cities was only 53 percent.

This category evaluates how micropolitan areas are faring in light of this trend. Each small city is ranked according to its total number of active, nongovernment doctors, projected to a rate per 100,000 residents.

Morgantown, West Virginia, has by far the most favorable situation. West Virginia University's medical center and school of medicine account for a large share of Morgantown's 485 doctors, a rate of 620 per 100,000. The national average, including metro areas, is only 197 per 100,000.

Hinesville, Georgia, on the other hand, has only 12 active physicians for its civilian population. Its rate is 29 doctors per 100,000.

Areas with good numbers of doctors are fairly evenly distributed around the country. Most of the cities with low rates are in the South.

Source. These statistics, published in 1988, are for 1985. U.S. Bureau of the Census, *County and City Data Book* (Washington: U.S. Government Printing Office, 1988).

Scoring. Twenty points for 240 or more physicians per 100,000; no points for 49 or less. The spacing is every 10 per 100,000.

       Doctor Availability: Highs and Lows

Highest	**Doctors Per 100,000 Residents**
1. Morgantown, W.Va.	620
2. Greenville, N.C.	382
3. Marshfield–Wisconsin Rapids, Wis.	341
4. Salisbury, Md.	247
4. Wenatchee, Wash.	247
6. Hattiesburg, Miss.	240
7. Mason City, Iowa	238
8. Missoula, Mont.	234
8. Traverse City, Mich.	234
10. Madisonville, Ky.	230

Lowest

219. Hinesville, Ga.	29
218. Del Rio, Tex.	46
217. Athens, Ala.	54
216. Minden, La.	59
213. Casa Grande–Apache Junction, Ariz.	60
213. Sidney, Ohio	60
213. Sierra Vista, Ariz.	60
211. Crowley, La.	64
211. Greenville, Tex.	64
210. Alamogordo, N.Mex.	65

(Figure following each area name indicates doctors per 100,000 residents; figure in parentheses represents rating points.)

Alabama

Athens	54	(1)
Auburn–Opelika	113	(7)
Decatur	98	(5)
Enterprise	74	(3)
Selma	126	(8)
Talladega	69	(2)

Alaska

Fairbanks	122	(8)

Arizona

Bullhead City– Lake Havasu City	97	(5)
Casa Grande– Apache Junction	60	(2)
Flagstaff	126	(8)
Prescott	112	(7)
Sierra Vista	60	(2)
Yuma	105	(6)

Arkansas

Blytheville	85	(4)
El Dorado	160	(12)
Hot Springs	174	(13)
Jonesboro	219	(17)
Rogers	101	(6)
Russellville	122	(8)

California

El Centro–Calexico– Brawley	74	(3)
Eureka	165	(12)
Hanford	76	(3)
Madera	79	(3)
San Luis Obispo– Atascadero	174	(13)

Colorado

Grand Junction	163	(12)

Connecticut

Torrington	161	(12)

Delaware

Dover	97	(5)

Florida

Key West	122	(8)
Vero Beach	187	(14)

Georgia

Brunswick	199	(15)
Carrollton	106	(6)
Dalton	132	(9)
Gainesville	155	(11)
Hinesville	29	(0)
La Grange	127	(8)
Rome	215	(17)
Valdosta	130	(9)

Idaho

Coeur d'Alene	128	(8)
Idaho Falls	154	(11)
Nampa–Caldwell	119	(7)
Pocatello	139	(9)
Twin Falls	176	(13)

Illinois

Carbondale	154	(11)
Danville	118	(7)
De Kalb	94	(5)
Freeport	119	(7)
Galesburg	153	(11)
Mattoon–Charleston	116	(7)
Ottawa	97	(5)
Quincy	176	(13)
Sterling	75	(3)

Indiana

Columbus	145	(10)
Marion	112	(7)
Michigan City–La Porte	131	(9)
New Castle	80	(4)
Richmond	130	(9)
Vincennes	140	(10)

Iowa

Ames	134	(9)
Burlington	161	(12)
Clinton	111	(7)
Fort Dodge	114	(7)
Marshalltown	142	(10)
Mason City	238	(19)
Muscatine	78	(3)

Kansas

Hutchinson	129	(8)
Manhattan	84	(4)
Salina	183	(14)

Kentucky

Bowling Green	145	(10)
Frankfort	130	(9)
Madisonville	230	(19)
Paducah	212	(17)
Radcliff–Elizabethtown	92	(5)
Richmond	121	(8)

Louisiana

Bogalusa	96	(5)
Crowley	64	(2)
Hammond	97	(5)
Minden	59	(1)
Morgan City	76	(3)
New Iberia	104	(6)
Opelousas	102	(6)
Ruston	89	(4)

Maine

Augusta–Waterville	191	(15)
Biddeford	90	(5)

Maryland

Salisbury	247	(20)

Michigan

Adrian	81	(4)
Marquette	179	(13)
Mount Pleasant	79	(3)
Owosso	73	(3)
Traverse City	234	(19)

Minnesota

Faribault	82	(4)
Mankato	156	(11)
Winona	94	(5)

Mississippi

Columbus	110	(7)
Greenville	109	(6)
Greenwood	94	(5)
Hattiesburg	240	(20)
Laurel	107	(6)
Meridian	192	(15)
Tupelo	189	(14)
Vicksburg	145	(10)

Missouri

Cape Girardeau	196	(15)
Jefferson City	125	(8)
Sikeston	82	(4)

Montana

Bozeman	164	(12)
Helena	161	(12)
Missoula	234	(19)

Nebraska

Grand Island	125	(8)

Nevada

Carson City	180	(14)

New Hampshire

Concord	165	(12)
Keene	147	(10)
Laconia	175	(13)

New Mexico

Alamogordo	65	(2)
Carlsbad	103	(6)
Clovis	85	(4)
Farmington	86	(4)
Gallup	111	(7)
Hobbs	75	(3)
Rio Rancho	95	(5)
Roswell	124	(8)

New York

Auburn	96	(5)
Batavia	103	(6)
Cortland	103	(6)
Gloversville	112	(7)
Ithaca	169	(12)
Jamestown	107	(6)
Kingston	150	(11)
Olean	130	(9)
Plattsburgh	118	(7)
Watertown	116	(7)

North Carolina

Eden	69	(2)
Goldsboro	105	(6)
Greenville	382	(20)
Havelock–New Bern	137	(9)
Kinston	137	(9)
Lumberton	78	(3)
Roanoke Rapids	86	(4)
Rocky Mount	102	(6)
Sanford	131	(9)
Shelby	99	(5)
Statesville	102	(6)
Wilson	132	(9)

North Dakota

Minot	155	(11)

Ohio

Ashland	78	(3)
Ashtabula	68	(2)
Athens	70	(3)
Chillicothe	96	(5)
East Liverpool	74	(3)
Findlay	111	(7)
Fremont	77	(3)
Marion	168	(12)
New Philadelphia	82	(4)
Portsmouth	89	(4)
Sandusky	149	(10)
Sidney	60	(2)
Tiffin	96	(5)
Wooster	83	(4)
Zanesville	130	(9)

Oklahoma

Ardmore	119	(7)
Bartlesville	180	(14)
Chickasha	82	(4)
Duncan	71	(3)
McAlester	118	(7)
Muskogee	121	(8)
Okmulgee	68	(2)
Ponca City	112	(7)
Stillwater	109	(6)

Oregon

Albany	96	(5)
Bend	185	(14)
Corvallis	209	(16)
Grants Pass	102	(6)
Klamath Falls	114	(7)
Roseburg	131	(9)

Pennsylvania

Butler	68	(2)
Chambersburg	110	(7)
New Castle	81	(4)
Pottsville	95	(5)

Rhode Island

Newport	124	(8)

South Carolina

Greenwood	188	(14)
Hilton Head Island	118	(7)
Myrtle Beach	109	(6)
Orangeburg	95	(5)
Sumter	85	(4)

Tennessee

Cleveland	119	(7)
Columbia	129	(8)
Cookeville	101	(6)
Morristown	104	(6)
Tullahoma	94	(5)

Texas

Alice	72	(3)
Bay City	75	(3)
Del Rio	46	(0)
Greenville	64	(2)
Huntsville	97	(5)
Lufkin	110	(7)
Nacogdoches	137	(9)
Palestine	78	(3)
Paris	168	(12)

Utah

Logan	120	(8)

Vermont

Rutland	153	(11)

Virginia

Blacksburg	146	(10)
Fredericksburg	206	(16)
Harrisonburg	135	(9)
Martinsville	95	(5)
Staunton–Waynesboro	160	(12)
Winchester	217	(17)

Washington

Aberdeen	95	(5)
Longview	143	(10)
Port Angeles	159	(11)
Pullman	102	(6)
Walla Walla	200	(16)
Wenatchee	247	(20)

West Virginia

Beckley	171	(13)
Clarksburg	156	(11)
Fairmont	97	(5)
Morgantown	620	(20)

Wisconsin

Fond du Lac	119	(7)
Manitowoc	105	(6)
Marshfield– Wisconsin Rapids	341	(20)
Stevens Point	113	(7)

Wyoming

Rock Springs	72	(3)

Specialist Availability

There are times when a general practitioner simply will not do. Many medical problems require the attention of specialists.

There are approximately 193,000 doctors in the United States who are classified as medical or surgical specialists and who work out of their own offices, not as part of hospital staffs. Included are physicians who specialize in allergies, cardiovascular diseases, dermatology, internal medicine, pediatrics, and all forms of surgery.

This category ranks each area according to its number of specialists, expressed as a rate per 100,000 residents. The average for the entire country is 80.0 per 100,000.

Marshfield–Wisconsin Rapids, Wisconsin, offers its population a broad choice of office-based specialists: 53 are surgeons and 90 are classified in other medical fields. The total of 143 translates to a rate of 185 per 100,000.

Rio Rancho, New Mexico, has only 6 medical or surgical specialists, a rate of 12 per 100,000. Most residents travel to nearby Albuquerque for health care.

All four regions of the country boast cities with strong availability rates for specialists. Most of the towns with poor records are in the South and the Midwest.

Source. These statistics, published in 1987, are for 1986. Derived from *Physician Characteristics and Distribution in the U.S.* (Chicago: American Medical Association, 1987).

Scoring. Twenty points for 153 or more specialists per 100,000; no points for 19 or fewer. The spacing is every 7 per 100,000.

Highest	Medical and Surgical Specialists Per 100,000 Residents
1. Marshfield–Wisconsin Rapids, Wis.	185
2. Morgantown, W.Va.	174
3. Salisbury, Md.	154
4. Paducah, Ky.	146
5. Hattiesburg, Miss.	142
6. Winchester, Va.	136
7. Missoula, Mont.	131
8. Mason City, Iowa	127
9. Wenatchee, Wash.	124
10. Traverse City, Mich.	123

Lowest	
219. Rio Rancho, N.Mex.	12
218. Crowley, La.	15
217. Faribault, Minn.	17
216. Athens, Ohio	19
215. New Castle, Ind.	20
213. Athens, Ala.	21
213. Casa Grande– Apache Junction, Ariz.	21
212. Hinesville, Ga.	24
210. Del Rio, Tex.	25
210. Sidney, Ohio	25

(Figure following each area name indicates the number of specialists per 100,000 residents; figure in parentheses represents rating points.)

Alabama

Athens	21	(1)
Auburn–Opelika	66	(7)
Decatur	59	(6)
Enterprise	47	(4)
Selma	61	(6)
Talladega	41	(4)

Alaska

Fairbanks	58	(6)

Arizona

Bullhead City– Lake Havasu City	43	(4)
Casa Grande– Apache Junction	21	(1)
Flagstaff	58	(6)
Prescott	63	(7)
Sierra Vista	31	(2)
Yuma	65	(7)

Arkansas

Blytheville	36	(3)
El Dorado	78	(9)
Hot Springs	94	(11)
Jonesboro	101	(12)
Rogers	34	(3)
Russellville	55	(6)

California

El Centro–Calexico– Brawley	42	(4)
Eureka	75	(8)
Hanford	30	(2)
Madera	35	(3)
San Luis Obispo– Atascadero	78	(9)

Colorado

Grand Junction	72	(8)

Connecticut

Torrington	76	(9)

Delaware

Dover	53	(5)

Florida

Key West	62	(7)
Vero Beach	116	(14)

Georgia

Brunswick	99	(12)
Carrollton	57	(6)
Dalton	75	(8)
Gainesville	100	(12)
Hinesville	24	(1)
La Grange	77	(9)
Rome	109	(13)
Valdosta	79	(9)

Idaho

Coeur d'Alene	58	(6)
Idaho Falls	92	(11)
Nampa–Caldwell	63	(7)
Pocatello	70	(8)
Twin Falls	99	(12)

Illinois

Carbondale	76	(9)
Danville	53	(5)
De Kalb	54	(5)
Freeport	83	(10)
Galesburg	69	(8)
Mattoon–Charleston	58	(6)
Ottawa	45	(4)
Quincy	98	(12)
Sterling	38	(3)

Indiana

Columbus	59	(6)
Marion	56	(6)
Michigan City–La Porte	60	(6)
New Castle	20	(1)
Richmond	57	(6)
Vincennes	72	(8)

Iowa

Ames	68	(7)
Burlington	85	(10)
Clinton	62	(7)
Fort Dodge	56	(6)
Marshalltown	74	(8)
Mason City	127	(16)
Muscatine	27	(2)

Kansas

Hutchinson	80	(9)
Manhattan	46	(4)
Salina	104	(13)

Kentucky

Bowling Green	75	(8)
Frankfort	57	(6)
Madisonville	101	(12)
Paducah	146	(19)
Radcliff–Elizabethtown	48	(5)
Richmond	58	(6)

Louisiana

Bogalusa	34	(3)
Crowley	15	(0)
Hammond	42	(4)
Minden	30	(2)
Morgan City	37	(3)
New Iberia	49	(5)
Opelousas	45	(4)
Ruston	61	(6)

Maine

Augusta–Waterville	83	(10)
Biddeford	40	(3)

Maryland

Salisbury	154	(20)

Michigan

Adrian	39	(3)
Marquette	91	(11)
Mount Pleasant	48	(5)
Owosso	41	(4)
Traverse City	123	(15)

Minnesota

Faribault	17	(0)
Mankato	92	(11)
Winona	52	(5)

Mississippi

Columbus	76	(9)
Greenville	66	(7)
Greenwood	48	(5)
Hattiesburg	142	(18)
Laurel	51	(5)
Meridian	113	(14)
Tupelo	122	(15)
Vicksburg	80	(9)

Missouri

Cape Girardeau	100	(12)
Jefferson City	66	(7)
Sikeston	50	(5)

Montana

Bozeman	77	(9)
Helena	88	(10)
Missoula	131	(16)

Nebraska

Grand Island	61	(6)

Nevada

Carson City	76	(9)

New Hampshire

Concord	87	(10)
Keene	64	(7)
Laconia	102	(12)

New Mexico

Alamogordo	36	(3)
Carlsbad	63	(7)
Clovis	53	(5)
Farmington	40	(3)
Gallup	43	(4)
Hobbs	35	(3)
Rio Rancho	12	(0)
Roswell	67	(7)

New York

Auburn	61	(6)
Batavia	48	(5)
Cortland	70	(8)
Gloversville	49	(5)
Ithaca	79	(9)
Jamestown	61	(6)
Kingston	60	(6)
Olean	79	(9)
Plattsburgh	63	(7)
Watertown	72	(8)

North Carolina

Eden	35	(3)
Goldsboro	49	(5)
Greenville	121	(15)
Havelock–New Bern	76	(9)
Kinston	78	(9)
Lumberton	35	(3)
Roanoke Rapids	48	(5)
Rocky Mount	53	(5)
Sanford	51	(5)
Shelby	57	(6)
Statesville	69	(8)
Wilson	82	(9)

North Dakota

Minot	83	(10)

Ohio

Ashland	39	(3)
Ashtabula	37	(3)
Athens	19	(0)
Chillicothe	56	(6)
East Liverpool	34	(3)
Findlay	64	(7)
Fremont	35	(3)
Marion	93	(11)
New Philadelphia	32	(2)
Portsmouth	39	(3)
Sandusky	66	(7)
Sidney	25	(1)
Tiffin	42	(4)
Wooster	41	(4)
Zanesville	69	(8)

Oklahoma

Ardmore	78	(9)
Bartlesville	78	(9)
Chickasha	45	(4)
Duncan	27	(2)
McAlester	59	(6)
Muskogee	67	(7)
Okmulgee	33	(2)
Ponca City	40	(3)
Stillwater	55	(6)

Oregon

Albany	43	(4)
Bend	93	(11)
Corvallis	110	(13)
Grants Pass	54	(5)
Klamath Falls	54	(5)
Roseburg	52	(5)

Pennsylvania

Butler	38	(3)
Chambersburg	44	(4)
New Castle	45	(4)
Pottsville	42	(4)

Rhode Island

Newport	57	(6)

South Carolina

Greenwood	91	(11)
Hilton Head Island	68	(7)
Myrtle Beach	54	(5)
Orangeburg	44	(4)
Sumter	51	(5)

Tennessee

Cleveland	69	(8)
Columbia	69	(8)
Cookeville	61	(6)
Morristown	51	(5)
Tullahoma	44	(4)

Texas

Alice	32	(2)
Bay City	32	(2)
Del Rio	25	(1)
Greenville	36	(3)
Huntsville	39	(3)
Lufkin	52	(5)
Nacogdoches	71	(8)
Palestine	42	(4)
Paris	109	(13)

Utah

Logan	75	(8)

Vermont

Rutland	87	(10)

Virginia

Blacksburg	77	(9)
Fredericksburg	110	(13)
Harrisonburg	61	(6)
Martinsville	55	(6)
Staunton–Waynesboro	70	(8)
Winchester	136	(17)

Washington

Aberdeen	40	(3)
Longview	67	(7)
Port Angeles	60	(6)
Pullman	39	(3)
Walla Walla	113	(14)
Wenatchee	124	(15)

West Virginia

Beckley	89	(10)
Clarksburg	63	(7)
Fairmont	55	(6)
Morgantown	174	(20)

Wisconsin

Fond du Lac	62	(7)
Manitowoc	54	(5)
Marshfield– Wisconsin Rapids	185	(20)
Stevens Point	61	(6)

Wyoming

Rock Springs	26	(1)

Hospital Availability

Many hospitals in metropolitan areas are overcrowded. A reporter visiting the Brookdale Hospital Medical Center in Brooklyn in 1988 found that not only were all 800 beds occupied but 31 patients were in the emergency room waiting to be admitted.

Such congestion underscores the need for adequate hospital facilities in all cities, large or small. This category calculates each area's number of available hospital beds in a rate per 100,000 residents. Included are all beds, cribs, and pediatric bassinets. The national average is 554 spaces per 100,000.

The Kinston, North Carolina, area has two hospitals with a combined total of 1,354 beds. Kinston's rate of 2,238 per 100,000 is particularly noteworthy because most of North Carolina's cities have figures below the national norm.

Rio Rancho, New Mexico, is the only micropolitan area without a hospital. Residents have no real concern, because adjacent Bernalillo County has 19 medical centers.

Midwestern cities generally offer the most favorable availability rates for hospital beds, Western cities the least.

Source. These statistics, published in 1988, are for 1985. U.S. Bureau of the Census, *County and City Data Book* (Washington: U.S. Government Printing Office, 1988).

Scoring. Twenty points for 1,150 spaces or more per 100,000; no points for 199 or fewer. The spacing is every 50 per 100,000.

Highest	Hospital Beds Per 100,000 Residents
1. Kinston, N.C.	2,238
2. Faribault, Minn.	2,171
3. Meridian, Miss.	1,892
4. Chillicothe, Ohio	1,792
5. Danville, Ill.	1,632
6. Staunton–Waynesboro, Va.	1,406
7. Marion, Ind.	1,357
8. Minot, N.Dak.	1,336
9. Augusta–Waterville, Maine	1,271
10. Richmond, Ind.	1,264

Lowest

219. Rio Rancho, N.Mex.	0
218. Madera, Calif.	140
217. Grants Pass, Oreg.	188
216. Muscatine, Iowa	190
215. Farmington, N.Mex.	191
214. Greenville, Tex.	193
213. New Castle, Ind.	205
212. Huntsville, Tex.	209
210. Palestine, Tex.	213
210. Pullman, Wash.	213

(Figure following each area name indicates hospital beds per 100,000 residents; figure in parentheses represents rating points.)

Alabama

Athens	266	(2)
Auburn–Opelika	353	(4)
Decatur	590	(8)
Enterprise	891	(14)
Selma	514	(7)
Talladega	394	(4)

Alaska

Fairbanks	347	(3)

Arizona

Bullhead City–		
Lake Havasu City	282	(2)
Casa Grande–		
Apache Junction	289	(2)
Flagstaff	277	(2)
Prescott	736	(11)
Sierra Vista	389	(4)
Yuma	269	(2)

Arkansas

Blytheville	488	(6)
El Dorado	582	(8)
Hot Springs	650	(10)
Jonesboro	568	(8)
Rogers	396	(4)
Russellville	337	(3)

California

El Centro–Calexico–		
Brawley	220	(1)
Eureka	301	(3)
Hanford	260	(2)
Madera	140	(0)
San Luis Obispo–		
Atascadero	825	(13)

Colorado

Grand Junction	703	(11)

Connecticut

Torrington	263	(2)

Delaware

Dover	756	(12)

Florida

Key West	359	(4)
Vero Beach	480	(6)

Georgia

Brunswick	680	(10)
Carrollton	438	(5)
Dalton	346	(3)
Gainesville	567	(8)
Hinesville	356	(4)
La Grange	739	(11)
Rome	1,113	(19)
Valdosta	583	(8)

Idaho

Coeur d'Alene	250	(2)
Idaho Falls	516	(7)
Nampa–Caldwell	369	(4)
Pocatello	398	(4)
Twin Falls	342	(3)

Illinois

Carbondale	354	(4)
Danville	1,632	(20)
De Kalb	348	(3)
Freeport	370	(4)
Galesburg	648	(9)
Mattoon–Charleston	366	(4)
Ottawa	540	(7)
Quincy	680	(10)
Sterling	345	(3)

Indiana

Columbus	345	(3)
Marion	1,357	(20)
Michigan City–La Porte	544	(7)
New Castle	205	(1)
Richmond	1,264	(20)
Vincennes	688	(10)

Iowa

Ames	525	(7)
Burlington	870	(14)
Clinton	669	(10)
Fort Dodge	452	(6)
Marshalltown	430	(5)
Mason City	822	(13)
Muscatine	190	(0)

Kansas

Hutchinson	353	(4)
Manhattan	288	(2)
Salina	718	(11)

Kentucky

Bowling Green	660	(10)
Frankfort	358	(4)
Madisonville	880	(14)
Paducah	1,100	(19)
Radcliff–Elizabethtown	402	(5)
Richmond	394	(4)

Louisiana

Bogalusa	522	(7)
Crowley	296	(2)
Hammond	473	(6)
Minden	423	(5)
Morgan City	317	(3)
New Iberia	350	(4)
Opelousas	440	(5)
Ruston	303	(3)

Maine

Augusta–Waterville	1,271	(20)
Biddeford	268	(2)

Maryland

Salisbury	767	(12)

Michigan

Adrian	385	(4)
Marquette	612	(9)
Mount Pleasant	227	(1)
Owosso	235	(1)
Traverse City	951	(16)

Minnesota

Faribault	2,171	(20)
Mankato	362	(4)
Winona	493	(6)

Mississippi

Columbus	608	(9)
Greenville	624	(9)
Greenwood	541	(7)
Hattiesburg	943	(15)
Laurel	576	(8)
Meridian	1,892	(20)
Tupelo	921	(15)
Vicksburg	863	(14)

Missouri

Cape Girardeau	867	(14)
Jefferson City	969	(16)
Sikeston	499	(6)

Montana

Bozeman	274	(2)
Helena	590	(8)
Missoula	473	(6)

Nebraska

Grand Island	925	(15)

Nevada

Carson City	272	(2)

New Hampshire

Concord	852	(14)
Keene	533	(7)
Laconia	339	(3)

New Mexico

Alamogordo	245	(1)
Carlsbad	347	(3)
Clovis	343	(3)
Farmington	191	(0)
Gallup	445	(5)
Hobbs	440	(5)
Rio Rancho	0	(0)
Roswell	662	(10)

New York

Auburn	368	(4)
Batavia	738	(11)
Cortland	373	(4)
Gloversville	319	(3)
Ithaca	217	(1)
Jamestown	507	(7)
Kingston	311	(3)
Olean	463	(6)
Plattsburgh	551	(8)
Watertown	916	(15)

North Carolina

Eden	334	(3)
Goldsboro	1,143	(19)
Greenville	659	(10)
Havelock–New Bern	355	(4)
Kinston	2,238	(20)
Lumberton	410	(5)
Roanoke Rapids	376	(4)
Rocky Mount	354	(4)
Sanford	351	(4)
Shelby	527	(7)
Statesville	517	(7)
Wilson	431	(5)

North Dakota

Minot	1,336	(20)

Ohio

Ashland	284	(2)
Ashtabula	433	(5)
Athens	739	(11)
Chillicothe	1,792	(20)
East Liverpool	477	(6)
Findlay	362	(4)
Fremont	671	(10)
Marion	636	(9)
New Philadelphia	329	(3)
Portsmouth	634	(9)
Sandusky	631	(9)
Sidney	257	(2)
Tiffin	284	(2)
Wooster	608	(9)
Zanesville	686	(10)

Oklahoma

Ardmore	540	(7)
Bartlesville	668	(10)
Chickasha	347	(3)
Duncan	345	(3)
McAlester	463	(6)
Muskogee	728	(11)
Okmulgee	383	(4)
Ponca City	316	(3)
Stillwater	388	(4)

Oregon

Albany	215	(1)
Bend	347	(3)
Corvallis	219	(1)
Grants Pass	188	(0)
Klamath Falls	335	(3)
Roseburg	790	(12)

Pennsylvania

Butler	450	(6)
Chambersburg	935	(15)
New Castle	479	(6)
Pottsville	462	(6)

Rhode Island
Newport	411	(5)

South Carolina
Greenwood	525	(7)
Hilton Head Island	272	(2)
Myrtle Beach	335	(3)
Orangeburg	332	(3)
Sumter	265	(2)

Tennessee
Cleveland	450	(6)
Columbia	444	(5)
Cookeville	353	(4)
Morristown	537	(7)
Tullahoma	722	(11)

Texas
Alice	223	(1)
Bay City	381	(4)
Del Rio	269	(2)
Greenville	193	(0)
Huntsville	209	(1)
Lufkin	538	(7)
Nacogdoches	699	(10)
Palestine	213	(1)
Paris	866	(14)

Utah
Logan	238	(1)

Vermont
Rutland	384	(4)

Virginia
Blacksburg	223	(1)
Fredericksburg	586	(8)
Harrisonburg	325	(3)
Martinsville	311	(3)
Staunton–Waynesboro	1,406	(20)
Winchester	731	(11)

Washington
Aberdeen	441	(5)
Longview	330	(3)
Port Angeles	282	(2)
Pullman	213	(1)
Walla Walla	858	(14)
Wenatchee	385	(4)

West Virginia
Beckley	878	(14)
Clarksburg	690	(10)
Fairmont	345	(3)
Morgantown	862	(14)

Wisconsin
Fond du Lac	541	(7)
Manitowoc	469	(6)
Marshfield– Wisconsin Rapids	1,029	(17)
Stevens Point	222	(1)

Wyoming
Rock Springs	224	(1)

Local Health Funding

A strong commitment by local government to medical care not only results in a healthier community but also saves money for consumers. A 1986 study by a branch of the National Academy of Sciences reported that both for-profit and nonprofit hospitals do their jobs well, but the private facilities typically charge patients anywhere from 8 to 24 percent more than the public centers do.

This category ranks each area according to the amount of money allocated to health care by its county and city governments. Included are all expenditures for hospitals, clinics, environmental health activities, and public health administration. The annual total is divided by the number of residents.

Muskogee, Oklahoma, devotes 47 percent of its public dollars to health, an astounding figure given the national average of 8 percent. Muskogee's annual total equals $713 for every man, woman, and child, compared with the U.S. norm of $92 per capita.

Alice, Texas, and Rio Rancho, New Mexico, both spend less than 50 cents per person on health care. Their totals round to zero.

Southern cities show the strongest financial commitment to health. But there are exceptions. Several communities in the South, as well as the West, devote few resources.

Source. These statistics, published in 1988, are for the 1981–1982 budget year. Derived from U.S. Bureau of the Census, *County and City Data Book* (Washington: U.S. Government Printing Office, 1988).

Scoring. Twenty points for $390 or more per capita; no points for $9 or less. The spacing is every $20 per capita.

**Annual Per Capita
Health-Related Spending
By Local Governments**

Highest	**$**
1. Muskogee, Okla.	713
2. Vincennes, Ind.	689
3. Greenwood, S.C.	530
4. Brunswick, Ga.	496
5. Hattiesburg, Miss.	472
6. Columbus, Ind.	466
7. Dalton, Ga.	421
8. La Grange, Ga.	410
9. Nacogdoches, Tex.	404
10. Gainesville, Ga.	402

Lowest	
218. Alice, Tex.	0
218. Rio Rancho, N.Mex.	0
210. Alamogordo, N.Mex.	1
210. Blacksburg, Va.	1
210. Clovis, N.Mex.	1
210. Galesburg, Ill.	1
210. Gallup, N.Mex.	1
210. Martinsville, Va.	1
210. Salisbury, Md.	1
210. Staunton–Waynesboro, Va.	1

(Figure following each area name indicates annual per capita health-related spending by local governments in dollars; figure in parentheses represents rating points.)

Alabama

Athens	116	(6)
Auburn–Opelika	240	(12)
Decatur	229	(11)
Enterprise	25	(1)
Selma	8	(0)
Talladega	154	(8)

Alaska

Fairbanks	27	(1)

Arizona

Bullhead City– Lake Havasu City	136	(7)
Casa Grande– Apache Junction	69	(3)
Flagstaff	28	(1)
Prescott	103	(5)
Sierra Vista	78	(4)
Yuma	52	(3)

Arkansas

Blytheville	179	(9)
El Dorado	213	(11)
Hot Springs	130	(7)
Jonesboro	6	(0)
Rogers	45	(2)
Russellville	9	(0)

California

El Centro–Calexico– Brawley	373	(19)
Eureka	72	(4)
Hanford	110	(6)
Madera	67	(3)
San Luis Obispo– Atascadero	94	(5)

Colorado

Grand Junction	19	(1)

Connecticut

Torrington	6	(0)

Delaware

Dover	4	(0)

Florida

Key West	125	(6)
Vero Beach	318	(16)

Georgia

Brunswick	496	(20)
Carrollton	324	(16)
Dalton	421	(20)
Gainesville	402	(20)
Hinesville	85	(4)
La Grange	410	(20)
Rome	334	(17)
Valdosta	366	(18)

Idaho

Coeur d'Alene	240	(12)
Idaho Falls	10	(1)
Nampa–Caldwell	6	(0)
Pocatello	204	(10)
Twin Falls	313	(16)

Illinois

Carbondale	30	(2)
Danville	10	(1)
De Kalb	64	(3)
Freeport	7	(0)
Galesburg	1	(0)
Mattoon–Charleston	11	(1)
Ottawa	11	(1)
Quincy	12	(1)
Sterling	202	(10)

Indiana

Columbus	466	(20)
Marion	3	(0)
Michigan City–La Porte	4	(0)
New Castle	258	(13)
Richmond	9	(0)
Vincennes	689	(20)

Iowa

Ames	287	(14)
Burlington	21	(1)
Clinton	17	(1)
Fort Dodge	8	(0)
Marshalltown	22	(1)
Mason City	10	(1)
Muscatine	191	(10)

Kansas

Hutchinson	11	(1)
Manhattan	12	(1)
Salina	15	(1)

Kentucky

Bowling Green	45	(2)
Frankfort	12	(1)
Madisonville	7	(0)
Paducah	26	(1)
Radcliff–Elizabethtown	175	(9)
Richmond	21	(1)

Louisiana

Bogalusa	163	(8)
Crowley	93	(5)
Hammond	156	(8)
Minden	22	(1)
Morgan City	286	(14)
New Iberia	183	(9)
Opelousas	242	(12)
Ruston	16	(1)

Maine

Augusta–Waterville	2	(0)
Biddeford	4	(0)

Maryland

Salisbury	1	(0)

Michigan

Adrian	149	(7)
Marquette	100	(5)
Mount Pleasant	80	(4)
Owosso	78	(4)
Traverse City	103	(5)

Minnesota

Faribault	308	(15)
Mankato	8	(0)
Winona	8	(0)

Mississippi

Columbus	241	(12)
Greenville	191	(10)
Greenwood	266	(13)
Hattiesburg	472	(20)
Laurel	283	(14)
Meridian	9	(0)
Tupelo	8	(0)
Vicksburg	8	(0)

Missouri

Cape Girardeau	2	(0)
Jefferson City	8	(0)
Sikeston	14	(1)

Montana

Bozeman	14	(1)
Helena	13	(1)
Missoula	25	(1)

Nebraska

Grand Island	4	(0)

Nevada

Carson City	221	(11)

New Hampshire

Concord	3	(0)
Keene	3	(0)
Laconia	5	(0)

New Mexico

Alamogordo	1	(0)
Carlsbad	3	(0)
Clovis	1	(0)
Farmington	3	(0)
Gallup	1	(0)
Hobbs	4	(0)
Rio Rancho	0	(0)
Roswell	129	(6)

New York

Auburn	55	(3)
Batavia	29	(1)
Cortland	31	(2)
Gloversville	19	(1)
Ithaca	36	(2)
Jamestown	88	(4)
Kingston	74	(4)
Olean	74	(4)
Plattsburgh	78	(4)
Watertown	19	(1)

North Carolina

Eden	29	(1)
Goldsboro	201	(10)
Greenville	14	(1)
Havelock–New Bern	362	(18)
Kinston	312	(16)
Lumberton	16	(1)
Roanoke Rapids	44	(2)
Rocky Mount	20	(1)
Sanford	217	(11)
Shelby	20	(1)
Statesville	13	(1)
Wilson	8	(0)

North Dakota

Minot	4	(0)

Ohio

Ashland	20	(1)
Ashtabula	22	(1)
Athens	85	(4)
Chillicothe	30	(2)
East Liverpool	20	(1)
Findlay	19	(1)
Fremont	11	(1)
Marion	271	(14)
New Philadelphia	27	(1)
Portsmouth	33	(2)
Sandusky	38	(2)
Sidney	16	(1)
Tiffin	42	(2)
Wooster	137	(7)
Zanesville	51	(3)

Oklahoma

Ardmore	210	(11)
Bartlesville	2	(0)
Chickasha	253	(13)
Duncan	3	(0)
McAlester	300	(15)
Muskogee	713	(20)
Okmulgee	17	(1)
Ponca City	5	(0)
Stillwater	263	(13)

Oregon

Albany	26	(1)
Bend	149	(7)
Corvallis	27	(1)
Grants Pass	37	(2)
Klamath Falls	27	(1)
Roseburg	52	(3)

Pennsylvania

Butler	23	(1)
Chambersburg	41	(2)
New Castle	16	(1)
Pottsville	81	(4)

Rhode Island

Newport	2	(0)

South Carolina

Greenwood	530	(20)
Hilton Head Island	101	(5)
Myrtle Beach	9	(0)
Orangeburg	329	(16)
Sumter	6	(0)

Tennessee

Cleveland	250	(13)
Columbia	319	(16)
Cookeville	316	(16)
Morristown	8	(0)
Tullahoma	158	(8)

Texas

Alice	0	(0)
Bay City	258	(13)
Del Rio	3	(0)
Greenville	101	(5)
Huntsville	13	(1)
Lufkin	57	(3)
Nacogdoches	404	(20)
Palestine	195	(10)
Paris	277	(14)

Utah

Logan	8	(0)

Vermont

Rutland	2	(0)

Virginia

Blacksburg	1	(0)
Fredericksburg	4	(0)
Harrisonburg	5	(0)
Martinsville	1	(0)
Staunton–Waynesboro	1	(0)
Winchester	2	(0)

Washington

Aberdeen	52	(3)
Longview	23	(1)
Port Angeles	248	(12)
Pullman	84	(4)
Walla Walla	24	(1)
Wenatchee	53	(3)

West Virginia

Beckley	3	(0)
Clarksburg	6	(0)
Fairmont	328	(16)
Morgantown	27	(1)

Wisconsin

Fond du Lac	122	(6)
Manitowoc	128	(6)
Marshfield– Wisconsin Rapids	138	(7)
Stevens Point	116	(6)

Wyoming

Rock Springs	235	(12)

Death Rate

The East has the highest death rate among the nation's four major regions, followed in order by the Midwest, the South, and the West. A listing of the percentage of elderly residents has the identical ranking, starting with the aging East and ending with the youthful West.

It is obvious the larger number of deaths in the East does not reflect on the competence of its doctors. The correlation between age and dying is a simple one. So why include the death rate as a category? The intent is to measure the strain placed on each area's health-care system. The greater the number of terminal patients, the less the attention that can be given to people with smaller complaints.

Manhattan, Kansas, is dominated by Kansas State University. Nearly 40 percent of its residents are between the ages of 15 and 24; the national figure is just 17 percent. Manhattan is typical of the college and military towns that crowd the list of those with the lowest death rates.

Pottsville, Pennsylvania, has a much older population than the country as a whole. Its annual death rate of 13.9 per 1,000 residents is also well above the national average of 8.6 per 1,000.

Source. These statistics, published in 1988, are for 1984. U.S. Bureau of the Census, *County and City Data Book* (Washington: U.S. Government Printing Office, 1988).

Scoring. Twenty points for a death rate of 3.9 or less per 1,000; no points for 13.5 or more. The spacing is every 0.5 per 1,000.

Lowest	Annual Deaths Per 1,000 Residents
1. Manhattan, Kans.	3.6
2. Fairbanks, Alaska	3.8
2. Hinesville, Ga.	3.8
4. Flagstaff, Ariz.	4.1
4. Rock Springs, Wyo.	4.1
6. Pullman, Wash.	4.7
7. Ames, Iowa	5.0
7. Farmington, N.Mex.	5.0
9. Bozeman, Mont.	5.2
9. Radcliff–Elizabethtown, Ky.	5.2

Highest

219. Pottsville, Pa.	13.9
218. Hot Springs, Ariz.	13.1
217. Okmulgee, Okla.	12.8
216. Paris, Tex.	12.0
214. Prescott, Ariz.	11.9
214. Quincy, Ill.	11.9
213. Minden, La.	11.8
212. Portsmouth, Ohio	11.7
211. Vincennes, Ind.	11.6
209. Clarksburg, W.Va.	11.5
209. Vero Beach, Fla.	11.5

(Figure following each area name indicates deaths per 1,000 residents; figure in parentheses represents rating points.)

Alabama

Athens	8.0 (11)
Auburn–Opelika	6.9 (14)
Decatur	8.4 (11)
Enterprise	8.6 (10)
Selma	10.4 (7)
Talladega	9.4 (9)

Alaska

Fairbanks	3.8 (20)

Arizona

Bullhead City– Lake Havasu City	9.7 (8)
Casa Grande– Apache Junction	8.3 (11)
Flagstaff	4.1 (19)
Prescott	11.9 (4)
Sierra Vista	7.1 (13)
Yuma	7.8 (12)

Arkansas

Blytheville	9.8 (8)
El Dorado	11.2 (5)
Hot Springs	13.1 (1)
Jonesboro	8.7 (10)
Rogers	10.0 (7)
Russellville	8.0 (11)

California

El Centro–Calexico– Brawley	7.7 (12)
Eureka	8.8 (10)
Hanford	7.0 (13)
Madera	8.1 (11)
San Luis Obispo– Atascadero	8.4 (11)

Colorado

Grand Junction	7.6 (12)

Connecticut

Torrington	9.2 (9)

Delaware

Dover	7.2 (13)

Florida

Key West	8.7 (10)
Vero Beach	11.5 (4)

Georgia

Brunswick	9.1 (9)
Carrollton	8.5 (10)
Dalton	7.7 (12)
Gainesville	7.4 (13)
Hinesville	3.8 (20)
La Grange	10.5 (6)
Rome	9.9 (8)
Valdosta	8.4 (11)

Idaho

Coeur d'Alene	8.2 (11)
Idaho Falls	6.2 (15)
Nampa–Caldwell	8.7 (10)
Pocatello	6.4 (15)
Twin Falls	8.4 (11)

Illinois

Carbondale	8.1 (11)
Danville	9.8 (8)
De Kalb	7.4 (13)
Freeport	9.4 (9)
Galesburg	11.2 (5)
Mattoon–Charleston	9.1 (9)
Ottawa	10.5 (6)
Quincy	11.9 (4)
Sterling	8.4 (11)

Indiana

Columbus	7.4	(13)
Marion	9.6	(8)
Michigan City–La Porte	9.3	(9)
New Castle	10.6	(6)
Richmond	9.7	(8)
Vincennes	11.6	(4)

Iowa

Ames	5.0	(17)
Burlington	9.8	(8)
Clinton	9.8	(8)
Fort Dodge	10.8	(6)
Marshalltown	10.1	(7)
Mason City	10.9	(6)
Muscatine	9.2	(9)

Kansas

Hutchinson	9.8	(8)
Manhattan	3.6	(20)
Salina	8.4	(11)

Kentucky

Bowling Green	7.0	(13)
Frankfort	9.0	(9)
Madisonville	10.3	(7)
Paducah	10.6	(6)
Radcliff–Elizabethtown	5.2	(17)
Richmond	6.7	(14)

Louisiana

Bogalusa	10.1	(7)
Crowley	9.6	(8)
Hammond	8.4	(11)
Minden	11.8	(4)
Morgan City	7.3	(13)
New Iberia	8.0	(11)
Opelousas	9.2	(9)
Ruston	7.5	(12)

Maine

Augusta–Waterville	9.0	(9)
Biddeford	9.0	(9)

Maryland

Salisbury	10.8	(6)

Michigan

Adrian	7.9	(12)
Marquette	6.8	(14)
Mount Pleasant	5.9	(16)
Owosso	7.8	(12)
Traverse City	7.6	(12)

Minnesota

Faribault	8.2	(11)
Mankato	7.5	(12)
Winona	8.6	(10)

Mississippi

Columbus	7.8	(12)
Greenville	10.1	(7)
Greenwood	11.0	(5)
Hattiesburg	9.3	(9)
Laurel	10.3	(7)
Meridian	10.6	(6)
Tupelo	9.0	(9)
Vicksburg	9.5	(8)

Missouri

Cape Girardeau	8.3	(11)
Jefferson City	7.3	(13)
Sikeston	9.4	(9)

Montana

Bozeman	5.2	(17)
Helena	7.2	(13)
Missoula	6.3	(15)

Nebraska

Grand Island	9.4	(9)

Nevada

Carson City	8.8	(10)

New Hampshire

Concord	9.1 (9)
Keene	8.5 (10)
Laconia	10.6 (6)

New Mexico

Alamogordo	5.6 (16)
Carlsbad	8.9 (10)
Clovis	7.2 (13)
Farmington	5.0 (17)
Gallup	5.8 (16)
Hobbs	6.4 (15)
Rio Rancho	7.5 (12)
Roswell	9.0 (9)

New York

Auburn	9.9 (8)
Batavia	9.2 (9)
Cortland	9.1 (9)
Gloversville	10.4 (7)
Ithaca	6.6 (14)
Jamestown	10.9 (6)
Kingston	9.7 (8)
Olean	10.7 (6)
Plattsburgh	7.2 (13)
Watertown	10.7 (6)

North Carolina

Eden	9.2 (9)
Goldsboro	8.2 (11)
Greenville	7.9 (12)
Havelock–New Bern	6.7 (14)
Kinston	9.4 (9)
Lumberton	8.6 (10)
Roanoke Rapids	10.6 (6)
Rocky Mount	9.4 (9)
Sanford	8.5 (10)
Shelby	9.1 (9)
Statesville	8.8 (10)
Wilson	9.2 (9)

North Dakota

Minot	6.6 (14)

Ohio

Ashland	8.0 (11)
Ashtabula	9.3 (9)
Athens	7.5 (12)
Chillicothe	8.9 (10)
East Liverpool	10.2 (7)
Findlay	8.3 (11)
Fremont	8.8 (10)
Marion	8.8 (10)
New Philadelphia	10.7 (6)
Portsmouth	11.7 (4)
Sandusky	8.5 (10)
Sidney	8.3 (11)
Tiffin	8.2 (11)
Wooster	7.9 (12)
Zanesville	10.3 (7)

Oklahoma

Ardmore	10.8 (6)
Bartlesville	10.1 (7)
Chickasha	9.0 (9)
Duncan	10.0 (7)
McAlester	11.3 (5)
Muskogee	11.3 (5)
Okmulgee	12.8 (2)
Ponca City	10.0 (7)
Stillwater	6.7 (14)

Oregon

Albany	8.4 (11)
Bend	7.6 (12)
Corvallis	5.4 (17)
Grants Pass	10.6 (6)
Klamath Falls	8.3 (11)
Roseburg	9.3 (9)

Pennsylvania

Butler	8.9 (10)
Chambersburg	9.1 (9)
New Castle	10.5 (6)
Pottsville	13.9 (0)

Rhode Island

Newport	8.6 (10)

South Carolina

Greenwood	8.9 (10)
Hilton Head Island	5.3 (17)
Myrtle Beach	7.5 (12)
Orangeburg	8.8 (10)
Sumter	6.9 (14)

Tennessee

Cleveland	7.1 (13)
Columbia	11.0 (5)
Cookeville	8.8 (10)
Morristown	8.2 (11)
Tullahoma	9.2 (9)

Texas

Alice	7.9 (12)
Bay City	8.3 (11)
Del Rio	6.5 (14)
Greenville	9.8 (8)
Huntsville	5.3 (17)
Lufkin	8.6 (10)
Nacogdoches	8.9 (10)
Palestine	9.8 (8)
Paris	12.0 (3)

Utah

Logan	5.3 (17)

Vermont

Rutland	10.6 (6)

Virginia

Blacksburg	5.3 (17)
Fredericksburg	6.7 (14)
Harrisonburg	7.7 (12)
Martinsville	8.8 (10)
Staunton–Waynesboro	10.0 (7)
Winchester	9.1 (9)

Washington

Aberdeen	10.1 (7)
Longview	8.0 (11)
Port Angeles	10.5 (6)
Pullman	4.7 (18)
Walla Walla	10.5 (6)
Wenatchee	10.8 (6)

West Virginia

Beckley	10.0 (7)
Clarksburg	11.5 (4)
Fairmont	10.5 (6)
Morgantown	6.5 (14)

Wisconsin

Fond du Lac	8.4 (11)
Manitowoc	9.7 (8)
Marshfield–Wisconsin Rapids	7.6 (12)
Stevens Point	7.3 (13)

Wyoming

Rock Springs	4.1 (19)

The Results

Hattiesburg, Mississippi, owes much to the longleaf pines that form a broad belt across the southeastern part of the state. The lumber boom of the 1920s established the community as the dominant city of its region. The state guidebook produced by the Federal Writers' Project in 1938 depicted Hattiesburg as "a town whose heart is in the noisy factory district from which rise the pungent odors of turpentine and cut pine."

But Hattiesburg differed from other Southern lumber cities in its push to diversify its economy. It consequently prospered despite increased foreign competition in the wood market. The city is the home of the University of Southern Mississippi and its 10,000 students. It also has more than 8,000 manufacturing jobs in a variety of industries.

Health care is another important component of the local economy. Hattiesburg bills itself as "the medical center of South Mississippi," but for once, a chamber of commerce is guilty of understatement. The city occupies first place nationally in the health-care section, with 82 of a possible 100 points.

The county government operates Forrest County General Hospital, a 443-bed facility. The Methodist Hospital of Hattiesburg adds another 201 beds. The area's availability ratios for both doctors and specialists are among the best in micropolitan America.

Hattiesburg is joined by six other Southern cities in this section's list of the ten best communities. Two Midwestern towns and one from the East round out the health-care honor roll.

The South also dominates at the other end of the scale, placing eight cities among the eleven with the worst scores in this section. The lowest position belongs to Okmulgee, Oklahoma, with only 11 points.

Okmulgee, which means "bubbling water," was once the capital of the Creek Indian Nation. It is now an oil-refining and glass-manufacturing center.

The local health-care system is not well developed. Okmulgee's two hospitals, which receive minimal local-government support, have only 153 beds. The city's availability ratios for doctors and specialists are substantially below the national norms.

Besides the eight Southern cities, there are two Midwestern towns and one Western community in the bottom eleven.

Highest	Rating Points
1. Hattiesburg, Miss.	82
2. Marshfield–Wisconsin Rapids, Wis.	76
3. Rome, Ga.	74
4. Morgantown, W.Va.	69
5. Traverse City, Mich.	67
6. Brunswick, Ga.	66
7. Gainesville, Ga.	64
8. Kinston, N.C.	63
9. Greenwood, S.C.	62
9. Paducah, Ky.	62
11. Greenville, N.C.	58
11. Salisbury, Md.	58
13. Missoula, Mont.	57
13. Nacogdoches, Tex.	57
15. Marion, Ohio	56
15. Paris, Tex.	56
17. Mason City, Iowa	55
17. Meridian, Miss.	55
17. Minot, N.Dak.	55
17. Twin Falls, Idaho	55
17. Valdosta, Ga.	55

Lowest	
219. Okmulgee, Okla.	11
218. Minden, La.	13
217. Duncan, Okla.	15
216. New Philadelphia, Ohio	16
212. Crowley, La.	17
212. Del Rio, Tex.	17
212. Rio Rancho, N.Mex.	17
212. Sidney, Ohio	17
209. Alice, Tex.	18
209. Eden, N.C.	18
209. Greenville, Tex.	18

	Hattiesburg, Miss.	Okmulgee, Okla.
Total Points in Section	82	11
Rank in Section	1	219
Results (and Rating Points)		
Doctor Availability		
Doctors per 100,000 residents	240 (20)	68 (2)
Specialist Availability		
Medical and surgical specialists per 100,000 residents	142 (18)	33 (2)
Hospital Availability		
Hospital beds per 100,000 residents	943 (15)	383 (4)
Local Health Funding		
Annual per capita health-related spending by local governments	$472 (20)	$17 (1)
Death Rate		
Annual deaths per 1,000 residents	9.3 (9)	12.8 (2)

(Figure following each area name indicates the composite score from the five categories in this section.)

Alabama

Athens	21
Auburn–Opelika	44
Decatur	41
Enterprise	32
Selma	28
Talladega	27

Alaska

Fairbanks	38

Arizona

Bullhead City– Lake Havasu City	26
Casa Grande– Apache Junction	19
Flagstaff	36
Prescott	34
Sierra Vista	25
Yuma	30

Arkansas

Blytheville	30
El Dorado	45
Hot Springs	42
Jonesboro	47
Rogers	22
Russellville	28

California

El Centro– Calexico– Brawley	39
Eureka	37
Hanford	26
Madera	20
San Luis Obispo– Atascadero	51

Colorado

Grand Junction	44

Connecticut

Torrington	32

Delaware

Dover	35

Florida

Key West	35
Vero Beach	54

Georgia

Brunswick	66
Carrollton	43
Dalton	52
Gainesville	64
Hinesville	29
La Grange	54
Rome	74
Valdosta	55

Idaho

Coeur d'Alene	39
Idaho Falls	45
Nampa–Caldwell	28
Pocatello	46
Twin Falls	55

Illinois

Carbondale	37
Danville	41
De Kalb	29
Freeport	30
Galesburg	33
Mattoon–Charleston	27
Ottawa	23
Quincy	40
Sterling	30

Indiana

Columbus	52
Marion	41
Michigan City– La Porte	31
New Castle	25
Richmond	43
Vincennes	52

Iowa

Ames	54
Burlington	45
Clinton	33
Fort Dodge	25
Marshalltown	31
Mason City	55
Muscatine	24

Kansas

Hutchinson	30
Manhattan	31
Salina	50

Kentucky

Bowling Green	43
Frankfort	29
Madisonville	52
Paducah	62
Radcliff– Elizabethtown	41
Richmond	33

Louisiana

Bogalusa	30
Crowley	17
Hammond	34
Minden	13
Morgan City	36
New Iberia	35
Opelousas	36
Ruston	26

Maine

Augusta–Waterville	54
Biddeford	19

Maryland

Salisbury	58

Michigan

Adrian	30
Marquette	52
Mount Pleasant	29
Owosso	24
Traverse City	67

Minnesota

Faribault	50
Mankato	38
Winona	26

Mississippi

Columbus	49
Greenville	39
Greenwood	35
Hattiesburg	82
Laurel	40
Meridian	55
Tupelo	53
Vicksburg	41

Missouri

Cape Girardeau	52
Jefferson City	44
Sikeston	25

Montana

Bozeman	41
Helena	44
Missoula	57

Nebraska

Grand Island	38

Nevada

Carson City	46

New Hampshire

Concord	45
Keene	34
Laconia	34

New Mexico

Alamogordo	22
Carlsbad	26
Clovis	25
Farmington	24
Gallup	32
Hobbs	26
Rio Rancho	17
Roswell	40

New York

Auburn	26
Batavia	32
Cortland	29
Gloversville	23
Ithaca	38
Jamestown	29
Kingston	32
Olean	34
Plattsburgh	39
Watertown	37

North Carolina

Eden	18
Goldsboro	51
Greenville	58
Havelock–New Bern	54
Kinston	63
Lumberton	22
Roanoke Rapids	21
Rocky Mount	25
Sanford	39
Shelby	28
Statesville	32
Wilson	32

North Dakota

Minot	55

Ohio

Ashland	20
Ashtabula	20
Athens	30
Chillicothe	43
East Liverpool	20
Findlay	30
Fremont	27
Marion	56
New Philadelphia	16
Portsmouth	22
Sandusky	38
Sidney	17
Tiffin	24
Wooster	36
Zanesville	37

Oklahoma

Ardmore	40
Bartlesville	40
Chickasha	33
Duncan	15
McAlester	39
Muskogee	51
Okmulgee	11
Ponca City	20
Stillwater	43

Oregon

Albany	22
Bend	47
Corvallis	48
Grants Pass	19
Klamath Falls	27
Roseburg	38

Pennsylvania

Butler	22
Chambersburg	37
New Castle	21
Pottsville	19

Rhode Island

Newport	29

South Carolina

Greenwood	62
Hilton Head Island	38
Myrtle Beach	26
Orangeburg	38
Sumter	25

Tennessee

Cleveland	47
Columbia	42
Cookeville	42
Morristown	29
Tullahoma	37

Texas

Alice	18
Bay City	33
Del Rio	17
Greenville	18
Huntsville	27
Lufkin	32
Nacogdoches	57
Palestine	26
Paris	56

Utah

Logan	34

Vermont

Rutland	31

Virginia

Blacksburg	37
Fredericksburg	51
Harrisonburg	30
Martinsville	24
Staunton–Waynesboro	47
Winchester	54

Washington

Aberdeen	23
Longview	32
Port Angeles	37
Pullman	32
Walla Walla	51
Wenatchee	48

West Virginia

Beckley	44
Clarksburg	32
Fairmont	36
Morgantown	69

Wisconsin

Fond du Lac	38
Manitowoc	31
Marshfield–Wisconsin Rapids	76
Stevens Point	33

Wyoming

Rock Springs	36

7

Housing

Owning one's home is an essential component of the American dream. It is also a wise investment. "In 99 percent of cases, if you can buy, you should," advises Adriane Berg, a New York City lawyer who wrote *Your Wealth-Building Years.* Housing seems to be virtually recession-proof. The average price of a home continued to rise nationally during the economic downturns of 1973–1974, 1976–1978, and 1980–1982.

Residents of crowded metropolitan areas are finding that owning a house in small-town America, whether a weekend retreat or a new residence, carries an additional benefit. It affords peace of mind. "My daughters were growing up. I started noticing my gray hair, started worrying about mortality," corporate lawyer Stanley Gulkin told the *New York Times.* "You ask yourself, 'What's it all for?' So instead of having a mid-life crisis, I bought a house in the country." Nor is he alone. "We are witnessing a national phenomenon that is tied to major metropolitan areas," observed John Tuccillo, chief economist for the National Association of Realtors, in 1987.

Small cities must meet this demand with an attractive inventory of homes. This section rates each area according to the age and size of available units, the cost of purchasing a house, and the severity of associated expenses, such as taxes and climate control.

The final decade of the twentieth century promises substantial changes in the national housing market. Thousands of apartment buildings and condominium complexes were constructed in both large and small cities during the 1980s. The nineties will be much different. The massive baby-boom generation is now having children of its own. An increasing number of these young adults will yearn to flee their tiny apartments for roomy homes with spacious yards. "The broad maturing middle-aged population is going to do to the upper end of the housing market what they did to the school systems in the 1960s: push it to the limits," predicts James Hughes, the chairman of the Department of Urban Planning and Policy Development at Rutgers University.

Many of these eager buyers will find their dream homes in micropolitan areas. Small towns offer a proportionately better supply of good-sized units. Fully 53 percent of the houses located outside of metropolitan areas have three or more bedrooms; just 49.5 percent of the homes in large cities and their suburbs can say the same.

Even more important is the bottom line on the mortgage. Metropolitan house hunters often suffer a form of "sticker shock." A 1989 survey by the American Chamber of Commerce Researchers Association found that the typical 1,800-square-foot house in Boston cost $290,000, in San Francisco $244,400, in Washington, D.C., $150,277. These prices are well beyond the means of many home buyers. Companies are noticing a greater difficulty in getting their employees to accept transfers into such expensive regions. Runzheimer International, a management-consulting firm, contacted 143 corporations in 1988. It found that 83 percent could cite instances when a worker refused to move to a city where he or she thought mortgages were too steep.

Small towns offer real bargains in comparison. The 1980 census reported that the typical house in a metro area cost 22.5 percent more than its non-metropolitan counterpart. The gap appears to have widened over the decade, if additional figures from the 1989 Chamber of Commerce Researchers Association study can be taken as proof. Consider these comparisons of average housing prices in metros and their micropolitan neighbors: a home in large Wilmington, Delaware, is 51 percent more expensive than the same 1,800-square-foot house in small Dover. The difference between Atlanta and Rome, Georgia, is more than 65 miles; there is also a difference of 47 percent in the cost of a home. And a house in Seattle will set you back 29 percent more than would the identical unit in Wenatchee, Washington.

Ranking micropolitan America. The perfect small city would boast a plentiful supply of new, large, reasonably priced houses that can be inexpensively maintained. Each area is tested in five categories:

1. Housing Age: Does the community have a nice selection of modern homes, or are most of the units more than a bit creaky?

2. Housing Size: Are there plenty of houses fit for growing families, or is space generally cramped?

3. Housing Costs: Could you afford to purchase a house in this area, or are prices too steep?

4. Property Taxes: Does the city impose a pleasantly light tax burden on houses, or will your annual bill be enormous?

5. Heating and Cooling: Will mild weather cut your utility bills, or will you be running your furnace or air conditioner virtually all the time?

Housing Age

If a modern house is your dream, go West. Or go South. It makes little difference. The Census Bureau last did a complete inventory of the age of American housing in 1980. Its findings still provide an important relative measure of the available supply of new and old homes. The West and South have plenty of new ones, since only 16 percent of the houses in each region were built before 1940. A third of the stock in the Midwest predates World War II. The figure in the East is a creaky 42 percent.

This category ranks each small city according to the proportion of its housing that was constructed in the 1930s or earlier. The national average is 25.8 percent of all year-round units.

Bullhead City–Lake Havasu City, Arizona, bloomed in the desert well after Pearl Harbor. Not a single house within the limits of Lake Havasu City existed in 1940; only 3.3 percent of the homes in the whole micropolitan area are that old.

A sluggish economy and a declining population base have limited construction in Pottsville, Pennsylvania. More than 70 percent of its units were built by 1939.

Source. These statistics, published in 1983, are for 1980. U.S. Bureau of the Census, *Census of Housing* (Washington: U.S. Government Printing Office, 1983).

Scoring. Twenty points for 4.9 percent or less; no points for 62.0 percent or more. The spacing is every 3.0 percent.

	Homes Built Before 1940
Lowest	%
1. Bullhead City– Lake Havasu City, Ariz.	3.3
2. Fairbanks, Alaska	3.4
3. Carson City, Nev.	4.6
4. Hilton Head Island, S.C.	4.7
5. Farmington, N.Mex.	5.2
6. Hobbs, N.Mex.	5.3
6. Vero Beach, Fla.	5.3
8. Yuma, Ariz.	5.7
9. Flagstaff, Ariz.	6.0
9. Hinesville, Ga.	6.0
Highest	
219. Pottsville, Pa.	70.2
218. Watertown, N.Y.	62.5
217. Jamestown, N.Y.	60.7
216. Gloversville, N.Y.	59.7
215. Auburn, N.Y.	59.0
214. Olean, N.Y.	58.9
213. Batavia, N.Y.	54.6
212. Cortland, N.Y.	53.4
211. Tiffin, Ohio	53.3
210. Rutland, Vt.	52.6

(Figure following each area name indicates percentage of homes built before 1940; figure in parentheses represents rating points.)

Alabama

Athens	15.7	(16)
Auburn–Opelika	10.7	(18)
Decatur	13.7	(17)
Enterprise	15.2	(16)
Selma	20.7	(14)
Talladega	18.5	(15)

Alaska

Fairbanks	3.4	(20)

Arizona

Bullhead City– Lake Havasu City	3.3	(20)
Casa Grande– Apache Junction	7.2	(19)
Flagstaff	6.0	(19)
Prescott	13.5	(17)
Sierra Vista	18.0	(15)
Yuma	5.7	(19)

Arkansas

Blytheville	18.1	(15)
El Dorado	24.5	(13)
Hot Springs	20.4	(14)
Jonesboro	14.7	(16)
Rogers	17.0	(15)
Russellville	16.1	(16)

California

El Centro–Calexico– Brawley	13.1	(17)
Eureka	23.9	(13)
Hanford	16.6	(16)
Madera	11.6	(17)
San Luis Obispo– Atascadero	11.5	(17)

Colorado

Grand Junction	17.6	(15)

Connecticut

Torrington	39.9	(8)

Delaware

Dover	19.5	(15)

Florida

Key West	10.4	(18)
Vero Beach	5.3	(19)

Georgia

Brunswick	12.5	(17)
Carrollton	18.9	(15)
Dalton	10.9	(18)
Gainesville	13.6	(17)
Hinesville	6.0	(19)
La Grange	28.0	(12)
Rome	21.9	(14)
Valdosta	13.0	(17)

Idaho

Coeur d'Alene	15.7	(16)
Idaho Falls	16.7	(16)
Nampa–Caldwell	20.9	(14)
Pocatello	21.9	(14)
Twin Falls	27.6	(12)

Illinois

Carbondale	22.7	(14)
Danville	43.6	(7)
De Kalb	33.3	(10)
Freeport	52.1	(4)
Galesburg	49.0	(5)
Mattoon–Charleston	39.0	(8)
Ottawa	49.4	(5)
Quincy	49.3	(5)
Sterling	39.7	(8)

Indiana

Columbus	22.3	(14)
Marion	36.7	(9)
Michigan City–La Porte	32.9	(10)
New Castle	42.3	(7)
Richmond	41.7	(7)
Vincennes	51.6	(4)

Iowa

Ames	28.4	(12)
Burlington	46.8	(6)
Clinton	51.6	(4)
Fort Dodge	47.2	(5)
Marshalltown	46.3	(6)
Mason City	42.2	(7)
Muscatine	49.0	(5)

Kansas

Hutchinson	36.2	(9)
Manhattan	19.9	(15)
Salina	30.3	(11)

Kentucky

Bowling Green	19.8	(15)
Frankfort	19.4	(15)
Madisonville	27.6	(12)
Paducah	21.9	(14)
Radcliff–Elizabethtown	12.2	(17)
Richmond	21.2	(14)

Louisiana

Bogalusa	22.4	(14)
Crowley	20.0	(14)
Hammond	15.8	(16)
Minden	13.7	(17)
Morgan City	15.5	(16)
New Iberia	17.0	(15)
Opelousas	16.4	(16)
Ruston	13.3	(17)

Maine

Augusta–Waterville	45.2	(6)
Biddeford	42.1	(7)

Maryland

Salisbury	24.7	(13)

Michigan

Adrian	41.7	(7)
Marquette	36.8	(9)
Mount Pleasant	27.6	(12)
Owosso	39.8	(8)
Traverse City	25.0	(13)

Minnesota

Faribault	41.0	(7)
Mankato	37.1	(9)
Winona	51.2	(4)

Mississippi

Columbus	13.6	(17)
Greenville	18.0	(15)
Greenwood	24.3	(13)
Hattiesburg	15.0	(16)
Laurel	18.0	(15)
Meridian	20.9	(14)
Tupelo	11.8	(17)
Vicksburg	18.7	(15)

Missouri

Cape Girardeau	23.2	(13)
Jefferson City	24.2	(13)
Sikeston	20.7	(14)

Montana

Bozeman	24.9	(13)
Helena	29.3	(11)
Missoula	19.4	(15)

Nebraska

Grand Island	32.7	(10)

Nevada

Carson City	4.6	(20)

New Hampshire

Concord	44.9	(6)
Keene	45.9	(6)
Laconia	42.8	(7)

New Mexico

Alamogordo	8.1	(18)
Carlsbad	10.4	(18)
Clovis	10.9	(18)
Farmington	5.2	(19)
Gallup	10.2	(18)
Hobbs	5.3	(19)
Rio Rancho	12.9	(17)
Roswell	13.7	(17)

New York

Auburn	59.0	(1)
Batavia	54.6	(3)
Cortland	53.4	(3)
Gloversville	59.7	(1)
Ithaca	40.3	(8)
Jamestown	60.7	(1)
Kingston	39.2	(8)
Olean	58.9	(2)
Plattsburgh	40.5	(8)
Watertown	62.5	(0)

North Carolina

Eden	25.7	(13)
Goldsboro	15.1	(16)
Greenville	16.4	(16)
Havelock–New Bern	15.4	(16)
Kinston	17.3	(15)
Lumberton	17.3	(15)
Roanoke Rapids	28.3	(12)
Rocky Mount	23.2	(13)
Sanford	14.4	(16)
Shelby	19.2	(15)
Statesville	20.5	(14)
Wilson	21.8	(14)

North Dakota

Minot	21.5	(14)

Ohio

Ashland	44.2	(6)
Ashtabula	44.3	(6)
Athens	43.1	(7)
Chillicothe	37.7	(9)
East Liverpool	45.1	(6)
Findlay	40.2	(8)
Fremont	45.2	(6)
Marion	40.2	(8)
New Philadelphia	49.2	(5)
Portsmouth	39.6	(8)
Sandusky	36.2	(9)
Sidney	39.4	(8)
Tiffin	53.3	(3)
Wooster	35.0	(9)
Zanesville	39.7	(8)

Oklahoma

Ardmore	23.9	(13)
Bartlesville	20.7	(14)
Chickasha	29.0	(11)
Duncan	18.0	(15)
McAlester	26.3	(12)
Muskogee	28.5	(12)
Okmulgee	39.5	(8)
Ponca City	36.4	(9)
Stillwater	20.3	(14)

Oregon

Albany	16.6	(16)
Bend	11.9	(17)
Corvallis	13.8	(17)
Grants Pass	12.6	(17)
Klamath Falls	25.2	(13)
Roseburg	12.5	(17)

Pennsylvania

Butler	33.6	(10)
Chambersburg	38.0	(8)
New Castle	48.4	(5)
Pottsville	70.2	(0)

Rhode Island

Newport	38.7	(8)

South Carolina

Greenwood	19.2	(15)
Hilton Head Island	4.7	(20)
Myrtle Beach	9.8	(18)
Orangeburg	16.2	(16)
Sumter	13.0	(17)

Tennessee

Cleveland	11.7	(17)
Columbia	25.6	(13)
Cookeville	11.6	(17)
Morristown	11.6	(17)
Tullahoma	11.9	(17)

Texas

Alice	13.0	(17)
Bay City	11.4	(17)
Del Rio	12.8	(17)
Greenville	18.2	(15)
Huntsville	10.3	(18)
Lufkin	12.7	(17)
Nacogdoches	16.5	(16)
Palestine	24.6	(13)
Paris	25.7	(13)

Utah

Logan	28.5	(12)

Vermont

Rutland	52.6	(4)

Virginia

Blacksburg	12.8	(17)
Fredericksburg	17.6	(15)
Harrisonburg	29.2	(11)
Martinsville	15.2	(16)
Staunton–Waynesboro	27.6	(12)
Winchester	25.2	(13)

Washington

Aberdeen	37.3	(9)
Longview	21.8	(14)
Port Angeles	16.8	(16)
Pullman	36.2	(9)
Walla Walla	32.7	(10)
Wenatchee	29.8	(11)

West Virginia

Beckley	25.7	(13)
Clarksburg	47.7	(5)
Fairmont	47.7	(5)
Morgantown	31.3	(11)

Wisconsin

Fond du Lac	45.9	(6)
Manitowoc	46.1	(6)
Marshfield– Wisconsin Rapids	32.1	(10)
Stevens Point	33.6	(10)

Wyoming

Rock Springs	22.7	(14)

Housing Size

The history of America is the story of people looking for room to grow. The first settlers arrived here with the hope of escaping the confinement of Europe. Their descendants, finding the Atlantic seaboard uncomfortably crowded, pushed westward across prairie, desert, and mountain to the Pacific.

The quest for space no longer entails such physical hardship. Most people would be content with a home large enough to house their families in comfort. This category assesses each city's supply of such units, computing the percentage of all houses that have three or more bedrooms. Slightly more than half of the nation's homes meet the test: 50.5 percent, to be exact.

Sidney, Ohio, offers the widest array of large houses. Fully 9,800 of its more than 14,900 homes have a minimum of three bedrooms, amounting to 65.7 percent. Nearly 2,400 of Sidney's units have four or more bedrooms.

Key West, Florida, is noted for its historic gingerbread architecture, but not for living space. Only 25.2 percent of the houses in the Key West area have at least three bedrooms.

Midwestern cities generally offer the best selections of spacious homes, Western towns the worst.

Source. These statistics, published in 1983, are for 1980. U.S. Bureau of the Census, *Census of Housing* (Washington: U.S. Government Printing Office, 1983).

Scoring. Twenty points for 65.0 percent or more; no points for 26.9 percent or less. The spacing is every 2.0 percent.

	Homes With 3+ Bedrooms
Highest	%
1. Sidney, Ohio	65.7
2. Enterprise, Ala.	64.7
3. Fremont, Ohio	64.4
4. Pottsville, Pa.	63.9
5. Owosso, Mich.	63.8
6. Batavia, N.Y.	63.2
6. Harrisonburg, Va.	63.2
8. Fond du Lac, Wis.	63.1
9. Orangeburg, S.C.	62.7
10. Ashland, Ohio	62.0
10. Tiffin, Ohio	62.0

Lowest	
219. Key West, Fla.	25.2
218. Vero Beach, Fla.	34.7
217. Gallup, N.Mex.	35.9
216. Carbondale, Ill.	36.6
215. Prescott, Ariz.	36.8
214. Bullhead City– Lake Havasu City, Ariz.	37.8
213. Fairbanks, Alaska	38.0
212. Hot Springs, Ark.	38.8
211. San Luis Obispo– Atascadero, Calif.	39.2
210. Yuma, Ariz.	39.8

(Figure following each area name indicates percentage of homes with three or more bedrooms; figure in parentheses represents rating points.)

Alabama

Athens	59.2	(17)
Auburn–Opelika	45.7	(10)
Decatur	61.5	(18)
Enterprise	64.7	(19)
Selma	52.1	(13)
Talladega	56.2	(15)

Alaska

Fairbanks	38.0	(6)

Arizona

Bullhead City– Lake Havasu City	37.8	(6)
Casa Grande– Apache Junction	43.5	(9)
Flagstaff	41.9	(8)
Prescott	36.8	(5)
Sierra Vista	49.8	(12)
Yuma	39.8	(7)

Arkansas

Blytheville	49.5	(12)
El Dorado	48.7	(11)
Hot Springs	38.8	(6)
Jonesboro	50.9	(12)
Rogers	51.8	(13)
Russellville	55.4	(15)

California

El Centro–Calexico– Brawley	41.6	(8)
Eureka	41.2	(8)
Hanford	53.2	(14)
Madera	51.8	(13)
San Luis Obispo– Atascadero	39.2	(7)

Colorado

Grand Junction	52.6	(13)

Connecticut

Torrington	56.9	(15)

Delaware

Dover	60.5	(17)

Florida

Key West	25.2	(0)
Vero Beach	34.7	(4)

Georgia

Brunswick	56.8	(15)
Carrollton	53.9	(14)
Dalton	50.4	(12)
Gainesville	55.8	(15)
Hinesville	52.6	(13)
La Grange	48.2	(11)
Rome	48.1	(11)
Valdosta	57.7	(16)

Idaho

Coeur d'Alene	48.9	(11)
Idaho Falls	56.6	(15)
Nampa–Caldwell	49.9	(12)
Pocatello	49.1	(12)
Twin Falls	52.1	(13)

Illinois

Carbondale	36.6	(5)
Danville	46.7	(10)
De Kalb	52.2	(13)
Freeport	56.6	(15)
Galesburg	50.1	(12)
Mattoon–Charleston	44.1	(9)
Ottawa	51.9	(13)
Quincy	47.6	(11)
Sterling	57.5	(16)

Indiana

Columbus	57.5	(16)
Marion	51.8	(13)
Michigan City–La Porte	55.3	(15)
New Castle	53.2	(14)
Richmond	51.8	(13)
Vincennes	41.9	(8)

Iowa

Ames	47.2	(11)
Burlington	49.5	(12)
Clinton	54.3	(14)
Fort Dodge	53.0	(14)
Marshalltown	53.9	(14)
Mason City	49.9	(12)
Muscatine	53.1	(14)

Kansas

Hutchinson	47.6	(11)
Manhattan	45.7	(10)
Salina	52.3	(13)

Kentucky

Bowling Green	52.6	(13)
Frankfort	50.5	(12)
Madisonville	49.1	(12)
Paducah	50.2	(12)
Radcliff–Elizabethtown	56.1	(15)
Richmond	50.9	(12)

Louisiana

Bogalusa	55.2	(15)
Crowley	55.0	(15)
Hammond	52.7	(13)
Minden	54.4	(14)
Morgan City	52.7	(13)
New Iberia	52.4	(13)
Opelousas	54.5	(14)
Ruston	56.0	(15)

Maine

Augusta–Waterville	51.2	(13)
Biddeford	52.5	(13)

Maryland

Salisbury	59.6	(17)

Michigan

Adrian	61.0	(18)
Marquette	51.4	(13)
Mount Pleasant	51.8	(13)
Owosso	63.8	(19)
Traverse City	56.0	(15)

Minnesota

Faribault	59.0	(17)
Mankato	52.8	(13)
Winona	51.8	(13)

Mississippi

Columbus	59.5	(17)
Greenville	50.8	(12)
Greenwood	48.3	(11)
Hattiesburg	52.9	(13)
Laurel	59.7	(17)
Meridian	52.2	(13)
Tupelo	57.6	(16)
Vicksburg	52.8	(13)

Missouri

Cape Girardeau	52.6	(13)
Jefferson City	56.6	(15)
Sikeston	51.1	(13)

Montana

Bozeman	46.3	(10)
Helena	45.6	(10)
Missoula	43.4	(9)

Nebraska

Grand Island	48.9	(11)

Nevada

Carson City	47.2	(11)

New Hampshire

Concord	51.2	(13)
Keene	53.1	(14)
Laconia	49.1	(12)

New Mexico

Alamogordo	58.3	(16)
Carlsbad	49.9	(12)
Clovis	57.0	(16)
Farmington	47.6	(11)
Gallup	35.9	(5)
Hobbs	53.0	(14)
Rio Rancho	51.5	(13)
Roswell	54.1	(14)

New York

Auburn	60.1	(17)
Batavia	63.2	(19)
Cortland	57.6	(16)
Gloversville	56.7	(15)
Ithaca	50.0	(12)
Jamestown	55.4	(15)
Kingston	51.7	(13)
Olean	60.6	(17)
Plattsburgh	57.0	(16)
Watertown	58.7	(16)

North Carolina

Eden	49.1	(12)
Goldsboro	57.1	(16)
Greenville	55.0	(15)
Havelock–New Bern	59.3	(17)
Kinston	56.2	(15)
Lumberton	59.4	(17)
Roanoke Rapids	55.3	(15)
Rocky Mount	54.5	(14)
Sanford	60.4	(17)
Shelby	55.8	(15)
Statesville	55.5	(15)
Wilson	52.6	(13)

North Dakota

Minot	57.6	(16)

Ohio

Ashland	62.0	(18)
Ashtabula	59.6	(17)
Athens	47.4	(11)
Chillicothe	52.0	(13)
East Liverpool	55.3	(15)
Findlay	60.2	(17)
Fremont	64.4	(19)
Marion	61.4	(18)
New Philadelphia	57.4	(16)
Portsmouth	50.9	(12)
Sandusky	59.6	(17)
Sidney	65.7	(20)
Tiffin	62.0	(18)
Wooster	61.6	(18)
Zanesville	52.0	(13)

Oklahoma

Ardmore	50.0	(12)
Bartlesville	56.5	(15)
Chickasha	51.0	(13)
Duncan	52.0	(13)
McAlester	49.8	(12)
Muskogee	48.2	(11)
Okmulgee	46.0	(10)
Ponca City	47.0	(11)
Stillwater	41.9	(8)

Oregon

Albany	52.1	(13)
Bend	48.7	(11)
Corvallis	51.0	(13)
Grants Pass	41.1	(8)
Klamath Falls	45.6	(10)
Roseburg	49.2	(12)

Pennsylvania

Butler	60.2	(17)
Chambersburg	60.7	(17)
New Castle	56.2	(15)
Pottsville	63.9	(19)

Rhode Island

Newport	51.9	(13)

South Carolina

Greenwood	51.6	(13)
Hilton Head Island	52.8	(13)
Myrtle Beach	56.9	(15)
Orangeburg	62.7	(18)
Sumter	60.8	(17)

Tennessee

Cleveland	56.2	(15)
Columbia	53.6	(14)
Cookeville	57.8	(16)
Morristown	59.2	(17)
Tullahoma	60.6	(17)

Texas

Alice	45.7	(10)
Bay City	43.6	(9)
Del Rio	47.7	(11)
Greenville	45.5	(10)
Huntsville	41.0	(8)
Lufkin	50.7	(12)
Nacogdoches	46.8	(10)
Palestine	51.4	(13)
Paris	48.1	(11)

Utah

Logan	53.5	(14)

Vermont

Rutland	59.3	(17)

Virginia

Blacksburg	48.6	(11)
Fredericksburg	59.8	(17)
Harrisonburg	63.2	(19)
Martinsville	55.0	(15)
Staunton–Waynesboro	60.5	(17)
Winchester	61.8	(18)

Washington

Aberdeen	48.4	(11)
Longview	50.8	(12)
Port Angeles	46.8	(10)
Pullman	47.8	(11)
Walla Walla	48.0	(11)
Wenatchee	45.4	(10)

West Virginia

Beckley	54.7	(14)
Clarksburg	51.6	(13)
Fairmont	49.4	(12)
Morgantown	46.9	(10)

Wisconsin

Fond du Lac	63.1	(19)
Manitowoc	60.3	(17)
Marshfield– Wisconsin Rapids	58.8	(16)
Stevens Point	61.2	(18)

Wyoming

Rock Springs	50.4	(12)

Housing Costs

The great American dream of owning a home seems increasingly elusive. Housing costs have risen at almost double the inflation rate since 1950. A report from the U.S. League of Savings Institutions says the typical first-time home buyer in 1977 was 26; the mortgage spiral pushed the age to 31½ by 1987.

Many house shoppers, dismayed by skyrocketing prices in large cities and their suburbs, are taking a serious look at smaller cities. This category ranks each area according to the median value of a single-family home occupied by its owner.

A note of caution: all figures are from 1980. Neither the Census Bureau nor any industry organization has conducted a comprehensive study of small-city housing prices since then. The National Association of Realtors reported in 1988 that the cost of the average house had risen almost 5 percent a year since 1980, although conditions vary by locality.

The 1980 list nonetheless provides an opportunity to compare an area's housing values both with other areas and with the national average, which was then $47,300.

Southern cities offer the best bargains, exemplified by Paris, Texas, at $21,500. Most of the small cities with the steepest mortgages are in the West, led by San Luis Obispo–Atascadero, California, with a median value of $77,600.

Source. These statistics, published in 1988, are for 1980. U.S. Bureau of the Census, *County and City Data Book* (Washington: U.S. Government Printing Office, 1988).

Scoring. Twenty points for $24,999 or less; no points for $63,000 or more. The spacing is every $2,000.

	Median Value of Owner-Occupied Homes
Lowest	**$**
1. Paris, Tex.	21,500
2. Okmulgee, Okla.	21,900
3. McAlester, Okla.	22,300
4. Pottsville, Pa.	22,600
5. Alice, Tex.	23,200
6. Roanoke Rapids, N.C.	24,600
7. Bogalusa, La.	25,300
8. Lumberton, N.C.	25,500
9. Greenville, Tex.	25,800
10. El Dorado, Ark.	25,900

Highest

219. San Luis Obispo–Atascadero, Calif.	77,600
218. Carson City, Nev.	75,200
217. Fairbanks, Alaska	66,000
216. Corvallis, Oreg.	65,800
215. Key West, Fla.	64,300
214. Rock Springs, Wyo.	62,300
213. Missoula, Mont.	60,900
211. Madera, Calif.	60,100
211. Torrington, Conn.	60,100
210. Bozeman, Mont.	59,800

(Figure following each area name indicates the median value in dollars of owner-occupied homes; figure in parentheses represents rating points.)

Alabama

Athens	30,300	(17)
Auburn–Opelika	39,300	(12)
Decatur	38,300	(13)
Enterprise	33,500	(15)
Selma	29,000	(17)
Talladega	26,700	(19)

Alaska

Fairbanks	66,000	(0)

Arizona

Bullhead City– Lake Havasu City	49,100	(7)
Casa Grande– Apache Junction	34,400	(15)
Flagstaff	55,600	(4)
Prescott	52,400	(6)
Sierra Vista	38,800	(13)
Yuma	40,400	(12)

Arkansas

Blytheville	28,500	(18)
El Dorado	25,900	(19)
Hot Springs	35,800	(14)
Jonesboro	31,600	(16)
Rogers	39,000	(12)
Russellville	32,700	(16)

California

El Centro–Calexico– Brawley	47,800	(8)
Eureka	57,000	(3)
Hanford	46,700	(9)
Madera	60,100	(2)
San Luis Obispo– Atascadero	77,600	(0)

Colorado

Grand Junction	59,000	(2)

Connecticut

Torrington	60,100	(2)

Delaware

Dover	42,000	(11)

Florida

Key West	64,300	(0)
Vero Beach	46,400	(9)

Georgia

Brunswick	36,700	(14)
Carrollton	32,000	(16)
Dalton	33,800	(15)
Gainesville	37,700	(13)
Hinesville	36,900	(14)
La Grange	29,000	(17)
Rome	30,500	(17)
Valdosta	35,500	(14)

Idaho

Coeur d'Alene	53,400	(5)
Idaho Falls	48,800	(8)
Nampa–Caldwell	43,000	(10)
Pocatello	44,700	(10)
Twin Falls	41,900	(11)

Illinois

Carbondale	36,800	(14)
Danville	33,000	(15)
De Kalb	55,200	(4)
Freeport	37,400	(13)
Galesburg	38,300	(13)
Mattoon–Charleston	36,500	(14)
Ottawa	42,400	(11)
Quincy	36,800	(14)
Sterling	39,600	(12)

Indiana

Columbus	43,600 (10)
Marion	32,100 (16)
Michigan City–La Porte	38,600 (13)
New Castle	30,600 (17)
Richmond	32,400 (16)
Vincennes	29,400 (17)

Iowa

Ames	57,300 (3)
Burlington	37,500 (13)
Clinton	39,100 (12)
Fort Dodge	39,500 (12)
Marshalltown	40,600 (12)
Mason City	40,700 (12)
Muscatine	43,500 (10)

Kansas

Hutchinson	35,300 (14)
Manhattan	46,800 (9)
Salina	35,900 (14)

Kentucky

Bowling Green	41,000 (11)
Frankfort	42,000 (11)
Madisonville	28,800 (18)
Paducah	33,300 (15)
Radcliff–Elizabethtown	39,200 (12)
Richmond	38,900 (13)

Louisiana

Bogalusa	25,300 (19)
Crowley	30,600 (17)
Hammond	35,700 (14)
Minden	26,500 (19)
Morgan City	45,100 (9)
New Iberia	40,000 (12)
Opelousas	28,200 (18)
Ruston	37,400 (13)

Maine

Augusta–Waterville	38,500 (13)
Biddeford	43,100 (10)

Maryland

Salisbury	38,100 (13)

Michigan

Adrian	36,700 (14)
Marquette	37,800 (13)
Mount Pleasant	37,500 (13)
Owosso	35,100 (14)
Traverse City	45,300 (9)

Minnesota

Faribault	49,300 (7)
Mankato	48,000 (8)
Winona	39,700 (12)

Mississippi

Columbus	36,700 (14)
Greenville	26,200 (19)
Greenwood	31,700 (16)
Hattiesburg	31,900 (16)
Laurel	30,000 (17)
Meridian	31,800 (16)
Tupelo	36,200 (14)
Vicksburg	35,900 (14)

Missouri

Cape Girardeau	40,100 (12)
Jefferson City	43,900 (10)
Sikeston	29,300 (17)

Montana

Bozeman	59,800 (2)
Helena	49,700 (7)
Missoula	60,900 (2)

Nebraska

Grand Island	43,600 (10)

Nevada

Carson City	75,200 (0)

New Hampshire

Concord	44,800	(10)
Keene	41,000	(11)
Laconia	43,600	(10)

New Mexico

Alamogordo	34,500	(15)
Carlsbad	32,000	(16)
Clovis	33,900	(15)
Farmington	48,000	(8)
Gallup	35,400	(14)
Hobbs	32,800	(16)
Rio Rancho	48,800	(8)
Roswell	30,500	(17)

New York

Auburn	31,100	(16)
Batavia	35,500	(14)
Cortland	35,600	(14)
Gloversville	28,700	(18)
Ithaca	42,900	(11)
Jamestown	31,900	(16)
Kingston	37,500	(13)
Olean	28,000	(18)
Plattsburgh	35,400	(14)
Watertown	28,300	(18)

North Carolina

Eden	29,200	(17)
Goldsboro	35,800	(14)
Greenville	41,200	(11)
Havelock–New Bern	37,800	(13)
Kinston	35,200	(14)
Lumberton	25,500	(19)
Roanoke Rapids	24,600	(20)
Rocky Mount	34,456	(15)
Sanford	34,300	(15)
Shelby	32,100	(16)
Statesville	35,100	(14)
Wilson	37,700	(13)

North Dakota

Minot	46,200	(9)

Ohio

Ashland	40,200	(12)
Ashtabula	39,600	(12)
Athens	31,900	(16)
Chillicothe	37,400	(13)
East Liverpool	34,800	(15)
Findlay	44,700	(10)
Fremont	42,400	(11)
Marion	38,300	(13)
New Philadelphia	37,300	(13)
Portsmouth	28,900	(18)
Sandusky	47,300	(8)
Sidney	39,500	(12)
Tiffin	38,100	(13)
Wooster	50,900	(7)
Zanesville	33,600	(15)

Oklahoma

Ardmore	27,800	(18)
Bartlesville	40,200	(12)
Chickasha	32,900	(16)
Duncan	32,200	(16)
McAlester	22,300	(20)
Muskogee	27,700	(18)
Okmulgee	21,900	(20)
Ponca City	33,400	(15)
Stillwater	38,300	(13)

Oregon

Albany	48,900	(8)
Bend	59,400	(2)
Corvallis	65,800	(0)
Grants Pass	58,500	(3)
Klamath Falls	44,200	(10)
Roseburg	51,000	(6)

Pennsylvania

Butler	45,200	(9)
Chambersburg	41,200	(11)
New Castle	33,400	(15)
Pottsville	22,600	(20)

Rhode Island
Newport	57,000	(3)

South Carolina
Greenwood	32,000	(16)
Hilton Head Island	50,600	(7)
Myrtle Beach	43,000	(10)
Orangeburg	29,400	(17)
Sumter	33,200	(15)

Tennessee
Cleveland	35,500	(14)
Columbia	31,700	(16)
Cookeville	36,900	(14)
Morristown	33,100	(15)
Tullahoma	35,200	(14)

Texas
Alice	23,200	(20)
Bay City	36,300	(14)
Del Rio	30,300	(17)
Greenville	25,800	(19)
Huntsville	43,100	(10)
Lufkin	32,200	(16)
Nacogdoches	34,600	(15)
Palestine	28,500	(18)
Paris	21,500	(20)

Utah
Logan	58,300	(3)

Vermont
Rutland	40,300	(12)

Virginia
Blacksburg	43,200	(10)
Fredericksburg	48,700	(8)
Harrisonburg	44,169	(10)
Martinsville	32,773	(16)
Staunton–Waynesboro	40,308	(12)
Winchester	44,626	(10)

Washington
Aberdeen	43,400	(10)
Longview	50,600	(7)
Port Angeles	58,400	(3)
Pullman	47,000	(8)
Walla Walla	46,300	(9)
Wenatchee	48,500	(8)

West Virginia
Beckley	38,500	(13)
Clarksburg	35,000	(14)
Fairmont	35,600	(14)
Morgantown	50,400	(7)

Wisconsin
Fond du Lac	41,300	(11)
Manitowoc	40,700	(12)
Marshfield–Wisconsin Rapids	39,100	(12)
Stevens Point	45,300	(9)

Wyoming
Rock Springs	62,300	(1)

Property Taxes

The arrival of the property-tax bill is never one of the highlights of the year. It is particularly painful in the East, where levies run an average of 44 percent above the national norm. But most home owners, regardless of region, are frustrated by the size of their bills. Voters in California and other states have eagerly seized the chance to approve referendums limiting local taxing powers.

This category weighs each area's property-tax burden, dividing the total levy by the number of residents. The average for the entire country is $340 per capita.

Athens, Alabama, has the lightest load among the nation's small cities. It taxes each person just $38.

Far on the other end of the scale is Rock Springs, Wyoming, with property taxes that are 34 times larger than those in Athens, $1,295 from every man, woman, and child. No other city is within $600 of the tax burden imposed by Rock Springs.

Southern cities offer a haven from high taxation, with few exceptions. Most of the small cities with high property-tax loads are either in the Northeast or the West.

Source. These statistics, published in 1988, are for the 1981–1982 budget year. U.S. Bureau of the Census, *County and City Data Book* (Washington: U.S. Government Printing Office, 1988).

Scoring. Twenty points for $50 or less per capita; no points for $526 or more. The spacing is every $25 per capita.

Property Taxes Per Capita

Lowest	$
1. Athens, Ala.	38
2. Talladega, Ala.	45
3. Radcliff–Elizabethtown, Ky.	46
4. Richmond, Ky.	48
5. Hammond, La.	53
6. Clovis, N.Mex.	56
7. Enterprise, Ala.	57
8. Opelousas, La.	60
9. Auburn–Opelika, Ala.	62
10. Alamogordo, N.Mex.	63

Highest

219. Rock Springs, Wyo.	1,295
218. Laconia, N.H.	668
217. Bay City, Tex.	624
216. Keene, N.H.	590
215. Kingston, N.Y.	575
214. Traverse City, Mich.	564
213. Missoula, Mont.	533
212. Concord, N.H.	519
211. Torrington, Conn.	501
210. Bend, Oreg.	490

(Figure following each area name indicates property taxes per capita in dollars; figure in parentheses represents rating points.)

Alabama

Athens	38	(20)
Auburn–Opelika	62	(19)
Decatur	103	(17)
Enterprise	57	(19)
Selma	79	(18)
Talladega	45	(20)

Alaska

Fairbanks	209	(13)

Arizona

Bullhead City– Lake Havasu City	417	(5)
Casa Grande– Apache Junction	345	(8)
Flagstaff	247	(12)
Prescott	333	(8)
Sierra Vista	254	(11)
Yuma	224	(13)

Arkansas

Blytheville	127	(16)
El Dorado	162	(15)
Hot Springs	157	(15)
Jonesboro	145	(16)
Rogers	185	(14)
Russellville	301	(9)

California

El Centro–Calexico– Brawley	216	(13)
Eureka	263	(11)
Hanford	236	(12)
Madera	297	(10)
San Luis Obispo– Atascadero	351	(7)

Colorado

Grand Junction	308	(9)

Connecticut

Torrington	501	(1)

Delaware

Dover	80	(18)

Florida

Key West	335	(8)
Vero Beach	340	(8)

Georgia

Brunswick	296	(10)
Carrollton	125	(17)
Dalton	227	(12)
Gainesville	202	(13)
Hinesville	77	(18)
La Grange	173	(15)
Rome	267	(11)
Valdosta	141	(16)

Idaho

Coeur d'Alene	270	(11)
Idaho Falls	221	(13)
Nampa–Caldwell	199	(14)
Pocatello	226	(12)
Twin Falls	214	(13)

Illinois

Carbondale	186	(14)
Danville	334	(8)
De Kalb	386	(6)
Freeport	319	(9)
Galesburg	375	(7)
Mattoon–Charleston	331	(8)
Ottawa	424	(5)
Quincy	245	(12)
Sterling	319	(9)

Indiana

Columbus	345	(8)
Marion	299	(10)
Michigan City–La Porte	383	(6)
New Castle	279	(10)
Richmond	277	(10)
Vincennes	225	(13)

Iowa

Ames	347	(8)
Burlington	408	(5)
Clinton	420	(5)
Fort Dodge	459	(3)
Marshalltown	474	(3)
Mason City	467	(3)
Muscatine	409	(5)

Kansas

Hutchinson	436	(4)
Manhattan	197	(14)
Salina	356	(7)

Kentucky

Bowling Green	77	(18)
Frankfort	94	(18)
Madisonville	106	(17)
Paducah	108	(17)
Radcliff–Elizabethtown	46	(20)
Richmond	48	(20)

Louisiana

Bogalusa	100	(18)
Crowley	90	(18)
Hammond	53	(19)
Minden	100	(18)
Morgan City	190	(14)
New Iberia	101	(17)
Opelousas	60	(19)
Ruston	72	(19)

Maine

Augusta–Waterville	296	(10)
Biddeford	346	(8)

Maryland

Salisbury	221	(13)

Michigan

Adrian	473	(3)
Marquette	425	(5)
Mount Pleasant	265	(11)
Owosso	377	(6)
Traverse City	564	(0)

Minnesota

Faribault	222	(13)
Mankato	376	(6)
Winona	233	(12)

Mississippi

Columbus	135	(16)
Greenville	191	(14)
Greenwood	170	(15)
Hattiesburg	169	(15)
Laurel	160	(15)
Meridian	160	(15)
Tupelo	173	(15)
Vicksburg	208	(13)

Missouri

Cape Girardeau	176	(14)
Jefferson City	203	(13)
Sikeston	131	(16)

Montana

Bozeman	353	(7)
Helena	433	(4)
Missoula	533	(0)

Nebraska

Grand Island	411	(5)

Nevada

Carson City	108	(17)

New Hampshire

Concord	519	(1)
Keene	590	(0)
Laconia	668	(0)

New Mexico

Alamogordo	63	(19)
Carlsbad	139	(16)
Clovis	56	(19)
Farmington	220	(13)
Gallup	85	(18)
Hobbs	185	(14)
Rio Rancho	74	(19)
Roswell	78	(18)

New York

Auburn	386	(6)
Batavia	369	(7)
Cortland	380	(6)
Gloversville	339	(8)
Ithaca	378	(6)
Jamestown	425	(5)
Kingston	575	(0)
Olean	374	(7)
Plattsburgh	312	(9)
Watertown	397	(6)

North Carolina

Eden	206	(13)
Goldsboro	129	(16)
Greenville	176	(14)
Havelock–New Bern	120	(17)
Kinston	154	(15)
Lumberton	123	(17)
Roanoke Rapids	164	(15)
Rocky Mount	147	(16)
Sanford	207	(13)
Shelby	138	(16)
Statesville	143	(16)
Wilson	201	(13)

North Dakota

Minot	212	(13)

Ohio

Ashland	270	(11)
Ashtabula	315	(9)
Athens	177	(14)
Chillicothe	245	(12)
East Liverpool	180	(14)
Findlay	292	(10)
Fremont	291	(10)
Marion	298	(10)
New Philadelphia	270	(11)
Portsmouth	165	(15)
Sandusky	400	(6)
Sidney	268	(11)
Tiffin	289	(10)
Wooster	285	(10)
Zanesville	225	(13)

Oklahoma

Ardmore	149	(16)
Bartlesville	161	(15)
Chickasha	131	(16)
Duncan	121	(17)
McAlester	92	(18)
Muskogee	178	(14)
Okmulgee	93	(18)
Ponca City	196	(14)
Stillwater	127	(16)

Oregon

Albany	419	(5)
Bend	490	(2)
Corvallis	391	(6)
Grants Pass	289	(10)
Klamath Falls	279	(10)
Roseburg	361	(7)

Pennsylvania

Butler	213	(13)
Chambersburg	191	(14)
New Castle	232	(12)
Pottsville	161	(15)

Rhode Island

Newport	476	(2)

South Carolina

Greenwood	201	(13)
Hilton Head Island	219	(13)
Myrtle Beach	249	(12)
Orangeburg	129	(16)
Sumter	124	(17)

Tennessee

Cleveland	153	(15)
Columbia	148	(16)
Cookeville	115	(17)
Morristown	193	(14)
Tullahoma	120	(17)

Texas

Alice	300	(10)
Bay City	624	(0)
Del Rio	85	(18)
Greenville	195	(14)
Huntsville	353	(7)
Lufkin	193	(14)
Nacogdoches	218	(13)
Palestine	237	(12)
Paris	150	(16)

Utah

Logan	156	(15)

Vermont

Rutland	417	(5)

Virginia

Blacksburg	150	(16)
Fredericksburg	225	(13)
Harrisonburg	140	(16)
Martinsville	148	(16)
Staunton–Waynesboro	171	(15)
Winchester	243	(12)

Washington

Aberdeen	180	(14)
Longview	223	(13)
Port Angeles	140	(16)
Pullman	176	(14)
Walla Walla	186	(14)
Wenatchee	181	(14)

West Virginia

Beckley	125	(17)
Clarksburg	162	(15)
Fairmont	162	(15)
Morgantown	140	(16)

Wisconsin

Fond du Lac	396	(6)
Manitowoc	261	(11)
Marshfield–Wisconsin Rapids	402	(5)
Stevens Point	316	(9)

Wyoming

Rock Springs	1,295	(0)

Heating and Cooling

Neither air conditioners nor furnaces receive much of a workout in San Luis Obispo–Atascadero, California. Mild Pacific Ocean breezes hold summertime temperatures below 80 degrees, while the warm California sun coaxes the average daily high past 62 degrees in January.

This category estimates the demands placed on a home climate–control system in each area, using a measure known as the degree day. It is calculated this way: First determine each day's average temperature. Every degree above 65 is called a cooling degree day; each degree below 65 is a heating degree day. For example, a temperature of 58 yields seven heating degree days. The higher the total, the greater the need for energy to keep a house comfortable.

San Luis Obispo–Atascadero averages 2,783 degree days a year: 2,498 for heating and just 285 for cooling. No other micropolitan area is within 995 degree days of this small total.

Fairbanks, Alaska, is a nightmare for anyone hoping to hold down utility bills. The temperature drops below zero 114 days a year, the major reason for Fairbanks's astronomical total of 14,344 degree days.

Southern cities dominate the list of towns with the lowest heating and cooling needs. The Midwest generally requires the most energy.

Source. These statistics, published in 1985, are averages of conditions from 1951 through 1980. Derived from *Climates of the States* (Detroit: Gale Research Co., 1985).

Scoring. Twenty points for 3,999 degree days or less; no points for 9,700 or more. The spacing is every 300 degree days.

Lowest Needs	Heating and Cooling Degree Days
1. San Luis Obispo–Atascadero, Calif.	2,783
2. Vero Beach, Fla.	3,779
3. Brunswick, Ga.	4,098
4. Valdosta, Ga.	4,102
5. Hilton Head Island, S.C.	4,128
5. Hinesville, Ga.	4,128
7. Opelousas, La.	4,146
8. Hammond, La.	4,157
9. Sierra Vista, Ariz.	4,197
10. New Iberia, La.	4,204

Highest Needs

219. Fairbanks, Alaska	14,344
218. Bozeman, Mont.	9,887
217. Minot, N.Dak.	9,838
216. Marquette, Mich.	9,668
215. Marshfield–Wisconsin Rapids, Wis.	8,854
214. Mankato, Minn.	8,621
213. Faribault, Minn.	8,616
212. Stevens Point, Wis.	8,533
211. Mason City, Iowa	8,500
210. Winona, Minn.	8,472

(Figure following each area name indicates heating and cooling degree days; figure in parentheses represents rating points.)

Alabama

Athens	4,987	(16)
Auburn–Opelika	4,532	(18)
Decatur	4,987	(16)
Enterprise	4,221	(19)
Selma	4,473	(18)
Talladega	4,581	(18)

Alaska

Fairbanks	14,344	(0)

Arizona

Bullhead City– Lake Havasu City	5,424	(15)
Casa Grande– Apache Junction	5,072	(16)
Flagstaff	7,381	(8)
Prescott	5,555	(14)
Sierra Vista	4,197	(19)
Yuma	5,227	(15)

Arkansas

Blytheville	5,435	(15)
El Dorado	4,864	(17)
Hot Springs	5,079	(16)
Jonesboro	5,467	(15)
Rogers	5,607	(14)
Russellville	5,203	(15)

California

El Centro–Calexico– Brawley	4,937	(16)
Eureka	4,725	(17)
Hanford	4,264	(19)
Madera	4,327	(18)
San Luis Obispo– Atascadero	2,783	(20)

Colorado

Grand Junction	6,888	(10)

Connecticut

Torrington	7,030	(9)

Delaware

Dover	5,535	(14)

Florida

Key West	4,870	(17)
Vero Beach	3,779	(20)

Georgia

Brunswick	4,098	(19)
Carrollton	4,538	(18)
Dalton	5,000	(16)
Gainesville	4,808	(17)
Hinesville	4,128	(19)
La Grange	4,413	(18)
Rome	4,957	(16)
Valdosta	4,102	(19)

Idaho

Coeur d'Alene	6,856	(10)
Idaho Falls	8,283	(5)
Nampa–Caldwell	6,544	(11)
Pocatello	7,568	(8)
Twin Falls	6,892	(10)

Illinois

Carbondale	5,958	(13)
Danville	6,608	(11)
De Kalb	7,470	(8)
Freeport	7,703	(7)
Galesburg	7,219	(9)
Mattoon–Charleston	6,691	(11)
Ottawa	6,959	(10)
Quincy	6,909	(10)
Sterling	7,330	(8)

Indiana

Columbus	6,473	(11)
Marion	7,052	(9)
Michigan City–La Porte	7,126	(9)
New Castle	6,919	(10)
Richmond	6,701	(10)
Vincennes	6,383	(12)

Iowa

Ames	7,666	(7)
Burlington	7,143	(9)
Clinton	7,354	(8)
Fort Dodge	7,960	(6)
Marshalltown	7,774	(7)
Mason City	8,500	(4)
Muscatine	7,181	(9)

Kansas

Hutchinson	6,482	(11)
Manhattan	6,644	(11)
Salina	6,753	(10)

Kentucky

Bowling Green	5,738	(14)
Frankfort	6,068	(13)
Madisonville	5,561	(14)
Paducah	5,703	(14)
Radcliff–Elizabethtown	5,657	(14)
Richmond	5,494	(15)

Louisiana

Bogalusa	4,402	(18)
Crowley	4,367	(18)
Hammond	4,157	(19)
Minden	4,741	(17)
Morgan City	4,226	(19)
New Iberia	4,204	(19)
Opelousas	4,146	(19)
Ruston	4,677	(17)

Maine

Augusta–Waterville	7,951	(6)
Biddeford	7,755	(7)

Maryland

Salisbury	5,216	(15)

Michigan

Adrian	7,254	(9)
Marquette	9,668	(1)
Mount Pleasant	7,626	(7)
Owosso	7,402	(8)
Traverse City	8,126	(6)

Minnesota

Faribault	8,616	(4)
Mankato	8,621	(4)
Winona	8,472	(5)

Mississippi

Columbus	4,863	(17)
Greenville	4,881	(17)
Greenwood	4,953	(16)
Hattiesburg	4,365	(18)
Laurel	4,576	(18)
Meridian	4,637	(17)
Tupelo	5,049	(16)
Vicksburg	4,507	(18)

Missouri

Cape Girardeau	5,796	(14)
Jefferson City	6,227	(12)
Sikeston	5,780	(14)

Montana

Bozeman	9,887	(0)
Helena	8,470	(5)
Missoula	8,055	(6)

Nebraska

Grand Island	7,510	(8)

Nevada

Carson City	6,139	(12)

New Hampshire

Concord	7,835	(7)
Keene	7,441	(8)
Laconia	7,835	(7)

New Mexico

Alamogordo	4,815	(17)
Carlsbad	4,988	(16)
Clovis	5,270	(15)
Farmington	6,470	(11)
Gallup	6,577	(11)
Hobbs	4,719	(17)
Rio Rancho	5,692	(14)
Roswell	4,989	(16)

New York

Auburn	7,293	(9)
Batavia	7,271	(9)
Cortland	7,697	(7)
Gloversville	7,673	(7)
Ithaca	7,505	(8)
Jamestown	7,618	(7)
Kingston	6,957	(10)
Olean	7,886	(7)
Plattsburgh	8,332	(5)
Watertown	7,904	(6)

North Carolina

Eden	5,141	(16)
Goldsboro	4,806	(17)
Greenville	4,848	(17)
Havelock–New Bern	4,516	(18)
Kinston	4,735	(17)
Lumberton	4,724	(17)
Roanoke Rapids	5,044	(16)
Rocky Mount	4,848	(17)
Sanford	4,925	(16)
Shelby	4,999	(16)
Statesville	5,057	(16)
Wilson	4,848	(17)

North Dakota

Minot	9,838	(0)

Ohio

Ashland	6,923	(10)
Ashtabula	6,883	(10)
Athens	6,213	(12)
Chillicothe	6,134	(12)
East Liverpool	6,125	(12)
Findlay	7,075	(9)
Fremont	6,887	(10)
Marion	6,845	(10)
New Philadelphia	6,546	(11)
Portsmouth	5,839	(13)
Sandusky	6,837	(10)
Sidney	6,882	(10)
Tiffin	6,696	(11)
Wooster	6,919	(10)
Zanesville	6,493	(11)

Oklahoma

Ardmore	5,144	(16)
Bartlesville	5,728	(14)
Chickasha	5,465	(15)
Duncan	5,344	(15)
McAlester	5,431	(15)
Muskogee	5,447	(15)
Okmulgee	5,346	(15)
Ponca City	6,165	(12)
Stillwater	5,713	(14)

Oregon

Albany	5,189	(16)
Bend	7,184	(9)
Corvallis	5,189	(16)
Grants Pass	4,918	(16)
Klamath Falls	6,894	(10)
Roseburg	4,823	(17)

Pennsylvania

Butler	6,904	(10)
Chambersburg	6,335	(12)
New Castle	6,527	(11)
Pottsville	6,641	(11)

Rhode Island
Newport	6,503	(11)

South Carolina
Greenwood	4,822	(17)
Hilton Head Island	4,128	(19)
Myrtle Beach	4,298	(19)
Orangeburg	4,557	(18)
Sumter	4,448	(18)

Tennessee
Cleveland	5,161	(16)
Columbia	5,258	(15)
Cookeville	5,694	(14)
Morristown	5,374	(15)
Tullahoma	5,007	(16)

Texas
Alice	4,475	(18)
Bay City	4,299	(19)
Del Rio	4,782	(17)
Greenville	5,161	(16)
Huntsville	4,556	(18)
Lufkin	4,581	(18)
Nacogdoches	4,581	(18)
Palestine	4,583	(18)
Paris	5,231	(15)

Utah
Logan	7,344	(8)

Vermont
Rutland	7,532	(8)

Virginia
Blacksburg	6,092	(13)
Fredericksburg	5,563	(14)
Harrisonburg	5,813	(13)
Martinsville	5,338	(15)
Staunton–Waynesboro	5,878	(13)
Winchester	5,808	(13)

Washington
Aberdeen	5,346	(15)
Longview	5,198	(16)
Port Angeles	5,729	(14)
Pullman	6,999	(10)
Walla Walla	5,670	(14)
Wenatchee	6,440	(11)

West Virginia
Beckley	6,043	(13)
Clarksburg	6,217	(12)
Fairmont	6,115	(12)
Morgantown	6,174	(12)

Wisconsin
Fond du Lac	8,089	(6)
Manitowoc	7,905	(6)
Marshfield– Wisconsin Rapids	8,854	(3)
Stevens Point	8,533	(4)

Wyoming
Rock Springs	8,159	(6)

Enterprise, Alabama, owes much to a grayish, one-quarter-inch-long beetle that destroyed what was once the region's cash crop. The boll weevil invaded the Enterprise area in 1915, killing 60 percent of its cotton in two short years. This costly lesson in the danger of relying on one major source of income inspired the desperate community to diversify. Other forms of agriculture flourished, notably peanuts. New factories sprang up. The government constructed massive Fort Rucker just seven miles northeast of Enterprise.

A grateful city decided to build a most unusual monument to its good fortune. A classical female figure holds aloft a basin, in which rests a large beetle. The inscription reads: "In profound appreciation of the boll weevil and what it has done as the herald of prosperity." The monument still stands today.

An important indicator of modern-day prosperity in Enterprise is the quality of the area's homes. Almost two-thirds of the houses have at least three bedrooms, a figure matched by few small cities. Property taxes are among the lowest in the country, as are heating and cooling costs. Mortgages are reasonable. These factors contribute to Enterprise's first-place showing in the housing section, with 88 of a possible 100 points.

The South has a virtual monopoly on the best scores in this section, holding nine of the top ten positions. The sole exception is Alamogordo, New Mexico.

Bozeman and Missoula, Montana, have much more in common than simply being cities in the same state. Both are tucked between the towering, snow-capped ridges of the Rocky Mountains. Both are the sites of large colleges: Bozeman with Montana State University, Missoula with the University of Montana. And both are tied for last place in the housing section, with just 32 points each.

It is expensive to buy and maintain a house in either town. Bozeman and Missoula are both among the ten small cities with the highest average mortgages in the country. Property taxes and heating bills are almost as steep as the nearby peaks. There is also a shortage of large homes, as developers keep in mind the smaller space needs of students. The result is a seemingly random mixture of apartment buildings, dormitories, and spacious houses. "[Missoula] has a tendency to straggle away with little apparent plan," noted the Federal Writers' Project guidebook as far back as 1939.

Cold-weather cities dominate the list of communities with the worst scores in the housing section. Five of the bottom eleven are from the East, another five from the West, and one from the Midwest.

Highest	**Rating Points**
1. Enterprise, Ala.	88
2. Talladega, Ala.	87
3. Athens, Ala.	86
3. Opelousas, La.	86
5. Alamogordo, N.Mex.	85
5. Lumberton, N.C.	85
5. Minden, La.	85
5. Orangeburg, S.C.	85
9. Bogalusa, La.	84
9. Sumter, S.C.	84
11. Clovis, N.Mex.	83
11. Hinesville, Ga.	83
13. Crowley, La.	82
13. Laurel, Miss.	82
13. Roswell, N.Mex.	82
13. Valdosta, Ga.	82
17. Columbus, Miss.	81
17. Decatur, Ala.	81
17. Hammond, La.	81
17. Havelock–New Bern, N.C.	81
17. Ruston, La.	81
17. Tullahoma, Tenn.	81

Lowest

218. Bozeman, Mont.	32
218. Missoula, Mont.	32
217. Rock Springs, Wyo.	33
216. Torrington, Conn.	35
215. Laconia, N.H.	36
212. Concord, N.H.	37
212. Helena, Mont.	37
212. Newport, R.I.	37
211. Mason City, Iowa	38
209. Fairbanks, Alaska	39
209. Keene, N.H.	39

	Enterprise, Ala.	Bozeman, Mont.	Missoula, Mont.
Total Points in Section	88	32	32
Rank in Section	1	218*	218*
Results (and Rating Points)			
Housing Age Percentage of homes built before 1940	15.2 (16)	24.9 (13)	19.4 (15)
Housing Size Percentage of homes with three or more bedrooms	64.7 (19)	46.3 (10)	43.4 (9)
Housing Costs Median value of owner- occupied homes	$33,500 (15)	$59,800 (2)	$60,900 (2)
Property Taxes Property taxes per capita	$57 (19)	$353 (7)	$533 (0)
Heating and Cooling Heating and cooling degree days	4,221 (19)	9,887 (0)	8,055 (6)

*There was a tie for last place.

(Figure following each area name indicates the composite score from the five categories in this section.)

Alabama

Athens	86
Auburn–Opelika	77
Decatur	81
Enterprise	88
Selma	80
Talladega	87

Alaska

Fairbanks	39

Arizona

Bullhead City– Lake Havasu City	53
Casa Grande– Apache Junction	67
Flagstaff	51
Prescott	50
Sierra Vista	70
Yuma	66

Arkansas

Blytheville	76
El Dorado	75
Hot Springs	65
Jonesboro	75
Rogers	68
Russellville	71

California

El Centro– Calexico– Brawley	62
Eureka	52
Hanford	70
Madera	60
San Luis Obispo– Atascadero	51

Colorado

Grand Junction	49

Connecticut

Torrington	35

Delaware

Dover	75

Florida

Key West	43
Vero Beach	60

Georgia

Brunswick	75
Carrollton	80
Dalton	73
Gainesville	75
Hinesville	83
La Grange	73
Rome	69
Valdosta	82

Idaho

Coeur d'Alene	53
Idaho Falls	57
Nampa–Caldwell	61
Pocatello	56
Twin Falls	59

Illinois

Carbondale	60
Danville	51
De Kalb	41
Freeport	48
Galesburg	46
Mattoon–Charleston	50
Ottawa	44
Quincy	52
Sterling	53

Indiana

Columbus	59
Marion	57
Michigan City– La Porte	53
New Castle	58
Richmond	56
Vincennes	54

Iowa

Ames	41
Burlington	45
Clinton	43
Fort Dodge	40
Marshalltown	42
Mason City	38
Muscatine	43

Kansas

Hutchinson	49
Manhattan	59
Salina	55

Kentucky

Bowling Green	71
Frankfort	69
Madisonville	73
Paducah	72
Radcliff– Elizabethtown	78
Richmond	74

Louisiana

Bogalusa	84
Crowley	82
Hammond	81
Minden	85
Morgan City	71
New Iberia	76
Opelousas	86
Ruston	81

Maine

Augusta–Waterville	48
Biddeford	45

Maryland

Salisbury	71

Michigan

Adrian	51
Marquette	41
Mount Pleasant	56
Owosso	55
Traverse City	43

Minnesota

Faribault	48
Mankato	40
Winona	46

Mississippi

Columbus	81
Greenville	77
Greenwood	71
Hattiesburg	78
Laurel	82
Meridian	75
Tupelo	78
Vicksburg	73

Missouri

Cape Girardeau	66
Jefferson City	63
Sikeston	74

Montana

Bozeman	32
Helena	37
Missoula	32

Nebraska

Grand Island	44

Nevada

Carson City	60

New Hampshire

Concord	37
Keene	39
Laconia	36

New Mexico

Alamogordo	85
Carlsbad	78
Clovis	83
Farmington	62
Gallup	66
Hobbs	80
Rio Rancho	71
Roswell	82

New York

Auburn	49
Batavia	52
Cortland	46
Gloversville	49
Ithaca	45
Jamestown	44
Kingston	44
Olean	51
Plattsburgh	52
Watertown	46

North Carolina

Eden	71
Goldsboro	79
Greenville	73
Havelock–New Bern	81
Kinston	76
Lumberton	85
Roanoke Rapids	78
Rocky Mount	75
Sanford	77
Shelby	78
Statesville	75
Wilson	70

North Dakota

Minot	52

Ohio

Ashland	57
Ashtabula	54
Athens	60
Chillicothe	59
East Liverpool	62
Findlay	54
Fremont	56
Marion	59
New Philadelphia	56
Portsmouth	66
Sandusky	50
Sidney	61
Tiffin	55
Wooster	54
Zanesville	60

Oklahoma

Ardmore	75
Bartlesville	70
Chickasha	71
Duncan	76
McAlester	77
Muskogee	70
Okmulgee	71
Ponca City	61
Stillwater	65

Oregon

Albany	58
Bend	41
Corvallis	52
Grants Pass	54
Klamath Falls	53
Roseburg	59

Pennsylvania

Butler	59
Chambersburg	62
New Castle	58
Pottsville	65

Rhode Island

Newport	37

South Carolina

Greenwood	74
Hilton Head Island	72
Myrtle Beach	74
Orangeburg	85
Sumter	84

Tennessee

Cleveland	77
Columbia	74
Cookeville	78
Morristown	78
Tullahoma	81

Texas

Alice	75
Bay City	59
Del Rio	80
Greenville	74
Huntsville	61
Lufkin	77
Nacogdoches	72
Palestine	74
Paris	75

Utah

Logan	52

Vermont

Rutland	46

Virginia

Blacksburg	67
Fredericksburg	67
Harrisonburg	69
Martinsville	78
Staunton– Waynesboro	69
Winchester	66

Washington

Aberdeen	59
Longview	62
Port Angeles	59
Pullman	52
Walla Walla	58
Wenatchee	54

West Virginia

Beckley	70
Clarksburg	59
Fairmont	58
Morgantown	56

Wisconsin

Fond du Lac	48
Manitowoc	52
Marshfield– Wisconsin Rapids	46
Stevens Point	50

Wyoming

Rock Springs	33

8

Public Safety

Violence has become an accepted way of life in America," insists Jerald Vaughn of the International Association of Chiefs of Police. "We seem to thrive on it."

Law-enforcement officers echo Vaughn's assertion from coast to coast. Police in Los Angeles County made 12,000 gang-related arrests in 1987, but scored no dramatic gain in the battle for the streets. Washington registered the nation's highest drug-homicide rate at the end of the eighties. "We arrested 43,000 people last year," said exasperated police chief Maurice Turner. "What the hell is the police department going to do?"

Statistics also dramatize the increasing tendency of Americans to resort to violent behavior. The federal government annually tabulates the number of murders, rapes, robberies, and aggravated assaults, expressing the total as a rate. There were 161 of these violent crimes per 100,000 U.S. residents in 1960; the figure had soared to 609.7 per 100,000 by 1987.

Many experts believe the penalties for these crimes are not sufficiently severe to discourage violent acts. A 1986 study by the Bureau of Justice Statistics reported that the average murderer spent about seven years behind bars, the average robber two and a half years. "We are incarcerating more people, but most get out before very long and many are worse than before,"

292 maintains Lyle Shannon, a criminologist at the University of Iowa.

It is important that a community do its best to combat the increasing rate of violent crime. This section evaluates each small city according to its rate of reported criminal offenses, the size of its police force, and its financial commitment to its police and fire departments.

Some experts believe that the nation's serious crime problem will lessen in intensity as the population grows older during the 1990s. But frightened urban residents can't wait that long. They must make choices now. One option is to fight back. "The community has to come forward," says Bill Hopkins of the New York State Substance Abuse Services Division. "If people keep running into their houses too afraid to say anything to police, the drug gangs are going to take over the streets." *Newsweek* documented a case of successful community involvement in Brooklyn in 1988, where a group of Muslims worked with police to shut down crack houses. But such instances remain rare.

Another course of action is flight. Many urbanites are carefully considering moves to safer parts of America. Their worries are understandable when viewed in light of the number of murders in five major metropolitan areas in 1987:

New York City	1,733
Los Angeles	1,412
Detroit	882
Chicago	757
Atlanta	361

The figures for both New York and Detroit compute to more than 20 murders annually per 100,000 residents. The lowest rate for these five metros belongs to Chicago: 12.3 murders per 100,000. Contrast that with the highest murder rate of any small town: Selma, Alabama, had three murders in 1987, or a rate of 11.7 per 100,000.

As you might expect, micropolitan areas are safer than metros from all types of criminals. The federal government says the typical large city and its suburbs experienced a total of 6,294.5 crimes per 100,000 residents in 1987; the typical small city had a rate of 4,898.5 per 100,000. The disparity becomes even larger when only violent crimes are considered. The metropolitan rate for 1987 was 720.0 offenses per 100,000. The micropolitan figure was not even half as large: just 350.8 violent crimes per 100,000 residents.

Ranking micropolitan America. The ideal small city would have a low crime rate, particularly when it comes to violent offenses. It would also have a large, well-funded police force and a professional fire department.

Each area is graded in five categories:

1. Total Crime Rate: Can you live free from the worry of any sort of crime, including the smallest, or is there a high rate of offenses?

2. Violent Crime Rate: Can you walk the streets without physical fear, or are violent incidents a daily occurrence?

3. Police Presence: Does the local force have adequate staffing, or is it badly understaffed?

4. Local Police Funding: Does the local government show a willingness to pay for superior police protection?

5. Local Fire Funding: Are local officials likewise free with their financial support for the fire department?

Total Crime Rate

Count to yourself: one thousand one, one thousand two. While you were counting, another crime was committed somewhere in the United States. The current rate is one incident every two seconds, with the greatest probability in big cities. Metropolitan areas average 28 percent more offenses than do small cities.

This category ranks each area according to its total crime rate. The figure is determined by adding the number of these incidents reported in a year: murder, rape, robbery, aggravated assault, burglary, larceny/theft, and motor-vehicle theft. The total is then projected to a rate per 100,000 residents. The national average, including metros, is 5,550 offenses per 100,000.

Most of these figures are for 1987. Some cities failed to report their records for that year to the government, so their most recent available rates are listed. The numbers have been adjusted, based on fluctuations in the state's rate, if they were for a year prior to 1986. -

Mattoon–Charleston, Illinois, offers a safe haven for those weary of big-city crime. Only 718 offenses were reported in Mattoon–Charleston over the year, for a rate of just 1,884 per 100,000.

Most of the highest figures belong to Southern towns. The prime example is Brunswick, Georgia. Its 3,477 crimes equal a rate of 17,408 per 100,000. There is an average of four and a half larceny/thefts in Brunswick daily.

Source. These statistics, published in 1988, are for 1987. Derived from U.S. Federal Bureau of Investigation, *Uniform Crime Reports* (Washington: U.S. Government Printing Office, 1988).

Scoring. Twenty points for 2,499.9 or less per 100,000; no points for 12,000.0 or more. The spacing is every 500 per 100,000.

Lowest	Reported Crimes Per 100,000 Residents
1. Mattoon–Charleston, Ill.	1,883.5
2. Ashland, Ohio	2,241.6
3. Pullman, Wash.	2,424.4
4. Rio Rancho, N.Mex.	2,667.2
5. Pottsville, Pa.	3,055.4
6. Athens, Ala.	3,083.2
7. Clarksburg, W.Va.	3,136.9
8. New Philadelphia, Ohio	3,151.9
9. Butler, Pa.	3,152.5
10. Cookeville, Tenn.	3,225.9

Highest	
219. Brunswick, Ga.	17,407.6
218. Valdosta, Ga.	15,036.6
217. Myrtle Beach, S.C.	14,194.1
216. Key West, Fla.	13,236.5
215. Gallup, N.Mex.	13,223.9
214. Salisbury, Md.	12,360.6
213. Paris, Tex.	12,343.6
212. Eureka, Calif.	12,085.9
211. Greenville, Tex.	12,060.6
210. Paducah, Ky.	11,661.7

(Figure following each area name indicates the number of reported crimes per 100,000 residents; figure in parentheses represents rating points.)

Alabama

Athens	3,083.2	(18)
Auburn–Opelika	7,878.0	(9)
Decatur	6,879.0	(11)
Enterprise	7,447.3	(10)
Selma	10,891.6	(3)
Talladega	3,872.8	(17)

Alaska

Fairbanks	3,719.5	(17)

Arizona

Bullhead City–Lake Havasu City	6,558.0	(11)
Casa Grande– Apache Junction	9,135.6	(6)
Flagstaff	9,182.3	(6)
Prescott	6,954.3	(11)
Sierra Vista	4,070.2	(16)
Yuma	10,094.1	(4)

Arkansas

Blytheville	9,451.9	(6)
El Dorado	5,609.8	(13)
Hot Springs	10,568.2	(3)
Jonesboro	5,132.4	(14)
Rogers	4,324.1	(16)
Russellville	7,041.5	(10)

California

El Centro–Calexico– Brawley	10,032.0	(4)
Eureka	12,085.9	(0)
Hanford	5,484.0	(14)
Madera	5,012.6	(14)
San Luis Obispo– Atascadero	4,743.2	(15)

Colorado

Grand Junction	8,029.1	(8)

Connecticut

Torrington	3,414.6	(18)

Delaware

Dover	10,132.2	(4)

Florida

Key West	13,236.5	(0)
Vero Beach	9,403.8	(6)

Georgia

Brunswick	17,407.6	(0)
Carrollton	8,152.9	(8)
Dalton	7,602.7	(9)
Gainesville	9,359.6	(6)
Hinesville	8,632.0	(7)
La Grange	7,830.3	(9)
Rome	7,154.2	(10)
Valdosta	15,036.6	(0)

Idaho

Coeur d'Alene	8,100.4	(8)
Idaho Falls	6,058.0	(12)
Nampa–Caldwell	8,356.6	(8)
Pocatello	5,816.2	(13)
Twin Falls	7,294.1	(10)

Illinois

Carbondale	6,274.5	(12)
Danville	8,086.1	(8)
De Kalb	4,570.1	(15)
Freeport	5,724.5	(13)
Galesburg	5,488.2	(14)
Mattoon–Charleston	1,883.5	(20)
Ottawa	3,316.2	(18)
Quincy	6,866.3	(11)
Sterling	4,757.9	(15)

Indiana

Columbus	6,581.8	(11)
Marion	5,257.3	(14)
Michigan City– La Porte	5,260.0	(14)
New Castle	5,720.2	(13)
Richmond	4,711.4	(15)
Vincennes	4,421.3	(16)

Iowa

Ames	4,965.3	(15)
Burlington	7,663.0	(9)
Clinton	7,828.6	(9)
Fort Dodge	9,643.3	(5)
Marshalltown	4,885.0	(15)
Mason City	7,684.4	(9)
Muscatine	4,261.8	(16)

Kansas

Hutchinson	7,197.8	(10)
Manhattan	4,934.6	(15)
Salina	5,185.4	(14)

Kentucky

Bowling Green	7,037.5	(10)
Frankfort	4,969.5	(15)
Madisonville	7,096.6	(10)
Paducah	11,661.7	(1)
Radcliff– Elizabethtown	4,745.9	(15)
Richmond	3,750.4	(17)

Louisiana

Bogalusa	5,636.2	(13)
Crowley	3,476.1	(18)
Hammond	4,366.0	(16)
Minden	3,480.8	(18)
Morgan City	3,745.4	(17)
New Iberia	3,442.4	(18)
Opelousas	4,366.0	(16)
Ruston	4,386.3	(16)

Maine

Augusta–Waterville	6,030.0	(12)
Biddeford	4,838.6	(15)

Maryland

Salisbury	12,360.6	(0)

Michigan

Adrian	7,095.5	(10)
Marquette	4,875.7	(15)
Mount Pleasant	4,114.2	(16)
Owosso	6,214.9	(12)
Traverse City	7,056.1	(10)

Minnesota

Faribault	6,247.3	(12)
Mankato	5,893.9	(13)
Winona	6,475.4	(12)

Mississippi

Columbus	6,041.2	(12)
Greenville	8,672.9	(7)
Greenwood	7,355.4	(10)
Hattiesburg	5,636.9	(13)
Laurel	9,292.7	(6)
Meridian	5,736.8	(13)
Tupelo	4,657.6	(15)
Vicksburg	4,954.1	(15)

Missouri

Cape Girardeau	6,599.1	(11)
Jefferson City	4,468.9	(16)
Sikeston	5,603.5	(13)

Montana

Bozeman	5,938.1	(13)
Helena	7,192.5	(10)
Missoula	9,484.9	(6)

Nebraska

Grand Island	6,752.6	(11)

Nevada

Carson City	5,094.9	(14)

New Hampshire

Concord	4,784.9	(15)
Keene	4,937.9	(15)
Laconia	6,425.8	(12)

New Mexico

Alamogordo	6,403.9	(12)
Carlsbad	6,705.6	(11)
Clovis	5,630.7	(13)
Farmington	7,058.6	(10)
Gallup	13,223.9	(0)
Hobbs	6,413.5	(12)
Rio Rancho	2,667.2	(19)
Roswell	6,917.6	(11)

New York

Auburn	5,460.7	(14)
Batavia	4,243.6	(16)
Cortland	5,478.3	(14)
Gloversville	5,059.5	(14)
Ithaca	8,185.5	(8)
Jamestown	5,414.6	(14)
Kingston	4,908.8	(15)
Olean	5,136.7	(14)
Plattsburgh	3,705.3	(17)
Watertown	4,572.3	(15)

North Carolina

Eden	5,471.8	(14)
Goldsboro	7,920.4	(9)
Greenville	7,992.3	(9)
Havelock–New Bern	4,385.7	(16)
Kinston	8,671.0	(7)
Lumberton	9,124.7	(6)
Roanoke Rapids	4,615.9	(15)
Rocky Mount	8,590.7	(7)
Sanford	8,054.5	(8)
Shelby	6,518.7	(11)
Statesville	7,760.4	(9)
Wilson	9,193.4	(6)

North Dakota

Minot	4,394.8	(16)

Ohio

Ashland	2,241.6	(20)
Ashtabula	6,990.2	(11)
Athens	4,293.1	(16)
Chillicothe	10,639.5	(3)
East Liverpool	5,772.4	(13)
Findlay	4,708.4	(15)
Fremont	3,684.7	(17)
Marion	7,369.1	(10)
New Philadelphia	3,151.9	(18)
Portsmouth	5,873.0	(13)
Sandusky	6,755.1	(11)
Sidney	5,597.9	(13)
Tiffin	4,778.1	(15)
Wooster	5,234.0	(14)
Zanesville	7,290.4	(10)

Oklahoma

Ardmore	7,961.3	(9)
Bartlesville	7,645.2	(9)
Chickasha	8,342.9	(8)
Duncan	5,443.5	(14)
McAlester	6,248.3	(12)
Muskogee	8,468.9	(8)
Okmulgee	8,750.6	(7)
Ponca City	3,845.5	(17)
Stillwater	4,512.1	(15)

Oregon

Albany	6,098.8	(12)
Bend	9,189.9	(6)
Corvallis	5,672.3	(13)
Grants Pass	11,353.3	(2)
Klamath Falls	9,482.6	(6)
Roseburg	9,830.8	(5)

Pennsylvania

Butler	3,152.5	(18)
Chambersburg	7,137.1	(10)
New Castle	4,137.0	(16)
Pottsville	3,055.4	(18)

Rhode Island

Newport	7,730.2	(9)

South Carolina

Greenwood	7,315.6	(10)
Hilton Head Island	6,569.0	(11)
Myrtle Beach	14,194.1	(0)
Orangeburg	9,894.5	(5)
Sumter	8,214.9	(8)

Tennessee

Cleveland	5,044.7	(14)
Columbia	4,551.2	(15)
Cookeville	3,225.9	(18)
Morristown	5,301.3	(14)
Tullahoma	3,784.9	(17)

Texas

Alice	9,746.3	(5)
Bay City	9,289.7	(6)
Del Rio	5,618.1	(13)
Greenville	12,060.6	(0)
Huntsville	5,885.2	(13)
Lufkin	7,616.3	(9)
Nacogdoches	5,351.9	(14)
Palestine	8,469.2	(8)
Paris	12,343.6	(0)

Utah

Logan	4,650.8	(15)

Vermont

Rutland	6,952.1	(11)

Virginia

Blacksburg	4,371.5	(16)
Fredericksburg	5,699.9	(13)
Harrisonburg	4,319.9	(16)
Martinsville	6,190.1	(12)
Staunton–		
Waynesboro	3,569.0	(17)
Winchester	6,232.1	(12)

Washington

Aberdeen	11,037.1	(2)
Longview	8,045.1	(8)
Port Angeles	7,952.1	(9)
Pullman	2,424.4	(20)
Walla Walla	10,409.9	(4)
Wenatchee	11,345.4	(2)

West Virginia

Beckley	3,542.2	(17)
Clarksburg	3,136.9	(18)
Fairmont	4,571.3	(15)
Morgantown	4,582.6	(15)

Wisconsin

Fond du Lac	5,719.5	(13)
Manitowoc	5,655.2	(13)
Marshfield–		
Wisconsin Rapids	4,914.4	(15)
Stevens Point	7,359.2	(10)

Wyoming

Rock Springs	6,272.1	(12)

Violent Crime Rate

The lurid headlines that blare from the front pages of its daily tabloids lead to the conclusion that New York City has more than its share of violence. The annual statistics confirm the impression, giving these New York City totals for 1987: 1,672 murders, 3,507 rapes, 78,890 robberies, and 64,244 aggravated assaults.

Anyone looking to escape this carnage merely needs to drive to the other end of the state. Olean, New York, had no murders or rapes in 1987. Its entire list of violent crimes consisted of two robberies and three aggravated assaults.

This category calculates the violent-crime rate for each area, projecting its annual totals in the four classifications listed above to a rate per 100,000 residents. These offenses are included in the total crime rate, but are also separated for their own figure because of the great concern about violent crime.

Olean is virtually free of violence, as its rate of 28.6 per 100,000 indicates. Compare it to the national average of 610 per 100,000, or New York City's figure of 2,036.

Brunswick, Georgia, is one of three small cities with a violent-crime rate higher than New York's. Its 2 murders, 32 rapes, 153 robberies, and 521 assaults compute to a rate of 3,545 per 100,000.

Southern cities are prominent on the list of towns with violent-crime problems. The Midwest offers the greatest safety.

Source. These statistics, published in 1988, are for 1987. Derived from U.S. Federal Bureau of Investigation, *Uniform Crime Reports* (Washington: U.S. Government Printing Office, 1988).

Scoring. Twenty points for 49.9 or less per 100,000; no points for 1,475 or more. The spacing is every 75.0 per 100,000.

	Lowest	Reported Violent Crimes Per 100,000 Residents
1.	Olean, N.Y.	28.6
2.	Minot, N.Dak.	31.0
3.	Batavia, N.Y.	37.6
4.	Muscatine, Iowa	42.7
5.	Clinton, Iowa	43.5
6.	Beckley, W.Va.	51.7
6.	Bozeman, Mont.	51.7
8.	Sidney, Ohio	54.2
9.	Pullman, Wash.	67.9
10.	Sierra Vista, Ariz.	71.9

Highest

219.	Brunswick, Ga.	3,544.6
218.	Selma, Ala.	3,189.8
217.	Greenville, Tex.	2,595.9
216.	Eureka, Calif.	1,928.7
215.	Paris, Tex.	1,539.2
214.	Greenwood, S.C.	1,517.2
213.	Salisbury, Md.	1,509.0
212.	Valdosta, Ga.	1,441.2
211.	Chambersburg, Pa.	1,421.2
210.	Orangeburg, S.C.	1,375.1

(Figure following each area name indicates the number of reported violent crimes per 100,000 residents; figure in parentheses represents rating points.)

Alabama

Athens	481.6	(14)
Auburn–Opelika	837.7	(9)
Decatur	498.4	(14)
Enterprise	687.1	(11)
Selma	3,189.8	(0)
Talladega	535.9	(13)

Alaska

Fairbanks	252.8	(17)

Arizona

Bullhead City–Lake Havasu City	872.2	(9)
Casa Grande–Apache Junction	581.2	(12)
Flagstaff	731.2	(10)
Prescott	311.7	(16)
Sierra Vista	71.9	(19)
Yuma	943.1	(8)

Arkansas

Blytheville	1,300.8	(3)
El Dorado	439.9	(14)
Hot Springs	927.7	(8)
Jonesboro	132.2	(18)
Rogers	84.0	(19)
Russellville	359.9	(15)

California

El Centro–Calexico–Brawley	630.0	(12)
Eureka	1,928.7	(0)
Hanford	423.0	(15)
Madera	1,245.6	(4)
San Luis Obispo–Atascadero	283.8	(16)

Colorado

Grand Junction	256.6	(17)

Connecticut

Torrington	565.4	(13)

Delaware

Dover	784.7	(10)

Florida

Key West	1,021.7	(7)
Vero Beach	1,244.0	(4)

Georgia

Brunswick	3,544.6	(0)
Carrollton	706.0	(11)
Dalton	451.3	(14)
Gainesville	433.4	(14)
Hinesville	601.3	(12)
La Grange	1,023.5	(7)
Rome	457.1	(14)
Valdosta	1,441.2	(1)

Idaho

Coeur d'Alene	398.7	(15)
Idaho Falls	168.9	(18)
Nampa–Caldwell	332.5	(16)
Pocatello	212.6	(17)
Twin Falls	264.3	(17)

Illinois

Carbondale	330.0	(16)
Danville	886.7	(8)
De Kalb	139.0	(18)
Freeport	636.9	(12)
Galesburg	253.7	(17)
Mattoon–Charleston	99.7	(19)
Ottawa	122.6	(19)
Quincy	274.4	(17)
Sterling	230.5	(17)

Indiana

Columbus	179.8	(18)
Marion	264.0	(17)
Michigan City–La Porte	220.5	(17)
New Castle	281.7	(16)
Richmond	130.0	(18)
Vincennes	231.4	(17)

Iowa

Ames	330.0	(16)
Burlington	657.4	(11)
Clinton	43.5	(20)
Fort Dodge	609.4	(12)
Marshalltown	459.2	(14)
Mason City	579.6	(12)
Muscatine	42.7	(20)

Kansas

Hutchinson	545.9	(13)
Manhattan	244.4	(17)
Salina	153.1	(18)

Kentucky

Bowling Green	644.0	(12)
Frankfort	631.4	(12)
Madisonville	941.8	(8)
Paducah	1,222.9	(4)
Radcliff–Elizabethtown	335.5	(16)
Richmond	551.7	(13)

Louisiana

Bogalusa	678.9	(11)
Crowley	384.9	(15)
Hammond	552.1	(13)
Minden	856.9	(9)
Morgan City	144.8	(18)
New Iberia	117.1	(19)
Opelousas	552.1	(13)
Ruston	287.1	(16)

Maine

Augusta–Waterville	260.1	(17)
Biddeford	324.8	(16)

Maryland

Salisbury	1,509.0	(0)

Michigan

Adrian	180.3	(18)
Marquette	125.7	(18)
Mount Pleasant	150.0	(18)
Owosso	567.9	(13)
Traverse City	251.8	(17)

Minnesota

Faribault	183.2	(18)
Mankato	149.6	(18)
Winona	86.6	(19)

Mississippi

Columbus	236.8	(17)
Greenville	720.0	(11)
Greenwood	375.1	(15)
Hattiesburg	304.5	(16)
Laurel	126.0	(18)
Meridian	146.6	(18)
Tupelo	143.2	(18)
Vicksburg	449.7	(14)

Missouri

Cape Girardeau	514.3	(13)
Jefferson City	323.5	(16)
Sikeston	315.7	(16)

Montana

Bozeman	51.7	(19)
Helena	183.0	(18)
Missoula	306.7	(16)

Nebraska

Grand Island	166.6	(18)

Nevada

Carson City	620.3	(12)

New Hampshire

Concord	183.8	(18)
Keene	212.8	(17)
Laconia	346.5	(16)

New Mexico

Alamogordo	392.1	(15)
Carlsbad	343.6	(16)
Clovis	455.6	(14)
Farmington	550.7	(13)
Gallup	1,268.8	(3)
Hobbs	671.1	(11)
Rio Rancho	253.0	(17)
Roswell	460.7	(14)

New York

Auburn	101.8	(19)
Batavia	37.6	(20)
Cortland	225.6	(17)
Gloversville	136.9	(18)
Ithaca	369.0	(15)
Jamestown	109.2	(19)
Kingston	808.5	(9)
Olean	28.6	(20)
Plattsburgh	244.5	(17)
Watertown	118.0	(19)

North Carolina

Eden	696.6	(11)
Goldsboro	826.7	(9)
Greenville	693.2	(11)
Havelock–New Bern	447.6	(14)
Kinston	942.0	(8)
Lumberton	1,016.7	(7)
Roanoke Rapids	215.8	(17)
Rocky Mount	673.0	(11)
Sanford	989.0	(7)
Shelby	630.2	(12)
Statesville	404.1	(15)
Wilson	692.2	(11)

North Dakota

Minot	31.0	(20)

Ohio

Ashland	420.9	(15)
Ashtabula	414.3	(15)
Athens	351.4	(15)
Chillicothe	556.2	(13)
East Liverpool	122.0	(19)
Findlay	277.4	(16)
Fremont	264.8	(17)
Marion	247.7	(17)
New Philadelphia	152.3	(18)
Portsmouth	363.0	(15)
Sandusky	554.0	(13)
Sidney	54.2	(19)
Tiffin	438.1	(14)
Wooster	138.3	(18)
Zanesville	633.3	(12)

Oklahoma

Ardmore	512.2	(13)
Bartlesville	292.9	(16)
Chickasha	479.3	(14)
Duncan	222.1	(17)
McAlester	402.6	(15)
Muskogee	573.2	(13)
Okmulgee	924.8	(8)
Ponca City	164.9	(18)
Stillwater	209.6	(17)

Oregon

Albany	208.2	(17)
Bend	130.3	(18)
Corvallis	99.3	(19)
Grants Pass	241.6	(17)
Klamath Falls	492.0	(14)
Roseburg	337.1	(16)

Pennsylvania

Butler	236.4	(17)
Chambersburg	1,421.2	(1)
New Castle	494.0	(14)
Pottsville	128.5	(18)

Rhode Island

Newport	327.3	(16)

South Carolina

Greenwood	1,517.2	(0)
Hilton Head Island	879.4	(8)
Myrtle Beach	630.9	(12)
Orangeburg	1,375.1	(2)
Sumter	1,139.2	(5)

Tennessee

Cleveland	420.1	(15)
Columbia	284.5	(16)
Cookeville	186.1	(18)
Morristown	297.0	(16)
Tullahoma	129.7	(18)

Texas

Alice	274.0	(17)
Bay City	1,021.4	(7)
Del Rio	326.4	(16)
Greenville	2,595.9	(0)
Huntsville	517.2	(13)
Lufkin	737.2	(10)
Nacogdoches	701.0	(11)
Palestine	874.0	(9)
Paris	1,539.2	(0)

Utah

Logan	120.1	(19)

Vermont

Rutland	284.0	(16)

Virginia

Blacksburg	148.4	(18)
Fredericksburg	387.0	(15)
Harrisonburg	98.0	(19)
Martinsville	608.0	(12)
Staunton– Waynesboro	217.8	(17)
Winchester	254.3	(17)

Washington

Aberdeen	350.6	(15)
Longview	388.1	(15)
Port Angeles	156.8	(18)
Pullman	67.9	(19)
Walla Walla	875.9	(8)
Wenatchee	511.1	(13)

West Virginia

Beckley	51.7	(19)
Clarksburg	167.2	(18)
Fairmont	172.7	(18)
Morgantown	184.7	(18)

Wisconsin

Fond du Lac	122.6	(19)
Manitowoc	96.2	(19)
Marshfield– Wisconsin Rapids	207.3	(17)
Stevens Point	187.9	(18)

Wyoming

Rock Springs	645.6	(12)

Police Presence

It has been demonstrated that there is a direct link between a community's crime rate and the size of its police force. "Modern America has too much crime and too little law enforcement to make punishment very certain," wrote Lawrence Sherman, a University of Maryland criminology professor, in 1986. "Since 1978, in fact, the total number of police officers in big cities has been declining, while both serious and minor crimes have surged."

This category rates each area according to the total of full-time law-enforcement .personnel in its central city, expressed as a rate per 100,000 residents. The average for the entire country, including large cities, is 262.8 police employees for every 100,000 citizens.

Gainesville, Georgia, boasts a force of 84, including 79 uniformed officers. That equals a rate of 485 people involved in law enforcement per 100,000.

Huntsville, Texas, has twice the central-city population of Gainesville, but its police force is half the size. Huntsville has 41 police employees, including 30 in uniform, for a rate of only 111 per 100,000.

Southern cities typically have the largest police departments. Those in the Midwest are the smallest.

Source. These statistics, published in 1988, are for 1987. Derived from U.S. Federal Bureau of Investigation, *Uniform Crime Reports* (Washington: U.S. Government Printing Office, 1988).

Scoring. Twenty points for 450 or more per 100,000; no points for 126.9 or less. The spacing is every 17 per 100,000.

	Police Employees
Highest	**Per 100,000 Residents**
1. Gainesville, Ga.	484.7
2. Vero Beach, Fla.	434.5
3. Gallup, N.Mex.	431.7
4. Laurel, Miss.	373.2
5. Myrtle Beach, S.C.	364.5
6. Newport, R.I.	351.3
7. Salisbury, Md.	349.5
8. Brunswick, Ga.	349.1
9. Statesville, N.C.	347.2
10. Prescott, Ariz.	329.9

Lowest

219. Huntsville, Tex.	110.7
218. Marion, Ohio	116.9
217. Logan, Utah	117.7
216. New Castle, Pa.	120.7
215. Owosso, Mich.	123.2
214. Mount Pleasant, Mich.	123.3
213. Athens, Ohio	124.6
212. Pullman, Wash.	125.2
211. Bozeman, Mont.	127.7
209. East Liverpool, Ohio	127.9
209. Grand Island, Nebr.	127.9

(Figure following each area name indicates the number of police employees per 100,000 residents; figure in parentheses represents rating points.)

Alabama

Athens	220.5	(6)
Auburn–Opelika	256.2	(8)
Decatur	213.3	(6)
Enterprise	222.3	(6)
Selma	296.1	(10)
Talladega	270.0	(9)

Alaska

Fairbanks	170.2	(3)

Arizona

Bullhead City– Lake Havasu City	326.9	(12)
Casa Grande– Apache Junction	308.9	(11)
Flagstaff	242.5	(7)
Prescott	329.9	(12)
Sierra Vista	143.2	(1)
Yuma	247.7	(8)

Arkansas

Blytheville	211.1	(5)
El Dorado	207.8	(5)
Hot Springs	222.0	(6)
Jonesboro	159.7	(2)
Rogers	202.0	(5)
Russellville	158.2	(2)

California

El Centro–Calexico– Brawley	212.2	(6)
Eureka	209.0	(5)
Hanford	200.1	(5)
Madera	170.3	(3)
San Luis Obispo– Atascadero	185.9	(4)

Colorado

Grand Junction	286.7	(10)

Connecticut

Torrington	225.2	(6)

Delaware

Dover	326.6	(12)

Florida

Key West	308.5	(11)
Vero Beach	434.5	(19)

Georgia

Brunswick	349.1	(14)
Carrollton	255.9	(8)
Dalton	268.6	(9)
Gainesville	484.7	(20)
Hinesville	321.6	(12)
La Grange	313.1	(11)
Rome	271.8	(9)
Valdosta	221.8	(6)

Idaho

Coeur d'Alene	226.8	(6)
Idaho Falls	203.1	(5)
Nampa–Caldwell	164.5	(3)
Pocatello	198.1	(5)
Twin Falls	162.2	(3)

Illinois

Carbondale	244.1	(7)
Danville	207.3	(5)
De Kalb	171.0	(3)
Freeport	185.8	(4)
Galesburg	201.1	(5)
Mattoon–Charleston	205.2	(5)
Ottawa	173.3	(3)
Quincy	209.6	(5)
Sterling	237.6	(7)

Indiana

Columbus	223.4	(6)
Marion	181.5	(4)
Michigan City–La Porte	221.6	(6)
New Castle	217.7	(6)
Richmond	248.5	(8)
Vincennes	163.0	(3)

Iowa

Ames	139.5	(1)
Burlington	153.6	(2)
Clinton	149.6	(2)
Fort Dodge	155.2	(2)
Marshalltown	214.8	(6)
Mason City	172.2	(3)
Muscatine	165.4	(3)

Kansas

Hutchinson	195.2	(5)
Manhattan	275.6	(9)
Salina	151.8	(2)

Kentucky

Bowling Green	220.3	(6)
Frankfort	208.0	(5)
Madisonville	241.0	(7)
Paducah	243.2	(7)
Radcliff–Elizabethtown	172.4	(3)
Richmond	183.9	(4)

Louisiana

Bogalusa	249.4	(8)
Crowley	190.1	(4)
Hammond	272.6	(9)
Minden	177.7	(3)
Morgan City	305.7	(11)
New Iberia	187.8	(4)
Opelousas	216.9	(6)
Ruston	167.9	(3)

Maine

Augusta–Waterville	223.2	(6)
Biddeford	207.7	(5)

Maryland

Salisbury	349.5	(14)

Michigan

Adrian	181.2	(4)
Marquette	177.8	(3)
Mount Pleasant	123.3	(0)
Owosso	123.2	(0)
Traverse City	202.4	(5)

Minnesota

Faribault	184.5	(4)
Mankato	140.6	(1)
Winona	157.7	(2)

Mississippi

Columbus	222.7	(6)
Greenville	260.0	(8)
Greenwood	243.5	(7)
Hattiesburg	265.1	(9)
Laurel	373.2	(15)
Meridian	274.6	(9)
Tupelo	267.1	(9)
Vicksburg	265.2	(9)

Missouri

Cape Girardeau	224.1	(6)
Jefferson City	198.8	(5)
Sikeston	295.3	(10)

Montana

Bozeman	127.7	(1)
Helena	186.5	(4)
Missoula	200.2	(5)

Nebraska

Grand Island	127.9	(1)

Nevada

Carson City	210.0	(5)

New Hampshire

Concord	250.2	(8)
Keene	183.3	(4)
Laconia	266.0	(9)

New Mexico

Alamogordo	275.7	(9)
Carlsbad	179.5	(4)
Clovis	219.1	(6)
Farmington	271.4	(9)
Gallup	431.7	(18)
Hobbs	289.6	(10)
Rio Rancho	252.6	(8)
Roswell	217.6	(6)

New York

Auburn	201.0	(5)
Batavia	213.4	(6)
Cortland	226.3	(6)
Gloversville	226.9	(6)
Ithaca	260.6	(8)
Jamestown	253.5	(8)
Kingston	281.3	(10)
Olean	200.8	(5)
Plattsburgh	230.8	(7)
Watertown	258.9	(8)

North Carolina

Eden	263.0	(9)
Goldsboro	265.8	(9)
Greenville	286.5	(10)
Havelock–New Bern	180.9	(4)
Kinston	315.4	(12)
Lumberton	261.4	(8)
Roanoke Rapids	238.4	(7)
Rocky Mount	280.5	(10)
Sanford	311.6	(11)
Shelby	325.8	(12)
Statesville	347.2	(13)
Wilson	236.7	(7)

North Dakota

Minot	184.1	(4)

Ohio

Ashland	179.3	(4)
Ashtabula	162.3	(3)
Athens	124.6	(0)
Chillicothe	230.6	(7)
East Liverpool	127.9	(1)
Findlay	174.6	(3)
Fremont	196.8	(5)
Marion	116.9	(0)
New Philadelphia	128.9	(1)
Portsmouth	147.4	(2)
Sandusky	160.6	(2)
Sidney	194.3	(4)
Tiffin	184.5	(4)
Wooster	205.2	(5)
Zanesville	240.0	(7)

Oklahoma

Ardmore	207.6	(5)
Bartlesville	236.6	(7)
Chickasha	234.2	(7)
Duncan	215.3	(6)
McAlester	217.9	(6)
Muskogee	204.8	(5)
Okmulgee	221.0	(6)
Ponca City	237.7	(7)
Stillwater	182.9	(4)

Oregon

Albany	151.6	(2)
Bend	210.5	(5)
Corvallis	168.0	(3)
Grants Pass	203.3	(5)
Klamath Falls	196.5	(5)
Roseburg	253.7	(8)

Pennsylvania

Butler	152.2	(2)
Chambersburg	166.3	(3)
New Castle	120.7	(0)
Pottsville	170.1	(3)

Rhode Island

Newport	351.3	(14)

South Carolina

Greenwood	224.9	(6)
Hilton Head Island	280.0	(10)
Myrtle Beach	364.5	(14)
Orangeburg	278.9	(9)
Sumter	288.8	(10)

Tennessee

Cleveland	218.1	(6)
Columbia	195.2	(5)
Cookeville	246.7	(8)
Morristown	259.5	(8)
Tullahoma	190.7	(4)

Texas

Alice	177.9	(3)
Bay City	170.5	(3)
Del Rio	167.1	(3)
Greenville	170.4	(3)
Huntsville	110.7	(0)
Lufkin	177.7	(3)
Nacogdoches	197.5	(5)
Palestine	252.1	(8)
Paris	194.6	(4)

Utah

Logan	117.7	(0)

Vermont

Rutland	287.6	(10)

Virginia

Blacksburg	184.3	(4)
Fredericksburg	312.8	(11)
Harrisonburg	166.7	(3)
Martinsville	294.1	(10)
Staunton–Waynesboro	257.6	(8)
Winchester	273.6	(9)

Washington

Aberdeen	279.3	(9)
Longview	192.2	(4)
Port Angeles	227.8	(6)
Pullman	125.2	(0)
Walla Walla	194.0	(4)
Wenatchee	224.3	(6)

West Virginia

Beckley	260.7	(8)
Clarksburg	210.4	(5)
Fairmont	179.7	(4)
Morgantown	212.4	(6)

Wisconsin

Fond du Lac	191.6	(4)
Manitowoc	212.0	(6)
Marshfield– 　　Wisconsin Rapids	228.9	(6)
Stevens Point	224.7	(6)

Wyoming

Rock Springs	245.8	(7)

Local Police Funding

Keeping law and order is an increasingly expensive task. New vehicles, the latest communications gear, up-to-date weapons, and secure detention facilities all cost money, lots of it. And that's before talking about salaries for police officers and their civilian support staffs.

This category evaluates the financial commitment of each area to its police. The amount of money allocated to law enforcement by both county and city governments is divided by the number of residents. Included are all expenditures for police patrols, equipment, custody of those awaiting trial, and traffic-safety operations. The national average is $60 from every man, woman, and child for police protection.

Western cities generally spend the most on law enforcement, led by Fairbanks, Alaska, which allocates $139 per capita. That is the highest figure for the nation's small cities, but is low for Alaska, which has a state average of $167 per capita.

Two micropolitan areas are tied for last place. Both Chambersburg, Pennsylvania, and Radcliff–Elizabethtown, Kentucky, spend just $14 per person on law enforcement. Eastern and Southern cities typically allocate less to their police than do communities in other regions.

Source. These statistics, published in 1988, are for the 1981–1982 budget year. Derived from U.S. Bureau of the Census, *County and City Data Book* (Washington: U.S. Government Printing Office, 1988).

Scoring. Twenty points for $96 or more per capita; no points for $19 or less. The spacing is every $4 per capita.

**Annual Per Capita
Police-Related Spending
By Local Governments**

Highest	$
1. Fairbanks, Alaska	139
2. Aberdeen, Wash.	98
3. Rock Springs, Wyo.	91
4. El Centro–Calexico–Brawley, Calif.	88
5. Brunswick, Ga.	86
5. Eureka, Calif.	86
7. Wenatchee, Wash.	84
8. Key West, Fla.	82
9. San Luis Obispo–Atascadero, Calif.	78
10. Hobbs, N.Mex.	76

Lowest	
218. Chambersburg, Pa.	14
218. Radcliff–Elizabethtown, Ky.	14
216. Butler, Pa.	16
216. Plattsburgh, N.Y.	16
215. Pottsville, Pa.	17
214. Richmond, Ky.	18
213. New Castle, Pa.	19
212. Hinesville, Ga.	20
209. Jonesboro, Ark.	21
209. Rutland, Vt.	21
209. Vincennes, Ind.	21

(Figure following each area name indicates annual per capita police-related spending by local government in dollars; figure in parentheses represents rating points.)

Alabama

Athens	26	(2)
Auburn–Opelika	42	(6)
Decatur	31	(3)
Enterprise	29	(3)
Selma	33	(4)
Talladega	30	(3)

Alaska

Fairbanks	139	(20)

Arizona

Bullhead City– Lake Havasu City	74	(14)
Casa Grande– Apache Junction	69	(13)
Flagstaff	74	(14)
Prescott	44	(7)
Sierra Vista	68	(13)
Yuma	53	(9)

Arkansas

Blytheville	42	(6)
El Dorado	29	(3)
Hot Springs	34	(4)
Jonesboro	21	(1)
Rogers	26	(2)
Russellville	31	(3)

California

El Centro–Calexico– Brawley	88	(18)
Eureka	86	(17)
Hanford	70	(13)
Madera	62	(11)
San Luis Obispo– Atascadero	78	(15)

Colorado

Grand Junction	42	(6)

Connecticut

Torrington	31	(3)

Delaware

Dover	27	(2)

Florida

Key West	82	(16)
Vero Beach	66	(12)

Georgia

Brunswick	86	(17)
Carrollton	30	(3)
Dalton	32	(4)
Gainesville	43	(6)
Hinesville	20	(1)
La Grange	55	(9)
Rome	44	(7)
Valdosta	37	(5)

Idaho

Coeur d'Alene	38	(5)
Idaho Falls	41	(6)
Nampa–Caldwell	34	(4)
Pocatello	45	(7)
Twin Falls	39	(5)

Illinois

Carbondale	43	(6)
Danville	43	(6)
De Kalb	49	(8)
Freeport	32	(4)
Galesburg	47	(7)
Mattoon–Charleston	52	(9)
Ottawa	41	(6)
Quincy	39	(5)
Sterling	46	(7)

Indiana

Columbus	31	(3)
Marion	32	(4)
Michigan City–La Porte	41	(6)
New Castle	26	(2)
Richmond	31	(3)
Vincennes	21	(1)

Iowa

Ames	36	(5)
Burlington	40	(6)
Clinton	41	(6)
Fort Dodge	44	(7)
Marshalltown	44	(7)
Mason City	50	(8)
Muscatine	39	(5)

Kansas

Hutchinson	41	(6)
Manhattan	28	(3)
Salina	42	(6)

Kentucky

Bowling Green	33	(4)
Frankfort	37	(5)
Madisonville	25	(2)
Paducah	26	(2)
Radcliff–Elizabethtown	14	(0)
Richmond	18	(0)

Louisiana

Bogalusa	44	(7)
Crowley	42	(6)
Hammond	50	(8)
Minden	35	(4)
Morgan City	70	(13)
New Iberia	50	(8)
Opelousas	46	(7)
Ruston	35	(4)

Maine

Augusta–Waterville	25	(2)
Biddeford	34	(4)

Maryland

Salisbury	31	(3)

Michigan

Adrian	42	(6)
Marquette	36	(5)
Mount Pleasant	27	(2)
Owosso	37	(5)
Traverse City	46	(7)

Minnesota

Faribault	43	(6)
Mankato	52	(9)
Winona	54	(9)

Mississippi

Columbus	24	(2)
Greenville	45	(7)
Greenwood	32	(4)
Hattiesburg	39	(5)
Laurel	35	(4)
Meridian	35	(4)
Tupelo	30	(3)
Vicksburg	34	(4)

Missouri

Cape Girardeau	40	(6)
Jefferson City	39	(5)
Sikeston	39	(5)

Montana

Bozeman	43	(6)
Helena	49	(8)
Missoula	46	(7)

Nebraska

Grand Island	30	(3)

Nevada

Carson City	61	(11)

New Hampshire

Concord	40	(6)
Keene	32	(4)
Laconia	57	(10)

New Mexico

Alamogordo	37	(5)
Carlsbad	57	(10)
Clovis	41	(6)
Farmington	60	(11)
Gallup	34	(4)
Hobbs	76	(15)
Rio Rancho	31	(3)
Roswell	55	(9)

New York

Auburn	33	(4)
Batavia	36	(5)
Cortland	31	(3)
Gloversville	35	(4)
Ithaca	30	(3)
Jamestown	44	(7)
Kingston	32	(4)
Olean	30	(3)
Plattsburgh	16	(0)
Watertown	29	(3)

North Carolina

Eden	44	(7)
Goldsboro	28	(3)
Greenville	35	(4)
Havelock–New Bern	31	(3)
Kinston	39	(5)
Lumberton	27	(2)
Roanoke Rapids	36	(5)
Rocky Mount	38	(5)
Sanford	46	(7)
Shelby	29	(3)
Statesville	32	(4)
Wilson	39	(5)

North Dakota

Minot	36	(5)

Ohio

Ashland	36	(5)
Ashtabula	35	(4)
Athens	22	(1)
Chillicothe	26	(2)
East Liverpool	29	(3)
Findlay	42	(6)
Fremont	39	(5)
Marion	38	(5)
New Philadelphia	32	(4)
Portsmouth	22	(1)
Sandusky	49	(8)
Sidney	38	(5)
Tiffin	37	(5)
Wooster	37	(5)
Zanesville	29	(3)

Oklahoma

Ardmore	26	(2)
Bartlesville	38	(5)
Chickasha	30	(3)
Duncan	33	(4)
McAlester	24	(2)
Muskogee	41	(6)
Okmulgee	33	(4)
Ponca City	49	(8)
Stillwater	29	(3)

Oregon

Albany	50	(8)
Bend	55	(9)
Corvallis	44	(7)
Grants Pass	57	(10)
Klamath Falls	33	(4)
Roseburg	54	(9)

Pennsylvania

Butler	16	(0)
Chambersburg	14	(0)
New Castle	19	(0)
Pottsville	17	(0)

Rhode Island

Newport	67	(12)

South Carolina

Greenwood	44	(7)
Hilton Head Island	33	(4)
Myrtle Beach	43	(6)
Orangeburg	22	(1)
Sumter	30	(3)

Tennessee

Cleveland	24	(2)
Columbia	33	(4)
Cookeville	33	(4)
Morristown	37	(5)
Tullahoma	33	(4)

Texas

Alice	40	(6)
Bay City	47	(7)
Del Rio	33	(4)
Greenville	27	(2)
Huntsville	36	(5)
Lufkin	25	(2)
Nacogdoches	30	(3)
Palestine	27	(2)
Paris	33	(4)

Utah

Logan	36	(5)

Vermont

Rutland	21	(1)

Virginia

Blacksburg	36	(5)
Fredericksburg	30	(3)
Harrisonburg	23	(1)
Martinsville	33	(4)
Staunton–Waynesboro	35	(4)
Winchester	38	(5)

Washington

Aberdeen	98	(20)
Longview	71	(13)
Port Angeles	58	(10)
Pullman	40	(6)
Walla Walla	54	(9)
Wenatchee	84	(17)

West Virginia

Beckley	33	(4)
Clarksburg	33	(4)
Fairmont	26	(2)
Morgantown	24	(2)

Wisconsin

Fond du Lac	73	(14)
Manitowoc	61	(11)
Marshfield– Wisconsin Rapids	67	(12)
Stevens Point	53	(9)

Wyoming

Rock Springs	91	(18)

Local Fire Funding

The willingness of small-city residents to help their neighbors has been historically tested by fires and other disasters. The volunteer fire department would hustle to the scene, or neighbors would form an impromptu "bucket brigade" to battle the flames. Today, a micropolitan area is less likely to rely on such spontaneity. Full-time firefighters are common.

This category ranks each area according to its financial commitment to fire protection. The total amount spent annually by county and city governments is divided by the number of residents. Among the expenditures included in this measure are those for fire-department facilities and employees, support of volunteer forces, and fire inspections. The country on the whole averages an allocation of $31 per person to pay these bills.

Fairbanks, Alaska, spent nearly $7.5 million on its fire department in the budget studied by the Census Bureau. That equals $138 for each resident of the area.

Three small cities—Ardmore, Oklahoma; Dover, Delaware; and Pottsville, Pennsylvania—each allocated just $4 per capita. Dover is one of two state capitals to still be served by a volunteer fire force.

Western cities generally spend the most on fire protection, Southern towns the least.

Source. These statistics, published in 1984, are for 1982. U.S. Bureau of the Census, *Census of Governments: Compendium of Government Finances* (Washington: U.S. Government Printing Office, 1984).

Scoring. Twenty points for $81 or more per capita; no points for $4 or less. The spacing is every $4 per capita.

**Annual Per Capita
Fire-Protection Spending
By Local Governments**

Highest	$
1. Fairbanks, Alaska	138
2. Bullhead City– Lake Havasu City, Ariz.	63
2. Rome, Ga.	63
4. Newport, R.I.	62
5. Bend, Oreg.	48
6. Hobbs, N.Mex.	47
7. Carson City, Nev.	46
8. Rock Springs, Wyo.	44
9. Laconia, N.H.	41
10. Auburn, N.Y.	40
10. Concord, N.H.	40
10. El Centro–Calexico–Brawley, Calif.	40
10. Hanford, Calif.	40

Lowest	
217. Ardmore, Okla.	4
217. Dover, Del.	4
217. Pottsville, Pa.	4
215. Bay City, Tex.	5
215. Hinesville, Ga.	5
214. Chambersburg, Pa.	6
210. Casa Grande– Apache Junction, Ariz.	7
210. Radcliff–Elizabethtown, Ky.	7
210. Sikeston, Mo.	7
210. Vero Beach, Fla.	7

(Figure following each area name indicates annual per capita fire-protection spending by local government in dollars; figure in parentheses represents rating points.)

Alabama

Athens	9	(2)
Auburn–Opelika	28	(6)
Decatur	18	(4)
Enterprise	9	(2)
Selma	16	(3)
Talladega	12	(2)

Alaska

Fairbanks	138	(20)

Arizona

Bullhead City– Lake Havasu City	63	(15)
Casa Grande– Apache Junction	7	(1)
Flagstaff	30	(7)
Prescott	34	(8)
Sierra Vista	23	(5)
Yuma	25	(6)

Arkansas

Blytheville	12	(2)
El Dorado	15	(3)
Hot Springs	18	(4)
Jonesboro	15	(3)
Rogers	17	(4)
Russellville	9	(2)

California

El Centro–Calexico– Brawley	40	(9)
Eureka	35	(8)
Hanford	40	(9)
Madera	14	(3)
San Luis Obispo– Atascadero	31	(7)

Colorado

Grand Junction	30	(7)

Connecticut

Torrington	18	(4)

Delaware

Dover	4	(0)

Florida

Key West	29	(7)
Vero Beach	7	(1)

Georgia

Brunswick	35	(8)
Carrollton	16	(3)
Dalton	23	(5)
Gainesville	28	(6)
Hinesville	5	(1)
La Grange	37	(9)
Rome	63	(15)
Valdosta	25	(6)

Idaho

Coeur d'Alene	19	(4)
Idaho Falls	32	(7)
Nampa–Caldwell	18	(4)
Pocatello	29	(7)
Twin Falls	22	(5)

Illinois

Carbondale	17	(4)
Danville	24	(5)
De Kalb	25	(6)
Freeport	24	(5)
Galesburg	23	(5)
Mattoon–Charleston	26	(6)
Ottawa	21	(5)
Quincy	31	(7)
Sterling	15	(3)

Indiana

Columbus	27	(6)
Marion	18	(4)
Michigan City–La Porte	24	(5)
New Castle	14	(3)
Richmond	24	(5)
Vincennes	19	(4)

Iowa

Ames	21	(5)
Burlington	25	(6)
Clinton	20	(4)
Fort Dodge	17	(4)
Marshalltown	20	(4)
Mason City	20	(4)
Muscatine	23	(5)

Kansas

Hutchinson	37	(9)
Manhattan	12	(2)
Salina	31	(7)

Kentucky

Bowling Green	29	(7)
Frankfort	33	(8)
Madisonville	26	(6)
Paducah	32	(7)
Radcliff–Elizabethtown	7	(1)
Richmond	23	(5)

Louisiana

Bogalusa	16	(3)
Crowley	10	(2)
Hammond	13	(3)
Minden	9	(2)
Morgan City	19	(4)
New Iberia	17	(4)
Opelousas	19	(4)
Ruston	18	(4)

Maine

Augusta–Waterville	21	(5)
Biddeford	29	(7)

Maryland

Salisbury	26	(6)

Michigan

Adrian	20	(4)
Marquette	19	(4)
Mount Pleasant	10	(2)
Owosso	19	(4)
Traverse City	23	(5)

Minnesota

Faribault	19	(4)
Mankato	25	(6)
Winona	35	(8)

Mississippi

Columbus	24	(5)
Greenville	21	(5)
Greenwood	23	(5)
Hattiesburg	29	(7)
Laurel	20	(4)
Meridian	20	(4)
Tupelo	23	(5)
Vicksburg	30	(7)

Missouri

Cape Girardeau	29	(7)
Jefferson City	25	(6)
Sikeston	7	(1)

Montana

Bozeman	21	(5)
Helena	16	(3)
Missoula	35	(8)

Nebraska

Grand Island	20	(4)

Nevada

Carson City	46	(11)

New Hampshire

Concord	40	(9)
Keene	29	(7)
Laconia	41	(10)

New Mexico

Alamogordo	10	(2)
Carlsbad	23	(5)
Clovis	32	(7)
Farmington	33	(8)
Gallup	23	(5)
Hobbs	47	(11)
Rio Rancho	8	(1)
Roswell	35	(8)

New York

Auburn	40	(9)
Batavia	26	(6)
Cortland	28	(6)
Gloversville	27	(6)
Ithaca	26	(6)
Jamestown	27	(6)
Kingston	30	(7)
Olean	23	(5)
Plattsburgh	22	(5)
Watertown	36	(8)

North Carolina

Eden	13	(3)
Goldsboro	22	(5)
Greenville	20	(4)
Havelock–New Bern	13	(3)
Kinston	22	(5)
Lumberton	9	(2)
Roanoke Rapids	13	(3)
Rocky Mount	18	(4)
Sanford	19	(4)
Shelby	15	(3)
Statesville	18	(4)
Wilson	27	(6)

North Dakota

Minot	20	(4)

Ohio

Ashland	18	(4)
Ashtabula	19	(4)
Athens	13	(3)
Chillicothe	23	(5)
East Liverpool	11	(2)
Findlay	24	(5)
Fremont	14	(3)
Marion	33	(8)
New Philadelphia	17	(4)
Portsmouth	20	(4)
Sandusky	27	(6)
Sidney	18	(4)
Tiffin	27	(6)
Wooster	15	(3)
Zanesville	14	(3)

Oklahoma

Ardmore	4	(0)
Bartlesville	33	(8)
Chickasha	22	(5)
Duncan	15	(3)
McAlester	20	(4)
Muskogee	29	(7)
Okmulgee	16	(3)
Ponca City	38	(9)
Stillwater	19	(4)

Oregon

Albany	27	(6)
Bend	48	(11)
Corvallis	27	(6)
Grants Pass	16	(3)
Klamath Falls	23	(5)
Roseburg	37	(9)

Pennsylvania

Butler	8	(1)
Chambersburg	6	(1)
New Castle	14	(3)
Pottsville	4	(0)

Rhode Island

Newport	62	(15)

South Carolina

Greenwood	16	(3)
Hilton Head Island	20	(4)
Myrtle Beach	17	(4)
Orangeburg	8	(1)
Sumter	14	(3)

Tennessee

Cleveland	21	(5)
Columbia	20	(4)
Cookeville	14	(3)
Morristown	20	(4)
Tullahoma	23	(5)

Texas

Alice	13	(3)
Bay City	5	(1)
Del Rio	14	(3)
Greenville	28	(6)
Huntsville	9	(2)
Lufkin	21	(5)
Nacogdoches	24	(5)
Palestine	13	(3)
Paris	19	(4)

Utah

Logan	20	(4)

Vermont

Rutland	22	(5)

Virginia

Blacksburg	8	(1)
Fredericksburg	15	(3)
Harrisonburg	10	(2)
Martinsville	9	(2)
Staunton–Waynesboro	18	(4)
Winchester	11	(2)

Washington

Aberdeen	39	(9)
Longview	28	(6)
Port Angeles	23	(5)
Pullman	16	(3)
Walla Walla	39	(9)
Wenatchee	33	(8)

West Virginia

Beckley	17	(4)
Clarksburg	18	(4)
Fairmont	19	(4)
Morgantown	14	(3)

Wisconsin

Fond du Lac	31	(7)
Manitowoc	36	(8)
Marshfield–Wisconsin Rapids	26	(6)
Stevens Point	27	(6)

Wyoming

Rock Springs	44	(10)

The Results

Fairbanks, Alaska, does not exactly have a history of excessive dedication to law and order. Fairbanks was born in the early days of the twentieth century as a gold-rush town. One needs only a passing acquaintance with western lore to know that the lack of decorum in such communities was surpassed only by the absence of support for organized law enforcement.

Such a past dies hard. Author Neal Peirce observed in 1972 that Fairbanks was "still a rough-and-tumble frontier town that sits on the edge of one of the world's great wildernesses." Joe McGinniss, writing a book on Alaska a few years later, thought Fairbanks was reverting to its lawless past as the Trans-Alaska Pipeline was being built. "There was virtually no police force left in the city," he wrote. "There were drugs and whores and trailer camps, and disputes among residents were less likely to be settled in small-claims court than by small-caliber—or large-caliber—pistol."

Fairbanks retains its frontier flavor, but it has curbed the excesses of the pipeline boom so effectively that it takes first place in the public safety section, with 77 of a possible 100 points. The city has greatly increased its spending on its police and fire departments, now leading all American small cities in both categories. Both the total crime rate and the violent-crime rate are substantially below the national average.

The West offers the best selection of cities with strong public safety scores, taking five of the twelve highest positions. Three of the remaining slots belong to Midwestern cities, two each to communities from the East and the South.

Greenville, Texas, gained a small measure of fame a few decades back as the birthplace of Audie Murphy, the nation's most decorated soldier of World War II. Fighting of the domestic kind earns it last place in the public safety section, with only 11 points.

Greenville has a serious crime problem. Both its total rate and its violent-crime rate are among the highest in micropolitan America. Greenville spends less than half the national average on its police department, devoting only slightly more money to fire protection.

The South dominates the list of small cities with low scores in the public safety section, holding eight slots in the bottom ten. They are joined by Chambersburg, Pennsylvania, and Salisbury, Maryland.

Highest	Rating Points
1. Fairbanks, Alaska	77
2. Newport, R.I.	66
3. Morgan City, La.	63
4. Bullhead City–Lake Havasu City, Ariz.	61
5. Hobbs, N.Mex.	59
5. Mattoon–Charleston, Ill.	59
5. Ponca City, Okla.	59
5. Rock Springs, Wyo.	59
9. Fond du Lac, Wis.	57
9. Laconia, N.H.	57
9. Manitowoc, Wis.	57
9. San Luis Obispo–Atascadero, Calif.	57
13. Concord, N.H.	56
13. Hanford, Calif.	56
13. Marshfield–Wisconsin Rapids, Wis.	56
16. Aberdeen, Wash.	55
16. Rome, Ga.	55
18. Jamestown, N.Y.	54
18. Prescott, Ariz.	54
18. Sierra Vista, Ariz.	54

Lowest	
219. Greenville, Tex.	11
218. Paris, Tex.	12
217. Chambersburg, Pa.	15
215. Orangeburg, S.C.	18
215. Valdosta, Ga.	18
214. Selma, Ala.	20
213. Paducah, Ky.	21
212. Blytheville, Ark.	22
211. Salisbury, Md.	23
210. Bay City, Tex.	24

	Fairbanks, Alaska	Greenville, Tex.
Total Points in Section	77	11
Rank in Section	1	219

Results (and Rating Points)

Total Crime Rate
Reported crimes per
100,000 residents   3,719.5 (17)   12,060.6 (0)

Violent Crime Rate
Reported violent crimes
per 100,000 residents   252.8 (17)   2,595.9 (0)

Police Presence
Police employees per
100,000 residents   170.2 (3)   170.4 (3)

Local Police Funding
Annual per capita police-
related spending by local
governments $139 (20) $27 (2)

Local Fire Funding
Annual per capita fire-
protection spending by
local governments $138 (20) $28 (6)

(Figure following each area name indicates the composite score from the five categories in this section.)

Alabama	
Athens	42
Auburn–Opelika	38
Decatur	38
Enterprise	32
Selma	20
Talladega	44

Alaska	
Fairbanks	77

Arizona	
Bullhead City–Lake Havasu City	61
Casa Grande–Apache Junction	43
Flagstaff	44
Prescott	54
Sierra Vista	54
Yuma	35

Arkansas	
Blytheville	22
El Dorado	38
Hot Springs	25
Jonesboro	38
Rogers	46
Russellville	32

California	
El Centro–Calexico–Brawley	49
Eureka	30
Hanford	56
Madera	35
San Luis Obispo–Atascadero	57

Colorado	
Grand Junction	48

Connecticut	
Torrington	44

Delaware	
Dover	28

Florida	
Key West	41
Vero Beach	42

Georgia	
Brunswick	39
Carrollton	33
Dalton	41
Gainesville	52
Hinesville	33
La Grange	45
Rome	55
Valdosta	18

Idaho	
Coeur d'Alene	38
Idaho Falls	48
Nampa–Caldwell	35
Pocatello	49
Twin Falls	40

Illinois	
Carbondale	45
Danville	32
De Kalb	50
Freeport	38
Galesburg	48
Mattoon–Charleston	59
Ottawa	51
Quincy	45
Sterling	49

Indiana	
Columbus	44
Marion	43
Michigan City–La Porte	48
New Castle	40
Richmond	49
Vincennes	41

Iowa	
Ames	42
Burlington	34
Clinton	41
Fort Dodge	30
Marshalltown	46
Mason City	36
Muscatine	49

Kansas	
Hutchinson	43
Manhattan	46
Salina	47

Kentucky	
Bowling Green	39
Frankfort	45
Madisonville	33
Paducah	21
Radcliff–Elizabethtown	35
Richmond	39

Louisiana	
Bogalusa	42
Crowley	45
Hammond	49
Minden	36
Morgan City	63
New Iberia	53
Opelousas	46
Ruston	43

Maine

Augusta–Waterville	42
Biddeford	47

Maryland

Salisbury	23

Michigan

Adrian	42
Marquette	45
Mount Pleasant	38
Owosso	34
Traverse City	44

Minnesota

Faribault	44
Mankato	47
Winona	50

Mississippi

Columbus	42
Greenville	38
Greenwood	41
Hattiesburg	50
Laurel	47
Meridian	48
Tupelo	50
Vicksburg	49

Missouri

Cape Girardeau	43
Jefferson City	48
Sikeston	45

Montana

Bozeman	44
Helena	43
Missoula	42

Nebraska

Grand Island	37

Nevada

Carson City	53

New Hampshire

Concord	56
Keene	47
Laconia	57

New Mexico

Alamogordo	43
Carlsbad	46
Clovis	46
Farmington	51
Gallup	30
Hobbs	59
Rio Rancho	48
Roswell	48

New York

Auburn	51
Batavia	53
Cortland	46
Gloversville	48
Ithaca	40
Jamestown	54
Kingston	45
Olean	47
Plattsburgh	46
Watertown	53

North Carolina

Eden	44
Goldsboro	35
Greenville	38
Havelock–New Bern	40
Kinston	37
Lumberton	25
Roanoke Rapids	47
Rocky Mount	37
Sanford	37
Shelby	41
Statesville	45
Wilson	35

North Dakota

Minot	49

Ohio

Ashland	48
Ashtabula	37
Athens	35
Chillicothe	30
East Liverpool	38
Findlay	45
Fremont	47
Marion	40
New Philadelphia	45
Portsmouth	35
Sandusky	40
Sidney	45
Tiffin	44
Wooster	45
Zanesville	35

Oklahoma

Ardmore	29
Bartlesville	45
Chickasha	37
Duncan	44
McAlester	39
Muskogee	39
Okmulgee	28
Ponca City	59
Stillwater	43

Oregon

Albany	45
Bend	49
Corvallis	48
Grants Pass	37
Klamath Falls	34
Roseburg	47

Pennsylvania

Butler	38
Chambersburg	15
New Castle	33
Pottsville	39

Rhode Island

Newport	66

South Carolina

Greenwood	26
Hilton Head Island	37
Myrtle Beach	36
Orangeburg	18
Sumter	29

Tennessee

Cleveland	42
Columbia	44
Cookeville	51
Morristown	47
Tullahoma	48

Texas

Alice	34
Bay City	24
Del Rio	39
Greenville	11
Huntsville	33
Lufkin	29
Nacogdoches	38
Palestine	30
Paris	12

Utah

Logan	43

Vermont

Rutland	43

Virginia

Blacksburg	44
Fredericksburg	45
Harrisonburg	41
Martinsville	40
Staunton–Waynesboro	50
Winchester	45

Washington

Aberdeen	55
Longview	46
Port Angeles	48
Pullman	48
Walla Walla	34
Wenatchee	46

West Virginia

Beckley	52
Clarksburg	49
Fairmont	43
Morgantown	44

Wisconsin

Fond du Lac	57
Manitowoc	57
Marshfield–Wisconsin Rapids	56
Stevens Point	49

Wyoming

Rock Springs	59

9

Transportation

Traveling through our major cities has become a nerve-wracking chore. Approximately 9 million residents of metropolitan areas consume more than one and a half hours each day just driving to and from work. Fully 600,000 of these stop-and-go commuters live in the Los Angeles region. They were given a chilling glimpse of the future on the fateful day of October 29, 1986. A single afternoon accident on the San Diego Freeway triggered a chain of events that resulted in virtual gridlock in much of the metro area. The ironically named expressways were not cleared for eight hours.

Traveling between our metropolitan centers also is often an exasperating test of patience. The vast majority of people headed from one city to another by public transportation choose to go by air. But they are spending more and more time on the ground. "We simply have too much aluminum and not enough concrete," concluded T. Allan McArtor, the chief of the Federal Aviation Administration, about the runway congestion in 1988. The situation has since become even worse. Flights scheduled for departure from Chicago's O'Hare Airport are annually delayed by a total of 133,000 hours, those at Hartsfield International Airport in Atlanta by 88,000 hours. It's no wonder that one Eastern Airlines pilot announced to his passengers, "I'm fed up. I'm sick and tired of the delays, tired of waiting." He taxied his plane

330 out of a long line at the Atlanta airport, went back to the terminal, and quit.

Small cities should offer their residents an escape from these metropolitan transportation woes. This section rates each area according to the ease of local travel, including the availability of public transit. It also measures the degree of difficulty in heading out of town, whether by car or by plane.

Rush hours are much shorter and more relaxed in micropolitan America. A 1983 Census Bureau study said the typical resident of a small city took 18.5 minutes to travel to work. His metropolitan counterpart needed an average of nearly 23 minutes.

Most small cities enjoy easy access to the world around them, thanks largely to the ubiquitous interstate highways. "These masochistic marvels have—along with telephones, television, and jet planes—reshaped American culture," wrote Robert Samuelson in *Newsweek*. "They have shrunk the nation, homogenized the landscape, and strengthened common lifestyles." Freeways have also made it possible for once-isolated residents of small cities to travel quickly and efficiently to metropolitan areas and other destinations.

A plane ticket is not as easily obtained in small cities, but the situation is becoming brighter. It is true that only 41 micropolitan areas receive direct service from national and major regional carriers, the legacy of airline deregulation in 1978. But commuter airlines, most of them affiliated with the majors, have moved to fill the void. They now provide efficient feeder service to large airports.

Perhaps the biggest drawback to commuter airlines is their use of small planes, many of which are propeller driven. Passengers expecting a jet are often taken by surprise. "There are a lot of businessmen who perhaps did not know the first time when they flew that 19-passenger plane," conceded John Doty, the manager of interline and industry affairs at Eastern Airlines. "But they certainly knew the next time. And we have a lot of repeat business." The good news is that commuter airlines are now moving toward larger craft as their business improves. *Aviation Week and Space Technology,* the industry's newsmagazine, reports that commuter carriers are anticipating an annual increase in passengers of 8 percent through the 1990s.

Ranking micropolitan America. The perfect small city would allow its residents to get to work quickly, whether by car or public transit. It would offer easy access to interstate highways and major airlines. Each area is tested in five categories:

1. Commuting Ease: Can you get where you are going without hassle, or is rush hour a smaller version of what you would find in a big city?

2. Public Transit Usage: Is there a bus system that local residents find to be reliable, or is it generally ignored?

3. Highway Availability: Is the area served by an interstate highway **331** and other major roads, or will you have a hard time driving to **another** city?

4. Local Highway Funding: Does the local government spend what it takes to maintain and expand the area's roads and bridges?

5. Aviation Availability: Can you easily get a flight to another town, or will you be grounded?

Commuting Ease

One of the joys of small-city life is the lack of traffic congestion. It is entirely possible to drive home after an exhausting day at work without enduring a mile-long backup on the expressway. Fully 29 percent of those who live in small cities can reach their jobs in less than 10 minutes; the figure in metropolitan areas is only 15 percent.

This category measures the ease with which one can commute in each area, based on the average time it takes residents to get from home to work.

Grand Island, Nebraska, is a commuter's paradise. One of every three persons is on the job less than 10 minutes after backing the car out of the driveway. Another 52 percent need only 10 to 19 minutes to make the trip to their offices or factories. The typical commute is just 12 minutes in Grand Island, compared with the national average of 21.7 minutes.

Fredericksburg, Virginia, has the highest figure, 28.8 minutes. More than a quarter of its residents drive more than 45 minutes to work, most heading north to Washington. There is talk of instituting special rush-hour train service from Fredericksburg to Washington's Union Station to handle this load.

Most of the cities with the shortest commuting times are in the Midwest. Residents of the South have the longest drives.

Source. These statistics, published in 1983, are for 1980. U.S. Bureau of the Census, *Census of Population* (Washington: U.S. Government Printing Office, 1983).

Scoring. Twenty points for 12.5 minutes or less; no points for 27.8 minutes or more. The spacing is every 0.8 minutes.

Lowest Times	Mean Travel Time to Work In Minutes
1. Grand Island, Nebr.	12.0
2. Clovis, N.Mex.	12.4
3. Bozeman, Mont.	12.6
4. Manhattan, Kans.	12.8
5. Pullman, Wash.	12.9
6. Fort Dodge, Iowa	13.0
7. Mason City, Iowa	13.1
7. Roswell, N.Mex.	13.1
7. Winona, Minn.	13.1
10. Marshalltown, Iowa	13.3

Highest

219. Fredericksburg, Va.	28.8
218. Opelousas, La.	27.1
217. Rio Rancho, N.Mex.	26.8
216. Hammond, La.	25.9
215. Crowley, La.	24.7
214. Rock Springs, Wyo.	24.4
213. Bogalusa, La.	24.2
212. Athens, Ala.	23.9
211. Idaho Falls, Idaho	23.6
210. Minden, La.	22.5

(Figure following each area name indicates mean travel time to work in minutes; figure in parentheses represents rating points.)

Alabama

Athens	23.9 (5)
Auburn–Opelika	17.4 (13)
Decatur	20.0 (10)
Enterprise	19.0 (11)
Selma	18.4 (12)
Talladega	19.8 (10)

Alaska

Fairbanks	15.9 (15)

Arizona

Bullhead City– Lake Havasu City	14.6 (17)
Casa Grande– Apache Junction	19.0 (11)
Flagstaff	15.1 (16)
Prescott	15.5 (16)
Sierra Vista	15.5 (16)
Yuma	15.0 (16)

Arkansas

Blytheville	13.9 (18)
El Dorado	15.9 (15)
Hot Springs	19.0 (11)
Jonesboro	16.1 (15)
Rogers	16.5 (15)
Russellville	17.8 (13)

California

El Centro–Calexico– Brawley	15.4 (16)
Eureka	15.5 (16)
Hanford	15.8 (15)
Madera	18.9 (12)
San Luis Obispo– Atascadero	17.1 (14)

Colorado

Grand Junction	16.1 (15)

Connecticut

Torrington	21.1 (9)

Delaware

Dover	17.8 (13)

Florida

Key West	14.4 (17)
Vero Beach	16.9 (14)

Georgia

Brunswick	16.7 (14)
Carrollton	21.3 (9)
Dalton	16.7 (14)
Gainesville	20.1 (10)
Hinesville	14.2 (17)
La Grange	17.0 (14)
Rome	19.5 (11)
Valdosta	16.0 (15)

Idaho

Coeur d'Alene	18.1 (13)
Idaho Falls	23.6 (6)
Nampa–Caldwell	16.3 (15)
Pocatello	14.5 (17)
Twin Falls	13.9 (18)

Illinois

Carbondale	15.5 (16)
Danville	16.1 (15)
De Kalb	15.7 (16)
Freeport	15.6 (16)
Galesburg	15.8 (15)
Mattoon–Charleston	13.8 (18)
Ottawa	16.2 (15)
Quincy	14.5 (17)
Sterling	15.7 (16)

Indiana

Columbus	15.8 (15)
Marion	15.6 (16)
Michigan City–La Porte	18.8 (12)
New Castle	20.4 (10)
Richmond	15.4 (16)
Vincennes	16.2 (15)

Iowa

Ames	14.5 (17)
Burlington	14.7 (17)
Clinton	15.3 (16)
Fort Dodge	13.0 (19)
Marshalltown	13.3 (19)
Mason City	13.1 (19)
Muscatine	15.3 (16)

Kansas

Hutchinson	14.5 (17)
Manhattan	12.8 (19)
Salina	13.8 (18)

Kentucky

Bowling Green	15.9 (15)
Frankfort	16.4 (15)
Madisonville	20.3 (10)
Paducah	17.2 (14)
Radcliff–Elizabethtown	16.1 (15)
Richmond	17.9 (13)

Louisiana

Bogalusa	24.2 (5)
Crowley	24.7 (4)
Hammond	25.9 (3)
Minden	22.5 (7)
Morgan City	19.7 (11)
New Iberia	21.4 (8)
Opelousas	27.1 (1)
Ruston	16.1 (15)

Maine

Augusta–Waterville	17.4 (13)
Biddeford	20.6 (9)

Maryland

Salisbury	17.2 (14)

Michigan

Adrian	19.3 (11)
Marquette	14.2 (17)
Mount Pleasant	16.2 (15)
Owosso	22.1 (8)
Traverse City	15.6 (16)

Minnesota

Faribault	14.9 (17)
Mankato	13.6 (18)
Winona	13.1 (19)

Mississippi

Columbus	16.6 (14)
Greenville	14.7 (17)
Greenwood	15.8 (15)
Hattiesburg	18.6 (12)
Laurel	19.8 (10)
Meridian	17.3 (14)
Tupelo	17.5 (13)
Vicksburg	19.0 (11)

Missouri

Cape Girardeau	16.2 (15)
Jefferson City	16.1 (15)
Sikeston	15.8 (15)

Montana

Bozeman	12.6 (19)
Helena	13.5 (18)
Missoula	14.8 (17)

Nebraska

Grand Island	12.0 (20)

Nevada

Carson City	15.5 (16)

New Hampshire

Concord	18.9 (12)
Keene	16.9 (14)
Laconia	18.3 (12)

New Mexico

Alamogordo	17.1 (14)
Carlsbad	18.2 (12)
Clovis	12.4 (20)
Farmington	21.3 (9)
Gallup	19.2 (11)
Hobbs	15.4 (16)
Rio Rancho	26.8 (2)
Roswell	13.1 (19)

New York

Auburn	19.1 (11)
Batavia	18.6 (12)
Cortland	16.1 (15)
Gloversville	18.4 (12)
Ithaca	15.7 (16)
Jamestown	15.4 (16)
Kingston	20.6 (9)
Olean	17.0 (14)
Plattsburgh	15.5 (16)
Watertown	16.3 (15)

North Carolina

Eden	18.8 (12)
Goldsboro	16.9 (14)
Greenville	17.1 (14)
Havelock–New Bern	17.9 (13)
Kinston	18.0 (13)
Lumberton	21.3 (9)
Roanoke Rapids	18.6 (12)
Rocky Mount	18.6 (12)
Sanford	17.6 (13)
Shelby	18.7 (12)
Statesville	18.7 (12)
Wilson	16.8 (14)

North Dakota

Minot	13.7 (18)

Ohio

Ashland	16.4 (15)
Ashtabula	19.3 (11)
Athens	18.5 (12)
Chillicothe	19.7 (11)
East Liverpool	19.4 (11)
Findlay	15.2 (16)
Fremont	15.7 (16)
Marion	16.1 (15)
New Philadelphia	17.4 (13)
Portsmouth	21.8 (8)
Sandusky	15.7 (16)
Sidney	15.4 (16)
Tiffin	15.3 (16)
Wooster	16.5 (15)
Zanesville	18.3 (12)

Oklahoma

Ardmore	15.7 (16)
Bartlesville	15.4 (16)
Chickasha	21.7 (8)
Duncan	16.9 (14)
McAlester	17.8 (13)
Muskogee	17.7 (13)
Okmulgee	20.7 (9)
Ponca City	13.5 (18)
Stillwater	14.5 (17)

Oregon

Albany	17.1 (14)
Bend	15.0 (16)
Corvallis	15.0 (16)
Grants Pass	17.0 (14)
Klamath Falls	14.5 (17)
Roseburg	18.4 (12)

Pennsylvania

Butler	20.7 (9)
Chambersburg	18.5 (12)
New Castle	18.1 (13)
Pottsville	20.8 (9)

Rhode Island

Newport	16.0 (15)

South Carolina

Greenwood	17.0 (14)
Hilton Head Island	15.4 (16)
Myrtle Beach	17.6 (13)
Orangeburg	21.5 (8)
Sumter	17.7 (13)

Tennessee

Cleveland	18.8 (12)
Columbia	19.8 (10)
Cookeville	16.5 (15)
Morristown	18.4 (12)
Tullahoma	18.2 (12)

Texas

Alice	20.1 (10)
Bay City	21.7 (8)
Del Rio	14.2 (17)
Greenville	21.7 (8)
Huntsville	17.2 (14)
Lufkin	17.5 (13)
Nacogdoches	17.0 (14)
Palestine	18.7 (12)
Paris	16.2 (15)

Utah

Logan	16.1 (15)

Vermont

Rutland	15.9 (15)

Virginia

Blacksburg	16.5 (15)
Fredericksburg	28.8 (0)
Harrisonburg	17.4 (13)
Martinsville	17.6 (13)
Staunton–Waynesboro	18.8 (12)
Winchester	20.1 (10)

Washington

Aberdeen	18.7 (12)
Longview	17.8 (13)
Port Angeles	17.1 (14)
Pullman	12.9 (19)
Walla Walla	14.5 (17)
Wenatchee	14.3 (17)

West Virginia

Beckley	22.4 (7)
Clarksburg	19.2 (11)
Fairmont	20.6 (9)
Morgantown	18.1 (13)

Wisconsin

Fond du Lac	14.6 (17)
Manitowoc	14.3 (17)
Marshfield– Wisconsin Rapids	13.4 (18)
Stevens Point	14.5 (17)

Wyoming

Rock Springs	24.4 (5)

Public Transit Usage

Mass transit is essential to the nation's metropolitan centers. Buses, subways, and elevated trains swiftly carry thousands who otherwise would be without transportation or would be forced to edge their cars onto already-jammed expressways.

Public transit is not as crucial to smaller cities. But it is nonetheless important to have bus service for the elderly, the disabled, and the second workers in one-car families. This category ranks each area according to the number of people who rely on public transit to get them to their jobs, expressed as a rate per 1,000 commuters.

Nearly 4,500 people take the bus to work each weekday in Idaho Falls, Idaho. That equals 158 of every 1,000 people traveling to employment in that area, much better than the national average of 64 transit users per 1,000 commuters. It even surpasses the figure for the country's metro areas, 81 per 1,000.

Residents of four small cities must use their own means to get around, having little or no bus service. These communities are Bozeman, Montana; Clovis, New Mexico; Coeur d'Alene, Idaho; and Prescott, Arizona.

Source. These statistics, published in 1983, are for 1980. U.S. Bureau of the Census, *Census of Population* (Washington: U.S. Government Printing Office, 1983).

Scoring. Twenty points for 78 or more public-transit users per 1,000; no points for 0 or 1. The spacing is every 4 per 1,000.

Highest	Users of Public Transit Per 1,000 Commuters
1. Idaho Falls, Idaho	158
2. Rock Springs, Wyo.	115
3. Carlsbad, N.Mex.	112
4. De Kalb, Ill.	39
5. Fairbanks, Alaska	35
6. Fredericksburg, Va.	34
7. Hanford, Calif.	33
8. La Grange, Ga.	32
9. Morgantown, W.Va.	31
10. Missoula, Mont.	29

Lowest

216. Bozeman, Mont.	0
216. Clovis, N.Mex.	0
216. Coeur d'Alene, Idaho	0
216. Prescott, Ariz.	0
209. Bay City, Tex.	1
209. Bullhead City–Lake Havasu City, Ariz.	1
209. Cookeville, Tenn.	1
209. Grants Pass, Oreg.	1
209. Hutchinson, Kans.	1
209. Stillwater, Okla.	1
209. Twin Falls, Idaho	1

(Figure following each area name indicates the number of users of public transit per 1,000 commuters; figure in parentheses represents rating points.)

Alabama

Athens	5	(1)
Auburn–Opelika	11	(3)
Decatur	3	(1)
Enterprise	7	(2)
Selma	27	(7)
Talladega	11	(3)

Alaska

Fairbanks	35	(9)

Arizona

Bullhead City– Lake Havasu City	1	(0)
Casa Grande– Apache Junction	6	(2)
Flagstaff	5	(1)
Prescott	0	(0)
Sierra Vista	15	(4)
Yuma	17	(4)

Arkansas

Blytheville	4	(1)
El Dorado	4	(1)
Hot Springs	14	(4)
Jonesboro	2	(1)
Rogers	3	(1)
Russellville	3	(1)

California

El Centro–Calexico– Brawley	10	(3)
Eureka	17	(4)
Hanford	33	(8)
Madera	4	(1)
San Luis Obispo– Atascadero	7	(2)

Colorado

Grand Junction	7	(2)

Connecticut

Torrington	12	(3)

Delaware

Dover	7	(2)

Florida

Key West	13	(3)
Vero Beach	2	(1)

Georgia

Brunswick	10	(3)
Carrollton	9	(2)
Dalton	5	(1)
Gainesville	8	(2)
Hinesville	10	(3)
La Grange	32	(8)
Rome	15	(4)
Valdosta	8	(2)

Idaho

Coeur d'Alene	0	(0)
Idaho Falls	158	(20)
Nampa–Caldwell	3	(1)
Pocatello	20	(5)
Twin Falls	1	(0)

Illinois

Carbondale	4	(1)
Danville	9	(2)
De Kalb	39	(10)
Freeport	5	(1)
Galesburg	7	(2)
Mattoon–Charleston	2	(1)
Ottawa	5	(1)
Quincy	8	(2)
Sterling	4	(1)

Indiana

Columbus	6	(2)
Marion	3	(1)
Michigan City–La Porte	13	(3)
New Castle	2	(1)
Richmond	11	(3)
Vincennes	9	(2)

Iowa

Ames	20	(5)
Burlington	21	(5)
Clinton	19	(5)
Fort Dodge	7	(2)
Marshalltown	5	(1)
Mason City	5	(1)
Muscatine	2	(1)

Kansas

Hutchinson	1	(0)
Manhattan	7	(2)
Salina	7	(2)

Kentucky

Bowling Green	5	(1)
Frankfort	2	(1)
Madisonville	3	(1)
Paducah	3	(1)
Radcliff–Elizabethtown	20	(5)
Richmond	3	(1)

Louisiana

Bogalusa	14	(4)
Crowley	9	(2)
Hammond	6	(2)
Minden	7	(2)
Morgan City	8	(2)
New Iberia	7	(2)
Opelousas	21	(5)
Ruston	7	(2)

Maine

Augusta–Waterville	6	(2)
Biddeford	11	(3)

Maryland

Salisbury	14	(4)

Michigan

Adrian	3	(1)
Marquette	7	(2)
Mount Pleasant	5	(1)
Owosso	2	(1)
Traverse City	3	(1)

Minnesota

Faribault	5	(1)
Mankato	27	(7)
Winona	12	(3)

Mississippi

Columbus	2	(1)
Greenville	21	(5)
Greenwood	17	(4)
Hattiesburg	23	(6)
Laurel	12	(3)
Meridian	21	(5)
Tupelo	7	(2)
Vicksburg	13	(3)

Missouri

Cape Girardeau	7	(2)
Jefferson City	13	(3)
Sikeston	7	(2)

Montana

Bozeman	0	(0)
Helena	5	(1)
Missoula	29	(7)

Nebraska

Grand Island	4	(1)

Nevada

Carson City	7	(2)

New Hampshire

Concord	6	(2)
Keene	6	(2)
Laconia	5	(1)

New Mexico

Alamogordo	10	(3)
Carlsbad	112	(20)
Clovis	0	(0)
Farmington	5	(1)
Gallup	15	(4)
Hobbs	10	(3)
Rio Rancho	3	(1)
Roswell	2	(1)

New York

Auburn	22	(6)
Batavia	6	(2)
Cortland	8	(2)
Gloversville	20	(5)
Ithaca	27	(7)
Jamestown	15	(4)
Kingston	20	(5)
Olean	7	(2)
Plattsburgh	6	(2)
Watertown	11	(3)

North Carolina

Eden	6	(2)
Goldsboro	4	(1)
Greenville	10	(3)
Havelock–New Bern	19	(5)
Kinston	7	(2)
Lumberton	4	(1)
Roanoke Rapids	5	(1)
Rocky Mount	12	(3)
Sanford	4	(1)
Shelby	6	(2)
Statesville	5	(1)
Wilson	13	(3)

North Dakota

Minot	22	(6)

Ohio

Ashland	7	(2)
Ashtabula	5	(1)
Athens	13	(3)
Chillicothe	5	(1)
East Liverpool	3	(1)
Findlay	3	(1)
Fremont	4	(1)
Marion	6	(2)
New Philadelphia	3	(1)
Portsmouth	6	(2)
Sandusky	3	(1)
Sidney	2	(1)
Tiffin	4	(1)
Wooster	5	(1)
Zanesville	5	(1)

Oklahoma

Ardmore	5	(1)
Bartlesville	5	(1)
Chickasha	3	(1)
Duncan	3	(1)
McAlester	4	(1)
Muskogee	3	(1)
Okmulgee	2	(1)
Ponca City	4	(1)
Stillwater	1	(0)

Oregon

Albany	3	(1)
Bend	4	(1)
Corvallis	3	(1)
Grants Pass	1	(0)
Klamath Falls	4	(1)
Roseburg	6	(2)

Pennsylvania

Butler	6	(2)
Chambersburg	4	(1)
New Castle	15	(4)
Pottsville	10	(3)

Rhode Island

Newport	21	(5)

South Carolina

Greenwood	6	(2)
Hilton Head Island	13	(3)
Myrtle Beach	6	(2)
Orangeburg	7	(2)
Sumter	8	(2)

Tennessee

Cleveland	2	(1)
Columbia	10	(3)
Cookeville	1	(0)
Morristown	5	(1)
Tullahoma	4	(1)

Texas

Alice	2	(1)
Bay City	1	(0)
Del Rio	5	(1)
Greenville	4	(1)
Huntsville	2	(1)
Lufkin	3	(1)
Nacogdoches	2	(1)
Palestine	7	(2)
Paris	2	(1)

Utah

Logan	8	(2)

Vermont

Rutland	7	(2)

Virginia

Blacksburg	3	(1)
Fredericksburg	34	(9)
Harrisonburg	7	(2)
Martinsville	6	(2)
Staunton–Waynesboro	13	(3)
Winchester	16	(4)

Washington

Aberdeen	23	(6)
Longview	9	(2)
Port Angeles	12	(3)
Pullman	18	(5)
Walla Walla	2	(1)
Wenatchee	2	(1)

West Virginia

Beckley	3	(1)
Clarksburg	27	(7)
Fairmont	15	(4)
Morgantown	31	(8)

Wisconsin

Fond du Lac	8	(2)
Manitowoc	9	(2)
Marshfield– Wisconsin Rapids	2	(1)
Stevens Point	7	(2)

Wyoming

Rock Springs	115	(20)

Highway Availability

It's wonderful if your small city is just 100 miles away from the bright lights of an attractive metropolitan center or the haunting silence of a spacious national forest. But such proximity means little if your only access is by way of a two-lane county road that specializes in stop signs and no-passing zones.

This category evaluates the quality of each area's highway system. It awards points on the following scale: 10 for a main (two-number) interstate highway, 5 for a spur   (three-number) interstate or a four-lane U.S. road, 3 for a two-lane U.S. highway, 2 for a limited-access state road, and 1 for any other state highway. To qualify for points, these roads merely need pass through any part of the micropolitan area, with the exception of the 1-point state roads, which must reach the central city.

Michigan City–La Porte, Indiana, and Orangeburg, South Carolina, lead the way with 46 points. Each area has access to two interstates.

Gloversville, New York, is isolated at the gateway to the Adirondack Mountains. It can be reached by a single state highway, earning it just one point.

Source. These statistics, published in 1988, are for 1988. Derived from *Rand McNally Road Atlas* (Chicago: Rand McNally and Co., 1988).

Scoring. Twenty points for 40 or more index points; no points for 0 or 1. The spacing is every two index points.

Highest	Highway Index
1. Michigan City–La Porte, Ind.	46
1. Orangeburg, S.C.	46
3. Butler, Pa.	43
4. Rocky Mount, N.C.	39
5. Concord, N.H.	38
6. Staunton–Waynesboro, Va.	36
7. Ottawa, Ill.	35
8. New Castle, Pa.	33
9. Flagstaff, Ariz.	32
10. Casa Grande–Apache Junction, Ariz.	31

Lowest

219. Gloversville, N.Y.	1
217. Bay City, Tex.	2
217. Bogalusa, La.	2
214. Fairbanks, Alaska	3
214. Madera, Calif.	3
214. Port Angeles, Wash.	3
212. Carbondale, Ill.	4
212. Newport, R.I.	4
203. Corvallis, Oreg.	5
203. Eureka, Calif.	5
203. Ithaca, N.Y.	5
203. Key West, Fla.	5
203. Marquette, Mich.	5
203. Marshalltown, Iowa	5
203. Marshfield–Wisconsin Rapids, Wis.	5
203. Morgan City, La.	5
203. Pullman, Wash.	5

(Figure following each area name indicates highway index; figure in parentheses represents rating points.)

Alabama

Athens	26	(13)
Auburn–Opelika	25	(12)
Decatur	27	(13)
Enterprise	7	(3)
Selma	8	(4)
Talladega	20	(10)

Alaska

| Fairbanks | 3 | (1) |

Arizona

Bullhead City–		
Lake Havasu City	30	(15)
Casa Grande–		
Apache Junction	31	(15)
Flagstaff	32	(16)
Prescott	30	(15)
Sierra Vista	20	(10)
Yuma	13	(6)

Arkansas

Blytheville	14	(7)
El Dorado	12	(6)
Hot Springs	12	(6)
Jonesboro	12	(6)
Rogers	8	(4)
Russellville	14	(7)

California

El Centro–Calexico–		
Brawley	14	(7)
Eureka	5	(2)
Hanford	12	(6)
Madera	3	(1)
San Luis Obispo–		
Atascadero	7	(3)

Colorado

| Grand Junction | 20 | (10) |

Connecticut

| Torrington | 15 | (7) |

Delaware

| Dover | 15 | (7) |

Florida

| Key West | 5 | (2) |
| Vero Beach | 18 | (9) |

Georgia

Brunswick	26	(13)
Carrollton	20	(10)
Dalton	17	(8)
Gainesville	17	(8)
Hinesville	17	(8)
La Grange	23	(11)
Rome	14	(7)
Valdosta	21	(10)

Idaho

Coeur d'Alene	16	(8)
Idaho Falls	19	(9)
Nampa–Caldwell	17	(8)
Pocatello	26	(13)
Twin Falls	7	(3)

Illinois

Carbondale	4	(2)
Danville	18	(9)
De Kalb	10	(5)
Freeport	7	(3)
Galesburg	19	(9)
Mattoon–Charleston	18	(9)
Ottawa	35	(17)
Quincy	9	(4)
Sterling	7	(3)

Indiana

Columbus	18	(9)
Marion	16	(8)
Michigan City–La Porte	46	(20)
New Castle	23	(11)
Richmond	23	(11)
Vincennes	12	(6)

Iowa

Ames	21	(10)
Burlington	11	(5)
Clinton	14	(7)
Fort Dodge	11	(5)
Marshalltown	5	(2)
Mason City	20	(10)
Muscatine	10	(5)

Kansas

Hutchinson	8	(4)
Manhattan	20	(10)
Salina	15	(7)

Kentucky

Bowling Green	26	(13)
Frankfort	28	(14)
Madisonville	16	(8)
Paducah	23	(11)
Radcliff–Elizabethtown	21	(10)
Richmond	20	(10)

Louisiana

Bogalusa	2	(1)
Crowley	17	(8)
Hammond	26	(13)
Minden	20	(10)
Morgan City	5	(2)
New Iberia	8	(4)
Opelousas	22	(11)
Ruston	20	(10)

Maine

Augusta–Waterville	21	(10)
Biddeford	19	(9)

Maryland

Salisbury	14	(7)

Michigan

Adrian	11	(5)
Marquette	5	(2)
Mount Pleasant	12	(6)
Owosso	13	(6)
Traverse City	11	(5)

Minnesota

Faribault	13	(6)
Mankato	11	(5)
Winona	19	(9)

Mississippi

Columbus	15	(7)
Greenville	11	(5)
Greenwood	9	(4)
Hattiesburg	24	(12)
Laurel	17	(8)
Meridian	30	(15)
Tupelo	12	(6)
Vicksburg	15	(7)

Missouri

Cape Girardeau	15	(7)
Jefferson City	11	(5)
Sikeston	26	(13)

Montana

Bozeman	22	(11)
Helena	18	(9)
Missoula	19	(9)

Nebraska

Grand Island	22	(11)

Nevada

Carson City	10	(5)

New Hampshire

Concord	38	(19)
Keene	7	(3)
Laconia	16	(8)

New Mexico

Alamogordo	11	(5)
Carlsbad	13	(6)
Clovis	11	(5)
Farmington	15	(7)
Gallup	16	(8)
Hobbs	14	(7)
Rio Rancho	13	(6)
Roswell	19	(9)

New York

Auburn	18	(9)
Batavia	22	(11)
Cortland	14	(7)
Gloversville	1	(0)
Ithaca	5	(2)
Jamestown	20	(10)
Kingston	23	(11)
Olean	12	(6)
Plattsburgh	18	(9)
Watertown	19	(9)

North Carolina

Eden	19	(9)
Goldsboro	14	(7)
Greenville	16	(8)
Havelock–New Bern	12	(6)
Kinston	12	(6)
Lumberton	24	(12)
Roanoke Rapids	22	(11)
Rocky Mount	39	(19)
Sanford	15	(7)
Shelby	18	(9)
Statesville	29	(14)
Wilson	28	(14)

North Dakota

Minot	13	(6)

Ohio

Ashland	29	(14)
Ashtabula	21	(10)
Athens	11	(5)
Chillicothe	14	(7)
East Liverpool	10	(5)
Findlay	23	(11)
Fremont	22	(11)
Marion	9	(4)
New Philadelphia	22	(11)
Portsmouth	11	(5)
Sandusky	24	(12)
Sidney	12	(6)
Tiffin	10	(5)
Wooster	24	(12)
Zanesville	20	(10)

Oklahoma

Ardmore	24	(12)
Bartlesville	6	(3)
Chickasha	23	(11)
Duncan	6	(3)
McAlester	13	(6)
Muskogee	30	(15)
Okmulgee	29	(14)
Ponca City	23	(11)
Stillwater	16	(8)

Oregon

Albany	14	(7)
Bend	6	(3)
Corvallis	5	(2)
Grants Pass	15	(7)
Klamath Falls	6	(3)
Roseburg	14	(7)

Pennsylvania

Butler	43	(20)
Chambersburg	27	(13)
New Castle	33	(16)
Pottsville	16	(8)

Rhode Island

Newport	4	(2)

South Carolina

Greenwood	8	(4)
Hilton Head Island	13	(6)
Myrtle Beach	24	(12)
Orangeburg	46	(20)
Sumter	29	(14)

Tennessee

Cleveland	21	(10)
Columbia	23	(11)
Cookeville	15	(7)
Morristown	20	(10)
Tullahoma	18	(9)

Texas

Alice	6	(3)
Bay City	2	(1)
Del Rio	12	(6)
Greenville	19	(9)
Huntsville	18	(9)
Lufkin	12	(6)
Nacogdoches	12	(6)
Palestine	13	(6)
Paris	11	(5)

Utah

Logan	9	(4)

Vermont

Rutland	10	(5)

Virginia

Blacksburg	22	(11)
Fredericksburg	25	(12)
Harrisonburg	24	(12)
Martinsville	13	(6)
Staunton–Waynesboro	36	(18)
Winchester	26	(13)

Washington

Aberdeen	9	(4)
Longview	12	(6)
Port Angeles	3	(1)
Pullman	5	(2)
Walla Walla	10	(5)
Wenatchee	8	(4)

West Virginia

Beckley	28	(14)
Clarksburg	19	(9)
Fairmont	16	(8)
Morgantown	22	(11)

Wisconsin

Fond du Lac	13	(6)
Manitowoc	21	(10)
Marshfield– Wisconsin Rapids	5	(2)
Stevens Point	10	(5)

Wyoming

Rock Springs	16	(8)

Local Highway Funding

America is losing the battle to keep its roads and bridges in acceptable condition. The National Council on Public Works Improvement, as part of its 1988 report card on the infrastructure, awarded the country's highway system the mediocre grade of C-plus. An earlier inventory by the federal government had determined that 12 percent of all interstate-highway miles were urgently in need of repair.

This category ranks each area according to its financial commitment to its transportation network. Total annual expenditures by county and city governments are divided by the number of residents. Included are all allocations for construction, maintenance, and operation of roads and bridges, as well as funding for street lighting and snow removal.

Cold-weather cities face the greatest problems with their highways and generally spend the most on them. Marshfield–Wisconsin Rapids, Wisconsin, shells out $192 per capita, more than three times the national average of $63. Marshfield–Wisconsin Rapids devotes 14 percent of its local budget to highways and bridges. The typical community uses only 5.5 percent.

Dover, Delaware, is one of the cities in warmer climates that give roads a lower priority. Dover spends just $8 per capita a year.

Source. These statistics, published in 1988, are for the 1981–1982 budget year. Derived from U.S. Bureau of the Census, *County and City Data Book* (Washington: U.S. Government Printing Office, 1988).

Scoring. Twenty points for $170 or more per capita; no points for $17 or less. The spacing is every $8 per capita.

Local Highway Funding: Highs and Lows

	Annual Per Capita Highway-Related Spending By Local Governments
Highest	**$**
1. Marshfield– Wisconsin Rapids, Wis.	192
2. Mankato, Minn.	187
3. Pullman, Wash.	185
4. Aberdeen, Wash.	178
5. Watertown, N.Y.	174
6. Olean, N.Y.	170
7. Manitowoc, Wis.	156
7. New Iberia, La.	156
9. Batavia, N.Y.	149
10. Longview, Wash.	148

Lowest	
219. Dover, Del.	8
218. Havelock–New Bern, N.C.	9
217. Martinsville, Va.	10
216. Kinston, N.C.	11
214. Hilton Head Island, S.C.	12
214. Shelby, N.C.	12
213. Orangeburg, S.C.	13
211. Greenwood, S.C.	14
211. Harrisonburg, Va.	14
210. Winchester, Va.	15

(Figure following each area name incidates annual per capita highway-related spending by local government in dollars; figure in parentheses represents rating points.)

Alabama

Athens	52	(5)
Auburn–Opelika	43	(4)
Decatur	57	(5)
Enterprise	52	(5)
Selma	36	(3)
Talladega	32	(2)

Alaska

Fairbanks	83	(9)

Arizona

Bullhead City– Lake Havasu City	69	(7)
Casa Grande– Apache Junction	62	(6)
Flagstaff	91	(10)
Prescott	48	(4)
Sierra Vista	59	(6)
Yuma	53	(5)

Arkansas

Blytheville	42	(4)
El Dorado	57	(5)
Hot Springs	42	(4)
Jonesboro	36	(3)
Rogers	31	(2)
Russellville	72	(7)

California

El Centro–Calexico– Brawley	67	(7)
Eureka	98	(11)
Hanford	65	(6)
Madera	62	(6)
San Luis Obispo– Atascadero	56	(5)

Colorado

Grand Junction	73	(7)

Connecticut

Torrington	72	(7)

Delaware

Dover	8	(0)

Florida

Key West	33	(2)
Vero Beach	46	(4)

Georgia

Brunswick	61	(6)
Carrollton	47	(4)
Dalton	49	(4)
Gainesville	49	(4)
Hinesville	24	(1)
La Grange	65	(6)
Rome	47	(4)
Valdosta	52	(5)

Idaho

Coeur d'Alene	54	(5)
Idaho Falls	40	(3)
Nampa–Caldwell	49	(4)
Pocatello	41	(3)
Twin Falls	72	(7)

Illinois

Carbondale	75	(8)
Danville	67	(7)
De Kalb	79	(8)
Freeport	70	(7)
Galesburg	90	(10)
Mattoon–Charleston	80	(8)
Ottawa	106	(12)
Quincy	122	(14)
Sterling	71	(7)

Indiana

Columbus	44	(4)
Marion	31	(2)
Michigan City–La Porte	44	(4)
New Castle	41	(3)
Richmond	47	(4)
Vincennes	45	(4)

Iowa

Ames	84	(9)
Burlington	94	(10)
Clinton	80	(8)
Fort Dodge	123	(14)
Marshalltown	146	(17)
Mason City	93	(10)
Muscatine	73	(7)

Kansas

Hutchinson	135	(15)
Manhattan	40	(3)
Salina	78	(8)

Kentucky

Bowling Green	26	(2)
Frankfort	26	(2)
Madisonville	25	(1)
Paducah	27	(2)
Radcliff–Elizabethtown	28	(2)
Richmond	28	(2)

Louisiana

Bogalusa	40	(3)
Crowley	69	(7)
Hammond	42	(4)
Minden	55	(5)
Morgan City	100	(11)
New Iberia	156	(18)
Opelousas	46	(4)
Ruston	55	(5)

Maine

Augusta–Waterville	53	(5)
Biddeford	52	(5)

Maryland

Salisbury	69	(7)

Michigan

Adrian	73	(7)
Marquette	94	(10)
Mount Pleasant	59	(6)
Owosso	68	(7)
Traverse City	66	(7)

Minnesota

Faribault	101	(11)
Mankato	187	(20)
Winona	109	(12)

Mississippi

Columbus	42	(4)
Greenville	77	(8)
Greenwood	86	(9)
Hattiesburg	60	(6)
Laurel	95	(10)
Meridian	92	(10)
Tupelo	67	(7)
Vicksburg	65	(6)

Missouri

Cape Girardeau	49	(4)
Jefferson City	44	(4)
Sikeston	30	(2)

Montana

Bozeman	39	(3)
Helena	66	(7)
Missoula	99	(11)

Nebraska

Grand Island	114	(13)

Nevada

Carson City	50	(5)

New Hampshire

Concord	57	(5)
Keene	75	(8)
Laconia	84	(9)

New Mexico

Alamogordo	29	(2)
Carlsbad	98	(11)
Clovis	43	(4)
Farmington	102	(11)
Gallup	43	(4)
Hobbs	70	(7)
Rio Rancho	34	(3)
Roswell	111	(12)

New York

Auburn	135	(15)
Batavia	149	(17)
Cortland	134	(15)
Gloversville	96	(10)
Ithaca	106	(12)
Jamestown	137	(15)
Kingston	116	(13)
Olean	170	(20)
Plattsburgh	109	(12)
Watertown	174	(20)

North Carolina

Eden	20	(1)
Goldsboro	17	(0)
Greenville	17	(0)
Havelock–New Bern	9	(0)
Kinston	11	(0)
Lumberton	19	(1)
Roanoke Rapids	22	(1)
Rocky Mount	23	(1)
Sanford	23	(1)
Shelby	12	(0)
Statesville	17	(0)
Wilson	18	(1)

North Dakota

Minot	55	(5)

Ohio

Ashland	69	(7)
Ashtabula	85	(9)
Athens	55	(5)
Chillicothe	57	(5)
East Liverpool	60	(6)
Findlay	83	(9)
Fremont	62	(6)
Marion	54	(5)
New Philadelphia	74	(8)
Portsmouth	55	(5)
Sandusky	69	(7)
Sidney	76	(8)
Tiffin	67	(7)
Wooster	58	(6)
Zanesville	62	(6)

Oklahoma

Ardmore	110	(12)
Bartlesville	46	(4)
Chickasha	89	(9)
Duncan	39	(3)
McAlester	78	(8)
Muskogee	35	(3)
Okmulgee	55	(5)
Ponca City	73	(7)
Stillwater	36	(3)

Oregon

Albany	97	(10)
Bend	95	(10)
Corvallis	106	(12)
Grants Pass	67	(7)
Klamath Falls	102	(11)
Roseburg	146	(17)

Pennsylvania

Butler	39	(3)
Chambersburg	35	(3)
New Castle	42	(4)
Pottsville	34	(3)

Rhode Island

Newport	43	(4)

South Carolina

Greenwood	14	(0)
Hilton Head Island	12	(0)
Myrtle Beach	26	(2)
Orangeburg	13	(0)
Sumter	25	(1)

Tennessee

Cleveland	36	(3)
Columbia	49	(4)
Cookeville	45	(4)
Morristown	42	(4)
Tullahoma	43	(4)

Texas

Alice	70	(7)
Bay City	66	(7)
Del Rio	17	(0)
Greenville	62	(6)
Huntsville	33	(2)
Lufkin	36	(3)
Nacogdoches	53	(5)
Palestine	43	(4)
Paris	59	(6)

Utah

Logan	49	(4)

Vermont

Rutland	71	(7)

Virginia

Blacksburg	23	(1)
Fredericksburg	24	(1)
Harrisonburg	14	(0)
Martinsville	10	(0)
Staunton–Waynesboro	26	(2)
Winchester	15	(0)

Washington

Aberdeen	178	(20)
Longview	148	(17)
Port Angeles	110	(12)
Pullman	185	(20)
Walla Walla	110	(12)
Wenatchee	73	(7)

West Virginia

Beckley	17	(0)
Clarksburg	26	(2)
Fairmont	30	(2)
Morgantown	27	(2)

Wisconsin

Fond du Lac	97	(10)
Manitowoc	156	(18)
Marshfield–Wisconsin Rapids	192	(20)
Stevens Point	138	(16)

Wyoming

Rock Springs	96	(10)

Aviation Availability

Travelers who decide not to drive themselves from one city to another have three choices of common carriers: plane, bus, and train. Fully 92 percent decide to fly. It's an attractive option for residents of metropolitan areas with large modern airports. But air service to small cities has been erratic since federal deregulation in 1978.

This category rates the ease of air travel from each area in two ways. It first totals the number of passengers boarding planes with 60 or more seats, operated by one of 46 national or regional airlines. Only 41 small cities are listed by the Federal Aviation Administration as air-traffic hubs offering such service. Vicksburg, Mississippi, is half of the Jackson/Vicksburg hub, which handles more than 427,000 passengers a year.

This statistic unfortunately provides an incomplete picture of local air operations, since it excludes commuter airlines, charter services, and private planes. This category therefore uses a second ranking: the total number of general-aviation craft, expressed as a rate per 100,000 residents. Small planes offer an easy way of crossing the vastness of Alaska, explaining Fairbanks's fleet of 928, or 1,373 per 100,000. Hinesville, Georgia, has the poorest concentration of general-aviation craft, just 26 per 100,000 residents.

Southern and Western cities generally offer the best chances of catching a commercial flight, with towns in the West also having the strongest fleets of small planes.

Sources. The commercial-aviation statistics, published in 1988, are for 1987. U.S. Federal Aviation Administration, *Airport Activity Statistics of Certificated Route Air Carriers* (Washington: U.S. Government Printing Office, 1988). The general-aviation statistics, published in 1988, are for 1987. Derived from U.S. Federal Aviation Administration, *Census of U.S. Civil Aircraft* (Washington: U.S. Government Printing Office, 1988).

Scoring. For commercial aviation: 10 points for 270,001 or more passengers; no points for 0. The spacing is every 30,000 passengers. For general aviation: 10 points for 400 or more per 100,000; no points for 39 or less. The spacing is every 40 per 100,000.

Highest	Enplaned Passengers on National And Major Regional Air Carriers
1. Vicksburg, Miss.	427,037
2. Decatur, Ala.	359,374
3. Frankfort, Ky.	336,610
4. Myrtle Beach, S.C.	217,842
5. Fairbanks, Alaska	200,167
6. Grand Junction, Colo.	171,685
7. Missoula, Mont.	132,717
8. Bozeman, Mont.	113,802
9. Concord, N.H.	111,501
10. Key West, Fla.	99,938

Lowest

42. 178 tied	0

General Aviation Availability: Highs and Lows

Highest	General Aviation Craft Per 100,000 Residents
1. Fairbanks, Alaska	1,373
2. Carson City, Nev.	485
3. Bend, Oreg.	431
4. Vero Beach, Fla.	426
5. Dover, Del.	403
6. Wenatchee, Wash.	361
7. Prescott, Ariz.	356
8. Coeur d'Alene, Idaho	353
9. Bullhead City–Lake Havasu City, Ariz.	349
10. Klamath Falls, Oreg.	348

Lowest

219. Hinesville, Ga.	26
217. Bogalusa, La.	38
217. Talladega, Ala.	38
215. New Castle, Pa.	40
215. Wilson, N.C.	40
214. Richmond, Ky.	42
213. Clinton, Iowa	43
211. Orangeburg, S.C.	44
211. Radcliff–Elizabethtown, Ky.	44
210. Athens, Ala.	46

(Number of enplaned commercial passengers on national and major regional air carriers is shown in brackets if applicable. Figure following each area name indicates the number of general aviation craft per 100,000 residents; figure in parentheses represents rating points.)

Alabama

Athens		46	(1)
Auburn–Opelika		59	(1)
Decatur	[359,374]	93	(12)
Enterprise		224	(5)
Selma		95	(2)
Talladega		38	(0)

Alaska

Fairbanks	[200,167]	1,373	(17)

Arizona

Bullhead City–Lake Havasu City		349	(8)
Casa Grande–Apache Junction		218	(5)
Flagstaff	[21,336]	321	(9)
Prescott		356	(8)
Sierra Vista		218	(5)
Yuma	[29,405]	273	(7)

Arkansas

Blytheville		122	(3)
El Dorado		159	(3)
Hot Springs		102	(2)
Jonesboro		200	(5)
Rogers		167	(4)
Russellville		99	(2)

California

El Centro–Calexico–Brawley		237	(5)
Eureka	[58,627]	158	(5)
Hanford		194	(4)
Madera		164	(4)
San Luis Obispo–Atascadero		239	(5)

Colorado

Grand Junction	[171,685]	164	(10)

Connecticut

Torrington		126	(3)

Delaware

Dover		403	(10)

Florida

Key West	[99,938]	323	(12)
Vero Beach		426	(10)

Georgia

Brunswick		149	(3)
Carrollton		89	(2)
Dalton		92	(2)
Gainesville		116	(2)
Hinesville		26	(0)
La Grange		63	(1)
Rome		79	(1)
Valdosta		136	(3)

Idaho

Coeur d'Alene		353	(8)
Idaho Falls	[67,050]	166	(7)
Nampa–Caldwell		195	(4)
Pocatello	[12,483]	137	(4)
Twin Falls	[8,488]	310	(8)

Illinois

Carbondale		139	(3)
Danville	[2,446]	124	(4)
De Kalb		177	(4)
Freeport		121	(3)
Galesburg	[2,191]	107	(3)
Mattoon–Charleston	[1,767]	77	(2)
Ottawa		157	(3)
Quincy	[3,513]	94	(3)
Sterling		89	(2)

Indiana

Columbus		122	(3)
Marion		74	(1)
Michigan City–La Porte		100	(2)
New Castle	[2,637]	96	(3)
Richmond		61	(1)
Vincennes		155	(3)

Iowa

Ames		152	(3)
Burlington	[6,259]	132	(4)
Clinton		43	(1)
Fort Dodge		108	(2)
Marshalltown		86	(2)
Mason City		123	(3)
Muscatine		157	(3)

Kansas

Hutchinson		124	(3)
Manhattan		135	(3)
Salina		194	(4)

Kentucky

Bowling Green		64	(1)
Frankfort	[336,610]	130	(13)
Madisonville		52	(1)
Paducah	[404]	109	(3)
Radcliff–Elizabethtown		44	(1)
Richmond		42	(1)

Louisiana

Bogalusa		38	(0)
Crowley		112	(2)
Hammond		81	(2)
Minden		52	(1)
Morgan City		117	(2)
New Iberia		107	(2)
Opelousas		89	(2)
Ruston		101	(2)

Maine

Augusta–Waterville	127	(3)
Biddeford	96	(2)

Maryland

Salisbury	[151]	94	(3)

Michigan

Adrian		130	(3)
Marquette		87	(2)
Mount Pleasant		135	(3)
Owosso		123	(3)
Traverse City	[515]	196	(5)

Minnesota

Faribault	131	(3)
Mankato	133	(3)
Winona	82	(2)

Mississippi

Columbus		135	(3)
Greenville		191	(4)
Greenwood		283	(7)
Hattiesburg		76	(1)
Laurel		111	(2)
Meridian		95	(2)
Tupelo		95	(2)
Vicksburg	[427,037]	68	(11)

Missouri

Cape Girardeau	[274]	98	(3)
Jefferson City	[653]	115	(3)
Sikeston	[274]	114	(3)

Montana

Bozeman	[113,802]	295	(11)
Helena	[33,716]	241	(8)
Missoula	[132,717]	180	(9)

Nebraska

Grand Island	106	(2)

Nevada

Carson City	485	(10)

New Hampshire

Concord	[111,501]	142	(7)
Keene		203	(5)
Laconia		316	(7)

New Mexico

Alamogordo		209	(5)
Carlsbad		141	(3)
Clovis		263	(6)
Farmington	[11,360]	189	(5)
Gallup		96	(2)
Hobbs		285	(7)
Rio Rancho		59	(1)
Roswell		213	(5)

New York

Auburn		63	(1)
Batavia		114	(2)
Cortland	[68,096]	82	(5)
Gloversville		71	(1)
Ithaca	[68,096]	91	(5)
Jamestown		92	(2)
Kingston		86	(2)
Olean		57	(1)
Plattsburgh		68	(1)
Watertown		85	(2)

North Carolina

Eden		69	(1)
Goldsboro		70	(1)
Greenville		76	(1)
Havelock–New Bern		111	(2)
Kinston	[50,506]	95	(4)
Lumberton		73	(1)
Roanoke Rapids		91	(2)
Rocky Mount		51	(1)
Sanford		87	(2)
Shelby		86	(2)
Statesville		96	(2)
Wilson		40	(1)

North Dakota

Minot	[81,124]	245	(9)

Ohio

Ashland	89	(2)
Ashtabula	68	(1)
Athens	113	(2)
Chillicothe	64	(1)
East Liverpool	114	(2)
Findlay	123	(3)
Fremont	132	(3)
Marion	67	(1)
New Philadelphia	73	(1)
Portsmouth	68	(1)
Sandusky	110	(2)
Sidney	59	(1)
Tiffin	106	(2)
Wooster	91	(2)
Zanesville	151	(3)

Oklahoma

Ardmore	160	(4)
Bartlesville	198	(4)
Chickasha	155	(3)
Duncan	139	(3)
McAlester	116	(2)
Muskogee	119	(2)
Okmulgee	70	(1)
Ponca City	167	(4)
Stillwater	156	(3)

Oregon

Albany		238	(5)
Bend	[43,755]	431	(12)
Corvallis		187	(4)
Grants Pass		202	(5)
Klamath Falls	[18,681]	348	(9)
Roseburg		224	(5)

Pennsylvania

Butler	90	(2)
Chambersburg	62	(1)
New Castle	40	(1)
Pottsville	54	(1)

Rhode Island

Newport	98	(2)

South Carolina

Greenwood		79	(1)
Hilton Head Island		114	(2)
Myrtle Beach	[217,842]	115	(10)
Orangeburg		44	(1)
Sumter		79	(1)

Tennessee

Cleveland	55	(1)
Columbia	78	(1)
Cookeville	78	(1)
Morristown	68	(1)
Tullahoma	286	(7)

Texas

Alice	127	(3)
Bay City	183	(4)
Del Rio	313	(7)
Greenville	128	(3)
Huntsville	52	(1)
Lufkin	88	(2)
Nacogdoches	113	(2)
Palestine	82	(2)
Paris	131	(3)

Utah

Logan	104	(2)

Vermont

Rutland	82	(2)

Virginia

Blacksburg	51	(1)
Fredericksburg	97	(2)
Harrisonburg	119	(2)
Martinsville	76	(1)
Staunton–Waynesboro	54	(1)
Winchester	59	(1)

Washington

Aberdeen		128	(3)
Longview		111	(2)
Port Angeles	[5,734]	279	(7)
Pullman	[19,572]	337	(9)
Walla Walla	[16,208]	281	(8)
Wenatchee	[17,064]	361	(10)

West Virginia

Beckley	51	(1)
Clarksburg	88	(2)
Fairmont	70	(1)
Morgantown	62	(1)

Wisconsin

Fond du Lac		144	(3)
Manitowoc		50	(1)
Marshfield– Wisconsin Rapids		80	(2)
Stevens Point	[78,346]	73	(4)

Wyoming

Rock Springs	102	(2)

The Results

Pullman, Washington, was originally called Three Forks, but was renamed in 1884 in honor of George Pullman, the inventor of the railroad sleeping car. The chamber of commerce makes the most of this connection. It distributes a brochure with a cover picture of the city's modest skyline as seen from the open rear door of a train. The town's slogan is printed across the photo, "Pullman: On The Right Track."

Such a proud statement certainly applies to the city's transportation system, which has blossomed from its first rail link to the outside world a century ago. A modern airport just east of Pullman now offers the quickest access to other cities. It is one of just 41 micropolitan facilities in America to be served by national or major regional airlines with jets for at least 60 passengers.

Travel within the Pullman area is relatively painless. The typical worker is able to drive to his or her job in less than 13 minutes; the national average is almost 22 minutes. And there is public transit: usage in Pullman could not be called high by any means, but it is more than double the norm for small towns. Cars and buses cruise on well-maintained highways. Few communities spend more per capita on their roads. All of these facts have contributed to Pullman's first-place finish in the transportation section, with 55 of a possible 100 points.

Western cities generally have the best transportation systems. Six of the twelve communities with the highest scores in this section are from that region. The Midwest lands four of the remaining slots, the East the other two.

Bogalusa, Louisiana, and Rio Rancho, New Mexico, have little in common. Bogalusa is an old industrial town in the yellow-pine belt near the Mississippi line. Its Great Southern Lumber Mill was once one of the largest in the world. Rio Rancho is a new bedroom community springing up on the open country near Albuquerque. "There used to be lots of coyotes when we first came out," remembers one resident, who has only been in the area since 1979.

But Bogalusa and Rio Rancho are alike in their transportation inadequacies. Neither city offers major airline service. Local roads are funded well below the national average in both communities, while commuters spend as much time behind the wheel as do their counterparts in big cities. Bogalusa and Rio Rancho consequently tie for last place in the transportation section, with just 13 points each.

The South holds eight of the eleven positions on the list of small cities with the worst scores. The East, Midwest, and West split the other three spots.

Transportation Scores: Highs and Lows

Highest	Rating Points
1. Pullman, Wash.	55
2. Mankato, Minn.	53
2. Missoula, Mont.	53
4. Carlsbad, N.Mex.	52
4. Flagstaff, Ariz.	52
6. Fairbanks, Alaska	51
7. Watertown, N.Y.	49
8. Manitowoc, Wis.	48
8. Ottawa, Ill.	48
10. Bullhead City–Lake Havasu City, Ariz.	47
10. Grand Island, Nebr.	47
10. Jamestown, N.Y.	47
13. Meridian, Miss.	46
13. Roswell, N.Mex.	46
15. Aberdeen, Wash.	45
15. Ardmore, Okla.	45
15. Concord, N.H.	45
15. Frankfort, Ky.	45
15. Idaho Falls, Idaho	45
15. Rock Springs, Wyo.	45
15. Winona, Minn.	45

Lowest

218. Bogalusa, La.	13
218. Rio Rancho, N.Mex.	13
217. Bay City, Tex.	20
214. Greenwood, S.C.	21
214. Madisonville, Ky.	21
214. Portsmouth, Ohio	21
213. Martinsville, Va.	22
209. Beckley, W.Va.	23
209. Crowley, La.	23
209. Goldsboro, N.C.	23
209. Opelousas, La.	23

	Pullman, Wash.	Bogalusa, La.	Rio Rancho, N.Mex.
Total Points in Section	55	13	13
Rank in Section	1	218*	218*
Results (and Rating Points)			
Commuting Ease Mean travel time to work in minutes	12.9 (19)	24.2 (5)	26.8 (2)
Public Transit Usage Users of public transit per 1,000 commuters	18 (5)	14 (4)	3 (1)
Highway Availability Highway index	5 (2)	2 (1)	13 (6)
Local Highway Funding Annual per capita highway-related spending by local governments	$185 (20)	$40 (3)	$34 (3)
Aviation Availability a. Enplaned commercial passengers on national and major regional air carriers	19,572	0	0
b. General aviation craft per 100,000 residents	337 (9)	38 (0)	59 (1)

*There was a tie for last place.

(Figure following each area name indicates the composite score from the five categories in this section.)

Alabama

Athens	25
Auburn–Opelika	33
Decatur	41
Enterprise	26
Selma	28
Talladega	25

Alaska

Fairbanks	51

Arizona

Bullhead City–Lake Havasu City	47
Casa Grande–Apache Junction	39
Flagstaff	52
Prescott	43
Sierra Vista	41
Yuma	38

Arkansas

Blytheville	33
El Dorado	30
Hot Springs	27
Jonesboro	30
Rogers	26
Russellville	30

California

El Centro–Calexico–Brawley	38
Eureka	38
Hanford	39
Madera	24
San Luis Obispo–Atascadero	29

Colorado

Grand Junction	44

Connecticut

Torrington	29

Delaware

Dover	32

Florida

Key West	36
Vero Beach	38

Georgia

Brunswick	39
Carrollton	27
Dalton	29
Gainesville	26
Hinesville	29
La Grange	40
Rome	27
Valdosta	35

Idaho

Coeur d'Alene	34
Idaho Falls	45
Nampa–Caldwell	32
Pocatello	42
Twin Falls	36

Illinois

Carbondale	30
Danville	37
De Kalb	43
Freeport	30
Galesburg	39
Mattoon–Charleston	38
Ottawa	48
Quincy	40
Sterling	29

Indiana

Columbus	33
Marion	28
Michigan City–La Porte	41
New Castle	28
Richmond	35
Vincennes	30

Iowa

Ames	44
Burlington	41
Clinton	37
Fort Dodge	42
Marshalltown	41
Mason City	43
Muscatine	32

Kansas

Hutchinson	39
Manhattan	37
Salina	39

Kentucky

Bowling Green	32
Frankfort	45
Madisonville	21
Paducah	31
Radcliff–Elizabethtown	33
Richmond	27

Louisiana

Bogalusa	13
Crowley	23
Hammond	24
Minden	25
Morgan City	28
New Iberia	34
Opelousas	23
Ruston	34

Maine
Augusta–Waterville	33
Biddeford	28

Maryland
Salisbury	35

Michigan
Adrian	27
Marquette	33
Mount Pleasant	31
Owosso	25
Traverse City	34

Minnesota
Faribault	38
Mankato	53
Winona	45

Mississippi
Columbus	29
Greenville	39
Greenwood	39
Hattiesburg	37
Laurel	33
Meridian	46
Tupelo	30
Vicksburg	38

Missouri
Cape Girardeau	31
Jefferson City	30
Sikeston	35

Montana
Bozeman	44
Helena	43
Missoula	53

Nebraska
Grand Island	47

Nevada
Carson City	38

New Hampshire
Concord	45
Keene	32
Laconia	37

New Mexico
Alamogordo	29
Carlsbad	52
Clovis	35
Farmington	33
Gallup	29
Hobbs	40
Rio Rancho	13
Roswell	46

New York
Auburn	42
Batavia	44
Cortland	44
Gloversville	28
Ithaca	42
Jamestown	47
Kingston	40
Olean	43
Plattsburgh	40
Watertown	49

North Carolina
Eden	25
Goldsboro	23
Greenville	26
Havelock–New Bern	26
Kinston	25
Lumberton	24
Roanoke Rapids	27
Rocky Mount	36
Sanford	24
Shelby	25
Statesville	29
Wilson	33

North Dakota
Minot	44

Ohio
Ashland	40
Ashtabula	32
Athens	27
Chillicothe	25
East Liverpool	25
Findlay	40
Fremont	37
Marion	27
New Philadelphia	34
Portsmouth	21
Sandusky	38
Sidney	32
Tiffin	31
Wooster	36
Zanesville	32

Oklahoma
Ardmore	45
Bartlesville	28
Chickasha	32
Duncan	24
McAlester	30
Muskogee	34
Okmulgee	30
Ponca City	41
Stillwater	31

Oregon
Albany	37
Bend	42
Corvallis	35
Grants Pass	33
Klamath Falls	41
Roseburg	43

Pennsylvania

Butler	36
Chambersburg	30
New Castle	38
Pottsville	24

Rhode Island

Newport	28

South Carolina

Greenwood	21
Hilton Head Island	27
Myrtle Beach	39
Orangeburg	31
Sumter	31

Tennessee

Cleveland	27
Columbia	29
Cookeville	27
Morristown	28
Tullahoma	33

Texas

Alice	24
Bay City	20
Del Rio	31
Greenville	27
Huntsville	27
Lufkin	25
Nacogdoches	28
Palestine	26
Paris	30

Utah

Logan	27

Vermont

Rutland	31

Virginia

Blacksburg	29
Fredericksburg	24
Harrisonburg	29
Martinsville	22
Staunton–Waynesboro	36
Winchester	28

Washington

Aberdeen	45
Longview	40
Port Angeles	37
Pullman	55
Walla Walla	43
Wenatchee	39

West Virginia

Beckley	23
Clarksburg	31
Fairmont	24
Morgantown	35

Wisconsin

Fond du Lac	38
Manitowoc	48
Marshfield–Wisconsin Rapids	43
Stevens Point	44

Wyoming

Rock Springs	45

10

Urban Proximity

Large cities might not be the greatest places to live, but they can be a lot of fun to visit. Metropolitan regions have the enormous resources needed to support cultural attractions and sports franchises that could not survive financially in small cities. Affluent suburbs boast gigantic malls that dwarf their micropolitan cousins. Big cities have the large numbers of viewers and advertisers required to sustain television stations whose signals can be received 50 miles away.

Small-city residents, anxious to avoid the congestion and confusion of urban life, can nonetheless benefit considerably from being close to a metropolitan center. Take the nation's capital for an example. Out-of-towners can enjoy the numerous historic sites, museums, and art galleries of Washington, D.C. Or they can shop in its large department stores. Or they can watch its professional teams play football, basketball, and hockey.

Most suburbanites no longer work in the central city. "For many, in fact, a trip into Washington has become a special occasion—a time to take a visiting relative to see the monuments," wrote John Milliken, the vice chairman of the Arlington (Virginia) County Board, in a 1987 *Washing-*

ton Post column. Residents of nearby micropolitan areas, such as Fredericksburg, Virginia, view both Washington *and* its suburbs in the same light. They make the 48-mile drive to see the sights, visit the shops, and watch the games. But at night, they head home to a community without Washington's crime or the suburbs' astronomically expensive housing. This section grades each area according to its proximity to urban centers that provide cultural activities, shopping, and big-league sporting events. It will be increasingly popular in the 1990s to view metro areas as resources for occasional use in these ways, rather than as full-time homes. Two trends support this prediction.

The first is the continuing decline of central cities. "For all the ballyhoo about the back-to-the-city movement and publicity about glittering new downtown office-hotel-apartment complexes, the hard figures still indicate decline and decay," says Púrdue University urban historian Jon Teaford. Cities will still have museums, zoos, and stadiums to attract visitors, but they will offer no compelling new arguments to draw permanent residents. Teaford suggests that the urban centers of the future will contain the poor, the childless, and those in such fields as banking and insurance.

The second important trend is the growing tendency of suburbs to follow the development patterns of the cities they surround. Purdue sociologist John Stahura notes that crime rates are rising in the nation's older suburbs, while their tax bases erode. Farther from the central city, many bedroom communities are being choked by unbridled growth. Insurance underwriter Joann Murphy told *Time* in 1987 that she had moved to Oak Brook, Illinois, in the 1960s "for the quiet and the country." Office buildings and shopping malls intruded on the peace, leading Murphy to complain, "This is like living in downtown Chicago."

It is little wonder that some suburbs are getting their own suburbs, or that many urban residents are gazing longingly beyond the confines of their metro areas. The exodus promises to be substantial. A 1988 report by the Metropolitan Washington Council of Governments, for example, predicted that the region's biggest growth will occur in an "outer ring" more than 20 miles from the city. This distant area is projected to add 129 percent more households and 96 percent more jobs by 2010.

Only one worry nags many of those considering a move: Can they survive being that far away from the city's attractions? Stuart Hollander, a tax lawyer who left San Francisco, contends that most people overstate their need for such immediate access. "A lot of people will say they miss the opera," he suggests. "I can't say that. We didn't go to the opera."

Ranking micropolitan America. The ideal small city would be reasonably close to regional centers for cultural activities, shopping, and professional sports. It would also receive television programming from a large city. Each area is evaluated in five categories:

1. Metro Center Proximity: Is the town near the central city of an officially designated metropolitan area?

2. Arts Center Proximity: Can you easily reach a city with museums, art galleries, orchestras, and live theater?

3. Retail Center Proximity: When you desire a change of pace, can you easily drive to a large city with a good variety of shops?

4. Sports Center Proximity: Can you quickly get to a professional sporting event?

5. Television Market: Does your town have access to a large choice of TV stations from a big market?

Metro Center Proximity

America's small cities are not lonely outposts in the boondocks, despite the stereotypes maintained by urbanites. More than half of all micropolitan areas—121 of 219, to be exact—are within 50 miles of the center of a metropolitan area. Merely 29 small cities are more than 100 miles from metropolitan amenities: in effect, more than a two-hour drive.

This category ranks each area according to the road mileage between it and the closest metro center. The dominant city of any of the nation's 333 metropolitan areas qualifies as a metro center, provided it is not also listed as a micropolitan area.

Rio Rancho, New Mexico, is the small city with the quickest access to a large neighbor. It is only an 11-mile drive across the county line to Albuquerque.

Fairbanks, Alaska, the northernmost micro in the nation, is also the most isolated. A resident heading for a metro center must drive 361 miles south to Anchorage.

The compact East has the largest number of small cities that are close to metropolitan areas. The vast West unsurprisingly has a virtual monopoly on cities that are distant from all metro centers.

Source. These statistics, published in 1988, are for 1988. Derived from *Rand McNally Road Atlas* (Chicago: Rand McNally and Co., 1988).

Scoring. Twenty points for 15 miles or less; no points for 206 miles or more. The spacing is every ten miles.

Lowest Road Mileage	Miles From Regional Center
1. Rio Rancho, N.Mex.	11
2. Ashland, Ohio	14
2. Torrington, Conn.	14
4. Hanford, Calif.	15
4. Nampa–Caldwell, Idaho	15
6. Vero Beach, Fla.	16
7. Rogers, Ark.	17
8. Biddeford, Maine	18
9. Kingston, N.Y.	19
9. New Castle, Pa.	19

Highest Road Mileage

219. Fairbanks, Alaska	361
218. Grand Junction, Colo.	236
217. Idaho Falls, Idaho	211
216. Farmington, N.Mex.	181
214. Marquette, Mich.	175
214. Yuma, Ariz.	175
213. Roswell, N.Mex.	173
212. Rock Springs, Wyo.	172
211. Missoula, Mont.	166
210. Pocatello, Idaho	162

(Figure following each area name indicates the number of miles from closest official metro area; figure in parentheses represents rating points.)

Alabama

Athens	24	(19)
Auburn–Opelika	32	(18)
Decatur	26	(18)
Enterprise	31	(18)
Selma	49	(16)
Talladega	23	(19)

Alaska

Fairbanks	361	(0)

Arizona

Bullhead City– Lake Havasu City	96	(11)
Casa Grande– Apache Junction	52	(16)
Flagstaff	137	(7)
Prescott	96	(11)
Sierra Vista	70	(14)
Yuma	175	(4)

Arkansas

Blytheville	68	(14)
El Dorado	85	(13)
Hot Springs	55	(16)
Jonesboro	66	(14)
Rogers	17	(19)
Russellville	76	(13)

California

El Centro–Calexico– Brawley	117	(9)
Eureka	158	(5)
Hanford	15	(20)
Madera	23	(19)
San Luis Obispo– Atascadero	94	(12)

Colorado

Grand Junction	236	(0)

Connecticut

Torrington	14	(20)

Delaware

Dover	46	(16)

Florida

Key West	161	(5)
Vero Beach	16	(19)

Georgia

Brunswick	71	(14)
Carrollton	49	(16)
Dalton	28	(18)
Gainesville	39	(17)
Hinesville	41	(17)
La Grange	45	(17)
Rome	54	(16)
Valdosta	78	(13)

Idaho

Coeur d'Alene	33	(18)
Idaho Falls	211	(0)
Nampa–Caldwell	15	(20)
Pocatello	162	(5)
Twin Falls	129	(8)

Illinois

Carbondale	96	(11)
Danville	35	(18)
De Kalb	31	(18)
Freeport	29	(18)
Galesburg	48	(16)
Mattoon–Charleston	44	(17)
Ottawa	45	(17)
Quincy	102	(11)
Sterling	57	(15)

Indiana

Columbus	39	(17)
Marion	32	(18)
Michigan City–La Porte	25	(19)
New Castle	20	(19)
Richmond	41	(17)
Vincennes	54	(16)

Iowa

Ames	28	(18)
Burlington	78	(13)
Clinton	37	(17)
Fort Dodge	91	(12)
Marshalltown	53	(16)
Mason City	82	(13)
Muscatine	30	(18)

Kansas

Hutchinson	52	(16)
Manhattan	54	(16)
Salina	90	(12)

Kentucky

Bowling Green	61	(15)
Frankfort	23	(19)
Madisonville	48	(16)
Paducah	96	(11)
Radcliff–Elizabethtown	36	(17)
Richmond	26	(18)

Louisiana

Bogalusa	64	(15)
Crowley	22	(19)
Hammond	41	(17)
Minden	31	(18)
Morgan City	37	(17)
New Iberia	20	(19)
Opelousas	22	(19)
Ruston	31	(18)

Maine

Augusta–Waterville	30	(18)
Biddeford	18	(19)

Maryland

Salisbury	102	(11)

Michigan

Adrian	34	(18)
Marquette	175	(4)
Mount Pleasant	53	(16)
Owosso	25	(19)
Traverse City	134	(8)

Minnesota

Faribault	48	(16)
Mankato	75	(14)
Winona	29	(18)

Mississippi

Columbus	61	(15)
Greenville	102	(11)
Greenwood	98	(11)
Hattiesburg	81	(13)
Laurel	85	(13)
Meridian	93	(12)
Tupelo	78	(13)
Vicksburg	44	(17)

Missouri

Cape Girardeau	113	(10)
Jefferson City	33	(18)
Sikeston	140	(7)

Montana

Bozeman	140	(7)
Helena	91	(12)
Missoula	166	(4)

Nebraska

Grand Island	98	(11)

Nevada

Carson City	32	(18)

New Hampshire

Concord	20	(19)
Keene	37	(17)
Laconia	46	(16)

New Mexico

Alamogordo	69	(14)
Carlsbad	142	(7)
Clovis	102	(11)
Farmington	181	(3)
Gallup	138	(7)
Hobbs	86	(12)
Rio Rancho	11	(20)
Roswell	173	(4)

New York

Auburn	27	(18)
Batavia	34	(18)
Cortland	34	(18)
Gloversville	50	(16)
Ithaca	34	(18)
Jamestown	54	(16)
Kingston	19	(19)
Olean	73	(14)
Plattsburgh	32	(18)
Watertown	74	(14)

North Carolina

Eden	26	(18)
Goldsboro	51	(16)
Greenville	74	(14)
Havelock–New Bern	50	(16)
Kinston	43	(17)
Lumberton	34	(18)
Roanoke Rapids	78	(13)
Rocky Mount	53	(16)
Sanford	36	(17)
Shelby	40	(17)
Statesville	27	(18)
Wilson	45	(17)

North Dakota

Minot	111	(10)

Ohio

Ashland	14	(20)
Ashtabula	42	(17)
Athens	39	(17)
Chillicothe	46	(16)
East Liverpool	25	(19)
Findlay	35	(18)
Fremont	32	(18)
Marion	39	(17)
New Philadelphia	26	(18)
Portsmouth	49	(16)
Sandusky	33	(18)
Sidney	34	(18)
Tiffin	46	(16)
Wooster	32	(18)
Zanesville	56	(15)

Oklahoma

Ardmore	72	(14)
Bartlesville	46	(16)
Chickasha	42	(17)
Duncan	33	(18)
McAlester	91	(12)
Muskogee	50	(16)
Okmulgee	39	(17)
Ponca City	68	(14)
Stillwater	64	(15)

Oregon

Albany	24	(19)
Bend	127	(8)
Corvallis	34	(18)
Grants Pass	28	(18)
Klamath Falls	76	(13)
Roseburg	71	(14)

Pennsylvania

Butler	35	(18)
Chambersburg	21	(19)
New Castle	19	(19)
Pottsville	35	(18)

Rhode Island

Newport	22	(19)

South Carolina

Greenwood	41	(17)
Hilton Head Island	31	(18)
Myrtle Beach	66	(14)
Orangeburg	44	(17)
Sumter	38	(17)

Tennessee

Cleveland	31	(18)
Columbia	44	(17)
Cookeville	76	(13)
Morristown	41	(17)
Tullahoma	58	(15)

Texas

Alice	43	(17)
Bay City	38	(17)
Del Rio	150	(6)
Greenville	50	(16)
Huntsville	56	(15)
Lufkin	83	(13)
Nacogdoches	70	(14)
Palestine	48	(16)
Paris	64	(15)

Utah

Logan	79	(13)

Vermont

Rutland	45	(17)

Virginia

Blacksburg	34	(18)
Fredericksburg	48	(16)
Harrisonburg	54	(16)
Martinsville	28	(18)
Staunton–Waynesboro	35	(18)
Winchester	41	(17)

Washington

Aberdeen	47	(16)
Longview	44	(17)
Port Angeles	79	(13)
Pullman	76	(13)
Walla Walla	56	(15)
Wenatchee	110	(10)

West Virginia

Beckley	59	(15)
Clarksburg	74	(14)
Fairmont	70	(14)
Morgantown	72	(14)

Wisconsin

Fond du Lac	38	(17)
Manitowoc	27	(18)
Marshfield– Wisconsin Rapids	47	(16)
Stevens Point	34	(18)

Wyoming

Rock Springs	172	(4)

Arts Center Proximity

Residents of Batavia, New York, find small-city life no barrier to artistic inspiration. Just 34 miles northeast of Batavia is Rochester, with its International Museum of Photography. Buffalo, home of the nationally recognized Albright-Knox Art Gallery, is only 36 miles west. Rochester and Buffalo each also has a regional theater company and one of the nation's 30 major orchestras.

This category evaluates each small city's proximity to the cultural treasures of a metropolitan area. Thirty large American cities have been classified as regional arts centers, based in part on their scores in the arts section of the *Places Rated Almanac*. Three major Canadian centers have also been placed on the list.

Micropolitan areas are ranked according to the road mileage to the nearest regional arts center. Batavia, with Rochester a mere 34 miles away, finishes first. Anyone in Fairbanks, Alaska, seeking a culture fix by car would be forced to drive 2,121 miles through the Yukon and British Columbia to Vancouver.

Midwestern cities generally have the best access to arts centers. Small towns in the West have the worst.

Sources. These statistics, published in 1988, are for 1988. Derived from *Rand McNally Road Atlas* (Chicago: Rand McNally and Co., 1988); Richard Boyer and David Savageau, *Places Rated Almanac* (New York: Prentice Hall, 1985).

Scoring. Twenty points for 40 miles or less; no points for 383 or more. The spacing is every 18 miles.

Atlanta, Ga. (ATL)
Baltimore, Md. (BAL)
Boston, Mass. (BOS)
Buffalo, N.Y. (BUF)
Chicago, Ill. (CHI)
Cincinnati, Ohio (CIN)
Cleveland, Ohio (CLE)
Columbus, Ohio (COL)
Dallas, Tex. (DAL)
Dayton, Ohio (DAY)
Denver, Colo. (DEN)
Detroit, Mich. (DET)
Honolulu, Hawaii (HON)
Houston, Tex. (HOU)
Indianapolis, Ind. (IND)
Los Angeles, Calif. (LA)
Milwaukee, Wis. (MIL)
Minneapolis, Minn. (MIN)
Montreal, Canada (MON)
New Haven, Conn. (NH)
New Orleans, La. (NO)
New York, N.Y. (NY)
Norfolk, Va. (NOR)
Philadelphia, Pa. (PHI)
Pittsburgh, Pa. (PIT)
Rochester, N.Y. (ROC)
Saint Louis, Mo. (STL)
San Diego, Calif. (SD)
San Francisco, Calif. (SF)
Seattle, Wash. (SEA)
Toronto, Canada (TOR)
Vancouver, Canada (VAN)
Washington, D.C. (WAS)

Lowest Road Mileage	Miles From Regional Center
1. Batavia, N.Y.	34
2. Butler, Pa.	38
3. Sidney, Ohio	39
4. Richmond, Ind.	41
5. East Liverpool, Ohio	44
6. Chillicothe, Ohio	46
6. Columbus, Ind.	46
8. Marion, Ohio	47
9. Faribault, Minn.	48
9. Fredericksburg, Va.	48
9. Hammond, La.	48
9. New Castle, Ind.	48
9. Torrington, Conn.	48

Highest Road Mileage

219. Fairbanks, Alaska	2,121
218. Key West, Fla.	821
217. Bozeman, Mont.	682
216. Idaho Falls, Idaho	658
215. Twin Falls, Idaho	646
214. Pocatello, Idaho	609
213. Helena, Mont.	593
212. Logan, Utah	561
211. Alamogordo, N.Mex.	546
210. Vero Beach, Fla.	531

(Figure following each area name indicates the number of miles from regional arts center; figure in parentheses represents rating points.)

Alabama

Athens (ATL)	201	(11)
Auburn–Opelika (ATL)	105	(16)
Decatur (ATL)	177	(12)
Enterprise (ATL)	217	(10)
Selma (ATL)	217	(10)
Talladega (ATL)	108	(16)

Alaska

Fairbanks (VAN)	2,121	(0)

Arizona

Bullhead City–Lake Havasu City (LA)	306	(5)
Casa Grande–Apache Junction (SD)	352	(2)
Flagstaff (LA)	476	(0)
Prescott (LA)	385	(0)
Sierra Vista (SD)	488	(0)
Yuma (SD)	175	(12)

Arkansas

Blytheville (STL)	216	(10)
El Dorado (DAL)	268	(7)
Hot Springs (DAL)	287	(6)
Jonesboro (STL)	265	(7)
Rogers (STL)	307	(5)
Russellville (DAL)	364	(2)

California

El Centro–Calexico–Brawley (SD)	117	(15)
Eureka (SF)	282	(6)
Hanford (LA)	182	(12)
Madera (SF)	154	(13)
San Luis Obispo–Atascadero (LA)	195	(11)

Colorado

Grand Junction (DEN)	246	(8)

Connecticut

Torrington (NH)	48	(19)

Delaware

Dover (PHI)	75	(18)

Florida

Key West (ATL)	821	(0)
Vero Beach (ATL)	531	(0)

Georgia

Brunswick (ATL)	281	(6)
Carrollton (ATL)	49	(19)
Dalton (ATL)	85	(17)
Gainesville (ATL)	50	(19)
Hinesville (ATL)	243	(8)
La Grange (ATL)	64	(18)
Rome (ATL)	65	(18)
Valdosta (ATL)	225	(9)

Idaho

Coeur d'Alene (SEA)	313	(4)
Idaho Falls (DEN)	658	(0)
Nampa–Caldwell (SEA)	502	(0)
Pocatello (DEN)	609	(0)
Twin Falls (SEA)	646	(0)

Illinois

Carbondale (STL)	99	(16)
Danville (IND)	91	(17)
De Kalb (CHI)	68	(18)
Freeport (CHI)	115	(15)
Galesburg (CHI)	184	(12)
Mattoon–Charleston (STL)	123	(15)
Ottawa (CHI)	90	(17)
Quincy (STL)	159	(13)
Sterling (CHI)	122	(15)

Indiana

Columbus (IND)	46	(19)
Marion (IND)	67	(18)
Michigan City– La Porte (CHI)	56	(19)
New Castle (IND)	48	(19)
Richmond (DAY)	41	(19)
Vincennes (IND)	121	(15)

Iowa

Ames (MIN)	217	(10)
Burlington (CHI)	230	(9)
Clinton (CHI)	150	(13)
Fort Dodge (MIN)	223	(9)
Marshalltown (MIN)	233	(9)
Mason City (MIN)	136	(14)
Muscatine (CHI)	202	(11)

Kansas

Hutchinson (DAL)	417	(0)
Manhattan (STL)	371	(1)
Salina (DEN)	404	(0)

Kentucky

Bowling Green (CIN)	213	(10)
Frankfort (CIN)	81	(17)
Madisonville (STL)	215	(10)
Paducah (STL)	170	(12)
Radcliff– Elizabethtown (CIN)	137	(14)
Richmond (CIN)	104	(16)

Louisiana

Bogalusa (NO)	64	(18)
Crowley (NO)	156	(13)
Hammond (NO)	48	(19)
Minden (DAL)	217	(10)
Morgan City (NO)	90	(17)
New Iberia (NO)	131	(14)
Opelousas (NO)	138	(14)
Ruston (DAL)	256	(8)

Maine

Augusta–Waterville (BOS)	163	(13)
Biddeford (BOS)	88	(17)

Maryland

Salisbury (BAL)	106	(16)

Michigan

Adrian (DET)	68	(18)
Marquette (MIL)	290	(6)
Mount Pleasant (DET)	149	(13)
Owosso (DET)	82	(17)
Traverse City (DET)	246	(8)

Minnesota

Faribault (MIN)	48	(19)
Mankato (MIN)	75	(18)
Winona (MIN)	116	(15)

Mississippi

Columbus (ATL)	270	(7)
Greenville (NO)	290	(6)
Greenwood (NO)	278	(6)
Hattiesburg (NO)	110	(16)
Laurel (NO)	135	(14)
Meridian (NO)	184	(12)
Tupelo (ATL)	292	(6)
Vicksburg (NO)	207	(10)

Missouri

Cape Girardeau (STL)	113	(15)
Jefferson City (STL)	126	(15)
Sikeston (STL)	145	(14)

Montana

Bozeman (SEA)	682	(0)
Helena (SEA)	593	(0)
Missoula (SEA)	481	(0)

Nebraska

Grand Island (DEN)	407	(0)

Nevada

Carson City (SF)	234	(9)

New Hampshire

Concord (BOS)	78	(17)
Keene (BOS)	83	(17)
Laconia (BOS)	103	(16)

New Mexico

Alamogordo (DEN)	546	(0)
Carlsbad (DAL)	460	(0)
Clovis (DAL)	418	(0)
Farmington (DEN)	399	(0)
Gallup (DEN)	515	(0)
Hobbs (DAL)	391	(0)
Rio Rancho (DEN)	433	(0)
Roswell (DAL)	487	(0)

New York

Auburn (ROC)	69	(18)
Batavia (ROC)	34	(20)
Cortland (ROC)	118	(15)
Gloversville (NH)	182	(12)
Ithaca (ROC)	92	(17)
Jamestown (BUF)	89	(17)
Kingston (NY)	104	(16)
Olean (BUF)	73	(18)
Plattsburgh (MON)	67	(18)
Watertown (ROC)	153	(13)

North Carolina

Eden (NOR)	219	(10)
Goldsboro (NOR)	167	(12)
Greenville (NOR)	130	(15)
Havelock–New Bern (NOR)	172	(12)
Kinston (NOR)	158	(13)
Lumberton (NOR)	244	(8)
Roanoke Rapids (NOR)	90	(17)
Rocky Mount (NOR)	112	(16)
Sanford (NOR)	207	(10)
Shelby (ATL)	203	(10)
Statesville (ATL)	281	(6)
Wilson (NOR)	131	(14)

North Dakota

Minot (MIN)	495	(0)

Ohio

Ashland (CLE)	65	(18)
Ashtabula (CLE)	58	(19)
Athens (COL)	74	(18)
Chillicothe (COL)	46	(19)
East Liverpool (PIT)	44	(19)
Findlay (COL)	95	(16)
Fremont (CLE)	85	(17)
Marion (COL)	47	(19)
New Philadelphia (CLE)	78	(17)
Portsmouth (COL)	99	(16)
Sandusky (CLE)	60	(18)
Sidney (DAY)	39	(20)
Tiffin (CLE)	90	(17)
Wooster (CLE)	62	(18)
Zanesville (COL)	56	(19)

Oklahoma

Ardmore (DAL)	110	(16)
Bartlesville (DAL)	309	(5)
Chickasha (DAL)	202	(11)
Duncan (DAL)	162	(13)
McAlester (DAL)	175	(12)
Muskogee (DAL)	239	(8)
Okmulgee (DAL)	226	(9)
Ponca City (DAL)	298	(5)
Stillwater (DAL)	258	(7)

Oregon

Albany (SEA)	241	(8)
Bend (SEA)	332	(3)
Corvallis (SEA)	253	(8)
Grants Pass (SF)	396	(0)
Klamath Falls (SF)	362	(2)
Roseburg (SEA)	350	(2)

Pennsylvania

Butler (PIT)	38	(20)
Chambersburg (BAL)	76	(18)
New Castle (PIT)	56	(19)
Pottsville (PHI)	97	(16)

Rhode Island
Newport (BOS)   74   (18)

South Carolina
Greenwood (ATL)	146	(14)
Hilton Head Island (ATL)	285	(6)
Myrtle Beach (NOR)	328	(4)
Orangeburg (ATL)	222	(9)
Sumter (ATL)	255	(8)

Tennessee
Cleveland (ATL)	112	(16)
Columbia (ATL)	252	(8)
Cookeville (ATL)	206	(10)
Morristown (ATL)	265	(7)
Tullahoma (ATL)	193	(11)

Texas
Alice (HOU)	232	(9)
Bay City (HOU)	79	(17)
Del Rio (HOU)	347	(2)
Greenville (DAL)	50	(19)
Huntsville (HOU)	72	(18)
Lufkin (HOU)	120	(15)
Nacogdoches (HOU)	139	(14)
Palestine (DAL)	112	(16)
Paris (DAL)	106	(16)

Utah
Logan (DEN)   561   (0)

Vermont
Rutland (BOS)   171   (12)

Virginia
Blacksburg (WAS)	257	(7)
Fredericksburg (WAS)	48	(19)
Harrisonburg (WAS)	126	(15)
Martinsville (NOR)	221	(9)
Staunton–Waynesboro (WAS)	152	(13)
Winchester (WAS)	71	(18)

Washington
Aberdeen (SEA)	108	(16)
Longview (SEA)	125	(15)
Port Angeles (SEA)	87	(17)
Pullman (SEA)	312	(4)
Walla Walla (SEA)	274	(7)
Wenatchee (SEA)	147	(14)

West Virginia
Beckley (COL)	243	(8)
Clarksburg (PIT)	111	(16)
Fairmont (PIT)	92	(17)
Morgantown (PIT)	77	(17)

Wisconsin
Fond du Lac (MIL)	63	(18)
Manitowoc (MIL)	82	(17)
Marshfield–Wisconsin Rapids (MIN)	171	(12)
Stevens Point (MIL)	154	(13)

Wyoming
Rock Springs (DEN)   360   (2)

Retail Center Proximity

Shopping is fine in most small cities. There is usually a mall near the outskirts of town, offering an array of national and regional chain stores. You can usually find just what you need.

But often shoppers need a broader selection. This category rates each area on its proximity to a large city that provides exactly such a range of choice. The *Rand McNally Commercial Atlas and Marketing Guide* splits the country into 47 major trading areas. The key cities of these regions, essentially their economic capitals, are listed here as retail centers.

Ames, Iowa, is the small city closest to a retail hub. Des Moines is just 28 miles south of Ames on Interstate 35. If you're skeptical about Des Moines being a shopping paradise, consider what it has to offer: 26 department stores, 91 women's clothing shops, 71 shoe stores, a total of 2,236 retail establishments.

Fairbanks, Alaska, is in Seattle's region. The road distance between the two communities is 2,265 miles.

Southern cities generally provide the best access to the joys of metropolitan shopping. Retail centers are farthest away in the West.

Sources. These statistics, published in 1988, are for 1988. Derived from *Rand McNally Road Atlas* (Chicago: Rand McNally and Co., 1988); *Rand McNally Commercial Atlas and Marketing Guide* (Chicago: Rand McNally and Co., 1988).

Scoring. Twenty points for 35 miles or less; no points for 264 or more. The spacing is every 12 miles.

Atlanta, Ga. (ATL)

Birmingham, Ala. (BIR)

Boston, Mass. (BOS)

Buffalo, N.Y. (BUF)

Charlotte, N.C. (CHA)

Chicago, Ill. (CHI)

Cincinnati, Ohio (CIN)

Cleveland, Ohio (CLE)

Columbus, Ohio (COL)

Dallas, Tex. (DAL)

Denver, Colo. (DEN)

Des Moines, Iowa (DM)

Detroit, Mich. (DET)

El Paso, Tex. (ELP)

Honolulu, Hawaii (HON)

Houston, Tex. (HOU)

Indianapolis, Ind. (IND)

Jacksonville, Fla. (JAC)

Kansas City, Mo. (KC)

Knoxville, Tenn. (KNO)

Little Rock, Ark. (LR)

Los Angeles, Calif. (LA)

Louisville, Ky. (LOU)

Memphis, Tenn. (MEM)

Miami, Fla. (MIA)

Milwaukee, Wis. (MIL)

Minneapolis, Minn. (MIN)

Nashville, Tenn. (NAS)

New Orleans, La. (NO)

New York, N.Y. (NY)

Oklahoma City, Okla. (OKC)

Omaha, Nebr. (OMA)

Philadelphia, Pa. (PHI)

Phoenix, Ariz. (PHO)

Pittsburgh, Pa. (PIT)

Portland, Oreg. (POR)

Richmond, Va. (RIC)

Saint Louis, Mo. (STL)

Salt Lake City, Utah (SLC)

San Antonio, Tex. (SA)

San Francisco, Calif. (SF)

Seattle, Wash. (SEA)

Spokane, Wash. (SPO)

Tampa, Fla. (TAM)

Tulsa, Okla. (TUL)

Washington, D.C. (WAS)

Wichita, Kans. (WIC)

Lowest Road Mileage	Miles From Regional Center
1. Ames, Iowa	28
2. Coeur d'Alene, Idaho	33
3. Batavia, N.Y.	36
3. Radcliff–Elizabethtown, Ky.	36
5. Butler, Pa.	38
6. Okmulgee, Okla.	39
7. Shelby, N.C.	40
8. Morristown, Tenn.	41
8. Statesville, N.C.	41
10. Chickasha, Okla.	42

Highest Road Mileage

219. Fairbanks, Alaska	2,265
218. Minot, N.Dak.	495
217. Farmington, N.Mex.	444
216. Clovis, N.Mex.	418
215. Bozeman, Mont.	402
214. Hobbs, N.Mex.	391
213. Gallup, N.Mex.	380
212. Rock Springs, Wyo.	360
211. Nampa–Caldwell, Idaho	351
210. Plattsburgh, N.Y.	319

(Figure following each area name indicates the number of miles from regional retail center; figure in parentheses represents rating points.)

Alabama

Athens (BIR)	98	(14)
Auburn–Opelika (ATL)	105	(14)
Decatur (BIR)	84	(15)
Enterprise (BIR)	178	(8)
Selma (BIR)	86	(15)
Talladega (BIR)	55	(18)

Alaska

Fairbanks (SEA)	2,265	(0)

Arizona

Bullhead City–Lake Havasu City (LA)	306	(0)
Casa Grande–Apache Junction (PHO)	52	(18)
Flagstaff (PHO)	137	(11)
Prescott (PHO)	96	(14)
Sierra Vista (PHO)	188	(7)
Yuma (PHO)	182	(7)

Arkansas

Blytheville (MEM)	68	(17)
El Dorado (LR)	116	(13)
Hot Springs (LR)	55	(18)
Jonesboro (LR)	126	(12)
Rogers (LR)	211	(5)
Russellville (LR)	76	(16)

California

El Centro–Calexico–Brawley (LA)	227	(4)
Eureka (SF)	282	(0)
Hanford (SF)	212	(5)
Madera (SF)	154	(10)
San Luis Obispo–Atascadero (LA)	195	(6)

Colorado

Grand Junction (DEN)	246	(2)

Connecticut

Torrington (NY)	103	(14)

Delaware

Dover (PHI)	75	(16)

Florida

Key West (MIA)	161	(9)
Vero Beach (MIA)	138	(11)

Georgia

Brunswick (JAC)	71	(17)
Carrollton (ATL)	49	(18)
Dalton (ATL)	85	(15)
Gainesville (ATL)	50	(18)
Hinesville (ATL)	243	(2)
La Grange (ATL)	64	(17)
Rome (ATL)	65	(17)
Valdosta (JAC)	120	(12)

Idaho

Coeur d'Alene (SPO)	33	(20)
Idaho Falls (SLC)	211	(5)
Nampa–Caldwell (SLC)	351	(0)
Pocatello (SLC)	162	(9)
Twin Falls (SLC)	209	(5)

Illinois

Carbondale (STL)	99	(14)
Danville (CHI)	137	(11)
De Kalb (CHI)	68	(17)
Freeport (CHI)	115	(13)
Galesburg (CHI)	184	(7)
Mattoon–Charleston (CHI)	184	(7)
Ottawa (CHI)	90	(15)
Quincy (STL)	159	(9)
Sterling (DM)	223	(4)

Indiana

Columbus (IND)	46	(19)
Marion (IND)	67	(17)
Michigan City– La Porte (CHI)	56	(18)
New Castle (IND)	48	(18)
Richmond (IND)	73	(16)
Vincennes (IND)	121	(12)

Iowa

Ames (DM)	28	(20)
Burlington (DM)	162	(9)
Clinton (DM)	199	(6)
Fort Dodge (DM)	91	(15)
Marshalltown (DM)	53	(18)
Mason City (DM)	120	(12)
Muscatine (DM)	148	(10)

Kansas

Hutchinson (WIC)	52	(18)
Manhattan (KC)	114	(13)
Salina (WIC)	90	(15)

Kentucky

Bowling Green (LOU)	112	(13)
Frankfort (LOU)	52	(18)
Madisonville (LOU)	158	(9)
Paducah (LOU)	220	(4)
Radcliff–Elizabethtown (LOU)	36	(19)
Richmond (LOU)	105	(14)

Louisiana

Bogalusa (NO)	64	(17)
Crowley (NO)	156	(9)
Hammond (NO)	48	(18)
Minden (DAL)	217	(4)
Morgan City (NO)	90	(15)
New Iberia (NO)	131	(12)
Opelousas (NO)	138	(11)
Ruston (NO)	289	(0)

Maine

Augusta–Waterville (BOS)	163	(9)
Biddeford (BOS)	88	(15)

Maryland

Salisbury (WAS)	115	(13)

Michigan

Adrian (DET)	68	(17)
Marquette (MIL)	290	(0)
Mount Pleasant (DET)	149	(10)
Owosso (DET)	82	(16)
Traverse City (DET)	246	(2)

Minnesota

Faribault (MIN)	48	(18)
Mankato (MIN)	75	(16)
Winona (MIL)	225	(4)

Mississippi

Columbus (MEM)	168	(8)
Greenville (MEM)	143	(11)
Greenwood (MEM)	127	(12)
Hattiesburg (NO)	110	(13)
Laurel (NO)	135	(11)
Meridian (MEM)	244	(2)
Tupelo (MEM)	106	(14)
Vicksburg (MEM)	222	(4)

Missouri

Cape Girardeau (STL)	113	(13)
Jefferson City (STL)	126	(12)
Sikeston (STL)	145	(10)

Montana

Bozeman (SPO)	402	(0)
Helena (SPO)	313	(0)
Missoula (SPO)	201	(6)

Nebraska

Grand Island (OMA)	136	(11)

Nevada

Carson City (SF)	234	(3)

New Hampshire

Concord (BOS)	78	(16)
Keene (BOS)	83	(16)
Laconia (BOS)	103	(14)

New Mexico

Alamogordo (ELP)	112	(13)
Carlsbad (ELP)	163	(9)
Clovis (DAL)	418	(0)
Farmington (ELP)	444	(0)
Gallup (ELP)	380	(0)
Hobbs (DAL)	391	(0)
Rio Rancho (ELP)	279	(0)
Roswell (ELP)	232	(3)

New York

Auburn (NY)	283	(0)
Batavia (BUF)	36	(19)
Cortland (NY)	257	(1)
Gloversville (NY)	206	(5)
Ithaca (NY)	267	(0)
Jamestown (BUF)	89	(15)
Kingston (NY)	104	(14)
Olean (BUF)	73	(16)
Plattsburgh (NY)	319	(0)
Watertown (NY)	317	(0)

North Carolina

Eden (CHA)	124	(12)
Goldsboro (CHA)	188	(7)
Greenville (CHA)	220	(4)
Havelock– New Bern (CHA)	265	(0)
Kinston (CHA)	214	(5)
Lumberton (CHA)	126	(12)
Roanoke Rapids (CHA)	221	(4)
Rocky Mount (CHA)	190	(7)
Sanford (CHA)	114	(13)
Shelby (CHA)	40	(19)
Statesville (CHA)	41	(19)
Wilson (CHA)	184	(7)

North Dakota

Minot (MIN)	495	(0)

Ohio

Ashland (CLE)	65	(17)
Ashtabula (CLE)	58	(18)
Athens (COL)	74	(16)
Chillicothe (COL)	46	(19)
East Liverpool (CLE)	89	(15)
Findlay (DET)	108	(13)
Fremont (DET)	98	(14)
Marion (COL)	47	(19)
New Philadelphia (CLE)	78	(16)
Portsmouth (CIN)	119	(13)
Sandusky (CLE)	60	(17)
Sidney (CIN)	92	(15)
Tiffin (DET)	116	(13)
Wooster (CLE)	62	(17)
Zanesville (COL)	56	(18)

Oklahoma

Ardmore (OKC)	97	(14)
Bartlesville (TUL)	46	(19)
Chickasha (OKC)	42	(19)
Duncan (OKC)	86	(15)
McAlester (OKC)	128	(12)
Muskogee (TUL)	50	(18)
Okmulgee (TUL)	39	(19)
Ponca City (OKC)	105	(14)
Stillwater (OKC)	64	(17)

Oregon

Albany (POR)	69	(17)
Bend (POR)	160	(9)
Corvallis (POR)	81	(16)
Grants Pass (POR)	246	(2)
Klamath Falls (POR)	280	(0)
Roseburg (POR)	178	(8)

Pennsylvania

Butler (PIT)	38	(19)
Chambersburg (WAS)	93	(15)
New Castle (PIT)	56	(18)
Pottsville (PHI)	97	(14)

Rhode Island

Newport (BOS)	74	(16)

South Carolina

Greenwood (CHA)	116	(13)
Hilton Head Island (ATL)	285	(0)
Myrtle Beach (CHA)	182	(7)
Orangeburg (CHA)	140	(11)
Sumter (CHA)	105	(14)

Tennessee

Cleveland (ATL)	112	(13)
Columbia (NAS)	44	(19)
Cookeville (NAS)	76	(16)
Morristown (KNO)	41	(19)
Tullahoma (NAS)	72	(16)

Texas

Alice (SA)	123	(12)
Bay City (HOU)	79	(16)
Del Rio (SA)	150	(10)
Greenville (DAL)	50	(18)
Huntsville (HOU)	72	(16)
Lufkin (HOU)	120	(12)
Nacogdoches (HOU)	139	(11)
Palestine (DAL)	112	(13)
Paris (DAL)	106	(14)

Utah

Logan (SLC)	79	(16)

Vermont

Rutland (NY)	257	(1)

Virginia

Blacksburg (RIC)	200	(6)
Fredericksburg (WAS)	48	(18)
Harrisonburg (WAS)	126	(12)
Martinsville (RIC)	173	(8)
Staunton–Waynesboro (RIC)	103	(14)
Winchester (WAS)	71	(17)

Washington

Aberdeen (SEA)	108	(13)
Longview (POR)	52	(18)
Port Angeles (SEA)	87	(15)
Pullman (SPO)	76	(16)
Walla Walla (SPO)	160	(9)
Wenatchee (SEA)	147	(10)

West Virginia

Beckley (CIN)	272	(0)
Clarksburg (PIT)	111	(13)
Fairmont (PIT)	92	(15)
Morgantown (PIT)	77	(16)

Wisconsin

Fond du Lac (MIL)	63	(17)
Manitowoc (MIL)	82	(16)
Marshfield–Wisconsin Rapids (MIL)	188	(7)
Stevens Point (MIL)	154	(10)

Wyoming

Rock Springs (DEN)	360	(0)

Sports Center Proximity

Green Bay, Wisconsin, is often cited as proof that a small city can support a major-league sports team. The football Packers are wildly popular, truly the pride of the community. But the fact remains that Green Bay is not really a small city. It is the 159th largest metro area in the country. No micropolitan area has a big-league professional franchise.

This category measures the distance from each area to the closest of 27 regional sports centers. Every center has teams in at least two of the following leagues: the National (baseball) League, the American (baseball) League, the National Football League, the National Basketball Association, and the National Hockey League.

Batavia, New York, is just 36 miles from Buffalo, home of the NFL Bills and the NHL Sabres. Buffalo is an avid sports town, holder of the all-time attendance records for the NFL and minor-league baseball. It has hopes of attracting a big-league baseball team in the 1990s. Faribault, Minnesota, is the micropolitan area closest to a major city with teams in all four sports, being 48 miles from Minneapolis.

Fairbanks, Alaska, is a 2,265-mile drive from its sports center, Seattle. Western towns are usually the farthest from big-league action. Southern and Midwestern cities are the nearest.

Source. These statistics, published in 1988, are for 1988. Derived from *Rand McNally Road Atlas* (Chicago: Rand McNally and Co., 1988).

Scoring. Twenty points for 38 miles or less; no points for 381 or more. The spacing is every 18 miles.

Atlanta, Ga. (ATL)

Boston, Mass. (BOS)

Buffalo, N.Y. (BUF)

Chicago, Ill. (CHI)

Cincinnati, Ohio (CIN)

Cleveland, Ohio (CLE)

Dallas, Tex. (DAL)

Denver, Colo. (DEN)

Detroit, Mich. (DET)

Houston, Tex. (HOU)

Indianapolis, Ind. (IND)

Kansas City, Mo. (KC)

Los Angeles, Calif. (LA)

Miami, Fla. (MIA)

Milwaukee, Wis. (MIL)

Minneapolis, Minn. (MIN)

Montreal, Canada (MON)

New York, N.Y. (NY)

Philadelphia, Pa. (PHI)

Phoenix, Ariz. (PHO)

Pittsburgh, Pa. (PIT)

Saint Louis, Mo. (STL)

San Diego, Calif. (SD)

San Francisco–Oakland, Calif. (SF)

Seattle, Wash. (SEA)

Toronto, Canada (TOR)

Washington, D.C. (WAS)

Lowest Road Mileage

Lowest Road Mileage	Miles From Regional Center
1. Batavia, N.Y.	36
2. Butler, Pa.	38
3. East Liverpool, Ohio	44
4. Columbus, Ind.	46
5. Faribault, Minn.	48
5. Fredericksburg, Va.	48
5. New Castle, Ind.	48
8. Carrollton, Ga.	49
9. Gainesville, Ga.	50
9. Greenville, Tex.	50

Highest Road Mileage

219. Fairbanks, Alaska	2,265
218. Bozeman, Mont.	682
217. Idaho Falls, Idaho	658
216. Twin Falls, Idaho	646
215. Pocatello, Idaho	609
214. Helena, Mont.	593
213. Logan, Utah	561
212. Nampa–Caldwell, Idaho	502
211. Minot, N.Dak.	495
210. Roswell, N.Mex.	487

(Figure following each area name indicates the number of miles from regional sports center; figure in parentheses represents rating points.)

Alabama

Athens (ATL)	201	(10)
Auburn–Opelika (ATL)	105	(16)
Decatur (ATL)	177	(12)
Enterprise (ATL)	217	(10)
Selma (ATL)	217	(10)
Talladega (ATL)	108	(16)

Alaska

Fairbanks (SEA)	2,265	(0)

Arizona

Bullhead City–Lake Havasu City (PHO)	217	(10)
Casa Grande–Apache Junction (PHO)	52	(19)
Flagstaff (PHO)	137	(14)
Prescott (PHO)	96	(16)
Sierra Vista (PHO)	188	(11)
Yuma (SD)	175	(12)

Arkansas

Blytheville (STL)	216	(10)
El Dorado (DAL)	268	(7)
Hot Springs (DAL)	287	(6)
Jonesboro (STL)	265	(7)
Rogers (KC)	215	(10)
Russellville (KC)	347	(2)

California

El Centro–Calexico–Brawley (SD)	117	(15)
Eureka (SF)	282	(6)
Hanford (LA)	182	(12)
Madera (SF)	154	(13)
San Luis Obispo–Atascadero (LA)	195	(11)

Colorado

Grand Junction (DEN)	246	(8)

Connecticut

Torrington (NY)	103	(16)

Delaware

Dover (PHI)	75	(17)

Florida

Key West (MIA)	161	(13)
Vero Beach (MIA)	138	(14)

Georgia

Brunswick (ATL)	281	(6)
Carrollton (ATL)	49	(19)
Dalton (ATL)	85	(17)
Gainesville (ATL)	50	(19)
Hinesville (ATL)	243	(8)
La Grange (ATL)	64	(18)
Rome (ATL)	65	(18)
Valdosta (ATL)	225	(9)

Idaho

Coeur d'Alene (SEA)	313	(4)
Idaho Falls (DEN)	658	(0)
Nampa–Caldwell (SEA)	502	(0)
Pocatello (DEN)	609	(0)
Twin Falls (SEA)	646	(0)

Illinois

Carbondale (STL)	99	(16)
Danville (IND)	91	(17)
De Kalb (CHI)	68	(18)
Freeport (CHI)	115	(15)
Galesburg (CHI)	184	(11)
Mattoon–Charleston (STL)	123	(15)
Ottawa (CHI)	90	(17)
Quincy (STL)	159	(13)
Sterling (CHI)	122	(15)

Indiana

Columbus (IND)	46	(19)
Marion (IND)	67	(18)
Michigan City–La Porte (CHI)	56	(19)
New Castle (IND)	48	(19)
Richmond (CIN)	62	(18)
Vincennes (IND)	121	(15)

Iowa

Ames (MIN)	217	(10)
Burlington (CHI)	230	(9)
Clinton (CHI)	150	(13)
Fort Dodge (MIN)	223	(9)
Marshalltown (MIN)	233	(9)
Mason City (MIN)	136	(14)
Muscatine (CHI)	202	(10)

Kansas

Hutchinson (KC)	208	(10)
Manhattan (KC)	114	(15)
Salina (KC)	171	(12)

Kentucky

Bowling Green (CIN)	213	(10)
Frankfort (CIN)	81	(17)
Madisonville (STL)	215	(10)
Paducah (STL)	170	(12)
Radcliff–Elizabethtown (CIN)	137	(14)
Richmond (CIN)	104	(16)

Louisiana

Bogalusa (HOU)	351	(2)
Crowley (HOU)	180	(12)
Hammond (HOU)	294	(5)
Minden (DAL)	217	(10)
Morgan City (HOU)	264	(7)
New Iberia (HOU)	223	(9)
Opelousas (HOU)	211	(10)
Ruston (DAL)	256	(7)

Maine

Augusta–Waterville (BOS)	163	(13)
Biddeford (BOS)	88	(17)

Maryland

Salisbury (WAS)	115	(15)

Michigan

Adrian (DET)	68	(18)
Marquette (MIL)	290	(6)
Mount Pleasant (DET)	149	(13)
Owosso (DET)	82	(17)
Traverse City (DET)	246	(8)

Minnesota

Faribault (MIN)	48	(19)
Mankato (MIN)	75	(17)
Winona (MIN)	116	(15)

Mississippi

Columbus (ATL)	270	(7)
Greenville (DAL)	396	(0)
Greenwood (ATL)	380	(0)
Hattiesburg (ATL)	388	(0)
Laurel (ATL)	363	(1)
Meridian (ATL)	302	(5)
Tupelo (ATL)	292	(5)
Vicksburg (DAL)	363	(1)

Missouri

Cape Girardeau (STL)	113	(15)
Jefferson City (STL)	126	(15)
Sikeston (STL)	145	(14)

Montana

Bozeman (SEA)	682	(0)
Helena (SEA)	593	(0)
Missoula (SEA)	481	(0)

Nebraska

Grand Island (KC)	335	(3)

Nevada

Carson City (SF)	234	(9)

New Hampshire

Concord (BOS)	78	(17)
Keene (BOS)	83	(17)
Laconia (BOS)	103	(16)

New Mexico

Alamogordo (PHO)	444	(0)
Carlsbad (DAL)	460	(0)
Clovis (DAL)	418	(0)
Farmington (DEN)	399	(0)
Gallup (PHO)	325	(4)
Hobbs (DAL)	391	(0)
Rio Rancho (DEN)	433	(0)
Roswell (DAL)	487	(0)

New York

Auburn (BUF)	128	(15)
Batavia (BUF)	36	(20)
Cortland (BUF)	169	(12)
Gloversville (NY)	206	(10)
Ithaca (BUF)	150	(13)
Jamestown (BUF)	89	(17)
Kingston (NY)	104	(16)
Olean (BUF)	73	(18)
Plattsburgh (MON)	67	(18)
Watertown (MON)	177	(12)

North Carolina

Eden (WAS)	277	(6)
Goldsboro (WAS)	269	(7)
Greenville (WAS)	260	(7)
Havelock– New Bern (WAS)	321	(4)
Kinston (WAS)	283	(6)
Lumberton (WAS)	338	(3)
Roanoke Rapids (WAS)	184	(11)
Rocky Mount (WAS)	225	(9)
Sanford (WAS)	299	(5)
Shelby (ATL)	203	(10)
Statesville (ATL)	281	(6)
Wilson (WAS)	243	(8)

North Dakota

Minot (MIN)	495	(0)

Ohio

Ashland (CLE)	65	(18)
Ashtabula (CLE)	58	(18)
Athens (CIN)	152	(13)
Chillicothe (CIN)	94	(16)
East Liverpool (PIT)	44	(19)
Findlay (DET)	108	(16)
Fremont (CLE)	85	(17)
Marion (CLE)	115	(15)
New Philadelphia (CLE)	78	(17)
Portsmouth (CIN)	119	(15)
Sandusky (CLE)	60	(18)
Sidney (CIN)	92	(17)
Tiffin (CLE)	90	(17)
Wooster (CLE)	62	(18)
Zanesville (PIT)	130	(14)

Oklahoma

Ardmore (DAL)	110	(16)
Bartlesville (KC)	204	(10)
Chickasha (DAL)	202	(10)
Duncan (DAL)	162	(13)
McAlester (DAL)	175	(12)
Muskogee (DAL)	239	(8)
Okmulgee (DAL)	226	(9)
Ponca City (KC)	255	(7)
Stillwater (DAL)	258	(7)

Oregon

Albany (SEA)	241	(8)
Bend (SEA)	332	(3)
Corvallis (SEA)	253	(8)
Grants Pass (SF)	396	(0)
Klamath Falls (SF)	362	(2)
Roseburg (SEA)	350	(2)

Pennsylvania

Butler (PIT)	38	(20)
Chambersburg (WAS)	93	(16)
New Castle (PIT)	56	(19)
Pottsville (PHI)	97	(16)

Rhode Island

Newport (BOS)	74	(18)

South Carolina

Greenwood (ATL)	146	(14)
Hilton Head Island (ATL)	285	(6)
Myrtle Beach (ATL)	360	(2)
Orangeburg (ATL)	222	(9)
Sumter (ATL)	255	(7)

Tennessee

Cleveland (ATL)	112	(15)
Columbia (ATL)	252	(8)
Cookeville (ATL)	206	(10)
Morristown (ATL)	265	(7)
Tullahoma (ATL)	193	(11)

Texas

Alice (HOU)	232	(9)
Bay City (HOU)	79	(17)
Del Rio (HOU)	347	(2)
Greenville (DAL)	50	(19)
Huntsville (HOU)	72	(18)
Lufkin (HOU)	120	(15)
Nacogdoches (HOU)	139	(14)
Palestine (DAL)	112	(15)
Paris (DAL)	106	(16)

Utah

Logan (DEN)	561	(0)

Vermont

Rutland (BOS)	171	(12)

Virginia

Blacksburg (WAS)	257	(7)
Fredericksburg (WAS)	48	(19)
Harrisonburg (WAS)	126	(15)
Martinsville (WAS)	279	(6)
Staunton–Waynesboro (WAS)	152	(13)
Winchester (WAS)	71	(18)

Washington

Aberdeen (SEA)	108	(16)
Longview (SEA)	125	(15)
Port Angeles (SEA)	87	(17)
Pullman (SEA)	312	(4)
Walla Walla (SEA)	274	(6)
Wenatchee (SEA)	147	(13)

West Virginia

Beckley (PIT)	247	(8)
Clarksburg (PIT)	111	(15)
Fairmont (PIT)	92	(17)
Morgantown (PIT)	77	(17)

Wisconsin

Fond du Lac (MIL)	63	(18)
Manitowoc (MIL)	82	(17)
Marshfield–Wisconsin Rapids (MIN)	171	(12)
Stevens Point (MIL)	154	(13)

Wyoming

Rock Springs (DEN)	360	(2)

Television Market

Perhaps nothing ties a small city tighter to a large community than television. Signals from distant stations expose small-town residents to a daily dose of big-city news, commercials, and sporting events. It is conceivable that many viewers may know more about happenings in the far-off metropolis than in their own town.

Arbitron has divided the continental U.S. into 212 "markets," regions that receive their television programs from the market's central city. This category evaluates each small city according to the relative size of the region in which it is included. Arbitron lists markets in the order of their total populations. It is generally true that the higher the rank, the greater the choice of stations and the better the quality of local programming.

Kingston, New York, is near the northern edge of the New York City market, ranked No. 1 on Arbitron's chart. There are 20 TV stations in the region, although not all can be received in Kingston.

Helena, Montana, is its own market, ranked 209th nationally. Helena has only two stations. Fairbanks, Alaska, is not included in Arbitron's analysis.

Small cities in the East are the most likely to be part of large television markets. Their Western counterparts are usually included in small markets.

Source. These statistics, published in 1988, are for 1988. *Broadcasting/Cablecasting Yearbook* (Washington: Broadcasting Publications, Inc., 1988).

Scoring. Twenty points for a rank of 1 to 10; no points for a rank of 201 to 212. The spacing is every 10 ranking positions.

Highest | **Market Rank**

1. Kingston, N.Y.	1
2. De Kalb, Ill.	3
2. Michigan City–La Porte, Ind.	3
2. Ottawa, Ill.	3
5. Dover, Del.	4
6. Concord, N.H.	6
6. Keene, N.H.	6
8. Greenville, Tex.	8
8. Palestine, Tex.	8
8. Paris, Tex.	8

Lowest*

219. Helena, Mont.	209
218. Mankato, Minn.	208
217. Bend, Oreg.	207
216. Flagstaff, Ariz.	205
215. Twin Falls, Idaho	202
214. Zanesville, Ohio	201
213. Harrisonburg, Va.	200
212. Hobbs, N.Mex.	194
212. Roswell, N.Mex.	194
210. Bowling Green, Ky.	191

*National rankings include only cities in the continental United States. Fairbanks, Alaska, is not assigned a market rank. It is awarded zero points in this category on the basis of relative population.

(Figure following each area name indicates national television market rank; figure in parentheses represents rating points.)

Alabama

Athens	89	(12)
Auburn–Opelika	118	(9)
Decatur	89	(12)
Enterprise	157	(5)
Selma	101	(10)
Talladega	49	(16)

Alaska

Fairbanks	NR	(0)

Arizona

Bullhead City– Lake Havasu City	21	(18)
Casa Grande– Apache Junction	21	(18)
Flagstaff	205	(0)
Prescott	21	(18)
Sierra Vista	83	(12)
Yuma	181	(2)

Arkansas

Blytheville	41	(16)
El Dorado	116	(9)
Hot Springs	55	(15)
Jonesboro	174	(3)
Rogers	119	(9)
Russellville	55	(15)

California

El Centro–Calexico– Brawley	181	(2)
Eureka	186	(2)
Hanford	63	(14)
Madera	63	(14)
San Luis Obispo– Atascadero	113	(9)

Colorado

Grand Junction	176	(3)

Connecticut

Torrington	23	(18)

Delaware

Dover	4	(20)

Florida

Key West	16	(19)
Vero Beach	53	(15)

Georgia

Brunswick	57	(15)
Carrollton	12	(19)
Dalton	80	(13)
Gainesville	12	(19)
Hinesville	103	(10)
La Grange	12	(19)
Rome	12	(19)
Valdosta	126	(8)

Idaho

Coeur d'Alene	79	(13)
Idaho Falls	159	(5)
Nampa–Caldwell	136	(7)
Pocatello	159	(5)
Twin Falls	202	(0)

Illinois

Carbondale	75	(13)
Danville	74	(13)
De Kalb	3	(20)
Freeport	114	(9)
Galesburg	77	(13)
Mattoon–Charleston	74	(13)
Ottawa	3	(20)
Quincy	154	(5)
Sterling	77	(13)

Indiana

Columbus	24	(18)
Marion	24	(18)
Michigan City–La Porte	3	(20)
New Castle	24	(18)
Richmond	48	(16)
Vincennes	129	(8)

Iowa

Ames	66	(14)
Burlington	77	(13)
Clinton	77	(13)
Fort Dodge	66	(14)
Marshalltown	66	(14)
Mason City	147	(6)
Muscatine	77	(13)

Kansas

Hutchinson	60	(15)
Manhattan	142	(6)
Salina	60	(15)

Kentucky

Bowling Green	191	(1)
Frankfort	76	(13)
Madisonville	90	(12)
Paducah	75	(13)
Radcliff–Elizabethtown	47	(16)
Richmond	76	(13)

Louisiana

Bogalusa	34	(17)
Crowley	112	(9)
Hammond	34	(17)
Minden	64	(14)
Morgan City	91	(11)
New Iberia	112	(9)
Opelousas	112	(9)
Ruston	116	(9)

Maine

Augusta–Waterville	69	(14)
Biddeford	69	(14)

Maryland

Salisbury	162	(4)

Michigan

Adrian	65	(14)
Marquette	184	(2)
Mount Pleasant	59	(15)
Owosso	59	(15)
Traverse City	138	(7)

Minnesota

Faribault	13	(19)
Mankato	208	(0)
Winona	134	(7)

Mississippi

Columbus	133	(7)
Greenville	168	(4)
Greenwood	168	(4)
Hattiesburg	161	(4)
Laurel	161	(4)
Meridian	175	(3)
Tupelo	133	(7)
Vicksburg	82	(12)

Missouri

Cape Girardeau	75	(13)
Jefferson City	152	(5)
Sikeston	75	(13)

Montana

Bozeman	189	(2)
Helena	209	(0)
Missoula	173	(3)

Nebraska

Grand Island	92	(11)

Nevada

Carson City	121	(8)

New Hampshire

Concord	6	(20)
Keene	6	(20)
Laconia	69	(14)

New Mexico

Alamogordo	56	(15)
Carlsbad	56	(15)
Clovis	117	(9)
Farmington	56	(15)
Gallup	56	(15)
Hobbs	194	(1)
Rio Rancho	56	(15)
Roswell	194	(1)

New York

Auburn	67	(14)
Batavia	38	(17)
Cortland	67	(14)
Gloversville	52	(15)
Ithaca	67	(14)
Jamestown	38	(17)
Kingston	1	(20)
Olean	38	(17)
Plattsburgh	96	(11)
Watertown	169	(4)

North Carolina

Eden	50	(16)
Goldsboro	35	(17)
Greenville	95	(11)
Havelock–New Bern	95	(11)
Kinston	95	(11)
Lumberton	150	(6)
Roanoke Rapids	35	(17)
Rocky Mount	35	(17)
Sanford	35	(17)
Shelby	31	(17)
Statesville	31	(17)
Wilson	35	(17)

North Dakota

Minot	146	(6)

Ohio

Ashland	11	(19)
Ashtabula	11	(19)
Athens	46	(16)
Chillicothe	33	(17)
East Liverpool	88	(12)
Findlay	65	(14)
Fremont	65	(14)
Marion	33	(17)
New Philadelphia	11	(19)
Portsmouth	46	(16)
Sandusky	11	(19)
Sidney	48	(16)
Tiffin	65	(14)
Wooster	11	(19)
Zanesville	201	(0)

Oklahoma

Ardmore	172	(3)
Bartlesville	54	(15)
Chickasha	37	(17)
Duncan	130	(8)
McAlester	54	(15)
Muskogee	54	(15)
Okmulgee	54	(15)
Ponca City	37	(17)
Stillwater	37	(17)

Oregon

Albany	26	(18)
Bend	207	(0)
Corvallis	26	(18)
Grants Pass	153	(5)
Klamath Falls	153	(5)
Roseburg	137	(7)

Pennsylvania

Butler	17	(19)
Chambersburg	9	(20)
New Castle	17	(19)
Pottsville	51	(15)

Rhode Island
Newport	44	(16)

South Carolina
Greenwood	36	(17)
Hilton Head Island	103	(10)
Myrtle Beach	130	(8)
Orangeburg	87	(12)
Sumter	87	(12)

Tennessee
Cleveland	80	(13)
Columbia	32	(17)
Cookeville	32	(17)
Morristown	61	(14)
Tullahoma	32	(17)

Texas
Alice	120	(9)
Bay City	10	(20)
Del Rio	42	(16)
Greenville	8	(20)
Huntsville	10	(20)
Lufkin	123	(8)
Nacogdoches	123	(8)
Palestine	8	(20)
Paris	8	(20)

Utah
Logan	40	(17)

Vermont
Rutland	96	(11)

Virginia
Blacksburg	73	(13)
Fredericksburg	9	(20)
Harrisonburg	200	(1)
Martinsville	73	(13)
Staunton–Waynesboro	62	(14)
Winchester	9	(20)

Washington
Aberdeen	15	(19)
Longview	26	(18)
Port Angeles	15	(19)
Pullman	79	(13)
Walla Walla	127	(8)
Wenatchee	15	(19)

West Virginia
Beckley	141	(6)
Clarksburg	162	(4)
Fairmont	17	(19)
Morgantown	17	(19)

Wisconsin
Fond du Lac	68	(14)
Manitowoc	68	(14)
Marshfield– Wisconsin Rapids	128	(8)
Stevens Point	128	(8)

Wyoming
Rock Springs	40	(17)

The Results

Butler is a small city that rests peacefully on the rolling hills of western Pennsylvania. It was laid out in 1803 on land originally owned by Robert Morris, the Philadelphia banker who won fame as the financier of the American Revolution. Butler prospered as an industrial center, thanks in no small part to the discoveries in the region of coal, gas, limestone, and oil.

Another nearby resource of great importance is the city of Pittsburgh, just 38 miles south of Butler. Once picturesquely described as "hell with the lid off," Pittsburgh has shed its image as a polluted, unsophisticated steel town. Its air now meets federal standards for cleanliness, while its economy has successfully diversified. Pittsburgh is currently tied with Dallas in having the nation's third-largest total of corporate headquarters. The 1985 edition of the *Places Rated Almanac,* citing Pittsburgh's "across-the-board strength in nearly all categories," declared that its metro area had the highest quality of life in the country.

Residents of the Butler area can drive to Pittsburgh in less than an hour. Once there, they might attend a performance of the Pittsburgh Symphony Orchestra or the Pittsburgh Opera. Or they could shop along the Golden Triangle, the center of the city's business district. Or they might take in a game of professional football, baseball, or hockey. This closeness to a wide array of metropolitan amenities earns Butler first place in the urban proximity section, with 96 of a possible 100 points.

Cities with high scores in this section are almost evenly divided between three regions of the country. Four of the top ten communities are in the Midwest, and three each in the East and the South.

Fairbanks, Alaska, is as far from metropolitan life as you can get among American small cities, which is why it settles in last place with 0 points. It is a five-and-a-half-hour drive from Fairbanks to the only metro area in Alaska, but an official brochure puts up a brave front. "Anchorage is only 365 [actually 361] miles away via the Parks Highway or the Alaska Railroad," it insists. Major cultural attractions, large shopping centers, and big-league sports are a long trip away to either Seattle or Vancouver, British Columbia.

The West, with its wide-open spaces, naturally has most of the small cities with low urban proximity scores. The only non-Western communities in the bottom eleven are Minot, North Dakota, and Marquette, Michigan.

Highest | Rating Points

		Rating Points
1.	Butler, Pa.	96
2.	Michigan City–La Porte, Ind.	95
3.	Batavia, N.Y.	94
3.	New Castle, Pa.	94
5.	New Castle, Ind.	93
6.	Ashland, Ohio	92
6.	Columbus, Ind.	92
6.	Fredericksburg, Va.	92
6.	Gainesville, Ga.	92
6.	Greenville, Tex.	92
11.	Ashtabula, Ohio	91
11.	Carrollton, Ga.	91
11.	De Kalb, Ill.	91
11.	Faribault, Minn.	91
15.	Sandusky, Ohio	90
15.	Winchester, Va.	90
15.	Wooster, Ohio	90
18.	Concord, N.H.	89
18.	La Grange, Ga.	89
18.	Marion, Ind.	89

Lowest

219.	Fairbanks, Alaska	0
218.	Roswell, N.Mex.	8
217.	Bozeman, Mont.	9
216.	Idaho Falls, Idaho	10
215.	Helena, Mont.	12
212.	Hobbs, N.Mex.	13
212.	Missoula, Mont.	13
212.	Twin Falls, Idaho	13
211.	Minot, N.Dak.	16
209.	Farmington, N.Mex.	18
209.	Marquette, Mich.	18

	Butler, Pa.	Fairbanks, Alaska
Total Points in Section	96	0
Rank in Section	1	219
Results (and Rating Points)		
Metro Center Proximity Miles from closest official metro area	35 (18)	361 (0)
Arts Center Proximity Miles from closest regional arts center	38 (20)	2,121 (0)
Retail Center Proximity Miles from regional retail center	38 (19)	2,265 (0)
Sports Center Proximity Miles from closest regional sports center	38 (20)	2,265 (0)
Television Market National rank of television market	17 (19)	NR (0)

(Figure following each area name indicates the composite score from the five categories in this section.)

Alabama

Athens	66
Auburn–Opelika	73
Decatur	69
Enterprise	51
Selma	61
Talladega	85

Alaska

Fairbanks	0

Arizona

Bullhead City–Lake Havasu City	44
Casa Grande–Apache Junction	73
Flagstaff	32
Prescott	59
Sierra Vista	44
Yuma	37

Arkansas

Blytheville	67
El Dorado	49
Hot Springs	61
Jonesboro	43
Rogers	48
Russellville	48

California

El Centro–Calexico–Brawley	45
Eureka	19
Hanford	63
Madera	69
San Luis Obispo–Atascadero	49

Colorado

Grand Junction	21

Connecticut

Torrington	87

Delaware

Dover	87

Florida

Key West	46
Vero Beach	59

Georgia

Brunswick	58
Carrollton	91
Dalton	80
Gainesville	92
Hinesville	45
La Grange	89
Rome	88
Valdosta	51

Idaho

Coeur d'Alene	59
Idaho Falls	10
Nampa–Caldwell	27
Pocatello	19
Twin Falls	13

Illinois

Carbondale	70
Danville	76
De Kalb	91
Freeport	70
Galesburg	59
Mattoon–Charleston	67
Ottawa	86
Quincy	51
Sterling	62

Indiana

Columbus	92
Marion	89
Michigan City–La Porte	95
New Castle	93
Richmond	86
Vincennes	66

Iowa

Ames	72
Burlington	53
Clinton	62
Fort Dodge	59
Marshalltown	66
Mason City	59
Muscatine	62

Kansas

Hutchinson	59
Manhattan	51
Salina	54

Kentucky

Bowling Green	49
Frankfort	84
Madisonville	57
Paducah	52
Radcliff–Elizabethtown	80
Richmond	77

Louisiana

Bogalusa	69
Crowley	62
Hammond	76
Minden	56
Morgan City	67
New Iberia	63
Opelousas	63
Ruston	42

Maine

Augusta–Waterville	67
Biddeford	82

Maryland

Salisbury	59

Michigan

Adrian	85
Marquette	18
Mount Pleasant	67
Owosso	84
Traverse City	33

Minnesota

Faribault	91
Mankato	65
Winona	59

Mississippi

Columbus	44
Greenville	32
Greenwood	34
Hattiesburg	46
Laurel	43
Meridian	34
Tupelo	45
Vicksburg	44

Missouri

Cape Girardeau	66
Jefferson City	65
Sikeston	58

Montana

Bozeman	9
Helena	12
Missoula	13

Nebraska

Grand Island	36

Nevada

Carson City	47

New Hampshire

Concord	89
Keene	87
Laconia	76

New Mexico

Alamogordo	42
Carlsbad	31
Clovis	20
Farmington	18
Gallup	26
Hobbs	13
Rio Rancho	35
Roswell	8

New York

Auburn	65
Batavia	94
Cortland	60
Gloversville	58
Ithaca	62
Jamestown	82
Kingston	85
Olean	83
Plattsburgh	65
Watertown	43

North Carolina

Eden	62
Goldsboro	59
Greenville	51
Havelock–New Bern	43
Kinston	52
Lumberton	47
Roanoke Rapids	62
Rocky Mount	65
Sanford	62
Shelby	73
Statesville	66
Wilson	63

North Dakota

Minot	16

Ohio

Ashland	92
Ashtabula	91
Athens	80
Chillicothe	87
East Liverpool	84
Findlay	77
Fremont	80
Marion	87
New Philadelphia	87
Portsmouth	76
Sandusky	90
Sidney	86
Tiffin	77
Wooster	90
Zanesville	66

Oklahoma

Ardmore	63
Bartlesville	65
Chickasha	74
Duncan	67
McAlester	63
Muskogee	65
Okmulgee	69
Ponca City	57
Stillwater	63

Oregon

Albany	70
Bend	23
Corvallis	68
Grants Pass	25
Klamath Falls	22
Roseburg	33

Pennsylvania

Butler	96
Chambersburg	88
New Castle	94
Pottsville	79

Rhode Island

Newport	87

South Carolina

Greenwood	75
Hilton Head Island	40
Myrtle Beach	35
Orangeburg	58
Sumter	58

Tennessee

Cleveland	75
Columbia	69
Cookeville	66
Morristown	64
Tullahoma	70

Texas

Alice	56
Bay City	87
Del Rio	36
Greenville	92
Huntsville	87
Lufkin	63
Nacogdoches	61
Palestine	80
Paris	81

Utah

Logan	46

Vermont

Rutland	53

Virginia

Blacksburg	51
Fredericksburg	92
Harrisonburg	59
Martinsville	54
Staunton–Waynesboro	72
Winchester	90

Washington

Aberdeen	80
Longview	83
Port Angeles	81
Pullman	50
Walla Walla	45
Wenatchee	66

West Virginia

Beckley	37
Clarksburg	62
Fairmont	82
Morgantown	83

Wisconsin

Fond du Lac	84
Manitowoc	82
Marshfield–Wisconsin Rapids	55
Stevens Point	62

Wyoming

Rock Springs	25

Conclusion:

The Report Cards

T here is no turning back. Life in America's metropolitan areas is already hectic, but large cities and their suburbs are becoming more and more crowded. The Census Bureau says the nation's metros are gaining approximately 2 million new residents every year! It is inevitable that the line at the bank will grow a bit longer, the wait for the doctor will require a few extra minutes, the nightly traffic jam will linger toward sunset.

Other metropolitan problems appear no closer to solution. The proliferation of drugs has led to virtual warfare in parts of Washington and other cities. Students in urban schools continue to score well below the national average on standardized tests. Suburban housing prices are spiraling well beyond the means of thousands upon thousands of families.

This book is inspired by the belief that there *is* an alternative to a chaotic metropolitan existence. A similar thought has already motivated many Americans, including some who had once fervently embraced an urban way of life. "A lot of yuppies have realized a very fast-paced lifestyle can't be kept up for a long time," says Douglas McCabe, a professor of industrial and labor relations at Georgetown University. "They're turning back to family values. They're leaving high-pressure corporations, high-pressure consulting firms, and establishing small family firms, moving to smaller cities and rural communities."

Yuppies, young families, and retired couples can all find happier, more relaxed existences in the smaller cities of America. But which of the country's 219 micropolitan areas should they choose to be their new homes?

The previous ten sections have given partial answers. Each section has graded all communities according to their performances in five relevant categories. The maximum possible score in any category is 20 points. The five category totals for each city are then combined for a section score, which represents the community's relative strength in a broad field, such as economics, health care, or transportation. The highest total in any section is obviously 100 points.

The overall desirability of any small city depends on a combination of factors. Adding each community's ten section totals yields a final score, which provides a measure of that town's quality of life. San Luis Obispo–Atascadero, California, leads the nation's micropolitan areas with 559 points. Nampa–Caldwell, Idaho, is in last place with 355.

Micropolitan Area	Rating Points	Micropolitan Area	Rating Points
1. San Luis Obispo–Atascadero, Calif.	559	37. Newport, R.I.	488
2. Corvallis, Oreg.	555	40. Traverse City, Mich.	486
3. Fredericksburg, Va.	541	41. Dover, Del.	483
4. Fairbanks, Alaska	533	41. Greenville, N.C.	483
4. Wenatchee, Wash.	533	41. Huntsville, Tex.	483
6. Hattiesburg, Miss.	527	41. Richmond, Ind.	483
7. Ames, Iowa	525	41. Walla Walla, Wash.	483
7. Port Angeles, Wash.	525	46. Auburn–Opelika, Ala.	482
9. Mankato, Minn.	523	47. Fond du Lac, Wis.	481
10. Aberdeen, Wash.	522	47. Jefferson City, Mo.	481
10. Brunswick, Ga.	522	49. Missoula, Mont.	480
12. Vero Beach, Fla.	520	50. Stevens Point, Wis.	479
13. Longview, Wash.	518	50. Stillwater, Okla.	479
14. Marshfield–Wisconsin Rapids, Wis.	517	52. Jamestown, N.Y.	478
15. Gainesville, Ga.	505	53. De Kalb, Ill.	477
16. Rome, Ga.	504	54. Kingston, N.Y.	476
17. Cape Girardeau, Mo.	503	55. Flagstaff, Ariz.	475
18. Key West, Fla.	502	56. Mattoon–Charleston, Ill.	474
19. Carson City, Nev.	501	57. Laconia, N.H.	473
19. Faribault, Minn.	501	57. Staunton–Waynesboro, Va.	473
21. Bartlesville, Okla.	498	59. Ashland, Ohio	470
22. Findlay, Ohio	497	59. Bowling Green, Ky.	470
23. Ithaca, N.Y.	496	59. Morgan City, La.	470
23. Salisbury, Md.	496	62. Albany, Oreg.	469
23. Winchester, Va.	496	63. Marion, Ohio	468
26. Pullman, Wash.	495	63. Roswell, N.Mex.	468
27. Columbus, Ind.	493	63. Tullahoma, Tenn.	468
27. Mason City, Iowa	493	66. Cookeville, Tenn.	467
27. Salina, Kans.	493	66. Decatur, Ala.	467
30. Concord, N.H.	492	66. Frankfort, Ky.	467
31. Plattsburgh, N.Y.	490	66. Manitowoc, Wis.	467
32. Batavia, N.Y.	489	66. Olean, N.Y.	467
32. Minot, N.Dak.	489	71. Meridian, Miss.	466
32. Morgantown, W.Va.	489	71. Ponca City, Okla.	466
32. Prescott, Ariz.	489	71. Tupelo, Miss.	466
32. Sandusky, Ohio	489	74. Ardmore, Okla.	465
37. Carbondale, Ill.	488	74. Marion, Ind.	465
37. La Grange, Ga.	488	74. Ottawa, Ill.	465
		74. Watertown, N.Y.	465

Micropolitan Area	Rating Points	Micropolitan Area	Rating Points
78. Augusta–Waterville, Maine	464	111. Kinston, N.C.	449
78. Myrtle Beach, S.C.	464	111. Mount Pleasant, Mich.	449
80. Keene, N.H.	463	111. Vicksburg, Miss.	449
80. Nacogdoches, Tex.	463	117. Carrollton, Ga.	448
80. New Iberia, La.	463	117. Cleveland, Tenn.	448
83. Marshalltown, Iowa	462	117. Clinton, Iowa	448
84. Muskogee, Okla.	461	117. Cortland, N.Y.	448
84. Quincy, Ill.	461	117. New Philadelphia, Ohio	448
86. Bend, Oreg.	460	122. Adrian, Mich.	447
86. Idaho Falls, Idaho	460	122. Hobbs, N.Mex.	447
86. Paducah, Ky.	460	124. Carlsbad, N.Mex.	446
86. Sanford, N.C.	460	125. Hanford, Calif.	445
90. Torrington, Conn.	459	125. Hot Springs, Ark.	445
90. Winona, Minn.	459	125. Sierra Vista, Ariz.	445
92. Helena, Mont.	458	128. Athens, Ohio	443
92. Richmond, Ky.	458	128. Hammond, La.	443
94. Rock Springs, Wyo.	457	128. Manhattan, Kans.	443
94. Valdosta, Ga.	457	131. Chillicothe, Ohio	442
96. Bozeman, Mont.	455	131. Grand Junction, Colo.	442
96. Hilton Head Island, S.C.	455	131. Ruston, La.	442
96. Roseburg, Oreg.	455	134. Galesburg, Ill.	441
99. Burlington, Iowa	453	135. Pocatello, Idaho	440
99. Eureka, Calif.	453	136. Hutchinson, Kans.	439
99. Greenwood, S.C.	453	137. Butler, Pa.	438
99. Vincennes, Ind.	453	138. Bay City, Tex.	437
103. Bullhead City–Lake Havasu City, Ariz.	452	138. Blacksburg, Va.	437
103. Jonesboro, Ark.	452	140. Alamogordo, N.Mex.	436
103. Paris, Tex.	452	140. El Dorado, Ark.	436
103. Rutland, Vt.	452	140. Radcliff– Elizabethtown, Ky.	436
103. Wooster, Ohio	452	143. Grand Island, Nebr.	435
108. Dalton, Ga.	451	144. McAlester, Okla.	434
109. Fort Dodge, Iowa	450	145. Auburn, N.Y.	433
109. Michigan City– La Porte, Ind.	450	145. Columbia, Tenn.	433
111. Fremont, Ohio	449	147. Columbus, Miss.	432
111. Harrisonburg, Va.	449	147. Danville, Ill.	432
111. Havelock– New Bern, N.C.	449	147. Statesville, N.C.	432
		147. Wilson, N.C.	432
		147. Zanesville, Ohio	432
		152. Biddeford, Maine	431

Micropolitan Area	Rating Points	Micropolitan Area	Rating Points
152. Logan, Utah	431	186. Sterling, Ill.	410
154. Enterprise, Ala.	430	188. Bogalusa, La.	407
154. Opelousas, La.	430	188. Rogers, Ark.	407
156. Clovis, N.Mex.	428	190. Madisonville, Ky.	406
156. Coeur d'Alene, Idaho	428	190. Sikeston, Mo.	406
158. Palestine, Tex.	426	192. Klamath Falls, Oreg.	405
159. El Centro–Calexico–		193. Farmington, N.Mex.	404
Brawley, Calif.	425	193. Greenwood, Miss.	404
159. Rocky Mount, N.C.	425	195. Talladega, Ala.	403
159. Tiffin, Ohio	425	196. Chambersburg, Pa.	402
162. Freeport, Ill.	424	197. Marquette, Mich.	401
162. Muscatine, Iowa	424	197. Portsmouth, Ohio	401
162. Sidney, Ohio	424	199. Sumter, S.C.	400
165. Chickasha, Okla.	423	200. Madera, Calif.	398
165. Clarksburg, W.Va.	423	201. East Liverpool, Ohio	397
165. Greenville, Tex.	423	202. Casa Grande–Apache	
168. New Castle, Ind.	422	Junction, Ariz.	396
169. Duncan, Okla.	420	202. Okmulgee, Okla.	396
169. Laurel, Miss.	420	204. Greenville, Miss.	391
171. Lufkin, Tex.	419	205. Eden, N.C.	387
171. New Castle, Pa.	419	206. Selma, Ala.	386
171. Twin Falls, Idaho	419	207. Gloversville, N.Y.	385
171. Yuma, Ariz.	419	208. Crowley, La.	383
175. Roanoke Rapids, N.C.	418	209. Alice, Tex.	381
176. Morristown, Tenn.	417	209. Pottsville, Pa.	381
177. Ashtabula, Ohio	416	211. Blytheville, Ark.	380
177. Orangeburg, S.C.	416	212. Hinesville, Ga.	373
179. Goldsboro, N.C.	414	212. Martinsville, Va.	373
179. Owosso, Mich.	414	214. Del Rio, Tex.	371
181. Russellville, Ark.	413	215. Minden, La.	370
181. Shelby, N.C.	413	216. Gallup, N.Mex.	367
183. Athens, Ala.	412	217. Rio Rancho, N.Mex.	366
183. Beckley, W.Va.	412	218. Lumberton, N.C.	364
185. Fairmont, W.Va.	411	219. Nampa–Caldwell,	
186. Grants Pass, Oreg.	410	Idaho	355

The Top Ten

1. San Luis Obispo–Atascadero, California

The easygoing charm of San Luis Obispo is most evident on Thursday nights. The town barricades its main thoroughfare, allows farmers and vendors to sell food, and stages a weekly street fair.

"Thursday night has become a ritual for the townspeople, like the ice-cream social in the old days," a local restaurant worker told the *New York Times*. "It's a chance for the people of San Luis Obispo to see each other." They crowd into the business district enveloped by the smell of barbecued ribs. People remain downtown long after dark.

This weekly community gathering is just one reason that many new-comers are finding San Luis Obispo and the nearby city of Atascadero to be an ideal place to live. The region offers a mild climate, marked by summertime temperatures in the upper 70s and winter highs in the mid-60s. It also scores well in the economics, public safety, and education sections, the latter thanks in large part to the presence in San Luis Obispo of California Polytechnic State University and its 16,000 students.

San Luis Obispo was established in 1772 by Father Junipero Serra as the fifth Spanish mission in California, midway between present-day Los Angeles and San Francisco. Atascadero is of much more recent origin. It was founded as a model community in 1913, 18 miles north of San Luis Obispo. Edward Gardner Lewis dreamed of developing a great metropolis in Atascadero, but he was forced into bankruptcy in 1924. An impressive rotunda and marble fountain in the town square date back to those early visions.

San Luis Obispo and Atascadero are located in small valleys bordered by wooded hills. The Pacific Ocean is a short drive to the west, as are William Randolph Hearst's opulent castle at San Simeon and the beaches at Morro Bay and Pismo Beach.

The region earned a footnote in American history when the Milestone Motel opened along the Pacific Coast Highway just outside of San Luis Obispo on December 12, 1925. It was the first inn designed specifically for motorists. A sign at the entrance told people how to pronounce the new word, *motel*.

San Luis Obispo–Atascadero is now looking to make its mark in another way as a fast-developing wine region. There are more than 50 wineries in the area, most only about a decade old. "This is a unique part of California," says one wine executive. "But I think a lot of people don't know it's here."

414 2. Corvallis, Oregon

Corvallis is nestled in the lush Willamette Valley; indeed, the city's name is loosely translated from the Latin phrase meaning "heart of the valley." The sharp crests of the Cascade Mountains are visible to the east, while green hills west of town rise gradually to the lower slopes of the Coast Range. The Pacific Ocean is beyond.

Corvallis's high scores in the education and sophistication sections are directly attributable to Oregon State University, Oregon's oldest state-supported college. OSU was once an agricultural school, but is now strong in science and engineering, among other subjects. Its campus is located at the west end of the city. More than 16,000 students attend classes there.

Corvallis is also blessed with a pleasant climate. The temperature will peak at a comfortable 80 degrees on a typical midsummer day. Readings surpass 90 degrees or fall below freezing on just 70 days a year.

The congenial weather and fertile soil of the Willamette Valley are boons to local farmers. Corvallis is the center of a rich dairy and fruit-producing region.

3. Fredericksburg, Virginia

The tree-lined streets and red-brick colonial buildings of Fredericksburg inspire thoughts of American history. One can picture George Washington visiting his mother at her city home, James Monroe practicing law at his downtown office, and soldiers from North and South battling fiercely for control of this strategically important town between Washington and Richmond.

Fredericksburg has done its best to keep its history alive. More than 350 buildings from the eighteenth and nineteenth centuries have been preserved in the city's National Historic District, Mary Washington's home and Monroe's office among them. The Civil War battlefields where more than 17,000 men died are now open to visitors, complete with museums. Those interested in purchasing a piece of the past can stroll the four-block "antique row" of shops along the Rappahannock River.

Fredericksburg does particularly well in the economics and housing sections. Many people who work in Washington prefer to take advantage of the charm and less expensive homes in Fredericksburg. They commute daily along Interstate 95.

4. Fairbanks, Alaska (tied with Wenatchee, Washington)   **415**

The local chamber of commerce tells the truth with its slogan, "Fairbanks: Extremely Alaska."

There seems to be no middle ground in America's northernmost small city. Summers are pleasant, with temperatures in the 70s and the sun shining on the horizon after midnight. Winters are brutal, marked by readings well below zero and as many as 19 hours of sub-Arctic darkness.

This tendency toward extremes is also apparent in the city's quality-of-life scores. Fairbanks stands at the top in three categories: economics, sophistication, and public safety. But it finishes dead last in urban proximity, a section in which it scores not a single point.

Fairbanks was born as a gold-rush camp in 1902, and long had the air of a rough frontier outpost. Its residents have tenaciously overcome steep odds by turning their community into one of the finest small cities in the country. One citizen told author Neal Peirce that the typical person living in Fairbanks "feels like the prospector out in the desert: it's tough, but it goes against his grain to pack up and move out."

4. Wenatchee, Washington

Wenatchee comes alive in late April and early May, when it hosts the annual Washington State Apple Blossom Festival. Fruit trees are everywhere, even on small cuts into the cliffs above the city. A visiting writer has described the region as "a sea of orchards, covered in spring with a pink foam of blossoms, mile upon mile, filling the valleys and covering the slopes; the air of the town is sweet with the fragrance."

Wenatchee's location on the Columbia River in the shadow of the Cascade Range makes it a recreational paradise. Summer is the time for boating on the Columbia or fishing in the high lakes of the Cascades. Winter sees local skiers heading to nearby Mission Ridge. Any time is right for a trip to Wenatchee National Forest. The 2 million-acre park has its headquarters in the city.

Wenatchee's highest score naturally comes in the diversions section. But this self-proclaimed Apple Capital of the World consistently receives above-average grades in most other fields.

416 6. Hattiesburg, Mississippi

The typical city trying to impress outsiders will cheerfully inflate any attribute, no matter how minor, to make itself look better on paper. Hattiesburg takes the opposite tack, bragging about how easy it is to *leave* town. It has adopted the name of the Hub City to stress its central location—70 miles from the Gulf of Mexico, 90 miles from Jackson, and 110 miles from both Mobile and New Orleans.

Urban proximity is actually not one of Hattiesburg's strong suits. It shines in health care, where it receives the best score of any small city, thanks to a high number of doctors and specialists. It also does well in the housing and climate/environment sections.

Hattiesburg was once a lumber town, depending on the region's abundance of longleaf pines. It has long since diversified its economy, with the University of Southern Mississippi among its most visible employers.

7. Ames, Iowa (tied with Port Angeles, Washington)

First there was the college: Iowa State University traces its origins to 1869. Then there was the city: Ames was incorporated a year later. This wooded town on the rolling prairie of central Iowa has always followed the lead of its university. Ames owes its prosperity to the stability of ISU, its leading employer. The city's population swells with 26,000 students. The university offers a vibrant array of cultural attractions at its modern Iowa State Center, which contains an auditorium, a gallery, a theater for plays, and an indoor athletic coliseum.

Ames also owes thanks to ISU for the city's strong scores in the education and sophistication categories. Those seeking a respite from life in a college town can take advantage of Ames's high score in urban proximity. Des Moines is just a 28-mile drive south on Interstate 35.

7. Port Angeles, Washington

No micropolitan area can match the breathtaking location of Port Angeles, nestled below the towering peaks of the Olympic Mountains on the coast of the Strait of Juan de Fuca. Its impressive natural harbor was discovered in 1791 by a Spanish captain, who named it "Port of Our Lady of the Angels." The U.S. Pacific fleet docked here during the 1920s and early 1930s. As many as 30,000 sailors crowded the town's small streets.

Port Angeles is much quieter these days. It serves as the headquarters for Olympic National Park, 1,400 square miles of mountains, lakes, glaciers, and a rain forest. The city itself avoids the heavy precipitation that swamps much of Washington. The Olympic Range acts as a shield, limiting Port Angeles to 24 inches of rain annually. Sea breezes keep temperatures mild year-round, contributing to the town's impressive score in the climate/environment section.

9. Mankato, Minnesota

The original white settlers set the tone for those who followed them to the area known as Mankato, the Sioux word for the bluish clay found on the banks of the Minnesota River. The founders disdained a summer arrival, choosing to establish a frontier outpost in February 1852. Modern residents exhibit a similar streak of hardiness, essential for surviving the brutally long Minnesota winter.

Mankato compensates for its climate with high scores in the education and sophistication categories, thanks to the presence of the 13,000-student Mankato State University. The welcome arrival of summer attracts residents to the 150 lakes within 15 minutes of the city. The metropolitan charms of Minneapolis and Saint Paul are a 90-minute drive to the northeast. Reaching the water, the Twin Cities, or other places is easy. Mankato earned second place nationally in the transportation section.

10. Aberdeen, Washington (tied with Brunswick, Georgia)

The Aberdeen area was self-sufficient from the beginning. The first settlers to make their homes in this coastal city were attracted by the excellent fishing in Grays Harbor and the Pacific Ocean. Lumber mills were constructed to harvest the massive stand of Douglas fir trees that covered the region. Walled off by mountains, forests, and the sea, residents realized the need to sustain their locally available livelihoods. The nation's first tree farm was planted near Aberdeen in 1941. Fishing and lumbering remain major industries today.

Tourism has also become important. Aberdeen bills itself as the Gateway to the Olympics, the rugged mountain range to the north. It also advertises its proximity to ocean beaches. The result is a strong score in the diversions section. Aberdeen also receives an excellent grade for its mild maritime climate.

418 10. Brunswick, Georgia

Brunswick offers a pleasant blend of the old and the new. A district known as Southend Brunswick evokes memories of the city's antebellum era with its moss-draped oaks and restored homes dating back as far as 1819. A glimpse of the shrimp fleet from Bay Street recalls Brunswick's proud history as a fishing port. It still claims the title of Shrimp Capital of the World.

There is much more than nostalgia to this southeastern Georgia city. Brunswick is a bustling resort community, the gateway to the Golden Isles, with their palm trees and miles of white-sand beaches. The combination of the warm Southern sun and cooling Atlantic breezes earns Brunswick a high score in the climate/environment section. It also does well in housing, health care, and—of course—diversions.

Regional and State Leaders

People have different tastes. It would be foolish to expect a stampede of newcomers to San Luis Obispo–Atascadero just because it stands No. 1 among the nation's small towns. Some folks simply don't want to live in California. Others might wish to confine their search for a congenial small city to a particular region of the country, say the East. A few people may narrow their plans still further, limiting themselves to a single state.

It is easy to determine the best micropolitan areas in each of the regions and states, using the same point totals employed for the national list. It is also possible to measure the distribution around the country of those small cities with the best and worst scores. All communities with more than 500 points are designated as superior; those below 400 points are rated as inferior. By coincidence, there are exactly 20 cities in each of the two groups.

The university town of Ithaca, New York, and the eastern shore community of Salisbury, Maryland, are tied for first place in the East. New York owns five of the ten best scores in the region. The East does not have any superior micros, while two are listed as inferior.

Fredericksburg, Virginia, which is third nationally, earns top billing in the South. Georgia offers the best selection of quality, having four of the region's top ten small towns. Seven Southern micropolitan areas are classified as superior, but 12 are inferior.

Ames, Iowa, edges out Mankato, Minnesota, for the highest honors in the Midwest. Three states—Iowa, Minnesota, and Ohio—have two cities on the region's list of the ten best. Five Midwestern towns qualify as superior. Only one is in the inferior group.

The West is naturally led by San Luis Obispo–Atascadero, California. **419** Washington holds five of the ten highest scores in the region. The West is the home of eight superior small cities and five inferior ones.

East	Rating Points	South	Rating Points
1. Ithaca, N.Y.	496	1. Fredericksburg, Va.	541
1. Salisbury, Md.	496	2. Hattiesburg, Miss.	527
3. Concord, N.H.	492	3. Brunswick, Ga.	522
4. Plattsburgh, N.Y.	490	4. Vero Beach, Fla.	520
5. Batavia, N.Y.	489	5. Gainesville, Ga.	505
5. Morgantown, W.Va.	489	6. Rome, Ga.	504
7. Newport, R.I.	488	7. Key West, Fla.	502
8. Dover, Del.	483	8. Bartlesville, Okla.	498
9. Jamestown, N.Y.	478	9. Winchester, Va.	496
10. Kingston, N.Y.	476	10. La Grange, Ga.	488

Midwest	Rating Points	West	Rating Points
1. Ames, Iowa	525	1. San Luis Obispo–Atascadero, Calif.	559
2. Mankato, Minn.	523	2. Corvallis, Oreg.	555
3. Marshfield–Wisconsin Rapids, Wis.	517	3. Fairbanks, Alaska	533
4. Cape Girardeau, Mo.	503	3. Wenatchee, Wash.	533
5. Faribault, Minn.	501	5. Port Angeles, Wash.	525
6. Findlay, Ohio	497	6. Aberdeen, Wash.	522
7. Columbus, Ind.	493	7. Longview, Wash.	518
7. Mason City, Iowa	493	8. Carson City, Nev.	501
7. Salina, Kans.	493	9. Pullman, Wash.	495
10. Minot, N.Dak.	489	10. Prescott, Ariz.	489
10. Sandusky, Ohio	489		

State	Top-Ranked Micropolitan Area	Rating Points	National Rank
Alabama	Auburn–Opelika	482	46
Alaska*	Fairbanks	533	4
Arizona	Prescott	489	32
Arkansas	Jonesboro	452	103
California	San Luis Obispo–Atascadero	559	1
Colorado*	Grand Junction	442	131
Connecticut*	Torrington	459	90
Delaware*	Dover	483	41
Florida	Vero Beach	520	12
Georgia	Brunswick	522	10
Idaho	Idaho Falls	460	86
Illinois	Carbondale	488	37
Indiana	Columbus	493	27
Iowa	Ames	525	7
Kansas	Salina	493	27
Kentucky	Bowling Green	470	59
Louisiana	Morgan City	470	59
Maine	Augusta–Waterville	464	78
Maryland*	Salisbury	496	23
Michigan	Traverse City	486	40
Minnesota	Mankato	523	9
Mississippi	Hattiesburg	527	6
Missouri	Cape Girardeau	503	17

*Only one micropolitan area in state. Four states do not have any micropolitan areas: Hawaii, Massachusetts, New Jersey, and South Dakota.

State	Top-Ranked Micropolitan Area	Rating Points	National Rank
Montana	Missoula	480	49
Nebraska*	Grand Island	435	143
Nevada*	Carson City	501	19
New Hampshire	Concord	492	30
New Mexico	Roswell	468	63
New York	Ithaca	496	23
North Carolina	Greenville	483	41
North Dakota*	Minot	489	32
Ohio	Findlay	497	22
Oklahoma	Bartlesville	498	21
Oregon	Corvallis	555	2
Pennsylvania	Butler	438	137
Rhode Island*	Newport	488	37
South Carolina	Myrtle Beach	464	78
Tennessee	Tullahoma	468	63
Texas	Huntsville	483	41
Utah*	Logan	431	152
Vermont*	Rutland	452	103
Virginia	Fredericksburg	541	3
Washington	Wenatchee	533	4
West Virginia	Morgantown	489	32
Wisconsin	Marshfield-Wisconsin Rapids	517	14
Wyoming*	Rock Springs	457	94

Individual Report Cards

It would be impetuous of you to select your new hometown or vacation spot solely on the basis of total points. You need to go beyond the numbers to find the community that will offer you the exact type of life you are seeking.

Let's say you have narrowed your list to Flagstaff, Arizona, and San Luis Obispo–Atascadero, California. The latter seems the obvious choice, having a healthy edge in points of 559 to 475. But keep in mind that all ten sections carry equal weight in those totals. That's the fairest way to compile an impartial national ranking for general use. However, these rankings may not address your particular concerns.

Feel free to tinker with the numbers. If climate/environment and urban proximity are especially important categories to your way of thinking, double those scores. Perhaps you really don't care about either area's offerings in education and diversions. Eliminate those scores, then refigure the totals. San Luis Obispo–Atascadero now has an even larger lead of 577 to 428.

Such alterations work both ways. Triple the diversions scores, double the transportation totals, and get rid of the climate/environment and urban proximity sections. Flagstaff is now a narrow winner, 571 to 556.

It is also a good idea to do further research about the communities that interest you. Check the report cards on the following pages for a start. There is an analysis of each of the country's 219 micropolitan areas, including overall scores and ranks, section totals, general information, and a summary of strengths and weaknesses. Each assessment lets you know how the small town in question compares with others. (A note of clarification: whenever a report card says a micro is the best or second-best or worst in a state in something, it actually means best or second-best or worst among all of that state's micropolitan areas.) Further information is always available from your library or the chambers of commerce in the towns you are studying.

Happy hunting!

Athens

General Information
Components: Limestone County
Area Population: 51,800
Central City Population: 15,870
Location: Extreme northern Alabama, west of Huntsville
Nearest Metro Center: Huntsville, 24 miles

Strengths: The Athens area has the lowest property taxes per capita of any micro. Metropolitan services are an easy drive down a four-lane U.S. highway to Huntsville.

Weaknesses: The area's residents have a low educational attainment: only slightly more than half of all adults are high-school graduates. Doctors are also in relatively short supply.

Scores by Sections	
Climate/Environment	68
Diversions	21
Economics	40
Education	24
Sophistication	19
Health Care	21
Housing	86
Public Safety	42
Transportation	25
Urban Proximity	66
Total Points	412

Auburn–Opelika

General Information
Components: Lee County
Area Population: 80,800
Central City Population: Auburn 29,760; Opelika 24,500
Location: East-central Alabama, near the Georgia line
Nearest Metro Center: Columbus, Ga., 32 miles

Strengths: The Auburn-Opelika area easily outpaces the other Alabama micros in education, thanks largely to Auburn University. The area's housing stock is modern and lightly taxed.

Weaknesses: Outside of college-related activities, there is little to do: concentrations of stores and amusement places are low.

Scores by Sections	
Climate/Environment	68
Diversions	26
Economics	36
Education	49
Sophistication	38
Health Care	44
Housing	77
Public Safety	38
Transportation	33
Urban Proximity	73
Total Points	482

Decatur

General Information
Components: Morgan County
Area Population: 98,800
Central City Population: 45,000
Location: Along the Tennessee River in northern Alabama, southwest of Huntsville
Nearest Metro Center: Huntsville, 26 miles

Strengths: The Decatur area has the highest per capita income of any Alabama micro. Access to commercial jet traffic is quick and easy.

Weaknesses: The education system, as with most Alabama micros, is a disappointment. It is often necessary to go to Huntsville for diversions, despite the fairly large size of Decatur.

Scores by Sections	
Climate/Environment	63
Diversions	28
Economics	46
Education	28
Sophistication	32
Health Care	41
Housing	81
Public Safety	38
Transportation	41
Urban Proximity	69
Total Points	467

Enterprise

Points: 430
National Rank: 154 of 219
State Rank: 3 of 6

General Information
Components: Coffee County
Area Population: 40,200
Central City Population: 19,790
Location: Extreme southeastern Alabama, northwest of Dothan
Nearest Metro Center: Dothan, 31 miles

Strengths: The Enterprise area's most dazzling jewel is its housing, ranked the best of any micro in the country. Enterprise also received the highest score of any Alabama micro when it comes to climate and the environment.

Weaknesses: Enterprise is relatively isolated, and hard to get out of: it has no interstates or major four-lane routes. Its scores are low in several other categories, notably sophistication, economics, health care, and public safety.

Scores by Sections	
Climate/Environment	70
Diversions	36
Economics	31
Education	36
Sophistication	28
Health Care	32
Housing	88
Public Safety	32
Transportation	26
Urban Proximity	51
Total Points	430

426 **Selma**

General Information
Components: Dallas County
Area Population: 52,700
Central City Population: 25,670
Location: Central Alabama, almost due west of Montgomery
Nearest Metro Center: Montgomery, 49 miles

Strengths: The Selma area does best in the three sections that are the strongest for all Alabama micros: climate/environment, housing, and urban proximity. But its score in each of those sections is in the state's bottom half.

Weaknesses: Selma's economy is distressing: only Greenwood, Miss., received a lower score in that section. The area is also plagued by a phenomenally high rate of violent crime.

Scores by Sections	
Climate/Environment	63
Diversions	28
Economics	18
Education	29
Sophistication	31
Health Care	28
Housing	80
Public Safety	20
Transportation	28
Urban Proximity	61
Total Points	386

Talladega

General Information
Components: Talladega County
Area Population: 76,500
Central City Population: 19,630
Location: East-central Alabama, east of Birmingham
Nearest Metro Center: Anniston, 23 miles

Strengths: Housing in the Talladega area is among the most inexpensive in the country. Taxes are low. Birmingham and Atlanta are easily accessible by freeway.

Weaknesses: Fewer than half of the adults in the Talladega micro had high-school diplomas, as of the last census. Incomes are generally low. The area's supply of doctors is substantially below the national average.

Scores by Sections	
Climate/Environment	46
Diversions	22
Economics	23
Education	24
Sophistication	20
Health Care	27
Housing	87
Public Safety	44
Transportation	25
Urban Proximity	85
Total Points	403

Fairbanks

Points: 533
National Rank: 4 of 219
State Rank: 1 of 1

General Information
Components: Fairbanks North Star Borough
Area Population: 67,600
Central City Population: 27,610
Location: Interior Alaska, northeast of Anchorage
Nearest Metro Center: Anchorage, 361 miles

Strengths: The Fairbanks area outscored all other micros in three sections: economics, sophistication, and public safety. The remaining seven sections were led by seven different micros. Fairbanks has an educated, industrious population.

Weaknesses: You can't get there from here: Fairbanks is easily the most isolated micro. The cost of living is high. And the climate? The average nightly low in January is –21°. Enough said.

Scores by Sections	
Climate/Environment	35
Diversions	68
Economics	78
Education	76
Sophistication	71
Health Care	38
Housing	39
Public Safety	77
Transportation	51
Urban Proximity	0
Total Points	533

ARIZONA

Bullhead City–Lake Havasu City

Points: 452
National Rank: 103 of 219
State Rank: 3 of 6

General Information
Components: Mohave County
Area Population: 76,600
Central City Population: Bullhead City 18,740; Lake Havasu City 18,280
Location: Along the Colorado River in extreme west-central Arizona
Nearest Metro Center: Las Vegas, Nev., 96 miles

Strengths: The Bullhead City–Lake Havasu City area has the highest proportion of new housing of any micro. Great news for Frostbelt refugees: this is one of the eight U.S. micros that never get snow.

Weaknesses: Summers are wickedly hot, low humidity or not. The average July high is 109°. Hospital-bed availability is low, compared to the national average.

Scores by Sections	
Climate/Environment	48
Diversions	49
Economics	49
Education	38
Sophistication	37
Health Care	26
Housing	53
Public Safety	61
Transportation	47
Urban Proximity	44
Total Points	452

428 Casa Grande–Apache Junction

Points: 396
National Rank: 202 of 219
State Rank: 6 of 6

General Information
Components: Pinal County
Area Population: 98,800
Central City Population: Casa Grande 15,790; Apache Junction 15,290
Location: South-central Arizona, southeast of Phoenix
Nearest Metro Center: Phoenix, 52 miles

Strengths: Phoenix is a quick drive up the interstate; Tucson isn't too much farther in the other direction. Housing is generally, modern and affordable.

Weaknesses: Urban proximity sometimes has its drawbacks. Residents of the Casa Grande–Apache Junction area must often go to Phoenix for health care. The local economy also looks to its big neighbor for help, consequently not gaining its own strength.

Scores by Sections	
Climate/Environment	46
Diversions	31
Economics	19
Education	33
Sophistication	26
Health Care	19
Housing	67
Public Safety	43
Transportation	39
Urban Proximity	73
Total Points	396

Flagstaff

Points: 475
National Rank: 55 of 219
State Rank: 2 of 6

General Information
Components: Coconino County
Area Population: 86,100
Central City Population: 39,180
Location: Central Arizona, north of Phoenix and south of the Grand Canyon
Nearest Metro Center: Phoenix, 137 miles

Strengths: There is plenty to do in the Flagstaff area, with the Grand Canyon leading the list of attractions. This micro also shows a stronger commitment to education than any comparable region in Arizona.

Weaknesses: Forget what the map says. Flagstaff has a northern climate. It receives almost 100 inches of snow a year; only six U.S. micros average more. The Flagstaff area is also isolated. It's a long drive to Phoenix or to anywhere.

Scores by Sections	
Climate/Environment	44
Diversions	60
Economics	49
Education	63
Sophistication	44
Health Care	36
Housing	51
Public Safety	44
Transportation	52
Urban Proximity	32
Total Points	475

Prescott

General Information
Components: Yavapai County
Area Population: 84,800
Central City Population: 21,520
Location: Central Arizona, northwest of Phoenix
Nearest Metro Center: Phoenix, 96 miles

Strengths: The Prescott area did not register an outstanding score in any of the ten sections, but consistently placed near or above the 50-point mark. This strong balance earned Prescott the highest total score of any Arizona micro.

Weaknesses: All of Arizona's micros did poorly in the section of health care; Prescott was no exception. It is below the national average for availability of doctors and specialists.

Scores by Sections	
Climate/Environment	57
Diversions	49
Economics	43
Education	52
Sophistication	48
Health Care	34
Housing	50
Public Safety	54
Transportation	43
Urban Proximity	59
Total Points	489

Sierra Vista

General Information
Components: Cochise County
Area Population: 91,800
Central City Population: 29,330
Location: Southeast Arizona, near the Mexican border
Nearest Metro Center: Tucson, 70 miles

Strengths: Sierra Vista has the lowest crime rate of any Arizona micro. It also strikes the best balance between the hot temperatures of the state's deserts and heavy snows of its mountains. Sierra Vista is the only Arizona micro below 5,000 total degree days.

Weaknesses: The Sierra Vista area has the same shortage of health services that afflicts the other micros in Arizona. The area's economy is sluggish. Incomes are below the national average.

Scores by Sections	
Climate/Environment	63
Diversions	37
Economics	31
Education	47
Sophistication	33
Health Care	25
Housing	70
Public Safety	54
Transportation	41
Urban Proximity	44
Total Points	445

430 Yuma

General Information
Components: Yuma County
Area Population: 86,800
Central City Population: 47,240
Location: Extreme southwestern Arizona, on the California line, near the Mexican border
Nearest Metro Center: San Diego, Calif., 175 miles

Strengths: Yuma has a good supply of relatively new housing. Property taxes are the lowest of any Arizona micro. This is another snow-free area.

Weaknesses: The average high temperature in July is 107°! Yuma has the lowest ratio of available hospital beds of the six micros in Arizona. The high-school dropout rate is among the worst in the country.

Scores by Sections	
Climate/Environment	52
Diversions	52
Economics	36
Education	33
Sophistication	40
Health Care	30
Housing	66
Public Safety	35
Transportation	38
Urban Proximity	37
Total Points	419

ARKANSAS

Blytheville

General Information
Components: Mississippi County
Area Population: 58,000
Central City Population: 23,210
Location: Northeastern Arkansas, near the Missouri line and the Mississippi River
Nearest Metro Center: Memphis, Tenn., 68 miles

Strengths: The Blytheville area has inexpensive housing, with the added attraction of low property taxes. The lights of Memphis are slightly more than an hour down river.

Weaknesses: Blytheville received the second-worst score in the entire country in the education section. Less than half of the area's adults have high-school diplomas. Blytheville's violent-crime rate is the worst among Arkansas's six micros.

Scores by Sections	
Climate/Environment	60
Diversions	27
Economics	24
Education	16
Sophistication	25
Health Care	30
Housing	76
Public Safety	22
Transportation	33
Urban Proximity	67
Total Points	380

El Dorado

General Information

Components: Union County
Area Population: 49,000
Central City Population: 25,510
Location: Extreme south-central Arkansas, near the Louisiana line
Nearest Metro Center: Monroe, La., 85 miles

Strengths: The El Dorado area registered the highest score of the six Arkansas micros in the economics section, thanks largely to strong industrial productivity. Housing is the least expensive in El Dorado, compared with the state's other micros.

Weaknesses: The educational system in El Dorado scores badly on the national scale. Teacher pay is low. The area is relatively isolated. It lacks access to an interstate.

Scores by Sections	
Climate/Environment	55
Diversions	34
Economics	50
Education	25
Sophistication	35
Health Care	45
Housing	75
Public Safety	38
Transportation	30
Urban Proximity	49
Total Points	436

Hot Springs

General Information

Components: Garland County
Area Population: 75,300
Central City Population: 36,930
Location: Central Arkansas, southwest of Little Rock
Nearest Metro Center: Little Rock, 55 miles

Strengths: The famous Hot Springs National Park attracts large numbers of tourists, guaranteeing plenty of diversions for residents as well. Urban amenities are available an hour up I-30 in Little Rock.

Weaknesses: Hot Springs's total crime rate is the highest of the six Arkansas micros. The area's spending on education is the lowest of the state's micros.

Scores by Sections	
Climate/Environment	63
Diversions	51
Economics	41
Education	25
Sophistication	45
Health Care	42
Housing	65
Public Safety	25
Transportation	27
Urban Proximity	61
Total Points	445

Jonesboro

Points: 452
National Rank: 103 of 219
State Rank: 1 of 6

General Information
Components: Craighead County
Area Population: 63,400
Central City Population: 30,050
Location: Northeastern Arkansas, near the Missouri line
Nearest Metro Center: Memphis, Tenn., 66 miles

Strengths: Jonesboro leads the state's six micros in just two sections, sophistication and health care, but it amassed Arkansas's highest total score by avoiding any major slip-ups.

Weaknesses: The Jonesboro area suffers from the same problems found across Arkansas. Its schools do poorly when compared on a national scale, and its transportation system is not well developed.

Scores by Sections	
Climate/Environment	61
Diversions	42
Economics	41
Education	30
Sophistication	45
Health Care	47
Housing	75
Public Safety	38
Transportation	30
Urban Proximity	43
Total Points	452

Rogers

Points: 407
National Rank: 188 of 219
State Rank: 5 of 6

General Information
Components: Benton County
Area Population: 89,000
Central City Population: 21,290
Location: Extreme northwestern Arkansas, near Missouri and Oklahoma
Nearest Metro Center: Fayetteville, 17 miles

Strengths: The Rogers area has the lowest crime rate of Arkansas's six micros. There is a good supply of new, large houses. The rate of income growth is among the fastest in the country.

Weaknesses: The educational system is a disappointment: the teachers in Rogers are among the lowest-paid in micropolitan America. The availability of medical specialists is the lowest of the state's micros.

Scores by Sections	
Climate/Environment	61
Diversions	27
Economics	47
Education	24
Sophistication	38
Health Care	22
Housing	68
Public Safety	46
Transportation	26
Urban Proximity	48
Total Points	407

Russellville

General Information
Components: Pope County
Area Population: 43,400
Central City Population: 19,590
Location: West-central Arkansas, east of Fort Smith
Nearest Metro Center: Little Rock, 76 miles

Strengths: The Russellville area offers a good stock of new, large houses at reasonable prices. Easy access to Little Rock is available by interstate.

Weaknesses: Russellville has the lowest ratio of available hospital beds among Arkansas's six micros. The area's education score is the best in the state, but is nonetheless poor when viewed in a national context.

Scores by Sections	
Climate/Environment	60
Diversions	35
Economics	43
Education	36
Sophistication	30
Health Care	28
Housing	71
Public Safety	32
Transportation	30
Urban Proximity	48
Total Points	413

CALIFORNIA

El Centro–Calexico–Brawley

Points: 425
National Rank: 159 of 219
State Rank: 4 of 5

General Information
Components: Imperial County
Area Population: 107,000
Central City Population: El Centro 27,880; Calexico 18,270; Brawley 17,940
Location: Extreme southeastern California, along the Mexican border
Nearest Metro Center: San Diego, 117 miles

Strengths: Few micros in the country surpass the financial commitment of El Centro–Calexico–Brawley to education. Most available houses are fairly new. Property taxes are the lowest of the five California micros.

Weaknesses: Both per capita income and the rate of income growth are lower than the figures for the state's other micros. The desert heat can be oppressive: the daily high in July averages 106°.

Scores by Sections	
Climate/Environment	51
Diversions	34
Economics	29
Education	51
Sophistication	27
Health Care	39
Housing	62
Public Safety	49
Transportation	38
Urban Proximity	45
Total Points	425

434 Eureka

General Information
Components: Humboldt County
Area Population: 114,200
Central City Population: 24,880
Location: Extreme northern California, along the Pacific coast
Nearest Metro Center: Redding, 158 miles

Strengths: Eureka has only five days a year where the temperature climbs over 90° or falls below 32°. No other U.S. micro has a climate anywhere near as mild. More than 76 percent of the area's adults have high-school diplomas. The dropout rate is low.

Weaknesses: Eureka keeps to itself. The closest metro area is a long, hard drive over the mountains. Only three micros in the country have violent-crime rates higher than Eureka's.

Scores by Sections	
Climate/Environment	78
Diversions	48
Economics	30
Education	68
Sophistication	53
Health Care	37
Housing	52
Public Safety	30
Transportation	38
Urban Proximity	19
Total Points	453

Hanford

General Information
Components: Kings County
Area Population: 85,900
Central City Population: 24,990
Location: Central California, south of Fresno
Nearest Metro Center: Visalia, 15 miles

Strengths: The average price of a home in the Hanford area is lower than the costs in California's other four micros. Fresno and Visalia are short freeway drives away.

Weaknesses: Hanford has the lowest ratio of available medical specialists among the state's five micros. Doctor and hospital-bed availability are well below national averages. Only Rio Rancho, N.Mex., has a lower rate of amusement places than Hanford.

Scores by Sections	
Climate/Environment	59
Diversions	29
Economics	33
Education	44
Sophistication	26
Health Care	26
Housing	70
Public Safety	56
Transportation	39
Urban Proximity	63
Total Points	445

Madera

General Information
Components: Madera County
Area Population: 77,900
Central City Population: 25,840
Location: Central California, northwest of Fresno
Nearest Metro Center: Fresno, 23 miles

Strengths: Madera's highest score came for its proximity to Fresno—less than a half hour away by freeway—and the San Francisco area, just 154 miles distant. Local education funding compares favorably with most micros in the country.

Weaknesses: Only Rio Rancho, N.Mex., has fewer hospital beds per 100,000 residents than does Madera. Daily newspaper readership is lower in Madera than in the state's four other micros; the area also has the fewest broadcast outlets.

Scores by Sections	
Climate/Environment	56
Diversions	31
Economics	32
Education	47
Sophistication	24
Health Care	20
Housing	60
Public Safety	35
Transportation	24
Urban Proximity	69
Total Points	398

San Luis Obispo–Atascadero

General Information
Components: San Luis Obispo County
Area Population: 196,700
Central City Population: San Luis Obispo 37,220; Atascadero 20,870
Location: Central coastal California, northwest of Santa Barbara
Nearest Metro Center: Santa Barbara, 94 miles

Strengths: The San Luis Obispo–Atascadero micro is America's finest. Its shining attribute is its pleasant climate, but its excellence is broad-based. The area received 48 or more points in nine of ten sections.

Weaknesses: The big quibble against San Luis Obispo–Atascadero is with its transportation system. Commercial jet traffic is not locally available, and the area has a limited choice of highways. Housing is the most expensive among U.S. micros.

Scores by Sections	
Climate/Environment	93
Diversions	55
Economics	57
Education	69
Sophistication	48
Health Care	51
Housing	51
Public Safety	57
Transportation	29
Urban Proximity	49
Total Points	559

Grand Junction

General Information
Components: Mesa County
Area Population: 89,000
Central City Population: 32,440
Location: West-central Colorado, near the Utah line
Nearest Metro Center: Provo, Utah, 236 miles

Strengths: Grand Junction has two television and eleven radio stations, broadcast power surpassed by only five micros. The area's violent-crime rate is among the nation's lowest 25 percent.

Weaknesses: Grand Junction is perched on the western rim of Colorado, nearly 250 miles removed from Denver. The weather tends to extremes: 200 days out of the year are below freezing or above 90°.

Scores by Sections	
Climate/Environment	44
Diversions	52
Economics	39
Education	44
Sophistication	57
Health Care	44
Housing	49
Public Safety	48
Transportation	44
Urban Proximity	21
Total Points	442

CONNECTICUT

Torrington

General Information
Components: Litchfield County
Area Population: 162,200
Central City Population: 31,090
Location: Northwest Connecticut, west of Hartford
Nearest Metro Center: Bristol, 14 miles

Strengths: The Torrington area's per capita income is the highest among all micros; the rate of income growth is third in the country. New York City is only 103 miles away.

Weaknesses: Housing is expensive, and is heavily taxed. The ratio of available hospital beds is well below the national norm. The local news media are weak.

Scores by Sections	
Climate/Environment	52
Diversions	34
Economics	56
Education	54
Sophistication	36
Health Care	32
Housing	35
Public Safety	44
Transportation	29
Urban Proximity	87
Total Points	459

Dover

Points: 483
National Rank: 41 of 219
State Rank: 1 of 1

General Information
Components: Kent County
Area Population: 105,200
Central City Population: 22,660
Location: Central Delaware
Nearest Metro Center: Wilmington, 46 miles

Strengths: Wilmington and Philadelphia can be quickly reached by US 13 and I-95. Dover's housing stock includes plenty of large, new units. Property taxes are low.

Weaknesses: Dover's crime rate is not among the nation's ten worst, but it is high. The highway system heading west toward Baltimore and Washington can be slow. Few communities spend fewer government dollars on parks than Dover.

Scores by Sections	
Climate/Environment	60
Diversions	34
Economics	57
Education	41
Sophistication	34
Health Care	35
Housing	75
Public Safety	28
Transportation	32
Urban Proximity	87
Total Points	483

FLORIDA

Key West

Points: 502
National Rank: 18 of 219
State Rank: 2 of 2

General Information
Components: Monroe County
Area Population: 72,500
Central City Population: 25,280
Location: The western tip of the Florida Keys
Nearest Metro Center: Miami, 161 miles

Strengths: No micro offers a wider array of things to do: Key West had the top score in the diversions section. The weather is usually pleasant: only 44 days annually climb above 90° or drop below 32°. Per capita income is fourth among all micros.

Weaknesses: Key West's spending on its schools is low; its dropout rate is high. Isolation can be a problem. There is only one road back to the mainland: US 1. Key West's total crime rate is among the steepest of all micros.

Scores by Sections	
Climate/Environment	89
Diversions	78
Economics	61
Education	32
Sophistication	41
Health Care	35
Housing	43
Public Safety	41
Transportation	36
Urban Proximity	46
Total Points	502

438 Vero Beach

General Information
Components: Indian River County
Area Population: 81,000
Central City Population: 17,720
Location: Central Florida's Atlantic coast, between Melbourne and Fort Pierce
Nearest Metro Center: Fort Pierce, 16 miles

Strengths: Only four of the nation's micros have higher per capita incomes than Vero Beach. Almost all of its available housing is less than 50 years old. No area east of California requires less energy to heat and cool homes, as measured by degree days, than Vero Beach.

Weaknesses: The high-school dropout problem is serious, with 26 percent of those between 16 and 19 not graduates and not in school. Vero Beach's violent-crime rate is high.

Scores by Sections	
Climate/Environment	79
Diversions	45
Economics	65
Education	29
Sophistication	49
Health Care	54
Housing	60
Public Safety	42
Transportation	38
Urban Proximity	59
Total Points	520

GEORGIA

Brunswick

General Information
Components: Glynn County
Area Population: 59,800
Central City Population: 19,190
Location: Extreme southeastern Georgia, on the Atlantic coast
Nearest Metro Center: Jacksonville, Fla., 71 miles

Strengths: The Brunswick area led all eight Georgia micros in three sections: climate/environment, diversions, and economics. A tourism-based economy yields the highest per capita income in micropolitan Georgia.

Weaknesses: Brunswick's total crime rate and violent-crime rate are both higher than the figures run up by every other micro in the country. The educational system is inadequate.

Scores by Sections	
Climate/Environment	75
Diversions	59
Economics	52
Education	27
Sophistication	32
Health Care	66
Housing	75
Public Safety	39
Transportation	39
Urban Proximity	58
Total Points	522

Carrollton

Points: 448
National Rank: 117 of 219
State Rank: 7 of 8

General Information
Components: Carroll County
Area Population: 64,900
Central City Population: 18,760
Location: Northwestern Georgia, southwest of Atlanta
Nearest Metro Center: Atlanta, 49 miles

Strengths: Downtown Atlanta is a quick jaunt away on I-20. Housing costs are reasonable, and property taxes are among the lowest in Georgia.

Weaknesses: Carrollton is lucky it isn't far away from Atlanta: there are few locally available diversions. Fewer than half of Carrollton's adults have high-school diplomas. Teacher pay is low even by Georgia's relaxed standards.

Scores by Sections	
Climate/Environment	65
Diversions	28
Economics	34
Education	26
Sophistication	21
Health Care	43
Housing	80
Public Safety	33
Transportation	27
Urban Proximity	91
Total Points	448

Dalton

Points: 451
National Rank: 108 of 219
State Rank: 6 of 8

General Information
Components: Whitfield County
Area Population: 69,300
Central City Population: 21,220
Location: Extreme northwestern Georgia, near the Tennessee line
Nearest Metro Center: Chattanooga, Tenn., 28 miles

Strengths: Chattanooga is a short ride north on I-75; Atlanta is only one and a half hours in the other direction. The Dalton area has a good stock of new homes. Housing costs are below the national average.

Weaknesses: Dalton's educational system is lacking: it was the lowest scorer in the country in the education section. Particularly serious is the high-school dropout problem, with 33.9 percent of those between 16 and 19 not graduates and not in school.

Scores by Sections	
Climate/Environment	69
Diversions	29
Economics	44
Education	13
Sophistication	21
Health Care	52
Housing	73
Public Safety	41
Transportation	29
Urban Proximity	80
Total Points	451

440

Gainesville

Points: 505
National Rank: 15 of 219
State Rank: 2 of 8

General Information
Components: Hall County
Area Population: 87,100
Central City Population: 16,300
Location: Northeastern Georgia, northeast of Atlanta
Nearest Metro Center: Athens, 39 miles

Strengths: Only five U.S. micros finished with better urban proximity scores than Gainesville. The bright lights of Atlanta and the university city of Athens are both relatively close. Gainesville has the lowest violent-crime rate of all Georgia micros.

Weaknesses: It's a familiar refrain in Georgia: Gainesville's schools are not what they should be, the same plight afflicting all of the state's micros. The local housing stock is modern, but costs are the highest in micropolitan Georgia.

Scores by Sections	
Climate/Environment	74
Diversions	28
Economics	48
Education	18
Sophistication	28
Health Care	64
Housing	75
Public Safety	52
Transportation	26
Urban Proximity	92
Total Points	505

Hinesville

Points: 373
National Rank: 212 of 219
State Rank: 8 of 8

General Information
Components: Liberty County
Area Population: 42,300
Central City Population: 16,480
Location: Southeastern Georgia, southwest of Savannah
Nearest Metro Center: Savannah, 41 miles

Strengths: In a state with excellent housing, Hinesville received the highest Georgia score in that section. Property taxes are lower than in any of Georgia's seven other micros.

Weaknesses: Hinesville's economy is dependent on the large military presence at Fort Stewart; the Pentagon thus casts a long shadow on local affairs. Per capita income is the lowest of Georgia's eight micros. Hinesville scored below 30 in six sections.

Scores by Sections	
Climate/Environment	69
Diversions	22
Economics	27
Education	16
Sophistication	20
Health Care	29
Housing	83
Public Safety	33
Transportation	29
Urban Proximity	45
Total Points	373

La Grange

General Information
Components: Troup County
Area Population: 54,200
Central City Population: 27,150
Location: West-central Georgia, southwest of Atlanta, near the Alabama line
Nearest Metro Center: Columbus, 45 miles

Strengths: La Grange residents have easy access to metropolitan amenities: Columbus is 45 miles away by freeway, Atlanta 64. Housing is less expensive in La Grange than in any of Georgia's other micros.

Weaknesses: Fewer than 42 percent of the adults in the La Grange area have received high-school diplomas; two micros in Louisiana are the only ones in America with lower figures.

Scores by Sections	
Climate/Environment	69
Diversions	32
Economics	39
Education	19
Sophistication	28
Health Care	54
Housing	73
Public Safety	45
Transportation	40
Urban Proximity	89
Total Points	488

Rome

General Information
Components: Floyd County
Area Population: 78,700
Central City Population: 30,910
Location: Northwestern Georgia, northwest of Atlanta
Nearest Metro Center: Gadsden, Ala., 54 miles

Strengths: The Rome area has higher ratios of doctors, specialists, and hospital beds than do any of Georgia's seven other micros. Rome's total crime rate is the smallest of the state's micros. Atlanta is just 65 miles away.

Weaknesses: Rome's school system is highly ranked among Georgia micros, but does badly when compared nationally. Only Bogalusa, La., spends less per capita on its parks than Rome does.

Scores by Sections	
Climate/Environment	67
Diversions	28
Economics	34
Education	29
Sophistication	33
Health Care	74
Housing	69
Public Safety	55
Transportation	27
Urban Proximity	88
Total Points	504

442 Valdosta

Points: 457
National Rank: 94 of 219
State Rank: 5 of 8

General Information
Components: Lowndes County
Area Population: 73,700
Central City Population: 36,970
Location: Extreme south-central Georgia, near the Florida line
Nearest Metro Center: Tallahassee, Fla., 78 miles

Strengths: Valdosta's housing stock is modern, reasonably priced, and lightly taxed. The area is a great one for shoppers; only Brunswick among Georgia micros has a higher ratio of retail outlets.

Weaknesses: Valdosta's total crime rate and violent-crime rate are both among the ten worst in micropolitan America. Teacher pay is extremely low, just one of the reasons Valdosta is marked down in the education section.

Scores by Sections	
Climate/Environment	64
Diversions	43
Economics	45
Education	31
Sophistication	33
Health Care	55
Housing	82
Public Safety	18
Transportation	35
Urban Proximity	51
Total Points	457

IDAHO

Coeur d'Alene

Points: 428
National Rank: 156 of 219
State Rank: 3 of 5

General Information
Components: Kootenai County
Area Population: 67,500
Central City Population: 24,690
Location: Western edge of the Idaho panhandle, near the Washington line
Nearest Metro Center: Spokane, Wash., 33 miles

Strengths: The other four Idaho micros are tucked far away from metropolitan life, but Coeur d'Alene is near Spokane. The climate in the Coeur d'Alene area is not as extreme, either in summer heat or winter cold, as that of the state's other micros.

Weaknesses: Coeur d'Alene received the worst score in the economics section of the five Idaho micropolitan areas. It also has the lowest ratio of hospital beds among the five, and spends the least per capita on education.

Scores by Sections	
Climate/Environment	52
Diversions	38
Economics	29
Education	45
Sophistication	41
Health Care	39
Housing	53
Public Safety	38
Transportation	34
Urban Proximity	59
Total Points	428

Idaho Falls

General Information
Components: Bonneville County
Area Population: 70,600
Central City Population: 42,830
Location: Southeastern Idaho, northeast of Pocatello
Nearest Metro Center: Salt Lake City, Utah, 211 miles

Strengths: Only three U.S. micros scored higher than Idaho Falls in the sophistication section. The local news media are strong. Commercial air traffic is available in greater quantity than elsewhere in Idaho micros. Per capita income tops the same group.

Weaknesses: It's a long drive to get anywhere: only two other American micros are farther from a metropolitan area than Idaho Falls is. Winters are fiercely cold: the average January nightly low is 9°.

Scores by Sections	
Climate/Environment	51
Diversions	44
Economics	58
Education	41
Sophistication	61
Health Care	45
Housing	57
Public Safety	48
Transportation	45
Urban Proximity	10
Total Points	460

Nampa–Caldwell

General Information
Components: Canyon County
Area Population: 90,200
Central City Population: Nampa 28,250; Caldwell 18,570
Location: Southwestern Idaho, west of Boise
Nearest Metro Center: Boise, 15 miles

Strengths: Nampa–Caldwell leads Idaho's micros in the housing section. The area's property taxes are lower than those of the state's other four micros. Boise is close, but sizeable metro areas are far away.

Weaknesses: The housing score was Nampa–Caldwell's only mark above 45. It received 35 or fewer points in seven of the ten sections, resulting in the area's last-place finish on the national total-points list.

Scores by Sections	
Climate/Environment	41
Diversions	24
Economics	31
Education	31
Sophistication	45
Health Care	28
Housing	61
Public Safety	35
Transportation	32
Urban Proximity	27
Total Points	355

444

Pocatello

General Information
Components: Bannock County
Area Population: 68,100
Central City Population: 44,420
Location: Southeastern Idaho, southeast of Boise
Nearest Metro Center: Salt Lake City, Utah, 162 miles

Strengths: An impressive number of Pocatello's adults have obtained high-school diplomas: 79.2 percent. The area's total crime rate is the lowest among Idaho's five micros.

Weaknesses: Gas up the car for a long trip down I-15 if you're seeking metropolitan diversions: Salt Lake City is about three hours away. The rate of income growth in Pocatello lags behind the figures for Idaho's other micros.

Scores by Sections	
Climate/Environment	43
Diversions	40
Economics	46
Education	51
Sophistication	48
Health Care	46
Housing	56
Public Safety	49
Transportation	42
Urban Proximity	19
Total Points	440

Twin Falls

Points: 419
National Rank: 171 of 219
State Rank: 4 of 5

General Information
Components: Twin Falls County
Area Population: 55,800
Central City Population: 27,750
Location: South-central Idaho, southeast of Boise
Nearest Metro Center: Boise, 129 miles

Strengths: The Twin Falls area has the highest ratio of doctors and medical specialists among any of Idaho's micros. Twin Falls also offers the most recreational opportunities in that group: it has the state's highest ratio of amusement places.

Weaknesses: Isolation is the biggest difficulty facing a Twin Falls resident. Boise is two hours by car in one direction, Salt Lake City three and a half hours in the other. The area has the worst score in the highway index of any Idaho micro.

Scores by Sections	
Climate/Environment	49
Diversions	49
Economics	38
Education	32
Sophistication	48
Health Care	55
Housing	59
Public Safety	40
Transportation	36
Urban Proximity	13
Total Points	419

Carbondale

General Information
Components: Jackson County
Area Population: 60,500
Central City Population: 24,170
Location: Extreme southern Illinois, southeast of Saint Louis
Nearest Metro Center: East Saint Louis, 96 miles

Strengths: The Carbondale area has the lowest property taxes of any Illinois micro; its housing is among the state's least expensive. Southern Illinois University accounts for Carbondale's educated population: 26.4 percent of its adults are college grads.

Weaknesses: Carbondale's per capita income is easily the lowest of the state's micros. Getting out of town is not quickly accomplished: there is no freeway toward Saint Louis.

Scores by Sections	
Climate/Environment	58
Diversions	39
Economics	34
Education	63
Sophistication	52
Health Care	37
Housing	60
Public Safety	45
Transportation	30
Urban Proximity	70
Total Points	488

Danville

General Information
Components: Vermilion County
Area Population: 91,300
Central City Population: 36,660
Location: East-central Illinois, near the Indiana line
Nearest Metro Center: Champaign, 35 miles

Strengths: Only four U.S. micros have a more favorable abundance of hospital beds than Danville does. The average price of a house is cheaper here than in any other micropolitan area in Illinois.

Weaknesses: Crime is a problem for the Danville area: it has both the highest total crime rate and the highest violent-crime rate in micropolitan Illinois. Teacher pay is lower in Danville than in all of the state's other micros but Mattoon–Charleston.

Scores by Sections	
Climate/Environment	57
Diversions	34
Economics	31
Education	39
Sophistication	34
Health Care	41
Housing	51
Public Safety	32
Transportation	37
Urban Proximity	76
Total Points	432

446 De Kalb

Points: 477
National Rank: 53 of 219
State Rank: 2 of 9

General Information
Components: De Kalb County
Area Population: 74,100
Central City Population: 31,570
Location: Northern Illinois, west of Chicago
Nearest Metro Center: Aurora, 31 miles

Strengths: De Kalb received the best score of any Illinois micro in the education section, tenth best in the country. Northern Illinois University deserves much of the credit. The amenities of Chicago are just 68 miles down the toll road.

Weaknesses: Housing is considerably more expensive in De Kalb than in any of the state's eight other micros. Availability of doctors and hospital beds are well below state norms. The local news media are weak.

Scores by Sections	
Climate/Environment	57
Diversions	32
Economics	28
Education	70
Sophistication	36
Health Care	29
Housing	41
Public Safety	50
Transportation	43
Urban Proximity	91
Total Points	477

Freeport

Points: 424
National Rank: 162 of 219
State Rank: 8 of 9

General Information
Components: Stephenson County
Area Population: 49,400
Central City Population: 25,830
Location: Extreme northwestern Illinois, west of Rockford
Nearest Metro Center: Rockford, 29 miles

Strengths: The Freeport area's per capita income is the highest among Illinois's micros; the same goes for its rate of income growth. Rockford is an easy drive; Chicago is only about two hours by tollway.

Weaknesses: Availability of hospital beds is well below the national average. Except for the four-lane highway to Rockford, Freeport's road system is inadequate.

Scores by Sections	
Climate/Environment	61
Diversions	35
Economics	35
Education	42
Sophistication	35
Health Care	30
Housing	48
Public Safety	38
Transportation	30
Urban Proximity	70
Total Points	424

Galesburg

General Information
Components: Knox County
Area Population: 56,300
Central City Population: 31,830
Location: West-central Illinois, northwest of Peoria
Nearest Metro Center: Davenport, Iowa, 48 miles

Strengths: Housing is among the less expensive in micropolitan Illinois. Citizens of the Galesburg area show a willingness to get involved in local affairs: their voter-turnout rate is the highest of the state's micros.

Weaknesses: Galesburg's economic base is shrinking: no other American micro had as great a rate of population decline from 1980 to 1986. Property taxes are among the highest in the state.

Scores by Sections	
Climate/Environment	57
Diversions	40
Economics	37
Education	43
Sophistication	39
Health Care	33
Housing	46
Public Safety	48
Transportation	39
Urban Proximity	59
Total Points	441

Mattoon–Charleston

General Information
Components: Coles County
Area Population: 52,000
Central City Population: Mattoon 19,150; Charleston 18,860
Location: East-central Illinois, southeast of Decatur
Nearest Metro Center: Decatur, 44 miles

Strengths: Feel free to walk the streets of Mattoon–Charleston: its total crime rate is the lowest of any U.S. micro. The area ranks third among Illinois's nine micros in education, thanks largely to Eastern Illinois University in Charleston.

Weaknesses: Mattoon–Charleston's ratio of available hospital beds is among the lower figures in micropolitan Illinois. Only two Illinois micros have lower per capita incomes.

Scores by Sections	
Climate/Environment	62
Diversions	39
Economics	33
Education	55
Sophistication	44
Health Care	27
Housing	50
Public Safety	59
Transportation	38
Urban Proximity	67
Total Points	474

448 Ottawa

General Information
Components: La Salle County
Area Population: 108,200
Central City Population: 17,890
Location: North-central Illinois, southwest of Chicago
Nearest Metro Center: Joliet, 45 miles

Strengths: The metropolitan comforts of Chicago are just 90 miles from Ottawa. And it's easy to get there: only six U.S. micros are served by better road systems than Ottawa, as measured by the highway index. The total crime rate is the state's second lowest.

Weaknesses: Ottawa's figures on the availability of doctors and medical specialists are near the bottom of micropolitan Illinois's list. No state micro has a lower percentage of adults with high-school diplomas than Ottawa's 62.1 percent.

Scores by Sections	
Climate/Environment	56
Diversions	42
Economics	38
Education	47
Sophistication	30
Health Care	23
Housing	44
Public Safety	51
Transportation	48
Urban Proximity	86
Total Points	465

Quincy

General Information
Components: Adams County
Area Population: 68,100
Central City Population: 39,600
Location: West-central Illinois, on the Mississippi River
Nearest Metro Center: Springfield, 102 miles

Strengths: With four television and five radio stations, Quincy has a stronger lineup of broadcast outlets than all but five U.S. micros. No Illinois micro has a better ratio of doctors and medical specialists than Quincy.

Weaknesses: This is Illinois's most isolated micro, the only one more than 100 miles from any metro center. Only Carbondale has a lower per capita income than Quincy among the nine state micros; none spends less per capita on education in the same group.

Scores by Sections	
Climate/Environment	56
Diversions	42
Economics	39
Education	43
Sophistication	53
Health Care	40
Housing	52
Public Safety	45
Transportation	40
Urban Proximity	51
Total Points	461

Sterling

Points: 410
National Rank: 186 of 219
State Rank: 9 of 9

General Information

Components: Whiteside County
Area Population: 62,800
Central City Population: 15,570
Location: Northwestern Illinois, southwest of Rockford
Nearest Metro Center: Rockford, 57 miles

Strengths: The Sterling area has a better selection of large homes than does any other Illinois micro. Property taxes are lighter than in most of micropolitan Illinois. No state micro spends more per capita on education than Sterling.

Weaknesses: The rate of personal income growth from 1979 to 1985 was slower in Sterling than in all but six U.S. micros. The Sterling area has the state's lowest figures for the availability of doctors, specialists, and hospital beds.

Scores by Sections	
Climate/Environment	55
Diversions	32
Economics	25
Education	47
Sophistication	28
Health Care	30
Housing	53
Public Safety	49
Transportation	29
Urban Proximity	62
Total Points	410

INDIANA

Columbus

Points: 493
National Rank: 27 of 219
State Rank: 1 of 6

General Information

Components: Bartholomew County
Area Population: 64,500
Central City Population: 30,890
Location: South-central Indiana, south of Indianapolis
Nearest Metro Center: Bloomington, 39 miles

Strengths: The Columbus area offers the chance to earn a good living: its per capita income ranks ninth among U.S. micros. Indianapolis is just 46 miles away, easily reached on I-65; Louisville is only slightly farther in the other direction.

Weaknesses: Housing is considerably more expensive in Columbus than in any other Indiana micro. The total crime rate, while not high on the national scale, is the highest among the state's six micros.

Scores by Sections	
Climate/Environment	58
Diversions	33
Economics	41
Education	45
Sophistication	36
Health Care	52
Housing	59
Public Safety	44
Transportation	33
Urban Proximity	92
Total Points	493

450

Marion

Points: 465
National Rank: 74 of 219
State Rank: 3 of 6

General Information
Components: Grant County
Area Population: 77,100
Central City Population: 35,810
Location: East-central Indiana, northeast of Indianapolis
Nearest Metro Center: Kokomo, 32 miles

Strengths: Indianapolis is slightly more than an hour away on Interstate 69. Teacher pay is higher in Marion than in any of Indiana's five other micros, helping this area attain the state's highest education score. Housing is inexpensive, hospital beds plentiful.

Weaknesses: The Marion area's base is declining: the local population dropped nearly 5 percent in the first half of the 1980s. Except for I-69, the highway system offers little more than slow state roads.

Scores by Sections	
Climate/Environment	56
Diversions	30
Economics	35
Education	51
Sophistication	35
Health Care	41
Housing	57
Public Safety	43
Transportation	28
Urban Proximity	89
Total Points	465

Michigan City–La Porte

Points: 450
National Rank: 109 of 219
State Rank: 5 of 6

General Information
Components: La Porte County
Area Population: 106,100
Central City Population: Michigan City 35,600; La Porte 21,720
Location: Extreme northwestern Indiana, between Chicago and South Bend
Nearest Metro Center: Gary, 25 miles

Strengths: Chicago is a scant 56 miles from Michigan City–La Porte, helping the area to the second-best urban proximity score in the country. Getting to Chicago or anywhere else is easy: Michigan City–La Porte rang up the nation's highest score in the highway index.

Weaknesses: The climate in Michigan City–La Porte is less forgiving than in the rest of the state: it receives two and a half times the snow of any other Indiana micro. The rate of income growth is the state's lowest.

Scores by Sections	
Climate/Environment	50
Diversions	27
Economics	31
Education	39
Sophistication	35
Health Care	31
Housing	53
Public Safety	48
Transportation	41
Urban Proximity	95
Total Points	450

New Castle

General Information
Components: Henry County
Area Population: 50,100
Central City Population: 18,370
Location: East-central Indiana, east of Indianapolis
Nearest Metro Center: Muncie, 20 miles

Strengths: An hour after stepping into your car in New Castle, you can be in downtown Indianapolis, 48 miles away. Only Vincennes has more inexpensive housing than New Castle among Indiana's micros.

Weaknesses: The New Castle area had the highest rate of population loss between 1980 and 1986 of any Indiana micro: 6.0 percent. New Castle also trails all other state micros in availability of doctors and hospital beds, and in teacher pay.

Scores by Sections	
Climate/Environment	59
Diversions	27
Economics	29
Education	35
Sophistication	28
Health Care	25
Housing	58
Public Safety	40
Transportation	28
Urban Proximity	93
Total Points	422

Richmond

General Information
Components: Wayne County
Area Population: 72,200
Central City Population: 39,030
Location: Extreme east-central Indiana, east of Indianapolis
Nearest Metro Center: Dayton, Ohio, 41 miles

Strengths: The Richmond area's violent-crime rate is the lowest among Indiana's six micros. Dayton is just 41 miles away, Cincinnati 62, Indianapolis 73. Richmond is tenth among all U.S. micros in availability of hospital beds.

Weaknesses: People are slipping away from Richmond: its population declined 5.1 percent from 1980 to 1986. Air traffic is less accessible from Richmond than from any other Indiana micro.

Scores by Sections	
Climate/Environment	65
Diversions	33
Economics	35
Education	43
Sophistication	38
Health Care	43
Housing	56
Public Safety	49
Transportation	35
Urban Proximity	86
Total Points	483

452 Vincennes

Points: 453
National Rank: 99 of 219
State Rank: 4 of 6

General Information
Components: Knox County
Area Population: 41,400
Central City Population: 20,550
Location: Southwestern Indiana, on the Wabash River
Nearest Metro Center: Evansville, 54 miles

Strengths: Housing is less expensive than in any other Indiana micro, and property taxes are lower. Vincennes has a much higher concentration of retail outlets than in the state's other micros. It also has the highest ratio of medical specialists in the group.

Weaknesses: In a state where micropolitan areas are noted for their proximity to large cities, Vincennes is the exception. Per capita income is much lower than in any of Indiana's five other micros.

Scores by Sections	
Climate/Environment	62
Diversions	41
Economics	27
Education	42
Sophistication	38
Health Care	52
Housing	54
Public Safety	41
Transportation	30
Urban Proximity	66
Total Points	453

IOWA

Ames

Points: 525
National Rank: 7 of 219
State Rank: 1 of 7

General Information
Components: Story County
Area Population: 72,500
Central City Population: 44,460
Location: Central Iowa, north of Des Moines
Nearest Metro Center: Des Moines, 28 miles

Strengths: The Ames area, with a major boost from Iowa State University, finished sixth in the nation in the education section. Almost 34 percent of the adults in Ames are college graduates. The local rate of income growth is higher than in all other Iowa micros.

Weaknesses: Housing is much more expensive than anywhere else in micropolitan Iowa. The weather is rugged everywhere in the state, but Ames has the highest number of extreme days, those with temperatures above 90° or below 32°.

Scores by Sections	
Climate/Environment	51
Diversions	42
Economics	49
Education	74
Sophistication	56
Health Care	54
Housing	41
Public Safety	42
Transportation	44
Urban Proximity	72
Total Points	525

Burlington

General Information
Components: Des Moines County
Area Population: 44,600
Central City Population: 28,000
Location: Extreme southeastern Iowa, on the Mississippi River
Nearest Metro Center: Iowa City, 78 miles

Strengths: It is less expensive to purchase a house in Burlington than in any of the other six micros in Iowa. No other state micro has a better ratio of available hospital beds. The local economy is well-balanced.

Weaknesses: Many micros in other parts of the country wouldn't mind having Burlington's violent-crime rate, but it is the highest among Iowa micros. Burlington has the lowest urban proximity score in the state.

Scores by Sections	
Climate/Environment	47
Diversions	45
Economics	48
Education	50
Sophistication	45
Health Care	45
Housing	45
Public Safety	34
Transportation	41
Urban Proximity	53
Total Points	453

Clinton

General Information
Components: Clinton County
Area Population: 53,600
Central City Population: 30,080
Location: Extreme east-central Iowa, on the Mississippi River
Nearest Metro Center: Davenport, 37 miles

Strengths: Clinton's violent-crime rate is the fifth lowest among all U.S. micros. No other area in micropolitan Iowa spends more per capita on education. Housing is less expensive than in any Iowa micro but Burlington.

Weaknesses: Only Fort Dodge has a lower per capita income than Clinton among Iowa micros. The Clinton area is also second lowest in the state when it comes to the availability of doctors, and third lowest in medical specialists.

Scores by Sections	
Climate/Environment	55
Diversions	44
Economics	39
Education	54
Sophistication	40
Health Care	33
Housing	43
Public Safety	41
Transportation	37
Urban Proximity	62
Total Points	448

Fort Dodge

Points: 450
National Rank: 109 of 219
State Rank: 5 of 7

General Information
Components: Webster County
Area Population: 42,700
Central City Population: 27,070
Location: Central Iowa, northwest of Des Moines
Nearest Metro Center: Des Moines, 91 miles

Strengths: Commuting is a snap in Fort Dodge: in only five U.S. micros does the average worker get to his place of employment more quickly. Fort Dodge's local newspaper reaches a higher percentage of readers than any other Iowa micro paper does.

Weaknesses: Fort Dodge's total crime rate is easily the worst in micropolitan Iowa. Availability of health-care services is below state norms. Per capita income is the lowest of Iowa's seven micros.

Scores by Sections	
Climate/Environment	55
Diversions	54
Economics	46
Education	53
Sophistication	46
Health Care	25
Housing	40
Public Safety	30
Transportation	42
Urban Proximity	59
Total Points	450

Marshalltown

Points: 462
National Rank: 83 of 219
State Rank: 3 of 7

General Information
Components: Marshall County
Area Population: 40,500
Central City Population: 26,070
Location: Central Iowa, northeast of Des Moines
Nearest Metro Center: Des Moines, 53 miles

Strengths: The Marshalltown area's per capita income falls just a few dollars short of being the highest in micropolitan Iowa. The percentage of high-school graduates is higher than in all Iowa micros but Ames. Marshalltown's crime rate is low.

Weaknesses: Marshalltown's ratio of available hospital beds is the second worst among Iowa micros. Property taxes are the highest in the same group.

Scores by Sections	
Climate/Environment	52
Diversions	43
Economics	46
Education	55
Sophistication	40
Health Care	31
Housing	42
Public Safety	46
Transportation	41
Urban Proximity	66
Total Points	462

Mason City

General Information
Components: Cerro Gordo County
Area Population: 48,800
Central City Population: 30,200
Location: North-central Iowa, northwest of Waterloo
Nearest Metro Center: Waterloo, 82 miles

Strengths: Mason City has micropolitan Iowa's best ratios of doctors and medical specialists. It also offers more diversions than any other Iowa micro, including a higher rate of both retail outlets and amusement places than the rest.

Weaknesses: Only eight U.S. micros place a greater strain on houses' heating and cooling bills than Mason City does, as measured by total degree days. Property taxes are relatively high.

Scores by Sections	
Climate/Environment	54
Diversions	57
Economics	43
Education	56
Sophistication	52
Health Care	55
Housing	38
Public Safety	36
Transportation	43
Urban Proximity	59
Total Points	493

Muscatine

General Information
Components: Muscatine County
Area Population: 41,300
Central City Population: 23,580
Location: Extreme eastern Iowa, on the Mississippi River, southwest of Davenport
Nearest Metro Center: Davenport, 30 miles

Strengths: Muscatine has the highest per capita income of any Iowa micro. Both its total crime rate and its violent-crime rate are the lowest in the state group; its violent rate is the fourth lowest among U.S. micros.

Weaknesses: Muscatine trails all other Iowa micros when it comes to the availability of doctors, medical specialists, and hospital beds. Its teacher pay is the lowest and its dropout rate is the highest in micropolitan Iowa.

Scores by Sections	
Climate/Environment	53
Diversions	38
Economics	55
Education	39
Sophistication	29
Health Care	24
Housing	43
Public Safety	49
Transportation	32
Urban Proximity	62
Total Points	424

Hutchinson

Points: 439
National Rank: 136 of 219
State Rank: 3 of 3

General Information
Components: Reno County
Area Population: 65,300
Central City Population: 41,500
Location: South-central Kansas, northwest of Wichita
Nearest Metro Center: Wichita, 52 miles

Strengths: No micro in the country has a daily newspaper that reaches a wider readership than the one in Hutchinson. Housing is less expensive here than in Kansas's two other micros.

Weaknesses: A combination of extreme temperatures, both hot and cold, and 22 waste sites undergoing cleanup landed Hutchinson with the second worst national score in the climate/environment section. The crime rate is the highest in micropolitan Kansas.

Scores by Sections	
Climate/Environment	32
Diversions	51
Economics	38
Education	47
Sophistication	51
Health Care	30
Housing	49
Public Safety	43
Transportation	39
Urban Proximity	59
Total Points	439

Manhattan

Points: 443
National Rank: 128 of 219
State Rank: 2 of 3

General Information
Components: Riley County
Area Population: 65,100
Central City Population: 33,750
Location: Northeastern Kansas, northwest of Topeka
Nearest Metro Center: Topeka, 54 miles

Strengths: More than 85 percent of Manhattan's adults have high-school diplomas: only four U.S. micros do better. Kansas State University provides a positive educational climate. The local housing stock is less heavily taxed than the state's other micros.

Weaknesses: Manhattan's per capita income is easily the lowest in micropolitan Kansas. Also at the bottom of the state's list are Manhattan's ratios of doctors, medical specialists, and hospital beds.

Scores by Sections	
Climate/Environment	47
Diversions	34
Economics	34
Education	58
Sophistication	46
Health Care	31
Housing	59
Public Safety	46
Transportation	37
Urban Proximity	51
Total Points	443

Salina

General Information
Components: Saline County
Area Population: 50,000
Central City Population: 42,830
Location: Central Kansas, north of Wichita
Nearest Metro Center: Wichita, 90 miles

Strengths: Salina's per capita income is the highest among the state's three micros. Salina also leads micropolitan Kansas in availability of doctors, specialists, and hospital beds, and has the lowest violent-crime rate.

Weaknesses: The rate of income growth in Salina is lower than in Kansas's two other micros. Teachers receive the least pay in the state group.

Scores by Sections	
Climate/Environment	47
Diversions	49
Economics	47
Education	51
Sophistication	54
Health Care	50
Housing	55
Public Safety	47
Transportation	39
Urban Proximity	54
Total Points	493

KENTUCKY

Bowling Green

Points: 470
National Rank: 59 of 219
State Rank: 1 of 6

General Information
Components: Warren County
Area Population: 82,400
Central City Population: 41,300
Location: South-central Kentucky, southwest of Louisville
Nearest Metro Center: Clarksville, Tenn., 61 miles

Strengths: The Bowling Green area's population grew 14.8 percent from 1980 to 1986: no other Kentucky micro had a rate even half as large. Western Kentucky University helps Bowling Green to the state's highest score in the education section.

Weaknesses: Despite its state victory in the education section, Bowling Green's financial commitment is poor: only four U.S. micros spend less per capita on their schools. Bowling Green has Kentucky's lowest urban proximity score, a sign of isolation.

Scores by Sections	
Climate/Environment	59
Diversions	38
Economics	52
Education	44
Sophistication	43
Health Care	43
Housing	71
Public Safety	39
Transportation	32
Urban Proximity	49
Total Points	470

458 Frankfort

Points: 467
National Rank: 66 of 219
State Rank: 2 of 6

General Information
Components: Franklin County
Area Population: 44,000
Central City Population: 26,920
Location: Northern Kentucky, between Louisville
and Lexington
Nearest Metro Center: Lexington, 23 miles

Strengths: Frankfort, Kentucky's capital, has an ideal location for those seeking metropolitan access: Lexington is 23 miles to the east, Louisville 52 to the west. The per capita income is the highest in micropolitan Kentucky.

Weaknesses: Housing is more expensive in the Frankfort area than in any of Kentucky's five other micros. Frankfort has the worst ratio of available hospital beds in the same state group.

Scores by Sections	
Climate/Environment	59
Diversions	31
Economics	38
Education	30
Sophistication	37
Health Care	29
Housing	69
Public Safety	45
Transportation	45
Urban Proximity	84
Total Points	467

Madisonville

Points: 406
National Rank: 190 of 219
State Rank: 6 of 6

General Information
Components: Hopkins County
Area Population: 46,600
Central City Population: 16,600
Location: West-central Kentucky, south of Evansville, Ind.
Nearest Metro Center: Owensboro, 48 miles

Strengths: Housing is much less expensive in Madisonville than in any other Kentucky micro. Madisonville also spends more per capita on education than its state counterparts, and has the most favorable availability ratio of doctors.

Weaknesses: Educational attainment is the lowest in the state: fewer than half of Madisonville's adults have high-school diplomas. The local road system is inferior to those of Kentucky's other micros, according to the highway index.

Scores by Sections	
Climate/Environment	60
Diversions	24
Economics	33
Education	21
Sophistication	32
Health Care	52
Housing	73
Public Safety	33
Transportation	21
Urban Proximity	57
Total Points	406

Paducah

Points: 460
National Rank: 86 of 219
State Rank: 3 of 6

General Information

Components: McCracken County
Area Population: 60,300
Central City Population: 28,370
Location: Extreme western Kentucky, on the Ohio River
Nearest Metro Center: Clarksville, Tenn., 96 miles

Strengths: Only Frankfort has a higher per capita income among Kentucky micros. Strong newspaper readership helped Paducah to Kentucky's highest score in the sophistication section. The area also has the state's best ratio of available hospital beds.

Weaknesses: Only nine U.S. micros have a higher total crime rate than Paducah, and its violent-crime rate is the worst in micropolitan Kentucky. Teacher pay is the lowest among the state's six micros.

Scores by Sections	
Climate/Environment	50
Diversions	38
Economics	49
Education	34
Sophistication	51
Health Care	62
Housing	72
Public Safety	21
Transportation	31
Urban Proximity	52
Total Points	460

Radcliff–Elizabethtown

Points: 436
National Rank: 140 of 219
State Rank: 5 of 6

General Information

Components: Hardin County
Area Population: 93,800
Central City Population: Radcliff 20,160; Elizabethtown 16,390
Location: North-central Kentucky, south of Louisville
Nearest Metro Center: Louisville, 36 miles

Strengths: Radcliff–Elizabethtown is a short drive from Louisville, with Cincinnati only about two and a half hours by car. Property taxes are the lowest among the state's six micros, while the housing stock is the newest.

Weaknesses: There is plenty of money in the Radcliff–Elizabethtown area, but most of it is in the vaults of Fort Knox: only Richmond has a lower per capita income among Kentucky micros. No U.S. micro spends less per capita on education.

Scores by Sections	
Climate/Environment	58
Diversions	22
Economics	35
Education	27
Sophistication	27
Health Care	41
Housing	78
Public Safety	35
Transportation	33
Urban Proximity	80
Total Points	436

460 Richmond

Points: 458
National Rank: 92 of 219
State Rank: 4 of 6

General Information
Components: Madison County
Area Population: 54,900
Central City Population: 23,380
Location: East-central Kentucky, southeast of Lexington
Nearest Metro Center: Lexington, 26 miles

Strengths: The Richmond area has a milder climate than the state's other micros, with at least 19 fewer days of extreme temperatures than any of the rest. Only three U.S. micros have lower property taxes. Lexington, Louisville, and Cincinnati are less than two hours away.

Weaknesses: Richmond's per capita income is easily the lowest in micropolitan Kentucky. Richmond has the state's second worst availability ratios of doctors and hospital beds.

Scores by Sections	
Climate/Environment	67
Diversions	34
Economics	37
Education	41
Sophistication	29
Health Care	33
Housing	74
Public Safety	39
Transportation	27
Urban Proximity	77
Total Points	458

LOUISIANA

Bogalusa

Points: 407
National Rank: 188 of 219
State Rank: 6 of 8

General Information
Components: Washington Parish
Area Population: 47,700
Central City Population: 17,240
Location: Southeastern Louisiana, northeast of New Orleans, near the Mississippi line
Nearest Metro Center: New Orleans, 64 miles

Strengths: Housing is less expensive in Bogalusa than in any of Louisiana's other micros; only six U.S. micros are more affordable. Bogalusa leads micropolitan Louisiana in availability of hospital beds.

Weaknesses: There are no major highways; air travel is tough to arrange. Those are two reasons Bogalusa received the nation's worst score in the transportation section. Only six U.S. micros have lower per capita incomes than Bogalusa.

Scores by Sections	
Climate/Environment	64
Diversions	23
Economics	19
Education	38
Sophistication	25
Health Care	30
Housing	84
Public Safety	42
Transportation	13
Urban Proximity	69
Total Points	407

Crowley

General Information
Components: Acadia Parish
Area Population: 59,600
Central City Population: 16,310
Location: South-central Louisiana, west of Lafayette
Nearest Metro Center: Lafayette, 22 miles

Strengths: Crowley's total crime rate is lower than that of any other state micro but New Iberia. Housing in the Crowley area is inexpensive and lightly taxed.

Weaknesses: Only four U.S. micros received worse scores in the health care section; only two did worse nationally in the economics section. Just 40.1 percent of Crowley's adults have high-school diplomas, the lowest figure in micropolitan America.

Scores by Sections	
Climate/Environment	70
Diversions	24
Economics	19
Education	21
Sophistication	20
Health Care	17
Housing	82
Public Safety	45
Transportation	23
Urban Proximity	62
Total Points	383

Hammond

General Information
Components: Tangipahoa Parish
Area Population: 92,100
Central City Population: 19,950
Location: Southeastern Louisiana, east of Baton Rouge
Nearest Metro Center: Baton Rouge, 41 miles

Strengths: Hammond has Louisiana's highest urban proximity score: Baton Rouge and New Orleans are both less than an hour away. Property taxes are the lowest in micropolitan Louisiana, lower than all but four U.S. micros.

Weaknesses: Hammond's per capita income is very low by national standards, and is the third worst among the state's eight micros. Teacher pay is the lowest in the same group of Louisiana micros.

Scores by Sections	
Climate/Environment	65
Diversions	30
Economics	31
Education	27
Sophistication	26
Health Care	34
Housing	81
Public Safety	49
Transportation	24
Urban Proximity	76
Total Points	443

462 Minden

General Information
Components: Webster Parish
Area Population: 46,100
Central City Population: 15,190
Location: Northwestern Louisiana, east of Shreveport
Nearest Metro Center: Shreveport, 31 miles

Strengths: Minden's housing is among the least expensive in America; only Bogalusa offers lower prices among Louisiana's micros. Minden's rate of income growth from 1979 to 1985 was the fastest in the state.

Weaknesses: Okmulgee, Okla., was the sole U.S. micro to receive a lower rating than Minden in the health care section. Minden's violent-crime rate is the highest among Louisiana's eight micros.

Scores by Sections	
Climate/Environment	49
Diversions	22
Economics	31
Education	30
Sophistication	23
Health Care	13
Housing	85
Public Safety	36
Transportation	25
Urban Proximity	56
Total Points	370

Morgan City

General Information
Components: Saint Mary Parish
Area Population: 64,300
Central City Population: 16,030
Location: Extreme south-central Louisiana, southwest of New Orleans
Nearest Metro Center: Houma, 37 miles

Strengths: Morgan City offers its residents plenty of diversions: no Louisiana micro spends more per capita on food and drink, or has a higher concentration of amusement places. Morgan City's per capita income is the highest in micropolitan Louisiana.

Weaknesses: Housing is considerably more expensive in Morgan City than in any other micro in the state; property taxes are also the highest. The high-school dropout rate is the worst in micropolitan Louisiana.

Scores by Sections	
Climate/Environment	72
Diversions	53
Economics	32
Education	27
Sophistication	21
Health Care	36
Housing	71
Public Safety	63
Transportation	28
Urban Proximity	67
Total Points	470

New Iberia

Points: 463
National Rank: 80 of 219
State Rank: 2 of 8

General Information
Components: Iberia Parish
Area Population: 69,000
Central City Population: 36,200
Location: South-central Louisiana, south of Lafayette
Nearest Metro Center: Lafayette, 20 miles

Strengths: Both New Iberia's total crime rate and its violent-crime rate are the lowest in micropolitan Louisiana. No state micro has a higher availability ratio of doctors or spends more to maintain its highways.

Weaknesses: Housing prices are steeper in the New Iberia area than in any Louisiana micro except Morgan City. Teacher pay is lower than in all but Hammond. Less than half of New Iberia's adults have high-school diplomas.

Scores by Sections	
Climate/Environment	70
Diversions	41
Economics	37
Education	27
Sophistication	27
Health Care	35
Housing	76
Public Safety	53
Transportation	34
Urban Proximity	63
Total Points	463

Opelousas

Points: 430
National Rank: 154 of 219
State Rank: 5 of 8

General Information
Components: Saint Landry Parish
Area Population: 88,400
Central City Population: 19,760
Location: South-central Louisiana, north of Lafayette
Nearest Metro Center: Lafayette, 22 miles

Strengths: Only two U.S. micros received higher scores in the housing section than Opelousas did. No Louisiana micro needs less energy for heating and cooling its homes, as measured by degree days.

Weaknesses: Opelousas's per capita income is the lowest among Louisiana micros, the fifth lowest among U.S. micros. Only 41.1 percent of the adults in the Opelousas area have high-school diplomas, the second lowest figure in the country.

Scores by Sections	
Climate/Environment	69
Diversions	22
Economics	30
Education	33
Sophistication	22
Health Care	36
Housing	86
Public Safety	46
Transportation	23
Urban Proximity	63
Total Points	430

464 **Ruston**

Points: 442
National Rank: 131 of 219
State Rank: 4 of 8

General Information
Components: Lincoln Parish
Area Population: 42,600
Central City Population: 21,440
Location: North-central Louisiana, west of Monroe
Nearest Metro Center: Monroe, 31 miles

Strengths: Thanks to the presence of Louisiana Tech and Grambling State University, the Ruston area easily amassed the state's highest score in the education section. Medical specialists are more easily available here than in any other state micro.

Weaknesses: Ruston is relatively isolated in northern Louisiana: it has the state's lowest urban proximity score. It is sometimes tough to find things to do: only nine U.S. micros have a lower concentration of amusement places.

Scores by Sections	
Climate/Environment	64
Diversions	30
Economics	26
Education	63
Sophistication	33
Health Care	26
Housing	81
Public Safety	43
Transportation	34
Urban Proximity	42
Total Points	442

MAINE

Augusta–Waterville

Points: 464
National Rank: 78 of 219
State Rank: 1 of 2

General Information
Components: Kennebec County
Area Population: 112,000
Central City Population: Augusta 20,640; Waterville 16,990
Location: South-central Maine, northeast of Lewiston
Nearest Metro Center: Lewiston, 30 miles

Strengths: Only eight U.S. micros have a better availability ratio of hospital beds than Augusta–Waterville does. This area made a strong showing in the sophistication section, thanks largely to excellent voter turnout.

Weaknesses: If you live in Augusta–Waterville, you had better like winter: nearly 80 inches of snow fall annually. Teacher pay is low by national standards. The area only grew by 1.9 percent in population between 1980 and 1986.

Scores by Sections	
Climate/Environment	50
Diversions	32
Economics	44
Education	43
Sophistication	51
Health Care	54
Housing	48
Public Safety	42
Transportation	33
Urban Proximity	67
Total Points	464

Biddeford

General Information
Components: York County
Area Population: 158,800
Central City Population: 20,700
Location: Extreme southern Maine, southwest of Portland
Nearest Metro Center: Portland, 18 miles

Strengths: Portland is just minutes away to the north, while Boston is only an hour and a half south of Biddeford. The total crime rate is low. The rate of income growth has been strong.

Weaknesses: Biddeford is far inferior to Maine's other micro, Augusta–Waterville, when it comes to health care. Availability figures for hospital beds and specialists are particularly small. Teacher pay falls well short of national norms.

Scores by Sections	
Climate/Environment	52
Diversions	38
Economics	44
Education	38
Sophistication	38
Health Care	19
Housing	45
Public Safety	47
Transportation	28
Urban Proximity	82
Total Points	431

MARYLAND

Salisbury

General Information
Components: Wicomico County
Area Population: 69,300
Central City Population: 17,740
Location: Extreme southeastern Maryland, on the Delmarva peninsula
Nearest Metro Center: Wilmington, Del., 102 miles

Strengths: Few U.S. micros can match Salisbury in strength of health care: only two have a higher ratio of specialists, only three have a better ratio of doctors. Salisbury has strong broadcast media, with three television and seven radio stations.

Weaknesses: Crime is a serious problem: Salisbury is among the seven worst micros in the country when it comes to both the total crime rate and the violent-crime rate. Washington and Baltimore are enticingly close, but difficult to reach on a limited choice of roads.

Scores by Sections	
Climate/Environment	60
Diversions	40
Economics	54
Education	46
Sophistication	50
Health Care	58
Housing	71
Public Safety	23
Transportation	35
Urban Proximity	59
Total Points	496

Adrian

Points: 447
National Rank: 122 of 219
State Rank: 3 of 5

General Information
Components: Lenawee County
Area Population: 88,800
Central City Population: 20,420
Location: Extreme southeastern Michigan, south-
west of Detroit
Nearest Metro Center: Jackson, 34 miles

Strengths: Detroit is only 68 miles by auto from
Adrian; the university metropolitan area of Ann
Arbor is even closer. Adrian has the highest per
capita income of Michigan's five micros; the rate
of income growth also leads the way.

Weaknesses: Adrian's total crime rate is the highest
in micropolitan Michigan. Availability ratios for
doctors, hospital beds, and specialists are all well
below national norms.

Scores by Sections	
Climate/Environment	59
Diversions	34
Economics	32
Education	57
Sophistication	30
Health Care	30
Housing	51
Public Safety	42
Transportation	27
Urban Proximity	85
Total Points	447

Marquette

Points: 401
National Rank: 197 of 219
State Rank: 5 of 5

General Information
Components: Marquette County
Area Population: 71,300
Central City Population: 21,370
Location: The north shore of Michigan's Upper
Peninsula, along Lake Superior
Nearest Metro Center: Green Bay, Wis., 175 miles

Strengths: Marquette's violent-crime rate is the
lowest among the state's five micros. The area
is second in the same group only to Traverse City
when it comes to health-care availability. Marquette's commitment to education is strong: 75.6
percent are high-school grads.

Weaknesses: Winters are only for the durable:
116.8 inches of snow annually and an average
nightly low of 4° in January. The Marquette area
is truly isolated: no micro east of the Mississippi
River is farther from its nearest metro center.

Scores by Sections	
Climate/Environment	41
Diversions	37
Economics	24
Education	68
Sophistication	42
Health Care	52
Housing	41
Public Safety	45
Transportation	33
Urban Proximity	18
Total Points	401

Mount Pleasant

General Information
Components: Isabella County
Area Population: 54,200
Central City Population: 21,890
Location: Central Michigan, northwest of Saginaw
Nearest Metro Center: Saginaw, 53 miles

Strengths: Central Michigan University helps Mount Pleasant to the highest education score in micropolitan Michigan. Property taxes are substantially lower than in the state's other micros. The total crime rate is the lowest in the same group.

Weaknesses: The Mount Pleasant area's per capita income is the lowest among Michigan's micros, as is its availability ratio for hospital beds. Its ratio of doctors is second worst.

Scores by Sections	
Climate/Environment	60
Diversions	34
Economics	29
Education	69
Sophistication	36
Health Care	29
Housing	56
Public Safety	38
Transportation	31
Urban Proximity	67
Total Points	449

Owosso

General Information
Components: Shiawassee County
Area Population: 69,000
Central City Population: 15,420
Location: South-central Michigan, west of Flint
Nearest Metro Center: Flint, 25 miles

Strengths: Flint is only 30 minutes from Owosso; much larger Detroit is just 82 miles away. Housing is less expensive in Owosso than in any of Michigan's four other micros. Per capita income is the second highest in the state.

Weaknesses: Shoppers find Owosso dull: only six U.S. micros have a lower concentration of retail outlets. Owosso trails Michigan's other micros when it comes to doctor availability and spending on parks. It also has a higher violent-crime rate.

Scores by Sections	
Climate/Environment	61
Diversions	23
Economics	27
Education	54
Sophistication	27
Health Care	24
Housing	55
Public Safety	34
Transportation	25
Urban Proximity	84
Total Points	414

468 Traverse City

Points: 486
National Rank: 40 of 219
State Rank: 1 of 5

General Information
Components: Grand Traverse County
Area Population: 59,200
Central City Population: 15,810
Location: Northwestern portion of Michigan's Lower Peninsula, north of Grand Rapids
Nearest Metro Center: Muskegon, 134 miles

Strengths: Traverse City has an excellent health-care system: only seven U.S. micros have a better ratio of doctors. Its tourism-based economy also provides diversions: Traverse City is among the national leaders in spending in restaurants and concentration of stores.

Weaknesses: Snow comes early and stays late: 96.3 inches a year. Getting to metropolitan areas is difficult, with the closest almost three hours away. Property taxes are substantial: only those of five U.S. micros are higher.

Scores by Sections	
Climate/Environment	48
Diversions	58
Economics	45
Education	61
Sophistication	53
Health Care	67
Housing	43
Public Safety	44
Transportation	34
Urban Proximity	33
Total Points	486

MINNESOTA

Faribault

Points: 501
National Rank: 19 of 219
State Rank: 2 of 3

General Information
Components: Rice County
Area Population: 47,500
Central City Population: 16,260
Location: Southeastern Minnesota, south of Minneapolis
Nearest Metro Center: Minneapolis, 48 miles

Strengths: Faribault is less than an hour from the Twin Cities by I-35: its urban proximity score was eleventh on the national list. Per capita income is the highest of Minnesota's three micros. Only Kinston, N.C., has a better ratio of hospital beds than Faribault.

Weaknesses: As with the other Minnesota micros, it gets brutally cold in Faribault. The average January low is 1°. Housing is more expensive than in the state's two other micros. The local news media are weak.

Scores by Sections	
Climate/Environment	51
Diversions	38
Economics	39
Education	68
Sophistication	34
Health Care	50
Housing	48
Public Safety	44
Transportation	38
Urban Proximity	91
Total Points	501

Mankato

Points: 523
National Rank: 9 of 219
State Rank: 1 of 3

General Information
Components: Blue Earth County
Area Population: 53,200
Central City Population: 29,870
Location: South-central Minnesota, southwest of Minneapolis
Nearest Metro Center: Minneapolis, 75 miles

Strengths: Mankato was among the nation's leaders in two sections. It was third in education, where Mankato State University was a big help. And it was second in transportation. Only Marshfield–Wisconsin Rapids, Wis., spends more per capita than Mankato on highways.

Weaknesses: Property taxes are higher in Mankato than in Minnesota's two other micros. Its rate of income growth is the lowest in the same group, as is its ratio of hospital beds.

Scores by Sections	
Climate/Environment	50
Diversions	50
Economics	46
Education	80
Sophistication	54
Health Care	38
Housing	40
Public Safety	47
Transportation	53
Urban Proximity	65
Total Points	523

Winona

Points: 459
National Rank: 90 of 219
State Rank: 3 of 3

General Information
Components: Winona County
Area Population: 46,300
Central City Population: 24,090
Location: Extreme southeastern Minnesota, on the Mississippi River
Nearest Metro Center: La Crosse, Wis., 29 miles

Strengths: Housing is less expensive in the Winona area than in Minnesota's two other micros. The local violent-crime rate is the lowest in the state, and among the lowest in the U.S.

Weaknesses: Winona's per capita income is the lowest in micropolitan Minnesota. It also trails the state's other two micros in the delivery of health-care services. The housing stock in Winona is much older than in Faribault or Mankato.

Scores by Sections	
Climate/Environment	51
Diversions	42
Economics	34
Education	63
Sophistication	43
Health Care	26
Housing	46
Public Safety	50
Transportation	45
Urban Proximity	59
Total Points	459

Columbus

Points: 432
National Rank: 147 of 219
State Rank: 5 of 8

General Information
Components: Lowndes County
Area Population: 60,200
Central City Population: 28,290
Location: East-central Mississippi, northeast of Jackson
Nearest Metro Center: Tuscaloosa, Ala., 61 miles

Strengths: Housing in the Columbus area is more expensive than in any other Mississippi micro, but that shouldn't obscure the fact that it is still very reasonable. Property taxes are the lightest in micropolitan Mississippi. The violent-crime rate is low.

Weaknesses: Only seven U.S. micros have lower teacher pay. Voter turnout is the lowest among Mississippi's micros. No other state micro spends less per capita to maintain its roads than Columbus.

Scores by Sections	
Climate/Environment	57
Diversions	33
Economics	35
Education	24
Sophistication	38
Health Care	49
Housing	81
Public Safety	42
Transportation	29
Urban Proximity	44
Total Points	432

Greenville

Points: 391
National Rank: 204 of 219
State Rank: 8 of 8

General Information
Components: Washington County
Area Population: 70,700
Central City Population: 40,000
Location: West-central Mississippi, on the Mississippi River
Nearest Metro Center: Pine Bluff, Ark., 102 miles

Strengths: Housing in Greenville is easily the least expensive in what is a low-priced state. Greenville is a communications center, with two television and five radio stations.

Weaknesses: Only two U.S. micros received lower total scores in the economics section. Per capita income is a big reason, with Greenville 216th of 219 areas. The Greenville area also scored badly in the education section, surpassing just five U.S. micros.

Scores by Sections	
Climate/Environment	64
Diversions	30
Economics	19
Education	19
Sophistication	34
Health Care	39
Housing	77
Public Safety	38
Transportation	39
Urban Proximity	32
Total Points	391

Greenwood

General Information
Components: Leflore County
Area Population: 41,300
Central City Population: 20,530
Location: Central Mississippi, north of Jackson
Nearest Metro Center: Jackson, 98 miles

Strengths: No Mississippi micro spends more per capita on education than Greenwood, nor does any pay its teachers higher wages, although Greenwood's scale is still poor in a national sense. Housing is less expensive here than in five of the state's other micros.

Weaknesses: Greenwood ranks dead last among the nation's micros in the economics section. Its per capita income is the lowest in micropolitan Mississippi, and is higher than only Gallup, N.Mex., nationally. Only 44.7 percent of Greenwood's adults graduated from high school.

Scores by Sections	
Climate/Environment	67
Diversions	39
Economics	16
Education	31
Sophistication	31
Health Care	35
Housing	71
Public Safety	41
Transportation	39
Urban Proximity	34
Total Points	404

Hattiesburg

General Information
Components: Forrest County
Area Population: 68,300
Central City Population: 40,740
Location: Southeastern Mississippi, southeast of Jackson
Nearest Metro Center: Biloxi, 81 miles

Strengths: Hattiesburg is easily the highest rated micro in Mississippi, leading the state in six of the ten sections. It leads the entire country in health care, placing among the best six U.S. micros in both doctor and specialist availability. Housing is inexpensive.

Weaknesses: Hattiesburg's per capita income is just middle-of-the-pack in micropolitan Mississippi. Only Columbus spends less than Hattiesburg among state micros for highway maintenance.

Scores by Sections	
Climate/Environment	63
Diversions	47
Economics	37
Education	39
Sophistication	48
Health Care	82
Housing	78
Public Safety	50
Transportation	37
Urban Proximity	46
Total Points	527

472 Laurel

Points: 420
National Rank: 169 of 219
State Rank: 6 of 8

General Information
Components: Jones County
Area Population: 63,000
Central City Population: 20,630
Location: Southeastern Mississippi, southeast of Jackson
Nearest Metro Center: Jackson, 85 miles

Strengths: The Laurel area received the highest score of any Mississippi micro in the fiercely competitive housing section. Laurel's violent-crime rate is the lowest in micropolitan Mississippi.

Weaknesses: Strangely, despite Laurel's success in avoiding violent crime, its total crime rate is the highest among the state's micros. Laurel has the smallest representation of college graduates of any Mississippi micro: just 10.1 percent of its adults qualify.

Scores by Sections	
Climate/Environment	64
Diversions	32
Economics	30
Education	23
Sophistication	26
Health Care	40
Housing	82
Public Safety	47
Transportation	33
Urban Proximity	43
Total Points	420

Meridian

Points: 466
National Rank: 71 of 219
State Rank: 2 of 8

General Information
Components: Lauderdale County
Area Population: 76,900
Central City Population: 42,970
Location: East-central Mississippi, east of Jackson
Nearest Metro Center: Jackson, 93 miles

Strengths: Meridian's per capita income is the second highest in micropolitan Mississippi; its rate of income growth is the highest. Meridian has the second strongest concentration of broadcast outlets of any U.S. micro: four TV stations, seven radio.

Weaknesses: No Mississippi micro spends less per capita on education than the Meridian area does. Teacher pay is among the lowest in the country. Metropolitan amenities are a long drive away.

Scores by Sections	
Climate/Environment	63
Diversions	37
Economics	37
Education	24
Sophistication	47
Health Care	55
Housing	75
Public Safety	48
Transportation	46
Urban Proximity	34
Total Points	466

Tupelo

General Information

Components: Lee County
Area Population: 62,100
Central City Population: 25,830
Location: Northeastern Mississippi, southeast of Memphis, Tenn.
Nearest Metro Center: Florence, Ala., 78 miles

Strengths: The Tupelo area leads all Mississippi micros in the economics section. While most of the state's micros are gaining population slowly, if at all, Tupelo was up 8.8 percent from 1980 to 1986. The total crime rate is the lowest among Mississippi micros.

Weaknesses: Teacher pay is among the lowest in the country: Tupelo ranks 215th out of 219 U.S. micros. Getting around is not easy: the highway index ranks Tupelo's road system as one of the three worst in micropolitan Mississippi.

Scores by Sections	
Climate/Environment	63
Diversions	39
Economics	43
Education	23
Sophistication	42
Health Care	53
Housing	78
Public Safety	50
Transportation	30
Urban Proximity	45
Total Points	466

Vicksburg

General Information

Components: Warren County
Area Population: 51,400
Central City Population: 26,020
Location: Western Mississippi, west of Jackson
Nearest Metro Center: Jackson, 44 miles

Strengths: Vicksburg's per capita income is the highest among the state's micros. The area has 22 fewer extreme-temperature days annually than any other Mississippi micro. Vicksburg's access to commercial jet traffic is better than that of any other U.S. micro.

Weaknesses: Only Hinesville, Ga., pays its teachers less than Vicksburg does. The violent-crime rate is the state's second highest. No other state micro has a weaker concentration of amusement places than Vicksburg.

Scores by Sections	
Climate/Environment	69
Diversions	37
Economics	34
Education	27
Sophistication	37
Health Care	41
Housing	73
Public Safety	49
Transportation	38
Urban Proximity	44
Total Points	449

Cape Girardeau

Points: 503
National Rank: 17 of 219
State Rank: 1 of 3

General Information
Components: Cape Girardeau County
Area Population: 61,300
Central City Population: 34,360
Location: Southeastern Missouri, on the Mississippi River
Nearest Metro Center: Saint Louis, 113 miles

Strengths: The Cape Girardeau area has the best availability ratios of doctors and medical specialists in micropolitan Missouri. It also has the best concentrations of retail outlets and amusement places among the state's three micros.

Weaknesses: The total crime rate and violent-crime rate in Cape Girardeau are both higher than the figures for Missouri's two other micros. Only seven U.S. micros spend less per capita on education than Cape Girardeau does.

Scores by Sections	
Climate/Environment	58
Diversions	46
Economics	50
Education	46
Sophistication	45
Health Care	52
Housing	66
Public Safety	43
Transportation	31
Urban Proximity	66
Total Points	503

Jefferson City

Points: 481
National Rank: 47 of 219
State Rank: 2 of 3

General Information
Components: Cole County
Area Population: 63,400
Central City Population: 36,210
Location: Central Missouri, south of Columbia
Nearest Metro Center: Columbia, 33 miles

Strengths: Jefferson City's per capita income is substantially larger than that of either of Missouri's two other micros. The area has micropolitan Missouri's highest percentage of high-school graduates and lowest total crime rate.

Weaknesses: Missouri's capital city falls well below the national norm for spending on education. Housing costs and property taxes exceed the figures in the state's other micros. Jefferson City lacks easy access to an interstate highway.

Scores by Sections	
Climate/Environment	55
Diversions	33
Economics	57
Education	39
Sophistication	47
Health Care	44
Housing	63
Public Safety	48
Transportation	30
Urban Proximity	65
Total Points	481

Sikeston

General Information
Components: Scott County
Area Population: 40,200
Central City Population: 17,610
Location: Extreme southeastern Missouri, south-west of Cairo, Ill.
Nearest Metro Center: Memphis, Tenn., 140 miles

Strengths: Housing in Sikeston is much less expensive than it is in Missouri's two other micros; property taxes are also lower. Two interstates run within miles of Sikeston, giving it the best highway index in micropolitan Missouri.

Weaknesses: Per capita income in Sikeston is much lower than the figures for the state's other micros. Only 51.4 percent of Sikeston's adults have earned high-school diplomas. Sikeston trails the other Missouri micros in availability of health services.

Scores by Sections	
Climate/Environment	60
Diversions	32
Economics	26
Education	25
Sophistication	26
Health Care	25
Housing	74
Public Safety	45
Transportation	35
Urban Proximity	58
Total Points	406

MONTANA

Bozeman

General Information
Components: Gallatin County
Area Population: 47,800
Central City Population: 23,490
Location: South-central Montana, west of Billings
Nearest Metro Center: Billings, 140 miles

Strengths: Bozeman is a shopper's paradise: only Myrtle Beach, S.C., has a greater concentration of retail outlets. Montana State University contributes to an outstanding educational climate. Just five U.S. micros have lower violent-crime rates than Bozeman.

Weaknesses: It takes a hardy person to withstand Bozeman's climate. The temperature is above 90° or below 32° an average of 241 days a year, the highest total in the country. Bozeman tied for last place nationally in the housing section, third lowest in urban proximity.

Scores by Sections	
Climate/Environment	41
Diversions	67
Economics	44
Education	73
Sophistication	60
Health Care	41
Housing	32
Public Safety	44
Transportation	44
Urban Proximity	9
Total Points	455

Helena

Points: 458
National Rank: 92 of 219
State Rank: 2 of 3

General Information

Components: Lewis and Clark County
Area Population: 46,400
Central City Population: 24,670
Location: West-central Montana, southwest of Great Falls
Nearest Metro Center: Great Falls, 91 miles

Strengths: Helena's per capita income is the highest in micropolitan Montana. Housing is substantially less expensive than in the state's two other micros. Helena also has the state's most favorable availability ratio of hospital beds.

Weaknesses: Montana's capital is remote from metropolitan America. Seattle is the closest sports and arts center: 593 miles from Helena. Property taxes are high. Winters are cold: January's average low is 8°.

Scores by Sections	
Climate/Environment	51
Diversions	62
Economics	40
Education	71
Sophistication	55
Health Care	44
Housing	37
Public Safety	43
Transportation	43
Urban Proximity	12
Total Points	458

Missoula

Points: 480
National Rank: 49 of 219
State Rank: 1 of 3

General Information

Components: Missoula County
Area Population: 77,700
Central City Population: 33,960
Location: Extreme western Montana, near the Idaho line
Nearest Metro Center: Great Falls, 166 miles

Strengths: The University of Montana is a major local influence, helping Missoula earn second place nationally in the sophistication section. Missoula has the state's best ratios of doctors and specialists. Only six U.S. micros have better jet service.

Weaknesses: High purchase prices, heavy taxation, large heating bills: these are all reasons Missoula tied for last place nationally in housing. Missoula is isolated: only eight U.S. micros are further from the nearest metro center.

Scores by Sections	
Climate/Environment	51
Diversions	61
Economics	36
Education	66
Sophistication	69
Health Care	57
Housing	32
Public Safety	42
Transportation	53
Urban Proximity	13
Total Points	480

Grand Island

Points: 435
National Rank: 143 of 219
State Rank: 1 of 1

General Information

Components: Hall County
Area Population: 48,900
Central City Population: 39,100
Location: Central Nebraska, west of Lincoln
Nearest Metro Center: Lincoln, 98 miles

Strengths: Grand Island is the place for anyone who wants to live close to work: the average commuting time of 12 minutes is the lowest in micropolitan America. Grand Island is tenth in the country in concentration of retail outlets.

Weaknesses: A combination of 108 waste sites being investigated and a high number of extreme-temperature days puts Grand Island in last place nationally in the climate/environment section. Metropolitan centers are a long drive away.

Scores by Sections	
Climate/Environment	31
Diversions	59
Economics	47
Education	49
Sophistication	47
Health Care	38
Housing	44
Public Safety	37
Transportation	47
Urban Proximity	36
Total Points	435

NEVADA

Carson City

Points: 501
National Rank: 19 of 219
State Rank: 1 of 1

General Information

Components: Carson City independent city
Area Population: 36,900
Central City Population: 36,900
Location: Extreme west-central Nevada, south of Reno
Nearest Metro Center: Reno, 32 miles

Strengths: Carson City's housing stock is among the newest in micropolitan America. Property taxes are relatively low. Carson City ranks third among U.S. micros in concentration of amusement places. Per capita income is tenth in the entire nation.

Weaknesses: Only San Luis Obispo–Atascadero, Calif., has more expensive housing than Carson City among U.S. micros. The availability ratio of hospital beds in Nevada's capital is low. The local news media have little clout.

Scores by Sections	
Climate/Environment	53
Diversions	54
Economics	53
Education	51
Sophistication	46
Health Care	46
Housing	60
Public Safety	53
Transportation	38
Urban Proximity	47
Total Points	501

Concord

General Information
Components: Merrimack County
Area Population: 109,700
Central City Population: 32,770
Location: Southern New Hampshire, north of Manchester
Nearest Metro Center: Manchester, 20 miles

Strengths: Not only is Manchester just 20 miles down the turnpike from Concord, but the brighter lights of Boston are only 58 miles beyond that. Only six U.S. micros have higher per capita incomes than Concord. Its crime rates are the lowest among New Hampshire micros.

Weaknesses: Concord spends the least per capita on education among New Hampshire micros. Housing here is slightly more expensive than elsewhere in the state. Property taxes are very high by national standards.

Scores by Sections	
Climate/Environment	38
Diversions	38
Economics	55
Education	45
Sophistication	44
Health Care	45
Housing	37
Public Safety	56
Transportation	45
Urban Proximity	89
Total Points	492

Keene

General Information
Components: Cheshire County
Area Population: 66,900
Central City Population: 22,370
Location: Extreme southwestern New Hampshire, west of Manchester
Nearest Metro Center: Fitchburg, Mass., 37 miles

Strengths: Even using slower state highways, one can get from Keene to Boston in two hours or less. Keene outspends the other two state micros when it comes to education. Housing in Keene is the least expensive in micropolitan New Hampshire.

Weaknesses: Tucked in a corner of New Hampshire without any expressways, Keene has a low highway index. Keene has lower availability ratios of doctors and specialists than the other state micros. Only three U.S. micros have higher property taxes.

Scores by Sections	
Climate/Environment	44
Diversions	34
Economics	48
Education	52
Sophistication	46
Health Care	34
Housing	39
Public Safety	47
Transportation	32
Urban Proximity	87
Total Points	463

Laconia

General Information
Components: Belknap County
Area Population: 47,100
Central City Population: 16,540
Location: Central New Hampshire, north of Manchester
Nearest Metro Center: Manchester, 46 miles

Strengths: Laconia is a lake-resort community that offers plenty of diversions, with high concentrations of retail stores and amusement places. Per capita income is substantial on a national scale. Boston is 103 miles away.

Weaknesses: Only Rock Springs, Wyo., has a higher property-tax rate than Laconia does. The total crime rate and violent-crime rate are the highest in micropolitan New Hampshire. Laconia's ratio of hospital beds is the lowest in the state.

Scores by Sections	
Climate/Environment	42
Diversions	62
Economics	56
Education	35
Sophistication	38
Health Care	34
Housing	36
Public Safety	57
Transportation	37
Urban Proximity	76
Total Points	473

NEW MEXICO

Alamogordo

General Information
Components: Otero County
Area Population: 50,200
Central City Population: 27,930
Location: South-central New Mexico, northeast of Las Cruces
Nearest Metro Center: Las Cruces, 69 miles

Strengths: Alamogordo's residents have the highest educational attainment in micropolitan New Mexico: 77.1 percent of the adults are high-school graduates. Alamogordo ranks fifth nationally in the housing section.

Weaknesses: Alamogordo does poorly in the health care section; its ratio of doctor availability is the lowest among New Mexico micros. Per capita income ranks in the state's bottom half. There are no interstate highways within 60 miles.

Scores by Sections	
Climate/Environment	53
Diversions	38
Economics	34
Education	53
Sophistication	37
Health Care	22
Housing	85
Public Safety	43
Transportation	29
Urban Proximity	42
Total Points	436

480 Carlsbad

Points: 446
National Rank: 124 of 219
State Rank: 3 of 8

General Information
Components: Eddy County
Area Population: 52,400
Central City Population: 27,850
Location: Extreme southeastern New Mexico, east of Las Cruces
Nearest Metro Center: Odessa, Tex., 142 miles

Strengths: One of the strongest public-transit systems in micropolitan America lands Carlsbad fourth place nationally in the transportation section. Only Roswell has less expensive housing than Carlsbad among New Mexico micros.

Weaknesses: Carlsbad's availability figures for doctors, hospital beds, and medical specialists are all well below national norms. Carlsbad is isolated, even for a vast state such as New Mexico: only two state micros are farther from a metro center.

Scores by Sections	
Climate/Environment	52
Diversions	45
Economics	41
Education	38
Sophistication	37
Health Care	26
Housing	78
Public Safety	46
Transportation	52
Urban Proximity	31
Total Points	446

Clovis

Points: 428
National Rank: 156 of 219
State Rank: 5 of 8

General Information
Components: Curry County
Area Population: 43,400
Central City Population: 33,780
Location: Extreme east-central New Mexico, near the Texas line
Nearest Metro Center: Lubbock, Tex., 102 miles

Strengths: Property taxes in Clovis are the lowest in micropolitan New Mexico, sixth lowest in the U.S. The total crime rate is the second lowest in the state, while Clovis's percentage of high-school graduates is surpassed in the state only by Alamogordo.

Weaknesses: Clovis has the same problem that afflicts most of New Mexico's micros: its health-care system is not up to par. It also shares isolation with its state counterparts: the nearest sports and arts center is Dallas, 418 miles to the east.

Scores by Sections	
Climate/Environment	55
Diversions	44
Economics	34
Education	46
Sophistication	40
Health Care	25
Housing	83
Public Safety	46
Transportation	35
Urban Proximity	20
Total Points	428

Farmington

General Information

Components: San Juan County
Area Population: 92,000
Central City Population: 39,050
Location: Extreme northwestern New Mexico, northwest of Santa Fe
Nearest Metro Center: Albuquerque, 181 miles

Strengths: Farmington's score in the economics section is boosted by high worker productivity, as measured by value added by manufacture. Farmington is well above the national average for spending on education. It is the only state micro served by major airlines.

Weaknesses: The weather can be tough: only nine U.S. micros have a larger annual average of extreme-temperature days. Farmington also has the standard difficulties in micropolitan New Mexico: below-average health care and isolation.

Scores by Sections	
Climate/Environment	49
Diversions	41
Economics	49
Education	41
Sophistication	36
Health Care	24
Housing	62
Public Safety	51
Transportation	33
Urban Proximity	18
Total Points	404

Gallup

Points: 367
National Rank: 216 of 219
State Rank: 7 of 8

General Information

Components: McKinley County
Area Population: 65,800
Central City Population: 22,470
Location: Extreme western New Mexico, near the Arizona line
Nearest Metro Center: Albuquerque, 138 miles

Strengths: Only five U.S. micros spend more per capita on their schools than Gallup does. Worker productivity is high. Gallup's road system, as measured by the highway index, is better than any New Mexico micro but Roswell.

Weaknesses: Poverty is a real problem in Gallup: both its per capita income and rate of income growth are the lowest in micropolitan America. The total crime rate is the fifth worst in the U.S. The school dropout rate is the state's worst.

Scores by Sections	
Climate/Environment	51
Diversions	39
Economics	39
Education	32
Sophistication	23
Health Care	32
Housing	66
Public Safety	30
Transportation	29
Urban Proximity	26
Total Points	367

482 Hobbs

General Information
Components: Lea County
Area Population: 64,900
Central City Population: 34,870
Location: Extreme southeastern New Mexico, near the Texas line
Nearest Metro Center: Odessa, Tex., 86 miles

Strengths: The Hobbs area has the highest per capita income of any New Mexico micro. Housing is inexpensive, and it takes less heating and cooling energy, as indicated by degree days, than any other place in micropolitan New Mexico.

Weaknesses: Hobbs does not offer easy access to metropolitan amenities: only five U.S. micros received lower scores in the urban proximity section. Only Alamogordo has a less favorable situation among state micros when it comes to doctor availability.

Scores by Sections	
Climate/Environment	56
Diversions	48
Economics	50
Education	40
Sophistication	35
Health Care	26
Housing	80
Public Safety	59
Transportation	40
Urban Proximity	13
Total Points	447

Rio Rancho

General Information
Components: Sandoval County
Area Population: 51,100
Central City Population: 26,520
Location: Central New Mexico, north of Albuquerque
Nearest Metro Center: Albuquerque, 11 miles

Strengths: The Rio Rancho area is substantially safer than New Mexico's other micros: both its total crime rate and violent-crime rate are the lowest in the group. Per capita income is the second highest in micropolitan New Mexico. Albuquerque is very close.

Weaknesses: Perhaps Albuquerque is too close: Rio Rancho relies on many of its services, rather than developing its own. That explains Rio Rancho's poor scores in sections such as diversions, health care, and transportation. The latter score was the nation's worst.

Scores by Sections	
Climate/Environment	48
Diversions	21
Economics	49
Education	40
Sophistication	24
Health Care	17
Housing	71
Public Safety	48
Transportation	13
Urban Proximity	35
Total Points	366

Roswell

General Information
Components: Chaves County
Area Population: 56,700
Central City Population: 44,110
Location: Southeastern New Mexico, northeast of Las Cruces
Nearest Metro Center: Lubbock, Tex., 173 miles

Strengths: Housing is less expensive in the Roswell area than anywhere else in micropolitan New Mexico. Roswell's health-care system is rated the best in the same group. The local array of broadcast outlets is the second strongest among U.S. micros: four TV stations, seven radio.

Weaknesses: For diehard urban dwellers, Roswell would be the end of the world: no micro in the continental U.S. received a lower score in the urban proximity section. Dallas, the closest sports and arts center, is 487 miles beyond the horizon.

Scores by Sections	
Climate/Environment	55
Diversions	47
Economics	43
Education	45
Sophistication	54
Health Care	40
Housing	82
Public Safety	48
Transportation	46
Urban Proximity	8
Total Points	468

NEW YORK

Auburn

General Information
Components: Cayuga County
Area Population: 79,900
Central City Population: 31,350
Location: Central New York, southwest of Syracuse
Nearest Metro Center: Syracuse, 27 miles

Strengths: The streets of Auburn are definitely safe: its violent-crime rate is very low. Housing is inexpensive by national standards. Syracuse is 30 minutes to the east; Rochester is less than one and a half hours to the west.

Weaknesses: Auburn has micropolitan New York's lowest concentrations of retail outlets and amusement places. No state micro has a less favorable ratio of doctor availability than Auburn. Watch out for the snow: almost 110 inches in an average winter.

Scores by Sections	
Climate/Environment	53
Diversions	28
Economics	38
Education	52
Sophistication	29
Health Care	26
Housing	49
Public Safety	51
Transportation	42
Urban Proximity	65
Total Points	433

484 Batavia

General Information
Components: Genesee County
Area Population: 58,800
Central City Population: 15,930
Location: Western New York, east of Buffalo
Nearest Metro Center: Rochester, 34 miles

Strengths: The Batavia area had the nation's third best score in the urban proximity section. Two of America's 40 largest metro areas, Buffalo and Rochester, are within 36 miles. Batavia's percentage of high-school graduates is second only to Ithaca among New York micros.

Weaknesses: Batavia's annual snowfall averages a hefty 93.4 inches. Only Auburn has a worse ratio of doctors to residents among New York micros. Outsiders are unusual: more than 89 percent of the residents of the Batavia area were born in New York.

Scores by Sections	
Climate/Environment	50
Diversions	37
Economics	33
Education	65
Sophistication	29
Health Care	32
Housing	52
Public Safety	53
Transportation	44
Urban Proximity	94
Total Points	489

Cortland

General Information
Components: Cortland County
Area Population: 47,400
Central City Population: 19,000
Location: Central New York, south of Syracuse
Nearest Metro Center: Syracuse, 34 miles

Strengths: Cortland, site of a campus of the State University of New York, has New York's second highest score in the education section. Cortland residents like to eat out: their area beats all other New York micros when it comes to spending at restaurants.

Weaknesses: Only Olean has a lower per capita income than Cortland in micropolitan New York. Figures for the availability of doctors, hospital beds, and medical specialists are all below national norms.

Scores by Sections	
Climate/Environment	51
Diversions	40
Economics	29
Education	69
Sophistication	34
Health Care	29
Housing	46
Public Safety	46
Transportation	44
Urban Proximity	60
Total Points	448

Gloversville

Points: 385
National Rank: 207 of 219
State Rank: 10 of 10

General Information
Components: Fulton County
Area Population: 54,600
Central City Population: 16,750
Location: Eastern New York, northwest of Albany
Nearest Metro Center: Albany, 50 miles

Strengths: Housing in the Gloversville area is among the least expensive in micropolitan New York. Only Plattsburgh has lower property taxes than Gloversville among the same group.

Weaknesses: No other U.S. micro has poorer connections to the outside world: Gloversville ranks dead last in the highway index. Gloversville generally has trouble keeping up with the rest of New York's .micros, finishing last in the state in six of ten sections.

Scores by Sections	
Climate/Environment	47
Diversions	25
Economics	31
Education	51
Sophistication	25
Health Care	23
Housing	49
Public Safety	48
Transportation	28
Urban Proximity	58
Total Points	385

Ithaca

Points: 496
National Rank: 23 of 219
State Rank: 1 of 10

General Information
Components: Tompkins County
Area Population: 87,600
Central City Population: 26,480
Location: South-central New York, northeast of Elmira
Nearest Metro Center: Elmira, 34 miles

Strengths: Cornell University is the only Ivy League school based in a U.S. micro. Its presence accounts for the fact that Ithaca received the nation's top score in the education section. No other New York micro has better ratios of doctors and medical specialists.

Weaknesses: Housing is much more expensive in Ithaca than anywhere else in micropolitan New York. Ithaca's total crime rate is much higher than the figures for the state's other micros. In New York, only Gloversville has a lower highway index than Ithaca.

Scores by Sections	
Climate/Environment	54
Diversions	36
Economics	40
Education	83
Sophistication	56
Health Care	38
Housing	45
Public Safety	40
Transportation	42
Urban Proximity	62
Total Points	496

486 Jamestown

Points: 478
National Rank: 52 of 219
State Rank: 4 of 10

General Information
Components: Chautauqua County
Area Population: 143,100
Central City Population: 34,710
Location: Extreme southwestern New York, southwest of Buffalo
Nearest Metro Center: Erie, Pa., 54 miles

Strengths: The arts, retail, and sports center of Buffalo is just one and a half hours by car from Jamestown; Erie, Pa., is about an hour away. Housing in the Jamestown area is inexpensive. The area's violent-crime rate is very low.

Weaknesses: Jamestown averages 142.4 inches of snow annually. Only two U.S. micros have older housing stocks: 60.7 percent of the Jamestown area's houses predate World War II, as of last count.

Scores by Sections	
Climate/Environment	52
Diversions	38
Economics	33
Education	62
Sophistication	37
Health Care	29
Housing	44
Public Safety	54
Transportation	47
Urban Proximity	82
Total Points	478

Kingston

Points: 476
National Rank: 54 of 219
State Rank: 5 of 10

General Information
Components: Ulster County
Area Population: 164,200
Central City Population: 24,170
Location: Southeastern New York, northwest of Poughkeepsie
Nearest Metro Center: Poughkeepsie, 19 miles

Strengths: Kingston leads micropolitan New York in per capita income and teacher pay. New York City is only 104 miles away. Kingston gets 42.6 inches of snow a year, which may seem like a lot to some people, but is easily the smallest total among New York micros.

Weaknesses: Crime and taxes are the biggest concerns in Kingston. The area's violent-crime rate is more than double the figure for any other micro in the state. Only four U.S. micros have higher property taxes than Kingston does.

Scores by Sections	
Climate/Environment	49
Diversions	35
Economics	44
Education	66
Sophistication	36
Health Care	32
Housing	44
Public Safety	45
Transportation	40
Urban Proximity	85
Total Points	476

Olean

General Information
Components: Cattaraugus County
Area Population: 85,300
Central City Population: 17,430
Location: Southwestern New York, southeast of Buffalo
Nearest Metro Center: Buffalo, 73 miles

Strengths: Olean is safe beyond question: its violent-crime rate is the lowest in micropolitan America. Only two U.S. micros spend more per capita on education than Olean. Housing is more inexpensive here than in any other New York micro.

Weaknesses: Winters are white: 165.5 inches of snow annually. Olean's per capita income is the lowest in micropolitan New York. There is no expressway toward Buffalo, the nearest metro.

Scores by Sections	
Climate/Environment	47
Diversions	40
Economics	29
Education	60
Sophistication	33
Health Care	34
Housing	51
Public Safety	47
Transportation	43
Urban Proximity	83
Total Points	467

Plattsburgh

General Information
Components: Clinton County
Area Population: 81,200
Central City Population: 20,800
Location: Extreme northeastern New York, on Lake Champlain
Nearest Metro Center: Burlington, Vt., 32 miles

Strengths: Plattsburgh's total crime rate is the lowest in micropolitan New York. Property taxes, while still a bit higher than the national average, are less than in any other state micro. Plattsburgh's rate of income growth leads the state.

Weaknesses: It gets cold and snowy on the shores of Lake Champlain: an average January low of 8° and 78.2 inches of snow a year. Plattsburgh doesn't offer much for shoppers with its low concentration of retail outlets.

Scores by Sections	
Climate/Environment	55
Diversions	35
Economics	53
Education	63
Sophistication	42
Health Care	39
Housing	52
Public Safety	46
Transportation	40
Urban Proximity	65
Total Points	490

488 Watertown

Points: 465
National Rank: 74 of 219
State Rank: 7 of 10

General Information
Components: Jefferson County
Area Population: 90,600
Central City Population: 27,040
Location: North-central New York, north of Syracuse
Nearest Metro Center: Syracuse, 74 miles

Strengths: The Watertown area ranks fourth among all U.S. micros when it comes to per capita spending on education. Watertown has micropolitan New York's best array of broadcast outlets and its best ratio of available hospital beds.

Weaknesses: The housing stock in Watertown is old: only Pottsville, Pa., has a higher percentage of units built before 1940. Annual snowfall is 101.3 inches. Watertown is isolated near the Canadian border: it has New York's lowest urban proximity score.

Scores by Sections	
Climate/Environment	51
Diversions	42
Economics	41
Education	58
Sophistication	45
Health Care	37
Housing	46
Public Safety	53
Transportation	49
Urban Proximity	43
Total Points	465

NORTH CAROLINA

Eden

Points: 387
National Rank: 205 of 219
State Rank: 11 of 12

General Information
Components: Rockingham County
Area Population: 85,500
Central City Population: 15,590
Location: Extreme north-central North Carolina, north of Greensboro
Nearest Metro Center: Danville, Va., 26 miles

Strengths: Housing in Eden is very inexpensive on the national scale. Eden's total crime rate is the third lowest in micropolitan North Carolina.

Weaknesses: Eden scored 25 or fewer points in five of ten sections. Its showing in the education section was the second lowest nationally; its sophistication score took the same low position. Eden's health-care total was better than only eight U.S. micros.

Scores by Sections	
Climate/Environment	69
Diversions	25
Economics	38
Education	16
Sophistication	19
Health Care	18
Housing	71
Public Safety	44
Transportation	25
Urban Proximity	62
Total Points	387

Goldsboro

General Information
Components: Wayne County
Area Population: 97,900
Central City Population: 34,990
Location: East-central North Carolina, southeast of Raleigh
Nearest Metro Center: Raleigh, 51 miles

Strengths: Goldsboro's property taxes are among the lowest in micropolitan North Carolina. The area's availability ratio of hospital beds is excellent.

Weaknesses: Having nine waste sites under investigation or cleanup, Goldsboro received the state's lowest score in the climate/environment section. No North Carolina micro spends less on its parks than Goldsboro does.

Scores by Sections	
Climate/Environment	50
Diversions	25
Economics	30
Education	36
Sophistication	26
Health Care	51
Housing	79
Public Safety	35
Transportation	23
Urban Proximity	59
Total Points	414

Greenville

Points: 483
National Rank: 41 of 219
State Rank: 1 of 12

General Information
Components: Pitt County
Area Population: 98,000
Central City Population: 38,740
Location: East-central North Carolina, east of Raleigh
Nearest Metro Center: Jacksonville, 74 miles

Strengths: Greenville owns North Carolina's highest score in the education section, thanks largely to East Carolina University. The Greenville area ranks second in the nation in doctor availability, and also leads state micros in the ratio of medical specialists.

Weaknesses: The average house costs more in Greenville than in any other North Carolina micro. Despite having the state's best education score, Greenville pays its teachers less than any other state micro.

Scores by Sections	
Climate/Environment	67
Diversions	37
Economics	46
Education	47
Sophistication	40
Health Care	58
Housing	73
Public Safety	38
Transportation	26
Urban Proximity	51
Total Points	483

490

Havelock–New Bern

Points: 449
National Rank: 111 of 219
State Rank: 3 of 12

General Information
Components: Craven County
Area Population: 81,100
Central City Population: Havelock 23,560; New Bern 19,010
Location: Extreme east-central North Carolina, near the Atlantic coast
Nearest Metro Center: Jacksonville, 50 miles

Strengths: The moderating influence of the Atlantic gives Havelock–New Bern the mildest climate in micropolitan North Carolina: it has 21 fewer extreme-temperature days than anyone else. Property taxes are the state's lowest.

Weaknesses: No North Carolina micro spends less per capita on education than Havelock–New Bern does. Housing is second highest in the state in total cost. Havelock–New Bern has the worst road system among state micros, according to the highway index.

Scores by Sections	
Climate/Environment	72
Diversions	29
Economics	43
Education	29
Sophistication	32
Health Care	54
Housing	81
Public Safety	40
Transportation	26
Urban Proximity	43
Total Points	449

Kinston

Points: 449
National Rank: 111 of 219
State Rank: 3 of 12

General Information
Components: Lenoir County
Area Population: 60,100
Central City Population: 25,050
Location: East-central North Carolina, southeast of Raleigh
Nearest Metro Center: Jacksonville, 43 miles

Strengths: Kinston leads micropolitan America in the ratio of hospital beds to residents. It offers the highest concentration of amusement places and the best access to major airlines of any North Carolina micro.

Weaknesses: Kinston's per capita income is one of the lowest in the state; its rate of income growth is the lowest. Both Kinston's total crime rate and its violent-crime rate are among the highest in micropolitan North Carolina.

Scores by Sections	
Climate/Environment	66
Diversions	38
Economics	30
Education	34
Sophistication	28
Health Care	63
Housing	76
Public Safety	37
Transportation	25
Urban Proximity	52
Total Points	449

Lumberton

General Information
Components: Robeson County
Area Population: 106,000
Central City Population: 19,130
Location: Southeastern North Carolina, south of Fayetteville
Nearest Metro Center: Fayetteville, 34 miles

Strengths: Housing is extremely reasonable in the Lumberton area: only seven U.S. micros have median prices that are lower. Only Roanoke Rapids spends more per capita on education among North Carolina micros than Lumberton does.

Weaknesses: Lumberton's inadequacies are broad-based: the area received fewer than 30 points in seven of ten sections. It ranks last in the nation in the sophistication section. Per capita income is the lowest among North Carolina micros, the violent-crime rate the highest.

Scores by Sections	
Climate/Environment	69
Diversions	24
Economics	22
Education	29
Sophistication	17
Health Care	22
Housing	85
Public Safety	25
Transportation	24
Urban Proximity	47
Total Points	364

Roanoke Rapids

General Information
Components: Halifax County
Area Population: 55,800
Central City Population: 15,100
Location: Northeastern North Carolina, northeast of Raleigh
Nearest Metro Center: Raleigh, 78 miles

Strengths: Roanoke Rapids has the least expensive housing among North Carolina micros, the sixth least expensive among U.S. micros. The violent-crime rate is the state's lowest. Roanoke Rapids leads North Carolina's micros in per capita spending on education.

Weaknesses: Only 42.6 percent of the adults in Roanoke Rapids have high-school diplomas, the fourth worst figure among U.S. micros. Per capita income ranks 211th in the country. Eden is the only North Carolina micro with a lower score than Roanoke Rapids in health care.

Scores by Sections	
Climate/Environment	65
Diversions	34
Economics	28
Education	31
Sophistication	25
Health Care	21
Housing	78
Public Safety	47
Transportation	27
Urban Proximity	62
Total Points	418

Rocky Mount

Points: 425
National Rank: 159 of 219
State Rank: 7 of 12

General Information
Components: Edgecombe and Nash counties
Area Population: 130,200
Central City Population: 48,120
Location: Northeastern North Carolina, northeast of Raleigh
Nearest Metro Center: Raleigh, 53 miles

Strengths: Access to and from the Rocky Mount area is greatly eased by its road system: only three U.S. micros scored better on the highway index. Rocky Mount's rate of income growth is just a shade behind Statesville, the North Carolina leader.

Weaknesses: Only 48.2 percent of the adults in Rocky Mount have graduated from high school. The area's availability ratios for doctors, specialists, and hospital beds are all below national averages. The local media have little clout.

Scores by Sections	
Climate/Environment	66
Diversions	33
Economics	38
Education	28
Sophistication	22
Health Care	25
Housing	75
Public Safety	37
Transportation	36
Urban Proximity	65
Total Points	425

Sanford

Points: 460
National Rank: 86 of 219
State Rank: 2 of 12

General Information
Components: Lee County
Area Population: 41,400
Central City Population: 17,970
Location: Central North Carolina, southwest of Raleigh
Nearest Metro Center: Fayetteville, 36 miles

Strengths: The per capita income of the Sanford area is higher than that of any other North Carolina micro. Sanford's housing stock has the highest proportion of new units in the state. The percentage of high-school graduates is second highest among North Carolina micros.

Weaknesses: Sanford's violent-crime rate is the second highest in micropolitan North Carolina. The availability ratios of hospital beds and specialists are among the state's lowest. Property taxes, while not steep, are the heaviest among North Carolina micros.

Scores by Sections	
Climate/Environment	66
Diversions	41
Economics	47
Education	39
Sophistication	28
Health Care	39
Housing	77
Public Safety	37
Transportation	24
Urban Proximity	62
Total Points	460

Shelby

General Information
Components: Cleveland County
Area Population: 86,500
Central City Population: 15,040
Location: Southwestern North Carolina, west of Charlotte
Nearest Metro Center: Charlotte, 40 miles

Strengths: Charlotte is less than an hour from Shelby on US 74 and I-85: Shelby has the best urban proximity score of any North Carolina micro. Housing is among the most reasonably priced in the state.

Weaknesses: It's lucky Charlotte is close: Shelby has the lowest diversions score among North Carolina micros. Only three areas in the same group have lower ratios of doctor availability than Shelby. Fewer than 48 percent of the local adults have high-school diplomas.

Scores by Sections	
Climate/Environment	63
Diversions	23
Economics	30
Education	29
Sophistication	23
Health Care	28
Housing	78
Public Safety	41
Transportation	25
Urban Proximity	73
Total Points	413

Statesville

General Information
Components: Iredell County
Area Population: 88,600
Central City Population: 19,300
Location: West-central North Carolina, north of Charlotte
Nearest Metro Center: Hickory, 27 miles

Strengths: Statesville leads North Carolina's micros in rate of income growth, and is second in per capita income. Located at the crossroads of two interstates, Statesville has North Carolina's second-best showing in the highway index.

Weaknesses: Statesville has micropolitan North Carolina's highest number of extreme-temperature days. Spending on local schools is below the national norm. The local news media are weak.

Scores by Sections	
Climate/Environment	65
Diversions	30
Economics	37
Education	27
Sophistication	26
Health Care	32
Housing	75
Public Safety	45
Transportation	29
Urban Proximity	66
Total Points	432

494 Wilson

General Information
Components: Wilson County
Area Population: 64,500
Central City Population: 35,060
Location: East-central North Carolina, east of Raleigh
Nearest Metro Center: Raleigh, 45 miles

Strengths: Wilson is second to Greenville among North Carolina micros in the availability of medical specialists; it is fourth in the state for doctors. An excellent highway system connects Wilson with the metro areas to the west and south.

Weaknesses: Only two North Carolina micros have more expensive housing than Wilson. Property taxes are also among the state's highest. Only 48 percent of Wilson's adults are high-school graduates. The total crime rate is the highest among the state's micros.

Scores by Sections	
Climate/Environment	67
Diversions	36
Economics	38
Education	32
Sophistication	26
Health Care	32
Housing	70
Public Safety	35
Transportation	33
Urban Proximity	63
Total Points	432

NORTH DAKOTA

Minot

General Information
Components: Ward County
Area Population: 61,300
Central City Population: 35,850
Location: North-central North Dakota, north of Bismarck
Nearest Metro Center: Bismarck, 111 miles

Strengths: Minot has the strongest complement of broadcast outlets in micropolitan America: four TV and nine radio stations. Minot is second among all U.S. micros in having high teacher pay and low violent-crime rates. It is eighth in the ratio of hospital beds.

Weaknesses: Minot is huddled by itself near the Canadian border: Minneapolis, 495 miles away, is the closest retail, arts, and sports center. Winters are only for the brave: the average low in January is –4°.

Scores by Sections	
Climate/Environment	50
Diversions	50
Economics	46
Education	68
Sophistication	59
Health Care	55
Housing	52
Public Safety	49
Transportation	44
Urban Proximity	16
Total Points	489

Ashland

Points: 470
National Rank: 59 of 219
State Rank: 3 of 15

General Information
Components: Ashland County
Area Population: 46,300
Central City Population: 19,520
Location: North-central Ohio, southwest of Cleveland
Nearest Metro Center: Mansfield, 14 miles

Strengths: Cleveland is just 65 miles up the interstate; three smaller metro centers are even closer to Ashland. Ashland's total crime rate is the second lowest in micropolitan America. The percentage of high-school grads ranks second among Ohio's micros.

Weaknesses: Ashland's level of health care is low: only Sidney has a less favorable ratio of available hospital beds among the state's micros. Housing in Ashland is more expensive than in most Ohio micros.

Scores by Sections	
Climate/Environment	63
Diversions	35
Economics	30
Education	53
Sophistication	32
Health Care	20
Housing	57
Public Safety	48
Transportation	40
Urban Proximity	92
Total Points	470

Ashtabula

Points: 416
National Rank: 177 of 219
State Rank: 13 of 15

General Information
Components: Ashtabula County
Area Population: 101,200
Central City Population: 22,180
Location: Extreme northeastern Ohio, northeast of Cleveland
Nearest Metro Center: Erie, Pa., 42 miles

Strengths: Ashtabula is about an hour's drive from Cleveland; Erie, Pa., is less than an hour in the other direction. The Ashtabula area is willing to spend for services: no Ohio micro offers higher teacher pay or spends more on highway maintenance.

Weaknesses: Ashtabula has micropolitan Ohio's second lowest ratio of available doctors, one sign of the inadequacies in local health care. Only East Liverpool has a lower rate of income growth among Ohio micros.

Scores by Sections	
Climate/Environment	49
Diversions	30
Economics	29
Education	47
Sophistication	27
Health Care	20
Housing	54
Public Safety	37
Transportation	32
Urban Proximity	91
Total Points	416

Athens

Points: 443
National Rank: 128 of 219
State Rank: 8 of 15

General Information
Components: Athens County
Area Population: 57,600
Central City Population: 20,870
Location: Southeastern Ohio, southeast of Columbus
Nearest Metro Center: Parkersburg, W.Va., 39 miles

Strengths: Athens, the home of Ohio University, holds the highest education score in micropolitan Ohio. Athens is second to Portsmouth in the state when it comes to both low housing costs and light property taxes.

Weaknesses: Athens's per capita income is easily the lowest among Ohio's micros. It can be difficult to find things to do: not one of the state's micros has a lighter concentration of amusement places. Only three U.S. micros have lower ratios of medical specialists.

Scores by Sections	
Climate/Environment	59
Diversions	25
Economics	23
Education	64
Sophistication	40
Health Care	30
Housing	60
Public Safety	35
Transportation	27
Urban Proximity	80
Total Points	443

Chillicothe

Points: 442
National Rank: 131 of 219
State Rank: 9 of 15

General Information
Components: Ross County
Area Population: 67,300
Central City Population: 23,420
Location: South-central Ohio, south of Columbus
Nearest Metro Center: Columbus, 46 miles

Strengths: Chillicothe is reasonably close to a couple of large metro centers: Columbus is 46 miles away, Cincinnati 94. Chillicothe ranks fourth in micropolitan America in the ratio of hospital beds to residents.

Weaknesses: Chillicothe's total crime rate is the highest among Ohio's micros; its violent-crime rate is the second highest. Chillicothe's spending on education ranks near the bottom of the state's list.

Scores by Sections	
Climate/Environment	61
Diversions	31
Economics	37
Education	38
Sophistication	31
Health Care	43
Housing	59
Public Safety	30
Transportation	25
Urban Proximity	87
Total Points	442

East Liverpool

General Information
Components: Columbiana County
Area Population: 110,100
Central City Population: 15,640
Location: Extreme east-central Ohio, south of Youngstown
Nearest Metro Center: Steubenville, 25 miles

Strengths: East Liverpool scores well in the urban proximity section because of the closeness of major centers: Pittsburgh is 44 miles away, Cleveland 89. Housing in East Liverpool is among the least expensive in micropolitan Ohio, taxes among the lowest.

Weaknesses: East Liverpool received only 25 points or less in five of ten sections. Its performance in the economics section was the third worst in the country. Only Marion among Ohio micros did worse in the highway index.

Scores by Sections	
Climate/Environment	60
Diversions	23
Economics	19
Education	41
Sophistication	25
Health Care	20
Housing	62
Public Safety	38
Transportation	25
Urban Proximity	84
Total Points	397

Findlay

General Information
Components: Hancock County
Area Population: 65,900
Central City Population: 36,660
Location: Northwestern Ohio, south of Toledo
Nearest Metro Center: Lima, 35 miles

Strengths: The Findlay area offers the highest per capita income of any Ohio micro. It also has the state's highest rate of educational attainment: 75.8 percent of Findlay's adults are high-school graduates. Detroit and Columbus are both about two hours away.

Weaknesses: Findlay's housing is among the most expensive in micropolitan Ohio: only Wooster and Sandusky are higher. Availability ratios of doctors, hospital beds, and medical specialists are all below national norms.

Scores by Sections	
Climate/Environment	67
Diversions	41
Economics	51
Education	54
Sophistication	38
Health Care	30
Housing	54
Public Safety	45
Transportation	40
Urban Proximity	77
Total Points	497

Fremont

Points: 449
National Rank: 111 of 219
State Rank: 6 of 15

General Information
Components: Sandusky County
Area Population: 62,200
Central City Population: 17,280
Location: North-central Ohio, southeast of Toledo
Nearest Metro Center: Toledo, 32 miles

Strengths: The Fremont area is one of three in micropolitan Ohio with per capita incomes of more than $10,000. Teacher pay is among the highest in the state. Fremont's total crime rate is the third lowest among Ohio micros.

Weaknesses: Fremont's ratios of doctor and specialist availability are among the lowest in the state. Housing is more expensive in Fremont than in most Ohio micros. The local media are weak.

Scores by Sections	
Climate/Environment	61
Diversions	29
Economics	36
Education	49
Sophistication	27
Health Care	27
Housing	56
Public Safety	47
Transportation	37
Urban Proximity	80
Total Points	449

Marion

Points: 468
National Rank: 63 of 219
State Rank: 4 of 15

General Information
Components: Marion County
Area Population: 65,300
Central City Population: 35,080
Location: Central Ohio, north of Columbus
Nearest Metro Center: Mansfield, 39 miles

Strengths: Marion has micropolitan Ohio's best availability ratios of doctors and medical specialists. The retail and arts center of Columbus is less than an hour away. Marion is among the state's bigger spenders on education.

Weaknesses: Marion has the worst road system, as measured by the highway index, among Ohio's micros. Only Portsmouth and Athens offer a smaller concentration of amusement places than Marion does in micropolitan Ohio.

Scores by Sections	
Climate/Environment	63
Diversions	28
Economics	35
Education	43
Sophistication	30
Health Care	56
Housing	59
Public Safety	40
Transportation	27
Urban Proximity	87
Total Points	468

New Philadelphia

General Information
Components: Tuscarawas County
Area Population: 85,500
Central City Population: 17,070
Location: East-central Ohio, south of Canton
Nearest Metro Center: Canton, 26 miles

Strengths: Just two U.S. micros spend more per capita on their parks than New Philadelphia does. Housing in this area is less expensive than in most Ohio micros. New Philadelphia's total crime rate is the second lowest in micropolitan Ohio.

Weaknesses: New Philadelphia's score in the health care section is the lowest in the state, fourth worst in the country. New Philadelphia's rate of income growth is the third lowest among Ohio's micros.

Scores by Sections	
Climate/Environment	66
Diversions	45
Economics	30
Education	41
Sophistication	28
Health Care	16
Housing	56
Public Safety	45
Transportation	34
Urban Proximity	87
Total Points	448

Portsmouth

General Information
Components: Scioto County
Area Population: 82,300
Central City Population: 23,070
Location: Extreme south-central Ohio, south of Columbus
Nearest Metro Center: Huntington, W.Va., 49 miles

Strengths: Portsmouth has the least expensive housing by far in micropolitan Ohio; its property taxes are also the lowest. Ohio's southernmost micro has fewer extreme-temperature days than any of its counterparts.

Weaknesses: The Portsmouth area has the state's lowest concentration of high-school graduates: just 54.2 percent. Per capita income is lower than in all Ohio micros but Athens. Commuting is a drag: it takes longer to get to work in Portsmouth than in any other Ohio micro.

Scores by Sections	
Climate/Environment	66
Diversions	26
Economics	21
Education	37
Sophistication	31
Health Care	22
Housing	66
Public Safety	35
Transportation	21
Urban Proximity	76
Total Points	401

500

Sandusky

General Information
Components: Erie County
Area Population: 77,100
Central City Population: 30,520
Location: Extreme north-central Ohio, west of Cleveland
Nearest Metro Center: Lorain, 33 miles

Strengths: Cleveland is slightly more than an hour to the east. Sandusky has the second-highest per capita income in micropolitan Ohio. No Ohio micro spends more on its educational system than Sandusky does.

Weaknesses: Property taxes are much higher in Sandusky than they are in any other Ohio micro, and only Wooster has more expensive houses. Sandusky's violent-crime rate is the third highest in the state.

Scores by Sections	
Climate/Environment	63
Diversions	33
Economics	44
Education	55
Sophistication	38
Health Care	38
Housing	50
Public Safety	40
Transportation	38
Urban Proximity	90
Total Points	489

Sidney

General Information
Components: Shelby County
Area Population: 44,000
Central City Population: 18,010
Location: West-central Ohio, north of Dayton
Nearest Metro Center: Lima, 34 miles

Strengths: Sidney has the eighth lowest violent-crime rate among all U.S. micros. The Sidney area offers the best selection of large homes in micropolitan America: 65.7 percent of all units have at least three bedrooms. Dayton is just 39 miles away.

Weaknesses: Sidney has the state's worst availability ratios for both doctors and hospital beds. The area's commercial sector does not fare well: Sidney has the lowest volume of retail sales per capita of any Ohio micro.

Scores by Sections	
Climate/Environment	59
Diversions	27
Economics	29
Education	41
Sophistication	27
Health Care	17
Housing	61
Public Safety	45
Transportation	32
Urban Proximity	86
Total Points	424

Tiffin

General Information
Components: Seneca County
Area Population: 61,600
Central City Population: 19,510
Location: North-central Ohio, southeast of Toledo
Nearest Metro Center: Toledo, 46 miles

Strengths: Cleveland, Detroit, and Toledo are all within two hours of Tiffin by car. More than 66 percent of Tiffin's adults have high-school diplomas, which ranks it sixth out of Ohio's 15 micros.

Weaknesses: The housing stock in the Tiffin area is the oldest in micropolitan Ohio: 53.3 percent of all units predate World War II. Only Sidney among Ohio micros has a lower ratio of hospital beds. The local news media have little clout.

Scores by Sections	
Climate/Environment	65
Diversions	31
Economics	27
Education	45
Sophistication	26
Health Care	24
Housing	55
Public Safety	44
Transportation	31
Urban Proximity	77
Total Points	425

Wooster

General Information
Components: Wayne County
Area Population: 101,200
Central City Population: 19,490
Location: North-central Ohio, southwest of Akron
Nearest Metro Center: Canton, 32 miles

Strengths: Wooster is a bit more than an hour from Cleveland; Akron and Canton are closer. Getting to those metros is easy: Wooster has Ohio's second-best score in the highway index. Per capita income is well above average for micropolitan Ohio.

Weaknesses: Housing is more expensive in Wooster than in any of the state's 14 other micros. Shopping can be tough: Wooster ranks dead last in Ohio when it comes to its concentration of retail outlets. The high-school dropout rate is the highest among state micros.

Scores by Sections	
Climate/Environment	63
Diversions	20
Economics	35
Education	44
Sophistication	29
Health Care	36
Housing	54
Public Safety	45
Transportation	36
Urban Proximity	90
Total Points	452

502 Zanesville

General Information
Components: Muskingum County
Area Population: 84,100
Central City Population: 27,920
Location: East-central Ohio, east of Columbus
Nearest Metro Center: Columbus, 56 miles

Strengths: Zanesville is outpaced by only Sandusky and Ashtabula among Ohio micros when it comes to spending on education. Housing is among the least expensive in the state. Zanesville ranks second among Ohio micros in medical specialist availability, third highest in availability of hospital beds.

Weaknesses: Ohio is a state where most micros are blessed with high urban proximity scores; Zanesville is the exception, finishing last in the state in that section. Zanesville's violent-crime rate is the highest in micropolitan Ohio.

Scores by Sections	
Climate/Environment	63
Diversions	35
Economics	29
Education	46
Sophistication	29
Health Care	37
Housing	60
Public Safety	35
Transportation	32
Urban Proximity	66
Total Points	432

OKLAHOMA

Ardmore

General Information
Components: Carter County
Area Population: 47,500
Central City Population: 25,050
Location: Extreme south-central Oklahoma, southeast of Oklahoma City
Nearest Metro Center: Sherman, Tex., 72 miles

Strengths: Ardmore has some of the more inexpensive housing in micropolitan America. No Oklahoma micro has a better ratio of medical specialists than Ardmore does, and none spends more to maintain its highways.

Weaknesses: Ardmore's violent-crime rate is higher than that of all but two of the state's micros. Spending on local parks is the lowest in micropolitan Oklahoma. Teacher pay, while average for the state, is nonetheless low.

Scores by Sections	
Climate/Environment	55
Diversions	43
Economics	44
Education	36
Sophistication	35
Health Care	40
Housing	75
Public Safety	29
Transportation	45
Urban Proximity	63
Total Points	465

Bartlesville

Points: 498
National Rank: 21 of 219
State Rank: 1 of 9

General Information
Components: Washington County
Area Population: 44,900
Central City Population: 30,010
Location: Northeastern Oklahoma, north of Tulsa
Nearest Metro Center: Tulsa, 46 miles

Strengths: Bartlesville is one of only three U.S. micros having per capita incomes above $13,000. More than 75 percent of Bartlesville's adults have high-school diplomas, the best figure in micropolitan Oklahoma. No micro in the state has a better ratio of doctors.

Weaknesses: The ways in and out of Bartlesville are limited: no Oklahoma micro scored lower on the highway index. Housing is more expensive here than in any other Oklahoma micro. Bartlesville has the state's highest number of extreme-temperature days.

Scores by Sections	
Climate/Environment	47
Diversions	44
Economics	52
Education	52
Sophistication	55
Health Care	40
Housing	70
Public Safety	45
Transportation	28
Urban Proximity	65
Total Points	498

Chickasha

Points: 423
National Rank: 165 of 219
State Rank: 7 of 9

General Information
Components: Grady County
Area Population: 44,500
Central City Population: 16,650
Location: South-central Oklahoma, southwest of Oklahoma City
Nearest Metro Center: Oklahoma City, 42 miles

Strengths: Chickasha has Oklahoma's highest score in the urban proximity section: Oklahoma City is less than an hour up the turnpike. No micro in the state is growing faster: the Chickasha area gained 12.8 percent in population from 1980 to 1986.

Weaknesses: No Oklahoma micro has a newspaper with less market penetration than Chickasha's. The total crime rate is the third highest among state micros. Availability ratios of doctors, specialists, and hospital beds are all low.

Scores by Sections	
Climate/Environment	53
Diversions	29
Economics	38
Education	31
Sophistication	25
Health Care	33
Housing	71
Public Safety	37
Transportation	32
Urban Proximity	74
Total Points	423

Duncan

Points: 420
National Rank: 169 of 219
State Rank: 8 of 9

General Information
Components: Stephens County
Area Population: 44,600
Central City Population: 22,290
Location: South-central Oklahoma, east of Lawton
Nearest Metro Center: Lawton, 33 miles

Strengths: No Oklahoma micro has a housing stock with a larger proportion of new units than Duncan. Housing costs are reasonable; property taxes are low. Per capita income is the third highest in micropolitan Oklahoma.

Weaknesses: Only two U.S. micros received lower scores than Duncan in the health care section. Duncan's rate of income growth is the lowest among micros in the state. In the highway index, Duncan tied Bartlesville for last place in micropolitan Oklahoma.

Scores by Sections	
Climate/Environment	51
Diversions	36
Economics	37
Education	37
Sophistication	33
Health Care	15
Housing	76
Public Safety	44
Transportation	24
Urban Proximity	67
Total Points	420

McAlester

Points: 434
National Rank: 144 of 219
State Rank: 6 of 9

General Information
Components: Pittsburg County
Area Population: 43,900
Central City Population: 18,820
Location: Southeastern Oklahoma, south of Tulsa
Nearest Metro Center: Tulsa, 91 miles

Strengths: Housing is extremely inexpensive in McAlester: only two U.S. micros have lower median prices. Property taxes are the lowest in the state. The rate of income growth in McAlester is the second highest in micropolitan Oklahoma.

Weaknesses: There is a down side to the money picture in McAlester: only one state micro has a lower per capita income. McAlester's percentage of high-school graduates is just a fraction away from being the state's lowest.

Scores by Sections	
Climate/Environment	59
Diversions	32
Economics	31
Education	33
Sophistication	31
Health Care	39
Housing	77
Public Safety	39
Transportation	30
Urban Proximity	63
Total Points	434

Muskogee

Points: 461
National Rank: 84 of 219
State Rank: 5 of 9

General Information
Components: Muskogee County
Area Population: 70,300
Central City Population: 42,480
Location: East-central Oklahoma, southeast of Tulsa
Nearest Metro Center: Tulsa, 50 miles

Strengths: No U.S. micro spends more government funds on health care than Muskogee does; no Oklahoma micro outspends Muskogee on education. The Muskogee area is well connected with the rest of the state: it received Oklahoma's best score in the highway index.

Weaknesses: Muskogee has the second highest total crime rate in micropolitan Oklahoma; its violent-crime rate holds the same position. Per capita income is relatively low.

Scores by Sections	
Climate/Environment	56
Diversions	35
Economics	37
Education	39
Sophistication	35
Health Care	51
Housing	70
Public Safety	39
Transportation	34
Urban Proximity	65
Total Points	461

Okmulgee

Points: 396
National Rank: 202 of 219
State Rank: 9 of 9

General Information
Components: Okmulgee County
Area Population: 40,000
Central City Population: 15,840
Location: East-central Oklahoma, south of Tulsa
Nearest Metro Center: Tulsa, 39 miles

Strengths: The average home in Okmulgee is less expensive than its counterpart in any U.S. micro but Paris, Tex. Property taxes are just a dollar away from being the state's lowest. Local workers score high for productivity. Tulsa is an easy drive away.

Weaknesses: No U.S. micro is a bigger disappointment in terms of health care: Okmulgee finished in last place nationally in that section. Per capita income is the lowest in micropolitan Oklahoma. Both the total and violent-crime rates are the state's highest.

Scores by Sections	
Climate/Environment	54
Diversions	27
Economics	40
Education	41
Sophistication	25
Health Care	11
Housing	71
Public Safety	28
Transportation	30
Urban Proximity	69
Total Points	396

506 Ponca City

General Information
Components: Kay County
Area Population: 52,200
Central City Population: 28,190
Location: North-central Oklahoma, northwest of Tulsa
Nearest Metro Center: Enid, 68 miles

Strengths: Ponca City's per capita income is surpassed only by Bartlesville among Oklahoma micros. Both the total crime rate and violent-crime rate are the state's lowest. No micro in the state offers a better concentration of amusement places.

Weaknesses: Ponca City's weakest point is health care: it has micropolitan Oklahoma's lowest ratio of hospital beds. This is also a somewhat isolated area: no micro in the state has a lower urban proximity score.

Scores by Sections	
Climate/Environment	52
Diversions	48
Economics	49
Education	40
Sophistication	39
Health Care	20
Housing	61
Public Safety	59
Transportation	41
Urban Proximity	57
Total Points	466

Stillwater

General Information
Components: Payne County
Area Population: 64,900
Central City Population: 36,630
Location: North-central Oklahoma, northeast of Oklahoma City
Nearest Metro Center: Oklahoma City, 64 miles

Strengths: Oklahoma State University is located in Stillwater, helping the area to the best education score among state micros. Stillwater has micropolitan Oklahoma's second-lowest total crime rate and violent-crime rate. The rate of income growth is the state's highest.

Weaknesses: Despite its high education score, Stillwater spends less per capita on its schools than any other Oklahoma micro does. Housing is more expensive here than anywhere but Bartlesville in micropolitan Oklahoma. The local news media have little clout.

Scores by Sections	
Climate/Environment	51
Diversions	40
Economics	36
Education	62
Sophistication	45
Health Care	43
Housing	65
Public Safety	43
Transportation	31
Urban Proximity	63
Total Points	479

Albany

Points: 469
National Rank: 62 of 219
State Rank: 2 of 6

General Information
Components: Linn County
Area Population: 89,000
Central City Population: 29,030
Location: West-central Oregon, south of Salem
Nearest Metro Center: Salem, 24 miles

Strengths: Albany shares the mild weather of nearby Corvallis, and they shared third place nationally in the climate/environment section. No Oregon micro and only eight micros across the country spend more on education than Albany does. Portland is only 69 miles away.

Weaknesses: Albany has micropolitan Oregon's lowest ratios of doctors and medical specialists. The rate of income growth is among the country's lowest. Property taxes are high.

Scores by Sections	
Climate/Environment	83
Diversions	37
Economics	23
Education	53
Sophistication	41
Health Care	22
Housing	58
Public Safety	45
Transportation	37
Urban Proximity	70
Total Points	469

Bend

Points: 460
National Rank: 86 of 219
State Rank: 3 of 6

General Information
Components: Deschutes County
Area Population: 68,700
Central City Population: 19,000
Location: Central Oregon, east of Eugene
Nearest Metro Center: Eugene, 127 miles

Strengths: Bend is second only to Corvallis among Oregon micros in both per capita income and percentage of high-school graduates. The violent-crime rate is the state's second lowest, again bested by Corvallis. Bend has micropolitan Oregon's best airline service.

Weaknesses: Bend is separated from the populated western spine of Oregon by the Cascade Mountains, explaining its low urban proximity score. The climate is harsher than in most of Oregon's micros, including 40.2 inches of snow a year. Housing is very costly.

Scores by Sections	
Climate/Environment	59
Diversions	59
Economics	32
Education	50
Sophistication	58
Health Care	47
Housing	41
Public Safety	49
Transportation	42
Urban Proximity	23
Total Points	460

508 Corvallis

General Information
Components: Benton County
Area Population: 64,600
Central City Population: 39,880
Location: West-central Oregon, southwest of Salem
Nearest Metro Center: Salem, 34 miles

Strengths: Corvallis performed very strongly in three sections, finishing second nationally in education, third in both climate/environment and sophistication. Oregon State University is a major local force. Corvallis also has the best health-care system among Oregon micros.

Weaknesses: Although the rate of income growth in the Corvallis area is the state's highest, it is still very low. Only three U.S. micros have housing more expensive than that in Corvallis. No Oregon micro has a lower volume of retail sales per capita.

Scores by Sections	
Climate/Environment	83
Diversions	44
Economics	28
Education	82
Sophistication	67
Health Care	48
Housing	52
Public Safety	48
Transportation	35
Urban Proximity	68
Total Points	555

Grants Pass

General Information
Components: Josephine County
Area Population: 68,200
Central City Population: 17,220
Location: Southwestern Oregon, northwest of Medford
Nearest Metro Center: Medford, 28 miles

Strengths: The Grants Pass area is the fastest-growing micro in Oregon, adding 15.8 percent to its population between 1980 and 1986. Property taxes are the second lowest among micros in the state. Teacher pay is much higher in Grants Pass than in any Oregon micro but Corvallis.

Weaknesses: Grants Pass has a shortage of hospital beds: its availability ratio is the third lowest in micropolitan America. The total crime rate is very high. Per capita income is the state's smallest. The closest arts and sports center, San Francisco, is 396 miles away.

Scores by Sections	
Climate/Environment	68
Diversions	46
Economics	32
Education	51
Sophistication	45
Health Care	19
Housing	54
Public Safety	37
Transportation	33
Urban Proximity	25
Total Points	410

Klamath Falls

Points: 405
National Rank: 192 of 219
State Rank: 6 of 6

General Information
Components: Klamath County
Area Population: 57,500
Central City Population: 18,320
Location: Extreme south-central Oregon, southeast of Medford
Nearest Metro Center: Medford, 76 miles

Strengths: Housing is less expensive in Klamath Falls than in any other Oregon micro. There is plenty of open room for outdoor activities: only six U.S. micros are less densely settled. More than 74 percent of Klamath Falls's adults are high-school graduates.

Weaknesses: Klamath Falls is isolated: it has Oregon's lowest urban proximity score. Its violent-crime rate is the state's highest. Per capita income in Klamath Falls is the second lowest in micropolitan Oregon. The level of health services is low.

Scores by Sections	
Climate/Environment	59
Diversions	46
Economics	21
Education	49
Sophistication	53
Health Care	27
Housing	53
Public Safety	34
Transportation	41
Urban Proximity	22
Total Points	405

Roseburg

Points: 455
National Rank: 96 of 219
State Rank: 4 of 6

General Information
Components: Douglas County
Area Population: 93,200
Central City Population: 16,160
Location: Southwestern Oregon, south of Eugene
Nearest Metro Center: Eugene, 71 miles

Strengths: Roseburg has only 72 extreme-temperature days, a major factor in placing it sixth among all U.S. micros in the climate/environment section. No Oregon micro has a better ratio of hospital beds than Roseburg; only Albany spends more per capita on education.

Weaknesses: Housing in Roseburg is relatively expensive. The total crime rate is the second highest in micropolitan Oregon. Per capita income is fairly low. Major urban centers are distant: it is 178 miles from Roseburg to Portland.

Scores by Sections	
Climate/Environment	81
Diversions	42
Economics	19
Education	50
Sophistication	43
Health Care	38
Housing	59
Public Safety	47
Transportation	43
Urban Proximity	33
Total Points	455

Butler

General Information
Components: Butler County
Area Population: 151,100
Central City Population: 16,430
Location: West-central Pennsylvania, north of Pittsburgh
Nearest Metro Center: Aliquippa, 35 miles

Strengths: No U.S. micro has a higher urban proximity score: it is a mere 38 miles from Butler to the arts, retail, and sports attractions of Pittsburgh. Butler ranks third in the nation in the highway index. More than 69 percent of Butler's adults are high-school graduates.

Weaknesses: Butler has micropolitan Pennsylvania's lowest ratios of doctors, hospital beds, and medical specialists. Housing is more expensive than in the state's three other micros.

Scores by Sections	
Climate/Environment	52
Diversions	24
Economics	31
Education	54
Sophistication	26
Health Care	22
Housing	59
Public Safety	38
Transportation	36
Urban Proximity	96
Total Points	438

Chambersburg

General Information
Components: Franklin County
Area Population: 118,700
Central City Population: 16,240
Location: Extreme south-central Pennsylvania, southwest of Harrisburg
Nearest Metro Center: Hagerstown, Md., 21 miles

Strengths: Washington and Baltimore are both less than two hours by car from Chambersburg. Per capita income is the highest among the state's four micros. Chambersburg has the most favorable ratios of hospital beds and doctors in micropolitan Pennsylvania.

Weaknesses: Chambersburg's score in the public safety section was the third lowest in the country: only eight U.S. micros have higher violent-crime rates. The rate of voter involvement is much lower in Chambersburg than in the state's other micros.

Scores by Sections	
Climate/Environment	51
Diversions	26
Economics	32
Education	39
Sophistication	22
Health Care	37
Housing	62
Public Safety	15
Transportation	30
Urban Proximity	88
Total Points	402

New Castle

Points: 419
National Rank: 171 of 219
State Rank: 2 of 4

General Information
Components: Lawrence County
Area Population: 101,900
Central City Population: 30,650
Location: Extreme west-central Pennsylvania, northwest of Pittsburgh
Nearest Metro Center: Youngstown, Ohio, 19 miles

Strengths: New Castle's urban proximity score ranks third in the nation: Youngstown is 19 miles away, Pittsburgh 56. Housing costs are reasonable. New Castle has a good road system: it ranked eighth nationally in the highway index.

Weaknesses: Finding recreational opportunities can be difficult: New Castle tied for last place among all U.S. micros in the diversions section. The rate of income growth is the state's smallest. Levels of health care in New Castle are below national norms.

Scores by Sections	
Climate/Environment	59
Diversions	18
Economics	26
Education	47
Sophistication	25
Health Care	21
Housing	58
Public Safety	33
Transportation	38
Urban Proximity	94
Total Points	419

Pottsville

Points: 381
National Rank: 209 of 219
State Rank: 4 of 4

General Information
Components: Schuylkill County
Area Population: 156,400
Central City Population: 17,050
Location: East-central Pennsylvania, northwest of Reading
Nearest Metro Center: Reading, 35 miles

Strengths: Housing in Pottsville is extremely inexpensive: only three U.S. micros have lower median prices. Both the total crime rate and the violent-crime rate are the lowest in micropolitan Pennsylvania. Philadelphia is only 97 miles away.

Weaknesses: Pottsville scored 24 or fewer points in five of ten sections, including a tie for last place nationally in the diversions section. No U.S. micro has a lower percentage of college graduates, a larger stock of old homes, or a higher death rate.

Scores by Sections	
Climate/Environment	57
Diversions	18
Economics	23
Education	35
Sophistication	22
Health Care	19
Housing	65
Public Safety	39
Transportation	24
Urban Proximity	79
Total Points	381

Newport

Points: 488
National Rank: 37 of 219
State Rank: 1 of 1

General Information

Components: Newport County
Area Population: 84,800
Central City Population: 29,320
Location: Southeastern Rhode Island, on the Atlantic coast
Nearest Metro Center: Fall River, Mass., 22 miles

Strengths: Newport's per capita income ranks sixth among all U.S. micros; its rate of income growth is second nationally. Of Newport's adults, 72 percent are high-school graduates. The violent-crime rate is low. Boston is just 74 miles away, Providence 35.

Weaknesses: Buying a home in Newport is much more expensive than in most U.S. micros. Property taxes are high. Only six U.S. micros have a worse choice of access roads than Newport, as measured by the highway index.

Scores by Sections	
Climate/Environment	48
Diversions	31
Economics	58
Education	61
Sophistication	43
Health Care	29
Housing	37
Public Safety	66
Transportation	28
Urban Proximity	87
Total Points	488

SOUTH CAROLINA

Greenwood

Points: 453
National Rank: 99 of 219
State Rank: 3 of 5

General Information

Components: Greenwood County
Area Population: 58,000
Central City Population: 22,230
Location: Northwestern South Carolina, southeast of Anderson
Nearest Metro Center: Anderson, 41 miles

Strengths: Only two U.S. micros spend more government funds per capita on health care than Greenwood does. Greenwood leads micropolitan South Carolina in availability of doctors and hospital beds. Housing is inexpensive. Atlanta is about three hours away.

Weaknesses: Greenwood has the sixth worst violent-crime rate among all U.S. micros. Access to and from the area is limited: Greenwood received South Carolina's lowest score on the highway index. Only 49.2 percent of local adults have high-school diplomas.

Scores by Sections	
Climate/Environment	67
Diversions	30
Economics	32
Education	34
Sophistication	32
Health Care	62
Housing	74
Public Safety	26
Transportation	21
Urban Proximity	75
Total Points	453

Hilton Head Island

General Information
Components: Beaufort County
Area Population: 85,600
Central City Population: 18,420
Location: Extreme southern South Carolina, on the Atlantic coast
Nearest Metro Center: Savannah, Ga., 31 miles

Strengths: Hilton Head Island leads all state micros in per capita income, rate of income growth, and percentage of high-school graduates. Only three U.S. micros have a larger stock of new housing: just 4.7 percent of Hilton Head Island's homes were built before 1940.

Weaknesses: The catch is that houses on Hilton Head Island are much more expensive than those in South Carolina's four other micros. No other micro in the state spends less per capita on education than Hilton Head Island does. Hospital-bed availability is very low.

Scores by Sections	
Climate/Environment	66
Diversions	47
Economics	55
Education	35
Sophistication	38
Health Care	38
Housing	72
Public Safety	37
Transportation	27
Urban Proximity	40
Total Points	455

Myrtle Beach

General Information
Components: Horry County
Area Population: 130,600
Central City Population: 27,980
Location: Northeastern South Carolina, on the Atlantic coast
Nearest Metro Center: Florence, 66 miles

Strengths: Myrtle Beach is a place to have fun: only Key West, Fla., received a higher score in the diversions section. The moderating influence of the Atlantic allows Myrtle Beach to have fewer extreme-temperature days than other South Carolina micros. The housing stock is new.

Weaknesses: Myrtle Beach's availability ratios of doctors, specialists, and hospital beds are well below national averages. With the large influx of visitors comes a crime problem: Myrtle Beach has the third-highest total crime rate in micropolitan America.

Scores by Sections	
Climate/Environment	61
Diversions	75
Economics	57
Education	31
Sophistication	30
Health Care	26
Housing	74
Public Safety	36
Transportation	39
Urban Proximity	35
Total Points	464

514 Orangeburg

General Information
Components: Orangeburg County
Area Population: 87,300
Central City Population: 15,420
Location: Central South Carolina, south of Columbia
Nearest Metro Center: Columbia, 44 miles

Strengths: The Orangeburg area has access to two interstates and several other major routes: its highway index is the highest in the country. Housing in Orangeburg is the most inexpensive among state micros. Property taxes are very low.

Weaknesses: Orangeburg has the lowest per capita income in micropolitan South Carolina. Its violent-crime rate is the tenth worst in the country; the total crime rate is also very high.

Scores by Sections	
Climate/Environment	66
Diversions	26
Economics	26
Education	40
Sophistication	28
Health Care	38
Housing	85
Public Safety	18
Transportation	31
Urban Proximity	58
Total Points	416

Sumter

Points: 400
National Rank: 199 of 219
State Rank: 5 of 5

General Information
Components: Sumter County
Area Population: 95,000
Central City Population: 28,740
Location: Central South Carolina, east of Columbia
Nearest Metro Center: Florence, 38 miles

Strengths: No South Carolina micro spends more per capita on education than Sumter does. Housing is inexpensive on the national scale; property taxes are the lowest in micropolitan South Carolina. Sumter has the state's second-best score in the highway index.

Weaknesses: Sumter scored 34 or fewer points in seven of ten sections. The area trails the other South Carolina micros when it comes to concentration of retail outlets, teacher pay, percentage of college graduates, doctor availability, and hospital-bed availability.

Scores by Sections	
Climate/Environment	60
Diversions	22
Economics	28
Education	34
Sophistication	29
Health Care	25
Housing	84
Public Safety	29
Transportation	31
Urban Proximity	58
Total Points	400

Cleveland

General Information
Components: Bradley County
Area Population: 72,300
Central City Population: 26,140
Location: Southeastern Tennessee, northeast of Chattanooga
Nearest Metro Center: Chattanooga, 31 miles

Strengths: Chattanooga is about 30 minutes by freeway from Cleveland; Atlanta is only about two hours away. Housing is relatively inexpensive. Cleveland's rate of income growth is the fastest in micropolitan Tennessee.

Weaknesses: Cleveland's violent-crime rate is the highest among the state's five micros. Spending on the local educational system is light. Cleveland's concentration of retail outlets is much lower than in any of Tennessee's other micros.

Scores by Sections	
Climate/Environment	65
Diversions	20
Economics	39
Education	25
Sophistication	31
Health Care	47
Housing	77
Public Safety	42
Transportation	27
Urban Proximity	75
Total Points	448

Columbia

General Information
Components: Maury County
Area Population: 53,900
Central City Population: 28,170
Location: Central Tennessee, southwest of Nashville
Nearest Metro Center: Nashville, 44 miles

Strengths: Buying a home in Columbia takes less money than it would elsewhere in micropolitan Tennessee; property taxes are also low. Nashville can be reached in an hour. Columbia has a better availability ratio of doctors than the state's other micros do.

Weaknesses: Columbia does not easily part with its money for schools: only six U.S. micros spend less per capita on education. Columbia's percentage of college graduates is the lowest in micropolitan Tennessee. Its rate of income growth is the state's slowest.

Scores by Sections	
Climate/Environment	61
Diversions	35
Economics	37
Education	21
Sophistication	21
Health Care	42
Housing	74
Public Safety	44
Transportation	29
Urban Proximity	69
Total Points	433

516 Cookeville

General Information
Components: Putnam County
Area Population: 51,100
Central City Population: 23,920
Location: Central Tennessee, east of Nashville
Nearest Metro Center: Nashville, 76 miles

Strengths: Cookeville's total crime rate is the lowest among state micros. Housing prices are the most expensive in micropolitan Tennessee, but are still reasonable. Property taxes are the state's lowest.

Weaknesses: Cookeville trails Tennessee's four other micros when it comes to per capita income. Only five U.S. micros spend less per capita on education. An even 50 percent of Cookeville's adults are high-school graduates, the state's lowest figure.

Scores by Sections	
Climate/Environment	70
Diversions	35
Economics	35
Education	32
Sophistication	31
Health Care	42
Housing	78
Public Safety	51
Transportation	27
Urban Proximity	66
Total Points	467

Morristown

General Information
Components: Hamblen County
Area Population: 52,900
Central City Population: 19,650
Location: Northeastern Tennessee, southwest of Johnson City
Nearest Metro Center: Knoxville, 41 miles

Strengths: Housing in Morristown is reasonably priced. No Tennessee micro spends more on education than Morristown does. The retail center of Knoxville is less than an hour away.

Weaknesses: Morristown has a dearth of outside activities: only two U.S. micros accumulated lower scores in the diversions section. Availability ratios of doctors, hospital beds, and specialists are below national norms.

Scores by Sections	
Climate/Environment	64
Diversions	19
Economics	37
Education	22
Sophistication	29
Health Care	29
Housing	78
Public Safety	47
Transportation	28
Urban Proximity	64
Total Points	417

Tullahoma

General Information
Components: Coffee County
Area Population: 41,300
Central City Population: 16,780
Location: South-central Tennessee, southeast of Nashville
Nearest Metro Center: Huntsville, Ala., 58 miles

Strengths: Tullahoma has the highest per capita income in micropolitan Tennessee. Slightly more than 56 percent of Tullahoma's adults are high-school graduates, the best figure among the state's micros. Property taxes are low; so are the crime rates.

Weaknesses: Tullahoma has the lowest ratios of doctors and medical specialists among Tennessee's five micros. No micro in the state has a lower concentration of amusement places. Tullahoma has no daily paper and only two radio stations.

Scores by Sections	
Climate/Environment	70
Diversions	36
Economics	40
Education	32
Sophistication	21
Health Care	37
Housing	81
Public Safety	48
Transportation	33
Urban Proximity	70
Total Points	468

TEXAS

Alice

General Information
Components: Jim Wells County
Area Population: 40,300
Central City Population: 22,480
Location: Extreme southern Texas, west of Corpus Christi
Nearest Metro Center: Corpus Christi, 43 miles

Strengths: Alice ranks fifth among all U.S. micros when it comes to inexpensive housing. The violent-crime rate in the Alice area is the lowest in micropolitan Texas. No micro in the state spends more than Alice to maintain its roads.

Weaknesses: Just 43.1 percent of Alice's adults own high-school diplomas, the fifth lowest mark in micropolitan America. The level of health care is very low. Only Del Rio has a lower per capita income than Alice among Texas micros.

Scores by Sections	
Climate/Environment	64
Diversions	33
Economics	30
Education	27
Sophistication	20
Health Care	18
Housing	75
Public Safety	34
Transportation	24
Urban Proximity	56
Total Points	381

518 Bay City

General Information
Components: Matagorda County
Area Population: 41,000
Central City Population: 19,360
Location: East-central Texas, southwest of Houston
Nearest Metro Center: Lake Jackson, 38 miles

Strengths: Houston and all of its arts, retail, and sports attractions are just 79 miles from Bay City. Per capita income in Bay City is substantially higher than in any other micro in the state. Only Huntsville spends more on education among Texas micros than Bay City.

Weaknesses: Property taxes in Bay City are heavy: only two U.S. micros have them higher. Housing is more expensive than in any Texas micro but Huntsville. Bay City has the nation's second-lowest score in the highway index. The crime rates are relatively high.

Scores by Sections	
Climate/Environment	66
Diversions	36
Economics	50
Education	38
Sophistication	24
Health Care	33
Housing	59
Public Safety	24
Transportation	20
Urban Proximity	87
Total Points	437

Del Rio

General Information
Components: Val Verde County
Area Population: 40,000
Central City Population: 34,700
Location: Southwestern Texas, on the Rio Grande, south of San Angelo
Nearest Metro Center: San Antonio, 150 miles

Strengths: Property taxes in Del Rio are easily the lowest in micropolitan Texas. Housing is reasonable based on the national scale. Del Rio's total crime rate is the state's second lowest; so is the violent-crime rate.

Weaknesses: Hinesville, Ga., is the only U.S. micro with a lower ratio of doctor availability than Del Rio's, and just two micros in the country have lower per capita incomes. Only 51.1 percent of Del Rio's adults are high-school graduates.

Scores by Sections	
Climate/Environment	58
Diversions	36
Economics	28
Education	23
Sophistication	23
Health Care	17
Housing	80
Public Safety	39
Transportation	31
Urban Proximity	36
Total Points	371

Greenville

Points: 423
National Rank: 165 of 219
State Rank: 6 of 9

General Information
Components: Hunt County
Area Population: 67,100
Central City Population: 24,650
Location: Northeastern Texas, northeast of Dallas
Nearest Metro Center: Dallas, 50 miles

Strengths: The nearness of Dallas has earned Greenville the best urban proximity score in the state, the sixth best in the country. Only eight U.S. micros have less expensive housing. Greenville has the second-highest per capita income in micropolitan Texas.

Weaknesses: Greenville took last place in the country in the public safety section: its violent-crime rate is higher than those of all but two U.S. micros. Greenville has the lowest ratio of available hospital beds of all the Texas micros.

Scores by Sections	
Climate/Environment	60
Diversions	29
Economics	46
Education	40
Sophistication	26
Health Care	18
Housing	74
Public Safety	11
Transportation	27
Urban Proximity	92
Total Points	423

Huntsville

Points: 483
National Rank: 41 of 219
State Rank: 1 of 9

General Information
Components: Walker County
Area Population: 54,100
Central City Population: 33,430
Location: East-central Texas, north of Houston
Nearest Metro Center: Bryan, 56 miles

Strengths: The presence of Sam Houston State University is largely responsible for the fact that Huntsville has Texas's highest score in the education section. Houston is less than one and a half hours away. Huntsville is the fastest-growing micro in Texas.

Weaknesses: The housing in Huntsville is the most expensive in micropolitan Texas. Only seven U.S. micros have a less favorable ratio of hospital beds than Huntsville. The local news media are weak.

Scores by Sections	
Climate/Environment	63
Diversions	39
Economics	59
Education	64
Sophistication	23
Health Care	27
Housing	61
Public Safety	33
Transportation	27
Urban Proximity	87
Total Points	483

520 Lufkin

General Information

Components: Angelina County
Area Population: 69,400
Central City Population: 32,080
Location: Extreme east-central Texas, southeast of Tyler
Nearest Metro Center: Tyler, 83 miles

Strengths: Lufkin trails only Bay City and Greenville among Texas micros when it comes to per capita income. No state micro has a higher concentration of amusement places. Housing in Lufkin is reasonable and lightly taxed.

Weaknesses: Lufkin's high-school dropout rate is higher than those of all Texas micros but Del Rio. Lufkin is somewhat isolated: its urban proximity score is one of the lowest in Texas. The local crime rates are relatively high.

Scores by Sections	
Climate/Environment	60
Diversions	36
Economics	41
Education	27
Sophistication	29
Health Care	32
Housing	77
Public Safety	29
Transportation	25
Urban Proximity	63
Total Points	419

Nacogdoches

General Information

Components: Nacogdoches County
Area Population: 50,600
Central City Population: 28,350
Location: Extreme east-central Texas, southeast of Tyler
Nearest Metro Center: Longview, 70 miles

Strengths: Nacogdoches, the home of Stephen F. Austin State University, has the highest percentage of college graduates of any Texas micro: 18.3 percent. Nacogdoches is second among Texas micros in availability of doctors and hospital beds. Its total crime rate is the state's lowest.

Weaknesses: No other area in micropolitan Texas spends less per capita on its educational system than Nacogdoches does. No state micro has a higher number of extreme-temperature days. Only Alice and Del Rio are more isolated in Texas, as measured by the urban proximity score.

Scores by Sections	
Climate/Environment	60
Diversions	34
Economics	36
Education	44
Sophistication	33
Health Care	57
Housing	72
Public Safety	38
Transportation	28
Urban Proximity	61
Total Points	463

Palestine

Points: 426
National Rank: 158 of 219
State Rank: 5 of 9

General Information
Components: Anderson County
Area Population: 47,500
Central City Population: 19,440
Location: East-central Texas, southwest of Tyler
Nearest Metro Center: Tyler, 48 miles

Strengths: Housing in Palestine is very inexpensive when compared to the typical U.S. micro. Only two state micros spend more per capita on their educational systems than Palestine does. Dallas is about two hours away by car.

Weaknesses: No Texas micro has a lower percentage of college graduates than Palestine's figure of 8.4 percent, nor does any micro in the state spend less per·capita in restaurants. The area is third lowest in the state in hospital-bed availability.

Scores by Sections	
Climate/Environment	65
Diversions	30
Economics	37
Education	37
Sophistication	21
Health Care	26
Housing	74
Public Safety	30
Transportation	26
Urban Proximity	80
Total Points	426

Paris

Points: 452
National Rank: 103 of 219
State Rank: 3 of 9

General Information
Components: Lamar County
Area Population: 45,000
Central City Population: 26,210
Location: Extreme northeastern Texas, northeast of Dallas
Nearest Metro Center: Sherman, 64 miles

Strengths: No Texas micro surpasses Paris in the availability of doctors, medical specialists, or hospital beds. If you're looking for a housing bargain, Paris is the place: no U.S. micro has a lower median price. Dallas is about two hours to the southwest.

Weaknesses: Paris's glaring weakness is in public safety: it finished with the nation's second-lowest score in that section. Only six U.S. micros have higher total crime rates. The Paris area has the slowest growth rate in micropolitan Texas, in terms of population.

Scores by Sections	
Climate/Environment	60
Diversions	37
Economics	47
Education	27
Sophistication	27
Health Care	56
Housing	75
Public Safety	12
Transportation	30
Urban Proximity	81
Total Points	452

Logan

Points: 431
National Rank: 152 of 219
State Rank: 1 of 1

General Information
Components: Cache County
Area Population: 65,500
Central City Population: 28,880
Location: Extreme northern Utah, north of Salt
   Lake City
Nearest Metro Center: Salt Lake City, 79 miles

Strengths: Utah State University casts a long
shadow over the Logan area, earning it sixth place
in the education section. Logan's violent-crime rate
is very low. The property-tax load is light.

Weaknesses: The smallness of Logan tax bills is
offset by the high cost of mortgages: housing is
expensive. The availability ratio of hospital beds
is very low. Getting in and out of Logan is not
always convenient: its score on the highway index
was relatively low.

Scores by Sections	
Climate/Environment	48
Diversions	32
Economics	30
Education	74
Sophistication	45
Health Care	34
Housing	52
Public Safety	43
Transportation	27
Urban Proximity	46
Total Points	431

VERMONT

Rutland

Points: 452
National Rank: 103 of 219
State Rank: 1 of 1

General Information
Components: Rutland County
Area Population: 60,000
Central City Population: 18,080
Location: Central Vermont, southeast of Burlington
Nearest Metro Center: Glens Falls, N.Y., 45 miles

Strengths: Rutland offers plenty of recreational
options: it finished 17th in the country in the
diversions section. Only six U.S. micros have a
higher concentration of retail outlets. The rate of
income growth is strong. An even 70 percent of
Rutland's adults are high-school graduates.

Weaknesses: The Green Mountains are beautiful,
but they slow down travelers: Rutland did not
do well in the highway index. Major urban centers are distant: Boston is 171
miles away. Hospital-bed availability and teacher pay are well below national norms.

Scores by Sections	
Climate/Environment	51
Diversions	56
Economics	46
Education	46
Sophistication	49
Health Care	31
Housing	46
Public Safety	43
Transportation	31
Urban Proximity	53
Total Points	452

Blacksburg

General Information
Components: Montgomery County
Area Population: 66,100
Central City Population: 30,380
Location: Southwestern Virginia, west of Roanoke
Nearest Metro Center: Roanoke, 34 miles

Strengths: Virginia Tech, based in Blacksburg, lifts the area to the top score in the education section among Virginia's six micros. Blacksburg has the state's best supply of new housing: only 12.8 percent of all units predate World War II. The rate of income growth leads the state.

Weaknesses: Per capita income in Blacksburg is lower than in any of the state's other micros. The ratio of hospital-bed availability is also the state's lowest. Besides college-related activities, little happens in Blacksburg: its diversions score is the state's second lowest.

Scores by Sections	
Climate/Environment	55
Diversions	29
Economics	38
Education	51
Sophistication	36
Health Care	37
Housing	67
Public Safety	44
Transportation	29
Urban Proximity	51
Total Points	437

Fredericksburg

General Information
Components: Spotsylvania County and Fredericksburg independent city
Area Population: 58,900
Central City Population: 19,500
Location: Northern Virginia, north of Richmond
Nearest Metro Center: Washington, D.C., 48 miles

Strengths: Fredericksburg is about an hour's drive on I-95 from Washington; Richmond is an hour in the other direction. No Virginia micro spends more on education than Fredericksburg. Per capita income stands at a healthy level. The diversions score is the state's highest.

Weaknesses: The high housing prices of metropolitan Washington are bleeding into the Fredericksburg area. The weather can be steamy: Fredericksburg leads the state's micros in the number of extreme-temperature days. Commuting time is higher than in any other U.S. micro.

Scores by Sections	
Climate/Environment	51
Diversions	52
Economics	68
Education	40
Sophistication	51
Health Care	51
Housing	67
Public Safety	45
Transportation	24
Urban Proximity	92
Total Points	541

524 Harrisonburg

Points: 449
National Rank: 111 of 219
State Rank: 4 of 6

General Information

Components: Rockingham County and Harrisonburg independent city
Area Population: 81,400
Central City Population: 27,000
Location: West-central Virginia, northwest of Charlottesville
Nearest Metro Center: Charlottesville, 54 miles

Strengths: Harrisonburg has micropolitan Virginia's lowest property taxes and best selection of large houses: 63.2 percent of all units have at least three bedrooms. The violent-crime rate is the state's lowest. Harrisonburg has a strong array of broadcast outlets: two TV and seven radio stations.

Weaknesses: The Blue Ridge Mountains separate Harrisonburg from the large urban centers of Virginia, as well as from Washington, D.C. Hospital-bed availability is well below the national average.

Scores by Sections	
Climate/Environment	61
Diversions	33
Economics	44
Education	39
Sophistication	44
Health Care	30
Housing	69
Public Safety	41
Transportation	29
Urban Proximity	59
Total Points	449

Martinsville

Points: 373
National Rank: 212 of 219
State Rank: 6 of 6

General Information

Components: Henry County and Martinsville independent city
Area Population: 74,900
Central City Population: 18,700
Location: Extreme south-central Virginia, south of Roanoke
Nearest Metro Center: Danville, 28 miles

Strengths: The average home in Martinsville is much less expensive than its counterparts in Virginia's other micros. Property taxes are light. Martinsville is closer than any of the state's other micros to a metro center.

Weaknesses: Martinsville's violent-crime rate is the highest in micropolitan Virginia; its highway index is the lowest. Only 45.7 percent of Martinsville's adults are high-school graduates. No state micro has a lower availability ratio of doctors or specialists.

Scores by Sections	
Climate/Environment	55
Diversions	22
Economics	31
Education	21
Sophistication	26
Health Care	24
Housing	78
Public Safety	40
Transportation	22
Urban Proximity	54
Total Points	373

Staunton–Waynesboro

General Information

Components: Augusta County and Staunton and Waynesboro independent cities

Area Population: 91,500

Central City Population: Staunton 21,500; Waynesboro 18,100

Location: West-central Virginia, west of Charlottesville

Nearest Metro Center: Charlottesville, 35 miles

Strengths: The Staunton–Waynesboro area ranks sixth among all U.S. micros when it comes to the availability of hospital beds; it is also sixth nationally in the highway index. Staunton–Waynesboro's total crime rate is the lowest in micropolitan Virginia.

Weaknesses: Staunton–Waynesboro trails the rest of the state's micros in teacher pay and rate of income growth. Only 54.3 percent of the area's adults have graduated from high school.

Scores by Sections	
Climate/Environment	62
Diversions	33
Economics	39
Education	30
Sophistication	35
Health Care	47
Housing	69
Public Safety	50
Transportation	36
Urban Proximity	72
Total Points	473

Winchester

General Information

Components: Frederick County and Winchester independent city

Area Population: 58,100

Central City Population: 21,200

Location: Extreme northwestern Virginia, northwest of Washington, D.C.

Nearest Metro Center: Hagerstown, Md., 41 miles

Strengths: Winchester has the highest per capita income in micropolitan Virginia. It leads the same group in availability of doctors and medical specialists. Washington is just 71 miles away, Baltimore only slightly farther.

Weaknesses: Winchester's total crime rate is higher than those of the state's other micros. Only Martinsville has a larger high-school dropout problem than Winchester among Virginia's micros. Property taxes are the highest in this group.

Scores by Sections	
Climate/Environment	55
Diversions	47
Economics	49
Education	27
Sophistication	35
Health Care	54
Housing	66
Public Safety	45
Transportation	28
Urban Proximity	90
Total Points	496

Aberdeen

General Information
Components: Grays Harbor County
Area Population: 62,700
Central City Population: 16,830
Location: Extreme western Washington, west of Olympia
Nearest Metro Center: Olympia, 47 miles

Strengths: Thanks to the Pacific Ocean, Aberdeen has only 48 extreme-temperature days annually. No other Washington micro pays its teachers more. Only three U.S. micros spend more on their highways; only one spends more for police protection.

Weaknesses: There's a good reason for heavy police expenditures: Aberdeen's total crime rate is very high. Per capita income is the second lowest among the state's six micros. No other area in micropolitan Washington has a lower ratio of doctors than Aberdeen.

Scores by Sections	
Climate/Environment	81
Diversions	62
Economics	28
Education	54
Sophistication	35
Health Care	23
Housing	59
Public Safety	55
Transportation	45
Urban Proximity	80
Total Points	522

Longview

General Information
Components: Cowlitz County
Area Population: 78,700
Central City Population: 29,140
Location: Southwestern Washington, on the Columbia River
Nearest Metro Center: Vancouver, Wash., 44 miles

Strengths: Longview is another of the Washington micros blessed with a mild climate, with just 62 extreme-temperature days a year. Portland, Oreg., is just an hour's drive down I-5. No state micro has a better stock of large homes or spends more per capita on education.

Weaknesses: Property taxes in Longview are the highest in micropolitan Washington; housing costs are also fairly steep. The rate of income growth is relatively low. Hospital-bed availability in Longview falls well below the national average.

Scores by Sections	
Climate/Environment	80
Diversions	46
Economics	34
Education	56
Sophistication	39
Health Care	32
Housing	62
Public Safety	46
Transportation	40
Urban Proximity	83
Total Points	518

Port Angeles

General Information
Components: Clallam County
Area Population: 53,700
Central City Population: 17,560
Location: The northern coast of Washington's
   Olympic peninsula, northwest of Seattle
Nearest Metro Center: Bremerton, 79 miles

Strengths: In a state boasting some outstanding
scores in the climate/environment section, Port
Angeles has the best, and is in fifth place nationally.
Per capita income is the highest in micropolitan
Washington, property taxes the lowest.

Weaknesses: Housing in Port Angeles is considerably more expensive than in any of Washington's
other micros. Only three U.S. micros scored lower
than Port Angeles on the highway index. The rate
of income growth is sluggish. The average daily
high in July is only 69°.

Scores by Sections	
Climate/Environment	82
Diversions	55
Economics	32
Education	54
Sophistication	40
Health Care	37
Housing	59
Public Safety	48
Transportation	37
Urban Proximity	81
Total Points	525

Pullman

General Information
Components: Whitman County
Area Population: 40,700
Central City Population: 23,160
Location: Extreme southeastern Washington,
   south of Spokane, near the Idaho line
Nearest Metro Center: Spokane, 76 miles

Strengths: Pullman, the location of Washington
State University, has the highest concentration of
college graduates of any U.S. micro: 36.8 percent
of its adults. Pullman led the nation in the transportation section. Only two U.S. micros have
lower total crime rates.

Weaknesses: Pullman is isolated in Washington's
southeastern corner: its diversions score is the state's
lowest, its urban proximity score is second lowest.
No Washington micro does as badly as Pullman
in per capita income and availability of hospital beds.

Scores by Sections	
Climate/Environment	66
Diversions	31
Economics	24
Education	80
Sophistication	57
Health Care	32
Housing	52
Public Safety	48
Transportation	55
Urban Proximity	50
Total Points	495

528 Walla Walla

General Information
Components: Walla Walla County
Area Population: 48,000
Central City Population: 25,260
Location: Southeastern Washington, southeast of
    Richland, near the Oregon line
Nearest Metro Center: Richland, 56 miles

Strengths: The Walla Walla area leads micropolitan Washington in the availability of hospital beds, and is second in doctors and medical specialists. Walla Walla is second in the state to Pullman in percentage of high-school graduates: 75.2 percent of its adults.

Weaknesses: Walla Walla has the highest violent-crime rate among Washington's micros; its total crime rate is also very high. No micro in the state has a lower concentration of amusement places. Major urban centers are distant, as shown by Walla Walla's low urban proximity score.

Scores by Sections	
Climate/Environment	65
Diversions	43
Economics	31
Education	63
Sophistication	50
Health Care	51
Housing	58
Public Safety	34
Transportation	43
Urban Proximity	45
Total Points	483

Wenatchee

General Information
Components: Chelan County
Area Population: 49,900
Central City Population: 18,280
Location: Central Washington, northeast of Yakima
Nearest Metro Center: Yakima, 110 miles

Strengths: Wenatchee offers many recreational choices: it is the least densely settled Washington micro, with a nearby national forest. It also has a higher concentration of retail outlets than all but five U.S. micros. Only three U.S. micros have a better ratio of doctors.

Weaknesses: Wenatchee's total crime rate is the highest in a state where most micros have high rates. No Washington micro is farther from a metropolitan center. The rate of income growth is slow. Housing is fairly expensive.

Scores by Sections	
Climate/Environment	57
Diversions	66
Economics	49
Education	53
Sophistication	55
Health Care	48
Housing	54
Public Safety	46
Transportation	39
Urban Proximity	66
Total Points	533

Beckley

Points: 412
National Rank: 183 of 219
State Rank: 3 of 4

General Information
Components: Raleigh County
Area Population: 84,200
Central City Population: 19,560
Location: Southern West Virginia, southeast of Charleston
Nearest Metro Center: Charleston, 59 miles

Strengths: Beckley has micropolitan West Virginia's best stock of new homes, as well as its largest percentage of homes with at least three bedrooms. Property taxes are the state's lowest. No West Virginia micro has a better ratio of hospital beds. Crime rates are small.

Weaknesses: Beckley is isolated to an extent unmatched by West Virginia's three other micros: its urban proximity score is much lower. Per capita income is next to the bottom in the state group. Only 53.6 percent of Beckley's adults are high-school graduates.

Scores by Sections	
Climate/Environment	63
Diversions	23
Economics	32
Education	31
Sophistication	37
Health Care	44
Housing	70
Public Safety	52
Transportation	23
Urban Proximity	37
Total Points	412

Clarksburg

Points: 423
National Rank: 165 of 219
State Rank: 2 of 4

General Information
Components: Harrison County
Area Population: 75,200
Central City Population: 19,960
Location: North-central West Virginia, east of Parkersburg
Nearest Metro Center: Parkersburg, 74 miles

Strengths: Clarksburg's total crime rate is the lowest in micropolitan West Virginia. Its housing costs are the most inexpensive among the state's four micros. None of the other areas in the state spends more on education than Clarksburg.

Weaknesses: Per capita income in Clarksburg is par for West Virginia, but is low on a national scale. Clarksburg has 25 more extreme-temperature days than any other West Virginia micro. The availability ratio of medical specialists is below the national norm.

Scores by Sections	
Climate/Environment	52
Diversions	27
Economics	25
Education	43
Sophistication	43
Health Care	32
Housing	59
Public Safety	49
Transportation	31
Urban Proximity	62
Total Points	423

530

Fairmont

General Information
Components: Marion County
Area Population: 64,100
Central City Population: 22,260
Location: North-central West Virginia, northeast
of Parkersburg
Nearest Metro Center: Wheeling, 70 miles

Strengths: Pittsburgh is less than two hours from Fairmont by I-79. Housing in Fairmont is inexpensive. The violent-crime rate is low. Fairmont is second to Morgantown in micropolitan West Virginia in percentage of high-school graduates.

Weaknesses: Fairmont's per capita income is the lowest among the state's four micros; the same is true of its rate of income growth. Fairmont's ratios of doctors, specialists, and hospital beds are all at the bottom of the state's list.

Scores by Sections	
Climate/Environment	44
Diversions	22
Economics	29
Education	44
Sophistication	29
Health Care	36
Housing	58
Public Safety	43
Transportation	24
Urban Proximity	82
Total Points	411

Morgantown

General Information
Components: Monongalia County
Area Population: 77,700
Central City Population: 26,840
Location: Extreme north-central West Virginia,
south of Pittsburgh, Pa.
Nearest Metro Center: Cumberland, Md., 72 miles

Strengths: West Virginia University is the reason Morgantown leads West Virginia in the education and sophistication sections. No U.S. micro has a better ratio of doctors than Morgantown; only one has better availability of specialists. Pittsburgh is just 77 miles away.

Weaknesses: Buying a house is much more expensive in Morgantown than in any of West Virginia's three other micros. The total crime and violent-crime rates, although not high in a national sense, are the highest in micropolitan West Virginia.

Scores by Sections	
Climate/Environment	46
Diversions	22
Economics	31
Education	58
Sophistication	45
Health Care	69
Housing	56
Public Safety	44
Transportation	35
Urban Proximity	83
Total Points	489

Fond du Lac

Points: 481
National Rank: 47 of 219
State Rank: 2 of 4

General Information
Components: Fond du Lac County
Area Population: 90,400
Central City Population: 36,530
Location: East-central Wisconsin, west of Sheboygan
Nearest Metro Center: Appleton, 38 miles

Strengths: Only seven U.S. micros have a better selection of large homes: 63.1 percent of the units in Fond du Lac have at least three bedrooms. Milwaukee is slightly more than an hour away. Fond du Lac's violent-crime rate is very low.

Weaknesses: Fond du Lac has long, cold winters: the average low in January is 7°. Property taxes are high. The local news media have little clout.

Scores by Sections	
Climate/Environment	60
Diversions	36
Economics	38
Education	54
Sophistication	28
Health Care	38
Housing	48
Public Safety	57
Transportation	38
Urban Proximity	84
Total Points	481

Manitowoc

Points: 467
National Rank: 66 of 219
State Rank: 4 of 4

General Information
Components: Manitowoc County
Area Population: 82,200
Central City Population: 32,070
Location: The Lake Michigan coast, southeast of Green Bay
Nearest Metro Center: Sheboygan, 27 miles

Strengths: Manitowoc is the most easily accessible micro in Wisconsin: it received the state's best score in the highway index. Milwaukee is about one and a half hours away. Manitowoc's violent-crime rate is the lowest in micropolitan Wisconsin. Property taxes are the state's lowest.

Weaknesses: Manitowoc trails the other state micros when it comes to education, spending the least on its schools. Its rate of income growth is the slowest in micropolitan Wisconsin. Manitowoc's ratios of doctors and specialists are the lowest of the state's micros.

Scores by Sections	
Climate/Environment	60
Diversions	35
Economics	28
Education	44
Sophistication	30
Health Care	31
Housing	52
Public Safety	57
Transportation	48
Urban Proximity	82
Total Points	467

532 Marshfield–Wisconsin Rapids

Points: 517
National Rank: 14 of 219
State Rank: 1 of 4

General Information
Components: Wood County
Area Population: 77,500
Central City Population: Marshfield 19,840; Wisconsin Rapids 19,050
Location: Central Wisconsin, southwest of Wausau
Nearest Metro Center: Wausau, 47 miles

Strengths: Marshfield–Wisconsin Rapids finished second nationally in the health care section: it has micropolitan America's best ratio of medical specialists. It has the highest per capita income, least expensive housing, and lowest crime rate in Wisconsin.

Weaknesses: Marshfield–Wisconsin Rapids has micropolitan Wisconsin's highest number of extreme-temperature days. In January, the average nightly low is 2°. Only eight U.S. micros scored lower than Marshfield–Wisconsin Rapids on the highway index.

Scores by Sections	
Climate/Environment	54
Diversions	44
Economics	49
Education	56
Sophistication	38
Health Care	76
Housing	46
Public Safety	56
Transportation	43
Urban Proximity	55
Total Points	517

Stevens Point

Points: 479
National Rank: 50 of 219
State Rank: 3 of 4

General Information
Components: Portage County
Area Population: 58,700
Central City Population: 22,250
Location: Central Wisconsin, south of Wausau
Nearest Metro Center: Wausau, 34 miles

Strengths: Stevens Point, which contains a campus of the University of Wisconsin, leads the state's micros in the percentage of high-school and college graduates. No area in micropolitan Wisconsin spends more per capita in restaurants than Stevens Point.

Weaknesses: Stevens Point has the lowest per capita income among the state's micros; it also trails in hospital-bed availability. Housing is more expensive in Stevens Point than in the other Wisconsin micros. The total crime rate is the state's highest.

Scores by Sections	
Climate/Environment	58
Diversions	47
Economics	40
Education	59
Sophistication	37
Health Care	33
Housing	50
Public Safety	49
Transportation	44
Urban Proximity	62
Total Points	479

Rock Springs

General Information
Components: Sweetwater County
Area Population: 47,000
Central City Population: 21,970
Location: Southwestern Wyoming, southwest of Casper
Nearest Metro Center: Salt Lake City, Utah, 172 miles

Strengths: The Rock Springs area is free with its pocketbook: it ranks first among all U.S. micros in spending on parks, second in education outlays, and third in spending on police. Rock Springs's per capita income ranks eighth nationally. The area offers wide-open spaces.

Weaknesses: Paying for all of its services takes a toll on Rock Springs: it has the highest property taxes in micropolitan America. Buying a home is also a very expensive matter. Metropolitan America is far away. There are 213 extreme-temperature days annually.

Scores by Sections	
Climate/Environment	47
Diversions	61
Economics	58
Education	54
Sophistication	39
Health Care	36
Housing	33
Public Safety	59
Transportation	45
Urban Proximity	25
Total Points	457

List of Tables

536

Health Care

Housing

Public Safety

ESSENTIALS
of Cash Flow

Essentials Series

The Essentials Series was created for busy business advisory and corporate professionals. The books in this series were designed so that these busy professionals can quickly acquire knowledge and skills in core business areas.

Each book provides need-to-have fundamentals for those professionals who must:

- Get up to speed quickly, because they have been promoted to a new position or have broadened their responsibility scope

- Manage a new functional area

- Brush up on new developments in their area of responsibility

- Add more value to their company or clients

Other books in this series include:

Essentials of Accounts Payable, Mary S. Schaeffer

Essentials of Capacity Management, Reginald Tomas Yu-Lee

Essentials of CRM: A Guide to Customer Relationship Management, Bryan Bergeron

Essentials of Credit, Collections, and Accounts Receivable, Mary S. Schaeffer

Essentials of Intellectual Property, Paul J. Lerner and Alexander I. Poltorak

Essentials of Trademarks and Unfair Competition, Dana Shilling

Essentials of XBRL: Financial Reporting in the 21st Century, Miklos A. Vasarhelyi, Liv A. Watson, Brian L. McGuire, and Rajendra P. Srivastava

Essentials of Corporate Performance Measurement, George T. Friedlob, Lydia L.F. Schleifer, and Franklin J. Plewa, Jr.

For more information on any of the above titles, please visit *www.wiley.com*.

ESSENTIALS
of Cash Flow

H. A. Schaeffer, Jr.

John Wiley & Sons, Inc.

To my two very special kids, Wendy Ann and Matthew, who I treasure greatly, and the Love of my Life, Mary, my darling wife, I dedicate this book: To the never ending love and joy that they bring me, and the will to always move forward in the face of all life's challenges.

Contents

Preface

Cash flow is often referred to as the lifeblood of an organization. With it, operations can proceed smoothly, allowing executives to make the best decisions possible without concerning themselves about the company's ability to pay. Without it, decisions are often hampered by the inability to pay and thus a company ends up implementing a plan or taking a course of action that is not optimal. The company that focuses on cash flow doing everything it can to squeeze the last bit out of each phase of its operations will have put itself on the best possible course for success—while simultaneously improving the bottom line.

The bottom-line impact of both good and bad cash flow management is often hidden from view because it doesn't show up as a specific line item. A company that improves the speed at which it collects its receivables might show a higher-than-expected investment income number or a lower interest expense. But few will be able to trace that back to the management of the accounts receivable portfolio—unless the controller or chief financial officer (CFO) or other financial executive carefully watches and measures the portfolio. And this is precisely what a number of world-class companies are doing.

It's not just the obvious cash items that can affect cash flow. Almost every step of the operation can have an impact. For example, how a company handles its billing can have a major impact on receivables. A company that bills just once a month has just given its customers an extra two weeks, on average, to hold onto its money. Conversely, one that bills every day has taken those two weeks back. The purpose of this book is to go through the entire business cycle, step by step and focus on areas that can be fine-tuned to enhance cash flow.

We start by taking a look at the order-to-cash cycle—the time frame and tasks that occur from the time your customer places its order until you actually have its cash in your bank account. There are quite a few places where a company can change its procedures to get that cash in the door just a little bit faster.

On the other side of the coin, Chapter 3 investigates the purchase-to-pay cycle—the timeframe between the time a company draws up a purchase order until the payment for those goods actually goes out the door. This long-ignored area is the latest area to come under scrutiny for cash flow enhancement practices.

When one of your company's customers files for bankruptcy protection, it can really do a number on your cash flow. Many people don't realize that a customer's bankruptcy filing doesn't necessarily mean they won't get their money. Chapter 4 investigates those times when a vendor can get paid and offers advice for those looking to solidify their position after a customer's bankruptcy filing. We also offer some advice on selling to a customer after such a filing—yes, it can be done sometimes, and occasionally quite profitably.

All sales are not created equal. In fact, some of them can be quite profitable, and some—well, your company may even book a loss by the time you are finished with them. A customer who pays months late, takes numerous deductions, and drives your staff crazy may actually cost you money, especially if you are in a business with thin profit margins. Unfortunately, many salespeople don't differentiate the customer just described from those who pay their bills on time and don't cause problems. Chapter 5 discusses methods you can use to keep your sales staff from impacting your cash flow in a negative manner.

Maverick purchasing can cost your company thousands, if not millions, of dollars when the purchasing staff doesn't operate within corporate guidelines. An even greater problem at some companies are employees who decide to avoid the purchasing department altogether and go out and buy what they need when they please. These individuals usually pay a higher price, cause the company to lose quantity discounts, and may even be acquiring items they don't need or are not entitled to purchase. Chapter 6 discusses ways that the purchasing function can be reengineered to maximize a company's purchasing dollars and improve its cash flow at the same time. Readers should note that the purchasing function at many companies has gone through massive changes in the last five years and many more are expected in the upcoming years.

Customer service is often overlooked when discussing cash flow. What some executives do not realize is that good customer service is an essential component of not only ongoing sales but also strong cash flow. Chapter 7 takes a look at how a well-run customer service department can enhance cash flow.

How your product is delivered to the customer also can affect cash flow. Put it in a shoddy box and it is likely to be damaged, causing the customer to either return it or take a deduction against the final payment. Additionally, such treatment may impact future sales negatively. Chapter 8 takes a look at how quality control, shipping, and returns can eat away at cash flow if not handled properly. It also contains suggestions on what savvy companies can do to ensure that these issues do not affect their cash flow.

Selling to dot-coms and other start-ups presents special problems to those companies concerned about their cash flow. Assuming the entity doesn't go out of business, vendors are likely to be paid slowly unless they handle these accounts correctly. Chapter 9 looks at ways that executives can make sales to start-ups without incurring cash flow deterioration.

Retailers present special problems to the vendors who supply them with product. Many are notorious for taking unauthorized, and often questionable, deductions when paying invoices. Some executives believe that certain customers start a dispute on some small issue to avoid paying a large invoice. Chapter 10 takes a look at what can be done to prevent cash flow deterioration that occurs when deductions are taken but not authorized and when disputes are not settled quickly. It takes a close look at what has become a huge problem—these issues when selling to retailers.

As you can see, some of the issues discussed require specialized knowledge or are too complicated for those with overstretched staffs to address adequately. Chapter 11 takes a look at some of the specialty service companies that have sprung up to help corporations deal with some of these narrow issues.

The Internet has invaded almost every aspect of our lives, especially our business lives. Chapter 12 discusses some of the recent innovations available through the Internet that can now be used to improve cash flow. There may be some surprises in that chapter for you—services you had never dreamed of.

Businesses today are often forced to operate on the narrowest of margins. The way a company's cash flow is handled can often mean the difference between a successful, thriving company and one that is at the mercy of the bankruptcy court and its creditors. It is my hope that, by implementing some of the techniques discussed in this book, you will firmly plant your company in the former category. Good luck.

Acknowledgments

I have had the privilege of working with many fine professionals in the business community and each of them had an impact on the creation of this book. They are too numerous to mention; however, I thank them all for their input.

John Wiley & Sons, Inc., and its editors, Sheck Cho and Tim Burgard, have been ideal partners for this and my last two book endeavors. They have helped make this project—as well as others—a reality.

## CHAPTER 1

The Lifeblood of the Organization: Why Cash Flow Is So Important

After reading this chapter, you will be able to

- See why cash flow is critical to the very existence of a company
- Know some of the external and internal factors that can affect the cash flow of a manufacturer
- Understand some of the external and internal factors that can affect the cash flow of a distributor
- Understand some of the external and internal factors that can affect the cash flow of a retailer
- Know some of the external and internal factors that can affect the cash flow of a service firm
- Understand what factors directly related to accounts receivables can affect the cash flow into a business

Why is cash critical to a business? Many an entrepreneur with a better "mousetrap" has asked that question and is now out of business. Many businesses that have not made a profit for many years but have solid cash flow continue to run while those that have great profit but no cash flow for a few years have filed for bankruptcy. Why is cash king? Companies need to buy goods such as raw materials, pay salaries, provide overhead, and so on. How can you obtain these without

1

working capital? While sales are the food that feeds the body of the business, a firm needs healthy cash flow (lifeblood) to keep it alive and moving forward.

Initial Cash Needed

Cash flow doesn't start with the collection of a receivable or the sale of an item for cash but actually starts with the creation of a business. Depending on the type of business that is started, basic supplies and services will be needed. Capital of some sort, whether in the form of a loan or cash investment by the owner(s), is needed to get the business off the ground. Once the necessary cash is obtained to clear the initial purchases and set up, cash is again needed to move the inventory or advertise the business. These can be in the form of salaries for sales and marketing staff, Web site creation, advertising in local papers, TV, radio, magazines, and so on. When sales are made, customers pay with credit cards or request open account credit. Once receivables are collected, cash is in hand to pay expenses, payables, loans, and buy new inventory in a never-ending cycle.

The Next Level of Cash Needs

Times occur in every growing business when cash is not "timely" enough to accommodate its needs. A firm may seek out cash in one of many ways:

One way is to shorten the time it takes to collect its receivables by offering its customers a cash discount for early payment of their debt. This will cost the firm profit and can cause other problems, which will be discussed in Chapter 2.

A business may ask its vendors to grant them longer credit terms or simply pay slower, which will be discussed in Chapter 3.

A business may go to its bank and request a working capital line of credit. This usually requires the business to pledge its assets as collateral and may require its officers to sign personal guarantees as well as pledging their personal assets to secure the loan.

As a business gets larger and has critical needs for cash especially if it is a retailer and has seasonal inventory, it may factor or sell its receivables to a third party for a discounted amount. A business may have major capital needs that typically do not fall under the day-to-day cash flow operation. The need of additional equipment, building space, and vehicles may require the leasing of these items. These leases require monthly payments plus interest, which needs to be addressed in the cash needs equation.

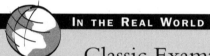

IN THE REAL WORLD

Classic Example of Lack of Cash Flow While Being Profitable: W. T. Grant

One of the largest bankruptcies of the 1970s was W.T. Grant for over $2 billion. During the years of 1966 to 1973, it reported increasing sales, with a total sales of $1.6 billion in 1973. It reported increasing sales each year with a consistent level of profits attached to those sales. Investors at the time paid attention only to the fact that sales and profits were up, not that cash flow was flat or decreasing. These cash shortages started in 1969, leading to W.T. Grant's surprise filing of bankruptcy on October 2, 1975. In this case each store had its own credit policy (credit was handled within the company since MasterCard/Visa did not exist at that time) and offered customer payment terms of 36 months with minimum payments being made. So while it had great sales, payment of the receivables was minimal, minimizing the company's ability to meet its day-to-day needs, let alone any long-term needs.

Items That Affect the Cash Flow of a Manufacturer

There are both internal and external factors that can directly affect the rate of cash flow of a company. Some internal and external factors for manufacturers include:

- Delays in receiving raw materials needed to complete a finished product
- Choosing the wrong firm to do assembly work or other customized work
- Choosing a supplier that has cash flow problems
- Price increases by suppliers
- Tightening up of credit terms by suppliers
- Defective raw materials
- Defective finished products
- Weak or poor computer systems capability
- Antiquated or poor manufacturing facilities and equipment or procedures that are not cost effective
- Overpurchasing of new equipment, additional facilities, or overhiring of staff to meet customers' demands
- Basic design problems
- Cost of borrowing to meet cash flow and capital needs versus leasing
- Competition
- Economic downturns
- War, acts of God, terrorism, fire, and so on
- Shipping delays and errors both of goods in and out
- Over- or underselling of products by the sales force
- Poor marketing campaign
- Selling credit terms instead of products

- Accepting customized jobs that are not cost effective
- Labor problems
- Fraud and theft
- Weather-related problems
- Changes in technology related to its product
- Changes in the law that affect how a company does business

Items That Affect the Cash Flow of a Distributor

Distributors may have internal and external problems such as:

- Receiving defective finished goods for resale from manufacturers
- Receiving the wrong goods rather than what was ordered
- Short shipments versus what was ordered
- Overshipment of goods that they ordered
- Being loaded up by their suppliers
- Choosing a supplier that has cash flow problems
- Tightening up of credit terms by suppliers
- Price increases that were increased by manufacturers and passed on to them
- Over- or underselling of a product by the sales force
- Poor marketing campaign
- The distributor's customers may have short paid what is owed and disputed the difference for various reasons
- Cost of borrowing to meet cash flow and capital needs versus leasing
- Competition
- Economic downturns
- War, acts of God, terrorism, fire, and so on

5

- Shipping delays of goods in or out
- Labor problems

Items That Affect the Cash Flow of a Retailer

Retailers, have similar but also other problems such as:

- Defective finished goods
- Wrong goods received
- Underbuying
- Overbuying
- No or few goods received in time to meet advertising schedule
- Price increases that may be difficult to pass on to the consumer due to competition
- Tightening up of credit terms by suppliers
- Choosing a supplier that has cash flow problems
- Short shipment of goods, especially if they are seasonal in nature
- Overshipment of goods, especially if they are seasonal in nature
- Damaged goods or packaging
- Internal and external theft
- Slow-moving inventory
- Whims of consumers
- Competition
- Economic downturns
- War, acts of God, terrorism, fire, and so on
- Shipping delays of goods in
- Wrong or delayed advertising
- Poor or badly timed marketing campaign
- Shortage of good low cost employees

- Overhead at locations that are not profitable
- Weather not conducive to seasonal products

Items That Affect the Cash Flow of a Service Firm

Service firms have slightly different problems such as:

- Meeting the demands of their customers
- Lacking the manpower to accommodate the customers' needs
- Subcontracting part of a project out to a firm that is experiencing cash flow problems
- Lack of the necessary equipment to start or complete the job
- Lack of necessary expertise for a custom order
- Pricing issues with the customer (what the customer is willing to pay versus their seller's needs and costs)
- Poor or antiquated computer systems
- Poor or antiquated capital equipment used in the production of the service being offered
- Cost of borrowing to meet cash flow and capital needs versus leasing
- Competition
- Initial costs incurred before any payments are received from the buyer
- Delays or costs in getting any raw materials needed to complete the service requirement of the buyer
- Economic conditions
- War, acts of God, terrorism, fire, and so on
- Labor problems
- Weather conditions that can affect service provided to the customer

Some of these internal and external obstacles to cash flow of a firm can be addressed by employing changes to its sales techniques or changing its pricing structure but others cannot be so easily overcome.

Items That Affect Cash Flow from Accounts Receivables

One factor that is listed occurs in all businesses (with the exception of retailers): slow payment or nonpayment of credit extensions, known as the collection of its accounts receivables. Some factors that can affect the collection of receivables include:

- Competition
- Written corporate policy that includes:
  - Terms of sale
  - When a customer is truly delinquent
  - Collection techniques incorporated
  - Support by upper management of its credit department versus sales department
  - When a customer is placed on credit hold
  - When a customer is placed with a collection agency and sued
- Corporate customer philosophy referring to how a customer is treated (i.e., customer is king, customer is important, etc.)
- Size and skill/experience level of the individuals in the credit and collections area
- Lack of computer systems that are conducive to improving cash flow efforts
- Sales support of cash flow as well as cooperation with the credit area and their integrity plus incentive to cooperate
- Actual top management support of cash flow, not just a written policy and procedures manual

A full review of the workings both in and outside of the credit and collections area will be reviewed in Chapter 2.

Summary

It is safe to say that making a sale is vital to a firm, but it is only the first step. If cash is not collected, the firm can be considered only a philanthropic organization. Always remember that a sale is not a sale until the cash register rings. Until that point, it is simply a gift.

Improving the Order-to-Cash Cycle

After reading this chapter, you will be able to

- Understand how order entry can directly affect cash flow
- See how credit review and decision making can directly affect cash flow and the cost effectiveness of a firm
- See the "carrot" and "stick" approaches to credit terms
- Use cash flow methods to prevent delinquency before it occurs
- Take steps to maximize collection efforts while staying cost effective
- Understand how to use collection agencies and collection attorneys for cash flow improvements and cost savings

Now we enter the area that most officers of a company consider the only part that has anything to do with the cash flow of a firm—the order-to-cash cycle. While this is probably one of the most critical parts of the cash flow focus, it is truly a misconception on their part. As you will see in the upcoming chapters, the order-to-cash cycle is just the beginning.

Order to Cash—A Simplistic View

Once an order is placed and the goods are shipped, assuming that the goods were sold on credit terms, it is now up to the firm's credit department to collect its money. This is a very simplistic view of the process, and between the start (placing the order) and the finish (cash), many things can be done to improve the process.

The Order Entry Process

Let's start with the order entry process. Many firms have very sophisticated computer systems that allow their customers to order goods directly through the seller's server system. Others provide access to ordering goods directly using a secure password-protected Web site, which gives them a universal access to automated ordering.

Depending on the complexity of the goods or services needed by the buyer, the intervention of an order entry expert or a salesperson will be required. Items such as customized goods; technically complex items; specialized service contracts; or carefully monitored items, such as some pharmaceuticals, hazardous chemicals, and so on, need individuals with additional training and understanding in the nature of the goods or services being offered for sale. The more technologically complex the order, the greater the skill, knowledge, and expertise of the order taker will need to be.

Credit Review and Decision

New Customer Application— Where Does It Come From?

A new customer will be required (in most companies) to submit a credit application. Depending on how your firm is set up, the application could come to the credit department from various locations such as:

- Through the salesperson covering that area or type of customer
- Forwarded by the customer directly to you after receiving a blank copy either from the salesperson, customer service department, or the credit department

- Credit department mails, faxes, or e-mails application directly to the customer and requests that they forward it back to the attention of the credit manager.

New Customer Application—What Information Should Be Requested?

Now that you know that the application will get to the credit department, what information should a good credit application contain? In many cases, the more detailed a credit application the better the credit decision, but the more difficult it will be to get it completed. It is sometimes wise to have more than one type of application based on whom you may be dealing with. If the firm is a large Fortune 500 firm, then it will be unlikely that you will get more than its name and address with possible mention of contact numbers for different departments. If it is a small firm, it may have limited information available on the company but a wealth of information on the owners.

 TIPS AND TECHNIQUES

What a Very Detailed Application Should Contain

- Customer's full legal name (a legal name, not a DBA [doing business as])

- Customer's physical address (the address where billing information is sent)

- Customer's phone/fax numbers and e-mail address as well as Web site address

- What type of business it is:
  - Proprietorship

- Partnership
- Limited liability partnership
- Limited liability company
- Corporation (state whether a "C" corporation or a Subchapter "S" corporation) (the date and state of incorporation and whether it is a private or public firm)
- Joint venture
- Nonprofit corporation
- Government agency (town, city, county, state, or federal)

- Phone/fax number and e-mail address of the accounts payable area that will have responsibility for paying this account

- If this is a proprietorship or partnership, the name(s), address(s) and home phone number(s) and e-mail address(s) of the owner(s)

- Corporate parent's name, address, phone/fax numbers and e-mail address

- Whether it is a division, subsidiary, or affiliate of the parent corporation

- Date firm started

- Type of firm that it is:
  - Manufacturer
  - Distributor
  - Retailer
  - Service firm
  - Other

- Credit limit requested

- Dun & Bradstreet Dun's # (identification number for companies)

- Bank reference information, including:

- Bank name
- Bank address where account is
- Bank account number(s)
- Type of account(s) with the bank
- What type(s) of collateral (if any) the bank has a lien on
- Whether a personal guarantee has been given to the bank by the officer(s) of the firm
- Bank officer's name in charge of its account
- Bank's phone/fax numbers as well as e-mail address
- Signed permission form to provide to bank to obtain a reference
- Trade references information, including (minimum 3, maximum 4):
  - Trade reference company name
  - Trade reference company's address where account is
  - Account number(s) with the trade reference company
  - Type of account(s) with the trade reference company
  - What type(s) of collateral (if any) the trade reference company has a lien on
  - Whether a personal guarantee has been given to the trade reference company by the officer(s) of the firm
  - Credit manager's name in charge of its account
  - Trade reference company's phone/fax numbers as well as e-mail address
  - Signed permission form to provide to trade reference company to obtain a reference
  - The credit application form should request the name of at least two references that would be similar in nature to the credit extender, such as (1) the supplier who previously provided the same or similar goods or services to the buyer

as the seller now offers, and (2) if a service vendor, the name of a firm that would be in a similar payment status as that of the vendor. (For example, to a restaurant with a broken refrigeration unit, the repair firm would be critical until the repair is made but not after; or a newspaper that published an ad for a restaurant would be important at the time that the ad is placed but not as important thereafter.)

- A request for audited financial statements on the firm (or at least financial statements if audited ones are not available)

- If this firm is a proprietorship or partnership, an authorization form at the bottom of the credit application must provide the permission to obtain a consumer credit report on either the owner or owners of the firm

- If this is a firm that is relatively new (less than one year in business) a personal guarantee may be needed. This must be a separate form from the credit application and should include in its body the permission to obtain consumer credit information on the parties signing it.

- If a personal guarantee is obtained, then the home address, phone number, and e-mail address should be obtained on all parties signing the personal guarantee.

- A final statement that the signor attests to the truthfulness of the above information

- Signatures and titles of those signing the credit application

New Customer Investigation

Now that you have a completed application, where do you go from here? The credit limit needed for a firm in order for it to become a viable and worthwhile customer will directly affect the level and intensity of the credit investigation. Defining what is a small, medium, and large credit extension for your firm will allow the company to set policy and procedures for level and costs for investigating a new customer.

Small Customers. The volume of new applications processed, credit limit systems controls in place, and cost involved with performing credit investigation (i.e., staff time, cost of credit reports, occasional bank fees for credit references, etc.) versus the risk of a loss from nonpayment by a

IN THE REAL WORLD

Considering Credit for High Volume Firms

If a firm receives hundreds of new requests for credit daily, which typically require small-dollar credit limits, then the entire application procedure and investigation may be very minimal. This is very commonplace in the telecommunications industry where hundreds of new customers sign up daily for service with suppliers of company local/long distance phone service. Credit limits may be for a few hundred dollars up to under $1,000.00. Some telecommunications firms have as many as 40,000 credit applications to consider in a month.

Credit review in these cases involves obtaining names and addresses of firms and running the firm through a sophisticated credit scoring system that "predicts" the likelihood of default of a firm and sets a limit comparable to the risk. These scoring systems are usually based on information supplied by credit reporting agencies and past experience of delinquency/losses of the credit grantor. The system would also check the customer against the credit grantor's own in-house accounts receivables to determine if any outstanding delinquency/losses exist for this new potential customer.

customer will help to determine the level of time and expense put into a credit investigation for a small customer.

Medium Customers. At this stage a certain level of investigation should be required as a part of the corporate credit policy and procedures manual. Reference checks should be performed as well as a check of both trade credit groups (if available) and/or a credit report from a credit reporting agency.

Large Customers—Obtaining Audited Data. While all the efforts that were made for the medium customer to check its creditworthiness were acceptable, a large credit extension needs far more attention paid to the credit decision process. Analysis of financial information should be made in all cases. Audited numbers should be obtained from the public as well as private firms. While it is very easy to obtain audited statements from public companies, it can be a real challenge to get this information from private firms. Public firms' financial statements can be obtained from the federal government's EDGAR Web site(http://www.sec.gov/edgar/searchedgar/formpick.htm) or directly from the customer's Web site. As for private firms, it is mandatory that a formal letter of confidentiality be provided stating who in the credit department (title only) will have access to its information, that it will be used for credit purposes only and that the sales department will have no access to this information. This may assist the credit grantor with the tough job of obtaining this information but will definitely not guarantee it.

Large Customers—Analyzing Financial Statements. Assuming that you are lucky enough to obtain a financial statement or truly blessed beyond all comprehension and receive a complete, audited financial statement, your work now begins. The ideal situation would be to have at least four years' worth of data but certainly settle for some rather than none. After obtaining the financial information, analysis of the business should be done to determine their present condition (present defined as the date of the financial report and not really as of today!). This status needs to be compared to previous years and against their peers to determine how they stack up.

TIPS AND TECHNIQUES

Four Methods Employed to Determine the Financial Strength of a Firm

Most credit professionals use one or more of the following approaches when analyzing the financial viability of a customer.

1 *Common size analysis.* Converts numbers from the balance sheet and income statement to percentages of a total (i.e., assets, liabilities and net worth, or net sales), allows companies of different sizes within an industry the ability to compare their results against that of other industry players, and allows a company to compare its percentages for each item against previous years' results

2 *Trend analysis.* Compares parts of the Balance Sheet, Income Statement, Statement of Cash Flows, and Ratios from the present year to those of previous years and works best when there are at least three to five years' worth of data to compare

3 *Comparison to industry standards.* Comparing the changes in "Key" ratios from each year against industry "Norms" to pinpoint movement toward improvement or decline in a business and to identify "unusual items"

4 *Ratio analysis.* Standardize financial data using mathematical relationships expressed as percentage or times which can be compared both against industry "Norms" or as part of trend (year-to-year) comparison

Completing this analysis provides the credit professional insight into the financial makeup of the customer. It can help to spot problems with cash flow, signs of debt overflow or signs of solid growth and profitability coupled with a strong cash position. This analysis coupled with the background credit investigation stated in looking at a medium customer provides a respectable amount of information in order to render a sound business credit decision.

New Customer

After all the analysis has been completed and a decision made, the potential customer will be granted a credit limit, a request for additional information or security will be made, or the customer will be rejected. At this point, we will discuss only the supposition that the customer has been approved for credit and proceed from there.

Credit-Approved (Established) Customer

Once a customer has an approved credit limit, the order will be processed and approved for shipping. This assumes that the order will not put the customer over its approved credit limit. It also assumes that any currently open invoices that exist for this firm are current. By current, we mean that they are within the corporate credit policy and procedures manual's definition of "current," which could be anywhere from 1 to 30 days past due depending on the firm's corporate philosophy (i.e., more sales oriented versus cash oriented). If both of these assumptions are correct, then the order will flow freely out the door.

Credit Terms

Cash Flow versus Profits: The Carrot Routine

There are many variations of credit terms offered by businesses and entire industries today. Credit terms can cost a seller both in terms of profit on sales and on cash flow. A firm that offers a cash discount may speed up cash flow by having customers who take advantage of it pay an amount that is less that the full amount of the invoice but get the payment in fewer days than it would if the buyer paid in the normal net time due. There is a definite cost to cash discount terms from the point of view of customers who take the discount but still pay in net terms. This type of "game playing" has existed since discount terms were first offered. The battle to recoup these disallowed discounts costs a company in terms of salaries of individuals needed to collect these small but quickly accruing dollars. Likewise, the company receives no benefit to its cash flow by having the customers pay beyond the date that was set for the legitimate date for taking the cash discount.

TIPS AND TECHNIQUES

Time-Tested Methods to Prevent Firms from Abusing Cash Discount Terms

- Set a definite policy approved and supported by top management as to the limit of what is accepted as the maximum time frame for receipt of payment in which the cash discount will be allowed.

- Set a definite policy approved and supported by top management as to a total amount or percentage of sales or receivables that can be accumulated, which will trigger a final warning letter to be sent to the head of the customer's purchasing department with a copy to the accounts payable manager, notifying them that if repayment of disallowed discounts are not made within 10 days, the customer's orders or service will be stopped.

- If the customer again takes a discount that is disallowed after being forced to repay under threat of credit hold, it will be notified that cash discount terms will no longer be offered to that customer.

- An automated dunning letter system will be set up, which notifies the customer every time that it takes a cash discount that is not justified.

- A letter of company policy in relation to cash discounts will be sent to the head of the purchasing departments of all of the seller's customers by the seller's president, notifying them about benefits of the cash discount program but advising them of the consequences of abusing the privilege of taking a cash discount.

- Disallowed cash discounts will not be written off just to keep a customer happy, for it will use this method to increase its profitability at the expense of the seller.

Cash Flow versus Profits: The Stick Routine

The direct opposite of a cash discount that is also employed as a means to keep profit intact and improve cash flow is late charges. When a customer pays beyond net credit terms, the seller adds a late fee, which will be billed to the customer against the dollar amount of the invoice versus the number of days beyond the due date of the invoice (plus grace period) times the interest rate allowed by the state that the seller is located. This fee typically more than offsets the time cost of money on these past due invoices and brings in additional cash when they are paid. A similar problem exists with the enforcement of the collection of these late fees as existed for collecting disallowed discounts. Customers (especially large ones) tend to pay slowly and refuse to pay late fees. The same steps that

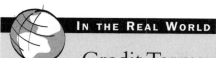

Credit Terms: Great Variance by Industry

Credit terms of industries vary greatly. In the food industry, in which the products are very perishable, the terms may be net 7 days from invoice date or net 10 or net 14 days. In the pharmaceuticals industry, typical terms are 2 percent 30 net 31 days, which means that if the invoice is paid in 30 days the customer may take 2 percent off the total invoice, but on the 31st day from invoice date the invoice is due in full. In the jewelry industry, terms of net 360 are common due to the slow turnover of jewelry. International terms of sale may extend out to net 180 days depending on the country in which the product is being shipped. In Canada net 30 days terms means 30 days from end of month or 30 days plus any time from the date that the goods were shipped to the end of that same month (i.e., goods shipped 4/15/02 would be due on 5/31/02).

were implemented and supported by top management must also be taken to keep the customer from abusing the system by increasing its profitability by paying late and keep cash flow intact for the seller.

One additional factor that must be looked into before deciding to charge late fees is the rate that your company plans to charge. In most if not all states there is a Usury Law ceiling established, which sets the maximum rate of interest that can be charged as a late fee. In New York State that rate is 24 percent but certainly is different in other localities. While not necessarily a proponent of this type of action, I do recommend it if all of your customers are businesses that tend to pay late and get an interest-free loan rather than use a credit card and get hit with interest if they don't pay the balance off in full when it is due.

IN THE REAL WORLD

Credit Cards versus Late Fees

Another alternative to charging late fees might be to accept credit cards as a means of payment. If you accept credit cards for payment, you can receive your payment in two to three days, automatically deposited into your account. The credit card firm does charge a fee for that service, which can run anywhere from 1.5 to 8 percent depending on the volume of business that you do, the average ticket sale size, the number of problems that you run into from charge backs on the credit card, and the type of clientele that you sell to (small proprietorships versus Fortune 500 firms). If your customer market is made up entirely of small types of firms and you can build the cost of the fee into the sale price, then you may be far better off than charging late fees. With late fees you still have to collect them and your past due balance, whereas you will always receive the money from the credit card company in two to three days plus you will not have to alienate your customer by constantly demanding your payment.

Cash Flow Improvement: Preventing Delinquency before It Can Occur

The PR Call

There are many ways to prevent delinquency before it can occur. One example is the Public Relations (PR) call. Let's assume that a firm has terms with its customers of 1 percent 10 days from invoice date net 30 days from invoice date. At 15 days from the invoice date a call is placed to the customer. They are immediately thanked for their business and asked to confirm receipt of the most recent invoice. (*Note:* This type of call is usually made only to major customers with large invoices outstanding.) After confirming receipt of invoice, determine if all goods were received, were

TIPS AND TECHNIQUES

Questions You Should Ask When Considering Accepting Credit Cards as Payment

Bank Concerns

- What banks are being considered for servicing your credit card needs?

- What is the discount rate that they will charge and is it a blended rate for MasterCard, Visa, and American Express? For how long is it good?

- What type of software package do they use, and is it compatible with your system?

- What reports will the bank provide to assist in the confirmation of acceptance of the credit card transaction?

- What means are needed by the bank to submit approved credit card transmissions for payment? Can an electronic submission of "payment tickets" be sent to the bank as well, or will paper ticket forms be required?

- If the bank that you use is not the credit card bank, how will these submissions for payment be tendered?

- If the bank that you use is not the bank that is the accepted provider, how will payments and data be transferred between the two banks and ultimately delivered to you?

- What reports are available to confirm payment by the bank into your lockbox?

- Can payments be automatically applied via an automated cash application system?

- What technical assistance can the bank provide in the setup of the software and use with your system?

- What training can the bank provide to those persons involved with the accepting of credit cards?

Internal Concerns

- At the time that the order is being taken, what credit card information will need to be inputted into the system? What screens or field blocks will need to be completed in order to finalize the sales order and generate the need for a nightly offline approval request? To reduce input errors, can the system be programmed to confirm certain checks of credit card numbers after a type of card has been chosen as being used for payment (i.e., MasterCard's always begin with a "5" and have 16 digits; Visa cards always begin with a "4" and have 16 digits; and American Express cards always begin with a "3" and have only 15 numbers.) .

- Orders need to be automatically held for one day until the approval is received. Who will release the approved orders? Can your system automatically release these orders from information that it receives from the bank? Once approval codes are downloaded from the bank, can these numbers be automatically added to the forms needing this information before the orders are released and the documents printed (i.e., sales orders, etc.)?

- How will the data need to be formatted to transmit to the bank a nightly offline batch request of credit card purchases for approval?

- Can your system generate a report each morning from information received from the bank the night before that lists the approved and disapproved credit card transactions?

- Who will reconcile the total dollars of credit orders taken daily to the total dollars of credit card orders approved and denied for payment to confirm balance of these numbers? Can this be automated?

- If the credit card is not approved, who will follow up the customer to either obtain a correct card number or a different card number or refer the customer to the credit department for submission of required credit information?

- If product is not available after the credit card order is approved, who will follow up with the customer as to the status of their order? If the customer wishes the order cancelled, who will reverse the credit card transaction?

- What documents will need to reflect the customer's credit card number, expiration date, name on credit card being used, and the approval number by the bank? What fields are available on the system to accommodate these needs?

- Can the customer's credit card information be retained on the system for future use and reference when the customer places additional orders? (This information should require an additional password for release of it to the user.)

- What information should the invoices reflect in connection with payment by credit card (i.e., paid by MasterCard, Visa, American Express, and date paid [Approval date])?

- Who will have the ability to accept credit cards for payment (i.e., customer service, credit, both)?

- Should the credit cards be used not only for new sales but also as a method to pay past due balances?

- Who should be designated as responsible for the security of the overall credit card operation?

- Who will have the authority to reverse a credit card transaction? (*Note:* This should not be the same individual as the person who accepts the cards.)

- Who will be doing the cash application of credit card payments if they cannot be automated? What information will be needed by them to minimize the efforts in its application (i.e., some means to identify a payment through possibly a sales order number, invoice number, etc.)?

- MasterCard and Visa transactions will be paid at 100 percent of face value in two banking days and the discount charges will be billed monthly. American Express deducts 2.95 percent from each transaction processed and pays the net amount in three banking days. Who will be responsible for the reconciliation of all three types of card billings and the approval and payment for the transactions processed for MasterCard and Visa sales?

- Can your system be programmed to automatically allow for the 2.95 percent deduction from each credit card transaction paid by American Express? Can these deductions be accrued in a general ledger account?

- Can reports be generated by your system to track customer type information and credit card type usage? Information needed, by customer type, will include the average dollar ticket size, percentage of type of card used, number of transactions by customer type with a total for each type, and total dollars of credit card sales by customer type versus that customer type's total sales. The reports needed for credit card type usage include total fees paid by each credit card type within a customer type and the percentage, total dollars with average ticket size, and the number of credit card type transactions used by each customer type. These reports should be made to reflect monthly and year to date statistics. See Exhibits 2.1 through 2.6.

TIPS AND TECHNIQUES CONTINUED

Special Note: The titles used on this form are for a company that mainly sells to these three types of buyers but could be altered for use in any type of customer base. (This type of information will be needed by the bank to use in the renegotiation of the discount rate and to track the costs involved with accepting each type of credit card. It will also help to determine if any credit card is being underutilized and acceptance should be discontinued.)

- What means will your firm use to notify their customers of their ability to now accept credit cards for payment? Will any special programs be offered to promote their use?

EXHIBIT 2.1

Credit Card Type: MasterCard

	Doctors	Government	Hospitals/Clinics
Total Fees Paid:			
This Month:			
YTD:			
% Used by			
Customer Type:			
This Month:			
YTD:			
$ Charged:			
This Month:			
YTD:			
Average Ticket Size:			
This Month:			
YTD:			
# Of Transactions:			
This Month:			
YTD:			

EXHIBIT 2.2

Credit Card Type: Visa

	Doctors	Government	Hospitals/Clinics
Total Fees Paid:			
This Month:			
YTD:			
% Used by			
Customer Type:			
This Month:			
YTD:			
$ Charged:			
This Month:			
YTD:			
Average Ticket Size:			
This Month:			
YTD:			
# Of Transactions:			
This Month:			
YTD:			

EXHIBIT 2.3

Credit Card Type: American Express

	Doctors	Government	Hospitals/Clinics
Total Fees Paid:			
This Month:			
YTD:			
% Used by			
Customer Type:			
This Month:			
YTD:			
$ Charged:			
This Month:			
YTD:			
Average Ticket Size:			
This Month:			
YTD:			
# Of Transactions:			
This Month:			
YTD:			

EXHIBIT 2.4

Customer Type: Doctors

	MasterCard	**Visa**	**American Express**

Average $ Ticket Size:
This Month:
YTD:

% of Usage:
This Month:
YTD:

# of Transactions:
This Month:
YTD:

Average Ticket Size:
This Month:
YTD:

Total $ of Credit Sales:
This Month:
YTD:

EXHIBIT 2.5

Customer Type: Government

	MasterCard	**Visa**	**American Express**

Average $ Ticket Size:
This Month:
YTD:

% of Usage:
This Month:
YTD:

# of Transactions:
This Month:
YTD:

Average Ticket Size:
This Month:
YTD:

Total $ of Credit Sales:
This Month:
YTD:

EXHIBIT 2.6

Customer Type: Hospitals/Clinics

	MasterCard	Visa	American Express
Average $ Ticket Size: This Month: YTD:			
% of Usage: This Month: YTD:			
# of Transactions: This Month: YTD:			
Average Ticket Size: This Month: YTD:			
Total $ of Credit Sales: This Month: YTD:			

satisfactory, and were received in a timely fashion. After confirming their knowledge of the credit terms and how cash discounts add to their bottom line, a confirmation of the due date should also be done.

If all responses are positive, with no questions or concerns, then thank the customer for their business and advise that their payment will be anticipated by the due date. If any problems with the shipment have arisen, then they can immediately be addressed and resolved before they get out of hand. If no invoice has been received, a replacement can immediately be sent to the customer. What has been accomplished by this action? Approximately 95 percent of all excuses for nonpayment have been eliminated as a result of this call. The only answer left as to why a customer hasn't paid you is that they don't have the funds to pay, which will result in a far different approach to handing extension of credit to them in the future.

Billing for Shipments or Services Rendered— Timing

When goods are shipped and services completed according to the terms of sale, an invoice is generated and typically mailed to the customer. Any delays in this process directly impact the cash flow of a business. Typical time for receipt of an invoice may be as little as one day to as much as seven days or more depending on the customer's location and the location and efficiency of the nearest main post office to your customer.

Many firms now electronically bill their customers or never create a real invoice but simply bill using the shipping documents. The faster that a bill or an electronic variation of it can be in the hands of those that need it to pay, the more likely your chances of being paid on time. If discount terms are offered, this likewise will improve the possibility that a customer will take advantage of this offer and pay you in shorter terms.

Depending on the industry to which you sell or offer services, the buyer may require that you bill electronically or bill off of the shipping documents. Assuming that there are not extreme costs in system hardware and software requirements, electronic billing is indeed the most cost effective from a cash flow perspective.

Financial Customer Service

Another way to prevent delinquency before it can occur is to create a "financial customer service" department. This would involve the merging of the customer service and credit areas into one operation. By doing this you have put those with the "finger on the pulse" of the customer together with the group that solves more problems with customers than any other area in the company. To obtain more details on how to create such a department, see *Financial Customer Service: A Guide to Making Smarter Business Decisions* (H.A. Schaeffer, New York: John Wiley & Sons, 1999).

What Information Should the Ideal Invoice Contain?

Having an invoice that has all the pertinent facts needed for payment and is easy to read can also improve the likelihood of swifter payment. Information that should be instantly noticeable to the eyes of the accounts payable person at the top of a *goods invoice* include:

- Customer's account number or ID
- Invoice number
- Invoice date
- The complete bill to location
- The complete ship to location
- The purchase order number
- The name of the shipping firm
- The date the goods were shipped
- The terms of sale
- The vendor's sales rep's name

Within the body of the goods invoice, it should include:

- Quantity of the item shipped
- An item number
- Description of the item with a serial number (if applicable)
- The unit price
- The total price of the line item

At the bottom of the goods invoice, it should include:

- The sales tax (if applicable)
- The freight amount

TIPS AND TECHNIQUES CONTINUED

- The total gross amount of the invoice

- The total net amount of the invoice if cash discount terms are being offered

Information that should be instantly noticeable to the eyes of the accounts payable person at the top of a *service invoice* includes:

- Customer's account number or ID

- Invoice number

- Invoice date

- The complete bill to location

- The complete ship to location (if applicable)

- The purchase order number

- The terms of sale

- The vendor's sales rep's name

Within the body of the service invoice, it should include:

- Complete (within reason) description of the service that was performed

- The total price of the line item

At the bottom of the service invoice, it should include:

- The sales tax (if applicable)

- The total gross amount of the invoice

- The total net amount of the invoice if cash discount terms are being offered

Communications and Education

The ultimate means to prevent delinquency before it can occur is to have a strong communications system that allows for all departments directly involved in the cash flow process to easily relay any problems that might occur that would delay or prevent payment. While many credit managers have an adversarial relationship with the sales and marketing groups, these situations must be at least minimized if not eliminated altogether. Many customers today will pit one department against the other in an effort to slow down their need to pay. Many other areas rarely know how their actions can directly affect the receipt of cash and loss of profitabil-

---

TIPS AND TECHNIQUES

Ways to Improve Communications and Cooperation between Departments

- Monthly open classes held by each department to instruct other areas on what their duties, responsibilities, and authority consists of should be held, as well as discussions as to how they can affect both the other department's goals and their own goals.

- The credit staff should attend all sales meetings both regional and national, to discuss customer problems, trends that are occurring that have slowed cash collections and reduced profitability, and a general brainstorming session to improve overall communications between these two areas.

- The credit department offers sales and marketing a service of prequalifying potential new customers to prevent a salesperson from putting out a large amount of effort to sell a customer only to find out that they do not qualify for credit terms.

TIPS AND TECHNIQUES CONTINUED

- Direct telephone and intranet communications of all areas (having a general copy of any customer or product problems sent to all areas directly affected by these problems)

- A required response time by each department to an inquiry sent to them by another area so as to prevent foot-dragging by another department versus problem solving

- Access (limited by password and need to know) to each department's database will allow all areas the ability to put the puzzle together when a customer either has problems or creates problems.

- Have all departments involved with the customer attend outside educational forums that cover not only their area of expertise but also the other departments' areas of expertise (i.e., credit staff attending a sales and marketing course, customer service attending a credit 101 seminar, etc.). This provides these areas with a view of the topic not originated by their counterparts in the same company and may bring new insights into their firm.

ity and don't understand what another area does or why cooperation is important to the entire company.

Communications between departments and education as to the responsibilities of each area of the firm can make the flow of critical internal information and degree of cooperation grow exponentially.

Improving Efficiency

One area that must always be addressed is efficiency. What are our weaknesses and what are our strengths? Before we can improve the cash flow outside of our world (that of the order entry area to the credit department), we must first look to ourselves for ways to improve. Compare now what you currently have in place and what you would like (within reason!) to achieve. The goal of being the most efficient in respect to cash flow should be measured against the following list of possibilities, which goes from worst to best. The areas to look at would be:

- How are orders taken?
  - Over the phone by an individual (least efficient and most prone to errors)
  - Through a salesperson at the customer's location
  - Direct access to the vendor's internal order entry system
  - Direct access to the vendor's internal order entry system via the Internet
  - Automatic order filling by the vendor for the customer via a direct link to the customer's online inventory system
  - Automatic order filling by the vendor for the customer via a direct link to the customer's online inventory system using an Internet-based connection (most efficient and least prone to errors)
- Credit processing
  - A credit application either is given to the customer by the salesperson, mailed out by the order entry/customer service person, or the credit department mails out the application (longest receipt time).
  - Application is mailed in when completed.
  - Application is faxed in when completed.
  - Application is on the Internet and can be printed out, completed, and mailed in to the credit department.
  - Application is on the Internet and can be completed online and immediately verified as to what firm sent it and who "signed" it (shortest receipt time).
- Credit investigation, time, and efficiency

- Call all references, obtain credit report by mail, and mail credit information request to industry trade group (slowest).

- Fax all references, obtain credit report by modem direct from credit reporting agency's outside phone line, and request that the trade group fax you the current references available on your potential customer.

- E-mail all references with e-mail request back, obtain credit report via the Internet, obtain industry trade information online via the Internet (fastest).

- *Credit investigation, cost versus limit.* This is an area that needs to be looked at on a case-by-case basis. What may be considered to be a large credit extension to one firm may be an automatic approval to another. Obviously, the more efficiently that a new applicant can be investigated the better, but there are certain cost factors involved with completing a credit investigation. The two most expensive parts of the investigation are manpower to do the work and the cost of credit reports. Manpower can be reduced if many of the functions are automated, such as e-mailing requests, Internet access to credit reports, and so on, but also credit scoring could reduce the costs involved with credit processing.

  While the creation of an automated credit scoring system can be very expensive, depending on the volume of new applicants, it may be the most cost-effective method. Credit reports vary greatly in both content and cost. Most are annual contracts and charge a scaled fee depending on the amount of information and the number of reports requested. For international reports, the speed at which you need a more customized report can likewise directly affect the cost.

  So what is the most cost-effective method for considering credit extension versus the risk of a loss? The best may be a combination of risk, acceptable losses, and reasonable costs to provide enough "peace of mind" to move forward with the sale of goods or services.

- Credit decision

  - *Poor.* Review all data, render decision, and mail out notification to all departments that the customer is approved; the customer's credit limit is listed on the system with no effect on orders or shipments.

  - *Better.* Review all data, render decision, and fax or voice mail all areas that need to know the credit decision; the customer's credit limit on the system monitors only shipments ready to go out but not orders pending.

  - *Best.* Review all data, render decision, and system immediately notifies all areas of the credit decision on all pending customers; the credit limit within the system acts as a ceiling for orders and shipments ready to go as well as an alert to all involved of any problem with releasing an order due to limit restrictions.

- Collection efforts

  - *Least efficient and effective.* Check a monthly detailed aged trial balance report of all customers; pick out delinquent customers; mail a past due notice to them, followed by form letters, followed by a call and more form letters; end by either collecting or placing for collection.

  - *Good.* Check a weekly detailed aged trial balance report of all customers; pick out delinquent customers; mail a past due notice to them, followed by form letters, followed by a call and more form letters; end by either collecting or placing for collection.

  - *Better.* The system provides a list of customers that are past due as of that day; mail a past due notice to them, followed by form letters, followed by a call and more form letters; end by either collecting or placing for collection.

- *Best.* System provides a list of customers that are past due that need follow up per the parameters set by the credit manager; e-mails are automatically sent to the accounts payable contacts with attached invoice and proof of delivery backup for new invoice delinquency; daily phone follow-up by collector is monitored going from highest dollar to lowest dollar in each aging category of delinquency; collection is made or final letter automatically prepared, forwarded to the credit manager for approval, and sent out by the system; the system determines if payment is made and, if not, account is automatically sent to the agency via the Internet with all documents needed for placement.

- Systems capability

  - *Worst.* All orders are manually keyed in; all customers are manually set up on the system; credit limits are not on the system or are merely a label on the system; the system provides no means to focus collection efforts of the collection staff.

  - *Better.* All orders are faxed in and still need to be keyed in; while orders are being entered, the customer set up data is also being entered; credit limits monitor orders ready to go; the system provides a list of customers who are past due of any amount or age on the system for the collection staff to contact.

  - *Best.* Orders are made online either through direct access to the vendor's system, through an Internet-based system, or through reverse supplying by the vendor to the customer via the customer's inventory control system; the setup data of the new customer is automatically uploaded when the customer places an order; the system provides a delinquency call list for each collector based on age of item and size of delinquency; the system automatically sends out e-mails to customers with backup needed for payment to be made; the system has ability to automatically refer any pending order or pending shipment to credit if set ceiling parameters of limit and delinquency are exceeded by the order or the pending shipment; the system will automatically notify all areas that shipments or orders are on hold if ceiling parameters are exceeded by the order or the pending shipment; the system, using the preset guidelines, will automatically notify the credit manager when to place an account for collections and, if approved, transmit all necessary documents to the agency.

Costs of Best Practices

Now that we have looked at what is ideal versus current practices, part of the cash flow considerations that must be looked at is the cost in implementing best practices, which may not be economically feasible. The key to solid cash flow management is not having the biggest and the best that money can buy but having the most efficient operation at the best possible cost. Let's now look at the costs involved in improving each of the preceding sections.

How Are Orders Taken? The type of business will directly affect what is the most cost-effective means for managing orders. Manufacturers or distributors selling large quantities of items on a regular basis to many customers would benefit the most from automated ordering. If the items to be sold are complicated or have the need of technical advice, an in-house or outside sales force may be needed. Specialized or customized products or services will likewise need hands-on help in placing an order. Although automating will decrease and nearly eliminate errors, it can also irritate and frustrate some customers. The most cost-effective method used may be a combination of order-taking methods, but each will need to be considered on a case-by-case basis.

Credit Processing. This is another case of how many new applicants are processed in a week. I have clients that process some 40,000 new customers a month and others that look at new applicants maybe once a month. So what is cost effective? Once again, the volume of new applicants will directly affect the need for automating the process. If your business has a very sophisticated Web site, the creation of a completely automated application system would be easily accomplished. If it is more of a "show and tell" type of Web site, then it would be a much more difficult task to automate the application process. Having the application available and able to be printed out online will save mailing time and prevent the problem of not having someone available with an application handy to give to the customer. A fax return would also speed up the process if an automated system were unavailable.

Credit Investigation, Time, and Efficiency. Internet and e-mail use by the credit staff are the most time-saving and cost-effective ways to handle credit investigation. Credit reports today can easily be obtained through the Internet, and e-mailing requests for both trade and bank references saves time and money in either mailing, faxing, or calling to request this information. Make sure the credit application has the e-mail address of those to contact in order to obtain these references.

Credit Investigation, Cost versus Limit. As noted earlier, this area truly needs to be looked at on a case-by-case basis. One additional area to be taken into consideration is that of the average ticket size of the goods or services that your firm offers. If you deal in small-dollar, high-volume sales, then automating the credit investigation and decision-making process using a credit scoring system may be the only answer.

Credit Decision. The cost factors involved with controlling the notification of all areas of credit decisions can be minimized greatly with an

Potential Losses from International Letters of Credit

A company without a limit control system can experience a loss on an international sale before the goods even leave the country. Sounds crazy? Consider the shipment of goods internationally that are to be paid for via a letter of credit. Each international letter of credit has its own terms and conditions built into the body of the L/C (letter of credit) that must be met in order for the seller to be paid. If only one item is not completely met exactly to the specification of the L/C, then payment will not be made and a discrepancy is created. Since letters of credit are drawn on banks and banks charge fees, each error is charged a discrepancy fee, which adds to the cost of the transaction.

The degree of difficulty in resolving the discrepancy will also add to the costs because an amendment may need to be added to the L/C to finally resolve this matter. This is assuming that the buyer is willing to agree to the change and that it doesn't already have the goods in its possession. The goods may have been automatically shipped out without credit approval due to a lack of credit limit control or verification that all terms and conditions of the L/C have been met. In this case, if a credit limit control was built into the system and required that for an order to be released all terms must be met (for an L/C, the credit limit would be $0), then no goods would leave the dock until all terms and conditions for payment by the L/C are reviewed and in compliance.

in-house e-mail system. A list of all that need to know can be preset, and a form e-mail can easily be sent. While an automated notice sent out by the system is a reduction in man-hours needed, it still may be nearly as cost effective to have a preset e-mail notice list available. The limit control, however, depending on the number of customers that you have, the volume of orders run through the system daily, and the dollars involved, can certainly cost justify a system that can monitor both the orders that are pending versus the approved limit and the shipments that are ready to leave the shipping dock or service that is about to commence.

Collection Efforts. Here is an area where a business that wishes to have the best cash flow should not spare the expenses. The easier it is for the collection staff to collect the firm's accounts receivables, the better the cash flow for the firm. While some firms tend to look down their noses at this aspect of the order-to-cash part of the cycle, it is far more than a necessary evil to have a well-seasoned, well-trained collection staff that has incentives to do their best beyond the veiled threat of job loss. Some firms have come out of the dark ages and are now sponsoring educational programs on the best way to collect the receivables while not alienating the customer and as an additional means to increase cash flow are offering bonus incentives to the collection staff for improved results.

Having a system that focuses the collection staff on the greatest dollar concentration of delinquency while not allowing the rest to age out further keeps balance to the collection efforts. Automating the e-mail of new delinquent invoices with proof of deliveries attached helps to substantially reduce the amount of casual delinquency that results from the lack of an invoice or the need of proof of delivery. Many firms use the need of an invoice copy or proof of delivery as a means to slow down their payment process and improve their cash flow.

The number of customers with balances, the volume of invoices, the dollar size of these invoices, and the staff available will directly affect the most cost effective approach. This likewise needs to be looked at on a case-by-case basis.

Systems Capability. There are many systems on the market today. They run the gamut of being little more than a cursory effort at providing some sort of coverage to each part of the operation in a company to the focused bolt-on system that manages all aspects of the credit and collection process. Needless to say, these packages are not cheap but they can pay for themselves in time saved, reduced manpower requirements, improved cash inflow, better credit decisions being rendered, and fewer losses materializing. These factors must be balanced against the same factors used in determining the maximum cash inflow versus the minimum cash outflow from expenses in maintaining the system, upgrades, setup, desired features (standard versus optional), and so on. As stated before, each consideration for both systems and hardware improvement must be looked at on a case-by-case basis and all factors weighed in determining the most efficient and cost-effective system.

Collection Efforts

Step One: Casual Delinquency Considerations

This area is the focal point for all delinquency control and the primary area for cash flow improvement. If delinquency can be controlled early on with minimal costs involved in keeping it maintained, then the business has achieved probably the greatest success in the war on cash flow problems. Assuming that a business bills daily for its shipments or services, delinquency results when an invoice exceeds the limits of the credit terms granted at the time credit was extended. Every day, this number moves out of the current column and into the first delinquency aging bucket that the business has established as the first level of delinquency. Depending on the credit terms extended the next aging bucket may be 1 to 30 days past due to as short as 1 to 7 days past due (typical in the food industry). This area now becomes (normally) the second largest dollar amount outstanding that is not current.

TIPS AND TECHNIQUES

Considerations that Must Be Addressed When a Buyer Dictates Payment Terms

- What are their annual purchases from your firm (i.e., are they a large customer, in the top five, or simply one of many customers)?

- What is the profit margin of the goods or services that you sell to them (substantial versus small)?

- What product or service do you provide to this firm (i.e., are your goods or services unique or are you one of many competitors offering this to the marketplace)?

- Can you build into your price the costs of carrying this sale for the longer time?

- Would a cash discount solve the problem and can it be cost justified?

- If there is no way to offset the costs of carrying them, the profit margin is not substantial and they purchase only minimally, can they either be referred to another supplier of your goods or services or simply dropped as a customer?

It is indeed a rare customer that pays for every invoice exactly on the due date that is on the invoice. Many firms set up policies that state all payments on net 30 days terms will be paid in 45 days. This is where a business needs to determine the factors to be considered before addressing this position.

TIPS AND TECHNIQUES

Steps for Reducing Delinquency

1 Automatic debit of the customer's bank account as the invoice comes due (not uncommon in many industries [e.g., tobacco and gasoline industries and many others])

2 Request that the customer pay you using an automated clearinghouse (ACH) transfer to your bank account.

3 For those not paying electronically, have a lockbox set up in the best strategic location to minimize float time for receipt of payment. (*Special note:* Shopping this cost with many banks, depending on your relationship with them, what services they offer, the areas that they cover, and fees that they charge can help to make this a more cost-effective proposition.)

4 Set a general maximum "grace period" deadline for payments to be received (can be from 1 day to as many as 15 days depending on the corporate philosophy, place in the market, profit margin, etc.) before:

- A late fee is assessed
- Customer is automatically e-mailed by the system a copy of the invoice with proof of delivery along with a request for immediate payment
- If your goods or services are in great demand, place the customer on credit hold and notify all internal parties that need to know, as well as e-mail the customer that this has occurred while requesting immediate payment of the past due invoice.

5 Depending on the size of the invoice, a phone call may be worthwhile to determine any problems or their reason for the nonpayment.

Assuming that you wish to keep them as a customer and none of the above suggestions helps to offset the problem, your choices are simple—either "grin and bear it" or actively pursue collection follow/hold orders to persuade them to change their policy. The one aspect that must be kept in mind at all times in taking either of the two actions is not to violate the Robinson–Patman Act, a federal antitrust law that governs the treatment of similar firms in the same equal manner. In essence, if you choose to "grin and bear it" for this customer, then you must do likewise for all the same types of customers. There are some exceptions to this law, but this book does not have the capacity to cover all of these areas. Before considering such actions, contact with in-house counsel or an outside counsel that specializes in antitrust issues is recommended.

Now that we have considered some of the factors that must be taken into consideration before pursuing our initial collection efforts, how do we reduce this form of delinquency?

Step Two: Interim Delinquency Reduction

How your aging buckets are set and your terms of sale will define what you consider as interim delinquency. For firms with typical credit terms of net 30 days delinquency beyond 15 days to 60 days past due are considered interim delinquency. This typically is where phone collection becomes solidly the order of the day, and the possibility of credit hold is definitely discussed. If your system has both the ability (as defined by the credit manager and corporate policy) to automatically place an account on hold and list the customers that need follow-up by largest dollar/oldest items, this will aid the credit staff in focusing their collection efforts. Pending orders to be shipped can be used as leverage to get the customer back on the prompt-paying track. If any documents (e.g., invoices, proof of deliveries, etc.) are needed, a system that allows for these to be e-mailed directly to the customer without the collector ever leaving his or her workstation adds to the cost effectiveness of the credit staff.

Steps for Reduction of Serious Delinquency

1 If there is a contract involved, such as with a manufacturer and a distributor, the possibility of termination of the right to sell your products is a definite leverage tool to resolve the delinquency issue.

2 Some contracts have built into them the right to automatically terminate the agreement if delinquency reaches a certain level. If this is not in place, it should be immediately added!

3 The reduction/elimination of the buyer's credit limit can also be used as a means to confirm the seriousness of the situation with the customer (this may be part of the system's capability as programmed by the credit manager and company philosophy).

4 The offering of a promissory note with interest and either additional security and/or personal guarantees by the owners of the firm can help to reduce the debt on a steady monthly basis. All interim sales made during the duration of the note would be made on a cash-on-delivery basis for goods and cash-in-advance for service sales.

Step Three: Serious Delinquency Reduction

Now that the account has exceeded 60 days past due, other actions/ factors must now be considered in the phone approach to resolving this delinquency.

Step Four: Last-Chance Delinquency Reduction

At this point (probably 90 to 120 days and beyond past due), the customer must be formally advised that they have lost all means to redeem themselves with your firm. A letter sent via certified mail with a return receipt requested should be sent notifying them that their credit limit has been revoked and that they have a 10-business-day deadline from the date of the letter for receipt of payment in full or be placed for collections and possible legal action. If no contact is made by the customer or payment in full received by the end of the 10 business days, the account should be automatically and immediately placed with a collection agency. If there is suspicion that the customer may have other creditors after them for delinquent debts, then the agency should be instructed to proceed with immediate legal action to resolve the overdue balance.

Collection Agencies and Outside Attorneys—Cost Effective Relationships

The number of placements, average size of the write-off balance, age of the balances, and degree of difficulty in collecting these debts (i.e., disputed versus nondisputed balances) will directly affect the ability of a firm to negotiate fees charged for collection of bad debts. While it is indeed worthwhile to be cost effective in looking at collection agencies and collection attorneys, it is far smarter to use firms that have been certified by certain watchdog agencies as adhering to certain ethical codes of practice. One such organization is the Commercial Law League, whose members must be monitored for their practices in dealing with not only their clients but with the debtors as well.

Typical fees vary from agency to agency and from attorney to attorney. Some are as high as 50 percent for small-balance accounts to as low as 10 percent for large-dollar balances. If your write-offs are substantial in dollars and large in volume, it is highly recommended that you put your bad debts out for contract bids and sign contracts with multiple firms to handle them. By doing this, you can then judge and compare the effectiveness of different agencies and direct more accounts to those that perform the best.

The last area of concern in placing accounts for collection with different agencies or attorney firms is that you should be willing to extend credit to one of these firms equal to the total outstanding of the accounts placed with them. This means that if you place $100,000 in total balances with a firm for collection, then you should feel comfortable in extending $100,000 in credit to that firm.

Why? Typically, when an account has been placed for collection, in order for a collection agency to keep track of payments and broken commitments, all payments are directed to the agency first, the check is cleared, and a monthly statement of payments is sent by the agency to the customer along with a check net of the fees owed to the agency/attorney. When an account cannot be collected by the agency, they typically notify the customer that it is deemed uncollectable and should be written off as a loss against taxes by the customer.

On a number of occasions, less reputable or financially troubled agencies or attorney firms may collect the debt but tell their clients that the debt is a loss. The only way that it was ever discovered was when the account was placed with a second agency and the debtor was contacted, they provided the agency with a front and back copy of their cancelled check showing payment in full being made to the first agency or attorney firm. While these types of unscrupulous firms do exist but are the exception to the rule, it is always smart to check out any firm before placing the account with them for collection.

External Factors that Can Directly Impact the Order-to-Cash Cycle

There are many events that can directly impact cash flow for a firm that is totally beyond their control. In recent times the events of September 11th, 2001, have caused many firms great grief and have presented new challenges to their very existence.

While it is definitely beyond the scope of this book to deal with all of the possibilities that could occur to directly affect the cash flow of a firm that is not internal in nature, it is highly recommended that the officers of the firm consult with their department managers in developing plans to address unusual or unpredictable events. Having emergency contingency plans in place, safe backup storage of needed documents and systems data, as well as new temporary locations for use in maintaining the effectiveness of the firm and the continuance of cash flow are all factors that need to be addressed long before a business-disruptive event can occur.

Summary

One area that was not touched on in this chapter that is definitely a factor in the collection process is bankruptcies, which, due to their very nature, deserve a chapter of their own and will be addressed exclusively in Chapter 4.

In the order-to-cash cycle there are many factors that can directly impact the cash flow and the cost effectiveness of a system or method of operation. Employees should strive to keep costs down and cash flow up and be aware of opportunities available to increase cash flow.

## CHAPTER 3

Improving the Purchase-to-Pay Cycle

After reading this chapter, you will be able to

- Improve the purchasing function to make sure your company pays as little as possible for the goods and services it buys
- Tighten procedures in your receiving facility
- Understand the importance of monitoring and avoiding duplicate payments
- Manage the accounts payable function so as to hold onto your cash as long as possible
- Understand why you should get purchasing and accounts payable to work together to wring the most concessions out of your suppliers.

The purchase-to-pay cycle is often overlooked in the quest to improve corporate cash flow. This is a shame because, as you will see, there are many ways to tighten policies and procedures to squeeze some additional cash out of the process.

The Requisition

In an ideal situation, purchasing does all the procuring for a company. This may seem self-evident to some, but as those in purchasing will readily attest, it is not always reality. (See *In the Real World*, "Requisitioning: The

Rogue Purchaser", for what frequently happens.) To make it easier for everyone in the company to order all goods through purchasing, many companies use a standardized form. *Tips and Techniques*, "Designing a Good Requisition Form", contains advice on designing a well-organized requisition form.

Getting All Purchases to Come Through Purchasing

While your goal should be to have as much of the corporate purchasing come through the purchasing department as possible, you should also be realistic in your expectations. Let's face it. If the president (or some other

IN THE REAL WORLD

Requisitioning: The Rogue Purchaser

Joe in accounting needs some colored pens for a presentation he is doing. Rather than order the pens through normal channels, he runs over to the local stationery store at lunchtime and selects the pens he wants. He pays $12.95 for pens that purchasing could have gotten through its standard contract with a national chain for $9.50. "What's the big deal?", you may be wondering. He spent an extra $3.45—so what? If Joe were the only rogue purchaser in the company, you would be right. However, multiply his actions by hundreds or even thousands, depending on the size of the company, and you can begin to see the extent of the problem. Worse, these purchasers are usually not buying one set of pens but rather product worth hundreds or even thousands of dollars. They purchase computers, special software, electronic gizmos, and so on, and the dollars start to add up.

high-level executive) of the company sends his or her secretary out to buy something, few employees are going to take exception to this action and try and change the behavior.

There are some huge advantages to having all orders come through purchasing. By aggregating purchases, many companies have been able to negotiate huge price discounts—often in areas not readily apparent. Let's look at a simple example of a company with 20 local branches. Each orders stationery goods from a local supply house. Some order from Staples, others from Kinkos, and still others from unaffiliated local stores. Each branch may not order significant enough amounts of goods to warrant a price discount, but when the orders are aggregated, the amount purchased is often significant and purchasing departments have been able to negotiate significant discounts. The stationery example is given because it is the most obvious and applies to most businesses. However, by looking at your company's purchasing patterns you will probably be able to uncover others. We'll take a look at how to do this further on in this chapter.

The Purchase Order

Once the decision to purchase has been made, the vendor contacted, and a deal struck, a purchase order (PO) is completed and sent to the vendor. It should be completely filled out, including all terms negotiated, freight arrangements, and any special deals. Often, purchasing does a spectacular job of negotiating a great deal and then does not fully document it or tell accounts payable. When the invoice eventually shows up, the vendor has conveniently "forgotten" to include the special terms on the invoice and has billed at the standard rate. If the company pays bills on the basis of the three-way match, and everything matches, accounts payable pays the invoice as billed, the savings are lost, and no one is aware of the lost savings.

Even if the invoice does come to purchasing for approval, what are the odds that the purchasing associate responsible for the transaction re-

Designing a Good Requisition Form

The following suggestions will help you design a user-friendly requisition form that meets the requirements of the purchasing staff:

- Have one form for everything so the purchasing staff can easily find the information needed.

- If it is an electronic form (and it should be), allow adequate spacing and use the tab function to make it easy for users completing the form.

- Include adequate space for the purchaser to make notations so the information does not have to be reentered.

- Use a preestablished numbering system for easy reference by all parties.

- Put instructions for completing the form on the corporate intranet site. If the form is preprinted, include the directions on the back of the form.

- Do not use preprinted forms. Make the form electronic to save printing costs and to remove the "You didn't send me any requisition forms" excuse from potential rogue purchasers.

- Have a space for the requisitioner's phone number and e-mail address. This will permit the purchasing associate to easily contact the requisitioner should there be a problem. It also allows purchasing to easily notify the person who ordered the goods of the potential delivery date and any potential delays.

- Include a space for purchasing to add the purchase order number for future reference.

members the special deal? In more than a few instances, purchasing associates approve such invoices, also forgetting the special deal they arranged. This can be avoided by including all the details on the PO initially. Many in purchasing hate this detail part of the job, but it is a best practice. Thus, many companies require that purchasing completely fill out the PO and that a copy be given to accounts payable.

Why Use Purchase Orders?

In addition to documenting the deal and as a device for sharing this information with all affected parties, some professionals see a PO as a tool to minimize risk. Thus, it is important to review the form used for the PO every few years to make sure that it not only meets the company's needs but also that it protects the company as much as possible. Since most orders, especially smaller ones, are not documented with a contract, the PO may be the only record you have of your agreement with the vendor. The PO does not completely protect you from a dishonest vendor. It could just be the first step in a battle of forms. Some companies take the additional step of having their attorneys review their PO forms.

Information to Be Included on Purchase Orders

By now you probably have determined that it is a good idea to include as much data as possible on the PO. The following items should be included:

- Company name, address, phone number, and e-mail address of contact person
- Supplier's name, address, and, if pertinent, phone number and e-mail address of contact person
- Date of order
- Terms, including any special arrangements for payment or freight
- Delivery date (scheduled)

- Description of goods ordered
- Quantity
- Units of measure (e.g., individual, dozen, gross etc.)
- Unit price
- Total amount
- Point at which title passes (e.g., free on board [FOB], etc.) *Note:* If buying internationally, make sure to use INCOTERMS and not U.S. terms. Always specify INCOTERMS if used.
- Terms and conditions
- Purchasing agent's name, phone number, and e-mail address
- Sales contact
- Item or part number (if applicable)
- Any relevant account numbers
- Bill-to address
- Ship-to address
- Sales tax status and any relevant exemption numbers
- Material classification code

Terms

Negotiating the best price is just the first step in squeezing the most cash flow out of the purchasing part of the cycle. Who pays for freight, insurance, and so on is sometimes set by industry custom and sometimes negotiated as part of the contract. Payment terms are an often-overlooked place where companies can squeeze out some additional cash flow. Let's look at a simple example. In many industries, standard open account terms call for payment 30 days after the invoice date. If this can be negotiated to 45 days, you have just improved not only the company's cash flow, but also its bottom line. The bottom-line improvement comes from the additional investment income earned on the money for 15 days if the company is a net investor, or the reduction in interest expense if the company is in a net borrowing position. This is just the first place where terms can be used to improve cash flow. Even more dramatically, early payment discounts can affect a company's bottom line.

Early payment terms are offered by some vendors to induce early payment, the most common being 2/10 net 30. These terms require that payment be made 30 days from the invoice date for the full amount or, if the customer is willing to pay in 10 days, it can take a 2 percent discount. Thus, a company with a $100 invoice could pay $100 after 30 days or $98 at the 10-day (or earlier) mark. At first glance, a $2 savings might not seem like much—but it is huge. Here's why. Without going through the mathematics, taking the discount and paying 20 days early turns into a 36 percent return, which few companies are able to match. Thus, most financial experts recommend taking the discount under these circumstances unless you can generate a return on your investments in excess of the 36 percent. Even a discount of 1 percent (1/20 net 30) would translate into an 18 percent return and in most cases would be worth taking—assuming there were no cash flow considerations.

However, cash flow considerations at some companies can be fierce. So, while the early payment discount may be attractive, some companies may find that they simply don't have the cash flow to make the early payment and thus must forgo the discount. Or do they? It's a dirty little secret that few financial executives will publicly admit, but many companies take the discount if they pay a few days after the discount period. Still others take the discount regardless of when they pay. Is this an ethical practice? This is a decision all executives must make for themselves. To put it in proper perspective, if you offer early payment discounts, check with your accounts receivable department and see how your customers are paying you.

Two Common Purchasing Problems and How to Solve Them

❶ *Duplicate orders for the same product.* Impeccable procedures combined with detailed record keeping are the first steps toward eliminating this issue. On a more global basis, aggregating the ordering of crucial supplies under one or several purchasing professionals from a limited number of vendors will reduce the chances of a duplicate erroneous order.

❷ *Conflicts between buyers and requisitioners.* For starters, making the purchasing department's policies and procedures clear to everyone within the company who might make a request of purchasing will go a long way to eliminating disputes. Prompt action on the part of purchasing will also help. Finally, let people know when they can expect the product. They may not be happy with what purchasing has to say—but the disagreement will be a lot less acrimonious than two weeks later down the road when they are informed that the goods they needed yesterday will not be arriving for another month.

Honest Buyers

Over 99 percent of the professionals involved in the purchasing process are honest and work very hard to get the best deal for their companies. In a few instances purchasers have been known to place an order with a vendor who offers under-the-table kickbacks. While no company condones this practice, it is difficult to police. Companies with written policy and procedures in place have taken the first step toward eliminating this conflict. An updated corporate ethics policy also helps. Other guidelines that will help prevent any misunderstanding in the purchasing decision include:

- All quotations should be received in writing, especially for major transactions.

- Contract should be awarded to the vendor that offers the lowest cost, not the lowest price. Some vendors make up on the back end what they give away on the front end. Something as simple as paying for freight or insurance can swing the equation. There are many valid reasons for not selecting the lowest-cost vendor. These reasons should be documented.

- Periodically, have existing contracts rebid to make sure that you continue to use the best cost/quality vendor.

- Watch the cars your buyers drive and other lifestyle issues that may indicate the buyer is living outside his or her income. The lifestyle issue is harder to monitor in an age of dual-income marriages but is one of the oldest signals that something is amiss in purchasing.

Receiving

The next step in the purchase-to-pay equation is the receiving dock. When goods are ordered, they are generally delivered to a company's receiving dock or its equivalent. The receiving department is supposed to log the shipment in, unpack it, and check the packing slip to the goods received. Any discrepancies should be noted and then forwarded, either electronically or in paper format, to the accounts payable department. In many, but not all, companies this is exactly how the process works.

Unfortunately, in some companies the receiving department does not closely monitor what is received and the employees do not check to see that what is on the packing slips was actually shipped. This is the first place where there can be cash slippage. If a dozen widgets were ordered and only 10 were sent, the company will pay for a dozen if that is what is on the packing slip *and* invoice and no one alerts accounts payable to the contrary.

Similarly, it is the task of the receiving department to note if any of the items received are damaged or are different from what was ordered. If green paint was ordered and red was received, the paint will be paid for unless someone returns it and makes a note of the return.

As companies move to payment alternatives different than the three-way match, the importance of the role played by the receiving department increases. This is especially true for companies using evaluated receipt settlement (ERS). It is crucial that incoming goods be checked against packing slips and discrepancies noted.

Manufacturing and Other Departments

Sometimes a product may look acceptable to the receiving staff but actually has a defect that is detected only when manufacturing closely inspects or uses the product. At that point, the goods are returned. Again, it is imperative that accounts payable be informed so the deduction can be taken before the invoice is paid. If the check has been mailed, it is then necessary to go after the vendor for a credit.

The Three-Way Match

Throughout this chapter there have been allusions to the three-way match and the importance of having accurate documents for this purpose. If the PO is filled out completely and the packing slip checked carefully by the receiving staff, accounts payable is in an excellent position to pay the invoice when it is received—if all three documents match. Theoretically, accounts payable should receive an invoice, match it to the packing slip and the PO, and then pay the invoice. In many cases, however, this is not how the process works.

Many companies require an approval from an appropriate executive before an invoice will be paid. Companies do this for numerous reasons. They include:

- A lack of confidence in the accounts payable staff
- A distrust that the receiving staff actually checked the packing slip against the product received
- The knowledge that the purchase order is rarely filled out completely or correctly
- A control-based corporate culture
- The fact that processing paper and approving invoices sometimes give staff the illusion of power.

Getting Invoices Approved

Mass confusion can result when the three-way match is not used for approval purposes, often causing a company to lose the early payment discount. In the best-case scenario, the invoice is mailed to the purchaser, who reviews it, approves it, and forwards it to accounts payable, where the invoice is then scheduled for payment according to the agreed-upon terms as indicated on the PO and the invoice. If this process is followed in a reasonably prompt fashion, the payment can be processed with adequate time to meet the early payment discount terms.

This is one of the bottlenecks where the process can break down. Not all purchasing executives will check incoming mail and invoice details as soon as they arrive. Many have been known to leave such documentation lying in their in-boxes until the vendor threatens to stop future shipments because payments are long past due. This is the first black hole that often houses invoices.

In the second scenario, the invoices are mailed directly to the accounts payable department, where a determination is made as to who ordered the goods. The invoice is then sent to that executive for approval, again sometimes disappearing into a black hole never to be seen again. Accounts payable associates who have dealt with this type of behavior know to keep track of to whom invoices were sent for approval and when. Of course, this entails additional paper-intensive work—not exactly the route efficient companies are looking to take in the twenty-first century.

A variation on the second scenario involves the invoices that show up in accounts payable with no PO number or reference to who ordered

IN THE REAL WORLD

The Overzealous Accounts Payable Associate

At the other end of the spectrum is the fastidious accounts payable associate who loves to keep his or her desk clean. Every night when he or she goes home every invoice that has come into the accounts payable department has been processed and scheduled for payment—immediately, regardless of whether an early payment discount is offered. The associate makes sure that all the bills get paid the minute they arrive. While the vendors may like this very much, it is a terrible practice from a cash flow (and financial) standpoint. Timely processing may be desirable, but paying vendors early should be a no-no.

Similarly, certain unscrupulous vendors will call accounts payable, demanding that an invoice be paid immediately, even though it is not yet due. Accounts payable associates should not take the vendor's word for it that an invoice is due. They should check it out and pay only if it is actually time to pay. If they uncover a vendor that makes this a regular practice, the vendor should be notified that you are aware of their behavior, and a note should be put in the vendor's file to alert any new employees to this trick.

the goods. These invoices are sometimes directed to accounts payable initially or wander around the corporation before eventually landing in accounts payable. Talk about a black hole. Then it falls on the shoulders of the accounts payable staff to try and ascertain who ordered the goods. In this situation, some companies have adopted a policy of sending these invoices back to the vendor, asking them to direct the invoice to the person who originally ordered the product.

Duplicate Payments

Although few companies like to admit it, duplicate and erroneous payments are a huge problem for many companies. Some experts estimate that approximately 1 percent of all payments made by corporate America are duplicate or excess. Whether this number is excessive or not, it brings home the point that controls need to be put in place to minimize duplicate payments. One side benefit of these controls is that many of them also guard against check fraud—a massive problem for corporate America. A number of the issues discussed in the following pages go to the heart of the duplicate payment issue, which clearly drains cash flow.

Why Invoices in the Black Hole Are a Problem

Aside from the obvious inefficiencies that waylaid invoices cause, they also can be a cash drain on a company. When a vendor does not receive a payment within a set number of days after the due date, one of its collectors will call the customer's accounts payable department to inquire about the payment status. After a quick review of the payments in progress, the vendor will be informed that no invoice was received. The vendor then prints out a new invoice and mails, faxes, or e-mails a copy of the invoice over to the customer. The copy is now rushed around for payment and a check is cut. Eventually, the original invoice finds its way into accounts payable, with the proper authorization, and is promptly paid—for a second time. You are probably thinking that your customers would return second payments, and you may be correct—if the customer realized it was a duplicate payment.

In reality, when the second check arrives and the accounts receivable associate tries to apply the cash, there is no outstanding invoice and the check gets deposited and credited to a suspense account for further research—when the associate has time. Needless to say, researching unapplied cash is a low priority at most companies. In reality, that research often doesn't get done, and, eventually, the amount is written off to miscellaneous income. Is this approach correct? Probably not, but that doesn't mean it does not happen.

Even if the customer realizes what happens, most simply issue a credit, which they may or may not tell the customer about. In the best of cases, the vendor informs the customer, who uses the credit on the next invoice. In the worst of cases—and this happens more frequently than most financial executives would care to admit—the vendor sends a credit notice to accounts payable and the accounts payable associate, not understanding what the credit notice is, pays it a second time. Thus, the invoice gets paid for a third time.

More often than not, the vendor does not send a notice and simply leaves the credit on the customer's account, never informing them of the balance. This is one reason why accounts payable is advised to ask all large vendors for a statement every six months or annually to verify outstanding invoices and balances. When this request is made, the vendor should be asked for a statement that shows all activity, not just outstanding invoices. Some companies will suppress the credit balances showing on statements unless specifically instructed not to do so.

Invoices without Invoice Numbers

One of the ways that companies check to make sure they are not making duplicate payments is to check against the invoice number. If an invoice doesn't have an invoice number, obviously this is not possible.

Thus, invoices without invoice numbers are often prime candidates for duplicate payments. Additionally, they are difficult to process because most accounting systems require an invoice number. To address this issue, most companies establish a set of rules for assigning an invoice number to such invoices. Ideally, the rules are set up so that no two invoices from the same vendor end up with the same invoice number. Thus, it is generally recommended to avoid using the date as an invoice number. Why? Because some vendors, such as overnight delivery services, temp agencies, and so on, might send two invoices on the same date.

Numerous Invoices from the Same Vendor

When a company receives many invoices from the same vendor, the invoice processing can get voluminous. Some companies have approached these vendors with a proposal to pay the vendor once a month (or week, depending on volume) from a statement rather than from individual invoices. When this approach is taken, the vendor should stop sending invoices. Unfortunately, not all vendors can suppress the printing and mailing of invoices. If your vendor falls into that category, it will be necessary to make changes to your procedures so that those vendors' invoices are never paid. This can be done by

- Alerting the staff
- Making a note in the file
- Making the necessary changes to the system so invoices cannot be processed

Paying from Copies

Let's face it—invoices do occasionally get lost in the mail. When that happens, it is necessary to have the vendor send a second invoice. In such instances, it is simplest to have the vendor fax over another copy of the invoice and use that to process the payment. The reality is that most lost in the mail invoices eventually show up, especially since most of them having been floating around your company or have been on someone's desk the whole time. When these invoices do show up, they look like an original invoice (because they are) and get paid. For this reason, many

Avoiding Duplicate Payments when Paying from Copies of Faxes

- Require an extra-level approval when paying from a copy. You will be surprised how many people will discover the original invoice when informed they are going to have to get their boss's approval for the payment.

- Thoroughly review the vendor's file to make sure the payment was not made.

- Pay from a copy only when the invoice is more than 60 days past due.

- Check the payment history of the vendor for the same invoice number or dollar amount.

- When purchasing makes the request, ask for an open PO and unmatched receiver.

- Mark the invoice "*Copy,*" and put it in the file.

- Since the duplicate payment is likely to occur when the original invoice eventually shows up in accounts payable, double check all severely late invoices to make sure they have not already been paid. Check against invoice number and dollar amount.

- Keep copies of all invoices paid from a copy or fax in a special tickler file for easy reference should one of those very old invoices find its way into the accounts payable department approved for payment.

companies refuse to pay from anything but an original invoice. What do you think a vendor does when informed of such a corporate policy? Most simply create a new "original" invoice. Thus, the ideal of never paying from copies doesn't work well in the real world. See *Tips and Techniques*, "Avoiding Duplicate Payments When Paying from Copies of Faxes" for some advice on paying from copies.

Rush Checks

Many in your accounts payable department consider rush checks, sometimes referred to as ASAP checks, a scourge. Not only does it cause a disruption in the work flow of the accounts payable department, but rush checks are also one of the leading causes of duplicate payments. What typically happens is that, for whatever reason, someone needs a check immediately. Either they didn't process an invoice in a timely manner, the invoice arrived late, or some other catastrophe occurred. The person arrives in accounts payable demanding a check. This requires someone to stop his or her work processing, process the invoice, and issue a check, often manually. Unfortunately, the invoice may be currently in the system awaiting a check or a check may have been cut very recently. Ultimately, two payments end up getting made.

The obvious, but often unrealistic, approach is to disallow all rush checks. A company with only weekly, or perhaps less frequent, check runs will find that such a policy is untenable to its senior executives. And what sane accounts payable associate is going to tell the president of the company that he or she cannot have a check because it is against company policy?

A more realistic approach regarding rush checks is to try to limit them. This can be done by:

- Making everyone aware of the accounts payable deadlines for checks
- Making it difficult (but not impossible) to get a rush check

- Thoroughly discussing the issue with the person requesting the immediate check. Often, the person will discover that he or she does not really need the check immediately and can wait for the next check run.

Accounts Payable Audit Firms

Duplicate payments have become such a problem that numerous firms have sprung up to help companies recover some of their lost funds. These audit firms (different from the accounting audit firms) generally work on a contingency basis. They keep a percentage of what they recover, anywhere from 33 to 50 percent, although there has been some pressure on prices. If the company recovers nothing, it costs you nothing. The best of these firms will also make recommendations on how and where you can tighten your procedures so duplicate and other types of erroneous payments are not made in the future.

Some financial executives look at the pricing and declare it too high, but their companies would have recovered nothing without the help of the audit firms. A few of these companies charge an hourly fee for their services, so those objecting to the cost might look at those firms. Others claim that their companies never make a duplicate payment. If that is the case, having one of these contingency firms will cost nothing, so there is little to lose.

Companies can locate audit firms by doing a search on the Internet using the key words accounts payable, audit, and recovery. Alternatively, many of these companies can be found exhibiting or speaking at accounts payable conferences.

Be aware that if you use one of these companies, your vendors will not be happy. When duplicate payments are uncovered, it is necessary to contact the vendor for repayment. Few vendors will repay the funds without researching the issues themselves. Since the audits are typically done a year or more after the fact, it means digging through the files and doing research on long-forgotten issues. Some will refuse to address items that are more than two or four years old.

Some companies hire audit firms and then do not recover the funds identified by the audit firm. They simply plug their procedures to stop losses in the future. Others go after only certain overpayments. They may, for example, not pursue a payment from a company that employs or is owned by a member of their board of directors.

When hiring such firms:

- Get several bids.

- Get references.

- Ideally select a firm with experience in your industry—they will know where the skeletons are hidden.

- Inquire how they are paid. Do they wait until you have been reimbursed or expect payment from you immediately? Be aware that, in all likelihood, you will not recover every claim they identify.

Payment Timing Issues

As was alluded to earlier, not all companies pay their bills on the due date. For starters, there is often a discussion of exactly what the due date is. The vendor typically thinks it is the invoice date, whether it's printed on the invoice or not. Many companies think the clock starts ticking the day the invoice arrives in the accounts payable department; from the previous discussion, you can see how late that can be. The longer a company takes to pay its bills, the better its cash flow position is. Of course, the downside of not paying invoices in a timely fashion is that your vendors might not appreciate it and might:

- Put your company on credit hold (ouch)

- Report your poor payment performance to the credit reporting agencies

- Require onerous payment terms in the future

However, there is a halfway point. Some companies undertake a formal or informal payment-stretching program. They might begin by making payments one day later than normal. They track their vendors' response, and those that do not complain are then stretched for two days, and so on.

Others are more straightforward about their plans. They talk to the vendors and tell them exactly what they are planning. If the vendors agree—and depending on who is the 800-pound gorilla in the relationship, they might—then new payment terms are agreed to.

Some big companies simply announce, "These are our terms." Take it or take your business elsewhere. If you are doing business with one of these giants, you may have already experienced this behavior.

Not everyone approves of payment stretching. It is a decision that each company must make for itself. It is an issue that should be addressed at a fairly senior level.

P-cards

Virtually everyone uses credit cards for their personal affairs. They are convenient and a great way for delaying payments for a few weeks. Businesses with many small invoices eventually reached the same conclusion, and many have started using what is referred to as p-cards, or corporate procurement cards, in their day-to-day operations. The beauty of these cards is that they allow employees to make small-dollar purchases needed for their everyday operations without going through the ordeal of filling out a requisition. They also save the purchasing department from having to chase after a lot of small-dollar orders. Accounts payable loves them because they replace hundreds, if not thousands, of small-dollar invoices with one large one.

From a cash flow standpoint they are wonderful as well. Rather than paying for goods immediately, a company often gets as much as 60 days' float on its money, and everyone wins. Companies have been moving to p-cards in droves. These cards, along with certain electronic initiatives, require fewer people in both purchasing and accounts payable to handle small-dollar transactions. Thus, this tool is not only a great cash flow enhancer, it also saves the company money through reduced head count.

There is another feature about these cards that not all card issuers will offer. Should your company use the card in sufficient volume, it may qualify for a rebate from the issuer.

The Purchasing and Accounts Payable Relationship

In some organizations, the relationship between purchasing and accounts payable is less than harmonious. Often, the two do not get along—and for understandable reasons. First, neither understands the other's problems. The simplest way to address that issue is to have the purchasing manager and the accounts payable manager spend a day (or week) in the other department to get a feel for what goes on. The old "walk a mile in the other party's shoes" will go a long way to improving the relationship.

Some experts recommend to accounts payable professionals that they invite the purchasing executive whose invoices give them the biggest headaches into the department for a visit. Let that executive try and process his own invoices. By actually seeing the problems encountered with seemingly easy invoices, the executive will gain new respect for those hard-working accounts payable professionals.

Similarly, by having the seemingly belligerent accounts payable associate spend a day with a purchasing professional, you may gain a more harmonious team once both parties understand the problems and issues the other encounters in the normal course of a business day.

Purchasing and Accounts Payable under One Umbrella

Some companies, especially those not in manufacturing, are starting to have the purchasing and accounts payable departments report to the same individual. This process immediately ends turf wars. Additionally, the two departments are then in a better position to work toward common goals, expand their horizons and skills, and work as a team. This approach has worked in a number of organizations and, as the two departments shrink, is likely to be viewed positively.

How Purchasing Can Use Accounts Payable Information

Often, accounts payable has data that would be useful to the purchasing professionals in negotiating better pricing and/or terms for the company. Until purchasing information is aggregated, companies sometimes don't have a clear idea of exactly how much they are spending on any one product. When the purchasing decision is made for a large quantity of a particular product, a better price can be negotiated than if a small amount is ordered—that is, if the corporation realizes how much it is spending on the item in question.

Typically, this data can be mined from the accounts payable system. In the hands of a competent purchasing professional, significant pricing concessions can often be negotiated. By having purchasing work closely with accounts payable and understand its systems, a better financial situation for the company overall can be had.

Summary

By focusing on all aspects of the purchase-to-pay cycle, innovative companies are finding ways to mine additional cash flow savings from their suppliers without making a huge investment in technology to do so. Don't overlook this unmined gold field when it comes to improving your company's cash flow position.

## CHAPTER 4

When a Customer Files for Bankruptcy Protection: How to Get Your Cash

After reading this chapter, you will be able to

- Become alert to potential bankruptcy filings

- Understand reclamation action, protecting your current receivables and cash flow in and out of a bankruptcy

- Understand preference payments—what they are and how they occur

- Understand preference payment vigilance—what are the pre-insolvency creditor's in-house actions

- Know what happens during the "90 days" prior to the bankruptcy filing

- Know how to deal with a preference action

- Understand settlement with a trustee—how to save some of the payment(s) received and keeping costs down

When we looked at the order-to-cash cycle, we looked at the process from the time the order was taken until the time that you got paid (or wrote off the account as a loss). One reality of today's world is the legal process known as bankruptcy. Bankruptcy filings in the past held a tremendous stigmatism for those that were left no alternative but to have the courts resolve the debts that were owed to many creditors.

As times changed and the bankruptcy legal process evolved from just a liquidation of the debtor's assets to a reorganization "fresh start" program to today's "creative accounting" method of problem solving for firms and some individuals, bankruptcy has lost its public ignominy and has become almost commonplace. Let's move on to dealing with the realities of bankruptcy and the ways we can keep the cash that we collect, minimize the loss of cash we will receive, or keep our expenses to a minimum in dealing with bankruptcy issues.

Becoming Alert to a Potential Bankruptcy Filing

There are many reasons why a firm will file for bankruptcy. Firms today file to break labor contracts or unprofitable leases and to defend against class-action lawsuits and insolvency. Along the "long and winding road"

TIPS AND TECHNIQUES

Warning Signs that Signal a Potential for Bankruptcy Filing

- Changes in payment habits: A customer who normally pays you on time or a few days late but now is paying you progressively slower and slower has a potential for bankruptcy.

- A request for longer terms of sale when never requested before or not for an excessively large year end or quarter end order

- Wholesale changes in top management

- Reduction in staff and phone access to the accounts payable area, making it generally more difficult to discuss past due items

TIPS AND TECHNIQUES CONTINUED

- In the case of goods, any return of large quantities of obsolete products

- In the case of goods, orders of very large quantities of needed goods to last during the "dry times"

- Bad publicity (larger and mid-sized firms)

- Deteriorating financial statements (*Special note:* A complete multiyear financial analysis comparing the results against industry standards and using such ratios as the Altman Z-score would be needed to determine the validity of a potential bankruptcy filing.)

- Excessive trade reference requests on your customer

- A refusal by your customer's bank to provide a reference when previously given

- Nonsufficient funds checks

- Payments made only to critical vendors while refusing or delaying all others

- Taking unjustified deductions to delay making payments

- Uncooperative and unreasonable behavior when attempting to resolve payment issues

- Announcement (depending on the size of the company) to creditors that they have changed their payment policy to longer terms than what are standard for the industry

- Offers to "trade dollars" as a way to get goods or services versus lowering of their total outstanding

- Getting an attorney involved or attempting to put together an unofficial creditors committee in the hopes of creating a "prepackaged bankruptcy" before the actual court filing

to the filing of bankruptcy, many tips are left to creditors that a filing may occur in the near future. As a general rule, there are a number of things that should "make our ears go up" to the potential filing of bankruptcy by a customer of ours.

IN THE REAL WORLD

Protecting New Value Defense

One step that should automatically be done at the time that a debtor is suspected of being a potential bankruptcy candidate if you are a seller of goods to them is to obtain proof of deliveries on all shipments made prior to 90 days and all future shipments. The reason for this is that one method a trustee uses to defeat a preference defense is to require a proof of delivery on all shipments made 90 days prior to the bankruptcy filing date.

There are two factors involved in this issue. The first is that in the new value, defense payments made by the debtor of existing debt can be offset by shipments made reasonably after the receipt of the payment (this will be defined in greater detail later in this chapter). If indeed no proof of delivery exists that the goods were ever received, then the defense will not hold water in court.

The other reason to obtain them immediately for the prior time and thereafter is that most proof of deliveries are only available for about 90 to 120 days after a shipment is received. Also, typically the trustee has exactly two years from the date of the bankruptcy filing to initiate legal action to recover a preference, and preference actions by a trustee rarely begin before the bankruptcy is at least a year into the bankruptcy. It would then be impossible for the vendor to obtain the necessary proof of deliveries to defend against the preference action. This is why it is vital to listen and take immediate action either before a filing or as soon as you have received notice of the filing regardless of whether a chapter 11 (reorganization) or a chapter 7 (liquidation) has been filed.

While it may be too late to prevent losses by the time we recognize some of these warning signs, we still need to react quickly when we do recognize the potential of a bankruptcy filing.

Reclamation Action—Protecting Your Current Receivables and Cash Flow in and out of a Bankruptcy

When a customer is first suspected of being potentially insolvent, your cash flow from receivables owed to you by them is at great risk. If the customer lacks the ability to pay you for the goods sold to them, an alternative is to retrieve your goods that they have in inventory related to the most recent billings. In order to accomplish this, a reclamation action must be commenced. What is reclamation? Reclamation is the right of a seller under the Uniform Commercial Code (UCC) to regain

TIPS AND TECHNIQUES

Essentials for a Valid Reclamation Claim

- The seller shipped product and extended credit to the debtor in the ordinary course of business of both.

- The debtor was insolvent at a time when the seller shipped, billed, and delivered the goods to them.

- A written demand was made by the vendor for the return of the goods within 10 days after the items were delivered to the debtor.

- The debtor had possession of the goods at the time of the reclamation demand, or the terms were not in the possession of a third-party buyer in the ordinary course of business or a good faith purchaser at the time of the reclamation demand.

Winning reclamation steps include:

1 The seller commences reclamation by conveying a reclamation letter within 10 days after the goods were received by the buyer.

2 The reclamation letter should include an in-depth account of the goods in question.

3 A confirmation of the date of delivery to the buyer

4 A demand for the immediate return of the items as referenced in your account

5 Demand an accounting of the items sold. (*Note:* An accounting is critical because the right to reclaim may be overcome by the debtor's resale of the goods to a buyer in the ordinary course of business.)

6 If accounting is not provided or is imprecise, the seller should be prepared to immediately demand a right to examine both the inventory on hand and the books and records related to the sales of said goods for the period between the delivery date of the goods and the date of the reclamation letter.

7 The letter should be delivered to the debtor by fax and certified mail, return receipt.

8 If the buyer files bankruptcy prior to the preparation of the reclamation letter (or at any time thereafter) the vendor should promptly contact buyer's attorney in order to demand from debtor either the immediate return of the goods or that the debtor sell the items, provided that the vendor has established an administrative claim or a lien under the Bankruptcy Code.

7 A seller should carry on with an adversary action through the bankruptcy court to put in force its rights so as to meet its onus of proof that the items subject to the reclamation demand were in the custody of the buyer at the time that the demand was made.

possession of goods shipped and delivered to an insolvent buyer. This is needed when an unsecured vendor is unable to retrieve goods or stop them in transit. Courts have agreed upon the certain essentials to establish a valid reclamation claim under the Bankruptcy Code (based on elements of the UCC).

IN THE REAL WORLD

Reclamation Claim: Is it Worth Filing?

Considering the day-to-day demands made on our time at work, the filing of a reclamation claim can be one of the things that least hit our "radar screen" when it comes to methods to protect our company's cash flow. This, however, can be a real mistake on our part, as typically companies that are contemplating bankruptcy tend to "load up" on goods that will carry them through the initial weeks of the bankruptcy proceedings. These large orders, though very enticing to our sales force, may be the last step before filing as part of the debtor's strategy to prepare for what lies ahead.

While little more than a few minutes of time are needed to cover the initial requirements for a reclamation action to begin, good timing and the filing of a motion of reclamation in court once bankruptcy has been filed will be needed in order to ensure either the return of goods or the establishment of an administrative claim. These claims are next in the "pecking order" for payment after all secured creditors are paid in full and are paid much faster than any unsecured trade creditors. Considering these factors, it may be wise, depending on the dollar size of the shipments and what your firm considers a "substantial order amount," once a customer starts running into continual delinquency problems to send a reclamation letter on a regular basis. These letters can act as a source of motivation for the debtor to pay on time or realize that the goods should be returned.

Preference Payments: What Are They and How Do They Occur?

When a debtor becomes insolvent the payment habits to the seller can vary greatly depending upon its need of either goods or services, which the seller provides. A critical vendor may be paid within terms right up until the day that bankruptcy is filed whereas an ordinary vendor may experience totally erratic payments.

Typically, to the ordinary creditor when payments become erratic, collection efforts increase and more pressure is placed on the debtor to pay on time or to better get them on track. This can change the recent payment pattern of the debtor as compared to its past payment history to the debtor.

Under the current bankruptcy law, all payments received 90 days prior to the filing of the bankruptcy while the debtor was insolvent may be deemed preferential in nature. This means that the seller may have received more than what they would have gotten in a liquidation action of the debtor and more than other creditors as well. A preference action against a creditor can be considered to be the definitive affront. A "successful mission" is accomplished in collecting the outstanding accounts receivable and then the seller is sued to recoup these payments.

Preference Payment Vigilance

The Preinsolvency Creditor's In-House Actions. Consistency in both credit extension and collection follow-up can help lessen the chances of alerting a trustee (chapter 7 liquidation bankruptcy) or debtor-in-possession (chapter 11 reorganization bankruptcy) to a potential preference payment(s). (*Special note:* It is beyond the scope of this book to delve into all the facets of the bankruptcy law, and it is highly recommended that, if you have specific legal questions related to a particular bankruptcy case, you confer with your counsel on the issue.) If all

IN THE REAL WORLD

Reality Check on the "90 Days Window"

Considering recent court actions, the 90 days window from date of bankruptcy filing is closer to 92 to 95 days. This is due to the courts deciding that the date that the check clears the debtor's bank is the actual date of payment not the date that the seller receives the check or the date of the check. Considering whether your customers' checks are processed through a lockbox or are manually taken or mailed by the seller to its bank daily will directly affect the payments considered in the time span of the preference action. It is thus recommended that when considering both preference actions and the defense of these, one should look at a range of time in the 95 days' range.

customers are treated the same (i.e., extended the same credit terms: same type of customers with no deviation due to size or annual purchases by the customer) and held to the same payment policies (i.e., charged late charges or held to the same limits on receipt of payment for the granting of a discount), then it is less likely that a seller will be the cause of a preference action. By enforcing credit terms unequally, differences occur in the payment patterns of similar customers, which make it very difficult to defend in court that the actions taken to collect payments were ordinary course of business.

Policies and procedures manuals that map out the typical steps used in the collection process help to define what actions are taken in dealing fairly with all types of customers. Consistency in following those steps prevents one customer from being treated differently than another. This does not mean blindly following these procedures as there are circumstances that can require special handling in many cases. However, allowing too many exceptions can cause problems. Depending on the size of your firm, receivables portfolio, staff size, volume of business, and so on, having a computer system in place that helps to consistently focus the credit staff in the type of follow-up reduces the likelihood of a preference. It also helps to alert the credit staff to potential problems of insolvency issues.

What Happens during the 90 Days Prior to the Bankruptcy Filing? If a customer is suspected of being a potential bankruptcy candidate, keep in mind how the customer has paid in the past and what steps both you and the customer are taking to pay currently. Many factors can actually enhance the possibility of a preference action's being taken against a seller.

This is not to say that any of the above would not be considered as a remedy in dealing with a delinquent or potentially insolvent customer. A wise person once said that "a bird in the hand is worth two in the bush" and "possession is nine tenths of the law." It is far better to face the possibility of a potential preference action and have your money or balance in hand than to try to avoid a preference action and never get any (or only a small amount) of your balance owed you. The trick is to balance the efforts used to collect the amount owed you while minimizing the potential for a preference action. This comes with many years of practice, solid systems support, a well-written policy and procedures manual, and knowing when to take a risk.

How to Deal with a Preference Action. Now that everything has been done to prevent a preference action or at least minimize the potential of it, what do you do to defend against giving up your hard-earned cash? Under the bankruptcy law, there are three defenses to a preference action (there is a fourth that is literally impossible to prove—

TIPS AND TECHNIQUES

Actions that Can Trigger a Preference Action

- Requiring additional security (i.e., standby letters of credit, security deposits, UCC filing, etc.) or personal or corporate guarantees when none were required before

- Demanding cash in advance or cash on delivery (COD) when the customer was granted credit in the past

- Requiring audited financial statements in order to grant any credit when none was required in the past

- Requiring payment of more than what was due in order to reduce the current balance outstanding

- Requiring that the customer "trade dollars for shipments" plus pay on past due in order to get additional product

- Charging late fees when none were charged in the past or enforcing collection of them when not enforced in the past

- Disallowing discounts when none were disallowed in the past

- Requiring a promissory note for the current balance and requiring that all future shipments be made on a cash in advance or COD basis until the note is paid in full

that the debtor was not insolvent at the time that payments were made to you). These defenses are:

1. *Contemporaneous exchange*, which is a simultaneous transfer of funds to a creditor at the same time that the goods are delivered, is the simplest example of a COD.

IN THE REAL WORLD

COD, the Ultimate Defense— Or Is It?

Since a COD payment is typically not considered a credit transaction, it is a definite defense against a preference action. There is, however, a situation that has occurred and has been contested in court, with the creditor ending up on the losing side of the battle. The events were as follows: A payment was received in a COD transaction and the check used for payment was returned for nonsufficient funds (bounced!). Once the vendor determined that the check was returned, they proceeded to contact the debtor and demand a replacement of the check with either a certified or cashier's check, which the debtor did.

When the trustee presented in court that the transaction was not a COD transaction but one in which credit was extended, the vendor countered that the payment was made as part of a COD sale. The court ruled that had the vendor simply redeposited the original check and it had cleared, then indeed this would have been simply a COD transaction. However, because they had required the debtor to replace the original check with that of a cashier's or certified check, that credit was extended until such time as the replacement check was received. This made the transaction no longer a contemporaneous transfer but simply a credit transaction that was subject to the possibility of a preference action.

The court did not rule out that the other two remaining defenses against a preference action would be valid in this case and would have to be looked at considering these types of preference defenses.

2. The second preference defense, *new value*, is simply the payment of an old debt in exchange for new goods or services. The payment, however, must be made before the release of new goods or ser-

vices and must be a related transaction. In this case, the courts have been reasonably flexible looking at the date the payment was received and considering one or multiple shipments as an offset to this payment. The courts will allow shipments or services that occurred within a two- to four-week period as an offset to a payment received, depending upon the nature of the relationship between the debtor and the creditor and what is typical for that type of industry.

3. The last defense and the hardest to prove is that of *ordinary course of business*. At best, it can be straightforward and easy to prove, and at its worst, it can be little more than creative accounting. The definition of the ordinary course of action defense is that the transfer was in payment of a debt incurred by the debtor in the ordinary course of its business or financial dealings of the debtor's business and financial interactions. The transfer itself was also made in a way that was common to both the debtor and the vendor.

Since this definition is as clear as mud, let me walk you through some possible scenarios to help define what ordinary course of business is.

- *Past payment history with the customer.* If a customer over the last one to two years paid on average in a certain number of days, this may be used as a "template" for a range of payments. If a customer pays on average between 45 and 50 days over a one- to two-year period and the customer has continued to pay that way during the 90 days prior to filing, then this is one possible type of proof using the ordinary course of business defense.

- *Past payment history with customers that are similar to the bankrupt firm.* If you sell products or services to other companies that are of a similar type and volume and these firms are in the same industry as the bankrupt firm, then how they paid you over the last one to two years on average can be used as an industry standard to compare to the payments made by the bankrupt company. If customers similar to the bankrupt firm paid you in 45 to 50 days over the last one to two years and the bankrupt firm has paid you in 45 to 50 days during the 90 days prior to the filing of bankruptcy, this is another possible type of proof using the ordinary course of business defense.

- *Outside industry standards to compare as an ordinary course of business defense.* If you are a member of a trade group that sells the same type of products to similar types of companies or if more than one of your members of the same trade group had sold to the same bankrupt firm and were paid on average in the same number of days as you were during the 90 days prior to the filing of bankruptcy, then this is a defense under ordinary course of business. The bankrupt firm paid other competitors in 45 to 50 days during the 90 days prior to filing, which is the same as how they paid you; thus, this is another possible type of proof using an ordinary course of business defense. Other sources of comparison can be used to establish an industry "norm" for payments for use in the comparison of the payments of the bankrupt firm to you. Dun & Bradstreet and the "Annual Statement Studies" book printed annually by Risk Management Association (RMA) could also be used as sources for comparison.

Settlement with a Trustee: How to Save Some of the Payment(s) Received and Keep Costs Down

If after examining your records you determine that a preference action could possibly exist, you have two possible actions that can be taken:

1. *Ignore the notice from the trustee demanding repayment of all payments made 90 days prior to the filing of bankruptcy (highly recommended in all cases!).* In some cases, trustees have a very limited budget from the estate to work from and will use a "bluff" technique to bring funds into the estate. A mass mailing to all firms that received checks prior to the 90 days from bankruptcy filing date demanding repayment of these payments to the estate may bring in some "easy" money. Some firms simply wishing to avoid a legal action

or those that are not well versed in preference defenses or procedures may simply pay to avoid a legal hassle. The trustee may make a settlement offer with a deadline attached to it giving the vendors a "quick settlement" figure that will change if they have to go to court.

By ignoring the letter you may call the trustee's bluff. If the amount is small (under $15,000), little or no action should be started to defend against this preference action. If the amount is large, a review of the facts of the action and initial compiling of documents should be performed. Depending on the size of the supposed preference amount, you now force the trustee to either drop the whole issue or actively pursue the matter in court. This will cost the estate money and the time of the trustee, which could be used for more profitable endeavors to bring funds into the estate. Trustees have not only a fiduciary responsibility to bring funds into the estate for disbursement to the unsecured creditors, but can also receive up to a minimum of 3 percent of all funds collected for disbursement to the unsecured creditors plus their expenses.

2. *Bring in outside help.* If your firm lacks the expertise necessary to successfully stave off a real preference action by the trustee or debtor-in-possession, you may call in an outside attorney firm or hire an individual or firm that specializes in preference defense. In 1996, the National Association of Credit Management (NACM) (a 106-year-old commercial credit association) created a program to instruct, examine, and certify its top credit executives to become expert witnesses in a bankruptcy preference action. These individuals were required to have had a minimum of 10 years' extensive experience in the credit field, met all educational and experience requirements, and finally pass a rigorous examination to become a Certified Credit Executive (CCE). At that time, membership for NACM was over 30,000, with over 800 individuals having the CCE credential. The first group to attempt to obtain the CEW (Certified Expert Witness) certification had over 140 in attendance. Of these, approximately 90 received the CEW designation.

These individuals, while not attorneys, have successfully examined the creditor's records, compiled suitable defenses, and negotiated a final resolution with trustees and debtors-in-possession at costs that are far lower than that of most legal counsel. While most counsel trained in bankruptcy law have the expertise to defend in court or negotiate with a trustee over preferences actions, they may lack the ability to compile and create a suitable defense that will be needed in court to defend a preference action. They may need to hire an outside audit firm to compile the necessary documents that they need to defend their case in court. This compounds the cost involved as most certified public accountant (CPA) firms as well as attorney firms bill by the hour at rates from $150 to $350 per hour.

It may be smart to always have the best defense, but that doesn't mean that the best defense is always the most expensive or prestigious. Before looking into the hiring of attorney/CPA firms to deal with a preference defense, talk to a firm that has been certified by the NACM to handle preferences. These firms and individuals can be located through NACM at their headquarters located in Columbia, Maryland, at (410) 740-5574.

If indeed you feel that an attorney needs to be involved in the action, the CEW can work closely with your counsel to defend against the preference action. They can even appear in court as expert witnesses to verify the validity of the defenses.

Summary

Bankruptcies cost firms millions every day and have been on the increase for the last few years. Firms look at bankruptcy not only as a means to eliminate debt, but also as a means to resolve problems. Some examples of these include dealing with class-action lawsuits (Johns Manville, asbestos litigation), break unprofitable leases (Loews theatres, leases), and dealing with high-interest junk bond debt (Covad, junk bonds).

Now that the stigma has been removed, vendors must be ever on their guard to prevent or minimize the loss of cash flow or the increase in expenses as a result of bankruptcy filings. While there is no way to stop this problem, every effort must be made both internally and externally to defend against this aggression and cavalier attitude of some firms to take the "quick and easy way out" of paying their just debts.

The next chapter discusses a more positive effort to improve cash flow—working with the sales and marketing departments.

## CHAPTER 5

How to Prevent Sales from Hurting Cash Flow

After reading this chapter, you will be able to

- Determine whether a sale is truly profitable
- Know what price is being charged for the goods or services being sold
- Know what direct expenses are tied to the creation of those goods or services
- Know what administrative expenses are incurred in the selling of these goods or services
- Understand the cost ramifications of selling goods or services for less than or equal to "cost"
- Know the cost factors related to the seasonality of goods and whether it is better to "fire sale" or inventory until the next appropriate season
- Understand the cost ramifications of selling terms versus selling products or services
- Determine the cost and cash flow ramifications of "playing games" to meet month-end, quarter-end, or year-end sales quotas
- Know the cost effectiveness or value of "customer perception and goodwill"
- Understand how sales fraud can cost a firm in terms of reputation, lawsuits, and criminal investigation

- Determine the cost effectiveness of both education and communication between all departments directly involved in the sales process

As stated in Chapter 1, a company can have a net loss from sales and still stay in business as long as it has solid cash flow. Does this mean that sales are not critical to the well-being of a firm? That idea is certainly ridiculous. A firm without sales will have no cash flow other than from investors or from borrowing, and this will hold up for only a short period of time. Sales are a critical part of operation of a firm, but smart and well-executed sales are the difference between a company that will not survive for long and one that will prosper and grow.

Is a Sale Truly Profitable?

This should be the first question that everyone involved with the sales function should ask before proceeding with a sale. The reality is the first question that most sales reps ask is "What is my commission?" Is it that they don't care if the sale is profitable, improves the cash flow of the firm,

TIPS AND TECHNIQUES

Factors to Be Considered when Assessing the Profitability of a Sale

- What price is being charged for the goods or services being sold?

- What direct expenses are tied to the creation of those goods or services?

- What administrative expenses are incurred in the selling of these goods or services?

TIPS AND TECHNIQUES CONTINUED

- What are the cost ramifications of selling goods or services for less than or equal to "cost"?

- What are the cost factors related to the seasonality of goods— is it better to "fire sale" or inventory until the next appropriate season?

- What are the cost ramifications of selling terms versus selling products or services?

- What are the cost and cash flow ramifications of "playing games" to meet month-end, quarter-end, or year-end sales quotas?

- How cost effective or valuable is "customer perception and goodwill"?

- How can sales fraud cost a firm in terms of reputation, lawsuits, and criminal investigation?

- How cost effective are both education and communication between all departments directly involved in the sales process?

or helps the firm to grow? Their principal task for the firm is to sell the company's goods or services to their customers. Most firms want their sales reps to only sell, sell, and sell some more. The firms that succeed, however, make their sales reps far more than an instrument to unload goods or services. They make them a member of the team that wants the business to grow and prosper, and they communicate freely with those involved in the day-to-day process that makes a company a success.

We will look at each one of the sale profitability assessment questions now and break down whether a sale is both profitable and cost effective, which is one side of the cash flow equation.

What Price Is Being Charged for the Goods or Services Sold?

Before selling any goods or services, a price needs to be set that will allow for the coverage of all expenses both directly related to the item or service to be sold and all other nondirect expenses that need to be taken into consideration. Some outside costs related to administrative costs are salaries, commissions, and bonuses of the sales force and management, and salary for nondirect sales personnel such as credit, customer service, order entry, accounting, human resources, purchasing, and so on.

Then there are the overhead costs that include, if a manufacturer, the creation of the finished product, storage of not only finished goods but also raw materials and work in process. For distributors and retailers there is the storage of finished goods only but if there are multiple locations then distribution networks may need to be considered in the cost equation. Shipping locally, regionally, nationally, or internationally as well as the need of special handling for certain types of goods on a regular basis must also be considered.

Competition may also affect the price of the goods for if there are many companies that sell similar products to the ones that you offer then you have far less to bargain with than if there are very few or no competitors.

As for service products, the cost factors include the same type of administrative costs as that of selling goods (i.e., sales force salaries and expenses, administrative sales and expenses, etc.) as well as special education of individuals to actually do the work required in performing the service and the expenses related to that work. Some special materials or capital equipment as well as maintenance of it may also be needed in order to perform the service work being sold.

On top of all of these expenses related to the goods or services, a reasonable profit needs to be added. How is this determined? One old adage is "whatever the market will bear." To a certain degree this adage is true for if your product or service is in great demand then prices can certainly be higher and vice versa. It was mentioned earlier that competition is a factor in pricing. Another is the customer base. Selling into a risky marketplace loaded with marginal customers may force a firm to sell at a higher price in order to offset the losses from writing off bad debt receivables. This is not to say that it is not cost effective to sell to marginal customers, for I was taught a long time ago that the customers that always pay you on time pay for your overhead but the marginal ones are your profit. So it is indeed wise to have a mixed receivable portfolio if you wish to be profitable.

What Direct Expenses Are Tied to the Creation of Those Goods or Services?

There are direct costs related to the creation of goods or services. Let's look at these in a little more detail.

Manufacturers' costs

Purchase of raw materials. For a manufacturer, keeping the prices that they pay for the initial materials down is crucial, for this is the foundation of the entire product that they are planning on selling. The other factor that must be considered, however, is not only whether the supplier can provide the necessary goods on a timely basis and at a good price, but also whether they will be there tomorrow. Working with the credit area to investigate new suppliers to determine their overall viability may prove to be extremely cost effective.

Work in process Goods that are not quite raw and not quite finished have labor and space costs to be considered in the overall cost equation. Until these goods are completed, they are of no real value to anyone other than the manufacturer.

Know Your Suppliers

In today's volatile world, it is smart to do business with a firm that can meet the supply needs of your firm. Firms that I worked in (such as Garlock Inc., a subsidiary of Coltec Industries, and Bausch & Lomb's Optical Systems Division) initiated annual or semiannual (most critical) vendor investigation to determine their financial strength, paying habits to their suppliers, and their pricing and delivery timing schedule. This provided the ability to monitor the vendor's status and to take aggressive actions if necessary to deal with any problems that might occur. Vendor investigation was instituted at Bausch & Lomb after one local vendor that provided a critical service of coating microscope parts was forced to file bankruptcy as a result of its bank taking all the funds in its payroll account. At both firms, it was required that all nonpublic firms provide financial data for analysis as well as bank and trade references. This minor cost analysis prevented many "surprises" that could have cost these firms many millions of dollars in orders that were canceled due to lateness and many dissatisfied customers.

Finished goods. Once completed, finished goods must be stored in inventory until they are sold or destroyed. There is a warehousing cost that also must be added into the cost equation based on how long this inventory remains on the manufacturer's shelves.

Distributors' and Retailers' Costs

Finished goods. The warehousing of product purchased for resale is one of the great indirect costs that both distributors and retailers carry. Having the necessary goods on hand in a timely basis may mean the difference between making and losing a major sale. The seasonality of some products directly affects how long some items should remain in inventory. Some items such as certain fashions related to a season may sell well one season but not sell at all thereafter. Depending on the type of item, shelf life may vary greatly and end up resulting in the selling of some goods at less than cost just to move them out of inventory.

IN THE REAL WORLD

Some Inventory Never "Fades Away"

How long is too long to keep goods in inventory? At Bausch & Lomb they learned that sometimes it is better to hang on to some inventory rather than get rid of it.

In the mid-1950s Bausch & Lomb had a pair of sunglasses that had a thick, heavy black frame and very dark lenses that were very popular at that time. By the late 1960s and all through the 1970s they still had a fair amount of this inventory that had been sitting on the shelves but not many were being sold. In 1980, when Bausch & Lomb was about to dispose of its remaining inventory of these glasses, out came a movie that changed the whole perspective of the firm's inventory policy. *The Blues Brothers* starring the late John Belushi and Dan Aykroyd hit the screen with both stars wearing these very same sunglasses. The movie, like the sunglasses, became an overnight hit. Bausch & Lomb had to pull its inventory out of the trash, pull its old machinery that manufactured these particular sunglasses out of mothballs, and fire up the process all over again. Thanks to this movie event, an old part of inventory went from obsolete to rare and in great demand! Bausch & Lomb used this same philosophy in the future and worked with Hollywood thereafter to promote the sale of its inventory. Some other examples of their working with Hollywood include the movie *Top Gun* and the television show *CHiPs*.

Distribution networks. Many large distributors and retailers have set up distribution networks across the country to meet the demands of their customers. Distributors have set these up to save on the transportation costs of getting goods to their customers on a more cost-effective, timely basis. Retailers have done this to save on the need to have large amounts of inventory at stores that are usually located at more expensive areas than the typical cost of warehouse storage costs. This gives them more space to exhibit more varieties of merchandise for sale rather than using more expensive space for inventory storage. It also allows retailers to buy more products at cheaper prices while keeping these distribution centers strategically located so as to minimize the turnaround time of getting needed inventory to their stores.

Service firms' costs

Capital equipment. The type of service that the firm provides will directly affect what capital equipment costs are involved. Some firms such as AT&T may have large areas that handle the switching of phone lines, managing of cell phone communications, and the controlling of high-speed Internet access. Other firms may have much smaller capital expenditures. For example, a local business that does plumbing contracting will have trucks, plumbing supplies, and the tools necessary to complete their contracted work.

Inventory costs. While typically not for resell, the inventory that a service provider may keep on hand will give them what they routinely need to complete normal expected daily contract work. Special needs may arise from time to time, and this is where having financially solid and reliable suppliers with diversified inventories available that can help them out on a moment's notice can come in handy. These same suppliers can be very cost effective by not requiring these service firms to maintain less infrequently used inventory on hand.

What Administrative Expenses Are Incurred in the Selling of These Goods or Services?

As mentioned earlier, there are administrative expenses related to the creation of goods or services. Looking at these in a little more detail, we find the following.

- Manufacturers', distributors', and retailers' costs
  - *Sales and marketing salaries, bonuses, commissions, and expenses.* Typical to all three of these types of firms, incentive programs were set up to encourage sales of the products (carrot routine). The other side of the coin was that the sales force had quotas to meet or become unemployed (stick routine). Proportionally, the moving of higher-margin goods had a better incentive program than those of lower-margin items. Occasionally, firms also set up incentive programs to move slow-selling merchandise or items that are seasonal in nature. Some firms even offer trips and large luxury items to the best sales effort. These likewise need to be added into the pricing structure.
  - *Administrative services.* Salaries and expenses covering areas that support the sales focus include credit, collections, accounts receivables, finance, human resources, purchasing, customer service, billing, shipping, and receiving. While all of these areas do not directly "sell product," each plays a vital role in the sales process and can be the real reason that a sale is made.
- *Service firms' other administrative expenses.* Since firms that sell service tend to deal in products that require specialized training, one of the additional expenses that they face is that of education costs. All service firms require that their employees are knowledgeable of the products and skilled in offering these services. Depending on the type of firm, the level of training that is required to perform the service task will vary.

Credit can be Creative

On many occasions, the credit manager may be the one to really make a sale happen. In one particular case, a sale of lower-margin (25 percent) goods totaling $250,000 was being considered to an extremely marginal firm with very poor credit. The firm had placed a custom, one-time order and was hoping to get credit terms for the purchase. When the credit manager was approached by the vice president of the product line to consider the sale, an investigation of the applicant was conducted. After determining the firm was an extremely high risk and that credit was highly unlikely, the credit manager advised the vice president that if he perhaps "sweetened" the deal to a local distributor, they might consider taking on the order and the risk. The vice president offered the local distributor an additional 5 percent incentive, which reduced the margin now down to 20 percent. After the distributor looked over the deal, they came back to the vice president and wanted 15 percent instead. Once informed of the distributor's counteroffer (no big surprise to the credit manager), the credit manager decided to take a second look at the investigation.

Looking at the historical payment record listed on the credit report showed that at certain times of the year this firm had paid within terms and all the rest of the year they paid extremely slow. They had always been offered net 30 days terms so there was no way to determine how they would react to cash discount terms. The credit manager contacted the vice president and asked him would he be still willing to give up the 5 percent that he had offered to the distributor. When he agreed, the credit manager contacted the chief financial officer (CFO) of the customer to discuss terms of sale. The credit manager proposed the following offer: 3 percent cash discount wire transfer the funds less the discount the day that the goods were ready to ship.

The CFO, after discussing the order and the terms with their president, called the credit manager and accepted the proposal. The credit

Firms such as cable and telephone installation and repair need employees that can learn the necessary skills to install cable systems or telecommunications systems in both homes and businesses. These training sessions are a major expense to a firm as employees are not productive until they are capable of performing the job on their own. The loss of highly trained employees can be a major cost to a firm, which is one reason why high turnover can be expensive. A firm must look to how they compensate their skilled employees and the work environment that these individuals have to deal with to minimize the loss of skilled staff to competitors.

What Are the Cost Ramifications of Selling Goods or Services for Less Than or Equal to "Cost"?

Why would any firm want to sell goods or services at a price that is equal to or less than their cost? In order to break into a new market in which there is a fair amount of competition, firms may need to initially "undercut" the market in order to get market share. While this can be expensive at first, in the long run this may prove to be the fastest way to get control of a market. There may be some backlash to this tactic that results in additional expenses. Depending on the size of the competition, the "new kid on the block" may not have the financial wherewithal to with-stand a market takeover. The other possibility is that of a class-action law-

David versus Goliath

One recent example of a major class action lawsuit claiming an attempt to quickly gain market share and virtual control of a market happened when small local pharmacies joined together to file a class-action lawsuit against Wal-Mart. According to the complaint, Wal-Mart had built stores in many small towns and proceeded to price their goods that were common to them and pharmacies to levels far below the prices of these small town stores. As a result, many of them initially tried to reduce products to match the competition but were eventually forced out of business because they did not have the financial strength to keep their prices that low for any great length of time. Once the competition was substantially reduced, Wal-Mart proceeded to raise its prices to levels that were more on a par with what they typically charge for the items.

When the class action lawsuit was filed, Wal-Mart countered by saying that they were able to charge lower prices by buying far larger quantities from suppliers than the small local pharmacies were and that they were not attempting to fix prices. The pharmacies countered this argument by saying that the prices charged were not just low but were lower than the cost of the best price Wal-Mart could get by buying the quantities that they bought—in other words, below their cost price. They also attempted to prove that once the competition was sufficiently eliminated, Wal-Mart proceeded to raise its prices on everything, which left their customers with nowhere else to go for their pharmaceutical needs.

The class action lawsuit was finally settled out of court, with no guilt admitted to and no details of the final settlement released.

suit, which could result from putting many small competitors out of business by selling at a loss temporarily, gaining control of the marketplace, and then substantially raising the prices on your products.

What Are the Cost Factors Related to the Seasonality of Goods—Is It Better to "Fire Sale" or Inventory until the Next Appropriate Season?

Seasonality of goods is a reality of life. We wear certain clothes in the summer or winter depending on where we live, we celebrate a variety of holidays and special days that require special merchandise, and we deal with fashion "ins" and "outs." All of these things affect our buying habits and our way of life, so what has this got to do with seasonality and cost controls for a firm? In a word, for those who are tied to certain markets—everything!

Firms that sell clothing must deal with whether items are popular and "in" or not popular and not saleable. Many firms do vast amounts of market research and invest heavily in advertising in order to sell their seasonal clothes before the season changes. This is why you may see winter coats being sold near the end of summer or spring and summer fashions being offered in the dead of winter. Companies make educated guesses as to what will be popular and what will not be popular for the upcoming season. Guess right and you turn over your inventory very well; guess wrong and you are stuck with merchandise that you almost can't give away.

Other merchandise beside clothes is extremely seasonal. Try the holidays. Retailers stock up on seasonal goods such as Christmas decorations, Halloween costumes, Easter rabbits, and so on. One of the hottest items that can make or break a firm is guessing which toy will be the hit of the Christmas season. Many manufacturers tie toys to cartoons and movies, and do massive television advertising to create a craze for their new toy. Guessing right can mean millions; guessing wrong can mean millions in sitting inventory.

Now that we have looked at what seasonality can do for a firm what is the right approach to inventory that exceeds its seasonal life? In the case of most holiday items, retailers tend to "fire sale" them at sometimes 50 percent off and pass on whatever remains to firms that sell close-out goods for pennies on the dollar just to get shelf space for other new merchandise. In this case, it is wiser to get something for your merchandise and free up shelf space than get nothing at all. For wholesalers and manufacturers in this position it may prove wiser to hold onto these items assuming that they are not perishable and that they don't take up too much space.

TIPS AND TECHNIQUES

Looking at Cost Factors of Seasonal Merchandise

- *Storage.* Reduction of warehouse space and nonmoving inventory (manufacturers, wholesalers, and retailers)

- *Shelf space blockage.* Past seasonal items versus new merchandise: keeping, disposing, or donating (retailers)

- *Perishable goods.* Fire sale, donate, or dispose of (manufacturers, wholesalers, and retailers)

- *Seasonal clothing.* Keeping, disposing, or donating (manufacturers, wholesalers, and retailers)

- *Fashion clothing.* Discounting and finally "fire selling" to a close-out firm (manufacturers, wholesalers, and retailers)

- *Transportation costs.* Returns of past merchandise (manufacturers and wholesalers)

- *Advertising costs.* Last attempt at getting rid of past seasonal merchandise (retailers)

As for perishable items, if they didn't get sold via a fire sale, then possible donation to a local charity may at least afford a firm a tax write-off.

In the case of seasonal clothing, some things may be worthwhile to carry over to the next year after many big sales, depending on the amount of space needed to store the items; otherwise selling them to a close-out firm may be a firm's only answer. If the clothing is very fashion sensitive, then it is all the more likely that it will be sold to a close-out store. Donations to charity may also be a way out to at least gain that very precious tax write-off.

IN THE REAL WORLD

Do Extended Terms Make Sense?

Many years ago, Bausch & Lomb offered a special terms promotion tied to the sale of its RayBan sunglasses to ski shops throughout the United States. Orders were taken in April and May from the shops and shipped in June. The ski-dating invoices had terms of 2 percent cash discount if paid by January 10th, net due January 30th. What happened in many cases was that many of the ski shops stocked up heavily in the RayBan sunglasses, sold all of them off either at regular prices or discounted them heavily as the season wound down, and finally closed their doors before the invoice was even 30 days past due. As a result, Bausch & Lomb suffered many losses from firms that were no longer in business. This was a very liberal sales promotion that allowed many small firms to overbuy goods and help them survive off of the funds that were due the manufacturer. While this program did help get the visibility that Bausch & Lomb wanted with the skiers, the losses that occurred offset the profits made on the total sales tied to the promotion. The following year Bausch & Lomb no longer offered this promotion.

What Are the Cost Ramifications of Selling Terms versus Selling Products or Services?

One of the oldest selling lines other than "I can get it for you wholesale" is "I can even get you a discount or longer credit terms if you buy this." Selling terms can be one surefire way to cut your profit margin down rapidly and could end up in some cases causing you not to get paid at all. Too long credit terms have tempted many firms from buying now and the seller suffering later when the funds that were meant for payment are all but gone.

How Much Does Cash Discount Cost (Cost of Capital)?

Typically, assets are allotted in the consideration that they will give a particular return. If this return is at a minimum, the same as the cost of the capital of that particular asset, then it will result in a damaging outcome on the total earnings. Vendors should be mindful of what they are losing versus what they are gaining when a cash discount is extended. On one side it loses the dollar total of the discount, and on the other it gains the extra days gained from early receipt of payment. If the terms of sale are 2 percent 10 days net 30 days, then the vendor would gain 20 days' availability of cash by extending this cash discount.

Only when the cost of capital exceeds the cost of extending a cash discount should discount terms be considered. The formula for computing the equivalent rate of cost of capital to that of a cash discount term offered for terms of 3 percent 10 days, net 30 days is:

$$\frac{\text{Discount rate} \times 365 \text{ days}}{\text{Number of days gain in early receipt of cash}}$$

$$\frac{.03 \times 365}{20} = .5475 \text{ or } 54.75\%$$

The offset of gaining 20 extra days of cash availability requires that the cost of capital be equal to or in excess of 54.75 percent to make the terms offered worthwhile to the vendor. The following table breaks down the cost of capital for some of the more common cash discount terms:

Comparative Annual Interest Rates

Cash Discount Percentage	?% 10 Days, Net 30 Days	?% 10 Days, Net 60 Days	?% 10 Days, Net 90 Days	?% 10 Days, Net 120 Days	?% 10 Days, Net 150 Days	?% 10 Days, Net 180 Days
0.50%	9.13%	3.65%	2.28%	1.66%	1.30%	1.07%
1.00%	18.25%	7.30%	4.56%	3.32%	2.61%	2.15%
1.50%	27.38%	10.95%	6.84%	4.98%	3.91%	3.22%
2.00%	36.50%	14.60%	9.13%	6.64%	5.21%	4.29%
2.50%	45.63%	18.25%	11.41%	8.30%	6.52%	5.37%
3.00%	54.75%	21.90%	13.69%	9.95%	7.82%	6.44%
4.00%	73.00%	29.20%	18.25%	13.27%	10.43%	8.59%
5.00%	91.25%	36.50%	22.81%	16.59%	13.04%	10.74%

Typical to some industries cash discounts are a way of life. A typical credit term in the pharmaceutical industry is 2 percent 30 days, net 31 days. The other downside to cash discounts is collecting the infamous disallowed cash discount.

Many firms will take the cash discount yet pay the vendor later than the designated discount due date or, worse than that, take the discount and pay later than the net due date. Many firms have a serious problem controlling disallowed discounts from their major customers who are usually the worst offenders. Some vendors have drawn a line in the sand and dared the buyer to cross it relating to cash discounts, while others have simply written off the deductions as a cost of doing business with some larger customers.

A real point of concern revolves around treating all firms equally when it comes to the resolution of cash discounts. The Robinson–Patman Act was enacted in 1936 and is one of three main federal antitrust laws. It requires all business-to-business vendors to sell their goods

Disallowed Discount Controls

One firm that had a problem with its customers blatantly taking cash discounts far after the discount due date set up a system to address this issue. A notice was sent to all customers advising them that each time that a discount was disallowed, the accounts payable manager would be sent a letter (with a copy to the buyer) with backup proving that the discount should be repaid. If the disallowed discount was not repaid, a follow-up letter was sent 30 days later demanding payment. When the total of disallowed cash discounts totaled either 1 percent of buyer's annual sales or $1,000 whichever was first, a final letter was sent, giving the buyer 20 days to repay the disallowed discounts or face being placed on credit hold. Copies of all previous correspondence and backup were attached to this letter.

If payment was not received, then the customer's orders were held until payment in full was received. As a kind of safety valve, the vendor allowed an unannounced 10-day grace period in addition to the original 10 days when the discount was due allowing any discounts if payment was received within the 20 days from the date of the invoice. With no legs to stand on, most customers that were not really using the cash discount as a means to increase their cash flow in order to survive repaid their disallowed cash discounts and monitored all future payments to stay within the boundaries set by the vendor. As for those that did not comply, orders were stopped and eventually they either repaid the disallowed cash discounts in order to get product or were sued for the outstanding balance due the vendor.

at the same price to all of their customers. One factor of price is cash discount terms. If one customer is forced to repay its disallowed discounts while other, more critical buyers are not, this is in direct violation of Robinson–Patman. The government rarely enforces the Robinson–

Patman Act, with the majority of suits being brought by buyers, who may be entitled to treble damages and attorneys' fees should they win. Though not as daunting as the other two federal antitrust laws, which include the threat of time in prison for officers of firms who violate them, the threat of treble damages if sued in a civil court may be sufficient to assuage a firm from ignoring it altogether.

The one remaining aspect of selling terms is in connection to granting extended terms and the time cost of money. While reviewing the details of how to compute the time cost of money is beyond the scope of this book, when determining the price that will be charged for goods or services the time it takes for a firm to be repaid for the sale should be taken into consideration. Obviously, the longer the terms extended, the higher the price should be and vice versa. While it is safe to say that no one can predict completely when each invoice will be repaid by a customer, at a minimum the cost of extending terms beyond what is normally granted should be considered in the pricing equation. As for dealing with the problem of late payments, consideration of late charges is one possible way to offset the cost of carrying a receivable beyond its standard terms.

What Are the Cost and Cash Flow Ramifications of "Playing Games" to Meet Month-End, Quarter-End, or Year-End Sales Quotas?

This, unfortunately, is all too common in big business today. While sales forces are pressured to meet the magic goals that coincidentally end at either month-end, quarter-end, and/or year-end, the push to get products out the door or service billings done always seems to fall during the last week to last few days at the end. This means that the lion's portion of all of the billings fall at the end of a month, with minimal billings occurring during the first few weeks of the month. Rare is the firm that bills steadily through the month, yet accounting for quite a few firms runs a "four-week, four-week, five-week" accounting cycle for each quarter. As a result of this, the accounting closing time for cash collections may vary greatly from as early as the 22nd of a month to as late as the 3rd of the following month. This causes great swings in the overall cash flow of the firm.

By billing the majority of the sales during the last few days of the month, against fairly standard terms of net 30 days, the likelihood is that a payment for the majority of the cash will not be received in the following month but more likely the month after. This tends to force a firm to live with limited cash flow literally three weeks out of every month. By doing this, a firm may be forced at times to borrow against its working capital line of credit in order to meet cash shortfall needs and add interest expense to cost of delaying cash that could be put to far more profitable endeavors than being tied up in receivables.

One additional cost that could also result from this type of last minute sales surge is the deterioration of the days' sales outstanding (DSO) ratio, which is the average time that it takes for a firm to collect its receivables. This is one of a few very important ratios that a bank will focus on when it considers a loan extension to a firm. Due to these late billings and the way that the accounting cycle is set up it will appear that the firm is carrying a fair amount of dead wood in its accounts receivable portfolio and will raise the interest rates that it will charge that customer for the loan. Under this same scenario, the bank may also reduce the amount that they will lend to the firm as well. This can be for many firms an extremely expensive proposition.

How Cost Effective or Valuable Is Customer Perception and Goodwill?

Many times, what people read in the press or hear on the evening news can make or break a firm. The quote that "the pen is mightier than the sword" applies even more today, in this age of instant information other-

IN THE REAL WORLD

Public Image: Expensive or Worth it?

Do you remember the Tylenol scare in the 1980s? Bottles of Tylenol were tampered with, and many consumers became sick or died as a result of the intentional poisoning by criminals. The manufacturer of the product, Johnson & Johnson, had many options that they could have taken but chose the one that was most difficult and expensive which happened to also be the moral and proper choice. Instead of pointing the finger at an unnamed madman and saying that they were not responsible for this problem, they stepped up and recalled all Tylenol from the shelves of every store and also from the shelves of every consumer who had bought it. They quickly developed a tamper-resistant bottle and issued coupons to consumers for a replacement of any bottles returned to them. Likewise, they restocked the shelves of all of their customers' stores with these replacements at no charge and absorbed millions of dollars of losses from the return of this product.

This type of action reflects the high caliber of moral responsibility that a firm can exhibit, which in the long run has made it one of the most respected firms in the consumers' eyes. This type of trusted reputation has paid off by making it one of the most recognized and trusted names in products.

Another less responsible reaction to a defective product has proven to tarnish the reputation of an old firm in the marketplace. Firestone, whose tires have been known to explode when used in conjunction with a Ford Explorer, has refused to deal with the problems that have occurred. They have instead pointed the finger at Ford, who in turn pointed the finger back. Needless to say, this has soured the average consumer on buying Firestone tires and Ford Explorers that were equipped with them and has cost both companies in tarnished reputation and millions of dollars of sales losses.

wise known as the Internet. The perception of the consumer can change whether a firm goes from being a wholesome part of the community or a villain to society.

While people buy stock and vote through their purchases of goods and services in all of their day-to-day activities, these same people take their perceptions to the workplace, which can cause havoc to firms that offer their goods or services to other businesses. Large investors, purchasing agents, and mutual fund holders base their decisions on more than a whim but they too are consumers and listen to what the public at large says and wants.

If a firm tends to look short term at the costs of dealing with a situation versus looking at the big picture and the future, they may pay the ultimate price. Many mighty firms have been quickly brought to their knees as a result of bad publicity. Corporate responsibility and reputation, while expensive to maintain, may be one cost factor that a firm should never underestimate and undervalue.

How Can Sales Fraud Cost a Firm in Terms of Reputation, Lawsuits, and Criminal Investigation?

Investors today like to see steady annual growth of the firms that they maintain stock in. This can put tremendous pressures on corporate boards to keep a firm always moving forward. Some firms may resort to creative accounting to attempt to mask what they perceive as a temporary financial setback when the reality may be just the opposite.

Public firms today must be audited in order for their stock to be sold on the three stock exchanges. The auditing firms have rules and guidelines to follow before issuing a clean bill of health to a firm, otherwise known as complete compliance to generally accepted accounting principles (GAAP). While these firms likewise are independent of the firms that they audit, the audit firms each vie for the honor and revenues of being the accounting firm of many major firms.

This can sometimes lead to problems with what is acceptable according to GAAP or overlooking certain practices that the auditors are led to believe are either not substantial or are very temporary. The federal government, through the Securities and Exchange Commission (SEC), acts as the watchdog of these accounting firms and the companies that they audit in order to make sure that investors are not cheated out of their investments in these firms.

IN THE REAL WORLD

The Games People (and Companies) Play

One recent example of corporate financial game playing was in the case of Xerox. In order to make their sales quotas for the year, tremendous pressure was placed on the executives in many country locations of Xerox to make sales numbers at all costs. In Mexico, they had machines shipped to warehouses for nonexistent customers and sales booked in order to make their sales quotas for many millions of dollars. After the beginning of the next year, the sales were reversed out and new real sales had to be made in order to make up the fictitious ones. This action was overlooked by the auditors and continued on until top Xerox officers were confronted by this practice by one of their top internal audit staff.

When this staff member was subsequently let go, he approached the SEC which began its own investigation. Xerox's own auditing firm refused to now grant a clean GAAP statement on their financials and after many months of back and forth negotiations the auditing firm has finally relented and signed off on the financials. To date Xerox is still being investigated by the SEC and may face charges brought by them. This has hurt the firm's reputation and caused them to recalculate years of financial statements.

Other firms today have faced even greater problems, with criminal actions being considered against the officers of the firm, bankruptcy being filed, criminal actions being considered against the auditing firm, and the firm being slowly dismantled and sold off piece by piece. The highest-profile story is the fall of Enron, a once highly admired and indeed a choice stock to own. There have been many cases in history of the financial games played by large firms and the use of bankruptcy to solve issues unrelated to excessive debt. Enron is just one of many.

While firms may only look short term in order to solve today's financial and shareholders' needs, the costs involved may be staggering if financial tricks are used instead of sound business sense and long-term planning. Fraud can cost not only the firm itself but the small investors who have many billions of dollars locked up in 401K savings plans for their retirements. The costs of financial fraud can go well beyond the corporate boardroom, depending upon the size of the firm, to society itself.

How Cost Effective Are Both Education and Communication between All Departments Directly Involved in the Sales Process?

In previous chapters we have talked about the need for educational departmental cross-training of job responsibilities, duties, and importance to the well-being of the firm of all areas that are directly involved with the customer. Each area's knowledge of the other allows for quicker resolution of problems, prevention of problems, and an appreciation of each other's jobs. Mutual training, both internally and externally, can prove to make firms more efficient and staffs more cooperative in accomplishing the two ultimate goals: serving the customer and making a profit.

While some educational programs can be expensive, preventing errors, finding better ways to solve a problem by seeing a much bigger picture, and being more cost effective in doing their jobs can save far

TIPS AND TECHNIQUES

Cost Savings from Cross-Department Education and Communication

- Prequalify new customers before efforts are made to sell them goods or services. If credit reviews a potential new customer before sales gets heavily involved in selling products or services, then time and effort can be better utilized on focusing on the most profitable sales.

- The credit function with its sources of information may be able to locate new potential customers to provide leads to the sales force.

- A credit review of major suppliers to your firm may prevent problems with firms that can meet the buyer's needs due to financial or credit problems.

- Customer service and sales generally hear about problems as they occur. By forwarding this information on to those that correct these issues, problems are reduced or eventually eliminated. Examples include:
  - Credit not holding orders due to defective goods
  - Returns areas issuing return authorizations and replacement orders
  - Billing areas adjusting pricing errors
  - Continuous problems with a certain type of product or service brought to the attention of the engineering or quality control area to determine how to stop these repetitive errors
  - Sales can adjust their selling strategies until problems are solved

more than the cost of these classes. This, however, is only half the battle. The one most cost effective and valuable tool in making a company successful is a free and quick means of communications between all areas. Firms today that employ an intranet system can quickly speed information to all parties and reduce if not eliminate costly errors before they can sometimes even occur.

Businesses use these and many other methods every day to make the most of education and communication as a means to grow successfully while keeping costs in line. Every problem solved so that it does not re-occur reduces the cost that a firm incurs and improves its reputation as a result of better education and communication.

Summary

While many areas see sales as being responsible for high costs and problems, the ultimate way to solve these issues and keep costs in line is through improved communication and interdepartmental education. With tools firmly in hand, Chapter 6 discusses how purchasing can maximize corporate cash.

How Purchasing Can Maximize Corporate Cash

After reading this chapter, you will be able to

- Know how sound current suppliers are
- Know when you should be suspicious that a supplier is in trouble
- Know what additional factors you should take into account when considering a new supplier
- Know how often you should look at suppliers

Purchasing is an integral part of the cash flow management process and should not be underrated in its importance. We've already discussed some of the implications in Chapter 3 on the purchase-to-pay cycle. In this chapter, we look at purchasing-related issues outside the aforementioned cycle. Without having the necessary parts and service contracts in place to get needed raw materials and service coverage on needed equipment, businesses would not have materials to sell nor the ability to offer their services to customers.

So how can purchasing improve cash flow? Let's look at the first step that they need to take in protecting their firms.

How Sound Are Current Suppliers?

Each supplier must offer the goods or services that the vendor needs in order to meet the needs of their customers. Current suppliers have a track record (good, bad, average) with the vendor that is always looked at first before any other concerns arise. This track record is reviewed regularly, and many suppliers have been dropped quickly if their efforts do not meet the needs and expectations of the vendor.

But what happens if the supplier that has always been there when you needed them suddenly goes out of business, files bankruptcy, or can't get materials or offer services to you because they are having cash flow problems of their own and have been put on credit hold by their suppliers? Now the vendor is left with nowhere to go but out into the cold, cruel world in search of another wonderful supplier of those very needed materials or services at a time that could prove crucial to have these items or services in place.

Obviously, the smaller the supplier, the less financial information and the smaller the number of trade references that will be available on the credit report. Their trade references should be available for review. If a vendor is a critical supplier, regardless of their size, it very wise to have at least one additional backup firm (if not more) to prevent your company from being left high and dry.

TIPS AND TECHNIQUES

Reviewing a Supplier for Financial Stability

- Obtain a new full credit report on the supplier.

- Review the payment pattern that the supplier has with their suppliers.

- If the majority of their suppliers, especially the larger ones, are paid 30 or more days slow, problems could be beginning.

- If the majority of their suppliers, especially the larger ones, are paid 60 or more days slow, problems definitely exist and an alternate source should be considered.

- If the majority of their suppliers, especially the larger ones, are paid 90 or more days slow, problems absolutely exist and a replacement must be found immediately.

- If the majority of their suppliers, especially the large ones, are paid promptly, then look to see if financial information is available, is current, and is audited

- If no financial information is available, look to see how long the firm has been in business (10 or more years is a plus; less than 10 is a minus) and if the owners and officers have a background in the products or services that they sell (10 or more years is a plus; less than 10 is a minus).

- If the officers have 10 or more years of background in the products or services that they sell, do they own their headquarters building or rent (own is a plus, lease from anyone other than the owner is a minus because this reflects stability).

- If the majority of their suppliers, especially the large ones, are paid promptly and the report has financial information but it is not current, contact the credit reporting agency and demand to see an update of the financial information.

- If the majority of their suppliers, especially the large ones, are paid promptly and if financial information is available and it is current but unaudited, then:

  - Ask the credit reporting agency to request audited financial information from the supplier and if refused.

  - Ask the supplier directly for them.

  - If they either don't have them available or refuse to provide them, consider looking for a alternate source.

- Review the unaudited financial data to determine annual sales, net worth, and total debt to net worth to see if it is increasing or decreasing (increase in sales and net worth is a plus, increase in total debt to net worth is a major minus)

- If the majority of their suppliers, especially the large ones, are paid promptly and if financial information is available, current, and audited, review it for:

  - Annual sales, net worth, and total debt to net worth to see if it is increasing or decreasing (increase in sales and net worth is a plus, increase in total debt to net worth is a major minus).

  - Check account payables turnover (average days that a firm takes to pay its trade vendors) and see if that has been increasing (a minus) or decreasing (a plus).

  - Scan the notes to the consolidated financial statement to see if there are any items that may put them into financial risk or default with their bank or trade vendors, any major or class-action lawsuits filed against them, or any other items that could jeopardize their existence.

  - Check recent articles on them on the Internet (if it is a public company, two areas available for current articles are Bloomberg.com [http://www.bloomberg.com/welcome.html] and Hoovers.com [http://www.hoovers.com/]) for any recent bad news that could put the company in precarious financial position.

  - Contact the supplier and request the names and telephone numbers of three other purchasing managers from firms similar to your firm that you can contact to see how good their on time delivery of parts and/or service is with them.

When Should You Be Suspicious That a Supplier Is in Trouble?

There are many danger signs that can tip the hand of a wayward supplier. (See *Tips and Techniques*, "Warning Signs that a Supplier Is in Trouble.") Any of these signs (with the exception of the last one) may not be a sure sign of trouble but definitely purport that ominous things are occurring in the life of this vendor. It is best to heed the signs of warning that appear and take steps to protect your business.

TIPS AND TECHNIQUES

Warning Signs that a Supplier Is in Trouble

- The receipt of goods has gradually slowed in recent times

- The supplier repeatedly complains of problems with their supplier, which has hurt them with all of their customers.

- Work on a service contract has slowed due to lack of materials.

- Supplier states that they no longer offer those parts but can substitute them with a different brand.

- Supplier has provided items that have consistently proven to be broken or defective.

- Service work has been unsatisfactory and repair crews constantly complain about their company.

- Service technicians have asked about a job with the buyer versus wanting to work for the company that the buyer has contracted to do the work.

- The supplier's sales rep talks to the buyer about being a sales rep for the buyer's firm.

- The service provider's technicians complain about the shoddy materials that they were given by their company to do the job.

- When trying to place an order, the buyer has gotten either nothing but busy signals or an answering machine to leave a message.

- After a message has been left, the seller or service provider does not return the call.

- Any newspaper, Internet, or television news article that advises that a firm's suppliers have slowed, shortened credit terms, or stop shipping altogether or that their loan covenant with their bank was violated by the supplier.

When Considering A New Supplier, What Additional Factors Should You Take into Account?

Before defining the additional questions that you may wish to ask a new vendor to your business, one factor may make a considerable difference as to how they will deal with you as a customer. While all customers were created equal, the truth of the matter is that they are not. The bigger buyer is more desirable from a sales rep's point of view. Bigger means more volume purchases, more variety of purchases, and quicker turnover of their product. It also can mean greater demands made of the supplier, better payment terms, intentionally (sometimes) slower paying habits, and the "jump when I yell" big buyer mentality that some large firms have.

The sales rep does feel the heat of this situation but still collects the commission at the end of the month when that big order goes through. The cash flow problems with larger customers that can sometimes force a smaller supplier to stretch farther with them than they would with other customers tends to make these types of firms less profitable and a cash flow hindrance rather than a major plus for cash flow.

Does this mean that you as a large buyer shouldn't take advantage of this position and demand better service from a supplier? Certainly not, but you should not expect the supplier to give you an unfair advantage over other customers that they sell to. If too much pressure is put on a small yet important supplier, you may end up forcing them out of business, leaving your business in a position of scrambling for a new supplier of a critical component of your business.

Another factor to be considered when looking into a new supplier is their ability to meet all of your supply or service needs. While a firm may be in great financial shape and may be top-notch at customer service, if their capacity to handle a large job is lacking, then you have two choices: find another supplier to back them up (which is highly recommended anyway) or discuss with them directly what their real capacity limit is. If they are one of the best in the business in what they do, then it may be worth the effort to discuss having them act as the central focus point for a larger purchase of goods or service and have them subcontract out the parts that they cannot handle. They would be the overseer of the job, and they would have to live up to their reputation for quality workmanship. This can improve your cash flow because there would be cost savings in having a large job filtered through one supplier versus many smaller ones, and they would also be grateful that your firm will help their company to grow substantially, which should help your firm in the long run.

Also to be considered when looking for a new vendor is the old saying "Location, Location, Location." Depending on the product or service that you are in need of, it is far better to have the vendor close and save on the shipping costs than to have to deal with one across the country or across the globe. While in many cases we have very little choice in where our suppliers are located, if given the opportunity to select one closer to home as long as prices are reasonably close, service is the same or better, and quality of products and services are equal or better, it makes sense to stay closer to home. Labor strikes and problems with shippers can create havoc when trying to meet your customers' needs if you don't get the parts or services that you need from a vendor.

An additional factor to be considered is the vendor's labor situation. If a vendor has a history of labor disputes or problems with the Equal Employment Opportunity Commission (EEOC), then they may be a firm that you may wish to steer clear of.

Finally, the area that should be considered before taking on a new vendor is its reputation, not only with other buyers but also with the public at large and the government. If a business is looked at as a bad neighbor, a polluter, or a general nuisance to the community where it is located, then this may ultimately affect their ability to service your company properly. Likewise, if the city, state, or federal government is investigating the business for reasons such as tax evasion, financial fraud, EEOC violations, or pollution violations, this too can be a great area of concern to a buyer. When a business is under siege from the community where it is located or is being investigated by the government for a number of reasons, then this firm has great potential for not being able to deliver on its product or service commitments. This factor must be heavily weighed against all the positives before any contract assignment is made with this vendor.

How Often Should You Look at Suppliers?

Typically, a full examination should be done on all major or critical vendors at least once a year. If quality of service declines during the year or if problems with defective goods increase rapidly, an immediate review is needed. If there is an increase in the number of short- or back-order shipments where there has been none in the past, or if there has been a substantial increase in defective goods, an interim review should be conducted. If the supplier increases its prices with little or no explanation, or shortens its credit terms when they are being paid on time, or offers cash discounts when none were offered in the past, an interim review is needed.

TIPS AND TECHNIQUES

Steps for Uncovering Potential Problems with Vendors Prior to Annual Review

If an interim review is needed, some of the areas that require checking include:

- An updated credit report if more than three months old to check on payment habits of the supplier with their suppliers

- Contacting other buyers that have dealt with this firm to determine if the quality of their workmanship or service has deteriorated

- Review any local or national news articles or check financial Web sites such as Bloomberg or Hoover (assuming that the vendor is large enough) for any new articles related to them that may hint of a problem or one on the horizon.

- If the vendor is a public company check the EDGAR (SEC) Web site (*http://www.sec.gov/edgar/searchedgar/formpick.htm*) to see if there have been any 8K filings. This form is required by the SEC to define any major change to a public company.

- If nothing out of the ordinary is reflected in this investigation, then the sales rep of the vendor along with the regional sales manager and/or vice president of sales should be asked to meet with the buyer to discuss current problems with their products or services.

If the problem is a temporary one, such as temporary shortages of raw materials needed by the supplier to provide its goods or services, and the situation has been corrected, then no further action should be taken but monitoring should continue. If the problems are extensive and may include a looming long-term labor strike, financial difficulties, government investigations, and the like, then locating at least one new source of matching goods or services is in order and should be given high priority.

Summary

While changes occur on a regular basis to firms that supply goods and services to buyers when a critical or major supplier of goods and services stumbles, we as vendors to our customers also stumble. We can ill afford to be careless and complacent with vendors who have been trustworthy in the past but now seem, at least on the surface, to be experiencing difficulty. It is vital that we take all necessary steps to be alert to a problem that may jeopardize our ability to perform at our best while keeping our cash flow sound by delivering quality goods and services at all times to our customers. We must always have a reliable second-string quarterback to support our hurt or injured superstar quarterback, whether it is permanently or temporarily. Being alert to the signals may mean the difference between having solid profit and cash flow or having losses and cash flow problems. Now we continue on to customer service enhancements to improve cash flow.

## CHAPTER 7

Customer Service Enhancements to Improve Cash Flow

After reading this chapter, you will be able to

- Understand how customer service saves a sale
- Take steps to sell more product or services
- Use customer service as a way to solve payment issues

Now we come to that part of the company that really is the frontline defense with the customer in keeping costs low. While everybody has heard those well-worn adages, "The customer is king" and "The customer is always right," both are not always true. Customers have one thought in mind when they call customer service—"What can I get out of them today along with what legitimate complaint that I have?"

Customer service has to deal with the upset, the screaming, the swearing, the abusive, and the rare understanding customer who has a problem. I take my hat off to them! With the exception of the credit department, I know of no area that has dealt with more problems or has been more poorly-treated than customer service.

So how do these poor souls aid the company in improving cash flow? They have the unique ability to not only keep a sale intact; but can make additional sales as well. Another great skill that they have is to resolve issues that cause customers not to pay their bills on time. Let's look at what customer service can do for you.

How Does Customer Service Save a Sale?

When a customer contacts customer service, it is with the intention of returning goods that they were sold or services that were not to their satisfaction. By having the right facts at their fingertips (i.e., access to order/account information or service logs), customer service can determine the history of the transaction, what was purchased, and when it was shipped and billed or serviced. They can immediately issue a return merchandise authorization (RMA) number if it is goods or determine what was not performed if a service sale and resolve the customer's problem immediately.

How does this cut costs and improve the company's cash flow? First, a customer that feels that they were treated fairly and professionally will purchase goods or services there again. Goodwill exhibited in this area can make or break a customer relationship. As for keeping costs down, an unhappy customer will not pay their invoice, which hurts cash flow. The need for someone to follow up in the credit department on a past due invoice that really isn't past due but disputed costs a company for the time lost by the collector, which could have been used to collect money from someone who truly is past due. If not properly handled by customer service, the situation now requires that the credit department act as customer service to investigate and follow up the salesperson as well as customer service in trying to resolve the disputed issue. This compounds the cost by bringing others into a situation that should have been resolved early on and now takes time away from the sales force that could have been used for selling.

While I don't encourage that customer service have complete power over what can be returned and how much or can force other areas to do work that will not be billed, I do encourage that they be empowered to take actions that can resolve most problems quickly while treating both the company and the customer fairly. The need for levels of approval should still be there but great time delays in getting approval must be eliminated at all costs. Solid training in how to be professional, fair, and cool under fire help a customer service rep deal with the irate and abusive customer. Education in the psychology of customers as well as training in how to deal with stress and knowledge of how other departments function within the firm will aid the rep in being the best at his or her job. This small expenditure can pay off in spades in time saved and goodwill restored.

How Do They Sell More?

Beyond their ability to salvage a sale, the well-trained and astute customer service person can turn an upset customer into a happy customer that not only gets their replacement goods or services but also buys additional goods or services. The customer ends up happy with the whole experience. It sounds too good to be true but it can be if customer service personnel are trained not only in resolving problems but also selling goods or services.

IN THE REAL WORLD

How Customer Service Increases Its Value

Apple Computer's customer service knows how to resolve issues with its computers as well as increasing its business. When a wireless card was installed into an IMac computer and the system would not recognize the card because it was defective, a call was placed to customer service to get an RMA for its return. When questioned about replacing the card, Apple was quick to offer a replacement. When asked about the incident service fee of $49.95 for the use of their technical support department, they were more than happy to credit that as well as the card proved defective and there may have been no need of technical support if the card had worked properly.

The replacement obviously kept the sale intact, but they lost the technical support revenue. That, however, is not the end of the story. At this point, the customer service person mentioned to the customer that for $149.00 they could have a three-year service agreement that would offer help with any aspect of their Apple computer and also offer them some additional software and educational assistance. When the replacement card came, they could simply call their special toll-free technical support line and schedule a person to do the installation. All future concerns that they may have or problems that they may run into would be easily handled by their technical support team free of charge.

This made a very satisfied customer and one that bought more than what they originally had planned to. It also left them with a feeling of security that Apple would be there if any problems occurred in the future.

How Can They Solve Payment Issues?

When a customer refuses to pay for goods or services, there are many reasons beyond what may be the real reason for nonpayment, which could be lack of cash flow.

Defective Goods

Customer service will typically replace defective goods, assuming that they were not sold as a "close out," "as is," or "final sale" merchandise. Immediate replacement of these goods is a matter of pride and reputation for a business, and that can be one of the most valuable assets a business has and can ill afford to tarnish. A new invoice is issued for the goods that

Reasons for Nonpayment
by a Customer

- Defective goods

- Incomplete or incorrect service work

- Pricing issues

- Short shipments (goods)

- Overshipments (goods)

- Never received goods or services

- Damaged goods

- Sales tax charged

- Freight charged when should have been shipped freight free

- Wrong goods shipped

- Did not meet all conditions in the purchase order

are sent to replace the defective ones. When the RMA has been issued, the invoice tied to it needs to be marked as disputed and the credit department notified to make sure that the customer is not contacted when it becomes overdue.

Once the goods have been received and inspected, then credit should immediately be issued. The final step that should be performed by the customer service group is to monitor the type and volume of product that was defective. This information, when forwarded to top management, gives them the insight into problems that are repetitively occurring with certain products and enables them to correct this situation. This type of communications can pay off in major dollar savings as it prevents a problem from getting out of hand, keeps customer satisfaction high by keeping defects low, and saves tremendously on the added time and expense to the repeated return of nonworking goods.

Incomplete or Incorrect Service Work

Incomplete or incorrect service work follows a similar path to defective goods. Similar procedures need to be followed as for defective goods with one major exception. If the problem of incorrect or incomplete service work is the result of one individual or group of individuals, they must be immediately dealt with. Retraining would be the first step and dismissal the second. Problems such as these cannot be tolerated for any length of time in order to keep a firm's reputation intact.

Pricing Issues, Short or Overshipments

Pricing issues and short or overshipments need to be handled in about the same manner. Credit needs to be issued or a return for the excess (or a possible price adjustment, which would be less than the cost of the freight charges to return the excess goods) needs to be granted. Areas that need to be notified that repetitive problems have been occurring in pricing errors include sales and marketing, billing, and systems staff, to make sure that all pricing is correct in the system. As for over- and undershipments, quality control and the shipping department need to be notified of any continuous quantity errors.

Never Received Goods

Never receiving the goods or the service contracted should be an area of major concern to both customer service and top management, for it can damage the reputation of a firm quickly and is symptomatic of other problems. There are a number of reasons why goods are not received. (See *Tips and Techniques*, "Main Reasons for Nonreceipt of Goods.")

TIPS AND TECHNIQUES

Main Reasons for Nonreceipt of Goods

- Freight carrier lost it.

- Freight carrier (driver) stole it.

- In-house theft

- Theft at customer's location

- Customer never checked goods in.

Customer service working with the shipping department can focus on carriers that have repeated missing shipments and after fair warnings stop using that carrier. The possibility of in-house theft can be corrected by many different means. The adding of surveillance cameras, additional security, and/or second counts made by another employee or spot counts made by the manager will seriously curb in-house theft. For suspected theft at a customer's location or a lost shipment within their location, a signed proof of delivery by the carrier will help to stem this problem.

Never Received Services

Customer service follow-ups with the service manager should solve most problems in this area. If there is a problem with an employee(s), additional training, supervision, and, if necessary, dismissal should be administered to rectify the issue. If there are problems relating to the customer in preventing the completion of the task, the credit department and sales and marketing should be notified and involved with the resolution of the issue. This could be an indication that the customer is using this as an excuse to prevent paying for the services.

The Case of the Missing Drugs!

One area that can ill afford to have its goods lost or stolen is in the pharmaceutical industry. One firm I had as a client reported that they were noticing small shipments of a level two narcotic were not reaching the customer. Initially, they were not concerned as this was an extremely large firm and had distribution locations set up for redelivery to their stores. After two shipments were lost, the pharmaceutical firm contacted the DEA (Drug Enforcement Agency) and had the shipment tracked by them to the customer.

The drugs were marked in a plain brown box with minimal indication as to what the contents of the package were. When the DEA followed the driver, he stopped at his house and proceeded to unload a few packages, including this one, into his garage and then continued on his route. The DEA followed for a few blocks and then arrested the driver and contacted the shipping firm to pick up their truck. With a warrant, the DEA searched the driver's garage and determined that he had taken over 400 packages that as yet had not been opened, with a total value of approximately $4 million dollars. The driver had no idea what he had been stealing but had felt that a few packages here or there would not have been missed. These kinds of losses can be extremely costly to a business and have grave potential for misuse, but in some industries it can be serious enough to deserve federal warrants and severe prison sentences as the goods could endanger large populations.

Damaged Goods

Having been notified that goods received are damaged, customer service needs to address this issue from two directions: from an in-house point of view and from a carrier's point of view. Communications with both quality control and the shipping area will alert them to the need to review how goods are packaged and reduce or eliminate the possibility of damage to the firm's products from shipping of these goods. Monitoring the number of damage reports from customers will help to determine if a specific carrier is causing the majority of the damaged shipments. Once this has been determined, if the problem persists after a reasonable warning the carrier is no longer used. During that time, insurance coverage of all goods shipped by the vendor using this carrier should be required.

Sales Tax Charged

The requirement of a sales tax exempt form and/or copy of the buyer's sales tax exempt form should be monitored and followed up with the customer by customer service. Until such time as the document is provided, no credit should be given for these charges. Annual reviews of these documents should be done and updated ones requested before they expire in order to prevent a firm from automatically being billed for sales tax. Letters can be system generated and follow-up dates can be incorporated into the customer service screen to alert them that these are coming due. If the document is not received before the expiration of the form, the seller's system will automatically reinstate the need to charge sales tax.

Freight Charged When It Should Have Been Shipped Freight Free

Some buyers use their own trucks for pickup of goods from vendors (especially for large shipments) or choose to use their own carriers instead of that of the vendor. The billing and shipping departments need this information so that the firm will not have goods shipped out improperly or be charged for shipping freight that never was done by the vendor's carriers. Customer service needs to make this information readily available to them from the customer's purchase order. Once this is verified, credit should be issued immediately for the charges.

Wrong Goods Shipped

This is similar in nature to the goods never received for in essence the correct goods have never been received. In this case, the customer service representative can correct the situation by simply issuing an RMA or trying to "sell" the customer on keeping the item (for a price that would be more than what it would cost if they returned it) and replacing it immediately. If this occurs on a regular basis, customer service needs to notify quality control as well as the shipping area that the wrong goods are being repeatedly pulled and shipped. Modifications to the procedures in place will need to be made in order to reduce the likelihood of this problem reoccurring. An automated picking and packing system tied to the customer's order should seriously reduce or eliminate these types of problems.

Did Not Meet All Conditions in the Purchase Order

This is an area that could cost the vendor the entire shipment if it is an international order and is tied to a letter of credit. Errors in following the terms and conditions of an international letter of credit can seriously reduce the chances of ever being paid. An international purchase order should always be reviewed to confirm that all terms and conditions as stated could be met to the letter. In dealing with some U.S. retailers, special markings on packaging and other unique requirements may be added to the purchase order, which can result in numerous deductions by them if these special terms are not met. In both cases, the credit department should be involved from the beginning in the international orders and alerted to constant problems with retailers' orders if this results in constant deductions and holding up of payments. This will be discussed in greater detail in Chapter 10.

Summary

Customer services duties should act as the focal point for the other departments as the department has the advantage of being the first contact point with the customer. In all of these cases, customer service has kept costs down by virtue of alerting primary areas to repetitive and persistent errors that cost the business millions of dollars over years in extra labor, merchandise, shipping costs, and time lost. Having them trained in not only servicing the customer but also selling additional goods or services likewise adds a new dimension to this extremely critical function. Having a department with its primary function being that of solving problems before they can become serious can make a firm not only more profitable but also much more cost efficient.

Chapter 8 discusses a related area, the shipping and receiving department, and determines how they can help improve cash flow.

Preventing Quality Control, Shipping, and Returns Problems that Drain Corporate Cash

After reading this chapter, you will be able to

- Improve the quality in quality control
- See where errors occur in shipping
- Take steps to correct these errors
- See where the errors occur in receiving
- Take steps to correct receiving errors
- Control employee theft in the shipping and receiving areas

This chapter discusses the critical task of getting the correct, working goods out the door to the customer intact as well as dealing with the returns of goods that prove less than acceptable to the customer. Many things can go wrong that result in the unnecessary return of goods, costing not only the vendor but the buyer as well. Too many of these problems can ultimately cause the loss of a customer due to vendor errors and the inability to service the customer properly. "To err is human, to forgive, divine" is not always the response that a vendor gets from a buyer when a mistake occurs, especially when it happens more than once. Let's look at each area where errors occur and see first how they cost the firm and what can be done to correct them.

Quality Control: Why Is the Quality So Bad?

Before goods are shipped to a customer, random checks are made by the quality control department to make sure that products meet the strict standards of quality of the vendor. Having said that, it is plain to see that a fair amount of defective goods do get shipped out every day.

One factor that typically is proportional to the volume of errors that occur is the profit margin of the product. The greater the profit margin, the higher the potential for errors and vice versa. Firms with extremely tight profit margins can ill afford to have mistakes that will cause them to literally lose money on the goods that they sell. There are some exceptions to this, which are tied to industries that are tightly regulated due to concerns over public safety such as in the case of the pharmaceuticals

IN THE REAL WORLD

Defective Goods: What Are the Costs?

There have been many headlines in the news lately dealing with product defects and recalls. One that brought a lot of public attention was that of Ford and Firestone. There were many headlines and lawsuits related to the alleged defects in the Firestone tires used on Ford Explorer trucks. It was alleged that these tires exploded at critical times and the accidents along with subsequent deaths of many individuals resulted from defects in them.

Unfortunately instead of working to address the problem and take responsibility for this situation, both companies digressed to finger-pointing at each other. As stated earlier in an In the Real World

Tips and Techniques continued

example (see "Public Image: Expensive or Worth It?" in Chapter 5), Johnson & Johnson addressed a problem of which they were never really at fault—that of the tampered Tylenol—and showed that they were a responsible member of the corporate community.

Manufacturing defects can occur at many different kinds of businesses. One such defect was almost comical, but certainly not to the firm that manufactured the item. One manufacturer created a new line of sunglasses that had plastic lenses instead of glass lenses. The frames for these new lenses were subcontracted out to another firm in Germany to produce. Unfortunately, the frames were made to specifications of a glass lens versus a plastic lens, which caused a rather embarrassing problem. When the first 50,000 pairs of sunglasses were assembled in the United States and shipped out to various customers, the buyers soon discovered the mysterious defect. The sunglasses were returned and replaced immediately by the manufacturer, as its reputation was indeed flawless with its customers. The defect was corrected and replacements shipped out with only minor delays. What was the defect? Internally, the sunglasses were quaintly described as the only pair of sunglasses on the market today with the optional pop-out lenses feature. It seemed that everyone who purchased these sunglasses and bent over to pick something up had both lenses immediately fall out into their hands.

The point is that how a company deals with its mistakes can drastically impact its customer base.

industry. Recalls are made extremely quickly if a problem arises with any drugs sold to the general public, and while this industry is one of the most profitable, it is also one of the most highly regulated.

If quality controls are in place, how do errors still occur? One reason may be related to the volume of goods created and shipped out every day by a vendor. Even with solid random sampling, some defects are bound to surface. Another possibility may be a design flaw in the goods themselves that has not been caught in the creation of the item to be sold but later turned up when used by the general public.

How Is the Quality Put Back into Quality Control?

Since quality control is the first line of defense in preventing problems with defective goods, it is indeed critical that sound testing methods be employed to prevent repetitive problems. The costs of recalls due to defects can be devastating to a firm. All new products to be sold need to be thoroughly tested under real-life conditions before being released for sale. As a way to improve and enhance a firm's products as well as its reputation, many employ outside firms to review and test their goods after internal testing has been completed and before being released to buyers for sale. Some organizations that act as watchdogs but also assist firms in preventing problems that can cause major recalls include:

- Underwriter's Laboratories
- National Association of State Public Interest Research Groups
- National Safe Kids Campaign
- National Safety Council (NSC)
- National Bureau of Standards (NBS)
- American National Standards Institute (ANSI)
- American Society for Testing and Materials (ASTM)
- International Organization for Standardization (ISO)
- U.S. Consumer Products Safety Commission

How Can Shipping Errors Occur?

Once again, volume can be one of the biggest reasons why shipping errors occur. As discussed earlier, when a business trickles shipments through all month and on the last days of the month opens the flood gates in order to make its month-end, quarter-end, or year-end goals, the shipping department must deal with this situation alone. Picking and packing goods when volumes are inconsistent can result in not having enough staff at critical times and having too much the rest of the time.

TIPS AND TECHNIQUES

Causes of Shipping Errors

- Shipping of the right goods to the wrong buyer

- Shipping of the wrong goods to the right buyer

- Shipping of the wrong goods to the wrong buyer

- Shipping the right goods to the right buyer but to a wrong location of theirs

- Shipping the wrong goods to the right buyer and to the right location of theirs

- Shipping out goods that are not properly packed which can allow for the damage of them

- Shipping out goods using the wrong shipper

- Shipping out an order that never had credit approval

- Shipping out goods to a buyer that had canceled its order

- Short shipping goods to the buyer

- Overshipping goods to the buyer

- Shipment is lost in transit

- Packaging is not marked as stated in the customer's purchase order

How Does Shipping Correct These Errors?

The number one culprit for shipping errors is volume. Only company-wide management of the order-shipment process can correct this problem. When a firm uses a "Turtle and the Hare" approach to sales/shipments, it ends up like the Hare racing madly at the end to win the race when steady-wins-the-race offers the most cost-effective means to manage their operation. This source of shipping errors is the one most easily corrected by simply smoothing out the level of daily shipments but the hardest to correct because it entails the changing of a corporate culture and philosophy. Until top management sees the errors of its ways, this problem will always exist. Now let's deal with the remaining twelve errors that can normally occur in a shipping area.

Errors In Shipping Goods

While this should be minimal if the firm has an automated system in place to pick goods, print a packing list and shipping label, and pack the correct shipment to the right buyer, errors can occur. Most typically, errors occur in a more hands-on manual system where shipping labels can become lost or out of place and end up on the wrong package. Spot inspections, even during busy times, as well as having a consistent process for handling larger inconsistent volumes of shipments need to be taught as well as enforced. After looking at the volume of errors, the costs involved with correcting them, as well as goodwill lost with a customer, the purchase of a more automated system may be in order.

Shipping Out Goods that Are Not Properly Packed, Thus Allowing Damage

With today's various means for insulating goods from shipping damage, it is inconceivable how anything can be damaged when packaged properly. Obviously, you have never seen the old Samsonite commercial with the ape banging the suitcase against the bars of its cage. If you have seen it, you will immediately realize that no one can guarantee 100 percent that something shipped will arrive unharmed. Having said this, however, it is safe to say that a company that properly packages its goods and clearly marks the boxes with "fragile, handle with care" labels and instructions as to the proper way to lift the package (hand trailer, forklift, etc.) should seriously reduce the chance of goods arriving at its customer damaged. Training in the art of proper packing of goods as well as making notes on both boxes and shipping documents as to the fragility of the goods being shipped will help to minimize these errors. Spot inspections as well as enforcement of proper packing procedures will keep them minimized.

Shipping Out Goods Using the Wrong Shipper

This can be caused by the customer asking for a last minute change getting goods to them to meet an urgent need or shortage. It can also occur through lack of communications within the shipping area, especially if shipping is done in three different eight-hour shifts daily. If a customer has its own shipper or uses its own trucks for pickup and delivery, then this more rare exception can result in goods going out via the wrong carrier.

The shipping requests of the customer need to be clearly inputted into the system by the order entry or customer service areas. Shipping documents should clearly state who the shipper is and areas set up at the loading docks for orders going out to the same shipper. This allows for a more centralized and efficient means for getting the goods on the truck of the shipper as quickly as possible. Once again, education and enforcement of procedures with unannounced spot checks must be done to keep errors to a minimum.

Shipping Out An Order that Never Had Credit Approval

This is the nightmare of every credit manager and can really come home to roost when the order ends up at a firm that files bankruptcy the day after the goods arrive or the shipment is tied to an international letter of credit and the goods were shipped out open account. How can this happen, you ask? It depends on how sophisticated and interconnected the computer system is between departments. Unless the credit department has the ability to stop shipping documents from being printed, or can even cancel orders out of the system altogether, these nightmares can occur on a fairly regular basis. Even with being able to stop the shipping documents from being printed, many cases have occurred where manual documents are created to get the goods out the door at a quarter-end or year-end closing.

There are two methods for dealing with this type of error:

1. The carrot

2. The stick

The *carrot approach* requires solid, free, and complete communications between the credit department, order entry, customer service, and the shipping department on all orders that are of a certain established dollar size and type (i.e., international shipment, marginal account, problem account, etc.). With this type of communications, orders that are an exception to the norm can be handled quickly and without manualizing the system. Access to each other's system also enables each area to have the latest information available on a customer, an order, or a shipment. This type of cooperation requires trust, openness, and education into the workings of each department. This is the foundation for a well-run cost-effective firm.

The *stick approach* makes the credit department the police department of the firm. This assignment requires that they have access and some control over these departments' system as well as input into the review, hiring, and firing of the management of these areas. Policies and procedures will need to be put into place with top management's complete backing that will help them to direct the way orders and shipments are handled from a credit perspective. Most communications will come from the credit department down versus completely interdepartmental. While this approach is rarely recommended in cases in which the customer base is mostly marginal, profit margins are relatively small, and cash flow is the number one agenda of the firm, it is the only way to keep this error from becoming rampant.

Shipping Out Goods to a Buyer that Had Canceled Its Order

Assuming that the shipping department didn't completely overlook the system, this error mainly falls on the back of the customer service department. Interdepartmental communications is the only way to keep this problem in check. Once the buyer has canceled an order, customer service should notify all departments, and if goods have been picked and packed, they should be immediately opened and returned to inventory by the shipping department. An in-house e-mail system can be one way to easily notify all areas as well as having notes added directly to the order on the system that is seen by the shipping department notifying them to cancel the order and return any pulled and packed goods to inventory.

Undershipping and Overshipping Goods to the Buyer and Shipments Lost in Transit

These types of errors occur more often when dealing with certain types of commodity products but can certainly happen to all firms from time to time. In the case of commodity products most firms have a standing agreement with their buyers to allow certain "flexibility" when it comes to filling their orders (usually plus or minus 10 percent). For the majority of typical vendors' shortages, overages, or missing shipments, these occur as a result of items being packed in odd quantities. Smaller items can be overlooked or mixed in with the packaging and either part of or an entire shipment can be delivered to the wrong address by a carrier who didn't obtain a signature.

Depending on the cost and profit margin related to the goods being shipped, this can be a negligible cost or an extremely costly one if it occurs frequently. Systems that keep daily audit counts of inventory and monitor orders to be shipped with inventory available help to keep these types of losses in check. Systematic audits of the picking and packing operation performed by the shipping department must be made.

In the case of continuous shortages or missing shipments altogether with a particular customer or of a particular product, special monitoring steps may need to be put into play, depending on the type of product being sold. As referenced earlier in an *In the Real World* example (see "The Case of the Missing Drugs!" in Chapter 7), the case of the missing drug is one that must be watched at all costs, and if a business does not react properly in this type of incident, then certainly a federal agency such as the DEA will. A business that does not take proper steps to correct this type of situation will be subject to a possible loss of its license to manufacture drugs and subject to possible fines and imprisonment of its officers in charge.

Packaging Is Not Marked as Stated in the Customer's Purchase Order

This will be discussed in somewhat more detail in Chapter 10, which discusses retailers. Suffice it to say that the only way to keep this type of problem in check is to keep communications flowing freely between the order entry, customer service, and the shipping departments. Easy access to the details of the customer's purchase order and the recording of particular packaging requirements visible to all departments helps to keep these types of problems in check.

How Do Receiving Errors Occur?

If you sell goods, it goes without saying that you will from time to time have returns of these items. There are many reasons for returns beyond

TIPS AND TECHNIQUES

Causes of Errors from Returns

- Returning defective goods to inventory

- Returning incomplete goods to inventory

- Returning damaged goods to inventory

- Improper disposal of defective, damaged, or expired goods

- Salvaging parts from defective or damaged returns that make other finished goods defective

- Returning good merchandise back to the wrong location in inventory

- Miscounting inventory and issuing paperwork for too much credit

- Miscounting inventory and issuing paperwork for too little credit

- Accepting back inventory that was not originally the vendor's

- Accepting back goods that were sold "as is"

- Accepting back goods beyond warranty

- Accepting back goods that were abused

the most obvious, which is that the goods were defective or damaged. If the items are consumer goods, other reasons include the wrong color was sent, the wrong size was ordered or received, the wrong item was received, it wasn't what they thought it would be, and so on. When dealing with other firms, reasons for returns include the item did not meet the specifications stated in the buyer's purchase order, overshipment, and the "sell by" date had expired (perishable items).

Now that we know that goods get returned, where do the errors occur? Before all goods that are received are either put back into inventory, scrapped, disassembled and used for parts, or specially disposed of (in the case of hazardous chemicals, drugs, etc.), they must be inspected by quality control. Quality control verifies these items for completeness (if multiple items in a box); correct quantities; proof that the materials belonged to the vendor originally; that their shelf life had truly expired; if damaged because of abuse or because of shipping; if defective, what was defective in the item; and if in good shape whether the goods are fit to return to inventory.

How Does Receiving Correct These Errors?

Returning Defective Goods, Incomplete Goods, and Damaged Goods to Inventory

These types of errors are ones that I classify as *compounded errors* as a time will come when the vendor will again sell those items and will once again face these items back in the receiving area. The only way to address this issue is to have areas specifically set up in the receiving area for each of these categories. Once an item is returned, it should be segregated according to the reason for return. For defective items, if there is any salvageable part(s), then those items should be separated out and returned to inventory for use. If the return is incomplete, all necessary parts should be available to complete the item and, once complete, it should be resealed and immediately returned to inventory. If the item is damaged, the same procedure used in defective goods is used for this type of return.

Improper Disposal of Defective, Damaged, or Expired Goods

Depending on the item being returned, the disposal may be as simple as loading into a dumpster, to selling scrap materials to a scrap dealer by the pound, to the extreme of destroying the materials according to either DEA or Environmental Protection Agency (EPA) rules.

Some firms dispose of a fair amount of items that can be sold to scrap dealers and bring income in from items that had lost all value. Assuming that it does not create a great expense to move this scrap or require any special labor or handling fees, this is a great way of bringing back some money into the firm.

As for improper disposal of drugs or hazardous chemicals, noncompliance with federal regulations could result in massive penalties including loss of license to sell these goods, substantial fines and possible prison time for the officers in charge of these operations. This does not take into

IN THE REAL WORLD

The Expense Caused by Dumping

Many cases have involved the dumping of hazardous materials either by accident, through carelessness, or through incompetence, as was the case of the Exxon Valdez. There, the captain commanding the oil tanker was suspected of being intoxicated at the time that he was commanding the ship.

In one case at a company where I was employed, the president asked me to meet with the president and owner of a firm that did metallic plating for our microscope bases. He was having financial problems and would have problems meeting our orders. Upon arriving there and meeting with the president, I determined that its bank had taken its payroll as payment against an outstanding loan that it had with the bank that was in default. He had requested that our company and two other Fortune 500 companies pay any balances due them not in advance of the expiration of the invoices' terms so he could meet payroll and finish the orders that he had for the three companies. I brought up other possibilities for obtaining money to meet their immediate and future needs, including mortgaging the building and the land.

He confided that he had invested every cent into his company and that when he bought the company 10 years earlier he was unaware that the previous owners had been dumping hazardous chemicals on the company grounds. Without investing many millions of dollars into cleaning up the land first, they would not be able to borrow a dime on the building or the land. Unfortunately, the bank was also aware of this and would not foreclose, as this would make them responsible for the cleanup. The bank chose to simply grab whatever assets they could find to reduce their overall exposure. The three companies did indeed pay their invoices and got their remaining orders completed and switched all future business elsewhere. The plating company was forced to file bankruptcy and let the courts deal with the situation of the hazardous materials dumped into the soil.

The total disregard for the welfare of the environment and the deceit that was used by the previous owners selling the firm to the current owner showed total lack of conscience by the previous owner. Also evident was the naiveté of the current owner to buy a firm without making a proper land condition check. This occurred some 16 years ago, and hopefully with tougher environmental dumping rules and penalties, individuals and firms have learned a valuable lesson that it is far smarter in terms of business and profitability to be a responsible neighbor.

account the cost of cleanup of the areas infected by these hazardous materials. If your firm plans to sell products that fall into these categories, it is mandatory that proper procedures for handing are documented and rigidly enforced.

Salvaging Parts from Defective or Damaged Returns that Make Other Finished Goods Defective

While it is smart business to make use of all goods that can be salvaged from defective or damaged goods, these components of themselves must indeed work; otherwise, your firm is simply recycling its problems. Before parts can be added back to inventory, a quality control check must be made. Checks for physical damage, electrical damage, or other less apparent problems should be made if it is cost effective to perform such an exercise. Batches of these items should be tested in completed units to confirm the overall working condition of the unit. As all parts used in assembly are inspected so too should these items be inspected, before returning them to a new life.

Returning Good Merchandise Back to the Wrong Location in Inventory

This type of error can be corrected easily if the firm has bar code scan ability as part of its overall inventory system. Bar code reading identifies the item and the location where these items are stored, and can aid in making sure that good inventory is returned to its proper location in the warehouse. This type of system can be sophisticated enough that it can keep an ongoing tally of what items are in inventory and how many are available for sale. Some systems can also help keep the inventory control department aware of current levels of inventory and what is needed in order to meet all current and pending orders.

Assuming that such a system is not available, then it is up to the receiving department personnel to properly return all good returned merchandise to their proper location in inventory control. These returns should be monitored and audited on a regular basis for accuracy.

Miscounting Inventory and Issuing Paperwork for Too Much Credit or Too Little Credit

These errors occur frequently and can make customer service and credit managers old before their time. The majority of the complaints that land at the feet of these two managers is the issuing of too little credit. Rarely does a customer ever comment when too much credit is issued (although I have to admit there are still a few honest ones out there that will notify you of this).

IN THE REAL WORLD

Value in Identifying Your Product

One company that I worked for sold wound rubber strips used for making gaskets. These were sold by the box.

Unbeknownst to its customers, the vendor had increased the width of these strips by an eighth of an inch throughout the length of the strip. This made its materials readily identifiable, as all other manufacturers' widths were different than theirs. One such customer who was a distributor of theirs had taken their boxes, switched in a competitor's product, and returned it for credit from the manufacturer. As part of their distributor agreement, this was considered grounds for immediate loss of ability to order products through this manufacturer. When these goods were received and checked, they were immediately discovered and the distributor was terminated as a customer. This type of fraud was not tolerated and should not be by any vendor.

The best way to help eliminate this problem is with bar code scanning of return merchandise, which helps to eliminate the need of counting the items (assuming that they are not too small to be counted this way). Without this ability, depending on the type of items being returned, using scales that perform a count by weight is one possibility, but the most likely is simply counting out the items. This should be immediately followed up by a second count by a different employee in the receiving area along with spot count checks by the receiving department manager.

Once the miscount is discovered, the only way to confirm how many were returned is to make a complete count of what was in inventory at the last count, less any sales, plus any additions other than this one, and if the difference does not match what is currently in inventory, the difference will determine what credit needs to be issued or reduced.

Accepting Back Inventory That Is Not Originally the Vendor's

This rarely happens except in the case of commodities-type goods being sold. A vendor should always be on its guard against this type of return as an unscrupulous buyer is defrauding it. Materials should be thoroughly inspected, and when credit is to be issued, the system should have the ability to confirm that a purchase was made by the buyer of this product from the vendor in recent days.

Accepting Back Goods That Were Sold "As Is," Beyond Warranty, and Abused

These three types of returns all have one thing in common: none of them are valid returns. Firms, however, accept these types of returns all the time. Why? Typically, it is due to keeping a large customer happy. This is especially true if the goods were sold to a major retailer chain that happens to be one of the vendor's top five customers. The retailers sell to the general consumer population, and in their eyes, "the customer is always right." Since it does not cost them anything to return an item to a manufacturer (freight costs are always included in the credit that is demanded by the retailer), they have little desire to argue with the customer about returning the goods to them. This area will be covered in far more detail in Chapter 10. For now, suffice it to say that the need by the retailer of your goods versus your need to sell them will make a major difference in how these types of returns are handled.

In the case of smaller nonretailers or one-time purchasers of large quantities of goods, returns from them should indeed be refused before delivery is accepted or returned at the buyer's expense. Items should be compared against past orders to determine if the goods were indeed bought from the vendor and the terms and conditions of the sale reviewed before credit is considered.

Controlling Employee Theft in the Shipping and Receiving Areas

One situation that occurs on a regular basis is loss to a firm due to employee theft. What the vendor sells is in direct proportion to the scale of employee theft that a firm experiences. Due to their nature, some firms take great pains in preventing any possibility of theft such as in the pharmaceutical industry.

Products that are consumer oriented versus industrial products that hold little interest to most individuals tend to be the main target of internal theft. More thefts occur in the shipping and receiving departments, as they are areas that are more prone to have goods flowing in and out of the area. Companies have taken many steps to keep these types of thefts from occurring by adding security cameras, guards, locking cages for inventory, and unannounced audits of inventory. All of this, as well as the costs of the thefts of the items themselves, add to the overall cost of

Employee Theft: What Does It Cost?

Recently, a firm that manufactured contact lenses had a $2 million theft perpetrated against it by three managers and the buyers who purchased the goods. The three managers were in charge of credit and billing, shipping and receiving, and regional sales. A number of large returns of contact lenses were not put back into inventory but shipped out to a small storage area rented by the three individuals. Credit was given for the returns with the notation that the goods were defective and destroyed. The sales manager approached a number of doctors, offering them prices for contact lenses that were half of the normal price that they paid to the manufacturer if they asked no questions. The sales manager delivered the goods, and the doctors paid for their purchase in cash.

As more and more lenses were returned, with none ever making it back into inventory, the corporate internal auditors started to get suspicious. They alerted security and began a covert monitoring of all goods going in and out of the Contact Lens Division. Customers who had large returns were questioned as to the condition of the merchandise that was returned. After determining that the goods were to be funneled off elsewhere, the police were brought in to make the arrest of the three individuals that were involved with the fraud and theft. The doctors who were buying the hot merchandise were likewise prosecuted.

Today, the firm has instituted very strict procedures for goods returns and has separated the credit and billing functions. Audits are now done on a regular but unscheduled basis of returns and shipments as well as all credits that are given to customers. While this breach in security cost them in the short term, in the long run it has made them a much smarter and better-run company.

the merchandise for sale, and some of this may not be able to be passed on to the buyer.

Summary

While these three areas can sometimes cause a drain on the cost effectiveness of a firm, proper management mixed with solid procedures and a good and reliable computer system can help rein in the effects of these problems. Many of the problems originate outside of these areas and must be dealt with by these sometimes overwhelmed and overworked areas. Human mistakes do happen but repetitive mistakes or intentional theft and fraud cannot be tolerated. Once again, cooperation and communications between interrelated departments that directly service the customer is mandatory to keep these costs well under control.

The next chapter discusses dealing with selling to dot-coms and other start-up companies.

## CHAPTER 9

Special Cash Considerations When Selling to Dot-coms and Other Start-ups

After reading this chapter, you will be able to

- Understand the first contact actions
- Determine the initial factors that are available to the credit department in making a decision that will protect the cash flow of the vendor
- Once the initial factors have been investigated and reviewed, understand how the credit department fortifies its position to keep the vendor's cash flow intact
- Know the next step after the order shipped or the service has been performed
- Understand the art of getting paid
- Collect on past due accounts
- Calculate the cost of placing an account for collections

The number one cash concern to selling to either a dot-com or a start-up firm is getting paid. The point of first-time sale for both types of firms is the best opportunity for the vendor to minimize the risk to cash flow involved with dealing with them. The life of the relationship between a vendor and its customers is like climbing a mountain. You begin at the bottom building a foundation in preparation for the climb up. As you proceed with sales and payments, the climb becomes smoother up the mountain. Occasionally, there may be problems with deductions from payments, product or service problems, and occasional payment problems that cause some slippage down the relationship mountain. If no real major problems occur, the climb is reasonably smooth and great peaks are reached in sales, cash flow, and profits for both firms. If, however, problems arise with continuously increasing deductions made as well as a slowdown in payments, major deterioration results in the ability to climb the mountain of sales, cash flow, and profits.

Ultimately, if the payments stop altogether and the customer closes its business, then all may be buried in an avalanche of debt and losses of sales, profit, and cash flow. Some smarter vendors take actions to protect themselves from the risk of climbing the mountain of success with less reliable and financially stable partners. Let's now look at the life cycle of a dot-com and start-up from the time that a first inquiry is made to the time that you either collect your money or write off your outstanding balance as a bad debt.

Sales/Order Entry: What Are the First Contact Actions?

When a firm first makes an inquiry into the purchase of a vendor's goods or services, there is no indication to the order entry person that the firm is a new business. The salesperson, however, either by being in the field or by visiting their location, will realize all too quickly that the firm is new or barely off the ground. Does this make a firm bad? Certainly not. Does this make the company a cash flow risk? Probably!

After providing all the necessary information to the new firm on the vendor's goods or services and answering any questions that the buyer may have, what are the first questions that the salesperson should ask?

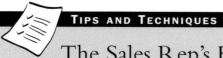

The Sales Rep's First Questions

- How long have they been in business?

- What type of product(s) or service(s) are they interested in?

- How do they intend to pay for their purchases?

- Are they willing to fill out and complete a credit application?

- Are they a proprietorship, partnership, limited liability company (LLC), or an incorporated business?

- How soon will they need delivery of their initial order?

- Will this be a one-time purchase or will regular purchases or services be needed? (The type of firm that they are and the type of vendor you are may make this question superfluous.)

- How much product or service will they need?

- If they will be a resaler on the Internet, do they have a sales tax exempt number yet?

- If not open for business yet (as in the case of a restaurant, boutique shop, etc.) when will their shop open for business?

- Are they prepared to place an order today, and, if so, in what amounts or for what services?

While it is important for the salesperson to "clinch the sale," it is also just as important to obtain as many facts as possible and communicate those to other areas in order to speed this order through the system. An order without the facts will go nowhere, and the salesperson will have wasted his or her time. After supplying them with a credit application and obtaining a signed purchase order, the salesperson should send all pertinent information (by e-mail if possible while it is still fresh in their mind) as well as a copy of the purchase order on to customer service with a copy to the credit department for review. With this information sent, the next step toward dealing with these types of firms can begin.

How Is Customer Service Involved in the Early Processing Stages?

The next step will be the setup of the firm on the vendor's computer system with a pending status and zero credit limit. The order will be entered and will have a date set for its pending shipment depending on credit approval and availability of goods or service timing. If any additional contact data is needed, they will contact the customer to complete the system's setup. Once this has been completed, they will await the final decision from the credit department on the new customer.

What Initial Factors Should the Credit Department Consider That Will Protect the Cash Flow of the Vendor?

With the information forwarded by the salesperson of the first meeting with the potential customer and customer's service notice of a pending account and order, the credit department will begin the initial investigation of the pending customer while awaiting the credit application. This could include obtaining a credit report (depending on the dollar amount of the order or anticipated volume of business) and if a member of an industrial credit trade group, they will clear the buyer's name to see if they have done business with any of the other members. Upon receiving the credit application, trade references will be contacted to determine if any credit history is available on the buyer.

If the firm is a new dot-com, check with the dot-com's or start-up's landlord. What terms were negotiated for the lease of space for the new dot-com? If they were given a regular lease with a security (single month) deposit, then they are very sound. If asked for many months'

TIPS AND TECHNIQUES

New Dot-com Credit Considerations

- Size of the initial order versus what the vendor considers is a small, medium, or large order

- Profit margin on the goods or services requested

- Whether this is a one-time order or purchases of goods or services continue on past the first order

- Any positive or negative information determined in the investigation

- If the customer has provided any financial information with their credit application

worth of security deposit (6 to 18 months) plus six months rent in advance as well as a one-year bank standby letter of credit, then be forewarned.

Assuming that this is either a new start-up firm or a relatively new dot-com, what is the next action that should be taken?

Size of Order

If the order is considered small, then a highly restricted and controlled credit limit will be established for the firm. If the order is larger, additional information and/or collateral may be needed.

Profit Margin on the Goods or Services Requested

If the profit margin is extremely high (better than 50 to 75 percent), then a highly restricted and controlled credit limit will be established for the firm. If the margin is less than 50 percent, additional information and/or collateral may be needed.

Whether This Is a One-Time Order or Purchases of Goods or Services Continue on Past the First Order

This has significant ramifications because for a one-time order, once the firm receives the goods or the services have been rendered, the buyer will have little or no real need of the vendor. This would substantially reduce the vendor's ability to collect its balance either on time or at all. An ongoing relationship provides the vendor with a means to enforce payment of their goods or services or the next order will not be allowed. This game of "hot potato" comes to an end, however, when the buyer runs out of money and closes its doors, leaving the vendor "holding the hot potato." Typically, the size of the orders tend to grow as the firm builds a relationship with the vendor, and the last one may indeed be the biggest one leaving the vendor with the greatest exposure at the most vulnerable time.

Any Positive or Negative Information Determined in the Investigation

With the newness of these types of firms, the likelihood of either positive or negative information will be minimal at best and nonexistent at worst. This could change if the customer provides authorization to perform a consumer credit check on the principal(s) of the firm. If they do provide this authorization and they offer a personal guarantee (if incorporated or are an LLC or LLP), then this reflects very favorably in considering granting credit to them. Assuming that the consumer credit information is positive, the possibility of approval has been greatly enhanced. If negative credit is found, depending on its nature, other factors such as additional information and/or collateral may be necessary.

Has the Customer Provided Any Financial Information with Their Credit Application?

While the likelihood of an audited financial statement accompanying the credit application for either a dot-com or a start-up firm is less than your being hit by lightning or winning the PowerBall lottery, providing financial information of a sort does show some concern on the buyer's part of the risk that is involved in extending credit to them. Looking at these financial statements may aid the credit department in determining if there is collateral available to be used to "prop up" the extension of credit.

TIPS AND TECHNIQUES

Two Financial Factors Related to Dot-coms

If a financial statement is obtained on the dot-com or start-up firm, one ratio that can be computed and considered is the *cash burn rate* of the firm. The formula is:

$$\frac{\text{Cash + Marketable Securities + Accounts Receivables}}{(\text{Cost of Goods Sold + Selling, General and Administrative Costs})/365} = \begin{array}{l}\text{number of days} \\ \text{until cash runs out} \\ \text{without profits}\end{array}$$

If the dot-coms or start-ups have a low number of days and have yet to make a profit, they will cease to exist very soon.

A second consideration is before accepting a dot-com's or a start-up's gross profit margin, check to see if it is inflated by the firm. This can be done by moving shipping and handling costs from marketing costs versus where they should be which is in cost of goods sold.

How Does the Credit Department Fortify Its Position to Keep the Vendor's Cash Flow Intact?

Assuming that the decision has been made to proceed with the extension of credit to this firm with some conditions, what are some possibilities to be discussed with the customer to shore up the vendor's position for being paid?

- *Additional information.* Assuming that financial data was not in- cluded with the credit application, a request for this data will aid in the determination of possible collateral that may be available to use to secure the vendor's position.

- *Personal guarantee(s).* If not offered at the time that the credit application was submitted, the signing of a personal guarantee (assuming that the buyer is an incorporated firm or an LLC or an LLP) and authorization to obtain a consumer credit report will allow the paying habits of the principal(s) to be considered in the overall credit decision equation. It may also add insight into other collateral owned by the principal(s) that could be used to shore up the vendor in extending credit to the buyer. See Exhibit 9.1.

- *Corporate guarantee.* This may be useful in the case of some start- ups that are subsidiaries or affiliates of larger corporations. In this situation, a firm that applies for credit may have a very large, financially sound and profitable parent company available to guarantee the debt. If the buyer is either a subsidiary or an affiliate of a larger firm, unless there is a corporate guarantee in place the parent has no responsibility for any debts incurred by the buyer. With a corporate guarantee in place the parent's standing is now the basis for credit extension and if substantial should more than cover any needs of the subsidiary or the affil- iate. See Exhibit 9.2.

- *Security deposit.* This is a type of collateral used frequently in credit extended by a firm that sells its services to another com- pany or individual. The amount of the security deposits vary

170

EXHIBIT 9.1

PERSONAL GUARANTEE

Your Company Name _____

Anywhere, N.Y.   (Date) _____

Gentlemen:

For value received, I hereby guarantee to you, your successors and assigns, the payment of all debts, liabilities and obligations of every nature, whether absolute or contingent, now or hereafter contracted or incurred by

(Name of Company)

a (an) _____ Corporation with its principal

office at _____ ("Customer")

(Street address, City, State, Zip)

and any and all renewals or extensions thereof, or of any part there-of, together with interest thereon and all expenses of collection.

You may without notice to me of any kind, change the rate of inter-est, grant any extensions of time to or make any compromise with or release and discharge Customer, or any other party liable with Customer, upon any instrument, indebtedness or obligation, and you may release or omit to collect or enforce or may compromise any collateral security held by you without thereby releasing me hereunder, or incurring any liability to me. You may, but you are not required to, realize on and apply any collateral held by you, to such obligations as you may elect, whether guaranteed hereby or not, without regard to any rights of mine in respect to the application thereof.

I expressly waive any rights to notice of acceptance from you or to any other notice or demand upon me or to any other actions or con-ditions prior to your reliance upon or enforcement of this guarantee. You may take or refrain from taking any of the actions authorized under this guarantee without notice of any kind to me.

EXHIBIT 9.1 CONTINUED

PERSONAL GUARANTEE

This guarantee shall be enforceable as to all of Customer's debts, liabilities and obligations despite Customer's discharge in bankruptcy or despite adjustment of such debts, liabilities and obligations in insolvency proceedings or pursuant to some other compromise with creditors.

If claim is ever made upon you for repayment or recovery of any amount or amounts received by you in payment or on account of any of the debts, liabilities and obligations of Customer and you repay all or part of said amount by reason of (a) any decree or order of any court or administrative body having jurisdiction over you or any of your property, or (b) any settlement or compromise of any such claim effected by you with any such claimant (including Customer) then in such event I agree that any such judgement, decree, order, settlement or compromise shall be binding upon me, notwithstanding any termination hereof or the cancellation of any note or other instrument evidencing any liability of Customer, and I shall be and remain liable to you hereunder for the amount so repaid or recovered to the same extent as if such amount had never originally been received by you.

This instrument shall be deemed to be a continuing guarantee and shall remain in full force and effect until you receive written notice from me by registered mail that I desire to be relieved of further liability hereunder or until I die or am adjudicated mentally incompetent and you have actual notice of the death or adjudication; such notice shall not, however, affect my liability, or that of my representatives or successors, for debts, liabilities or obligations then existing, whether absolute or contingent, or subsequent renewals or extensions thereof.

This instrument shall be binding upon my legal representatives and all persons claiming through or under me and shall inure to the benefit of your successors and assigns. No failure by you to exercise any right hereunder shall operate as a waiver of any other right.

EXHIBIT 9.1 CONTINUED

PERSONAL GUARANTEE

This agreement shall be deemed to be a contract under the laws of the state of _____ , and for all purposes shall be construed in accordance with the laws of said state. This guarantee contains the entire agreement between us and cannot be changed without the written assent of the party against whom such change is sought to be enforced.

Dated this _____ day of _____, 20_____.

Residence of Guarantor _____

STATE OF _____)

COUNTY OF _____: SS.

CITY OF _____)

On this _____ day of _____, 20_____ before me, the sub-scriber, personally appeared _____, to me personally known and known to me to be the same person described in and who executed the within instrument and he duly acknowledged to me that he executed the same.

_____ NOTARY PUBLIC

EXHIBIT 9.2

CORPORATE GUARANTEE

For value received, in the consideration of your selling and delivering unto _____ presently of _____, the "Customer", on credit such goods or performing such services for the Customer as said Customer may order from time to time on orders accepted by you, the undersigned, the "Guarantor" hereby agrees as follows:

1. The Guarantor hereby unconditionally guarantees to you the prompt payment and discharge when due of each and all obligations and indebtedness on account of the Customer and all notes, trade acceptance or other evidences of such indebtedness, for goods or services supplied by you. The Guarantor's liability hereunder shall extend to and include all costs of collection and reasonable counsel fees.

2. In the event of default by the Customer in payment and discharge when due to any of the Customer's obligations or of any installments due thereon, the Guarantor agrees to pay and otherwise made good, upon demand in whatever form or however evidenced then, owing by the Customer to you. This is a guaranty of payment.

3. The Guarantor waives notice of shipments, notice of non-performance on the Customer's part, notice of adjustment between you and the Customer and notice of default, extension, demand for payment and action to collect, if any, against the Customer, and notice of acceptance of this guaranty by you. The Guarantor further waives any and all defenses the Guarantor might have by reason of any extension of time given to the Customer, or the acceptance by you of any security, guarantees or collateral, release or modifications made with respect to the Customer's indebtedness. This guaranty shall not be affected by the amount of credit extended hereunder nor by any change in the form of said indebtedness, by note or otherwise, nor by any extension or renewal of said indebtedness.

4. The guaranty hereby given is an absolute continuing guaranty and shall continue in full force until all amounts owing by the Customer to you for which the Guarantor is liable hereunder have been paid in full.

EXHIBIT 9.2 CONTINUED

CORPORATE GUARANTEE

5. The Guarantor acknowledges and affirms that this guaranty is being made to induce you to extend credit to the customer, knowing that you are relying upon this guaranty in extending such credit.

Signed at _____ on _____ 20_____

Signed By _____

Typed Name _____

ATTEST:

Signed By _____

Typed Name _____

EXHIBIT 9.2 CONTINUED

CERTIFICATE OF CORPORATE RESOLUTION
SECRETARY'S CERTIFICATE

I, _____, Secretary of _____, a _____ corporation, do hereby duly adopted by the Board of Directors of _____ at a meeting duly held on the _____ day of _____, 20____. The said Resolution has not been altered, modified or rescinded, but remains in full force and effect as of the date hereof.

RESOLVED, That is this corporation in exercise of certain of the powers granted to it by its Charter and in furtherance of its business and for the benefit of its stockholders, and for the good and valuable consideration and in order to assist in accomplishing the objects for which this company was created, all of which reasons are understood, acknowledged, and concurred in by the board of directors of this corporation, shall execute a Guarantee in a form supplied by _____, which shall be an absolute, continuing, unconditional, and limited guarantee of all of the debts and accounts and obligations due from _____ of _____ debtor (an individual d/b/a (a partnership) (a _____ corporation) to _____. The guaranty hereby given is an absolute continuing guaranty and shall continue in full force and effect until all amounts owing by the Customer to you for which the Guarantor is liable hereunder have been paid in full.

FURTHER RESOLVED, The officers of this corporation are hereby authorized to execute said Guarantee and to take all other steps necessary to effectuate said Guarantee.

IN WITNESS WHEREOF, I have hereunto set my hand and affixed the seal _____, this _____ day of _____,20____.

_____
Secretary

greatly depending upon the volume of business done with the service provider or if a seller of goods needs some additional collateral to justify the risk that they are accepting from the buyer. Some firms offer interest on the money that they hold as collateral; others do not.

- *Standby bank letter of credit (L/C).* By pledging certain assets to a bank, a bank will issue in their customer's behalf a commercial paper guarantee. It will be for an exact amount good for a specific time, which is irrevocable (not necessarily but if not it is

IN THE REAL WORLD

Security Deposits: What Is Their Value?

The telecommunications industry is one area that regularly requires security deposits to enable them to extend credit to marginal customers and protect themselves from losses that can happen quickly and totally unexpectedly. A marginal business may be asked for as much as three times the monthly credit limit extended paid in advance and placed in an interest-bearing account to use as collateral before credit will be approved.

Considering the range in services that this industry offers to its commercial customers and the speed at which outstanding balances can be run up, it is critical for them to have this type of security in place to protect themselves when dealing with marginal customers.

Even if a firm files for bankruptcy since this industry is classified as a utility under the bankruptcy code they cannot terminate service immediately upon the customer filing but must be given "adequate assurances of payment" in exchange for this continuance. A new security deposit that will cover future credit extension may be one way that this assurance is granted.

worthless) and is payable if the customer defaults on payment of an invoice(s). A draft along with specific documents (invoice(s), bill of lading, statement of delinquency, etc.) can be presented to the bank for immediate payment. One thing that is typically common to a dot-com firm and sometimes to a start-up firm as well is that bulk of their initial assets consists mainly of cash. Banks will set aside a portion of this in order to issue a bank standby letter of credit on their behalf. Even if a firm files for bankruptcy, the vendor will be paid up to the amount of the L/C less any draws previously made against it by the vendor.

- *Filing a lien on the assets of a firm.* Under the Uniform Commercial Code (UCC) a company using a security agreement that defines the terms and conditions of a sale of goods may take as collateral either all or part of the assets of a firm as collateral in extending credit to a buyer. The lien is date and time sensitive to when the UCC-1 form with all proper documents is filed in accordance with the procedures stated in the Uniform Commercial Code. This means that those who have properly filed a lien as little as one minute before your filing has a prior lien to yours.

   A vendor can also choose to file a lien solely on the inventory that the buyer has in its inventory and any proceeds generated from the sale of these goods. This is called a Purchase Money Security Interest under the UCC and if all procedures are followed properly a first lien will be granted to the vendor regardless of those who have filed prior to this lien being filed. There are some fees involved with filing of these types of lien, which must be taken into account in the cost of doing business using this type of security but the costs may be far outweighed by the protection that it may offer. The exact details as to the proper way liens are filed, the fees involved, and pros and cons of filing a lien are beyond the scope of this book. Suffice it to say that assuming there are assets left in the business to cover your lien and that of anyone else that may be ahead of you (if any), all documents have been properly filed, and lien has not expired (as it is good for five years and is renewable), then your firm will be paid first in a bankruptcy proceeding in the order that the properly filed liens were filed.

As for a service provider, the taking of a general UCC-1 filing on all the assets of a buyer could be very valuable to them in that a dot-com or a start-up company is unlikely to have a bank loan that would be secured by the same type of lien on all assets. With this being the case the lien assuming that it was filed properly will guarantee you first crack at all remaining assets if the firm does file for bankruptcy or is forced into an involuntary bankruptcy by three unsecured creditors having a total outstanding undisputed balance of $10,000 or more. The problem with this situation is that unless the vendor stays very much on top of this buyer most of the assets could "disappear" before they have a chance to foreclose on them.

- *Direct debit of customer's checking account.* While this may be useful in helping to keep a dot-com or start-up company paying and keeping cash flow to the vendor steady, it is with the assumption that these firms have money readily available in their checking accounts sufficient to cover what is currently due. By using this collateral in conjunction with other forms of collateral such as a bank standby letter of credit or UCC filing it may help to keep the vendors' exposure down and also serve to immediately alert them to the fact that the buyer may be in financial trouble. This knowledge can be extremely valuable when dealing with marginal firms.

Order Shipped, Service Performed: What Next?

At this point, assuming that the goods were shipped according to the customer's purchase order or all service that was requested to the satisfaction of the customer, now comes the time that companies like best—billing for their labors. One of the most important aspects to keeping cash flow at its peak is to always make sure that billing is done the same day that the goods have been shipped or the work completed satisfactorily. Any delays in billing cost the company needless money.

TIPS AND TECHNIQUES

Expediting Invoices to Increase Cash Flow

Depending on the makeup, size, and diversity of location of your business, the faster you can get your invoices in the hands of payables staff of your customer, the sooner you will be paid. If your firm has locations based all over the country and your customer base is the same, the mailing of invoices from a location nearest to the customer is one way of getting it into their hands quicker.

If your customers have a sufficient degree of sophistication in their computer system, then an alternative may be to bill them electronically. This eliminates mail float altogether and guarantees that the customer always receives their invoices.

A third way that is being used by the automotive industry is to eliminate the invoice altogether and bill off of the packing slip and receiving documents. This saves both firms the time and expense of an extra step in the process and cuts down paperwork by a third in order to pay for the goods or services received.

In the case of goods being sent, if a customer is always in need of proof of deliveries in order to pay you, this same information can also be sent electronically, depending on who your shipper is. Most freight firms have online systems that allow proof of deliveries to be generated over the Internet and can be electronically forwarded on to the customer for their records.

Now That the Bill Is Out, When Do We Get Paid?

Your terms, whether you offer a cash discount, or if extended terms were offered will directly affect the initial follow-up made of this outstanding invoice. At this point in the life of the invoice, most firms await payment from the customer. Some customers will take advantage of the cash discounts and some firms will pay on time. Others will test the "ouch limits" of a firm. This means that a customer will see how long they can go before you will send them a delinquency notice, start charging late fees, and/or start holding their orders. Others will simply pay according to their company policy and, if a big enough customer, will dare you to put them on credit hold. Still others will pay you when they have money and only if you squeak louder ("the squeaky wheel gets the grease") than other creditors. Finally, those in deep trouble will either pay you when they are in desperate need of you or not at all.

TIPS AND TECHNIQUES

Cost Savings: Preventing Delinquency before It Can Occur

For first invoice, new customers (especially dot-coms or start-up companies), or for customers with very large invoices, some businesses will make a PR call about 15 days after the goods have been shipped and billed (this assumes some variation of a 30 days term). It the vendor offers terms of 2 percent 10 days, net 30 days, the call will be made after the acceptable date for allowance of the cash discount. The call will cover the following items:

- Were all of the goods received as listed on their purchase order?

- Was everything received intact?

- If there were any problems, what were they?

- Was the invoice received and the terms, prices, total, and description on it correct?

- Do they know that a cash discount was offered, they had missed the cutoff date, and that in the future it is in their best interest to take advantage of it?

- Do they understand when the net amount of the invoice is due and where they need to send their payment?

- It is important that payment be received on time so that all future shipments will go out on time and that they keep their credit rating with them sterling?

- Is there any other service or items that they need at this time?

- If they need anything in the future or have any problems, they should feel free to contact the vendor's contact person (provide his or her name, title, and phone number).

- Thank them for their business and advise them that you look forward to working with them in the future.

This call eliminates 95 percent of all reasons for delays in making a payment on this account. The only remaining reason is that the customer has no money to pay the invoice, which leads to other problems, addressed later in this chapter.

The Invoice Is Past Due—What Does the Vendor Do Now?

Many techniques have been employed over the years in the collection of invoices, especially from marginal customers such as start-ups and some dot-coms. Much of how a firm addresses the delinquency depends on (1) their company's philosophy (marketing oriented versus cash is king); (2)

TIPS AND TECHNIQUES

Time Savings/Cost Savings

Where a system can save time is in the ability to e-mail an original copy of a past due invoice, the Internet copy of the proof of delivery, and a cover letter (mostly a template form letter) to the customer without the collector ever leaving his or her desk. The most used excuse to delay a payment being made is lack of invoice and/or proof of delivery.

the personnel available to perform the task of collecting past due receivables, their skill level, and the support that top management gives them; and (3) the system's capability to assist the collection staff in focusing their efforts, reminding them of the need for follow-up of certain customers and saving them time to use for more cost-effective collection work.

In a credit department's policies and procedures manual under the procedures section, the typical steps for follow-up of delinquent customers should be outlined and what tools or strategies followed in order to limit delays to being paid. Some firms incorporate the use of dunning form letters, notices, or e-mails as a means of reducing the number of initial contacts that are needed by the collection staff. Others hit the ground running by getting on the phone with customers immediately and will not let up until payment is received. Considering the size of the staff versus the volume of customers that are past due may at times preclude the need of some form of nonvoice contact in order to cover the daily contact needs.

When a customer reaches certain levels of delinquency, more serious discussions of problems and how to resolve them must take place to prevent the reoccurrence of these customers in the follow-up list. Although certain firms handle the placing of customers on credit hold on a case-by-case basis, others automate the entire process as well as a system-wide notification of all departments that have direct contact with the customer that the customer has been placed on credit hold. So what is the magical number of days past due when a firm should place a customer on credit hold? Your position within an industry (one of many, one of few, the only one), your relationship with your customers (they need you more than you need them), and the support granted by top management (they will go to the mat with you versus don't alienate the customer or you are unemployed) will help you to determine the right time to place a firm on credit hold. In the case of start-ups and marginal dot-coms, the earlier the better. Once a line has been drawn in the sand and the customer understands that they must not cross it, then the need to follow them up will not arise until something very serious occurs.

The account now is over 30 days past due, the customer has broken a few commitments to pay and may now be on credit hold. At this point, it is worthwhile to get sales and marketing involved with future actions taken against this customer. The one thing that is always critical for the customer to understand is that all the people in your firm are a team that always works together and speaks the same language: "We offer quality products or services on a timely basis and ask only one thing in return—the prompt payment of our invoices." Now comes the reality! It is a rare situation indeed when a salesperson wants a customer cut off and stripped of their ability to buy from you.

However, if a salesperson has as part of his overall bonus objectives keeping delinquency low in his territories or, even worse, he does not get his commission until the customer pays the vendor, then you will indeed have all of his cooperation. While in some cases I feel that the latter is highly recommended, in most cases the former is more than sufficient reason to get the cooperation of most of the sales force.

IN THE REAL WORLD

Cash versus Marketing
Corporate Philosophy

Two firms that I have been associated with have had remarkably different strategies related to the collection of past due accounts. One firm, which I will call "Cash King," was a leveraged buyout firm that survived on its cash flow. It had very large interest and debt payments and needed consistent cash flow to meet these demands. It had one major advantage over its customers in that it was the only manufacturer of a product that was in great demand as its predecessor product was banned by the government. Customers either paid for their products on time or found themselves without it and waiting a fair amount of time before they got it again. At 15 days past due the customer was placed on credit hold and no orders were released until their account was completely current. Needless to say, the collection staff had the full support of top management in their collection efforts.

The second firm was extremely marketing oriented and was a *Fortune* 500 company with many competitors. Even though they sold a far superior product to that of their competition they believed that the "Customer Is King." They sold to their customers on credit terms of 2 percent 10 days, net 30 days, and did not even send a delinquency notice until their customers were 30 days past due.

In general, I would rate these two firms as being at both ends of the collection spectrum and somewhere in the middle but closer to the cash firm makes for a more balanced collection effort.

Now that the collection staff has the full attention of the sales force, the dollars that are involved, the distance to the customer, and need or lack thereof of this particular customer will determine whether a joint meeting at the customer's location or a joint conference call is in order. Especially if the customer is new and has a potential of being a major customer for the vendor, then it is a wise move to invest the extra dollars now to prevent future continuous problems down the road. In the case in which a vendor is the major supplier to a dot-com or start-up, the vendor is critical to them and must be given clear instructions from all areas of the vendor (credit, sales, top management, customer service, etc.) that, in order to do business with the vendor, payments must be made on time.

If the customer does not qualify for a direct visit by the collection staff, then a visit by the salesperson and a prearranged conference call made from the customer's office should be set up. This prevents the customer from trying to pit the salesperson against the collection staff and shows them that your company's sales and payment efforts are united.

If the account now hits 60 days past due, the possibility of a promissory note is one means to be used to help get payments made, receiving interest for the extra time for carrying the balance and helps to reduce the total exposure over a set period of time. Some promissory notes also include a personal guarantee signed by the owner/top shareholder of the firm, which opens up other collection possibilities if the start-up/dot-com defaults on the promissory note. During the time that the account is on the promissory note, all sales will be made on either a COD, cash-with-order, or cash-in-advance basis. See Exhibit 9.3 for a sample promissory note.

If the account hits 90 days past due, a final letter of demand should be sent giving them 15 days from the date of the letter to pay the balance in full or be placed for collections. If the customer does not pay, then the account must be placed for collections and, depending on the

EXHIBIT 9.3

PROMISSORY NOTE

$ _____

_____, _____, _____, 20_____
       (City or Town)   (State)

The undersigned, for value received, promise to pay to

YOUR COMPANY NAME

or order, located at _____

_____

in lawful money of the United States, the sum of   _____

_____ Dollars

in installments in the amounts and at the times stated in the Repayment Schedule(s) located and filled in on the reverse side hereof and made a part hereof, together with interest, payable on each installment date, on unpaid principal at the rate of _____ percent per year.

YOUR FIRM'S NAME may at any time, at its option, set off the amount due or to become due hereon against any claim of any of the parties directly or indirectly liable for the payment hereof against YOUR FIRM'S NAME.

This note and all other obligations owing by the undersigned to YOUR FIRM'S NAME shall become due and payable, without notice or demand, all of which are waived, (1) forthwith (a) upon any action of any kind being taken by or against any of the persons directly or indirectly liable for the payment hereof based on his inability to meet his obligations in full as they mature; or (b) upon the death or legal incapacity of any such person; or (2) at the option of YOUR FIRM'S NAME (a) upon the nonperformance by any of the undersigned of any of the agreements or conditions herein or in any other obligation of the undersigned to YOUR FIRM'S NAME or to any other person, firm or corporation, including, but not limited to, the failure to make

EXHIBIT 9.3 CONTINUED

any payment provided for herein, or (b) upon any change in the place, management or character of the business of any of the undersigned, or (c) upon any change in the place of employment of any of the undersigned, or (d) upon the sale, exchange, or depletion of all or a substantial portion of the assets of any of the persons directly or indirectly liable for the payment hereof.

No waiver by YOUR FIRM'S NAME of any default hereunder shall operate as a waiver of any other default.

If it becomes necessary to place this note in the hands of an attorney for collection, the undersigned agree to pay YOUR FIRM'S NAME actual expenditures of collection including reasonable attorney's fees.

If only one maker, this note shall be read in the singular. If more than one maker, the obligation of such makers shall be joint and several.

(If maker is a corporation, sign below.)

_____

BY _____ , _____

(Signature of an officer)   (Title)

Address of corporation: _____

_____

(If maker is an individual or a partnership, sign below.
All partners must sign this note.)

_____

(Signature)

Address: _____

_____

_____

(Signature)

Address: _____

_____

EXHIBIT 9.3 CONTINUED

REPAYMENT SCHEDULE

Date Due	Principal Payment	Interest Payment	Total Payment

GUARANTEE

For value received, the undersigned, jointly, and severally if more than one, guarantee the payment of the within note, agree to the terms thereof, and waive all demands and notices whatsoever, whether of presentment, demand for payment, non-payment or otherwise, and agree that the holder may at any time or from time to time modify or extend the terms of payment or any other provision thereof or release any party liable thereon without notice to and without affecting the liability of the undersigned hereunder.

size of the balance, a placement for legal action should be given after the agency has had 30 days to effect collection. See Exhibit 9.4 for a sample letter of demand.

What Does It Cost to Place an Account for Collection?

There are many collection agencies and collection law firms all over the world today. The variety of fees charged are almost as many as the number of firms that offer these services. Some charge a flat fee including court costs and attorney fees if later placed with an attorney for legal action. Some charge a fee based on the number of accounts that you place with them as well as the dollar size of the accounts and how far past due they are.

Before settling on an agency or legal firm, it is simply smart to know whom you are dealing with. If you are going to place accounts for collections, then you should be prepared to extend to that firm an amount equal to the total of all accounts that you wish to place. This may seem a bit silly since it is rare that your firm will be extending credit to a collection agency. The truth is that when you place an account for collections, you relinquish control of the account to this firm. If this firm is not reputable they may collect the account and advise you that it was deemed uncollectable after much effort on their part. Since you will likely not make any further attempts at collecting your balance, you will be totally unaware that the balance was ever collected.

The reputable firms belong to various associations that monitor their behavior and require certain standards of professionalism. Two such associations are:

1. The National Association of Credit Management, which oversees the professionalism of its affiliate members
2. The Commercial Law League, which requires members to always maintain specific standards or lose their ties to the association

EXHIBIT 9.4

Attn:

Balance:

EFFECTIVE IMMEDIATELY—CREDIT REVOKED!

This is a step I am always reluctant to take, but the past due condition of your account leaves me no choice.

This balance must be sent to:

> Your Company Name
> 123 Anywhere Street
> Anywhere, N.Y. 12345
> Attn: Mr. P. O. Invoices
> Credit Manager

If I do not have the balance by _____, your account will be referred to a collection agency for further action.

Very truly yours,

P.O. Invoices
Credit Manager

Once you have determined that you are dealing with a reputable firm, the next step will be to negotiate the rates that will be charged for their services. While many may think that it is smart to do business with one firm, this can sometimes come back to haunt you at a time when you least expect it. While that one-to-one relationship does give you a certain amount of control, it could leave you with no one to turn to if you don't have a reliable backup firm in an emergency. The downside to doing business with many collection agencies is that you will not be substantial enough of an account for them to make it worth their while to go the extra mile to collect that account versus using only one or two firms. Not all firms handle accounts everywhere or all types of accounts (commercial versus consumer), and sometimes it is simply better to have a reputable firm that is more local to the customer than thousands of miles away. This is definitely true when it comes to dealing directly with collection attorney firms, as some firms may not have attorneys that are licensed to practice law in the state when the customer resides.

One last possible action that may be considered if you are an unsecured creditor of a start-up firm or a dot-com as well as any seriously past due firm is contacting two other unsecured creditors of the firm and filing an involuntary bankruptcy petition with the bankruptcy court. In order to do this, the three unsecured trade creditors must have a total outstanding balance of at least $10,000. The reason for filing an involuntary petition for bankruptcy is to prevent the disappearance of the assets of the firm as well as determining if fraud was intended with the creation of this firm. While this action may be useful in preserving some assets before they can disappear, depending on how long it takes to wrap up this action, locate and sell all the assets, and disburse the funds after administrative expenses, there may be no cash left to distribute to the unsecured trade creditors. If fraud was the motive behind the company, though, this action may at least help to bring certain unscrupulous individuals to their just rewards in a federal penitentiary.

TIPS AND TECHNIQUES

Cost Savings: Flat versus Variable Rate with a Collection Agency

If a company wishes to offer a flat rate for all placements versus a variable rate, it could be worthwhile if the majority of its accounts placed for collection tend to be smaller and high volume versus larger and low volume. If it also has a fair amount of disputed accounts placed for collection, this too may be a good reason to use a firm that offers a fixed rate. When the account goes to court, the attorney representing the agency may require that they be paid on an hourly basis for their work versus a collection percentage, as they know that it will require a great deal more work to win the case.

Summary

When dealing with marginal customers such as start-up firms and some dot-coms, it is wise to be thorough and cautious when extending credit to them. Due diligence should be practiced and the consideration of security to protect your firm's position in case of a bankruptcy or "disappearance into the night" should always be a major factor in the granting of credit.

As for collection efforts, these firms should be treated with the same respect and dignity that all other customers are but should be monitored more carefully for the potential of a default on their balance due. Knowing when to push for payments, hold orders, and finally take serious action such as placing for collection or suing for your balance will help to make sales and keep cash flowing and costs down while controlling losses.

## CHAPTER 10

What Can Be Done to Prevent Cash-flow Deterioration Problems Due to Deductions/ Disputes and When Selling to Retailers

After reading this chapter, you will be able to

- Understand the origins of deductions/disputes
- Define deductions/disputes
- Understand vendor deductions/disputes
- Understand freight forwarder deductions/disputes
- Understand buyer deductions/disputes
- Understand retailer deductions/disputes

Whenever the words *deductions/disputes* are uttered around a person that manages accounting, cash flow, credit, customer service, and even sales and marketing, chills run down their spines. In computing the profit margin on a sale, rarely does the cost of deductions ever get added into the equation, but it can be one of the most costly expenses related to a sale.

While some industries are less prone to the effects of deductions/disputes, any business that has retailers as customers knows firsthand what it is like to deal with these types of problems. They come in many shapes (types) and in many sizes (dollars) and when added together can be extremely expensive.

Where do they come from? What are these items? Why do they occur? How can they be reduced or controlled? We will address where they come from and look at the many types of deductions that can occur. Once you know the face of the enemy, then you can deal with it.

Where Do Deductions/Disputes Come From?

Deductions/disputes can only originate from three sources:

1. Internal mistakes made by the vendor

2. Freight carriers

3. Unjustified items generated by the buyer

While having these items originate from the customer is bad enough, it is far worse when a company shoots itself in the foot, either by accident or through carelessness. Many departments within a vendor can generate errors that on the whole can cost the firm many millions of dollars yearly in expenses.

Human errors occur at the best of firms and the areas most frequently involved with these types of items are purchasing, engineering, manufacturing, order entry, sales and marketing, billing, quality control, shipping, customer service, receiving, and those areas that perform the service work for the vendor. Freight forwarders can likewise cause deductions/disputes due to goods not being delivered at all, delivered with less than what was picked up at the vendor, or delivering it in a damaged state. The buyer has areas that likewise get involved with deductions/disputes, including purchasing, accounts payables, receiving, top management, quality control, and shipping. Other areas of the buyer could also be involved especially if service work is involved, or the goods sold to them are for their internal use.

Types of Deductions/Disputes

Many types of deductions/disputes can occur, including:

- Defective goods
- Goods never received
- Incorrect packaging
- Order entry error
- Short shipments
- Overshipment of goods
- Incomplete shipments
- Wrong goods shipped
- Damaged goods
- Goods were not in compliance with the terms and conditions of the purchase order
- Goods beyond shelf-life date
- Pricing error
- Payment terms error
- Quantity billed error
- Wrong carrier used for delivery
- Freight charges error
- Sales tax charges error
- Wrong service provided
- Incomplete service provided
- Wrong materials or parts used in the service work performed
- Damage to the buyer from service work performed

- Service work not completed by the time specified on the service contract

- Service work does not meet the standards agreed to in the service contract

- Service work did not pass governmental inspection as required in the service contract

How Do Vendor Deductions/Disputes Occur?

Now that we have listed the most common forms of deduction/disputes that can occur, let's look at each one in detail and determine how they can occur from the point of view of the vendor.

Defective Goods

Defective goods deductions/disputes can occur for a number of reasons:

- One that is fairly common may simply be a design flaw in the item. Even though a product may be thoroughly tested under many possible circumstances and situations, most firms cannot guarantee that one of their products will not fail under all conditions.

- Another possible source for failure of a product could be parts purchased from a third party that were not up to the vendor's standard of quality. If one of these parts fail, then the product produced by the vendor may fail.

- The way that a product is assembled may be the reason the finished product fails. This likewise may cause a finished product to end up on the scrap heap.

- Insufficient testing of finished goods can allow a far greater number of defective items to slip through the cracks.

Sometimes defective goods are returned to inventory after being refurbished, but the goods are still not sufficiently repaired. While these goods typically are resold as used and carry a limited warranty, they still may prove to be unable to hold up as advertised.

TIPS AND TECHNIQUES

Recognizing Abuse versus Defective

Typically, when the reason for the return of goods is that it is defective, it is rare that it is the fault of the buyer that the product failed with one major exception—abuse of the goods outside of the manufacturer's specifications. When dealing with return of defective goods, it is smart to have open lines of communication among quality control, engineering, purchasing, sales, customer service, and the credit department. If complaints that come in to the customer service area and the credit department by many different buyers are focused on one particular product constantly being defective, then there is obvious reason for concern. Engineering and quality control must look into the assembly process, the quality of the goods purchased from a third party, the basic design, and the quantity and methods used to test that particular product. Changes may be needed in the product specs, the vendor who supplies parts, the assembly process, and the final testing procedure. Communication is the key to keeping these problems to a minimum.

Goods Never Received

This problem can have many different reasons for occurring and can be tied to the vendor, the shipping firm, and the buyer. The possible reasons for the goods never being received by the buyer include:

- Goods were shipped to the wrong customer.
- Goods were shipped to the wrong ship to location of the buyer.
- Goods were logged in as shipped but never left the loading dock.

199

- Goods were stolen by someone working for the vendor.
- The order was never entered into the vendor's system.

The majority of these errors center around the shipping area, while the remaining one involves the order entry area. The first three errors usually end up being human mistakes and may be related to having too many goods being shipped out at the same time. The degree of sophistication of the vendor's computer system may also directly be responsible for errors such as these occurring. As previously discussed, mistakes such as these are the result of having month-end, quarter-end, and year-end sales rushes to meet sales forecasts versus smooth, consistent daily sales being encouraged by top management.

TIPS AND TECHNIQUES

Dealing with Theft

In the case of internal theft, this type of problem must be monitored closely. If the customer service/credit department receives many complaints from customers repeatedly reporting that their shipments were not received, this information should be conveyed to both the shipping manager, top management, and if your company is large enough, the internal audit department. It is particularly important for the two areas getting the complaints to note what type of products were to be received by the buyer. This information may help in the apprehension of the suspected thief or thieves involved.

This issue, when tied to the freight forwarder, will be addressed later in this chapter. Additional security equipment will be needed and, if it still continues, the hiring of a security team to monitor goods leaving the shipping department will also be necessary. Internal audit will need to monitor paperwork and make spot checks of packages after they leave the inventory area.

As for orders never making it into the vendor's order entry system, there can be only two culprits to this problem: human error or system error. Orders that were never entered can result in payments not being made, especially if the order is the last part of a buyer's "ship complete" sale to their customer. Since the buyer will not be paid by their customer and the majority of the goods to be shipped to their customer is your product, then you will not be paid as well. Proper training and monitoring of complaints by customers should help the order entry manager keep these errors to a precious few.

In the case of systems error, an update to the system including on-line ordering over the Internet may be the answer. Backups of all orders received that day should be double-checked against the shipments that went out and orders still pending as means of checks and balances against errors.

Incorrect Packaging

This can be a problem from a few directions. The first is that the packaging does not follow the specifications of the buyer. They may have certain requirements to make the goods more sellable at their location (this is especially true of large retailers). Some retailers require certain types of markings on the shipping boxes themselves to better fit their needs. Before a firm should agree to the special packaging requirements of a retailer, they need to confirm that they can accommodate the retailer's request and that the costs for such special requirements are passed on to the retailer. Errors in these areas can originate at the order entry area, the sales area, the quality control area, and the shipping area. If the orders are not properly inputted into the system, the mistake is guaranteed. If the sales force does not pass on the unique specs of the customer, once again the error is guaranteed. Assuming that the information is in the system, it is up to quality control to make sure that the proper packaging and/or shipping markings are there. Finally, it is up to shipping to pull the correct inventory to send to the customer and not the stock that is generally used by all of the other customers.

Order Entry Error

This area and the sales force are the beginning points for a considerable number of errors that can occur to a vendor. If the order is not precisely the same as what is on the purchase order submitted by the buyer, all kinds of deductions can result. Any reduction of human error in the entering of an order drastically diminishes deductions/disputes. This saves a firm a fair amount of time and money fighting fires and allows them to better invest these things into more profitable efforts.

By monitoring the errors that occur, it can be determined if there is a pattern to them. If one individual in order entry or sales is the cause of the increase in these errors, additional training and monitoring initially will be needed. If it continues, replacement of these individuals may be required.

Short Shipments/Overshipment of Goods

Depending on the type of merchandise that a vendor is selling, shortages and overages within a 10 percent range may be totally acceptable. This is fairly common when the products are commodities, such as flour or sugar, or bulk shipments of chemicals. When the goods are more specific in nature and more expensive per item, however, shortages/overages are rarely condoned. The order entry, shipping, quality control, information technology, customer service, inventory control, and internal audit areas need to keep a tight rein on this type of error. In a system in which bar coding monitors the inventory and matches it with the orders entered, a nearly correct count should be maintained at all times.

Initially, errors could originate when the order is incorrectly entered into the system (manually) by order entry. Shipping needs to monitor how much is packed into the boxes that they ship. It is more likely that they would undership the order versus overship, assuming that the inventory area is monitored by others than shipping. If shipping has control over both areas, then both types of human errors could result in a non–bar-coded system. Internal audit needs to review procedures and monitor the errors that can occur in the inventory-shipping system. The tip that a fair amount of these errors are occurring should come from customer service and through their own spot checks of the operation.

Incomplete Shipments and Wrong Goods Shipped

The first error can occur as a result of shipments going out when the order specifically states "ship complete only." If it is a manual order, order entry needs to make sure that this request from the customer is clearly stated within the computer system so that shipping will not pull the inventory until all is available. Incomplete shipments, however, that are not

TIPS AND TECHNIQUES

Separation of Control Responsibility: Inventory and Shipping

Depending on the size of the firm, it is wise to have inventory control managed separately from the shipping area. This reduces the likelihood of theft and gives far better control over the possibility of human errors. If both areas are held responsible for the controlling of both of these types of errors, a system of checks and balances will have been established. Having a bar code system in place also helps in keeping controls in place and inventory and shipments correct. Customer service needs to monitor the calls and keep records that shortages or overages are occurring as well as what products are most frequently involved with these errors. This information needs to be quickly forwarded to internal audit (if one exists) or top management for their review and investigation.

listed as "ship complete" often occur as a result of back orders. The specific goods requested by the customer may not always be in stock and partials are sent out until all goods are available. This can sometimes cause problems for the collections area, as some customers are reluctant to pay invoices that they cannot bill to their customers due to not having a complete order sent to the end user. Either the sales, customer service, or the credit function need to carefully advise their customers if the only way that the vendor can get paid is if the order is shipped complete, then all orders in the future will be handled that way for the particular buyer. This should eliminate the problem of not being paid by the buyer or prompt them to use another excuse for not paying a proper invoice.

The second error is similar to the shortages/overages error. The error can originate in the order entry area if orders are manually taken. The only way to control these types of errors is to monitor to determine if the majority originate from one or more individuals or at a specific time of the day, week, month, and the like. Once a determination is made either additional training or better managing of work flow will be needed to reduce this error. The introduction of a completely automated order entry system will eliminate this error from originating here.

In the shipping area, this type of error can result from a poorly trained or careless employee or having too many shipments going out at the same time. The first reason can only be monitored, and if the employee needs training, then an appropriate and thorough review of procedures is in order. If the employee is simply careless, he or she must be warned and dismissed if improvement does not result.

Having too many shipments going out at the same time to meet a deadline is a problem that needs to be addressed by top management. As stated earlier, the proper management of a steady flow of daily billings/shipments versus the month-end madhouse of billings and shipments vastly improves cash flow from many different areas. This one reduces the likelihood of shipping errors occurring, payments not being made by the buyers, and customers' goodwill being lost.

Finally, both of these types of errors should be monitored and top management notified weekly as to the type of error and the timing of it. Armed with this type of information, top management will have the ability to act quickly and decisively in keeping these errors under control and cash flow moving at peak efficiency.

Damaged Goods and Goods Not in Compliance with the Terms and Conditions of the Purchase Order

These two types of errors do have some commonality to them. The first can occur from all three areas involved with goods errors: the vendor, the freight forwarder, and the buyer. In this section, we will address the error due to the vendor and will address the other two areas later in this chapter.

If goods are not properly packed or materials are not used to safeguard the merchandise from the transport and handling, breakage can occur. If proper markings are not made on boxes to direct both shippers and buyers in the proper way that these boxes are handled, lifted, moved, and stored, breakage will occur. Improper packaging can be controlled through proper training of the shipping department staff and monitoring by customer service of complaints. The vendor's purchasing department should monitor for errors of handling and storage markings printed on boxes purchased by the vendor for use by the vendor for shipping. If the continual breakage occurs as a result in the vendor's boxes not having the proper labels printed clearly in red for everyone to see, a different box and crate supplier must be found. Likewise, shipping needs to audit these materials for correctness and strength in handing the shipment of their goods and alert purchasing to any problems that they may encounter.

In the case of an international shipment tied to a letter of credit, errors of noncompliance to a purchase order that ties completely to a letter of credit will virtually eliminate the possibility of payment being made by the buyer. When a purchase order is received, if it is for a sizeable purchase (as defined by your firm as a large purchase), is complex in nature and requirements, or is attached to a payment by a letter of credit, it is critical to determine if all terms and conditions can be met.

Noninternational shipments tied to a letter of credit should be reviewed by all areas that need to be in compliance with it. This should include the engineering department (if it is custom made or different from normal product specs), sales and marketing, billing (if special invoicing

IN THE REAL WORLD

International Letters of Credit Problems

Many countries and many international companies, when shipping and billing goods between a buyer that isn't bound by the same laws and political and monetary conditions as the seller, use letters of credit. The credit of the buyer's bank is substituted for that of the buyer. Each customer and the country that they reside in have requirements to be met in order for goods to be brought into their country. Depending on the country location of the buyer, the seller's country may have laws governing the sale of certain types of goods. The origin of the goods may also directly affect whether the seller's goods can be accepted into the buyer's country.

Finally, some countries that have a shortage of the currency of the seller's country may put pressure on the buyer's bank (or may even own the banks) to slow down or prevent the payment of these letters of credit. All of these factors and many more must be taken into account when accepting an order that is complicated and payment will be made through a letter of credit. It is beyond the scope of this book to completely define terms and conditions related to international credit, but suffice it to say that it is a very complex operation. Thorough and continuously updated education, solid experience, reliable sources of events in foreign countries, sound knowledge of international laws and customs, and strict monitoring of the process as well as complete review of all documents both before, during, and after the shipment has left the dock must be done for payment to be received on time and in its entirety.

A rather unusual international sale that tested the mettle of the firm that made it occurred a few years ago by a firm that sold large water treatment pumps to firms all over the world. They had an order from the Kuwait government for a $1.2 million shipment to them that would be paid by a confirmed letter of credit payable by one of the largest U.S. banks. The vendor felt very comfortable with the terms and conditions of the letter of credit and, seeing that it was confirmed by one of the largest U.S. banks, they proceeded with the order. The goods were delivered the day after Iraq invaded and took over Kuwait. The vendor had delivered all the necessary paperwork to the U.S. bank for payment, but they were told that the bank would not be paying as the goods were delivered to a country that no longer existed, namely Kuwait. After about a month and half of threats and lawyers getting involved, the bank did the proper thing and paid the letter of credit.

While this was a rare and unusual event that occurred as a result of a very tragic international crisis, it is not unusual for all the players involved with the letter of credit sometimes using both the ordinary (misspelled information on shipping documents versus what was on the letter of credit) to the extremely unusual to delay or prevent payment. It is always worthwhile to spend that extra minute to double- and sometimes triple-check everything and continue to monitor the events in the life of the letter of credit until the payment is indeed in the vendor's hands.

procedures are requested such as additional copies of the invoice), inventory control, and shipping to determine if all goods are available and if any special packaging requirements were met.

For smaller orders, a review by order entry for product availability and special shipping requests needs to be made.

For international orders tied to a letter of credit, if an international marketing group does not exist in the firm, the responsibility to monitor and manage the entire order process should fall to the credit department, as they have the most to lose if the order is not in compliance and all requirements are not met. They will need to follow through to make sure that payment is made.

Goods beyond Shelf-Life Date

This is a very unusual error that rarely does occur. It exists only for those types of industries that deal in perishable products such as food, drugs, and so on. As most of these industries also must have inspections by such government agencies as the Food and Drug Administration (FDA) and the Drug Enforcement Administration (DEA), the monitoring of inventory is very careful. Close monitoring of goods for sale must be done by the inventory control and quality control areas to prevent any outdated products from being replaced on their shelves.

Pricing Error, Payment Terms Error, and Quantity Billed Error

These types of errors originate from either the sales and marketing or the billing areas. Price and terms of sale have been sold by the sales staff on many occasions at many firms throughout the world. When a sales force sells the price and terms versus selling the product, the vendor always suffers. While buying in volume deserves some breaks in price due to the cost savings that a vendor may gain from quantity selling, these prices must be offered across the board to all customers buying the same type of product. Credit terms should never be available for the sales force to offer as a means for making a sale. Terms of sale must be the same for all customers that buy the same type of product. Larger quantities may be offered better credit terms if they too likewise are offered across the board.

Pricing and credit terms are governed by a federal antitrust law (the Robinson–Patman Act), which makes it illegal to give better pricing, terms, and the like to one versus all similar customers. All exceptions or changes to credit terms of sale should be approved by a consensus of top management, including the sales and marketing vice president, the vice president of finance, and the chief financial officer (CFO). This is to make sure that the terms being offered are smart both from a sales and industry point of view and from a cost-effectiveness point of view.

From the point of view of the billing area, errors can occur in all three places if data for pricing, terms, and quantity are entered manually. Errors in credit terms are less likely if only one term of sale is ever offered by a firm. If entered manually, monitoring of errors to determine if repetitive errors are occurring due to one person or a few persons needs to be done by customer service and the information forwarded on to top management. If the errors are due to lack of training, additional hands-on work will need to be done by the billing manager. If the errors are due to large quantities of invoices being billed on the same day monthly, then this goes hand-in-hand with what was stated earlier as to the smoothing-out of orders being shipped and billed during the month.

The third, more worrisome possibility of pricing errors results from information from sales and marketing not being updated into the system, thus making billing errors rampant and the customers' view of the vendor as being incompetent. Pricing changes can occur for many reasons: increases or decreases in prices for raw materials, more efficient ways of creating the products, and so on. Once a change has been approved by top management and a date set for it to go into effect, every effort must be made to correct the pricing on the system as well as notifying the customers of it as well as its start date.

Wrong Carrier Used for Delivery

Typically, this error occurs only when the customer's purchase order specifically states the use of one particular carrier or if the customer has always used a particular carrier and changes this procedure on one occasion or very infrequently. This type of error ties to order entry, shipping, and, on rare occasions, the sales area. In the case of a manual system, the order from the customer specifically designates the shipper and this information is not inputted into the system. As discussed earlier, international shipments tied to a letter of credit could spell doom for the chances of payment if the shipping instructions were not followed to the letter.

Shipping could also be responsible for these types of errors if they habitually fail to read the order instructions and ship based on their normal procedures for that customer. This is most likely to occur when times are busiest and it is critical to get all shipments out quickly. As for sales being involved with this error, when an order is taken by the salesperson and he or she is notified either then or in writing at an earlier time that the customer has changed the carrier they wish to use for their shipments and this information is not passed on to order entry, errors will occur. It is imperative that the changes to all orders or special orders taken by a sales rep be forwarded on to order entry to be entered into the system and make it effective immediately to prevent errors from occurring.

The overall way to prevent this error from occurring is to counsel all three areas on the importance of passing along changes to the appropriate areas. Monitoring and focusing on staff that continuously make repetitive errors needs to be corrected either by additional training or dismissal.

Freight Charges Error

This error can be the result of lack of communication between shipping and order entry or can result from the wrong information being entered into the system by order entry. Once shipping has received notification from a shipper that their prices will be changed effective on a specific date, this information must be relayed to order entry in order to have it available for the system to enter into the billing data and quote information.

Human error once again could be the culprit for errors occurring to order entry when choosing the correct charge (assuming that the system does not do this automatically). If this error is monitored and once again it is the result of overload at month-end, then top management needs to be made aware of this so that they may take the appropriate steps to smooth out the shipping and billing process. Repetitive errors must also be managed either by automating the system, additional training, or dismissal of the problem employee.

Sales Tax Charges Error

In many firms, customer service is responsible for obtaining, maintaining, and following up sales tax exempt forms. In some larger firms, an accounting area, billing area, or the credit department may have that responsibility. A customer should always be charged sales tax if no current sales tax exempt form is on file with the vendor. Even though more work may be generated as a result of the need of issuing credit for previously billed invoices that were charged sales tax, the expenses involved from a state sales tax audit, penalties, and fines that can result would be far greater in both time and money.

While no error occurs when sales tax is charged and later credited once the form is received, even though additional paperwork and time are used to make everything correct, the real error occurs when either

211

sales tax is not charged when the exemption form is not received (either when promised or misfiled) or when the sales tax is charged and the form had been in hand from the very beginning. If the sales force is involved with obtaining these forms at the time when the credit application is submitted or follows up regularly when notified by customer service that the current sales tax exempt form will expire shortly, it must be made a high priority to them as well as the customer service staff that these forms are correct, not expired, and cover all states that the vendor ships product to for the buyer. Monitoring and auditing of these files should be done by internal audit as well as any outside auditing firm that creates the quarterly or year-end financial reports.

Wrong Service Provided and Incomplete Service Provided

When it comes to errors, we have been looking at firms that sell goods, not service providers. This industry brings with it a whole different breed

TIPS AND TECHNIQUES

Reasons for Incomplete Work

- Paperwork for project not entered properly in the system either by order entry or sales reps

- Materials needed for job are unavailable

- Labor problems of the contractor or subcontractor

- Financial difficulty, bankruptcy, or closure of the contractor or subcontractor

- Financial difficulty, bankruptcy, or closure of the buyer

- Slow or nonpayment of invoices by the buyer

of errors that can occur. As far as wrong service provided, this error can originate from the sales and order entry areas and also the team that performs the service work. The size and dollar amount of the service work to be performed and what the service provider considers a large job will directly affect the need for monitoring the costs and errors that can occur. Where materials are needed and could be readily wasted if the work is not properly performed to the customer's satisfaction, managerial monitoring of the work should be required.

When a service requires extensive knowledge of a more technical nature and certain expertise/credentials are needed to perform the service, a more knowledgeable sales rep should be involved with the entire order entry procedure. This should help to prevent misinforming the actual technician who will do the work. In more simple and repetitive work, a well-trained but less knowledgeable order entry person can man-

IN THE REAL WORLD

Construction Industry Progress Payments

In the construction industry, one common practice used by contractors to prevent losing all the money that was invested into a particular construction contract is to require progress payments over the life of the job. If the majority of the costs involved with the performing of the construction service are materials, then a substantial payment may be required up front to begin work on the project. If materials are minimal compared to the labor costs, then payments may be more evenly spread out and may have set event completions that trigger a progress billing.

Assuming that there are no financial problems involved with a job's being incomplete, the first three reasons could easily be the cause of most errors on service work. A true error revolves around the in-

TIPS AND TECHNIQUES CONTINUED

correct entering of all pertinent details of the order by order entry or the sales rep. If errors continuously occur with one individual, then additional training at first, and with no marked improvements, possible dismissal may resolve the issue.

As for unavailability of materials, multiple sources of these goods should be readily available. This is an area where communication between the purchasing and sales staff needs to be at its peak. Before an order is accepted, the ease of obtaining the necessary materials should be well in hand.

Labor issues, while not pleasant, typically revolve around a contract with a particular date for the union contract to expire. This does not mean that a firm should not accept a service job if its labor contract is due to expire within the life of that job. It should, however, have contingency plans to contend with a possible strike and walkout.

Finally, as for financial difficulties of any of the parties involved with the service work, this is rarely an error and is far beyond the scope of this book to address these issues. Suffice it to say that these situations occur daily and all precautions need to be taken to prevent these types of problems from occurring.

age the order-taking process. If a firm provides a purchase order detailing the service work to be done, it needs to be looked at to determine if the work is something that their firm normally does and whether the job is one that they can readily handle or additional outside help will be needed. While human errors can occur in every firm and though trust builds between a contractor and a subcontractor when they regularly use the same firm for many jobs that the contractor cannot completely handle, the chances for errors occurring outside of the main service provider increases when parts of a job are subcontracted out. Assuming that a reputable firm is selected and the job is audited by the contractor's engineers, the correct and proper work should be performed or corrected if an error has been made by the subcontractor.

Service Work Performed: Wrong Materials or Parts Used, and Damage to the Buyer

These two errors go hand-in-hand with each other. Even if the only damage caused to the buyer is a delay in the work being completed on time, this alone can easily injure the reputation of a service provider.

Going back again the main sources of errors for wrong materials or parts used in the service work performed revolves around either the order entry area or the sales rep that took the order. Focusing on what needs to be done and whether it is being done on a certain instrument or item can help to determine the materials or parts required to complete the job. In the case of repairs on a mechanical device, most manufacturers have a parts list for the item, which will aid in correctly ordering the proper parts for the job.

In the case of a type of construction job, a detailed list of items needed in the proper quantities should be reviewed not only with the service rep but also with the sales rep and chief engineer connected to the job. Once all have discussed the job requirements and material needs, a detailed proposal with cost should be approved by the buyer and the buyer's engineering staff tied to the work being done.

As to damage done to the buyer from work done by the service vendor, every effort to involve the buyer's engineering staff (major job) in the step-by-step performance of the work requested should be insisted upon so as to have agreement by both parties that the work met the specifications of the contract. In the case of smaller, less technical jobs, the work should be tested by both the service rep performing the work and a supervisor, and both should sign the work completion ticket. Repetitive human errors should be monitored by customer service and reported to top management for their review and correction of the situation. Additional training or a complete review of the work process should be done to prevent errors in the future. In both cases, the service provider should stand behind their work and be prepared to correct the situation to the customer's satisfaction once it is proved that there was any fault involved in the work of the vendor.

Service Contract: Service Work Not Completed by the Time Specified, Service Work Not Meeting the Agreed Standards, and Service Work Not Passing Required Governmental Inspection

These errors need to be addressed from the very beginning when the contract is first negotiated. In all three of these problems, the service work performed will be extensive and not completed in a matter of hours.

These errors can originate only from a company-wide acceptance of an order. The sales rep, chief engineer, CFO, purchasing manager, and service staff all would be involved with the estimates for this size of job, time of completion, labor and materials requirements, need of government inspection, compliance with customer's purchase order, and negotiation of the final terms and conditions of the contract. These types of errors can be prevented only by building into the contract sufficient time and profit to allow for problems that could occur. Being fully aware of all of the governmental codes that must be met in order to pass inspection should be the responsibility of the chief engineer of the job. As before, step-by-step inspections by the buyer's chief engineer with his or her signoff of the approved work should be one requirement in the contract to protect both parties that work is meeting the buyer's expectations.

In the case of a job out for bids, it is wise to have the vendor's staff review the contract in detail before submitting the company's bid to determine if there are any hidden costs or problems with meeting all the buyer's requirements. When the job out for bids looks too good to be true, it usually is.

How Do Freight Forwarder Deductions/Disputes Occur?

Since we have looked at how the vendor has had to deal with all types of deductions/disputes, we need to look into how these types of problems can be caused by the freight forwarder. Obviously, not all problems have a direct relationship to the freight forwarder; the list that they may have influence over includes:

- Goods never received
- Incomplete shipments
- Damaged goods

Goods Never Received

Once it has been determined that the goods have not been received, a tracer needs to be conducted. Today, most shippers provide Internet access to anyone with a tracking number to find where a shipment is, when it was delivered, and who signed for it. If indeed there is no receipt or delivery of a shipment, the shipper's customer service group will need to begin the investigation.

In one case, repetitive loss of packages did occur. It happened to be level two drugs that were closely watched by the firm as well as the DEA. If a buyer has continuous complaints related to nonreceipt of goods and signed proofs of delivery are not available on these shipments, it is time to begin a discussion with the carrier. While most carriers provide insurance coverage for lost or damaged goods, the reputation of the vendor as well as the freight forwarder is at stake. If the carrier does not

The World Traveler

At one time or another, we have all used an overnight shipper to get a package to someone who needed it immediately. Considering the millions of packages that get shipped daily through these carriers, it is amazing that so few are ever lost.

On one such occasion, a package was really lost! A package bound for Pittsburgh, Pennsylvania, sent from Rochester, New York, left on a world tour. Having lost its original shipping label, it had somehow been mixed in with packages bound for London, England. After the shipper's sales rep that handled our firm's contract was contacted, he had managed to locate the lost wanderer on its way from London to Tokyo, Japan. Their Japanese facility was contacted, and the package was rerouted by way of Honolulu, Hawaii, to San Francisco, California, and finally on to Pittsburgh, with an arrival date only five days late. Needless to say, we did not pay for the delivery or the world tour that our package took, but did receive some free shipments for the future due to our inconvenience.

follow through on monitoring the delivery of its goods and has repeated lost or missing deliveries, it is time to look for a new carrier.

Incomplete Shipments

This can occur if multiple shipments are made to a customer for delivery on the same day. Smaller packages may be mislaid or get separated from the original scheduled shipment. Monitoring the shipper for complaints of incomplete shipments, customer service can readily provide top management and the shipping area manager can alert their sales rep at the freight forwarder to these problems and reduce or eliminate them from reoccurring. If it continues and there are other freight forwarders that offer the same service at similar prices, a switch may be in order.

Damaged Goods

Assuming that goods were not damaged within the vendor's place of business and the buyer was not responsible for the goods being damaged, then the freight forwarder will need to address problems with damaged goods. Most carriers offer insurance to cover damaged goods, and some offer a deductible amount to keep the rate down to their customers.

When a vast amount of packages are transported daily, it is inevitable that even with the best of packaging some breakage will occur. While this is not unusual, it can become a problem if a specific or numerous buyers complain the goods are being delivered damaged on a regular basis. If indeed this is the case, then similar action taken in the case of lost or incomplete shipments will need to be addressed with the carrier. If improvements are not immediate, replacement will become mandatory to protect the reputation of the vendor.

How Do Buyer Deductions/Disputes Occur?

Now that we have reviewed and resolved the vendor and the freight forwarder deductions/disputes problems, we need to look into how these types of problems can be caused by the buyer. Obviously, not all problems have a direct relationship to the buyer; the list that they may have influence over includes:

- Defective goods
- Goods never received
- Short shipments
- Incomplete shipments
- Damaged goods

- Goods were not in compliance with the terms and conditions of the purchase order
- Pricing error
- Payment terms error
- Sales tax charges error
- Service work does not meet the standards agreed to in the service contract

Defective Goods

In theory, defective goods are the responsibility of the vendor, not the buyer. A number of firms, especially many retailers, will take back some larger consumer goods that have been used for a period of time that are in perfect working order and return them to the vendor as defective. Why? The answer is simple: It is easier to argue with a supplier than it is to argue with a consumer. Unhappy consumers will make their feelings known in the store where they bought the item and will spread the word to many that they were ripped off by a retailer who sold them shoddy goods. If the buyer is a very large customer of theirs, an unhappy vendor will simply "grin and bear it" as a cost of doing business. Unless the vendor provides products that are in great demand by the general public and supply is short or limited, the vendor has very little to bargain with when dealing with an "800-pound gorilla" retailer.

In defense of some retailers, due to pressure from many vendors they have cleaned up their act and have pulled the reins in on some abusive consumers that try to beat the system. Many are now requiring returns to be made within 15 days or they will be assessed a 25 percent restocking charge. Others demand that all packaging be returned intact along with the original sales receipt in order to receive credit. This prevents some less scrupulous consumers from sending in for rebates to the manufacturer that demand the original sales receipt and then returning the item for full credit.

In the case of larger consumer products that reflect signs of wear and tear or are blatantly abused, most retailers will simply offer extended warranty contracts that will cover problems with goods that need service repair versus simply taking the goods back.

While it is very illegal for vendors to conspire together and refuse to sell to certain retailers or buyers, it is still legal for credit managers to share the fact that certain firms take excessive deductions. This may help the vendor to negotiate a better deal with the buyer and, if nothing else, will offer a means to determine pricing across the board for all similar customers.

Goods Never Received

As all three of the parties involved with a sale (vendor, freight forwarder, and buyer) can be guilty of this error and we have looked at how the first two were responsible, now it is time that we look at the end of the chain—the buyer—and how they can be at fault.

The type of goods shipped (consumer goods versus a freight car full of flour) is in direct proportion to the probability that the goods will not be received. While it may be very difficult to make a freight car full of flour disappear, it is not unusual for an entire shipment of small toys or costume jewelry to vanish completely, especially if no signature was required when the goods were delivered.

Once a vendor has eliminated the possibility that errors of lost goods were not caused by either the freight forwarder or themselves, then the only other possibility is at the buyer's location. Safeguards such as requiring that all goods shipped have a signed receipt when delivered and weight checks being done on shipments to verify contents on a spot-check basis will help to eliminate any reasonable doubts that the loss of goods resulted after they were received at the buyer's location. If a buyer then continues to complain of lost shipments, they should be informed that the police and/or FBI, if it is interstate transportation, or other federal agencies (if drugs, the DEA or FDA may be contacted) will be called in to investigate these missing shipments.

Short Shipments, Incomplete Shipments, and Damaged Goods

All of these problems can be caused once again by the three parties involved with the buying and selling of goods. In the case of buyer shortages, incomplete shipments and damaged items may result once the goods have been in the custody of the buyer.

Some retailers have central distribution warehouses set up to store their excess inventory and use their own trucks instead of freight forwarders. Some of these firms will not place the goods in inventory at the time they arrive at the warehouse, but instead leave them on the trailers until the goods are needed. This means that at times there is no confirmation that all goods were received other than the trucker's signing for a load at the time of pickup.

Incomplete shipments can occur due to the buyer's purchase order stipulating "ship complete" and the buyer's receiving area staff not checking in all goods together. If goods come in multiple boxes and one or more are not counted in as being received on the same day, then a deduction can result for noncompliance with the terms of the purchase order. The one way to prevent this type of problem from occurring is for the vendor to have all goods listed as one shipment on the freight forwarder's manifest. This assumes that all goods can be loaded together either in one box or on one pallet. If the shipment is too great for this, all pallets and boxes must be marked with the same purchase order number and be reflected as part of the same shipment on the bill of lading and the packing slip.

Damaged goods can result from mishandling of the boxes by the buyer's receiving area staff, through carelessness in transporting the boxes into inventory, stacking the boxes improperly, or by leaving the items on

IN THE REAL WORLD

Miscount?

In a recent case, one retailer who also maintained a pharmacy at each store's location had ordered four pallets of a nonprescription drug that was packaged in bottles within their normal retail shelf boxes. These drugs were packed 24 to a box and were arranged on the pallet such that there were four boxes across, four boxes down, and four boxes high to make a square shipment. The retailer had counted the boxes as four boxes across, three boxes down, and four boxes high for a total of 48 versus 64 that were being shipped on a pallet ($4 \times 3 \times 4 = 48$ versus $4 \times 4 \times 4 = 64$).

After customer service was notified the third time that a pallet had shown up short they noticed that the shortages were consistently 16 missing boxes. This information was forwarded on to both the shipping area and the sales rep in charge of the account, who determined that indeed 64 boxes were being shipped on every pallet. Armed with this information, the sales rep visited the customer's distribution warehouse where the goods were stored. Since none of the pallets had been opened and still remained completely covered by shrink-wrap, the sales rep asked the retailer's receiving manager to remove the plastic and physically count the boxes on the pallets. Once the first pallet was opened, the receiving manager immediately acknowledged that all 64 boxes had been received.

To prevent this oversight from reoccurring, all boxes were shipped with different bright color stripes on opposite sides of each box. They were packed on the pallet with each box reversed to the box next to it and the pallet was wrapped in clear plastic to make sure that the colors were plainly seen.

Human errors can occur when a vast number of goods are received on a daily basis. It is wise to make sure that the chances of a human error occurring are kept to a minimum.

the trailer truck that they were shipped in. When a buyer uses its own trucks for the shipping of goods from vendors they may leave the inventory in the trailer until they have time to check it in. Some goods cannot be maintained in a noninsulated environment for long. While some items can withstand short periods of time exposed to transport conditions, not all can endure it for longer periods of time. Exposed to excessive heat or cold, or possible contact with water if the trailer is not completely intact or on high enough ground to prevent being damaged by flooding, goods can indeed be damaged when it is time to finally bring them into the buyer's inventory.

This is a more difficult problem for the vendor to deal with. Added packing and clear, bright labeling of boxes and pallets should help to prevent some of the problems with mishandling by the buyer's receiving area. By clearly stating in any agreement or amending all purchase orders such that the customer accepts any damage due to excessive storage (a limited number of days should be established for any outside storage that is less than the maximum that the goods can withstand) in an outside trailer beyond a designated date. Water damage caused as the result of extended outside storage in a trailer will likewise not be covered as damaged. These exemptions and precautions will prevent the vendor from being charged for unjustified damage made by the buyer.

Goods Not in Compliance with the Terms and Conditions of the Purchase Order

While this certainly can be a suitable reason for a deduction by a buyer, it is wise for the vendor to "read the fine print." Some buyers and especially many retailers have used vague or nondefined clauses on a purchase order to justify a deduction and reduce the price that they will have to pay for their purchase.

Many buyers will add a general statement that all terms and conditions of the purchase order must be met or a penalty charge equal to some percentage of the purchase order will be accessed. When the goods are received, a deduction is taken from the payment for noncompliance with the terms and conditions of the purchase order. It rarely states what the cause of the noncompliance was, and the amount is small enough that it may not be worth the effort of the vendor to chase after the buyer to explain it. Once this has occurred and has been successful for the buyer, they may proceed to make these charges at first on an irregular basis and then finally on a fairly regular basis. This may go on indefinitely until the vendor complains and demands an accounting for these items. If the buyer is a considerable customer of the vendor and the buyer has other options to purchase similar products from a competitor, it is most likely that the buyer will refuse to comply with the demands of an explanation and threaten to pull their account if the harassment continues.

So what is a poor vendor to do? Literally, there are only two recourses left to a vendor: stand and fight or bite the bullet. In the former, a vendor must be prepared to lose the buyer as a customer. They need to demand in writing a complete explanation for each deduction and provide all documentation that they have on these items to the buyer's purchasing manager. In the letter, the vendor must give the buyer a deadline to either explain their actions or repay the items by a set date. If no payment or explanation is provided, the next step is to ascend the chain of command within the customer. Ultimately, if no reasonable explanation is received by the time it is necessary to contact the buyer's president, the final letter should be addressed from one president to the other to see if a reasonable settlement can be reached before it is placed for legal action and all sales to the buyer ceases. If no response is given, the vendor must proceed with the actions stated in their letter to the president.

In the case of the latter, though in direct violation of the Robinson–Patman Act, the vendor will continue to write off these charges. They may look into raising their prices due to their suppliers' raising their costs of raw materials in order to offset these deduction items. If this buyer is the only one taking these illegitimate deductions and they are the only ones that are being charged the higher prices, then the cost of doing business with them will be offset by the higher prices that they will be paying for the vendor's goods. While not the norm, this may bring the situation back into compliance with the Robinson–Patman Act.

Pricing Error

This is a very old way of improving the cash flow of a buyer at the expense of their vendors. When a vendor changes their pricing structure to their customers, they have an obligation to make sure that not only have they received the notification but also that it has been updated in the buyer's accounts payable system. A letter sent by certified mail with a return receipt covering all changes made to the pricing should be sent not only to the purchasing manager, but also to the accounts payable manager of the buyer. This covers the two areas that sometimes don't communicate well with each other. The effective date as well as acknowledgment that any purchase orders already in the system will be honored at the previous prices should be included in this cover letter.

When a vendor relies on their sales reps to verbally advise the buyer's purchasing rep or manager of an upcoming price increase, yet never confirms this in writing to both purchasing and accounts payable, it becomes a license to steal from the vendor until this situation is rectified. Either the vendor's marketing or customer service areas should do this notification. Copies of all price changes should likewise be sent in advance of the notification to the buyers to the credit and billing areas.

Payment Terms Error

For the firm that offers only one credit term of sale, this is not a problem. Many firms, however, offer many terms to suit a special situation or a particular product or to introduce a new product. If new terms are for a limited time only, such as for the introduction of a new product, this type of information needs to be formally conveyed to both the purchasing and accounts payable managers. As in the case of the pricing changes, these notices need to be sent by certified mail with a return receipt required, and all of these should be sent to the attention of a named manager, not just to the attention of the purchasing or accounts payable manager. This eliminates the excuse that they never heard of any expiration date of the payment term.

If special payment terms are offered only for one particular product, this likewise needs to be addressed in the same manner as the introduction of a new product. In the case of a special situation such as a quarter-end large-volume sale or a special term offered to a seasonal product,

TIPS AND TECHNIQUES

Correcting Payment Terms Errors

If a customer continues to take advantage of the temporary payment term beyond the expiration time, a formal letter to both the purchasing and accounts payable managers needs to be sent with all backup pertaining to the incorrect terms (i.e., if a cash discount was offered, longer payment terms, etc.). In the case of a cash discount being taken when no longer offered, repayment of the discount needs to be requested immediately. As for extended terms, the customer needs to be made aware that the invoice(s) need to be paid now because they are overdue. If the customer doesn't respond, then a follow-up call should be made by the collection staff. If the customer either doesn't pay the invoice(s) or repays the disallowed discount and continues to take the expired terms, the account should be put on credit hold until the buyer's purchasing and accounts payable manager understand that such action will no longer be tolerated. Prior to this point, the sales rep tied to this account should make a call on the purchasing manager to try and rectify the situation in conjunction with the actions of the collection staff.

these likewise demand formal notification to prevent errors. Without this pronouncement it is highly likely that either the buyer will continue taking advantage of the terms beyond their expiration date or will ignore the change altogether. While the latter is doubtful, the former is a daily fact of life when new temporary terms are introduced.

Sales Tax Charges Error

As stated earlier, the managing of who gets the sales tax exempt forms from buyers falls to various parts of the company. Ultimately, if the credit area is responsible for keeping the accounts receivables clean of deduction/disputed items, then they will have to live with the consequences.

 TIPS AND TECHNIQUES

Sales Tax Exemption Forms— Costly if Not Current

Depending on the size of your firm and how often you bill your customers (I recommend daily), the follow-up of these firms should be conducted at least monthly, but weekly would be better. Since these forms have expiration dates that are not uniformly the same, a continuous effort to get them must be conducted in order to keep your billing correct. At least one month prior to the expiration of the sales tax exemption form(s), follow-up contact must be made. It can be made by e-mail, phone, letter, or fax, whichever is easiest and requires the least amount of effort. If any follow-up can be systems generated rather than requiring manual follow-up so much the better. Ultimately if no response is received within two weeks of the first attempt at obtaining the document(s), direct phone contact must be made. When the month is up and no forms are in hand, billing must be notified to start charging sales tax, or if the system is capable it can automatically start charging sales tax when the expiration date ends.

TIPS AND TECHNIQUES CONTINUED

If the customer continues to take a deduction for sales tax after the expiration of their form(s), then a disallowed deduction notice covering all sales tax deductions taken on their check must be sent to the purchasing and accounts payable manager. A follow-up one is again generated 30 days later if payment or the form(s) have not been received. When the total of these deductions reach either 1 percent of the customer's annual purchases or $1,000, whichever is less, a final letter is generated, giving them 20 days to deliver the form(s) or repay all sales tax deductions or the account will be placed on credit hold. If no paperwork or payment is received at 20 days, the account is placed on credit hold until either is received.

This is one area where it is vital to get this matter resolved early and make it automatic that the customer will forward all proper tax forms to keep them in compliance with sales tax laws. It is also vital to make sure that the customer knows that they will indeed be charged sales tax if the proper forms are not in the hands of the vendor.

Service Work Does Not Meet the Standards Agreed to in the Service Contract

This type of error is used by some buyers as a means to improve their cash flow. Due to its vagueness in meaning, the interpretation of what really was a problem remains undefined. Whether the deduction is for a small amount (as defined by what the vendor considers small versus large) or a considerable portion of the contract, there may be some tense negotiations.

Once this type of deduction in payment has been taken, immediate contact should be made initially by either the sales rep or customer service to determine the background on it. Once the reasons behind the deduction are clear, a determination needs to be made by the vendor for the validity of the claim. Some possible reasons for this deduction may be:

- Minor part(s) of a job have yet to be completed.
- Appearance of the job does not match exactly what was described in the purchase order.
- Materials listed in the purchase order were not delivered.
- Work was not completed in a timely manner.
- The finished job as depicted in the service contract does not perform in the manner described.

Due to the very nature of the deduction and the broadness of this topic, it is beyond the scope of this book to describe every possible reason behind this deduction. This may be an area where both parties are equally at fault or where it is smarter to simply eat the deduction as a cost of doing business with a potential of additional future sales to this buyer, which will more than offset the cost of this item. If, however, it is totally unreasonable and worth the cost to pursue this matter, normal collection procedures should be applied to it, ending with a possible lawsuit.

Why Are Retailer Deductions/Disputes a Problem?

Having gone through the three participants in the deduction hierarchy (vendor, freight forwarder, and buyer) and referenced on occasions the actions of retailers, it is time to look at two particular deductions not yet discussed here but employed as a sometimes desperate means to improve cash flow. The more commonplace and mostly legitimate ones that have been discussed earlier in this chapter include incorrect packaging, defective goods, short shipments, incomplete shipments, damaged goods, and goods not in compliance with terms and conditions of purchase order.

Retailers live and die on the whims of the consumers, the amount of advertising that they or the manufacturers do on goods that they sell, and the level of competition that they experience. Any way that they can lower their costs or overhead is one more step to survival at worst and financial stability and profitability at best. The key here is not only to sell goods and make profits, but to maximize profits so that investors also look favorably on them. Cash flow to them is critical, as has been proven in the past. Even the most profitable firms can file for bankruptcy if they lack cash. (See *In the Real World*, "Classic Example of Lack of Cash Flow . . .," in Chapter 1). One way to conserve cash is to reduce the amount that must be paid to your vendors, and this philosophy has been an age-old and time-honored practice of many retailers.

What can be done to keep this time-tested practice from jeopardizing the vendor's cash flow? To answer that question, we need to look at two additional areas and address each issue individually.

Disallowed Cash Discounts

The number one area to gain both time and additional cash flow for a retailer is tied to vendors that sell to them and offer cash discount credit terms. Not only do some pay late beyond the net terms time, but they also take off the discount amount from the payment. This type of abuse builds up deductions quickly and has caused many vendors to stop offering these types of credit terms to retailers in general. The problem with stopping, however, is that although the terms are no longer offered to the retailer, their system still maintains these payment terms and continues taking the deduction regardless of what the invoices reflect as terms of sale.

The procedure for dealing with disallowed deductions was discussed earlier, but one further note needs to be added here. When dealing with a firm that blatantly abuses the system, immediate and decisive action must be taken or improvements will never materialize. A code of business ethics should exist between a buyer and a seller, and this is a direct violation of that ethical boundary.

The Year-End Mystery Deduction

This deduction occurs when some retailers are in need of improving their year-end numbers by reducing their outstanding accounts payable without using their cash on hand or working capital lines of credit. Some firms in the past have used a general reason for the deduction such as damaged goods, yet not supplied any corresponding details of what the deduction relates to. This leaves the vendor with no recourse but to request documentation from the retailer, which goes back and forth for many months. Once the new year has begun and the financial data completed for the previous year, the retailers will slowly start to supply information on the deductions, which rarely result in any credit being issued.

IN THE REAL WORLD

Dealing with Nondescript Deductions by Retailers

One of the worst examples of the mystery year-end deduction occurred at the end of 1998 and was reported by a large financial newspaper in March 1999 about the Rite Aid Corporation. After interviewing many credit executives on the topic of deductions with Rite Aid, the newspaper discovered that at the end of 1998 Rite Aid had taken a number of large deductions while supplying little or no detail on either the reason for the deductions or where they were tied to sales of merchandise to them. This gave the credit executives of the vendors no real recourse but to start contacting Rite Aid and demanding backup information on these items.

The financial newspaper reported in September 1999 that Rite Aid had now started to repay these items to the vendors, which in essence gave Rite Aid a free loan for millions of dollars for a period of almost a year.

Summary

Deduction abuses may also be a sign of unpleasant things to come. If the customer or retailer is in financial difficulty and now uses less scrupulous methods to reduce payments, can nonpayment and bankruptcy be far behind? Vendors must always be on their guard and ever ready to take unwavering steps to bring the violators in line and prevent them from increasing the vendor's overall receivables exposure. By keeping well informed of any changes in the financial position of a customer and monitoring closely the performance of these firms' prevention of customer problems will improve.

The vendor likewise has a responsibility to make sure that its own house is in order. They need to also operate ethically and professionally and not use any undue clout that they may have with a product to blackmail a customer into accepting unjust terms and conditions. These types of behavior will come back to haunt the vendor in the long run when the demand of the market changes by virtue of increased competition.

It is on this note that we now proceed to Chapter 11, "Outside Services that Can Enhance Cash Flow."

Outside Services that Can Enhance Cash Flow

After reading this chapter, you will be able to

- Decide if factoring is relevant for your business
- Determine if outsourcing will make your business more or less cost effective
- Understand how receivables outsourcing affects cash flow
- Decide if deduction/disputes resolution outsourcing is worthwhile for your business
- Determine if accounts payable duplicate payment/overpayment outsourcing is worthwhile to your business

For the most part we have looked at ways to improve or enhance cash flow from an internal point of view. Now it is time to look at outside financial services that can be employed to improve cash flow.

In today's world those magic words still ring out from the corporate towers on high—*downsizing*, *rightsizing*, and so on. While in some cases they may be necessary, this may not always be the silver bullet that solves the problem. As a result of downsizing of many firms, new (and some very old) forms of business have made an appearance on the horizon to try to put the cash flow problems back on track.

Factoring: Does It Still Work?

A type of financing that has been around for hundreds of years and originated in Europe is a program of financing of receivables called factoring. Today's version of factoring is more in line with the needs of firms to get cash out of their receivables immediately rather than wait until payment arrives from their customers.

Factoring has been used for many years by the garment industry to address their seasonal changes and need of cash for the next selling period. These manufacturers sell their receivables to the factors for a discounted amount with a percentage held back until payment is received on the receivables from which their fees are deducted and the net amount is forwarded to the manufacturers. This holdback amount could be anywhere from 10 to 30 percent, depending on the nature of the business, whom they are selling to, and what type of products they are selling. It has become a growing area of business for helping small and some start-up firms generate cash quickly in order to meet their daily needs.

Not having the expertise or the resources to manage these receivables, many firms find this an easy way to generate cash without the headaches that can occur with trying to collect delinquent accounts. Many firms likewise do not qualify for bank working capital lines of credit that can help tide them over when cash demands arise yet receivables collections has not materialized. Some smaller service firms that now avail themselves of this advantage include employment agencies, printing shops, architects and engineers, and some consultants.

When negotiating a factoring agreement, there are a number of factors that must be considered that can directly affect the costs and benefits of the service.

While there are obvious advantages to this program, the costs may at times far outweigh the advantages. For those that can find other sources of additional cash during critical times, it is more cost effective to use them versus this form of receivables management.

TIPS AND TECHNIQUES

Cost and Benefit Considerations

- *Nonrecourse.* When a receivable is sold to a factor under this option, the sale is permanent and more risky for them. If the receivable becomes noncollectible, the factor has no means to recoup the money it provided up front to the client. For a factor to agree to a nonrecourse agreement, they will make a credit review of all of the client's customers to determine their credit-worthiness. Once a credit limit is determined, the factor will be willing to buy receivables from their client up to the amount of the limit set by them for each of the client's customers on a nonrecourse basis. The client bears no risk for the receivable and the factor since they are not extending credit to the client and will not require a credit evaluation and approval of the client.

- *Recourse.* When the client wishes to sell its customers more than the limit set by the factor, collection service will be provided for the client for a fee. These receivables will be held for a set number of days and then returned to the client for handling. While it is in the best interest of the factor to collect all nonrecourse receivables, there is little or no real incentive for them to collect those with full recourse since they will ultimately be returning these to the client.

- *Fees.* The fees charged for these factoring services run from 2 to 7 percent, and the amount that is held back varies with the type of customer that the client is selling.

Outsourcing: Is This New Idea More or Less Cost Effective?

With the reduction of the workforce in many firms, highly skilled professionals have created new firms that offer many of the services that they

Things to Expect from an Outsourcing Firm

- They will contact the clients' customers and make the contact completely "cosmetic," giving no hint that anyone other than the client is calling on past due receivables.

- The contract is for a specific length of time (typically more than a year) and not for just a quick "hit and run" collection effort.

- They may do short-term problem solving (such as cleaning up an in-house mess) if requested but tend to encourage long-term relationships.

- They can provide specialized knowledge to the client as a means to solve problems that may be constantly occurring.

- They have specialized tools and procedure that have been time tested under all conditions that they can offer the client as a means of putting the "house back in order."

- They can offer consulting help when dealing with unique or unusual situations.

What does Outsourcing cost?

- It could be a fixed (monthly or some other regular period) fee.

- It could be based on a percent of sales.

- It could be based on a percent (contingency) of the savings.

- It could be based on a combination of any of these.

- It will also require the cooperation of the credit staff.

- It will also require that a manager oversee their work and determine their effectiveness based on:

  - Lower bad debts
  - Improved DSO (days' sales outstanding)

used to provide to their previous employer. Three such types of firms include:

1. Receivables outsourcing firms
2. Deduction/Disputes resolution firms
3. Accounts Payable duplicate payment/overpayment firms

All of these firms can have a direct impact on cash flow by improving receivables collections, recouping deductions that were improperly taken by a customer, and recouping duplicate payments or overpayments made by the accounts payable area of a company. The last company may also include in their services the auditing of purchases and contracts between a buyer and vendor to determine if all credits due them were indeed given.

Is Receivables Outsourcing Worthwhile?

In a number of firms today, managers are expected to do more with less. While this may be practical if all the necessary tools are in place to handle this additional workload, it is rare that the credit function is ever in a position to be underworked and overpaid. One way that a competent credit manager can compensate for the additional workload is to outsource some of the more menial and repetitive follow-up to an outplacement firm.

Is Deduction/Dispute Resolution Outsourcing Worthwhile?

There are many reasons to use a deduction/dispute resolution firm. Some are more valid than others. The industry that your firm is part of will also directly influence the effectiveness of this type of service. A word of caution: If you have not made an effort to correct the internal sources of these types of deductions, then no amount of help from this type of firm will ever bear any fruit.

TIPS AND TECHNIQUES

Wrong and Right Reasons for Hiring a Deduction/Dispute Resolution Firm

Wrong Reasons

- *Eliminate headcount.* This merely exchanges one workforce for another and may actually slow down progress as your firm's people are more familiar with the claims and your system than the resolution firm

- *Expense savings.* By hiring the resolution firm, your firm may save on overhead expenses such as benefits of employees but in the long run the costs may be nearly the same.

- *Eliminate deductions.* This is an impossibility as your company's customers will always want to use deductions as a very profitable way to add to their bottom line. Deductions that are not valid are merely an interest-free loan and customers would be loath to give them up and hurt their bottom line.

- *Alternative to enforcing policy.* This likewise will not work for the same reason as stated above. By not enforcing policy, you offer your customers a wide-open door to take as many deductions (justified or not) as they wish with no ramifications.

Right Reasons

- *Adjusting resources to enhance results.* The benefit here is to put your staff to their best use dealing with the day-to-day problems and keeping resolution time short while the resolution firm handles the older, more labor-intensive older items. This helps the staff get a handle on the problem and stay on top of it.

- *Improve collections of unjustified deductions.* By keeping the time tight for deduction resolution, monies taken that were unjustified will be repaid more quickly and will keep your customers from living off of your profits.

TIPS AND TECHNIQUES CONTINUED

- *Headcount control.* By supplementing your staff with a resolution firm, additional staff will not be necessary. Once the backlog is cleaned up and a better handle over the deduction picture is established, any temporary increase of deductions should easily be handled by the current staff.

- *Put customers back on track.* By going after deductions quickly and chasing them on the older items all at once, the customer will recognize that you will no longer be accepting deductions that are not valid.

- *Improve policy enforcement.* By putting deduction management back on track, customers will see that there is a much more even and consistent management of these deduction items.

- *Improve customer service.* By clearing up these items faster, justified credits due a customer will be issued far more expeditiously and will help to improve the relationship that your firm shares with its customers.

While it is indeed worthwhile to consider the use of a deduction/dispute resolution firm, make sure that the one that you hire has had experience in your industry type and can supply references of other satisfied firms that have used their services. Don't be lax and not check those references for if they do a poor job for you, any money that you have paid them will go up in smoke.

Accounts Payable Duplicate Payment/Overpayment Outsourcing

Duplicate payment audit firms can be every credit and accounts receivable manager's nightmare. They can resurrect items that can be as old as six to seven years and demand payment for the benefit of your customer, so why not use them for your own firm?

The answer to that question is you should. Firms such as these will do the research work going back over as many years as you have records available for and will make every effort to collect duplicate payments, credits due you, and other items that would add cash and improve your bottom line.

The good news about them is that they typically work on a contingency basis, getting between 30 and 50 cents on the dollar that they collect. But since your firm has neither the manpower nor the time to do this type of work and they are willing to do it for free until they locate something for which credit or payment is due, it just makes sense to hire them.

The other good piece of news is that they will also act as an auditing firm of how efficient your accounts payable staff is in doing their job. If a high volume of duplicate payments or missed credits are located, this is an area where better systems, increased staff, increased training, and possible disciplinary action may be necessary to keep this problem from escalating. Often the audit firm discovers that the source of the problem is not in accounts payable, but in purchasing, or some other department.

The other benefit is that they can also help to identify the weaknesses in your system and where they are possibly being exploited. While taking credits twice by a customer's accounts payable staff can infuriate a credit and accounts receivable manager as a way to prevent this from occurring, some of these managers simply do not provide copies of any credits presently sitting on their customer's account. If after a relatively long period of time they are not taken (typically over two years), they may either be matched up against old items that they were not intended for or are written off. While they should be escheated, many firms will slowly clear out these smaller items over time so as to not set off alarm bells with the state. Having one of these firms do an audit helps to bring this practice by the vendor's credit department to the attention of the accounts payable staff and will help them keep the vendor honest in the future.

Summary

While all of these different methods to improve cash flow have merit, they are not perfect for all types of firms. Each must be considered on their own merits and looked at from the point of view of any hidden costs that may arise. It is also smart to use only a firm that is reputable, financially solid, and sufficiently large enough to meet the needs of your firm. In-house problems must be addressed first before automatically going outside to look for help. If internal problems are left to languish, no amount of outside help can ever hope to increase cash flow. Finally, it is just plain smart to know all the terms and conditions of the agreement that you sign with one of these firms as well as what the bottom-line costs will be.

Now we move on to Chapter 12, "Internet Innovations to Improve Cash Flow."

Internet Innovations to Improve Cash Flow

After reading this chapter, you will be able to

- Understand the basics of electronic invoicing
- See how collection agencies are using the Internet to improve their services
- Use the Internet to reduce (drastically) the number of phone calls coming into the accounts payable department
- Understand the benefits of XML

The Internet provides innovative ways for companies to improve productivity and squeeze out additional cash flow from virtually every cash flow–related function. The controller or chief financial officer (CFO) looking to improve cash flow can ask department experts for their best ideas. These professionals should know what's hot and what's not in their fields. This chapter takes a look at a few of the newest innovations.

Electronic Invoicing Advantages

The billing, accounts receivable, and accounts payable functions are all heavily paper intensive and could benefit greatly from any process that reduces that aspect. Electronic billing has long been a part of the electronic data interchange (EDI) equation, but not very many companies participate in EDI in a meaningful way. As might be expected, the Internet offers a solution. Electronic billing, e-invoicing, and invoices over the Internet are just a few of the monikers being given this latest phenomenon. Companies are turning to electronic invoicing in growing numbers because it:

- Reduces paper
- Lowers costs
- Reduces errors
- Provides a clear audit trail
- Improves operational efficiencies
- Offers an alternative to physically handling mail (important after the anthrax scare)

What Is Electronic Invoicing?

Electronic invoicing permits the creation of an electronic document (invoice) in a standard format that can be transmitted over the Internet from seller to buyer. The document can then be routed electronically for matching and approvals within the buying organization. In the best of all worlds, the payment is ultimately made electronically, usually through the automated clearing house (ACH) sometimes with the electronic invoice still attached. The last part does not happen as often as many experts would like because, for a variety of reasons outside the scope of this book, it is a battle to get companies in the United States to pay by any means other than a check.

The simplest form of electronic invoicing is the seller's creating an invoice and then simply e-mailing it, either in the body of the message or as an attachment to the purchaser. Most companies take a slightly more sophisticated approach, using one of the numerous products on the market today. These products are either:

- Driven by the purchasing side, which means the seller must go to a prespecified Web site and load the invoice information. Once that is done the information is transmitted, either immediately or once a day, to the buyer.

- Driven by the selling side, which means the buyer must go to a prespecified Web site to pick up the information provided by the seller.

TIPS AND TECHNIQUES

Selecting an Electronic Invoicing Service Provider

Some of the products allow both sides to see the status of all their transactions on the Web sites. Since this area is so new, the products are not standardized and the players are often names you will not recognize. Before signing up with one of these companies:

- Get proposals from several vendors.

- Ask for references and thoroughly check them out, being cognizant of the fact that you will be offered only good references.

- Make sure there are no hidden costs.

- If possible, get financials of the companies offering the products. Some are well capitalized, and others don't have much financial backing. Be aware that, even though you might not recognize the names, a few of the products have big name investors.

There are quite a few new players in this exciting area. Inevitably, some of them will not make it. Others, in all likelihood, will be bought out by bigger players in the financial community. Unfortunately, it is too early to tell who the survivors will be—so proceed with care.

Disseminating Payment Information

Many accounts payable managers complain that their staff spends an inordinate amount of time on the phone answering phone calls regarding payment status. Companies looking for their money waste an equal amount of time on the other end making those calls. These phone calls take extra time because most people feel the need to at least be a little polite and thus spend some time making small talk about the weather and so on (heaven forbid it's Super Bowl or World Series time!).

The first innovation in this area was interactive voice response (IVR) systems. These let vendors dial into an 800 number and with a few numbers (password, vendor number, invoice number, and possible invoice date) obtain information regarding when their invoice was scheduled for payment. These systems were a giant step in the right direction as they cut into the number of phone calls, thus making the accounts payable staff more efficient. Unfortunately, these systems were not exactly cheap and only a few larger companies adopted them, although those that did swear by them.

Posting Payment Information on The Internet

The next innovation in this area came when companies realized that this information could be posted on a corporate Web site. Again, guarded by a password security system, companies have begun posting this information on their Web sites. In addition to cutting out an enormous amount of phone calls and wasted time, these systems also assist companies in projecting their cash flow. By regularly checking the status of large invoices, a company can pinpoint its cash inflow.

Some companies that started with an IVR have switched to putting the information on the Internet, and some maintain both systems. Many of those that maintain both do so because:

- They have already made the capital investment in the hardware and software.

- Some of their vendors are comfortable with the IVR and they don't want to force another change.
- They can provide a backup system in case their Web site is down.

It should be noted that, while it is possible to spend a nice sum of money to add this feature to the Web site, especially if highly experienced personnel are hired for the project, some companies have done it without any help from their information technology (IT) departments. The financial investment made by the companies that "went it alone" was well within the reach of virtually every company reading this book (i.e., only a few thousand dollars). Please note, however, that this financial equation works only if the company has its own web site to start with.

Thus, companies can benefit from the Internet approach on both sides of the financial coin. By putting its own payment information up, the accounts payable department can greatly reduce the number of phone calls and resources devoted to answering these calls. On the other side of the house, the accounts receivable folks should inquire of all major customers if this feature is available and then use it with whichever customers offer the function.

There is one last note regarding the use of the Internet for payment information. A few companies refuse to answer phone calls about payment status, referring all such inquiries to their Web site. This stance might seem a little harsh, especially to customer service–driven companies, but it is one way to drive down the costs of the accounts payable function.

Collection Agencies and the Internet

Many collection agencies give their clients access to information via the Internet. With password protection, companies can submit new accounts or check on the status of existing referrals. Using such a service reduces paper use, saves postal fees, and also reduces the number of phone calls needed to be made to a collection agency to check on the status of accounts.

Additionally, it makes it easier for the referring company to check the activity of the accounts that have been referred. When using the phone, the company has to take the word of the processor on the other end that the work has been done. With Internet access, it is possible to check whenever a company feels like it. This checking ability also makes it easier to monitor the care that the collection agency has been giving to your accounts.

A company that has its activity on the Internet will also be able to tell when little or no work has been done on its accounts and can then pick up the phone and talk to a manager at the collection agency. All things being equal (and they rarely are) I would choose an agency with the ability to monitor accounts over the Internet over one that does not have this capability. With this ability the collectors at the agency can spend more of their time chasing your deadbeat customers and less time updating customers on account status.

Bank Lockbox Information on the Internet

Many professionals within an organization have the need to have information relating to lockbox collections as early in the day as possible. While the treasury staff needs to know the total collections for the day so the investment/borrowing decision can be made, the accounts receivable staff needs the details of the daily collections so that cash can be applied correctly. If cash is applied on a timely basis, the collection staff will not waste valuable time chasing after customers who have already paid, thus improving both customer relationships and collection results, each of which has a positive impact on cash flow.

Many banks now make this information available over the Internet. Not only can the company get the total dollars collected, but it can get that much needed information about what exactly was collected making everyone impacted more efficient.

Imaged Positive Pay

We haven't talked much in this book about positive pay. Virtually every expert will tell you that it is a company's best defense against check fraud—something that definitely has a negative impact on cash flow. Imaged positive pay permits the bank to put images of checks presented for payment on the Internet. Then, when a check is questioned, a representative of the company can view online the actual check in question. The company's representative can see if the signature is valid and if the check resembles those currently in use by the company. This visual image makes the positive pay approach more effective.

Electronic Catalogs

Many companies put their catalogs up on the Internet for consumers to view and place orders. This is old hat. However, companies have taken this approach one step further. Let's look at a simple example—the case of a company ordering stationery goods. If a corporation wishes to limit its employees' purchasing options, it can feature on its intranet site only those items it wishes to make available to the employees. For example, it might allow employees to order certain types of paper (but not expensive letterhead), certain kinds of pens (but not fancy fountain pens), small calculators (but not computers), and so on.

Companies have taken this electronic catalog approach several steps farther. Some companies use it to order goods for production, while others use it to order parts. Depending on the amount of goods available, a company may significantly reduce its purchasing and/or sales staff.

Information Found on the Internet

Research is now being conducted on the Internet by all sorts of departments. Whether it be financial data regarding a potential customer or supplier, information about new products and services, or simply breaking news, the Internet puts information in the hands of those who need it on a very timely basis. There is also a wide variety of relatively inexpensive or free newsletters available. These come from organizations as well as individuals or small companies looking to get their foot in your door.

Caveat

The Internet is sometimes referred to as the great equalizer, and that is an understatement. The Internet lets Mom-and-Pop companies compete with Fortune 500 firms. Well, perhaps that is an overstatement, but it does give you an idea of what's out there. This means that corporations must be doubly careful about new customers and new suppliers. Anyone with a few dollars and a little technical expertise can create a nifty looking Web site.

XML

Extensible markup language (XML) is the latest innovation to hit the corporate world. An in-depth discussion of the topic is well beyond the scope of this work. There are many fine books written on the topic and readers interested in learning more should refer to one of them. Suffice it to say that XML will revolutionize the way information is shared on the Internet and between companies. A few companies are already starting to submit their 10K reports to the Securities and Exchange Commission (SEC) in XML. Within the next few years it is expected that there will be a deluge of applications in XML, dwarfing the hypertext markup language (HTML) explosion of the last few years.

Summary

This chapter has just touched on the topic of how professionals concerned about cash flow can use the Internet. There are numerous applications, and those looking to increase cash flow and improve departmental productivity will investigate all that they find and make use of the very best techniques.

Conclusion

There are many creative ways to improve cash flow, reduce costs, and keep those expenses that need to be paid under control. Some businesses have gone to the extreme of using bankruptcy to improve their cash flow, while most responsible firms use much more reasonable methods to improve their day-to-day existence in the real world. There are tangible ways to improve our cash flow and we have even looked at a few intangible things that can affect a firm's cash flow and profitability. The cost involved with maintaining a solid reputation can sometimes pay off greatly in the long run even though it doesn't look that way in the beginning. Corporations need to look at themselves to determine if they are truly being responsible when they act or if they are merely trying to cover up their mistakes, hoping that they will never get caught. We have seen many headlines screaming out at us over firms such as Enron, Firestone, Ford, and many others that tried to hide but were eventually found out. Then there are firms like Johnson & Johnson. During a very bleak time, they addressed the issue bravely and now savor the honor of being one of the most respected firms in the United States. It is not always enough to just save money and cut costs; Corporate America needs to be cognizant of the effect they can have on the very lives of not only those that they service but also on those that depend on them every day for a daily living. While cash flow can be measured in dollars and cents, the value of teamwork, solid communications, and the support of those greatest of all assets of a corporation—their people—can be measured only in the success or failure of the firm.

One final thought deals with ethical behavior among firms. For all companies to maintain solid cash flow, a high level of ethical professionalism must be maintained at all times. Large firms should not live off of what they can wring out of their smaller suppliers and use deduction wizardry to improve their cash flow (sometimes only temporarily) for their investors. These types of cheap parlor tricks will always come back to haunt those that use them. It is a wise individual or firm that works on an equal footing with suppliers and customers to make all involved successful and profitable.

Index